PLATO

VII

LCL 123

LOEB CLASSICAL LIBRARY

EDITED BY
JEFFREY HENDERSON

PLATO

VII

LCL

PLATO

THEAETETUS · SOPHIST

WITH AN ENGLISH TRANSLATION BY
HAROLD NORTH FOWLER

HARVARD UNIVERSITY PRESS
CAMBRIDGE, MASSACHUSETTS
LONDON, ENGLAND

First published 1921

LOEB CLASSICAL LIBRARY® is a registered trademark
of the President and Fellows of Harvard College

ISBN 978-0-674-99137-8

*Printed on acid-free paper and bound by
The Maple-Vail Book Manufacturing Group*

CONTENTS

PREFACE

THE Greek text in this volume is based upon the
Codex Clarkianus and the Codex Venetus. Devia-
tions from the readings of these manuscripts are
noted in the margin at the foot of the page. In
most instances disagreement between these two manuscripts, and occasionally readings found in inferior
manuscripts or in ancient quotations, as well as
emendations offered by modern scholars, are noted,
even when they have not affected the text chosen.
The following abbreviations are employed :

B = Codex Clarkianus or Bodleianus, written A.D. 895.
T = Codex Venetus, Append. class. 4, cod. 1 ; twelfth
       century.
W = Codex Vindobonensis '54, Suppl. graec. 7.
D = Codex Venetus 185.
G = Codex Venetus, Append. class 4, cod. 54.
b t w = later hands of B T W.

    The brief introductions aim merely at supplying
such information as may aid the reader to appreciate
these particular dialogues.

HAROLD N. FOWLER

LIST OF PLATO'S WORKS showing their division
into volumes in this edition and their place in the
edition of H. Stephanus (vols. I–III, Paris, 1578).

LIST OF PLATO'S WORKS

THEAETETUS

INTRODUCTION TO THE *THEAETETUS*

In the *Theaetetus* Eucleides the Megarian repeats to his friend Terpsion a conversation between Socrates, the mathematician Theodorus, and the youth Theaetetus, who was himself a mathematician of note. The subject is the nature of knowledge, and the discussion is interrupted and furthered by two digressions, one concerning midwives, in which Socrates likens his method of investigation to the activities of the midwife, the other contrasting the lawyer and the philosopher.

The definition of knowledge is hard to attain, and is, in fact, not attained in this dialogue. The confusion between knowledge and various kinds or applications of knowledge is first cleared up, and then the discussion centres upon three definitions: (1) Knowledge is sensible perception; (2) Knowledge is true opinion; (3) Knowledge is true opinion with reasoned explanation.

The discussion of the first definition contains as one of its most important parts the refutation of the doctrine of Protagoras that "man is the measure of all things"; but it includes also a discussion of the doctrine of Heracleitus, that all things are always in

motion. Here Plato distinguishes two kinds of motion—movement in space and change of quality—and asserts that constant motion of the first kind must be accompanied by change, because otherwise the same things would be at the same time both in motion and at rest. This obvious fallacy Plato appears to ascribe to Heracleitus and his school. The result of this discussion is that if nothing is at rest, every answer on whatever subject is equally correct.

The possibility of false opinion is discussed in connexion with the second definition. This part of the dialogue contains many subtle distinctions and interesting comparisons. The errors of memory are illustrated by the wax tablets which, on account of their imperfections, fail to receive and preserve clear impressions from sensible objects, and the confusion of our recollections by the aviary, the possessor of which takes in his hand one bird when he wishes to take another, though all the birds have previously been caught and imprisoned by him.

The third definition is explained in various ways, none of which is found to be satisfactory, and the dialogue closes with its avowed purpose—the complete definition of knowledge — unaccomplished, Nevertheless the rejection of the definitions proposed is a gain in itself, and the dialogue may be said to prepare the way for the acceptance of the theory of ideas. It serves also as an example of the importance of the dialectic method, and shows Plato's interest in combating the theories of other philosophers.

The *Theaetetus* contains many interesting similes and comparisons, and is, like the *Sophist* and the

Statesman, pervaded by a subtle and at the same time ponderous kind of humour which is rather irritating to some, at least, among modern readers. The reasoning is careful and accurate, but the exposition is somewhat too prolix for modern taste.

The date of the *Theaetetus* is uncertain, but it cannot be one of the early dialogues. The mention of the Athenian army at Corinth makes any date much earlier than 390 impossible. At the very end the reader is prepared for a continuation of the conversation, and this takes place in the *Sophist,* but that dialogue and the *Statesman* may very well have been written some years later than the *Theaetetus,* from which they differ considerably in style.

There are separate editions of the *Theaetetus* by Lewis Campbell (Oxford, 1861 and 1883) and B. H. Kennedy (Cambridge, 1881 and 1894), both with translation and notes.

ΘΕΑΙΤΗΤΟΣ

[Η ΠΕΡΙ ΕΠΙΣΤΗΜΗΣ, ΠΕΙΡΑΣΤΙΚΟΣ]

ΤΑ ΤΟΥ ΔΙΑΛΟΓΟΥ ΠΡΟΣΩΠΑ

ΕΥΚΛΕΙΔΗΣ, ΤΕΡΨΙΩΝ, ΣΩΚΡΑΤΗΣ, ΘΕΟΔΩΡΟΣ, ΘΕΑΙΤΗΤΟΣ

A I. ΕΥ. Ἄρτι, ὦ Τερψίων, ἢ πάλαι ἐξ ἀγρου;

ΤΕΡ. Ἐπιεικῶς πάλαι. καὶ σέ γε ἐζήτουν κατ'
ἀγορὰν καὶ ἐθαύμαζον ὅτι οὐχ οἷός τ' ἦ εὑρεῖν.

ΕΥ. Οὐ γὰρ ἦ κατὰ πόλιν.

ΤΕΡ. Ποῦ μήν;

ΕΥ. Εἰς λιμένα καταβαίνων Θεαιτήτῳ ἐνέτυχον
φερομένῳ ἐκ Κορίνθου ἀπὸ τοῦ στρατοπέδου Ἀθήναζε.

ΤΕΡ. Ζῶντι ἢ τετελευτηκότι ;

B ΕΥ. Ζῶντι καὶ μάλα μόλις· χαλεπῶς μὲν γὰρ
ἔχει καὶ ὑπὸ τραυμάτων τινῶν, μᾶλλον μὴν αὐτὸν
αἱρεῖ τὸ γεγονὸς νόσημα ἐν τῷ στρατεύματι.

ΤΕΡ. Μῶν ἡ δυσεντηρία;

ΕΥ. Ναί.

ΤΕΡ. Οἷον ἄνδρα λέγεις ἐν κινδύνῳ εἶναι.

ΕΥ. Καλόν τε καὶ ἀγαθόν, ὦ Τερψίων, ἐπεί τοι

6

THEAETETUS

[OR ON KNOWLEDGE, TENTATIVE]

CHARACTERS

EUCLEIDES, TERPSION, SOCRATES, THEODORUS, THEAETETUS

EU. Just in from the country, Terpsion, or did you come some time ago?

TERP. Quite a while ago; and I was looking for you in the market-place and wondering that I could not find you.

EU. Well, you see, I was not in the city.

TERP. Where then?

EU. As I was going down to the harbour I met Theaetetus being carried to Athens from the camp at Corinth.

TERP. Alive or dead?

EU. Just barely alive; for he is suffering severely from wounds, and, worse than that, he has been taken with the sickness that has broken out in the army.

TERP. You mean the dysentery?

EU. Yes.

TERP. What a man he is who you say is in danger!

EU. A noble man, Terpsion, and indeed just now I

καὶ νῦν ἤκουόν τινων μάλα ἐγκωμιαζόντων αὐτὸν
περὶ τὴν μάχην.

ΤΕΡ. Καὶ οὐδέν γ' ἄτοπον, ἀλλὰ καὶ πολὺ θαυ-
μαστότερον, εἰ μὴ τοιοῦτος ἦν. ἀτὰρ πῶς οὐκ
C αὐτοῦ Μεγαροῖ κατέλυεν;

ΕΤ. Ἠπείγετο οἴκαδε· ἐπεὶ ἔγωγ' ἐδεόμην καὶ
συνεβούλευον, ἀλλ' οὐκ ἤθελεν. καὶ δῆτα προπέμ-
ψας αὐτόν, ἀπιὼν πάλιν ἀνεμνήσθην καὶ ἐθαύμασα
Σωκράτους, ὡς μαντικῶς ἄλλα τε δὴ εἶπε καὶ περὶ
τούτου. δοκεῖ γάρ μοι ὀλίγον πρὸ τοῦ θανάτου
ἐντυχεῖν αὐτῷ μειρακίῳ ὄντι, καὶ συγγενόμενός
τε καὶ διαλεχθεὶς πάνυ ἀγασθῆναι αὐτοῦ τὴν
φύσιν. καί μοι ἐλθόντι Ἀθήναζε τούς τε λόγους οὓς
D διελέχθη αὐτῷ διηγήσατο, καὶ μάλα ἀξίους ἀκοῆς,
εἶπέ τε, ὅτι πᾶσα ἀνάγκη εἴη τοῦτον ἐλλόγιμον
γενέσθαι, εἴπερ εἰς ἡλικίαν ἔλθοι.

ΤΕΡ. Καὶ ἀληθῆ γε, ὡς ἔοικεν, εἶπεν. ἀτὰρ
τίνες ἦσαν οἱ λόγοι; ἔχοις ἂν διηγήσασθαι;

ΕΤ. Οὐ μὰ τὸν Δία, οὔκουν οὕτω γε ἀπὸ στό-
143 ματος· ἀλλ' ἐγραψάμην τότ' εὐθὺς οἴκαδ' ἐλθὼν
ὑπομνήματα, ὕστερον δὲ κατὰ σχολὴν ἀναμιμνη-
σκόμενος ἔγραφον, καὶ ὁσάκις Ἀθήναζε ἀφικοίμην,
ἐπανηρώτων τὸν Σωκράτη ὃ μὴ ἐμεμνήμην, καὶ
δεῦρο ἐλθὼν ἐπηνορθούμην· ὥστε μοι σχεδόν
τι πᾶς ὁ λόγος γέγραπται.

ΤΕΡ. Ἀληθῆ· ἤκουσά σου καὶ πρότερον, καὶ
μέντοι ἀεὶ μέλλων κελεύσειν ἐπιδεῖξαι διατέτριφα
δεῦρο. ἀλλὰ τί κωλύει νῦν ἡμᾶς διελθεῖν; πάντως
ἔγωγε καὶ ἀναπαύσασθαι δέομαι, ὡς ἐξ ἀγροῦ
ἥκων.

B ΕΤ. Ἀλλὰ μὲν δὴ καὶ αὐτὸς μέχρι Ἐρινοῦ

heard some people praising him highly for his conduct in the battle.

TERP. That is not at all strange; it would have been much more remarkable if he had not so conducted himself. But why did he not stop here in Megara?

EU. He was in a hurry to get home; for I begged and advised him to stop, but he would not. So I went along with him, and as I was coming back I thought of Socrates and wondered at his prophetic gift, especially in what he said about him. For I think he met him a little before his own death, when Theaetetus was a mere boy, and as a result of acquaintance and conversation with him, he greatly admired his qualities. When I went to Athens he related to me the conversation he had with him, which was well worth hearing, and he said he would surely become a notable man if he lived.

TERP. And he was right, apparently. But what was the talk? Could you relate it?

EU. No, by Zeus, at least not offhand. But I made notes at the time as soon as I reached home, then afterwards at my leisure, as I recalled things, I wrote them down, and whenever I went to Athens I used to ask Socrates about what I could not remember, and then I came here and made corrections; so that I have pretty much the whole talk written down.

TERP. That is true. I heard you say so before; and really I have been waiting about here all along intending to ask you to show it to me. What hinders us from reading it now? Certainly I need to rest, since I have come from the country.

EU. And I myself went with Theaetetus as far as

9

Θεαίτητον προύπεμψα, ὥστε οὐκ ἂν ἀηδῶς ἀνα-
παυοίμην. ἀλλ' ἴωμεν, καὶ ἡμῖν ἅμα ἀναπαυομένοις
ὁ παῖς ἀναγνώσεται.

ΤΕΡ. Ὀρθῶς λέγεις.

ΕΤ. Τὸ μὲν δὴ βιβλίον, ὦ Τερψίων, τουτί·
ἐγραψάμην δὲ δὴ οὑτωσὶ τὸν λόγον, οὐκ ἐμοὶ
Σωκράτη διηγούμενον ὡς διηγεῖτο, ἀλλὰ δια-
λεγόμενον οἷς ἔφη διαλεχθῆναι. ἔφη δὲ τῷ τε
γεωμέτρῃ Θεοδώρῳ καὶ τῷ Θεαιτήτῳ. ἵνα οὖν
C ἐν τῇ γραφῇ μὴ παρέχοιεν πράγματα αἱ μεταξὺ
τῶν λόγων διηγήσεις περὶ αὑτοῦ τε ὁπότε λέγοι ὁ
Σωκράτης, οἷον, καὶ ἐγὼ ἔφην ἢ καὶ ἐγὼ εἶπον,
ἢ αὖ περὶ τοῦ ἀποκρινομένου, ὅτι συνέφη ἢ οὐχ
ὡμολόγει, τούτων ἕνεκα ὡς αὐτὸν αὐτοῖς διαλεγό-
μενον ἔγραψα, ἐξελὼν τὰ τοιαῦτα.

ΤΕΡ. Καὶ οὐδέν γε ἀπὸ τρόπου, ὦ Εὐκλείδη.

ΕΤ. Ἀλλά, παῖ, λαβὲ τὸ βιβλίον καὶ λέγε.

D 2. ΣΩ. Εἰ μὲν τῶν ἐν Κυρήνῃ μᾶλλον ἐκη-
δόμην, ὦ Θεόδωρε, τὰ ἐκεῖ ἄν σε καὶ περὶ ἐκείνων
ἂν ἠρώτων, εἴ τινες αὐτόθι περὶ γεωμετρίαν ἤ τινα
ἄλλην φιλοσοφίαν εἰσὶ τῶν νέων ἐπιμέλειαν ποιού-
μενοι· νῦν δὲ ἧττον γὰρ ἐκείνους ἢ τούσδε φιλῶ,
καὶ μᾶλλον ἐπιθυμῶ εἰδέναι τίνες ἡμῖν τῶν νέων
ἐπίδοξοι γενέσθαι ἐπιεικεῖς· ταῦτα δὴ αὐτός τε
σκοπῶ καθ' ὅσον δύναμαι, καὶ τοὺς ἄλλους ἐρωτῶ
οἷς ἂν ὁρῶ τοὺς νέους ἐθέλοντας συγγίγνεσθαι.
σοὶ δὴ οὐκ ὀλίγιστοι πλησιάζουσι, καὶ δικαίως·
E ἄξιος γὰρ τά τε ἄλλα καὶ γεωμετρίας ἕνεκα. εἰ

Erineum,[1] so I also should not be sorry to take a rest. Come, let us go, and while we are resting, the boy shall read to us.

TERP. Very well.

EU. Here is the book, Terpsion. Now this is the way I wrote the conversation: I did not represent Socrates relating it to me, as he did, but conversing with those with whom he told me he conversed. And he told me they were the geometrician Theodorus and Theaetetus. Now in order that the explanatory words between the speeches might not be annoying in the written account, such as "and I said" or "and I remarked," whenever Socrates spoke, or "he agreed" or "he did not agree," in the case of the interlocutor, I omitted all that sort of thing and represented Socrates himself as talking with them.

TERP. That is quite fitting, Eucleides.

EU. Come, boy, take the book and read.

SOC. If I cared more for Cyrene and its affairs, Theodorus, I should ask you about things there and about the people, whether any of the young men there are devoting themselves to geometry or any other form of philosophy; but as it is, since I care less for those people than for the people here, I am more eager to know which of our own young men are likely to gain reputation. These are the things I myself investigate, so far as I can, and about which I question those others with whom I see that the young men like to associate. Now a great many of them come to you, and rightly, for you deserve it on account of your geometry, not to speak of other

[1] Erineum was between Eleusis and Athens, near the Cephissus. Apparently Eucleides had walked some thirty miles.

143

δὴ οὖν τινι ἐνέτυχες ἀξίῳ λόγου, ἡδέως ἂν πυ-
θοίμην.

ΘΕΟ. Καὶ μήν, ὦ Σώκρατες, ἐμοί τε εἰπεῖν καὶ
σοὶ ἀκοῦσαι πάνυ ἄξιον, οἵῳ ὑμῖν τῶν πολιτῶν
μειρακίῳ ἐντετύχηκα. καὶ εἰ μὲν ἦν καλός,
ἐφοβούμην ἂν σφόδρα λέγειν, μὴ καί τῳ δόξω ἐν
ἐπιθυμίᾳ αὐτοῦ εἶναι· νῦν δέ—καὶ μή μοι ἄχθου—
οὐκ ἔστι καλός, προσέοικε δὲ σοὶ τήν τε σιμότητα
καὶ τὸ ἔξω τῶν ὀμμάτων· ἧττον δὲ ἢ σὺ ταῦτ'
144 ἔχει. ἀδεῶς δὴ λέγω. εὖ γὰρ ἴσθι ὅτι ὧν δὴ
πώποτε ἐνέτυχον—καὶ πάνυ πολλοῖς πεπλησίακα—
οὐδένα πω ᾐσθόμην οὕτω θαυμαστῶς εὖ πεφυκότα.
τὸ γὰρ εὐμαθῆ ὄντα, ὡς ἄλλῳ χαλεπόν, πρᾷον αὖ
εἶναι διαφερόντως, καὶ ἐπὶ τούτοις ἀνδρεῖον παρ'
ὁντινοῦν, ἐγὼ μὲν οὔτ' ἂν ᾠόμην γενέσθαι οὔτε
ὁρῶ γιγνόμενον[1]· ἀλλ' οἵ τε ὀξεῖς ὥσπερ οὗτος
καὶ ἀγχίνοι καὶ μνήμονες ὡς τὰ πολλὰ καὶ πρὸς
τὰς ὀργὰς ὀξύρροποί εἰσι, καὶ ᾄττοντες φέρονται
B ὥσπερ τὰ ἀνερμάτιστα πλοῖα, καὶ μανικώτεροι
ἢ ἀνδρειότεροι φύονται, οἵ τε αὖ ἐμβριθέστεροι
νωθροί πως ἀπαντῶσι πρὸς τὰς μαθήσεις καὶ
λήθης γέμοντες. ὁ δὲ οὕτω λείως τε καὶ ἀπταίστως
καὶ ἀνυσίμως ἔρχεται ἐπὶ τὰς μαθήσεις τε καὶ
ζητήσεις μετὰ πολλῆς πρᾳότητος, οἷον ἐλαίου
ῥεῦμα ἀψοφητὶ ῥέοντος, ὥστε θαυμάσαι τὸ τηλι-
κοῦτον ὄντα οὕτως ταῦτα διαπράττεσθαι.

ΣΩ. Εὖ ἀγγέλλεις. τίνος δὲ καὶ ἔστι τῶν
πολιτῶν;

ΘΕΟ. Ἀκήκοα μὲν τοὔνομα, μνημονεύω δὲ οὔ.
C ἀλλὰ γάρ ἐστι τῶνδε τῶν προσιόντων ὁ ἐν τῷ

[1] γιγνόμενον T ut videtur, Burnet; γιγνομένους B, Berol.

12

reasons. So if you have met with any young man who is worth mentioning, I should like to hear about him.

THEO. Truly, Socrates, it is well worth while for me to talk and for you to hear about a splendid young fellow, one of your fellow-citizens, whom I have met. Now if he were handsome, I should be very much afraid to speak, lest someone should think I was in love with him. But the fact is—now don't be angry with me—he is not handsome, but is like you in his snub nose and protruding eyes, only those features are less marked in him than in you. You see I speak fearlessly. But I assure you that among all the young men I have ever met—and I have had to do with a great many—I never yet found one of such marvellously fine qualities. He is quick to learn, beyond almost anyone else, yet exceptionally gentle, and moreover brave beyond any other; I should not have supposed such a combination existed, and I do not see it elsewhere. On the contrary, those who, like him, have quick, sharp minds and good memories, have usually also quick tempers; they dart off and are swept away, like ships without ballast; they are excitable rather than courageous; those, on the other hand, who are steadier are somewhat dull when brought face to face with learning, and are very forgetful. But this boy advances toward learning and investigation smoothly and surely and successfully, with perfect gentleness, like a stream of oil that flows without a sound, so that one marvels how he accomplishes all this at his age.

SOC. That is good news; but which of our citizens is his father?

THEO. I have heard the name, but do not remember it. However, it does not matter, for the youth is

13

μέσῳ. ἄρτι γὰρ ἐν τῷ ἔξω δρόμῳ ἠλείφοντο
ἑταῖροί τέ τινες οὗτοι αὐτοῦ καὶ αὐτός, νῦν δέ μοι
δοκοῦσιν ἀλειψάμενοι δεῦρο ἰέναι. ἀλλὰ σκόπει,
εἰ γιγνώσκεις αὐτόν.

ΣΩ. Γιγνώσκω· ὁ τοῦ Σουνιέως Εὐφρονίου
ἐστίν, καὶ πάνυ γε, ὦ φίλε, ἀνδρὸς οἷον καὶ σὺ
τοῦτον διηγεῖ, καὶ ἄλλως εὐδοκίμου, καὶ μέντοι
καὶ οὐσίαν μάλα πολλὴν κατέλιπεν. τὸ δ᾽ ὄνομα
οὐκ οἶδα τοῦ μειρακίου.

D ΘΕΟ. Θεαίτητος, ὦ Σώκρατες, τό γε ὄνομα·
τὴν μέντοι οὐσίαν δοκοῦσί μοι ἐπίτροποί τινες
διεφθαρκέναι· ἀλλ᾽ ὅμως καὶ πρὸς τὴν τῶν
χρημάτων ἐλευθεριότητα θαυμαστός, ὦ Σώκρατες.

ΣΩ. Γεννικὸν λέγεις τὸν ἄνδρα. καί μοι κέλευε
αὐτὸν ἐνθάδε παρακαθίζεσθαι.

ΘΕΟ. Ἔσται ταῦτα. Θεαίτητε, δεῦρο παρὰ
Σωκράτη.

ΣΩ. Πάνυ μὲν οὖν, ὦ Θεαίτητε, ἵνα κἀγὼ ἐμαυτὸν ἀνασκέψωμαι, ποῖόν τι ἔχω τὸ πρόσωπον.
E φησὶν γὰρ Θεόδωρος ἔχειν με σοὶ ὅμοιον. ἀτὰρ
εἰ νῷν ἐχόντοιν ἑκατέρου λύραν ἔφη αὐτὰς ἡρμόσθαι
ὁμοίως, πότερον εὐθὺς ἂν ἐπιστεύομεν ἢ ἐπεσκε-
ψάμεθ᾽ ἄν, εἰ μουσικὸς ὢν λέγει;

ΘΕΑΙ. Ἐπεσκεψάμεθ᾽ ἄν.

ΣΩ. Οὐκοῦν τοιοῦτον μὲν εὑρόντες ἐπειθόμεθ᾽
ἄν, ἄμουσον δέ, ἠπιστοῦμεν;

ΘΕΑΙ. Ἀληθῆ.

ΣΩ. Νῦν δέ γ᾽, οἶμαι, εἴ τι μέλει ἡμῖν τῆς τῶν
145 προσώπων ὁμοιότητος, σκεπτέον, εἰ γραφικὸς ὢν
λέγει ἢ οὔ.

the middle one of those who are now coming toward
us. He and those friends of his were anointing themselves in the outer course,[1] and now they seem to
have finished and to be coming here. See if you
recognize him.

soc. Yes, I do. He is the son of Euphronius of
Sunium, who is a man of just the sort you describe,
and of good repute in other respects; moreover he
left a very large property. But the youth's name I
do not know.

theo. Theaetetus is his name, Socrates; but I
believe the property was squandered by trustees.
Nevertheless, Socrates, he is remarkably liberal with
his money, too.

soc. It is a noble man that you describe. Now
please tell him to come here and sit by us.

theo. I will. Theaetetus, come here to Socrates.

soc. Yes, do so, Theaetetus, that I may look at
myself and see what sort of a face I have; for Theodorus says it is like yours. Now if we each had
a lyre, and he said we had tuned them to the same
key, should we take his word for it without more ado,
or should we inquire first whether he who said it
was a musician?

theaet. We should inquire.

soc. Then if we found that he was a musician,
we should believe him, but if not, we should refuse
to take his word?

theaet. Yes.

soc. But now, if we are concerned about the likeness of our faces, we must consider whether he who
speaks is a painter, or not.

[1] The scene is evidently laid in a gymnasium; the young
men have been exercising.

ΘΕΑΙ. Δοκεῖ μοι.

ΣΩ. Ἦ οὖν ζωγραφικὸς Θεόδωρος;

ΘΕΑΙ. Οὔχ, ὅσον γέ με εἰδέναι.

ΣΩ. Ἆρ᾽ οὐδὲ γεωμετρικός;

ΘΕΑΙ. Πάντως δήπου, ὦ Σώκρατες.

ΣΩ. Ἦ καὶ ἀστρονομικὸς καὶ λογιστικός τε καὶ μουσικὸς καὶ ὅσα παιδείας ἔχεται;

ΘΕΑΙ. Ἔμοιγε δοκεῖ.

ΣΩ. Εἰ μὲν ἄρα ἡμᾶς τοῦ σώματός τι ὁμοίους φησὶν εἶναι ἐπαινῶν πῃ ἢ ψέγων, οὐ πάνυ αὐτῷ ἄξιον τὸν νοῦν προσέχειν.

ΘΕΑΙ. Ἴσως οὔ.

B ΣΩ. Τί δ᾽, εἰ ποτέρου τὴν ψυχὴν ἐπαινοῖ πρὸς ἀρετήν τε καὶ σοφίαν; ἆρ᾽ οὐκ ἄξιον τῷ μὲν ἀκούσαντι προθυμεῖσθαι ἀνασκέψασθαι τὸν ἐπαινεθέντα, τῷ δὲ προθύμως ἑαυτὸν ἐπιδεικνύναι;

ΘΕΑΙ. Πάνυ μὲν οὖν, ὦ Σώκρατες.

3. ΣΩ. Ὥρα τοίνυν, ὦ φίλε Θεαίτητε, σοὶ μὲν ἐπιδεικνύναι, ἐμοὶ δὲ σκοπεῖσθαι· ὡς εὖ ἴσθι ὅτι Θεόδωρος πολλοὺς δὴ πρός με ἐπαινέσας ξένους τε καὶ ἀστοὺς οὐδένα πω ἐπήνεσεν ὡς σὲ νῦν δή.

ΘΕΑΙ. Εὖ ἂν ἔχοι, ὦ Σώκρατες· ἀλλ᾽ ὅρα μὴ C παίζων ἔλεγεν.

ΣΩ. Οὐχ οὗτος ὁ τρόπος Θεοδώρου· ἀλλὰ μὴ ἀναδύου τὰ ὡμολογημένα σκηπτόμενος παίζοντα λέγειν τόνδε, ἵνα μὴ καὶ ἀναγκασθῇ μαρτυρεῖν· πάντως γὰρ οὐδεὶς ἐπισκήψει αὐτῷ. ἀλλὰ θαρρῶν ἔμμενε τῇ ὁμολογίᾳ.

ΘΕΑΙ. Ἀλλὰ χρὴ ταῦτα ποιεῖν, εἰ σοὶ δοκεῖ.

ΣΩ. Λέγε δή μοι· μανθάνεις που παρὰ Θεοδώρου γεωμετρίας ἄττα;

ΘΕΑΙ. Ἔγωγε.

THEAET. I think we must.

soc. Well, is Theodorus a painter?

THEAET. Not so far as I know.

soc. Nor a geometrician, either?

THEAET. Oh yes, decidedly, Socrates.

soc. And an astronomer, and an arithmetician, and a musician, and in general an educated man?

THEAET. I think so.

soc. Well then, if he says, either in praise or blame, that we have some physical resemblance, it is not especially worth while to pay attention to him.

THEAET. Perhaps not.

soc. But what if he should praise the soul of one of us for virtue and wisdom? Is it not worth while for the one who hears to examine eagerly the one who is praised, and for that one to exhibit his qualities with eagerness?

THEAET. Certainly, Socrates.

soc. Then, my dear Theaetetus, this is just the time for you to exhibit your qualities and for me to examine them; for I assure you that Theodorus, though he has praised many foreigners and citizens to me, never praised anyone as he praised you just now.

THEAET. A good idea, Socrates; but make sure that he was not speaking in jest.

soc. That is not Theodorus's way. But do not seek to draw back from your agreement on the pretext that he is jesting, or he will be forced to testify under oath; for certainly no one will accuse him of perjury. Come, be courageous and hold to the agreement.

THEAET. I suppose I must, if you say so.

soc. Now tell me; I suppose you learn some geometry from Theodorus?

THEAET. Yes.

D ΣΩ. Καὶ τῶν περὶ ἀστρονομίαν τε καὶ ἁρμονίας καὶ λογισμούς;

ΘΕΑΙ. Προθυμοῦμαί γε δή.

ΣΩ. Καὶ γὰρ ἐγώ, ὦ παῖ, παρά γε τούτου καὶ παρ' ἄλλων, οὓς ἂν οἴωμαί τι τούτων ἐπαΐειν. ἀλλ' ὅμως τὰ μὲν ἄλλα ἔχω περὶ αὐτὰ μετρίως, σμικρὸν δέ τι ἀπορῶ, ὃ μετὰ σοῦ τε καὶ τῶνδε σκεπτέον. καί μοι λέγε· ἆρ' οὐ τὸ μανθάνειν ἐστὶν τὸ σοφώτερον γίγνεσθαι περὶ ὃ μανθάνει τις;

ΘΕΑΙ. Πῶς γὰρ οὔ;

ΣΩ. Σοφίᾳ δέ γ', οἶμαι, σοφοὶ οἱ σοφοί.

ΘΕΑΙ. Ναί.

E ΣΩ. Τοῦτο δὲ μῶν διαφέρει τι ἐπιστήμης;

ΘΕΑΙ. Τὸ ποῖον;

ΣΩ. Ἡ σοφία. ἢ οὐχ ἅπερ ἐπιστήμονες, ταῦτα καὶ σοφοί;

ΘΕΑΙ. Τί μήν;

ΣΩ. Ταὐτὸν ἄρα ἐπιστήμη καὶ σοφία;

ΘΕΑΙ. Ναί.

ΣΩ. Τοῦτ' αὐτὸ τοίνυν ἐστὶν ὃ ἀπορῶ καὶ οὐ δύναμαι λαβεῖν ἱκανῶς παρ' ἐμαυτῷ, ἐπιστήμη ὅ τί
146 ποτε τυγχάνει ὄν. ἆρ' οὖν δὴ ἔχομεν λέγειν αὐτό; τί φατέ; τίς ἂν ἡμῶν πρῶτος εἴποι; ὁ δὲ ἁμαρτών, καὶ ὃς ἂν ἀεὶ ἁμαρτάνῃ, καθεδεῖται, ὥσπερ φασὶν οἱ παῖδες οἱ σφαιρίζοντες, ὄνος· ὃς δ' ἂν περιγένηται ἀναμάρτητος, βασιλεύσει ἡμῶν καὶ ἐπιτάξει ὅ τι ἂν βούληται ἀποκρίνεσθαι. τί σιγᾶτε; οὔ τί που, ὦ Θεόδωρε, ἐγὼ ὑπὸ φιλο-λογίας ἀγροικίζομαι, προθυμούμενος ἡμᾶς[1] ποιῆσαι διαλέγεσθαι καὶ φίλους τε καὶ προσηγόρους ἀλλή-λοις γίγνεσθαι;

[1] ἡμᾶς] ὑμᾶς Τ.

18

soc. And astronomy and harmony and arithmetic?

THEAET. I try hard to do so.

soc. And so do I, my boy, from him and from any others who I think know anything about these things. But nevertheless, although in other respects I get on fairly well in them, yet I am in doubt about one little matter, which should be investigated with your help and that of these others. Tell me, is not learning growing wiser about that which one learns?

THEAET. Of course.

soc. And the wise, I suppose, are wise by wisdom.

THEAET. Yes.

soc. And does this differ at all from knowledge?

THEAET. Does what differ?

soc. Wisdom. Or are not people wise in that of which they have knowledge?

THEAET. Of course.

soc. Then knowledge and wisdom are the same thing?

THEAET. Yes.

soc. Well, it is just this that I am in doubt about and cannot fully grasp by my own efforts—what knowledge really is. Can we tell that? What do you say? Who of us will speak first? And he who fails, and whoever fails in turn, shall go and sit down and be donkey, as the children say when they play ball; and whoever gets through without failing shall be our king and shall order us to answer any questions he pleases. Why are you silent? I hope, Theodorus, I am not rude, through my love of discussion and my eagerness to make us converse and show ourselves friends and ready to talk to one another.

B ΘΕΟ. Ἥκιστα μέν, ὦ Σώκρατες, τὸ τοιοῦτον
ἂν εἴη ἄγροικον, ἀλλὰ τῶν μειρακίων τι κέλευέ σοι
ἀποκρίνεσθαι· ἐγὼ μὲν γὰρ ἀήθης τῆς τοιαύτης
διαλέκτου, καὶ οὐδ' αὖ συνεθίζεσθαι ἡλικίαν ἔχω·
τοῖσδε δὲ πρέποι τε ἂν τοῦτο καὶ πολὺ πλέον
ἐπιδιδοῖεν· τῷ γὰρ ὄντι ἡ νεότης εἰς πᾶν ἐπίδοσιν
ἔχει. ἀλλ', ὥσπερ ἤρξω, μὴ ἀφίεσο τοῦ Θεαιτήτου,
ἀλλ' ἐρώτα.

ΣΩ. Ἀκούεις δή, ὦ Θεαίτητε, ἃ λέγει Θεόδωρος,
C ᾧ ἀπειθεῖν,[1] ὡς ἐγὼ οἶμαι, οὔτε σὺ ἐθελήσεις,
οὔτε θέμις περὶ τὰ τοιαῦτα ἀνδρὶ σοφῷ ἐπιτάττοντι
νεώτερον ἀπειθεῖν. ἀλλ' εὖ καὶ γενναίως εἰπέ·
τί σοι δοκεῖ εἶναι ἐπιστήμη;

ΘΕΑΙ. Ἀλλὰ χρή, ὦ Σώκρατες, ἐπειδήπερ ὑμεῖς
κελεύετε. πάντως γάρ, ἄν τι καὶ ἁμάρτω, ἐπαν-
ορθώσετε.

4. ΣΩ. Πάνυ μὲν οὖν, ἄν πέρ γε οἷοί τε ὦμεν.

ΘΕΑΙ. Δοκεῖ τοίνυν μοι καὶ ἃ παρὰ Θεοδώρου
ἄν τις μάθοι ἐπιστῆμαι εἶναι, γεωμετρία τε καὶ
ἃς νῦν δὴ σὺ διῆλθες, καὶ αὖ σκυτοτομική τε καὶ
D αἱ τῶν ἄλλων δημιουργῶν τέχναι, πᾶσαί τε καὶ
ἑκάστη τούτων, οὐκ ἄλλο τι ἢ ἐπιστήμη εἶναι.

ΣΩ. Γενναίως γε καὶ φιλοδώρως, ὦ φίλε, ἓν
αἰτηθεὶς πολλὰ δίδως καὶ ποικίλα ἀνθ' ἁπλοῦ.

ΘΕΑΙ. Πῶς τί τοῦτο λέγεις, ὦ Σώκρατες;

ΣΩ. Ἴσως μὲν οὐδέν· ὃ μέντοι οἶμαι, φράσω.
ὅταν λέγῃς σκυτικήν, μή τι ἄλλο φράζεις ἢ ἐπιστήμην ὑποδημάτων ἐργασίας;

ΘΕΑΙ. Οὐδέν.

E ΣΩ. Τί δ', ὅταν τεκτονικήν; μή τι ἄλλο ἢ
ἐπιστήμην τῆς τῶν ξυλίνων σκευῶν ἐργασίας;

---

[1] ἀπειθεῖν W; ἀπιστεῖν BT; ἀπελθεῖν al.

THEO. That sort of thing would not be at all rude, Socrates; but tell one of the youths to answer your questions; for I am unused to such conversation and, moreover, I am not of an age to accustom myself to it. But that would be fitting for these young men, and they would improve much more than I; for the fact is, youth admits of improvement in every way. Come, question Theaetetus as you began to do, and do not let him off.

SOC. Well, Theaetetus, you hear what Theodorus says, and I think you will not wish to disobey him, nor is it right for a young person to disobey a wise man when he gives instructions about such matters. Come, speak up well and nobly. What do you think knowledge is?

THEAET. Well, Socrates, I must, since you bid me. For if I make a mistake, you are sure to set me right.

SOC. Certainly, if we can.

THEAET. Well then, I think the things one might learn from Theodorus are knowledge—geometry and all the things you spoke of just now—and also cobblery and the other craftsmen's arts; each and all of these are nothing else but knowledge.

SOC. You are noble and generous, my friend, for when you are asked for one thing you give many, and a variety of things instead of a simple answer.

THEAET. What do you mean by that, Socrates?

SOC. Nothing, perhaps; but I will tell you what I think I mean. When you say " cobblery " you speak of nothing else than the art of making shoes, do you?

THEAET. Nothing else.

SOC. And when you say " carpentry "? Do you mean anything else than the art of making wooden furnishings?

ΘΕΑΙ. Οὐδὲ τοῦτο.

ΣΩ. Οὐκοῦν ἐν ἀμφοῖν, οὗ ἑκατέρα ἐπιστήμη, τοῦτο ὁρίζεις;

ΘΕΑΙ. Ναί.

ΣΩ. Τὸ δέ γ' ἐρωτηθέν,[1] ὦ Θεαίτητε, οὐ τοῦτο ἦν, τίνων ἡ ἐπιστήμη, οὐδὲ ὁπόσαι τινές· οὐ γὰρ ἀριθμῆσαι αὐτὰς βουλόμενοι ἠρόμεθα, ἀλλὰ γνῶναι ἐπιστήμην αὐτὸ ὅ τί ποτ' ἐστίν. ἢ οὐδὲν λέγω;

ΘΕΑΙ. Πάνυ μὲν οὖν ὀρθῶς.

147 ΣΩ. Σκέψαι δὴ καὶ τόδε. εἴ τις ἡμᾶς τῶν φαύλων τι καὶ προχείρων ἔροιτο, οἷον περὶ πηλοῦ, ὅ τί ποτ' ἐστίν, εἰ ἀποκριναίμεθα αὐτῷ πηλὸς ὁ τῶν χυτρέων καὶ πηλὸς ὁ τῶν ἱπνοπλαθῶν καὶ πηλὸς ὁ τῶν πλινθουργῶν, οὐκ ἂν γελοῖοι εἶμεν;

ΘΕΑΙ. Ἴσως.

ΣΩ. Πρῶτον μέν γέ που οἰόμενοι συνιέναι ἐκ τῆς ἡμετέρας ἀποκρίσεως τὸν ἐρωτῶντα, ὅταν εἴπωμεν πηλός, εἴτε ὁ τῶν κοροπλαθῶν προσθέντες B εἴτε ἄλλων ὡντινωνοῦν δημιουργῶν. ἤ, οἴει, τίς τι συνίησίν τινος ὄνομα, ὃ μὴ οἶδεν τί ἐστιν;

ΘΕΑΙ. Οὐδαμῶς.

ΣΩ. Οὐδ' ἄρα ἐπιστήμην ὑποδημάτων συνίησιν ὁ ἐπιστήμην μὴ εἰδώς.

ΘΕΑΙ. Οὐ γάρ.

ΣΩ. Σκυτικὴν ἄρα οὐ συνίησιν ὃς ἂν ἐπιστήμην ἀγνοῇ, οὐδέ τινα ἄλλην τέχνην.

ΘΕΑΙ. Ἔστιν οὕτως.

ΣΩ. Γελοία ἄρα ἡ ἀπόκρισις τῷ ἐρωτηθέντι ἐπιστήμη τί ἐστιν, ὅταν ἀποκρίνηται τέχνης τινὸς

[1] τὸ δέ γ' ἐρωτηθέν Burnet; τὸ δέ γε ἐρωτηθέν W, Berol.; τὸ δ' ἐπερωτηθέν BT.

THEAETETUS

THEAET. Nothing else by that, either.

SOC. Then in both cases you define that to which each form of knowledge belongs?

THEAET. Yes.

SOC. But the question, Theaetetus, was not to what knowledge belongs, nor how many the forms of knowledge are; for we did not wish to number them, but to find out what knowledge itself really is. Or is there nothing in what I say?

THEAET. Nay, you are quite right.

SOC. Take this example. If anyone should ask us about some common everyday thing, for instance, what clay is, and we should reply that it is the potters' clay and the oven‑makers' clay and the brickmakers' clay, should we not be ridiculous?

THEAET. Perhaps.

SOC. Yes; in the first place for assuming that the questioner can understand from our answer what clay is, when we say "clay," no matter whether we add "the image-makers' " or any other craftsmen's. Or does anyone, do you think, understand the name of anything when he does not know what the thing is?

THEAET. By no means.

SOC. Then he does not understand knowledge of shoes if he does not know knowledge.

THEAET. No.

SOC. Then he who is ignorant of knowledge does not understand cobblery or any other art.

THEAET. That is true.

SOC. Then it is a ridiculous answer to the question "what is knowledge?" when we give the name of

C ὄνομα. τινὸς γὰρ ἐπιστήμην ἀποκρίνεται οὐ τοῦτ'
ἐρωτηθείς.

ΘΕΑΙ. Ἔοικεν.

ΣΩ. Ἔπειτά γέ που ἐξὸν φαύλως καὶ βραχέως
ἀποκρίνασθαι περιέρχεται ἀπέραντον ὁδόν. οἷον
καὶ ἐν τῇ τοῦ πηλοῦ ἐρωτήσει φαῦλόν που καὶ
ἁπλοῦν εἰπεῖν ὅτι γῆ ὑγρῷ φυραθεῖσα πηλὸς ἂν
εἴη, τὸ δ' ὅτου ἐᾶν χαίρειν.

5. ΘΕΑΙ. Ῥᾴδιον, ὦ Σώκρατες, νῦν γε οὕτω
φαίνεται· ἀτὰρ κινδυνεύεις ἐρωτᾶν οἷον καὶ
αὐτοῖς ἡμῖν ἔναγχος εἰσῆλθε διαλεγομένοις, ἐμοί
D τε καὶ τῷ σῷ ὁμωνύμῳ τούτῳ Σωκράτει.

ΣΩ. Τὸ ποῖον δή, ὦ Θεαίτητε;

ΘΕΑΙ. Περὶ δυνάμεών τι ἡμῖν Θεόδωρος ὅδε
ἔγραφε, τῆς τε τρίποδος πέρι καὶ πεντέποδος
ἀποφαίνων [1] ὅτι μήκει οὐ σύμμετροι τῇ ποδιαίᾳ,
καὶ οὕτω κατὰ μίαν ἑκάστην προαιρούμενος μέχρι
τῆς ἑπτακαιδεκάποδος· ἐν δὲ ταύτῃ πως ἐνέσχετο.
ἡμῖν οὖν εἰσῆλθέ τι τοιοῦτον, ἐπειδὴ ἄπειροι τὸ
πλῆθος αἱ δυνάμεις ἐφαίνοντο, πειραθῆναι συλλαβεῖν
E εἰς ἕν, ὅτῳ πάσας ταύτας προσαγορεύσομεν τὰς
δυνάμεις.

---

[1] ἀποφαίνων om. T; Burnet brackets.

---

[1] A simple form of the first statement would be: The
square roots of 3, 5, etc., are irrational numbers or surds.
The word δύναμις has not the meaning which we give in
English to "power," namely the result of multiplication of
a number by itself, but that which we give to "root," i.e.
the number which, when multiplied by itself, produces a
given result. Here Theaetetus is speaking of square roots
only ; and when he speaks of numbers and of equal factors

some art; for we give in our answer something that knowledge belongs to, when that was not what we were asked.

THEAET. So it seems.

soc. Secondly, when we might have given a short, everyday answer, we go an interminable distance round; for instance, in the question about clay, the everyday, simple thing would be to say "clay is earth mixed with moisture" without regard to whose clay it is.

THEAET. It seems easy just now, Socrates, as you put it; but you are probably asking the kind of thing that came up among us lately when your namesake, Socrates here, and I were talking together.

soc. What kind of thing was that, Theaetetus?

THEAET. Theodorus here was drawing some figures for us in illustration of roots, showing that squares containing three square feet and five square feet are not commensurable in length with the unit of the foot, and so, selecting each one in its turn up to the square containing seventeen square feet; and at that he stopped. Now it occurred to us, since the number of roots appeared to be infinite, to try to collect them under one name, by which we could henceforth call all the roots.[1]

he evidently thinks of rational whole numbers only, not of irrational numbers or fractions. He is not giving an exhaustive presentation of his investigation, but merely a brief sketch of it to illustrate his understanding of the purpose of Socrates. Toward the end of this sketch the word δύναμις is limited to the square roots of "oblong" numbers, i.e. to surds. The modern reader may be somewhat confused because Theaetetus seems to speak of arithmetical facts in geometrical terms. (Cf. Gow, *Short History of Greek Mathematics*, p. 85.)

ΣΩ. Ἦ καὶ ηὕρετέ τι τοιοῦτον;

ΘΕΑΙ. Ἔμοιγε δοκοῦμεν· σκόπει δὲ καὶ σύ.

ΣΩ. Λέγε.

ΘΕΑΙ. Τὸν ἀριθμὸν πάντα δίχα διελάβομεν· τὸν μὲν δυνάμενον ἴσον ἰσάκις γίγνεσθαι τῷ τετραγώνῳ τὸ σχῆμα ἀπεικάσαντες τετράγωνόν τε καὶ ἰσόπλευρον προσείπομεν.

ΣΩ. Καὶ εὖ γε.

ΘΕΑΙ. Τὸν τοίνυν μεταξὺ τούτου, ὧν καὶ τὰ 148 τρία καὶ τὰ πέντε καὶ πᾶς ὃς ἀδύνατος ἴσος ἰσάκις γενέσθαι, ἀλλ' ἢ πλείων ἐλαττονάκις ἢ ἐλάττων πλεονάκις γίγνεται, μείζων δὲ καὶ ἐλάττων ἀεὶ πλευρὰ αὐτὸν περιλαμβάνει, τῷ προμήκει αὖ σχήματι ἀπεικάσαντες προμήκη ἀριθμὸν ἐκαλέσαμεν.

ΣΩ. Κάλλιστα. ἀλλὰ τί τὸ μετὰ τοῦτο;

ΘΕΑΙ. Ὅσαι μὲν γραμμαὶ τὸν ἰσόπλευρον καὶ ἐπίπεδον ἀριθμὸν τετραγωνίζουσι, μῆκος ὡρισάμεθα, ὅσαι δὲ τὸν ἑτερομήκη, δυνάμεις, ὡς μήκει B μὲν οὐ ξυμμέτρους ἐκείναις, τοῖς δ' ἐπιπέδοις ἃ δύνανται. καὶ περὶ τὰ στερεὰ ἄλλο τοιοῦτον.

ΣΩ. Ἄριστά γ' ἀνθρώπων, ὦ παῖδες· ὥστε μοι δοκεῖ ὁ Θεόδωρος οὐκ ἔνοχος τοῖς ψευδομαρτυρίοις ἔσεσθαι.

ΘΕΑΙ. Καὶ μήν, ὦ Σώκρατες, ὅ γε ἐρωτᾷς περὶ ἐπιστήμης, οὐκ ἂν δυναίμην ἀποκρίνασθαι, ὥσπερ περὶ τοῦ μήκους καὶ τῆς δυνάμεως. καίτοι σύ γέ μοι δοκεῖς τοιοῦτόν τι ζητεῖν· ὥστε πάλιν αὖ φαίνεται ψευδὴς ὁ Θεόδωρος.

THEAETETUS

soc. And did you find such a name?

THEAET. I think we did. But see if you agree.

soc. Speak on.

THEAET. We divided all number into two classes. The one, the numbers which can be formed by multiplying equal factors, we represented by the shape of the square and called square or equilateral numbers.

soc. Well done!

THEAET. The numbers between these, such as three and five and all numbers which cannot be formed by multiplying equal factors, but only by multiplying a greater by a less or a less by a greater, and are therefore always contained in unequal sides, we represented by the shape of the oblong rectangle and called oblong numbers.

soc. Very good; and what next?

THEAET. All the lines which form the four sides of the equilateral or square numbers we called lengths, and those which form the oblong numbers we called surds, because they are not commensurable with the others in length, but only in the areas of the planes which they have the power to form. And similarly in the case of solids.[1]

soc. Most excellent, my boys! I think Theodorus will not be found liable to an action for false witness.

THEAET. But really, Socrates, I cannot answer that question of yours about knowledge, as we answered the question about length and square roots. And yet you seem to me to want something of that kind. So Theodorus appears to be a false witness after all.

[1] That is, cubes and cube roots.

C ΣΩ. Τί δέ; εἴ σε πρὸς δρόμον ἐπαινῶν μηδενὶ οὕτω δρομικῷ ἔφη τῶν νέων ἐντετυχηκέναι, εἶτα διαθέων τοῦ ἀκμάζοντος καὶ ταχίστου ἡττήθης, ἡττόν τι ἂν οἴει ἀληθῆ τόνδ᾽ ἐπαινέσαι;

ΘΕΑΙ. Οὐκ ἔγωγε.

ΣΩ. Ἀλλὰ τὴν ἐπιστήμην, ὥσπερ νῦν δὴ ἐγὼ ἔλεγον, σμικρόν τι οἴει εἶναι ἐξευρεῖν καὶ οὐ τῶν πάντῃ ἄκρων;

ΘΕΑΙ. Νὴ τὸν Δί᾽ ἔγωγε καὶ μάλα γε τῶν ἀκροτάτων.

ΣΩ. Θάρρει τοίνυν περὶ σαυτῷ καὶ τὶ οἴου

D Θεόδωρον λέγειν, προθυμήθητι δὲ παντὶ τρόπῳ τῶν τε ἄλλων πέρι καὶ ἐπιστήμης λαβεῖν λόγον, τί ποτε τυγχάνει ὄν.

ΘΕΑΙ. Προθυμίας μὲν ἕνεκα, ὦ Σώκρατες, φανεῖται.

6. ΣΩ. Ἴθι δή—καλῶς γὰρ ἄρτι ὑφηγήσω—πειρῶ μιμούμενος τὴν περὶ τῶν δυνάμεων ἀπόκρισιν, ὥσπερ ταύτας πολλὰς οὔσας ἑνὶ εἴδει περιέλαβες, οὕτω καὶ τὰς πολλὰς ἐπιστήμας ἑνὶ λόγῳ προσειπεῖν.

E ΘΕΑΙ. Ἀλλ᾽ εὖ ἴσθι, ὦ Σώκρατες, πολλάκις δὴ αὐτὸ ἐπεχείρησα σκέψασθαι, ἀκούων τὰς παρὰ σοῦ ἀποφερομένας ἐρωτήσεις· ἀλλὰ γὰρ οὔτ᾽ αὐτὸς δύναμαι πεῖσαι ἐμαυτὸν ὡς ἱκανῶς τι λέγω, οὔτ᾽ ἄλλου ἀκοῦσαι λέγοντος οὕτως ὡς σὺ διακελεύει· οὐ μὲν δὴ αὖ οὐδ᾽ ἀπαλλαγῆναι τοῦ μέλειν.[1]

ΣΩ. Ὠδίνεις γάρ, ὦ φίλε Θεαίτητε, διὰ τὸ μὴ κενὸς ἀλλ᾽ ἐγκύμων εἶναι.

ΘΕΑΙ. Οὐκ οἶδα, ὦ Σώκρατες· ὃ μέντοι πέπονθα λέγω.

---

[1] μέλειν B, Berol. et γρ. W (and Burnet); μέλλειν T: εὑρεῖν W.

soc. Nonsense! If he were praising your running and said he had never met any young man who was so good a runner, and then you were beaten in a race by a full grown man who held the record, do you think his praise would be any less truthful?

THEAET. Why, no.

soc. And do you think that the discovery of knowledge, as I was just now saying, is a small matter and not a task for the very ablest men?

THEAET. By Zeus, I think it is a task for the very ablest.

soc. Then you must have confidence in yourself, and believe that Theodorus is right, and try earnestly in every way to gain an understanding of the nature of knowledge as well as of other things.

THEAET. If it is a question of earnestness, Socrates, the truth will come to light.

soc. Well then—for you pointed out the way admirably just now—take your answer about the roots as a model, and just as you embraced them all in one class, though they were many, try to designate the many forms of knowledge by one definition.

THEAET. But I assure you, Socrates, I have often tried to work that out, when I heard reports of the questions that you asked, but I can neither persuade myself that I have any satisfactory answer, nor can I find anyone else who gives the kind of answer you insist upon; and yet, on the other hand, I cannot get rid of a feeling of concern about the matter.

soc. Yes, you are suffering the pangs of labour, Theaetetus, because you are not empty, but pregnant.

THEAET. I do not know, Socrates; I merely tell you what I feel.

PLATO

149 ΣΩ. Εἶτα, ὦ καταγέλαστε, οὐκ ἀκήκοας, ὡς
ἐγώ εἰμι ὑὸς μαίας μάλα γενναίας τε καὶ βλοσυρᾶς,
Φαιναρέτης;

ΘΕΑΙ. Ἤδη τοῦτό γε ἤκουσα.

ΣΩ. Ἆρα καί, ὅτι ἐπιτηδεύω τὴν αὐτὴν τέχνην,
ἀκήκοας;

ΘΕΑΙ. Οὐδαμῶς.

ΣΩ. Ἀλλ' εὖ ἴσθ' ὅτι· μὴ μέντοι μου κατείπῃς
πρὸς τοὺς ἄλλους. λέληθα γάρ, ὦ ἑταῖρε, ταύτην
ἔχων τὴν τέχνην· οἱ δέ, ἅτε οὐκ εἰδότες, τοῦτο
μὲν οὐ λέγουσι περὶ ἐμοῦ, ὅτι δὲ ἀτοπώτατός εἰμι
καὶ ποιῶ τοὺς ἀνθρώπους ἀπορεῖν. ἢ καὶ τοῦτο
ἀκήκοας;

B ΘΕΑΙ. Ἔγωγε.

ΣΩ. Εἴπω οὖν σοι τὸ αἴτιον;

ΘΕΑΙ. Πάνυ μὲν οὖν.

ΣΩ. Ἐννόησον δὴ τὸ περὶ τὰς μαίας ἅπαν ὡς
ἔχει, καὶ ῥᾷον μαθήσει ὃ βούλομαι. οἶσθα γάρ
που ὡς οὐδεμία αὐτῶν ἔτι αὐτὴ κυϊσκομένη τε
καὶ τίκτουσα ἄλλας μαιεύεται, ἀλλ' αἱ ἤδη ἀδύνατοι
τίκτειν.

ΘΕΑΙ. Πάνυ μὲν οὖν.

ΣΩ. Αἰτίαν δέ γε τούτου φασὶν εἶναι τὴν Ἄρ-
τεμιν, ὅτι ἄλοχος οὖσα τὴν λοχείαν εἴληχε. στερί-
C φαις μὲν οὖν ἄρα οὐκ ἔδωκε μαιεύεσθαι, ὅτι ἡ
ἀνθρωπίνη φύσις ἀσθενεστέρα ἢ λαβεῖν τέχνην
ὧν ἂν ᾖ ἄπειρος· ταῖς δὲ δι' ἡλικίαν ἀτόκοις
προσέταξε τιμῶσα τὴν αὑτῆς ὁμοιότητα.

ΘΕΑΙ. Εἰκός.

ΣΩ. Οὐκοῦν καὶ τόδε εἰκός τε καὶ ἀναγκαῖον,

soc. Have you then not heard, you absurd boy, that I am the son of a noble and burly midwife, Phaenarete?

THEAET. Yes, I have heard that.

soc. And have you also heard that I practise the same art?

THEAET. No, never.

soc. But I assure you it is true; only do not tell on me to the others; for it is not known that I possess this art. But other people, since they do not know it, do not say this of me, but say that I am a most eccentric person and drive men to distraction. Have you heard that also?

THEAET. Yes, I have.

soc. Shall I tell you the reason then?

THEAET. Oh yes, do.

soc. Just take into consideration the whole business of the midwives, and you will understand more easily what I mean. For you know, I suppose, that no one of them attends other women while she is still capable of conceiving and bearing, but only those do so who have become too old to bear.

THEAET. Yes, certainly.

soc. They say the cause of this is Artemis, because she, a childless goddess, has had childbirth allotted to her as her special province. Now it would seem she did not allow barren women to be midwives, because human nature is too weak to acquire an art which deals with matters of which it has no experience, but she gave the office to those who on account of age were not bearing children, honouring them for their likeness to herself.

THEAET. Very likely.

soc. Is it not, then, also likely and even necessary,

31

τὰς κυούσας καὶ μὴ γιγνώσκεσθαι μᾶλλον ὑπὸ τῶν μαιῶν ἢ τῶν ἄλλων;

ΘΕΑΙ. Πάνυ γε.

ΣΩ. Καὶ μὴν καὶ διδοῦσαί γε αἱ μαῖαι φαρμάκια D καὶ ἐπάδουσαι δύνανται ἐγείρειν τε τὰς ὠδῖνας καὶ μαλθακωτέρας, ἂν βούλωνται, ποιεῖν, καὶ τίκτειν τε δὴ τὰς δυστοκούσας, καὶ ἐὰν νέον ὂν[1] δόξῃ ἀμβλίσκειν, ἀμβλίσκουσιν;

ΘΕΑΙ. Ἔστι ταῦτα.

ΣΩ. Ἆρ᾽ οὖν ἔτι καὶ τόδε αὐτῶν ᾔσθησαι, ὅτι καὶ προμνήστριαί εἰσι δεινόταται, ὡς πάσσοφοι οὖσαι περὶ τοῦ γνῶναι ποίαν χρὴ ποίῳ ἀνδρὶ συνοῦσαν ὡς ἀρίστους παῖδας τίκτειν;

ΘΕΑΙ. Οὐ πάνυ τοῦτο οἶδα.

ΣΩ. Ἀλλ᾽ ἴσθ᾽ ὅτι ἐπὶ τούτῳ μεῖζον φρονοῦσιν E ἢ ἐπὶ τῇ ὀμφαλητομίᾳ. ἐννόει γάρ· τῆς αὐτῆς ἢ ἄλλης οἴει τέχνης εἶναι θεραπείαν τε καὶ συγκομιδὴν τῶν ἐκ γῆς καρπῶν καὶ αὖ τὸ γιγνώσκειν εἰς ποίαν γῆν ποῖον φυτόν τε καὶ σπέρμα καταβλητέον;

ΘΕΑΙ. Οὔκ, ἀλλὰ τῆς αὐτῆς.

ΣΩ. Εἰς γυναῖκα δέ, ὦ φίλε, ἄλλην μὲν οἴει τοῦ τοιούτου, ἄλλην δὲ συγκομιδῆς;

ΘΕΑΙ. Οὔκουν εἰκός γε.

150 ΣΩ. Οὐ γάρ. ἀλλὰ διὰ τὴν ἄδικόν τε καὶ ἄτεχνον συναγωγὴν ἀνδρὸς καὶ γυναικός, ᾗ δὴ προαγωγία ὄνομα, φεύγουσι καὶ τὴν προμνηστικὴν ἅτε σεμναὶ οὖσαι αἱ μαῖαι, φοβούμεναι μὴ εἰς ἐκείνην τὴν αἰτίαν διὰ ταύτην ἐμπέσωσιν· ἐπεὶ

---

[1] νέον ὂν of the mss. is impossible; Schanz suggests νόμιμον " lawful," Adam νηδὺν " the womb." Possibly Plato wrote ἀνετέον " permissible."

that midwives should know better than anyone else who are pregnant and who are not?

THEAET. Certainly.

soc. And furthermore, the midwives, by means of drugs and incantations, are able to arouse the pangs of labour and, if they wish, to make them milder, and to cause those to bear who have difficulty in bearing; and they cause miscarriages if they think them desirable.

THEAET. That is true.

soc. Well, have you noticed this also about them, that they are the most skilful of matchmakers, since they are very wise in knowing what union of man and woman will produce the best possible children?

THEAET. I do not know that at all.

soc. But be assured that they are prouder of this than of their skill in cutting the umbilical cord. Just consider. Do you think the knowledge of what soil is best for each plant or seed belongs to the same art as the tending and harvesting of the fruits of the earth, or to another?

THEAET. To the same art.

soc. And in the case of a woman, do you think, my friend, that there is one art for the sowing and another for the harvesting?

THEAET. It is not likely.

soc. No; but because there is a wrongful and un-scientific way of bringing men and women together, which is called pandering, the midwives, since they are women of dignity and worth, avoid match-making, through fear of falling under the charge of pander-

ταῖς γε ὄντως μαίαις μόναις που προσήκει καὶ
προμνήσασθαι ὀρθῶς.

ΘΕΑΙ. Φαίνεται.

ΣΩ. Τὸ μὲν τοίνυν τῶν μαιῶν τοσοῦτον, ἔλαττον
δὲ τοῦ ἐμοῦ δράματος. οὐ γὰρ πρόσεστι γυναιξὶν
B ἐνίοτε μὲν εἴδωλα τίκτειν, ἔστι δ' ὅτε ἀληθινά,
τοῦτο δὲ μὴ ῥᾴδιον εἶναι διαγνῶναι. εἰ γὰρ
προσῆν, μέγιστόν τε καὶ κάλλιστον ἔργον ἦν ἂν
ταῖς μαίαις τὸ κρίνειν τὸ ἀληθές τε καὶ μή· ἢ
οὐκ οἴει;

ΘΕΑΙ. Ἔγωγε.

7. ΣΩ. Τῇ δέ γ' ἐμῇ τέχνῃ τῆς μαιεύσεως
τὰ μὲν ἄλλα ὑπάρχει ὅσα ἐκείναις, διαφέρει δὲ τῷ
τε ἄνδρας ἀλλὰ μὴ γυναῖκας μαιεύεσθαι καὶ τῷ
τὰς ψυχὰς αὐτῶν τικτούσας ἐπισκοπεῖν ἀλλὰ μὴ
τὰ σώματα. μέγιστον δὲ τοῦτ' ἔνι τῇ ἡμετέρᾳ
C τέχνῃ, βασανίζειν δυνατὸν εἶναι παντὶ τρόπῳ,
πότερον εἴδωλον καὶ ψεῦδος ἀποτίκτει τοῦ νέου ἡ
διάνοια ἢ γόνιμόν τε καὶ ἀληθές. ἐπεὶ τόδε γε
καὶ ἐμοὶ ὑπάρχει, ὅπερ ταῖς μαίαις· ἄγονός εἰμι
σοφίας, καὶ ὅπερ ἤδη πολλοί μοι ὠνείδισαν, ὡς
τοὺς μὲν ἄλλους ἐρωτῶ, αὐτὸς δὲ οὐδὲν ἀποκρί-
νομαι περὶ οὐδενὸς διὰ τὸ μηδὲν ἔχειν σοφόν,
ἀληθὲς ὀνειδίζουσιν. τὸ δὲ αἴτιον τούτου τόδε·
μαιεύεσθαί με ὁ θεὸς ἀναγκάζει, γεννᾶν δὲ ἀπεκώ-
λυσεν. εἰμὶ δὴ οὖν αὐτὸς μὲν οὐ πάνυ τις σοφός,
D οὐδέ τί μοι ἔστιν εὕρημα τοιοῦτον γεγονὸς τῆς
ἐμῆς ψυχῆς ἔκγονον· οἱ δ' ἐμοὶ συγγιγνόμενοι τὸ
μὲν πρῶτον φαίνονται ἔνιοι μὲν καὶ πάνυ ἀμαθεῖς,
πάντες δὲ προϊούσης τῆς συνουσίας, οἷσπερ ἂν ὁ
θεὸς παρείκῃ, θαυμαστὸν ὅσον ἐπιδιδόντες, ὡς

ing. And yet the true midwife is the only proper
match-maker.

THEAET. It seems so.

soc. So great, then, is the importance of midwives; but their function is less important than
mine. For women do not, like my patients, bring
forth at one time real children and at another mere
images which it is difficult to distinguish from the
real. For if they did, the greatest and noblest part
of the work of the midwives would be in distinguishing between the real and the false. Do you not
think so?

THEAET. Yes, I do.

soc. All that is true of their art of midwifery is
true also of mine, but mine differs from theirs in
being practised upon men, not women, and in tending
their souls in labour, not their bodies. But the
greatest thing about my art is this, that it can test
in every way whether the mind of the young man
is bringing forth a mere image, an imposture, or a
real and genuine offspring. For I have this in
common with the midwives: I am sterile in point of
wisdom, and the reproach which has often been
brought against me, that I question others but make
no reply myself about anything, because I have no
wisdom in me, is a true reproach; and the reason of
it is this: the god compels me to act as midwife,
but has never allowed me to bring forth. I am,
then, not at all a wise person myself, nor have I any
wise invention, the offspring born of my own soul;
but those who associate with me, although at first
some of them seem very ignorant, yet, as our
acquaintance advances, all of them to whom the
god is gracious make wonderful progress, not only

35

αὐτοῖς τε καὶ τοῖς ἄλλοις δοκοῦσι· καὶ τοῦτο
ἐναργὲς ὅτι παρ' ἐμοῦ οὐδὲν πώποτε μαθόντες,
ἀλλ' αὐτοὶ παρ' αὑτῶν πολλὰ καὶ καλὰ εὑρόντες
τε καὶ τεκόντες.[1] τῆς μέντοι μαιείας ὁ θεός
τε καὶ ἐγὼ αἴτιος. ὧδε δὲ δῆλον· πολλοὶ ἤδη
E τοῦτο ἀγνοήσαντες καὶ ἑαυτοὺς αἰτιασάμενοι, ἐμοῦ
δὲ καταφρονήσαντες, ἢ αὐτοὶ ἢ ὑπ' ἄλλων πεισθέντες ἀπῆλθον πρωαίτερον τοῦ δέοντος, ἀπελθόντες
δὲ τά τε λοιπὰ ἐξήμβλωσαν διὰ πονηρὰν συνουσίαν
καὶ τὰ ὑπ' ἐμοῦ μαιευθέντα κακῶς τρέφοντες
ἀπώλεσαν, ψευδῆ καὶ εἴδωλα περὶ πλείονος ποιησά-
μενοι τοῦ ἀληθοῦς, τελευτῶντες δ' αὑτοῖς τε καὶ
τοῖς ἄλλοις ἔδοξαν ἀμαθεῖς εἶναι. ὧν εἷς γέγονεν
151 Ἀριστείδης ὁ Λυσιμάχου καὶ ἄλλοι πάνυ πολλοί·
οἷς, ὅταν πάλιν ἔλθωσι δεόμενοι τῆς ἐμῆς συνουσίας καὶ θαυμαστὰ δρῶντες, ἐνίοις μὲν τὸ γι-
γνόμενόν μοι δαιμόνιον ἀποκωλύει συνεῖναι, ἐνίοις
δὲ ἐᾷ, καὶ πάλιν οὗτοι[2] ἐπιδιδόασι. πάσχουσι δὲ
δὴ οἱ ἐμοὶ συγγιγνόμενοι καὶ τοῦτο ταὐτὸν ταῖς
τικτούσαις· ὠδίνουσι γὰρ καὶ ἀπορίας ἐμπίμ-
πλανται νύκτας τε καὶ ἡμέρας πολὺ μᾶλλον ἢ
ἐκεῖναι[3]. ταύτην δὲ τὴν ὠδῖνα ἐγείρειν τε καὶ
ἀποπαύειν ἡ ἐμὴ τέχνη δύναται. καὶ οὗτοι μὲν
B δὴ οὕτως. ἐνίοις[4] δέ, ὦ Θεαίτητε, οἳ ἄν μοι μὴ
δόξωσί πως ἐγκύμονες εἶναι, γνοὺς ὅτι οὐδὲν
ἐμοῦ δέονται, πάνυ εὐμενῶς προμνῶμαι καί, σὺν

---

[1] καὶ τεκόντες W, Berol.; κατέχοντες BT.
[2] οὗτοι T; αὐτοὶ B.
[3] ἐκεῖναι B; κεῖναι T.
[4] ἐνίοις Berol., Burnet; ἐνίοτε BT : ἔνιοι W.

in their own opinion, but in that of others as well. And it is clear that they do this, not because they have ever learned anything from me, but because they have found in themselves many fair things and have brought them forth. But the delivery is due to the god and me. And the proof of it is this: many before now, being ignorant of this fact and thinking that they were themselves the cause of their success, but despising me, have gone away from me sooner than they ought, whether of their own accord or because others persuaded them to do so. Then, after they have gone away, they have miscarried thenceforth on account of evil companionship, and the offspring which they had brought forth through my assistance they have reared so badly that they have lost it; they have considered impostures and images of more importance than the truth, and at last it was evident to themselves, as well as to others, that they were ignorant. One of these was Aristeides, the son of Lysimachus, and there are very many more. When such men come back and beg me, as they do, with wonderful eagerness to let them join me again, the spiritual monitor that comes to me forbids me to associate with some of them, but allows me to converse with others, and these again make progress. Now those who associate with me are in this matter also like women in childbirth; they are in pain and are full of trouble night and day, much more than are the women; and my art can arouse this pain and cause it to cease. Well, that is what happens to them. But in some cases, Theaetetus, when they do not seem to me to be exactly pregnant, since I see that they have no need of me, I act with perfect goodwill

θεῷ εἰπεῖν, πάνυ ἱκανῶς τοπάζω οἷς ἂν συγ-
γενόμενοι ὄναιντο· ὧν πολλοὺς μὲν δὴ ἐξέδωκα
Προδίκῳ, πολλοὺς δὲ ἄλλοις σοφοῖς τε καὶ θεσ-
πεσίοις ἀνδράσι.

Ταῦτα δή σοι, ὦ ἄριστε, ἕνεκα τοῦδε ἐμήκυνα,
ὑποπτεύων¹ σε, ὥσπερ καὶ αὐτὸς οἴει, ὠδίνειν τι
κυοῦντα ἔνδον. προσφέρου οὖν πρός με ὡς πρὸς
C μαίας ὑὸν καὶ αὐτὸν μαιευτικόν, καὶ ἃ ἂν ἐρωτῶ
προθυμοῦ ὅπως οἷός τ᾿ εἶ οὕτως ἀποκρίνασθαι·
καὶ ἐὰν ἄρα σκοπούμενός τι ὧν ἂν λέγῃς ἡγήσω-
μαι εἴδωλον καὶ μὴ ἀληθές, εἶτα ὑπεξαιρῶμαι καὶ
ἀποβάλλω,² μὴ ἀγρίαινε ὥσπερ αἱ πρωτότοκοι
περὶ τὰ παιδία. πολλοὶ γὰρ ἤδη, ὦ θαυμάσιε,
πρός με οὕτω διετέθησαν, ὥστε ἀτεχνῶς δάκνειν
ἕτοιμοι εἶναι, ἐπειδάν τινα λῆρον αὐτῶν ἀφ-
αιρῶμαι, καὶ οὐκ οἴονταί με εὐνοίᾳ τοῦτο ποιεῖν,
D πόρρω ὄντες τοῦ εἰδέναι ὅτι οὐδεὶς θεὸς δύσνους
ἀνθρώποις, οὐδ᾿ ἐγὼ δυσνοίᾳ τοιοῦτον οὐδὲν δρῶ,
ἀλλά μοι ψεῦδός τε συγχωρῆσαι καὶ ἀληθὲς
ἀφανίσαι οὐδαμῶς θέμις. πάλιν δὴ οὖν ἐξ ἀρχῆς,
ὦ Θεαίτητε, ὅ τί ποτ᾿ ἐστὶν ἐπιστήμη, πειρῶ
λέγειν· ὡς δ᾿ οὐχ οἷός τ᾿ εἶ, μηδέποτ᾿ εἴπῃς.
ἐὰν γὰρ θεὸς ἐθέλῃ καὶ ἀνδρίζῃ, οἷός τ᾿ ἔσει.

8. ΘΕΑΙ. Ἀλλὰ μέντοι, ὦ Σώκρατες, σοῦ γε
οὕτω παρακελευομένου αἰσχρὸν μὴ οὐ παντὶ
E τρόπῳ προθυμεῖσθαι ὅ τί τις ἔχει λέγειν. δοκεῖ
οὖν μοι ὁ ἐπιστάμενός τι αἰσθάνεσθαι τοῦτο ὃ
ἐπίσταται, καὶ ὥς γε νυνὶ φαίνεται, οὐκ ἄλλο τί
ἐστιν ἐπιστήμη ἢ αἴσθησις.

¹ ὑποπτεύων Β; ὑποπτεύω al.
² ἀποβάλλω Τ; ὑποβάλω Β; ἀποβάλω W.

as match-maker and, under God, I guess very successfully with whom they can associate profitably, and I
have handed over many of them to Prodicus, and
many to other wise and inspired men.

Now I have said all this to you at such length, my
dear boy, because I suspect that you, as you yourself believe, are in pain because you are pregnant
with something within you. Apply, then, to me,
remembering that I am the son of a midwife and
have myself a midwife's gifts, and do your best to
answer the questions I ask as I ask them. And if,
when I have examined any of the things you say, it
should prove that I think it is a mere image and
not real, and therefore quietly take it from you and
throw it away, do not be angry as women are when
they are deprived of their first offspring. For many,
my dear friend, before this have got into such a state
of mind towards me that they are actually ready to
bite me, if I take some foolish notion away from
them, and they do not believe that I do this in
kindness, since they are far from knowing that no
god is unkind to mortals, and that I do nothing of
this sort from unkindness, either, and that it is quite
out of the question for me to allow an imposture or
to destroy the true. And so, Theaetetus, begin
again and try to tell us what knowledge is. And
never say that you are unable to do so; for if God
wills it and gives you courage, you will be able.

THEAET. Well then, Socrates, since you are so
urgent it would be disgraceful for anyone not to
exert himself in every way to say what he can. I
think, then, that he who knows anything perceives
that which he knows, and, as it appears at present,
knowledge is nothing else than perception.

ΣΩ. Εὖ γε καὶ γενναίως, ὦ παῖ· χρὴ γὰρ οὕτως ἀποφαινόμενον λέγειν. ἀλλὰ φέρε δὴ αὐτὸ κοινῇ σκεψώμεθα, γόνιμον ἢ ἀνεμιαῖον τυγχάνει ὄν. αἴσθησις, φής, ἐπιστήμη;

ΘΕΑΙ. Ναί.

ΣΩ. Κινδυνεύεις μέντοι λόγον οὐ φαῦλον εἰρη-
152 κέναι περὶ ἐπιστήμης, ἀλλ' ὃν ἔλεγε καὶ Πρωτ-
αγόρας. τρόπον δέ τινα ἄλλον εἴρηκε τὰ αὐτὰ ταῦτα. φησὶ γάρ που πάντων χρημάτων μέτρον ἄνθρωπον εἶναι, τῶν μὲν ὄντων, ὡς ἔστι, τῶν δὲ μὴ ὄντων, ὡς οὐκ ἔστιν. ἀνέγνωκας γάρ που;

ΘΕΑΙ. ᾿Ανέγνωκα καὶ πολλάκις.

ΣΩ. Οὐκοῦν οὕτω πως λέγει, ὡς οἷα μὲν ἕκα-
στα ἐμοὶ φαίνεται, τοιαῦτα μὲν ἔστιν ἐμοί, οἷα δὲ σοί, τοιαῦτα δὲ αὖ σοί· ἄνθρωπος δὲ σύ τε κἀγώ;

ΘΕΑΙ. Λέγει γὰρ οὖν οὕτω.

B ΣΩ. Εἰκὸς μέντοι σοφὸν ἄνδρα μὴ ληρεῖν· ἐπ-
ακολουθήσωμεν οὖν αὐτῷ. ἆρ' οὐκ ἐνίοτε πνέον-
τος ἀνέμου τοῦ αὐτοῦ ὁ μὲν ἡμῶν ῥιγοῖ, ὁ δ' οὔ; καὶ ὁ μὲν ἠρέμα, ὁ δὲ σφόδρα;

ΘΕΑΙ. Καὶ μάλα.

ΣΩ. Πότερον οὖν τότε αὐτὸ ἐφ' ἑαυτοῦ[1] τὸ πνεῦμα ψυχρὸν ἢ οὐ ψυχρὸν φήσομεν; ἢ πεισόμεθα τῷ Πρωταγόρᾳ ὅτι τῷ μὲν ῥιγοῦντι ψυχρόν, τῷ δὲ μὴ οὔ;

ΘΕΑΙ. ᾿Έοικεν.

ΣΩ. Οὐκοῦν καὶ φαίνεται οὕτω ἑκατέρῳ;

ΘΕΑΙ. Ναί.

[1] ἑαυτοῦ W, Berol. ; ἑαυτὸ ΒΤ.

soc. Good! Excellent, my boy! That is the way one ought to speak out. But come now, let us examine your utterance together, and see whether it is a real offspring or a mere wind-egg. Perception, you say, is knowledge?

THEAET. Yes.

soc. And, indeed, if I may venture to say so, it is not a bad description of knowledge that you have given, but one which Protagoras also used to give. Only, he has said the same thing in a different way For he says somewhere that man is "the measure of all things, of the existence of the things that are and the non-existence of the things that are not." You have read that, I suppose?

THEAET. Yes, I have read it often.

soc. Well, is not this about what he means, that individual things are for me such as they appear to me, and for you in turn such as they appear to you —you and I being "man"?

THEAET. Yes, that is what he says.

soc. It is likely that a wise man is not talking nonsense; so let us follow after him. Is it not true that sometimes, when the same wind blows, one of us feels cold, and the other does not? or one feels slightly and the other exceedingly cold?

THEAET. Certainly.

soc. Then in that case, shall we say that the wind is in itself cold or not cold; or shall we accept Protagoras's saying that it is cold for him who feels cold and not for him who does not?

THEAET. Apparently we shall accept that.

soc. Then it also seems cold, or not, to each of the two?

THEAET. Yes.

ΣΩ. Τὸ δέ γε φαίνεται αἰσθάνεσθαί ἐστιν;

ΘΕΑΙ. Ἔστιν γάρ.

C ΣΩ. Φαντασία ἄρα καὶ αἴσθησις ταὐτὸν ἔν τε θερμοῖς καὶ πᾶσι τοῖς τοιούτοις. οἷα γὰρ αἰσθάνεται ἕκαστος, τοιαῦτα ἑκάστῳ καὶ κινδυνεύει εἶναι.

ΘΕΑΙ. Ἔοικεν.

ΣΩ. Αἴσθησις ἄρα τοῦ ὄντος ἀεί ἐστιν καὶ ἀψευδὲς ὡς ἐπιστήμη οὖσα.

ΘΕΑΙ. Φαίνεται.

ΣΩ. Ἆρ' οὖν πρὸς Χαρίτων πάσσοφός τις ἦν ὁ Πρωταγόρας, καὶ τοῦτο ἡμῖν μὲν ᾐνίξατο τῷ πολλῷ συρφετῷ, τοῖς δὲ μαθηταῖς ἐν ἀπορρήτῳ τὴν ἀλήθειαν ἔλεγεν;

D ΘΕΑΙ. Πῶς δή, ὦ Σώκρατες, τοῦτο λέγεις;

ΣΩ. Ἐγὼ ἐρῶ καὶ μάλ' οὐ φαῦλον λόγον, ὡς ἄρα ἓν μὲν αὐτὸ καθ' αὑτὸ οὐδέν ἐστιν, οὐδ' ἄν τι προσείποις ὀρθῶς οὐδ' ὁποιονοῦν τι, ἀλλ', ἐὰν ὡς μέγα προσαγορεύῃς, καὶ σμικρὸν φανεῖται, καὶ ἐὰν βαρύ, κοῦφον, ξύμπαντά τε οὕτως, ὡς μηδενὸς ὄντος ἑνὸς μήτε τινὸς μήτε ὁποιουοῦν· ἐκ δὲ δὴ φορᾶς τε καὶ κινήσεως καὶ κράσεως πρὸς ἄλληλα γίγνεται πάντα ἃ δή φαμεν εἶναι, οὐκ ὀρθῶς προσαγορεύοντες· ἔστι μὲν γὰρ οὐδέποτ' οὐδέν, ἀεὶ E δὲ γίγνεται. καὶ περὶ τούτου πάντες ἑξῆς οἱ σοφοὶ πλὴν Παρμενίδου συμφερέσθων,[1] Πρωταγόρας τε καὶ Ἡράκλειτος καὶ Ἐμπεδοκλῆς, καὶ τῶν ποιητῶν οἱ ἄκροι τῆς ποιήσεως ἑκατέρας, κωμῳδίας μὲν Ἐπίχαρμος, τραγῳδίας δὲ Ὅμηρος, ὃς [2] εἰπὼν

Ὠκεανόν τε θεῶν γένεσιν καὶ μητέρα Τηθύν

[1] συμφερέσθων B (ut videtur), Burnet; συμφέρεσθον TW, Berol., Eus.; συμφέροντα Stobaeus.
[2] ὃς add. Heindorf.

soc. But "seems" denotes perceiving?

THEAET. It does.

soc. Then seeming and perception are the same thing in matters of warmth and everything of that sort. For as each person perceives things, such they are to each person.

THEAET. Apparently.

soc. Perception, then, is always of that which exists and, since it is knowledge, cannot be false.

THEAET. So it seems.

soc. By the Graces! I wonder if Protagoras, who was a very wise man, did not utter this dark saying to the common herd like ourselves, and tell the truth [1] in secret to his pupils.

THEAET. Why, Socrates, what do you mean by that?

soc. I will tell you and it is not a bad description, either, that nothing is one and invariable, and you could not rightly ascribe any quality whatsoever to anything, but if you call it large it will also appear to be small, and light if you call it heavy, and everything else in the same way, since nothing whatever is one, either a particular thing or of a particular quality; but it is out of movement and motion and mixture with one another that all those things become which we wrongly say "are"—wrongly, because nothing ever is, but is always becoming. And on this subject all the philosophers, except Parmenides, may be marshalled in one line—Protagoras and Heracleitus and Empedocles—and the chief poets in the two kinds of poetry, Epicharmus, in comedy, and in tragedy, Homer, who, in the line

Oceanus the origin of the gods, and Tethys their mother [2]

---

[1] An allusion to the title of Protagoras's book, *Truth.*
[2] Homer, *Iliad*, xiv. 201, 302.

πάντα εἴρηκεν ἔκγονα ῥοῆς τε καὶ κινήσεως· ἢ
οὐ δοκεῖ τοῦτο λέγειν;

ΘΕΑΙ. Ἔμοιγε.

9. ΣΩ. Τίς οὖν ἂν ἔτι πρός γε τοσοῦτον
153 στρατόπεδον καὶ στρατηγὸν Ὅμηρον δύναιτο
ἀμφισβητήσας μὴ οὐ [1] καταγέλαστος γενέσθαι;

ΘΕΑΙ. Οὐ ῥᾴδιον, ὦ Σώκρατες.

ΣΩ. Οὐ γάρ, ὦ Θεαίτητε. ἐπεὶ καὶ τάδε τῷ
λόγῳ σημεῖα ἱκανά, ὅτι τὸ μὲν εἶναι δοκοῦν καὶ τὸ
γίγνεσθαι κίνησις παρέχει, τὸ δὲ μὴ εἶναι καὶ
ἀπόλλυσθαι ἡσυχία· τὸ γὰρ θερμόν τε καὶ πῦρ,
ὃ δὴ καὶ τἆλλα γεννᾷ καὶ ἐπιτροπεύει, αὐτὸ γεννᾶ-
ται ἐκ φορᾶς καὶ τρίψεως· τούτω [2] δὲ κινήσει.
ἢ οὐχ αὗται γενέσεις πυρός;

B   ΘΕΑΙ. Αὗται μὲν οὖν.

ΣΩ. Καὶ μὴν τό γε τῶν ζῴων γένος ἐκ τῶν
αὐτῶν τούτων φύεται.

ΘΕΑΙ. Πῶς δ᾽ οὔ;

ΣΩ. Τί δέ; ἡ τῶν σωμάτων ἕξις οὐχ ὑπὸ ἡσυχίας μὲν καὶ ἀργίας διόλλυται, ὑπὸ γυμνασίων δὲ
καὶ κινήσεων ἐπὶ τὸ πολὺ [3] σῴζεται;

ΘΕΑΙ. Ναί.

ΣΩ. Ἡ δ᾽ ἐν τῇ ψυχῇ ἕξις οὐχ ὑπὸ μαθήσεως
μὲν καὶ μελέτης, κινήσεων ὄντων, [4] κτᾶταί τε
μαθήματα καὶ σῴζεται καὶ γίγνεται βελτίων, ὑπὸ
δ᾽ ἡσυχίας, ἀμελετησίας τε καὶ ἀμαθίας οὔσης,
C οὔτε τι μανθάνει ἅ τε ἂν μάθῃ ἐπιλανθάνεται;

---

[1] μὴ οὐ W, Eus., Stobaeus; μὴ BT.
[2] τούτω B²W, Berol.; τοῦτο BT, Stobaeus.
[3] ἐπὶ τὸ πολὺ B, Stobaeus; ὡς ἐπὶ πολὺ T (ὡς above the
line); ἐπὶ πολὺ Burnet.
[4] κινήσεων οὐσῶν Stobaeus; κινησίοιν ὄντοιν Buttmann.

has said that all things are the offspring of flow and motion; or don't you think he means that?

THEAET. I think he does.

soc. Then who could still contend with such a great host, led by Homer as general, and not make himself ridiculous?

THEAET. It is not easy, Socrates.

soc. No, Theaetetus, it is not. For the doctrine is amply proved by this, namely, that motion is the cause of that which passes for existence, that is, of becoming, whereas rest is the cause of non-existence and destruction; for warmth or fire, which, you know, is the parent and preserver of all other things, is itself the offspring of movement and friction, and these two are forms of motion. Or are not these the source of fire?

THEAET. Yes, they are.

soc. And furthermore, the animal kingdom is sprung from these same sources.

THEAET. Of course.

soc. Well, then, is not the bodily habit destroyed by rest and idleness, and preserved, generally speaking, by gymnastic exercises and motions?

THEAET. Yes.

soc. And what of the habit of the soul? Does not the soul acquire information and is it not preserved and made better through learning and practice, which are motions, whereas through rest, which is want of practice and of study, it learns nothing and forgets what it has learned?

ΘΕΑΙ. Καὶ μάλα.

ΣΩ. Τὸ μὲν ἄρα ἀγαθὸν κίνησις κατά τε ψυχὴν καὶ κατὰ σῶμα, τὸ δὲ τοὐναντίον;

ΘΕΑΙ. Ἔοικεν.

ΣΩ. Ἔτι οὖν σοι λέγω νηνεμίας τε καὶ γαλήνας καὶ ὅσα τοιαῦτα, ὅτι αἱ μὲν ἡσυχίαι σήπουσι καὶ ἀπολλύασι, τὰ δ' ἕτερα σῴζει; καὶ ἐπὶ τούτοις τὸν κολοφῶνα ἀναγκάζω προσβιβάζων,[1] τὴν χρυσῆν σειρὰν ὡς οὐδὲν ἄλλο ἢ τὸν ἥλιον Ὅμηρος λέγει,
D καὶ δηλοῖ ὅτι ἕως μὲν ἂν ἡ περιφορὰ ᾖ κινουμένη καὶ ὁ ἥλιος, πάντα ἔστι καὶ σῴζεται τὰ ἐν θεοῖς τε καὶ ἀνθρώποις, εἰ δὲ σταίη τοῦτο ὥσπερ δεθέν, πάντα χρήματ' ἂν διαφθαρείη καὶ γένοιτ' ἂν τὸ λεγόμενον ἄνω κάτω πάντα;

ΘΕΑΙ. Ἀλλ' ἔμοιγε δοκεῖ, ὦ Σώκρατες, ταῦτα δηλοῦν, ἅπερ λέγεις.

10. ΣΩ. Ὑπόλαβε τοίνυν, ὦ ἄριστε, οὑτωσί· κατὰ τὰ ὄμματα πρῶτον, ὃ δὴ καλεῖς χρῶμα λευκόν, μὴ εἶναι αὐτὸ ἕτερόν τι ἔξω τῶν σῶν ὀμμάτων μηδ' ἐν τοῖς ὄμμασι· μηδέ τιν' αὐτῷ
E χώραν ἀποτάξῃς· ἤδη γὰρ ἂν εἴη τε δήπου[2] ἐν τάξει καὶ μένον[3] καὶ οὐκ ἂν ἐν γενέσει γίγνοιτο.

ΘΕΑΙ. Ἀλλὰ πῶς;

[1] ἀναγκάζω προσβιβάζων TW, Berol.; ἀναγκάζω προβιβάζων B, Stobaeus; προσβιβάζω (omitting ἀναγκάζω) Cobet, followed by Burnet. Possibly ἀναγράφω προσβιβάζων.
[2] δήπου Schanz; ἄν που BT.
[3] καὶ μένον Stobaeus; κείμενοι pr. B (corr. καὶ μένοι); κείμενον T.

THEAET. Certainly.

soc. Then the good, both for the soul and for the body, is motion, and rest is the opposite?

THEAET. Apparently.

soc. Now shall I go on and mention to you also windless air, calm sea, and all that sort of thing, and say that stillness causes decay and destruction and that the opposite brings preservation? And shall I add to this the all-compelling and crowning argument that Homer by "the golden chain"[1] refers to nothing else than the sun, and means that so long as the heavens and the sun go round everything exists and is preserved, among both gods and men, but if the motion should stop, as if bound fast, everything would be destroyed and would, as the saying is, be turned upside down?

THEAET. Yes, Socrates, I think he means what you say he does.

soc. Then, my friend, you must apply the doctrine in this way: first as concerns vision, the colour that you call white is not to be taken as something separate outside of your eyes, nor yet as something inside of them; and you must not assign any place to it, for then it would at once be in a definite position and stationary and would have no part in the process of becoming.

THEAET. But what do you mean?

[1] Homer, *Iliad*, viii. 18 ff., especially 26. In this passage Zeus declares that all the gods and goddesses together could not, with a golden chain, drag him from on high, but that if he pulled, he would drag them, with earth and sea, would then bind the chain round the summit of Olympus, and all the rest would hang aloft. This "crowning argument" is a *reductio ad absurdum* of the habit of using texts from Homer in support of all kinds of doctrine.

47

ΣΩ. Ἑπώμεθα τῷ ἄρτι λόγῳ, μηδὲν αὐτὸ καθ᾿ αὑτὸ ἓν ὂν τιθέντες· καὶ ἡμῖν οὕτω μέλαν τε καὶ λευκὸν καὶ ὁτιοῦν ἄλλο χρῶμα ἐκ τῆς προσβολῆς τῶν ὀμμάτων πρὸς τὴν προσήκουσαν φορὰν φανεῖται γεγενημένον, καὶ ὃ δὴ ἕκαστον εἶναί φαμεν χρῶμα, οὔτε τὸ προσβάλλον οὔτε τὸ προσβαλλόμενον ἔσται, ἀλλὰ μεταξύ τι ἑκάστῳ ἴδιον γεγονός· ἢ σὺ διισχυρίσαιο ἂν ὡς, οἷον σοὶ φαίνεται ἕκαστον χρῶμα, τοιοῦτον καὶ κυνὶ καὶ ὁτῳοῦν ζῴῳ;

ΘΕΑΙ. Μὰ Δί᾿ οὐκ ἔγωγε.

ΣΩ. Τί δέ; ἄλλῳ ἀνθρώπῳ ἆρ᾿ ὅμοιον καὶ σοὶ φαίνεται ὁτιοῦν; ἔχεις τοῦτο ἰσχυρῶς, ἢ πολὺ μᾶλλον, ὅτι οὐδὲ σοὶ αὐτῷ ταὐτὸν διὰ τὸ μηδέποτε ὁμοίως αὐτὸν σεαυτῷ ἔχειν;

ΘΕΑΙ. Τοῦτο μᾶλλόν μοι δοκεῖ ἢ ἐκεῖνο.

ΣΩ. Οὐκοῦν εἰ μὲν ᾧ[1] παραμετρούμεθα ἢ οὗ ἐφαπτόμεθα, μέγα ἢ λευκὸν ἢ θερμὸν ἦν, οὐκ ἄν ποτε ἄλλῳ προσπεσὸν ἄλλο ἂν ἐγεγόνει, αὐτό γε μηδὲν μεταβάλλον· εἰ δὲ αὖ τὸ παραμετρούμενον ἢ ἐφαπτόμενον ἕκαστον ἦν τούτων, οὐκ ἂν αὖ ἄλλου προσελθόντος ἤ τι παθόντος αὐτὸ μηδὲν παθὸν ἄλλο ἂν ἐγένετο. ἐπεὶ νῦν γε, ὦ φίλε, θαυμαστά τε καὶ γελοῖα εὐχερῶς πως ἀναγκαζόμεθα λέγειν, ὡς φαίη ἂν Πρωταγόρας τε καὶ πᾶς ὁ τὰ αὐτὰ ἐκείνῳ ἐπιχειρῶν λέγειν.

---

[1] ᾧ mss. ; ὃ Cornarius.

soc. Let us stick close to the statement we made a moment ago, and assume that nothing exists by itself as invariably one: then it will be apparent that black or white or any other colour whatsoever is the result of the impact of the eye upon the appropriate motion, and therefore that which we call colour will be in each instance neither that which impinges nor that which is impinged upon, but something between, which has occurred, peculiar to each individual. Or would you maintain that each colour appears to a dog, or any other animal you please, just as it does to you?

THEAET. No, by Zeus, I wouldn't.

soc. Well, does anything whatsoever appear the same to any other man as to you? Are you sure of this? Or are you not much more convinced that nothing appears the same even to you, because you yourself are never exactly the same?

THEAET. Yes, I am much more convinced of the last.

soc. Then, if that with which I compare myself in size, or which I touch, were really large or white or hot, it would never have become different by coming in contact with something different, without itself changing; and if, on the other hand, that which did the comparing or the touching were really large or white or hot, it would not have become different when something different approached it or was affected in some way by it, without being affected in some way itself. For nowadays, my friend, we find ourselves rather easily forced to make extraordinary and absurd statements, as Protagoras and everyone who undertakes to agree with him would say.

ΘΕΑΙ. Πῶς δὴ καὶ ποῖα λέγεις;

C ΣΩ. Σμικρὸν λαβὲ παράδειγμα, καὶ πάντα εἴσει ἃ βούλομαι. ἀστραγάλους γάρ που ἕξ, ἂν μὲν τέτταρας αὐτοῖς προσενέγκῃς, πλείους φαμὲν εἶναι τῶν τεττάρων καὶ ἡμιολίους, ἐὰν δὲ δώδεκα, ἐλάττους καὶ ἡμίσεις· καὶ οὐδὲ ἀνεκτὸν ἄλλως λέγειν· ἢ σὺ ἀνέξει;

ΘΕΑΙ. Οὐκ ἔγωγε.

ΣΩ. Τί οὖν; ἄν σε Πρωταγόρας ἔρηται ἤ τις ἄλλος· ὦ Θεαίτητε, ἔσθ᾽ ὅπως τι μεῖζον ἢ πλέον γίγνεται ἄλλως ἢ αὐξηθέν; τί ἀποκρινεῖ;

ΘΕΑΙ. Ἐὰν μέν, ὦ Σώκρατες, τὸ δοκοῦν πρὸς D τὴν νῦν ἐρώτησιν ἀποκρίνωμαι, ὅτι οὐκ ἔστιν. ἐὰν δὲ πρὸς τὴν προτέραν, φυλάττων μὴ ἐναντία εἴπω, ὅτι ἔστιν.

ΣΩ. Εὖ γε νὴ τὴν Ἥραν, ὦ φίλε, καὶ θείως. ἀτάρ, ὡς ἔοικεν, ἐὰν ἀποκρίνῃ ὅτι ἔστιν, Εὐριπί-δειόν τι ξυμβήσεται· ἡ μὲν γὰρ γλῶττα ἀνέλεγκτος ἡμῖν ἔσται, ἡ δὲ φρὴν οὐκ ἀνέλεγκτος.

ΘΕΑΙ. Ἀληθῆ.

ΣΩ. Οὐκοῦν εἰ μὲν δεινοὶ καὶ σοφοὶ ἐγώ τε καὶ σὺ ἦμεν, πάντα τὰ τῶν φρενῶν ἐξητακότες, ἤδη ἂν τὸ λοιπὸν ἐκ περιουσίας ἀλλήλων ἀποπειρώμενοι, E συνελθόντες σοφιστικῶς εἰς μάχην τοιαύτην, ἀλλή-λων τοὺς λόγους τοῖς λόγοις ἐκρούομεν· νῦν δὲ ἅτε ἰδιῶται πρῶτον βουλησόμεθα θεάσασθαι αὐτὰ πρὸς αὑτά, τί ποτ᾽ ἐστὶν ἃ διανοούμεθα, πότερον ἡμῖν ἀλλήλοις ξυμφωνεῖ ἢ οὐδ᾽ ὁπωστιοῦν.

THEAETETUS

THEAET. What do you mean? What statements?

soc. Take a little example and you will know all I have in mind. Given six dice, for instance, if you compare four with them, we say that they are more than the four, half as many again, but if you compare twelve with them, we say they are less, half as many; and any other statement would be inadmissible; or would you admit any other?

THEAET. Not I.

soc. Well then, if Protagoras, or anyone else, ask you, "Theaetetus, can anything become greater or more in any other way than by being increased?" what reply will you make?

THEAET. If I am to say what I think, Socrates, with reference to the present question, I should say "no," but if I consider the earlier question, I should say "yes," for fear of contradicting myself.

soc. Good, by Hera! Excellent, my friend! But apparently, if you answer "yes" it will be in the Euripidean spirit; for our tongue will be unconvinced, but not our mind.[1]

THEAET. True.

soc. Well, if you and I were clever and wise and had found out everything about the mind, we should henceforth spend the rest of our time testing each other out of the fulness of our wisdom, rushing together like sophists in a sophistical combat, battering each other's arguments with counter arguments. But, as it is, since we are ordinary people, we shall wish in the first place to look into the real essence of our thoughts and see whether they harmonize with one another or not at all.

[1] Eurip. *Hippol.* 612, ἡ γλῶσσ' ὀμώμοχ', ἡ δὲ φρὴν ἀνώμοτος, "my tongue has sworn, but my mind is unsworn."

ΘΕΑΙ. Πάνυ μὲν οὖν ἔγωγε τοῦτ᾽ ἂν βουλοίμην.

II. ΣΩ. Καὶ μὴν ἐγώ. ὅτε δ᾽ οὕτως ἔχει, ἄλλο τι ἢ ἠρέμα, ὡς πάνυ πολλὴν σχολὴν ἄγοντες, 155 πάλιν ἐπανασκεψόμεθα, οὐ δυσκολαίνοντες, ἀλλὰ τῷ ὄντι ἡμᾶς αὐτοὺς ἐξετάζοντες, ἄττα ποτ᾽ ἐστὶ ταῦτα τὰ φάσματα ἐν ἡμῖν; ὧν πρῶτον ἐπισκοποῦντες φήσομεν, ὡς ἐγὼ οἶμαι, μηδέποτε μηδὲν ἂν μεῖζον μηδὲ ἔλαττον γενέσθαι μήτε ὄγκῳ μήτε ἀριθμῷ, ἕως ἴσον εἴη αὐτὸ ἑαυτῷ. οὐχ οὕτως;

ΘΕΑΙ. Ναί.

ΣΩ. Δεύτερον δέ γε, ᾧ μήτε προστιθοῖτο μήτε ἀφαιροῖτο, τοῦτο μήτε αὐξάνεσθαί ποτε μήτε φθίνειν, ἀεὶ δὲ ἴσον εἶναι.

ΘΕΑΙ. Κομιδῇ μὲν οὖν.

B ΣΩ. Ἆρ᾽ οὖν οὐ καὶ τρίτον, ὃ μὴ πρότερον ἦν, ὕστερον ἀλλὰ [1] τοῦτο εἶναι ἄνευ τοῦ γενέσθαι καὶ γίγνεσθαι ἀδύνατον;

ΘΕΑΙ. Δοκεῖ γε δή.

ΣΩ. Ταῦτα δή, οἶμαι, ὁμολογήματα τρία μάχεται αὐτὰ αὑτοῖς ἐν τῇ ἡμετέρᾳ ψυχῇ, ὅταν τὰ περὶ τῶν ἀστραγάλων λέγωμεν, ἢ ὅταν φῶμεν ἐμὲ τηλικόνδε ὄντα, μήτε αὐξηθέντα μήτε τοὐναντίον παθόντα, ἐν ἐνιαυτῷ σοῦ τοῦ νέου νῦν μὲν μείζω εἶναι, ὕστερον δὲ ἐλάττω, μηδὲν τοῦ ἐμοῦ ὄγκου ἀφαιρεθέντος C ἀλλὰ σοῦ αὐξηθέντος. εἰμὶ γὰρ δὴ ὕστερον ὃ πρότερον οὐκ ἦ, οὐ γενόμενος· ἄνευ γὰρ τοῦ γίγνεσθαι γενέσθαι ἀδύνατον, μηδὲν δὲ ἀπολλὺς τοῦ ὄγκου οὐκ ἄν ποτε ἐγιγνόμην ἐλάττων. καὶ ἄλλα δὴ μυρία ἐπὶ μυρίοις οὕτως ἔχει, εἴπερ καὶ ταῦτα

---

[1] ὕστερον ἀλλὰ BT (schol. ὁ Πρόκλος τὸ ἀλλὰ παρέλκειν λέγει, i.e. ἀλλά is transposed to the second place); ἀλλὰ ὕστερον Stephanus et al.

THEAET. Certainly that is what I should like.

SOC. And so should I. But since this is the case, and we have plenty of time, shall we not quietly, without any impatience, but truly examining ourselves, consider again the nature of these appearances within us? And as we consider them, I shall say, I think, first, that nothing can ever become more or less in size or number, so long as it remains equal to itself. Is it not so?

THEAET. Yes.

SOC. And secondly, that anything to which nothing is added and from which nothing is subtracted, is neither increased nor diminished, but is always equal.

THEAET. Certainly.

SOC. And should we not say thirdly, that what was not previously could not afterwards be without becoming and having become?

THEAET. Yes, I agree.

SOC. These three assumptions contend with one another in our minds when we talk about the dice, or when we say that I, who do not, at my age, either increase in size or diminish, am in the course of a year first larger than you, who are young, and afterwards smaller, when nothing has been taken from my size, but you have grown. For I am, it seems, afterwards what I was not before, and I have not become so; for it is impossible to have become without becoming, and without losing anything of my size I could not become smaller. And there are countless myriads of such contradictions, if we are to accept these that I have mentioned. You follow

παραδεξόμεθα. ἔπει[1] γάρ που, ὦ Θεαίτητε·
δοκεῖς γοῦν μοι οὐκ ἄπειρος τῶν τοιούτων εἶναι.

ΘΕΑΙ. Καὶ νὴ τοὺς θεούς γε, ὦ Σώκρατες, ὑπερφυῶς ὡς θαυμάζω τί ποτ' ἐστὶ ταῦτα, καὶ ἐνίοτε
ὡς ἀληθῶς βλέπων εἰς αὐτὰ σκοτοδινιῶ.

D ΣΩ. Θεόδωρος γάρ, ὦ φίλε, φαίνεται οὐ κακῶς
τοπάζειν περὶ τῆς φύσεώς σου. μάλα γὰρ φιλο-
σόφου τοῦτο τὸ πάθος, τὸ θαυμάζειν· οὐ γὰρ
ἄλλη ἀρχὴ φιλοσοφίας ἢ αὕτη, καὶ ἔοικεν ὁ τὴν
Ἶριν Θαύμαντος ἔκγονον φήσας οὐ κακῶς γενεα-
λογεῖν. ἀλλὰ πότερον μανθάνεις ἤδη δι' ὃ ταῦτα
τοιαῦτ' ἐστὶν ἐξ ὧν τὸν Πρωταγόραν φαμὲν
λέγειν, ἢ οὔπω;

ΘΕΑΙ. Οὔπω μοι δοκῶ.

ΣΩ. Χάριν οὖν μοι εἴσει, ἐάν σοι ἀνδρός, μᾶλ-
E λον δὲ ἀνδρῶν ὀνομαστῶν τῆς διανοίας τὴν ἀλήθειαν
ἀποκεκρυμμένην συνεξερευνήσωμαι αὐτῶν;

ΘΕΑΙ. Πῶς γὰρ οὐκ εἴσομαι, καὶ πάνυ γε πολλήν;

12. ΣΩ. Ἄθρει δὴ περισκοπῶν μή τις τῶν
ἀμυήτων ἐπακούῃ. εἰσὶν δὲ οὗτοι οἱ οὐδὲν ἄλλο
οἰόμενοι εἶναι ἢ οὗ ἂν δύνωνται ἀπρὶξ τοῖν χεροῖν
λαβέσθαι, πράξεις δὲ καὶ γενέσεις καὶ πᾶν τὸ ἀόρα-
τον οὐκ ἀποδεχόμενοι ὡς ἐν οὐσίας μέρει.

ΘΕΑΙ. Καὶ μὲν δή, ὦ Σώκρατες, σκληρούς γε
156 λέγεις καὶ ἀντιτύπους ἀνθρώπους.

ΣΩ. Εἰσὶν γάρ, ὦ παῖ, μάλ' εὖ ἄμουσοι· ἄλλοι
δὲ πολὺ κομψότεροι, ὧν μέλλω σοι τὰ μυστήρια
λέγειν. ἀρχὴ δέ, ἐξ ἧς[2] καὶ ἃ νῦν δὴ ἐλέγομεν
πάντα ἤρτηται, ἥδε αὐτῶν, ὡς τὸ πᾶν κίνησις ἦν
καὶ ἄλλο παρὰ τοῦτο οὐδέν, τῆς δὲ κινήσεως δύο

---

[1] ἔπει Heindorf; εἰπὲ BT.
[2] ἐξ ἧς W²b; ἐξῆς BTW.

me, I take it, Theaetetus, for I think you are not
new at such things.

THEAET. By the gods, Socrates, I am lost in wonder
when I think of all these things, and sometimes
when I regard them it really makes my head swim.

soc. Theodorus seems to be a pretty good guesser
about your nature. For this feeling of wonder
shows that you are a philosopher, since wonder is
the only beginning of philosophy, and he who said
that Iris was the child of Thaumas[1] made a good
genealogy. But do you begin to understand why
these things are so, according to the doctrine we
attribute to Protagoras, or do you not as yet?

THEAET. Not yet, I think.

soc. And will you be grateful to me if I help you
to search out the hidden truth of the thought of a
famous man or, I should say, of famous men?

THEAET. Of course I shall be grateful, very
grateful.

soc. Look round and see that none of the uninitiated is listening. The uninitiated are those
who think nothing is except what they can grasp
firmly with their hands, and who deny the existence
of actions and generation and all that is invisible.

THEAET. Truly, Socrates, those you speak of are
very stubborn and perverse mortals.

soc. So they are, my boy, quite without culture.
But others are more clever, whose secret doctrines I
am going to disclose to you. For them the beginning,
upon which all the things we were just now speaking of depend, is the assumption that everything
is really motion and that there is nothing besides this,

---

[1] Hes. *Theog.* 780. Iris is the messenger of heaven, and
Plato interprets the name of her father as "Wonder" ($\theta\alpha\hat{u}\mu\alpha$).

εἴδη, πλήθει μὲν ἄπειρον ἑκάτερον, δύναμιν δὲ τὸ
μὲν ποιεῖν ἔχον, τὸ δὲ πάσχειν. ἐκ δὲ τῆς τούτων
ὁμιλίας τε καὶ τρίψεως πρὸς ἄλληλα γίγνεται
ἔκγονα πλήθει μὲν ἄπειρα, δίδυμα δέ, τὸ μὲν
B αἰσθητόν, τὸ δὲ αἴσθησις, ἀεὶ συνεκπίπτουσα καὶ
γεννωμένη μετὰ τοῦ αἰσθητοῦ. αἱ μὲν οὖν αἰσθήσεις τὰ τοιάδε ἡμῖν ἔχουσιν ὀνόματα, ὄψεις τε καὶ
ἀκοαὶ καὶ ὀσφρήσεις καὶ ψύξεις τε καὶ καύσεις
καὶ ἡδοναί γε δὴ καὶ λῦπαι καὶ ἐπιθυμίαι καὶ φόβοι
κεκλημέναι καὶ ἄλλαι, ἀπέραντοι μὲν αἱ ἀνώνυμοι,
παμπληθεῖς δὲ αἱ ὠνομασμέναι· τὸ δ᾽ αὖ αἰσθητὸν
γένος τούτων ἑκάσταις ὁμόγονον, ὄψεσι μὲν χρώματα παντοδαπαῖς παντοδαπά, ἀκοαῖς δὲ ὡσαύτως
C φωναί, καὶ ταῖς ἄλλαις αἰσθήσεσι τὰ ἄλλα αἰσθητὰ
ξυγγενῆ γιγνόμενα. τί δὴ οὖν ἡμῖν βούλεται
οὗτος ὁ μῦθος, ὦ Θεαίτητε, πρὸς τὰ πρότερα; ἆρα
ἐννοεῖς;

ΘΕΑΙ. Οὐ πάνυ, ὦ Σώκρατες.

ΣΩ. ᾿Αλλ᾽ ἄθρει, ἐάν πως ἀποτελεσθῇ. βούλεται
γὰρ δὴ λέγειν ὡς ταῦτα πάντα μέν, ὥσπερ λέγομεν,
κινεῖται, τάχος δὲ καὶ βραδυτὴς ἔνι τῇ κινήσει
αὐτῶν. ὅσον μὲν οὖν βραδύ, ἐν τῷ αὐτῷ καὶ πρὸς
τὰ πλησιάζοντα τὴν κίνησιν ἴσχει καὶ οὕτω δὴ
D γεννᾷ, τὰ δὲ γεννώμενα οὕτω δὴ θάττω ἐστίν.
φέρεται γὰρ καὶ ἐν φορᾷ αὐτῶν ἡ κίνησις πέφυκεν.
ἐπειδὰν οὖν ὄμμα καὶ ἄλλο τι τῶν τούτῳ ξυμ-
μέτρων πλησιάσαν γεννήσῃ τὴν λευκότητά τε καὶ
αἴσθησιν αὐτῇ ξύμφυτον, ἃ οὐκ ἄν ποτε ἐγένετο
ἑκατέρου ἐκείνων πρὸς ἄλλο ἐλθόντος, τότε δὴ
μεταξὺ φερομένων τῆς μὲν ὄψεως πρὸς τῶν ὀφθαλ-

but that there are two kinds of motion, each infinite in the number of its manifestations, and of these kinds one has an active, the other a passive force. From the union and friction of these two are born offspring, infinite in number, but always twins, the object of sense and the sense which is always born and brought forth together with the object of sense. Now we give the senses names like these: sight and hearing and smell, and the sense of cold and of heat, and pleasures and pains and desires and fears and so forth. Those that have names are very numerous, and those that are unnamed are innumerable. Now the class of objects of sense is akin to each of these; all sorts of colours are akin to all sorts of acts of vision, and in the same way sounds to acts of hearing, and the other objects of sense spring forth akin to the other senses. What does this tale mean for us, Theaetetus, with reference to what was said before? Do you see?

THEAET. Not quite, Socrates.

SOC. Just listen; perhaps we can finish the tale. It means, of course, that all these things are, as we were saying, in motion, and their motion has in it either swiftness or slowness. Now the slow element keeps its motion in the same place and directed towards such things as draw near it, and indeed it is in this way that it begets. But the things begotten in this way are quicker; for they move from one place to another, and their motion is naturally from one place to another. Now when the eye and some appropriate object which approaches beget whiteness and the corresponding perception—which could never have been produced by either of them going to anything else—then, while sight from the eye and white-

Ε μῶν, τῆς δὲ λευκότητος πρὸς τοῦ συναποτίκτοντος
τὸ χρῶμα, ὁ μὲν ὀφθαλμὸς ἄρα ὄψεως ἔμπλεως
ἐγένετο καὶ ὁρᾷ δὴ τότε καὶ ἐγένετο οὔ τι ὄψις
ἀλλ᾽ ὀφθαλμὸς ὁρῶν, τὸ δὲ ξυγγεννῆσαν τὸ χρῶμα
λευκότητος περιεπλήσθη καὶ ἐγένετο οὐ λευκότης αὖ
ἀλλὰ λευκόν, εἴτε ξύλον εἴτε λίθος εἴτε ὁτουοῦν [1]
ξυνέβη χρῶμα [2] χρωσθῆναι τῷ τοιούτῳ χρώματι.
καὶ τἆλλα δὴ οὕτω, σκληρὸν καὶ θερμὸν καὶ πάντα
τὸν αὐτὸν τρόπον ὑποληπτέον, αὐτὸ μὲν καθ᾽ αὑτὸ
157 μηδὲν εἶναι, ὃ δὴ καὶ τότε ἐλέγομεν, ἐν δὲ τῇ
πρὸς ἄλληλα ὁμιλίᾳ πάντα γίγνεσθαι καὶ παντοῖα
ἀπὸ τῆς κινήσεως, ἐπεὶ καὶ τὸ ποιοῦν εἶναί τι καὶ
τὸ πάσχον αὐτῶν ἐπὶ ἑνὸς νοῆσαι, ὥς φασιν, οὐκ
εἶναι παγίως. οὔτε γὰρ ποιοῦν ἐστί τι, πρὶν ἂν
τῷ πάσχοντι συνέλθῃ, οὔτε πάσχον, πρὶν ἂν τῷ
ποιοῦντι· τό τέ τινι συνελθὸν καὶ ποιοῦν ἄλλῳ
αὖ προσπεσὸν πάσχον ἀνεφάνη. ὥστε ἐξ ἁπάντων
τούτων, ὅπερ ἐξ ἀρχῆς ἐλέγομεν, οὐδὲν εἶναι ἓν αὐτὸ
καθ᾽ αὑτό, ἀλλά τινι ἀεὶ γίγνεσθαι, τὸ δ᾽ εἶναι
Β πανταχόθεν ἐξαιρετέον, οὐχ ὅτι ἡμεῖς πολλὰ καὶ
ἄρτι ἠναγκάσμεθα ὑπὸ συνηθείας καὶ ἀνεπιστημο-
σύνης χρῆσθαι αὐτῷ. τὸ δ᾽ οὐ δεῖ, ὡς ὁ τῶν
σοφῶν λόγος, οὔτε τι συγχωρεῖν οὔτε του οὔτ᾽
ἐμοῦ οὔτε τόδε οὔτ᾽ ἐκεῖνο οὔτε ἄλλο οὐδὲν ὄνομα
ὅ τι ἂν ἱστῇ, ἀλλὰ κατὰ φύσιν φθέγγεσθαι γιγνόμενα
καὶ ποιούμενα καὶ ἀπολλύμενα καὶ ἀλλοιούμενα
ὡς ἐάν τί τις στήσῃ τῷ λόγῳ, εὐέλεγκτος ὁ τοῦτο

---

[1] ὁτουοῦν Schanz; ὅτου οὖν BT; ὁτῳοῦν Campbell; ὁτιοῦν
vulg., Burnet.
[2] χρῶμα BT; χρῆμα Heindorf, Burnet; σχῆμα Schanz.

ness from that which helps to produce the colour are moving from one to the other, the eye becomes full of sight and so begins at that moment to see, and becomes, certainly not sight, but a seeing eye, and the object which joined in begetting the colour is filled with whiteness and becomes in its turn, not whiteness, but white, whether it be a stick or a stone, or whatever it be the hue of which is so coloured. And all the rest—hard and hot and so forth—must be regarded in the same way: we must assume, we said before, that nothing exists in itself, but all things of all sorts arise out of motion by intercourse with each other; for it is, as they say, impossible to form a firm conception of the active or the passive element as being anything separately; for there is no active element until there is a union with the passive element, nor is there a passive element until there is a union with the active; and that which unites with one thing is active and appears again as passive when it comes in contact with something else. And so it results from all this, as we said in the beginning, that nothing exists as invariably one, itself by itself, but everything is always becoming in relation to something, and "being" should be altogether abolished, though we have often—and even just now—been compelled by custom and ignorance to use the word. But we ought not, the wise men say, to permit the use of "something" or "somebody's" or "mine" or "this" or "that" or any other word that implies making things stand still, but in accordance with nature we should speak of things as "becoming" and "being made" and "being destroyed" and "changing"; for anyone who by his mode of speech makes things

ποιῶν. δεῖ δὲ καὶ κατὰ μέρος οὕτω λέγειν καὶ
περὶ πολλῶν ἀθροισθέντων, ᾧ δὴ ἀθροίσματι
C ἄνθρωπόν τε τίθενται καὶ λίθον καὶ ἕκαστον ζῷόν
τε καὶ εἶδος. ταῦτα δή, ὦ Θεαίτητε, ἆρ᾿ ἡδέα
δοκεῖ σοι εἶναι, καὶ γεύοιο ἂν αὐτῶν ὡς ἀρεσ-
κόντων;

ΘΕΑΙ. Οὐκ οἶδα ἔγωγε, ὦ Σώκρατες· καὶ γὰρ
οὐδὲ περὶ σοῦ δύναμαι κατανοῆσαι, πότερα δοκοῦντά
σοι λέγεις αὐτὰ ἢ ἐμοῦ ἀποπειρᾷ.

ΣΩ. Οὐ μνημονεύεις, ὦ φίλε, ὅτι ἐγὼ μὲν οὔτ᾿
οἶδα οὔτε ποιοῦμαι τῶν τοιούτων οὐδὲν ἐμόν, ἀλλ᾿
εἰμὶ αὐτῶν ἄγονος, σὲ δὲ μαιεύομαι καὶ τούτου ἕνεκα
ἐπᾴδω τε καὶ παρατίθημι ἑκάστων τῶν σοφῶν ἀπο-
D γεύσασθαι, ἕως ἂν εἰς φῶς τὸ σὸν δόγμα ξυν-
εξαγάγω· ἐξαχθέντος δὲ τότ᾿ ἤδη σκέψομαι εἴτ᾿
ἀνεμιαῖον εἴτε γόνιμον ἀναφανήσεται. ἀλλὰ
θαρρῶν καὶ καρτερῶν εὖ καὶ ἀνδρείως ἀποκρίνου
ἃ ἂν φαίνηταί σοι περὶ ὧν ἂν ἐρωτῶ.

ΘΕΑΙ. Ἐρώτα δή.

13. ΣΩ. Λέγε τοίνυν πάλιν, εἴ σοι ἀρέσκει
τὸ μή τι εἶναι ἀλλὰ γίγνεσθαι ἀεὶ ἀγαθὸν καὶ
καλὸν [1] καὶ πάντα ἃ ἄρτι διῇμεν.

ΘΕΑΙ. Ἀλλ᾿ ἔμοιγε, ἐπειδὴ σοῦ ἀκούω οὕτω
διεξιόντος, θαυμασίως φαίνεται ὡς ἔχειν λόγον
καὶ ὑποληπτέον ᾗπερ διελήλυθας.

E ΣΩ. Μὴ τοίνυν ἀπολίπωμεν ὅσον ἐλλεῖπον
αὐτοῦ. λείπεται δὲ ἐνυπνίων τε πέρι καὶ νόσων,
τῶν τε ἄλλων καὶ μανίας, ὅσα τε παρακούειν
ἢ παρορᾶν ἤ τι ἄλλο παραισθάνεσθαι λέγεται.

---

[1] ἀγαθὸν καὶ καλὸν mss.; secl. Ast.

stand still is easily refuted. And we must use such expressions in relation both to particular objects and collective designations, among which are " mankind " and " stone " and the names of every animal and class. Do these doctrines seem pleasant to you, Theaetetus, and do you find their taste agreeable ?

THEAET. I don't know, Socrates ; besides, I can't tell about you, either, whether you are preaching them because you believe them or to test me.

SOC. You forget, my friend, that I myself know nothing about such things, and claim none of them as mine, but am incapable of bearing them and am merely acting as a midwife to you, and for that reason am uttering incantations and giving you a taste of each of the philosophical theories, until I may help to bring your own opinion to light. And when it is brought to light, I will examine it and see whether it is a mere wind-egg or a real offspring. So be brave and patient, and in good and manly fashion tell what you think in reply to my questions.

THEAET. Very well ; ask them.

SOC. Then say once more whether the doctrine pleases you that nothing is, but is always becoming —good or beautiful or any of the other qualities we were just enumerating.

THEAET. Why, when I hear you telling about it as you did, it seems to me that it is wonderfully reasonable and ought to be accepted as you have presented it.

SOC. Let us, then, not neglect a point in which it is defective. The defect is found in connexion with dreams and diseases, including insanity, and everything else that is said to cause illusions of sight and hearing and the other senses. For of course

61

157

οἶσθα γάρ που ὅτι ἐν πᾶσι τούτοις ὁμολογουμένως
ἐλέγχεσθαι δοκεῖ ὃν ἄρτι διῇμεν λόγον, ὡς παντὸς
158 μᾶλλον ἡμῖν ψευδεῖς αἰσθήσεις ἐν αὐτοῖς γιγνομένας,
καὶ πολλοῦ δεῖ¹ τὰ φαινόμενα ἑκάστῳ ταῦτα καὶ
εἶναι, ἀλλὰ πᾶν τοὐναντίον οὐδὲν ὧν φαίνεται εἶναι.

ΘΕΑΙ. Ἀληθέστατα λέγεις, ὦ Σώκρατες.

ΣΩ. Τίς δὴ οὖν, ὦ παῖ, λείπεται λόγος τῷ τὴν
αἴσθησιν ἐπιστήμην τιθεμένῳ καὶ τὰ φαινόμενα
ἑκάστῳ ταῦτα καὶ εἶναι τούτῳ ᾧ φαίνεται;

ΘΕΑΙ. Ἐγὼ μέν, ὦ Σώκρατες, ὀκνῶ εἰπεῖν ὅτι
οὐκ ἔχω τί λέγω, διότι μοι νῦν δὴ ἐπέπληξας εἰπόντι
B αὐτό. ἐπεὶ ὡς ἀληθῶς γε οὐκ ἂν δυναίμην ἀμφισβητῆσαι ὡς οἱ μαινόμενοι ἢ οἱ ὀνειρώττοντες οὐ
ψευδῆ δοξάζουσιν, ὅταν οἱ μὲν θεοὶ αὐτῶν οἴωνται
εἶναι, οἱ δὲ πτηνοί τε καὶ ὡς πετόμενοι ἐν τῷ ὕπνῳ
διανοῶνται.

ΣΩ. Ἆρ᾽ οὖν οὐδὲ τὸ τοιόνδε ἀμφισβήτημα ἐννοεῖς περὶ αὐτῶν, μάλιστα δὲ περὶ τοῦ ὄναρ τε καὶ
ὕπαρ;

ΘΕΑΙ. Τὸ ποῖον;

ΣΩ. Ὃ πολλάκις σε οἶμαι ἀκηκοέναι ἐρωτώντων,
τί ἄν τις ἔχοι τεκμήριον ἀποδεῖξαι, εἴ τις ἔροιτο
νῦν οὕτως ἐν τῷ παρόντι, πότερον καθεύδομεν καὶ
πάντα ἃ διανοούμεθα ὀνειρώττομεν, ἢ ἐγρηγόραμέν
C τε καὶ ὕπαρ ἀλλήλοις διαλεγόμεθα.

ΘΕΑΙ. Καὶ μήν, ὦ Σώκρατες, ἄπορόν γε ὅτῳ
χρὴ² ἐπιδεῖξαι τεκμηρίῳ· πάντα γὰρ ὥσπερ
ἀντίστροφα τὰ αὐτὰ παρακολουθεῖ. ἅ τε γὰρ νυνὶ
διειλέγμεθα, οὐδὲν κωλύει καὶ ἐν τῷ ὕπνῳ δοκεῖν

¹ δεῖ mss. ; δεῖν Heindorf, followed by Schanz and
Wohlrab.
² χρὴ TW ; χρόνῳ χρὴ B ; χρεὼν Hultsch.

you know that in all these the doctrine we were just presenting seems admittedly to be refuted, because in them we certainly have false perceptions, and it is by no means true that everything is to each man which appears to him ; on the contrary, nothing is which appears.

THEAET. What you say is very true, Socrates.

soc. What argument is left, then, my boy, for the man who says that perception is knowledge and that in each case the things which appear are to the one to whom they appear ?

THEAET. I hesitate to say, Socrates, that I have no reply to make, because you scolded me just now when I said that. But really I cannot dispute that those who are insane or dreaming have false opinions, when some of them think they are gods and others fancy in their sleep that they have wings and are flying.

soc. Don't you remember, either, the similar dispute about these errors, especially about sleeping and waking ?

THEAET. What dispute ?

soc. One which I fancy you have often heard. The question is asked, what proof you could give if anyone should ask us now, at the present moment, whether we are asleep and our thoughts are a dream, or whether we are awake and talking with each other in a waking condition.

THEAET. Really, Socrates, I don't see what proof can be given ; for there is an exact correspondence in all particulars, as between the strophe and antistrophe of a choral song. Take, for instance, the conversation we have just had : there is nothing to prevent us from imagining in our sleep also that we

63

ἀλλήλοις διαλέγεσθαι· καὶ ὅταν δὴ ὄναρ ὀνείρατα
δοκῶμεν διηγεῖσθαι, ἄτοπος ἡ ὁμοιότης τούτων
ἐκείνοις.

ΣΩ. Ὁρᾷς οὖν ὅτι τό γε ἀμφισβητῆσαι οὐ χαλεπόν, ὅτε καὶ πότερόν ἐστιν ὕπαρ ἢ ὄναρ ἀμφισβη-
D τεῖται, καὶ δὴ ἴσου ὄντος τοῦ χρόνου ὃν καθεύδομεν
ᾧ ἐγρηγόραμεν, ἐν ἑκατέρῳ διαμάχεται ἡμῶν ἡ
ψυχὴ τὰ ἀεὶ παρόντα δόγματα παντὸς μᾶλλον εἶναι
ἀληθῆ, ὥστε ἴσον μὲν χρόνον τάδε φαμὲν ὄντα
εἶναι, ἴσον δὲ ἐκεῖνα, καὶ ὁμοίως ἐφ' ἑκατέροις
διισχυριζόμεθα.

ΘΕΑΙ. Παντάπασι μὲν οὖν.

ΣΩ. Οὐκοῦν καὶ περὶ νόσων τε καὶ μανιῶν ὁ
αὐτὸς λόγος, πλὴν τοῦ χρόνου ὅτι οὐχὶ ἴσος;

ΘΕΑΙ. Ὀρθῶς.

ΣΩ. Τί οὖν; πλήθει χρόνου καὶ ὀλιγότητι τὸ
ἀληθὲς ὁρισθήσεται;

E ΘΕΑΙ. Γελοῖον μέντ' ἂν εἴη πολλαχῇ.

ΣΩ. Ἀλλά τι ἄλλο ἔχεις σαφὲς ἐνδείξασθαι,
ὁποῖα τούτων τῶν δοξασμάτων ἀληθῆ;

ΘΕΑΙ. Οὔ μοι δοκῶ.

14. ΣΩ. Ἐμοῦ τοίνυν ἄκουε οἷα περὶ αὐτῶν
ἂν λέγοιεν οἱ τὰ ἀεὶ δοκοῦντα ὁριζόμενοι τῷ δοκοῦντι
εἶναι ἀληθῆ. λέγουσι δέ, ὡς ἐγὼ οἶμαι, οὕτως
ἐρωτῶντες· " ὦ Θεαίτητε, ὃ ἂν ἕτερον ᾖ παντάπασιν, μή πή τινα δύναμιν τὴν αὐτὴν ἕξει τῷ
ἑτέρῳ; καὶ μὴ ὑπολάβωμεν τῇ μὲν ταὐτὸν εἶναι
ὃ ἐρωτῶμεν, τῇ δὲ ἕτερον, ἀλλ' ὅλως ἕτερον."

ΘΕΑΙ. Ἀδύνατον τοίνυν ταὐτόν τι ἔχειν ἢ ἐν
64

are carrying on this conversation with each other, and when in a dream we imagine that we are relating dreams, the likeness between the one talk and the other is remarkable.

soc. So you see it is not hard to dispute the point, since it is even open to dispute whether we are awake or in a dream. Now since the time during which we are asleep is equal to that during which we are awake, in each state our spirit contends that the semblances that appear to it at any time are certainly true, so that for half the time we say that this is true, and for half the time the other, and we maintain each with equal confidence.

THEAET. Certainly.

soc. And may not, then, the same be said about insanity and the other diseases, except that the time is not equal?

THEAET. Yes.

soc. Well, then, shall truth be determined by the length or shortness of time?

THEAET. That would be absurd in many ways.

soc. But can you show clearly in any other way which of the two sets of opinions is true?

THEAET. I do not think I can.

soc. Listen, then, while I tell you what would be said about them by those who maintain that what appears at any time is true for him to whom it appears. They begin, I imagine, by asking this question: "Theaetetus, can that which is wholly other in any way the same quality as its alternative? And we must not assume that the thing in question is partially the same and partially other, but wholly other."

THEAET. It is impossible for it to be the same in

159 δυνάμει ἢ ἐν ἄλλῳ ὁτῳοῦν, ὅταν ᾖ κομιδῇ
ἕτερον.

ΣΩ. Ἆρ' οὖν οὐ καὶ ἀνόμοιον ἀναγκαῖον τὸ
τοιοῦτον ὁμολογεῖν;

ΘΕΑΙ. Ἔμοιγε δοκεῖ.

ΣΩ. Εἰ ἄρα τι συμβαίνει ὅμοιόν τῳ γίγνεσθαι
ἢ ἀνόμοιον, εἴτε ἑαυτῷ εἴτε ἄλλῳ, ὁμοιούμενον
μὲν ταὐτὸν φήσομεν γίγνεσθαι, ἀνομοιούμενον δὲ
ἕτερον;

ΘΕΑΙ. Ἀνάγκη.

ΣΩ. Οὐκοῦν πρόσθεν ἐλέγομεν ὡς πολλὰ μὲν
εἴη τὰ ποιοῦντα καὶ ἄπειρα, ὡσαύτως δέ γε τὰ πάσχοντα;

ΘΕΑΙ. Ναί.

ΣΩ. Καὶ μὴν ὅτι γε ἄλλο ἄλλῳ συμμιγνύμενον
καὶ ἄλλῳ οὐ ταὐτὰ ἀλλ' ἕτερα γεννήσει;

B ΘΕΑΙ. Πάνυ μὲν οὖν.

ΣΩ. Λέγωμεν δὴ ἐμέ τε καὶ σὲ καὶ τἆλλα ἤδη
κατὰ τὸν αὐτὸν λόγον, Σωκράτη ὑγιαίνοντα καὶ
Σωκράτη αὖ ἀσθενοῦντα. πότερον ὅμοιον τοῦτ'
ἐκείνῳ ἢ ἀνόμοιον φήσομεν;

ΘΕΑΙ. Ἆρα τὸν ἀσθενοῦντα Σωκράτη, ὅλον
τοῦτο λέγεις ὅλῳ ἐκείνῳ, τῷ ὑγιαίνοντι Σωκράτει;

ΣΩ. Κάλλιστα ὑπέλαβες· αὐτὸ τοῦτο λέγω.

ΘΕΑΙ. Ἀνόμοιον δήπου.

ΣΩ. Καὶ ἕτερον ἄρα οὕτως ὥσπερ ἀνόμοιον;

ΘΕΑΙ. Ἀνάγκη.

ΣΩ. Καὶ καθεύδοντα δὴ καὶ πάντα ἃ νῦν δὴ[1]
C διήλθομεν, ὡσαύτως φήσεις;

[1] νῦν δὴ Heindorf; νῦν BT.

anything, either in quality or in any other respect whatsoever, when it is wholly other.

soc. Must we not, then, necessarily agree that such a thing is also unlike?

THEAET. It seems so to me.

soc. Then if anything happens to become like or unlike anything—either itself or anything else—we shall say that when it becomes like it becomes the same, and when it becomes unlike it becomes other?

THEAET. We must.

soc. Well, we said before, did we not, that the active elements were many—infinite in fact—and likewise the passive elements?

THEAET. Yes.

soc. And furthermore, that any given element, by uniting at different times with different partners, will beget, not the same, but other results?

THEAET. Certainly.

soc. Well, then, let us take me, or you, or anything else at hand, and apply the same principle—say Socrates in health and Socrates in illness. Shall we say the one is like the other, or unlike?

THEAET. When you say "Socrates in illness" do you mean to compare that Socrates as a whole with Socrates in health as a whole?

soc. You understand perfectly; that is just what I mean.

THEAET. Unlike, I imagine.

soc. And therefore other, inasmuch as unlike?

THEAET. Necessarily.

soc. And you would say the same of Socrates asleep or in any of the other states we enumerated just now?

ΘΕΑΙ. Ἔγωγε.

ΣΩ. Ἕκαστον δὴ τῶν πεφυκότων τι ποιεῖν ἄλλο τι, ὅταν μὲν λάβῃ ὑγιαίνοντα Σωκράτη, ὡς ἑτέρῳ μοι χρήσεται, ὅταν δὲ ἀσθενοῦντα, ὡς ἑτέρῳ;

ΘΕΑΙ. Τί δ' οὐ μέλλει;

ΣΩ. Καὶ ἕτερα δὴ ἐφ' ἑκατέρου γεννήσομεν ἐγώ τε ὁ πάσχων καὶ ἐκεῖνο τὸ ποιοῦν;

ΘΕΑΙ. Τί μήν;

ΣΩ. Ὅταν δὴ οἶνον πίνω ὑγιαίνων, ἡδύς μοι φαίνεται καὶ γλυκύς;

ΘΕΑΙ. Ναί.

ΣΩ. Ἐγέννησε γὰρ δὴ ἐκ τῶν προωμολογημένων
D τό τε ποιοῦν καὶ τὸ πάσχον γλυκύτητά τε καὶ αἴσθησιν, ἅμα φερόμενα ἀμφότερα, καὶ ἡ μὲν αἴσθησις πρὸς τοῦ πάσχοντος οὖσα αἰσθανομένην τὴν γλῶτταν ἀπειργάσατο, ἡ δὲ γλυκύτης πρὸς τοῦ οἴνου περὶ αὐτὸν φερομένη γλυκὺν τὸν οἶνον τῇ ὑγιαινούσῃ γλώττῃ ἐποίησεν καὶ εἶναι καὶ φαίνεσθαι.

ΘΕΑΙ. Πάνυ μὲν οὖν τὰ πρότερα ἡμῖν οὕτως ὡμολόγητο.

ΣΩ. Ὅταν δὲ ἀσθενοῦντα, ἄλλο τι πρῶτον μὲν τῇ ἀληθείᾳ οὐ τὸν αὐτὸν ἔλαβεν; ἀνομοίῳ γὰρ δὴ προσῆλθεν.

ΘΕΑΙ. Ναί.

E ΣΩ. Ἕτερα δὴ αὖ ἐγεννησάτην ὅ τε τοιοῦτος Σωκράτης καὶ ἡ τοῦ οἴνου πόσις, περὶ μὲν τὴν γλῶτταν αἴσθησιν πικρότητος, περὶ δὲ τὸν οἶνον

THEAET. Yes.

soc. Then each of those elements which by the law of their nature act upon something else, will, when it gets hold of Socrates in health, find me one object to act upon, and when it gets hold of me in illness, another?

THEAET. How can it help it?

soc. And so, in the two cases, that active element and I, who am the passive element, shall each produce a different object?

THEAET. Of course.

soc. So, then, when I am in health and drink wine, it seems pleasant and sweet to me?

THEAET. Yes.

soc. The reason is, in fact, that according to the principles we accepted a while ago, the active and passive elements produce sweetness and perception, both of which are simultaneously moving from one place to another, and the perception, which comes from the passive element, makes the tongue perceptive, and the sweetness, which comes from the wine and pervades it, passes over and makes the wine both to be and to seem sweet to the tongue that is in health.

THEAET. Certainly, such are the principles we accepted a while ago.

soc. But when it gets hold of me in illness, in the first place, it really doesn't get hold of the same man, does it? For he to whom it comes is certainly unlike.

THEAET. True.

soc. Therefore the union of the Socrates who is ill and the draught of wine produces other results: in the tongue the sensation or perception of bitter-

γιγνομένην καὶ φερομένην πικρότητα, καὶ τὸν μὲν
οὐ πικρότητα ἀλλὰ πικρόν, ἐμὲ δὲ οὐκ αἴσθησιν
ἀλλ' αἰσθανόμενον;

ΘΕΑΙ. Κομιδῇ μὲν οὖν.

ΣΩ. Οὔκουν ἐγώ τε οὐδὲν ἄλλο ποτὲ γενήσομαι
οὕτως αἰσθανόμενος· τοῦ γὰρ ἄλλου ἄλλη αἴσθησις,
160 καὶ ἀλλοῖον καὶ ἄλλον ποιεῖ τὸν αἰσθανόμενον·
οὔτ' ἐκεῖνο τὸ ποιοῦν ἐμὲ μήποτ' ἄλλῳ συνελθὸν
ταὐτὸν γεννῆσαν τοιοῦτον γένηται· ἀπὸ γὰρ
ἄλλου ἄλλο γεννῆσαν ἀλλοῖον γενήσεται.

ΘΕΑΙ. Ἔστι ταῦτα.

ΣΩ. Οὐδὲ μὴν ἔγωγε ἐμαυτῷ τοιοῦτος, ἐκεῖνό
τε ἑαυτῷ τοιοῦτον γενήσεται.

ΘΕΑΙ. Οὐ γὰρ οὖν.

ΣΩ. Ἀνάγκη δέ γε ἐμέ τε τινὸς γίγνεσθαι, ὅταν
αἰσθανόμενος γίγνωμαι· αἰσθανόμενον γάρ, μηδενὸς δὲ αἰσθανόμενον ἀδύνατον γίγνεσθαι· ἐκεῖνό
B τέ τινι γίγνεσθαι, ὅταν γλυκὺ ἢ πικρὸν ἤ τι τοιοῦτον γίγνηται· γλυκὺ γάρ, μηδενὶ δὲ γλυκὺ ἀδύνατον γενέσθαι.

ΘΕΑΙ. Παντάπασι μὲν οὖν.

ΣΩ. Λείπεται δή, οἶμαι, ἡμῖν ἀλλήλοις, εἴτ'
ἐσμέν, εἶναι, εἴτε γιγνόμεθα, γίγνεσθαι, ἐπείπερ
ἡμῶν ἡ ἀνάγκη τὴν οὐσίαν συνδεῖ μέν, συνδεῖ δὲ
οὐδενὶ τῶν ἄλλων, οὐδ' αὖ ἡμῖν αὐτοῖς. ἀλλήλοις
δὴ λείπεται συνδεδέσθαι· ὥστε εἴτε τις εἶναί τι
ὀνομάζει, τινὶ εἶναι ἢ τινὸς ἢ πρός τι ῥητέον αὐτῷ,

ness, and in the wine—a bitterness which is engen-
dered there and passes over into the other; the wine
is made, not bitterness, but bitter, and I am made,
not perception, but perceptive.

THEAET. Certainly.

soc. Then I shall never have this perception of
any other thing; for a perception of another thing
is another perception, and makes the percipient
different and other: nor can that which acts on me
ever by union with another produce the same result
or become the same in kind; for by producing
another result from another passive element it will
become different in kind.

THEAET. That is true.

soc. And neither shall I, furthermore, ever again
become the same as I am, nor will that ever become
the same as it is.

THEAET. No.

soc. And yet, when I become percipient, I must
necessarily become percipient of something, for it
is impossible to become percipient and perceive
nothing; and that which is perceived must become
so to someone, when it becomes sweet or bitter or
the like; for to become sweet, but sweet to no one,
is impossible.

THEAET. Perfectly true.

soc. The result, then, I think, is that we (the active
and the passive elements) are or become, whichever
is the case, in relation to one another, since we are
bound to one another by the inevitable law of our
being, but to nothing else, not even to ourselves.
The result, then, is that we are bound to one
another; and so if a man says anything "is," he
must say it is to or of or in relation to something,

71

εἴτε γίγνεσθαι· αὐτὸ δὲ ἐφ' αὑτοῦ τι ἢ ὂν ἢ
C γιγνόμενον οὔτε αὐτῷ λεκτέον οὔτ' ἄλλου λέγοντος
ἀποδεκτέον, ὡς ὁ λόγος ὃν διεληλύθαμεν σημαίνει.

ΘΕΑΙ. Πανταπασι μὲν οὖν, ὦ Σώκρατες.

ΣΩ. Οὐκοῦν ὅτε δὴ τὸ ἐμὲ ποιοῦν ἐμοί ἐστιν
καὶ οὐκ ἄλλῳ, ἐγὼ καὶ αἰσθάνομαι αὐτοῦ, ἄλλος
δ' οὔ;

ΘΕΑΙ. Πῶς γὰρ οὔ;

ΣΩ. Ἀληθὴς ἄρα ἐμοὶ ἡ ἐμὴ αἴσθησις· τῆς γὰρ
ἐμῆς οὐσίας ἀεί ἐστιν· καὶ ἐγὼ κριτὴς κατὰ τὸν
Πρωταγόραν τῶν τε ὄντων ἐμοί, ὡς ἔστι, καὶ τῶν
μὴ ὄντων, ὡς οὐκ ἔστιν.

ΘΕΑΙ. Ἔοικεν.

D 15. ΣΩ. Πῶς ἂν οὖν ἀψευδὴς ὢν καὶ μὴ
πταίων τῇ διανοίᾳ περὶ τὰ ὄντα ἢ γιγνόμενα οὐκ
ἐπιστήμων ἂν εἴην ὧνπερ αἰσθητής;

ΘΕΑΙ. Οὐδαμῶς ὅπως οὔ.

ΣΩ. Παγκάλως ἄρα σοι εἴρηται ὅτι ἐπιστήμη
οὐκ ἄλλο τί ἐστιν ἢ αἴσθησις, καὶ εἰς ταὐτὸν συμ-
πέπτωκεν, κατὰ μὲν Ὅμηρον καὶ Ἡράκλειτον καὶ
πᾶν τὸ τοιοῦτον φῦλον οἷον ῥεύματα κινεῖσθαι τὰ
πάντα, κατὰ δὲ Πρωταγόραν τὸν σοφώτατον
πάντων χρημάτων ἄνθρωπον μέτρον εἶναι, κατὰ
E δὲ Θεαίτητον τούτων οὕτως ἐχόντων αἴσθησιν
ἐπιστήμην γίγνεσθαι. ἢ γάρ, ὦ Θεαίτητε; φῶμεν
τοῦτο σὸν μὲν εἶναι οἷον νεογενὲς παιδίον, ἐμὸν
δὲ μαίευμα; ἢ πῶς λέγεις;

ΘΕΑΙ. Οὕτως ἀνάγκη, ὦ Σώκρατες.

ΣΩ. Τοῦτο μὲν δή, ὡς ἔοικεν, μόλις ποτὲ ἐγεν-

THEAETETUS

and similarly if he says it "becomes"; but he must not say it is or becomes absolutely, nor can he accept such a statement from anyone else. That is the meaning of the doctrine we have been describing.

THEAET. Yes, quite so, Socrates.

soc. Then, since that which acts on me is to me and to me only, it is also the case that I perceive it, and I only?

THEAET. Of course.

soc. Then to me my perception is true; for in each case it is always part of my being; and I am, as Protagoras says, the judge of the existence of the things that are to me and of the non-existence of those that are not to me.

THEAET. So it seems.

soc. How, then, if I am an infallible judge and my mind never stumbles in regard to the things that are or that become, can I fail to know that which I perceive?

THEAET. You cannot possibly fail.

soc. Therefore you were quite right in saying that knowledge is nothing else than perception, and there is complete identity between the doctrine of Homer and Heracleitus and all their followers—that all things are in motion, like streams—the doctrine of the great philosopher Protagoras that man is the measure of all things—and the doctrine of Theaetetus that, since these things are true, perception is knowledge. Eh, Theaetetus? Shall we say that this is, so to speak, your new-born child and the result of my midwifery? Or what shall we say?

THEAET. We must say that, Socrates.

soc. Well, we have at last managed to bring this

νήσαμεν, ὅ τι δή ποτε τυγχάνει ὄν. μετὰ δὲ τὸν
τόκον τὰ ἀμφιδρόμια αὐτοῦ ὡς ἀληθῶς ἐν κύκλῳ
περιθρεκτέον τῷ λόγῳ, σκοπουμένους μὴ λάθῃ
ἡμᾶς οὐκ ἄξιον ὂν τροφῆς τὸ γιγνόμενον, ἀλλὰ
161 ἀνεμιαῖόν τε καὶ ψεῦδος. ἢ σὺ οἴει πάντως δεῖν
τό γε σὸν τρέφειν καὶ μὴ ἀποτιθέναι, ἢ καὶ ἀνέξει
ἐλεγχόμενον ὁρῶν, καὶ οὐ σφόδρα χαλεπανεῖς,
ἐάν τις σοῦ ὡς πρωτοτόκου αὐτὸ ὑφαιρῇ;

ΘΕΟ. ’Ανέξεται, ὦ Σώκρατες, Θεαίτητος· οὐδαμῶς γὰρ δύσκολος. ἀλλὰ πρὸς θεῶν εἰπέ, ἦ αὖ
οὐχ οὕτως ἔχει;

ΣΩ. Φιλόλογός γ’ εἶ ἀτεχνῶς καὶ χρηστός, ὦ
Θεόδωρε, ὅτι με οἴει λόγων τινὰ εἶναι θύλακον καὶ
ῥαδίως ἐξελόντα ἐρεῖν ὡς οὐκ αὖ ἔχει οὕτω ταῦτα·
B τὸ δὲ γιγνόμενον οὐκ ἐννοεῖς, ὅτι οὐδεὶς τῶν
λόγων ἐξέρχεται παρ’ ἐμοῦ ἀλλ’ ἀεὶ παρὰ τοῦ ἐμοὶ
προσδιαλεγομένου, ἐγὼ δὲ οὐδὲν ἐπίσταμαι πλέον
πλὴν βραχέος, ὅσον λόγον παρ’ ἑτέρου σοφοῦ
λαβεῖν καὶ ἀποδέξασθαι μετρίως. καὶ νῦν τοῦτο
παρὰ τοῦδε πειράσομαι, οὔ τι αὐτὸς εἰπεῖν.

ΘΕΟ. Σὺ κάλλιον, ὦ Σώκρατες, λέγεις· καὶ
ποίει οὕτως.

16. ΣΩ. Οἶσθ’ οὖν, ὦ Θεόδωρε, ὃ θαυμάζω
τοῦ ἑταίρου σου Πρωταγόρου;

C   ΘΕΟ. Τὸ ποῖον;

---

¹ The rite called *amphidromia* took place a few days
after the birth of a child. After some ceremonies of purification the nurse, in the presence of the family, carried the
74

forth, whatever it turns out to be; and now that it is born, we must in very truth perform the rite of running round with it in a circle [1]—the circle of our argument—and see whether it may not turn out to be after all not worth rearing, but only a wind-egg, an imposture. But, perhaps, you think that any offspring of yours ought to be cared for and not put away; or will you bear to see it examined and not get angry if it is taken away from you, though it is your first-born?

THEO. Theaetetus will bear it, Socrates, for he is not at all ill-tempered. But for heaven's sake, Socrates, tell me, is all this wrong after all?

SOC. You are truly fond of argument, Theodorus, and a very good fellow to think that I am a sort of bag full of arguments and can easily pull one out and say that after all the other one was wrong; but you do not understand what is going on: none of the arguments comes from me, but always from him who is talking with me. I myself know nothing, except just a little, enough to extract an argument from another man who is wise and to receive it fairly. And now I will try to extract this thought from Theaetetus, but not to say anything myself.

THEO. That is the better way, Socrates; do as you say.

SOC. Do you know, then, Theodorus, what amazes me in your friend Protagoras?

THEO. What is it?

infant rapidly about the family hearth, thereby introducing him, as it were, to the family and the family deities. At this time the father decided whether to bring up the child or to expose it. Sometimes, perhaps, the child was named on this occasion. In the evening relatives assembled for a feast at which shell-fish were eaten.

ΣΩ. Τὰ μὲν ἄλλα μοι πάνυ ἡδέως εἴρηκεν, ὡς
τὸ δοκοῦν ἑκάστῳ τοῦτο καὶ ἔστιν· τὴν δ' ἀρχὴν
τοῦ λόγου τεθαύμακα, ὅτι οὐκ εἶπεν ἀρχόμενος
τῆς ἀληθείας ὅτι πάντων χρημάτων μέτρον ἐστὶν
ὗς ἢ κυνοκέφαλος ἤ τι ἄλλο ἀτοπώτερον τῶν
ἐχόντων αἴσθησιν, ἵνα μεγαλοπρεπῶς καὶ πάνυ
καταφρονητικῶς ἤρξατο ἡμῖν λέγειν, ἐνδεικνύμενος
ὅτι ἡμεῖς μὲν αὐτὸν ὥσπερ θεὸν ἐθαυμάζομεν ἐπὶ
σοφίᾳ, ὁ δ' ἄρα ἐτύγχανεν ὢν εἰς φρόνησιν οὐδὲν
D βελτίων βατράχου γυρίνου, μὴ ὅτι ἄλλου του
ἀνθρώπων. ἢ πῶς λέγωμεν,[1] ὦ Θεόδωρε; εἰ γὰρ
δὴ ἑκάστῳ ἀληθὲς ἔσται ὃ ἂν δι' αἰσθήσεως δοξάζῃ,
καὶ μήτε τὸ ἄλλου πάθος ἄλλος βέλτιον διακρινεῖ,[2]
μήτε τὴν δόξαν κυριώτερος ἔσται ἐπισκέψασθαι
ἕτερος τὴν ἑτέρου, ὀρθὴ ἢ ψευδής, ἀλλ' ὃ πολλάκις
εἴρηται, αὐτὸς τὰ αὐτοῦ ἕκαστος μόνος δοξάσει,
ταῦτα δὲ πάντα ὀρθὰ καὶ ἀληθῆ, τί δή ποτε, ὦ
ἑταῖρε, Πρωταγόρας μὲν σοφός, ὥστε καὶ ἄλλων
E διδάσκαλος ἀξιοῦσθαι δικαίως μετὰ μεγάλων μι-
σθῶν, ἡμεῖς δὲ ἀμαθέστεροί τε καὶ φοιτητέον ἡμῖν
ἦν παρ' ἐκεῖνον, μέτρῳ ὄντι αὐτῷ ἑκάστῳ τῆς
αὑτοῦ σοφίας; ταῦτα πῶς μὴ φῶμεν δημούμενον
λέγειν τὸν Πρωταγόραν; τὸ δὲ δὴ ἐμόν τε καὶ
τῆς ἐμῆς τέχνης τῆς μαιευτικῆς σιγῶ, ὅσον
γέλωτα ὀφλισκάνομεν· οἶμαι δὲ καὶ ξύμπασα ἡ
τοῦ διαλέγεσθαι πραγματεία. τὸ γὰρ ἐπισκοπεῖν
καὶ ἐπιχειρεῖν [3] ἐλέγχειν τὰς ἀλλήλων φαντασίας
τε καὶ δόξας, ὀρθὰς ἑκάστου οὔσας, οὐ μακρὰ

---

[1] λέγωμεν BT ; λέγομεν vulg.
[2] διακρινεῖ most editors ; διακρίνῃ B (emendation) T.
[3] ἐπιχειρεῖν TW ; om. B.

soc. In general I like his doctrine that what appears to each one is to him, but I am amazed by the beginning of his book. I don't see why he does not say in the beginning of his *Truth* [1] that a pig or a dog-faced baboon or some still stranger creature of those that have sensations is the measure of all things. Then he might have begun to speak to us very imposingly and condescendingly, showing that while we were honouring him like a god for his wisdom, he was after all no better in intellect than any other man, or, for that matter, than a tadpole. What alternative is there, Theodorus? For if that opinion is true to each person which he acquires through sensation, and no one man can discern another's condition better than he himself, and one man has no better right to investigate whether another's opinion is true or false than he himself, but, as we have said several times, each man is to form his own opinions by himself, and these opinions are always right and true, why in the world, my friend, was Protagoras wise, so that he could rightly be thought worthy to be the teacher of other men and to be well paid, and why were we ignorant creatures and obliged to go to school to him, if each person is the measure of his own wisdom? Must we not believe that Protagoras was "playing to the gallery" in saying this? I say nothing of the ridicule that I and my science of midwifery deserve in that case,—and, I should say, the whole practice of dialectics, too. For would not the investigation of one another's fancies and opinions, and the attempt to refute them, when each man's must be

[1] *Truth* was apparently the title, or part of the title, of Protagoras's book.

162 μὲν καὶ διωλύγιος φλυαρία, εἰ ἀληθὴς ἡ ἀλήθεια
Πρωταγόρου, ἀλλὰ μὴ παίζουσα ἐκ τοῦ ἀδύτου
τῆς βίβλου ἐφθέγξατο;

ΘΕΟ. Ὦ Σώκρατες, φίλος ἀνήρ, ὥσπερ σὺ νῦν
δὴ εἶπες. οὐκ ἂν οὖν δεξαίμην δι' ἐμοῦ ὁμολο-
γοῦντος ἐλέγχεσθαι Πρωταγόραν, οὐδ' αὖ σοὶ παρὰ
δόξαν ἀντιτείνειν. τὸν οὖν Θεαίτητον πάλιν λαβέ·
πάντως καὶ νῦν δὴ μάλ' ἐμμελῶς σοι ἐφαίνετο
ὑπακούειν.

ΣΩ. Ἆρα κἂν εἰς Λακεδαίμονα ἐλθών, ὦ Θεό-
Β δωρε, πρὸς τὰς παλαίστρας ἀξιοῖς ἂν ἄλλους
θεώμενος γυμνούς, ἐνίους φαύλους, αὐτὸς μὴ ἀντ-
επιδεικνύναι τὸ εἶδος παραποδυόμενος;

ΘΕΟ. Ἀλλὰ τί μὴν δοκεῖς, εἴπερ μέλλοιέν μοι
ἐπιτρέψειν καὶ πείσεσθαι; ὥσπερ νῦν οἶμαι ὑμᾶς
πείσειν ἐμὲ μὲν ἐᾶν θεᾶσθαι καὶ μὴ ἕλκειν πρὸς τὸ
γυμνάσιον σκληρὸν ἤδη ὄντα, τῷ δὲ δὴ νεωτέρῳ
τε καὶ ὑγροτέρῳ ὄντι προσπαλαίειν.

17. ΣΩ. Ἀλλ' εἰ οὕτως, ὦ Θεόδωρε, σοὶ
C φίλον, οὐδ' ἐμοὶ ἐχθρόν, φασὶν οἱ παροιμιαζόμενοι.
πάλιν δὴ οὖν ἐπὶ τὸν σοφὸν Θεαίτητον ἰτέον. λέγε
δή, ὦ Θεαίτητε, πρῶτον μὲν ἃ νῦν δὴ διήλθομεν,
ἆρα οὐ συνθαυμάζεις[1] εἰ ἐξαίφνης οὕτως ἀναφανήσει
μηδὲν χείρων εἰς σοφίαν ὁτουοῦν ἀνθρώπων ἢ καὶ
θεῶν; ἢ ἧττόν τι οἴει τὸ Πρωταγόρειον μέτρον
εἰς θεοὺς ἢ εἰς ἀνθρώπους λέγεσθαι;

ΘΕΑΙ. Μὰ Δί' οὐκ ἔγωγε· καὶ ὅπερ γε ἐρωτᾷς,
πάνυ θαυμάζω. ἡνίκα γὰρ διῇμεν ὃν τρόπον
D λέγοιεν τὸ δοκοῦν ἑκάστῳ τοῦτο καὶ εἶναι τῷ
δοκοῦντι, πάνυ μοι εὖ ἐφαίνετο λέγεσθαι· νῦν δὲ
τοὐναντίον τάχα μεταπέπτωκεν.

[1] συνθαυμάζεις ΒΤ ; σὺ θαυμάζεις W.

78

right, be tedious and blatant folly, if the *Truth* of
Protagoras is true and he was not jesting when he
uttered his oracles from the shrine of his book?

THEO. Socrates, the man was my friend, as you
just remarked. So I should hate to bring about the
refutation of Protagoras by agreeing with you, and
I should hate also to oppose you contrary to
my real convictions. So take Theaetetus again;
especially as he seemed just now to follow your
suggestions very carefully.

soc. If you went to Sparta, Theodorus, and visited
the wrestling-schools, would you think it fair to look
on at other people naked, some of whom were of
poor physique, without stripping and showing your
own form, too?

THEO. Why not, if I could persuade them to allow
me to do so? So now I think I shall persuade you
to let me be a spectator, and not to drag me into the
ring, since I am old and stiff, but to take the younger
and nimbler man as your antagonist.

soc. Well, Theodorus, if that pleases you, it does
not displease me, as the saying is. So I must attack
the wise Theaetetus again. Tell me, Theaetetus,
referring to the doctrine we have just expounded, do
you not share my amazement at being suddenly
exalted to an equality with the wisest man, or even
god? Or do you think Protagoras's "measure"
applies any less to gods than to men?

THEAET. By no means; and I am amazed that you
ask such a question at all; for when we were discussing the meaning of the doctrine that whatever
appears to each one really is to him, I thought it
was good; but now it has suddenly changed to
the opposite.

ΣΩ. Νέος γὰρ εἶ, ὦ φίλε παῖ· τῆς οὖν δημηγο-
ρίας ὀξέως ὑπακούεις καὶ πείθει. πρὸς γὰρ ταῦτα
ἐρεῖ Πρωταγόρας ἤ τις ἄλλος ὑπὲρ αὐτοῦ· ὦ
γενναῖοι παῖδές τε καὶ γέροντες, δημηγορεῖτε
συγκαθεζόμενοι, θεούς τε εἰς τὸ μέσον ἄγοντες,
οὓς ἐγὼ ἔκ τε τοῦ λέγειν καὶ τοῦ γράφειν περὶ
Ε αὐτῶν, ὡς εἰσὶν ἢ ὡς οὐκ εἰσίν, ἐξαιρῶ, καὶ ἃ οἱ
πολλοὶ ἂν ἀποδέχοιντο ἀκούοντες, λέγετε ταῦτα,
ὡς δεινὸν εἰ μηδὲν διοίσει εἰς σοφίαν ἕκαστος τῶν
ἀνθρώπων βοσκήματος ὁτουοῦν· ἀπόδειξιν δὲ
καὶ ἀνάγκην οὐδ' ἡντινοῦν λέγετε, ἀλλὰ τῷ εἰκότι
χρῆσθε, ᾧ εἰ ἐθέλοι Θεόδωρος ἢ ἄλλος τις τῶν γεω-
μετρῶν χρώμενος γεωμετρεῖν, ἄξιος οὐδ' ἑνὸς
μόνου[1] ἂν εἴη. σκοπεῖτε οὖν σύ τε καὶ Θεόδωρος,
εἰ ἀποδέξεσθε πιθανολογίᾳ τε καὶ εἰκόσι περὶ
163 τηλικούτων[2] λεγομένους λόγους.

ΘΕΑΙ. Ἀλλ' οὐ δίκαιον, ὦ Σώκρατες, οὔτε σὺ
οὔτε ἂν ἡμεῖς φαῖμεν.

ΣΩ. Ἄλλη δὴ σκεπτέον, ὡς ἔοικεν, ὡς ὅ τε σὸς
καὶ ὁ Θεοδώρου λόγος.

ΘΕΑΙ. Πάνυ μὲν οὖν ἄλλη.

ΣΩ. Τῇδε δὴ σκοπῶμεν εἰ ἄρα ἐστὶν ἐπιστήμη
τε καὶ αἴσθησις ταὐτὸν ἢ ἕτερον. εἰς γὰρ τοῦτό
που πᾶς ὁ λόγος ἡμῖν ἔτεινεν, καὶ τούτου χάριν τὰ
πολλὰ καὶ ἄτοπα ταῦτα ἐκινήσαμεν. οὐ γάρ;

ΘΕΑΙ. Παντάπασι μὲν οὖν.

Β ΣΩ. Ἦ οὖν ὁμολογήσομεν, ἃ τῷ ὁρᾶν αἰσθανόμεθα ἢ τῷ ἀκούειν, πάντα ταῦτα ἅμα καὶ ἐπίστασθαι; οἷον τῶν βαρβάρων πρὶν μαθεῖν τὴν φωνὴν
πότερον οὐ φήσομεν ἀκούειν, ὅταν φθέγγωνται, ἢ

---

[1] μόνου] Adam, *Class. Rev.* iv. p. 103, suggests νόμου, "a
coin, a copper."   [2] τηλικούτων Τ; τούτων Β.

soc. You are young, my dear boy; so you are quickly moved and swayed by popular oratory. For in reply to what I have said, Protagoras, or someone speaking for him, will say, "Excellent boys and old men, there you sit together declaiming to the people, and you bring in the gods, the question of whose existence or non-existence I exclude from oral and written discussion, and you say the sort of thing that the crowd would readily accept—that it is a terrible thing if every man is to be no better than any beast in point of wisdom; but you do not advance any cogent proof whatsoever; you base your statements on probability. If Theodorus, or any other geometrician, should base his geometry on probability, he would be of no account at all. So you and Theodorus had better consider whether you will accept arguments founded on plausibility and probabilities in such important matters.

theaet. That would not be right, Socrates; neither you nor we would think so.

soc. Apparently, then, you and Theodorus mean we must look at the matter in a different way.

theaet. Yes, certainly in a different way.

soc. Well, then, let us look at it in this way, raising the question whether knowledge is after all the same as perception, or different. For that is the object of all our discussion, and it was to answer that question that we stirred up all these strange doctrines, was it not?

theaet. Most assuredly.

soc. Shall we then agree that all that we perceive by sight or hearing we know? For instance, shall we say that before having learned the language of foreigners we do not hear them when they speak,

ἀκούειν τε καὶ ἐπίστασθαι ἃ λέγουσι; καὶ αὖ
γράμματα μὴ ἐπιστάμενοι, βλέποντες εἰς αὐτὰ
πότερον οὐχ ὁρᾶν ἢ ἐπίστασθαι εἴπερ ὁρῶμεν δι-
ισχυριούμεθα;

ΘΕΑΙ. Αὐτό γε, ὦ Σώκρατες, τοῦτο αὐτῶν,
ὅπερ ὁρῶμέν τε καὶ ἀκούομεν, ἐπίστασθαι φήσομεν·
τῶν μὲν γὰρ τὸ σχῆμα καὶ τὸ χρῶμα ὁρᾶν τε καὶ
C ἐπίστασθαι, τῶν δὲ τὴν ὀξύτητα καὶ βαρύτητα
ἀκούειν τε ἅμα καὶ εἰδέναι· ἃ δὲ οἵ τε γραμματι-
σταὶ περὶ αὐτῶν καὶ οἱ ἑρμηνεῖς διδάσκουσιν, οὔτε
αἰσθάνεσθαι τῷ ὁρᾶν ἢ ἀκούειν οὔτε ἐπίστασθαι.

18. ΣΩ. Ἄριστά γ', ὦ Θεαίτητε, καὶ οὐκ
ἄξιόν σοι πρὸς ταῦτα ἀμφισβητῆσαι, ἵνα καὶ αὐξάνῃ.
ἀλλ' ὅρα δὴ καὶ τόδε ἄλλο προσιόν, καὶ σκόπει πῇ
αὐτὸ διωσόμεθα.

ΘΕΑΙ. Τὸ ποῖον δή;

ΣΩ. Τὸ τοιόνδε· εἴ τις ἔροιτο, " ἆρα δυνατόν,
ὅτου τις ἐπιστήμων γένοιτό ποτε, ἔτι ἔχοντα
D μνήμην αὐτοῦ τούτου καὶ σῳζόμενον, τότε ὅτε
μέμνηται μὴ ἐπίστασθαι αὐτὸ τοῦτο ὃ μέμνηται ; "
μακρολογῶ δέ, ὡς ἔοικε, βουλόμενος ἐρέσθαι, εἰ
μαθών τίς τι μεμνημένος μὴ οἶδε.

ΘΕΑΙ. Καὶ πῶς, ὦ Σώκρατες; τέρας γὰρ ἂν εἴη
ὃ λέγεις.

ΣΩ. Μὴ οὖν ἐγὼ ληρῶ; σκόπει δέ. ἆρα τὸ
ὁρᾶν οὐκ αἰσθάνεσθαι λέγεις καὶ τὴν ὄψιν αἴσθησιν;

ΘΕΑΙ. Ἔγωγε.

ΣΩ. Οὐκοῦν ὁ ἰδών τι ἐπιστήμων ἐκείνου γέγονεν
E ὃ εἶδεν κατὰ τὸν ἄρτι λόγον;

or that we both hear and know what they say?
And again, if we do not know the letters, shall we
maintain that we do not see them when we look
at them or that if we really see them we know them?

THEAET. We shall say, Socrates, that we know
just so much of them as we hear or see: in the
case of the letters, we both see and know the form
and colour, and in the spoken language we both
hear and at the same time know the higher and
lower notes of the voice; but we do not perceive
through sight or hearing, and we do not know, what
the grammarians and interpreters teach about them.

soc. First-rate, Theaetetus! and it is a pity to
dispute that, for I want you to grow. But look out
for another trouble that is yonder coming towards
us, and see how we can repel it.

THEAET. What is it?

soc. It is like this: If anyone should ask, "Is it
possible, if a man has ever known a thing and still
has and preserves a memory of that thing, that he
does not, at the time when he remembers, know that
very thing which he remembers?" I seem to be
pretty long winded; but I merely want to ask if a
man who has learned a thing does not know it
when he remembers it.

THEAET. Of course he does, Socrates; for what
you suggest would be monstrous.

soc. Am I crazy, then? Look here. Do you not
say that seeing is perceiving and that sight is perception?

THEAET. I do.

soc. Then, according to what we have just said,
the man who has seen a thing has acquired knowledge of that which he has seen?

ΘΕΑΙ. Ναί.

ΣΩ. Τί δέ; μνήμην οὐ λέγεις μέντοι τι;

ΘΕΑΙ. Ναί.

ΣΩ. Πότερον οὐδενὸς ἢ τινός;

ΘΕΑΙ. Τινὸς δήπου.

ΣΩ. Οὐκοῦν ὧν ἔμαθε καὶ ὧν ἤσθετο, τοιου·τωνί τινων;

ΘΕΑΙ. Τί μήν;

ΣΩ. ῝Ο δὴ εἶδέ τις, μέμνηταί που ἐνίοτε;

ΘΕΑΙ. Μέμνηται.

ΣΩ. ῏Η καὶ μύσας; ἢ τοῦτο δράσας ἐπελάθετο;

ΘΕΑΙ. Ἀλλὰ δεινόν, ὦ Σώκρατες, τοῦτό γε φάναι.

164 ΣΩ. Δεῖ γε μέντοι, εἰ σώσομεν[1] τὸν πρόσθε λόγον· εἰ δὲ μή, οἴχεται.

ΘΕΑΙ. Καὶ ἐγώ, νὴ τὸν Δία, ὑποπτεύω, οὐ μὴν ἱκανῶς γε συννοῶ· ἀλλ᾽ εἰπὲ πῇ.

ΣΩ. Τῇδε· ὁ μὲν ὁρῶν ἐπιστήμων, φαμέν, τούτου γέγονεν οὗπερ ὁρῶν· ὄψις γὰρ καὶ αἴσθησις καὶ ἐπιστήμη ταὐτὸν ὡμολόγηται.

ΘΕΑΙ. Πάνυ γε.

ΣΩ. Ὁ δέ γε ὁρῶν καὶ ἐπιστήμων γεγονὼς οὗ ἑώρα, ἐὰν μύσῃ, μέμνηται μέν, οὐχ ὁρᾷ δὲ αὐτό. ἢ γάρ;

ΘΕΑΙ. Ναί.

B ΣΩ. Τὸ δέ γε οὐχ ὁρᾷ οὐκ ἐπίσταταί ἐστιν, εἴπερ καὶ τὸ ὁρᾷ ἐπίσταται.

ΘΕΑΙ. Ἀληθῆ.

ΣΩ. Συμβαίνει ἄρα, οὗ τις ἐπιστήμων ἐγένετο,

_____
[1] σώσομεν Dissen; σώσοιμεν BT.

THEAET. Yes.

soc. Well, then, do you not admit that there is such a thing as memory?

THEAET. Yes.

soc. Memory of nothing or of something?

THEAET. Of something, surely.

soc. Of things he has learned and perceived— that sort of things?

THEAET. Of course.

soc. A man sometimes remembers what he has seen, does he not?

THEAET. He does.

soc. Even when he shuts his eyes, or does he forget if he does that?

THEAET. It would be absurd to say that, Socrates.

soc. We must, though, if we are to maintain our previous argument; otherwise, it is all up with it.

THEAET. I too, by Zeus, have my suspicions, but I don't fully understand you. Tell me how it is.

soc. This is how it is: he who sees has acquired knowledge, we say, of that which he has seen; for it is agreed that sight and perception and knowledge are all the same.

THEAET. Certainly.

soc. But he who has seen and has acquired knowledge of what he saw, if he shuts his eyes, remembers it, but does not see it. Is that right?

THEAET. Yes.

soc. But "does not see" is the same as "does not know," if it is true that seeing is knowing.

THEAET. True.

soc. Then this is our result. When a man has acquired knowledge of a thing and still remembers

85

ἔτι μεμνημένον αὐτὸν μὴ ἐπίστασθαι, ἐπειδὴ οὐχ ὁρᾷ· ὃ τέρας ἔφαμεν ἂν εἶναι εἰ γίγνοιτο.

ΘΕΑΙ. Ἀληθέστατα λέγεις.

ΣΩ. Τῶν ἀδυνάτων δή τι συμβαίνειν φαίνεται, ἐάν τις ἐπιστήμην καὶ αἴσθησιν ταὐτὸν φῇ εἶναι.

ΘΕΑΙ. Ἔοικεν.

ΣΩ. Ἄλλο ἄρα ἑκάτερον φατέον.

ΘΕΑΙ. Κινδυνεύει.

C ΣΩ. Τί οὖν δῆτ᾽ ἂν εἴη ἐπιστήμη; πάλιν ἐξ ἀρχῆς, ὡς ἔοικεν, λεκτέον. καίτοι τί ποτε μέλλομεν, ὦ Θεαίτητε, δρᾶν;

ΘΕΑΙ. Τίνος πέρι;

ΣΩ. Φαινόμεθά μοι ἀλεκτρυόνος ἀγεννοῦς δίκην πρὶν νενικηκέναι ἀποπηδήσαντες ἀπὸ τοῦ λόγου ᾄδειν.

ΘΕΑΙ. Πῶς δή;

ΣΩ. Ἀντιλογικῶς ἐοίκαμεν πρὸς τὰς τῶν ὀνομάτων ὁμολογίας ἀνομολογησάμενοι καὶ τοιούτῳ τινὶ περιγενόμενοι τοῦ λόγου ἀγαπᾶν, καὶ οὐ φάσκοντες ἀγωνισταὶ ἀλλὰ φιλόσοφοι εἶναι λαν-
D θάνομεν ταὐτὰ ἐκείνοις τοῖς δεινοῖς ἀνδράσιν ποιοῦντες.

ΘΕΑΙ. Οὔπω μανθάνω ὅπως λέγεις.

ΣΩ. Ἀλλ᾽ ἐγὼ πειράσομαι δηλῶσαι περὶ αὐτῶν ὅ γε δὴ νοῶ. ἠρόμεθα γὰρ δή, εἰ μαθὼν καὶ μεμνημένος τίς τι μὴ ἐπίσταται, καὶ τὸν ἰδόντα καὶ μύσαντα μεμνημένον ὁρῶντα δὲ οὐ ἀποδείξαντες, οὐκ εἰδότα ἀπεδείξαμεν καὶ ἅμα μεμνημένον· τοῦτο δ᾽ εἶναι ἀδύνατον. καὶ οὕτω δὴ μῦθος ἀπώλετο ὁ Πρωταγόρειος, καὶ ὁ σὸς ἅμα ὁ τῆς ἐπιστήμης καὶ αἰσθήσεως, ὅτι ταὐτόν ἐστιν.

it, he does not know it, since he does not see it; but we said that would be a monstrous conclusion.

THEAET. Very true.

soc. So, evidently, we reach an impossible result if we say that knowledge and perception are the same.

THEAET. So it seems.

soc. Then we must say they are different.

THEAET. I suppose so.

soc. Then what can knowledge be? We must, apparently, begin our discussion all over again. And yet, Theaetetus, what are we on the point of doing?

THEAET. About what?

soc. It seems to me that we are behaving like a worthless game-cock; before winning the victory we have leapt away from our argument and begun to crow.

THEAET. How so?

soc. We seem to be acting like professional debaters; we have based our agreements on the mere similarity of words and are satisfied to have got the better of the argument in such a way, and we do not see that we, who claim to be, not contestants for a prize, but lovers of wisdom, are doing just what those ingenious persons do.

THEAET. I do not yet understand what you mean.

soc. Well, I will try to make my thought clear. We asked, you recollect, whether a man who has learned something and remembers it does not know it. We showed first that the one who has seen and then shuts his eyes remembers, although he does not see, and then we showed that he does not know, although at the same time he remembers; but this, we said, was impossible. And so the Protagorean tale was brought to naught, and yours also about the identity of knowledge and perception.

E   ΘΕΑΙ. Φαίνεται.

ΣΩ. Οὔ τι ἄν, οἶμαι, ὦ φίλε, εἴπερ γε ὁ πατὴρ
τοῦ ἑτέρου μύθου ἔζη, ἀλλὰ πολλὰ[1] ἂν ἤμυνε·
νῦν δὲ ὀρφανὸν αὐτὸν ἡμεῖς προπηλακίζομεν. καὶ
γὰρ οὐδ' οἱ ἐπίτροποι, οὓς Πρωταγόρας κατέλιπεν,
βοηθεῖν ἐθέλουσιν, ὧν Θεόδωρος εἷς[2] ὅδε. ἀλλὰ
δὴ αὐτοὶ κινδυνεύσομεν τοῦ δικαίου ἕνεκ' αὐτῷ
βοηθεῖν.

ΘΕΟ. Οὐ γὰρ ἐγώ, ὦ Σώκρατες, ἀλλὰ μᾶλλον
165 Καλλίας ὁ Ἱππονίκου τῶν ἐκείνου ἐπίτροπος·
ἡμεῖς δέ πως θᾶττον ἐκ τῶν ψιλῶν λόγων πρὸς
τὴν γεωμετρίαν ἀπενεύσαμεν. χάριν γε μέντοι
σοὶ[3] ἕξομεν, ἐὰν αὐτῷ βοηθῇς.

ΣΩ. Καλῶς λέγεις, ὦ Θεόδωρε. σκέψαι οὖν
τήν γ' ἐμὴν βοήθειαν. τῶν γὰρ ἄρτι δεινότερα
ἄν τις ὁμολογήσειεν μὴ προσέχων τοῖς ῥήμασι
τὸν νοῦν, ᾗ τὸ πολὺ εἰθίσμεθα φάναι τε καὶ ἀπ-
αρνεῖσθαι. σοὶ λέγω ὅπῃ, ἢ Θεαιτήτῳ;

ΘΕΟ. Εἰς τὸ κοινὸν μὲν οὖν, ἀποκρινέσθω δὲ ὁ
B νεώτερος· σφαλεὶς γὰρ ἧττον ἀσχημονήσει.

19. ΣΩ. Λέγω δὴ τὸ δεινότατον ἐρώτημα·
ἔστι δέ, οἶμαι, τοιόνδε τι· ἆρα οἷόν τε τὸν αὐτὸν
εἰδότα τι τοῦτο ὃ οἶδεν μὴ εἰδέναι;

ΘΕΟ. Τί δὴ οὖν ἀποκρινούμεθα, ὦ Θεαίτητε;

ΘΕΑΙ. Ἀδύνατόν που, οἶμαι ἔγωγε.

ΣΩ. Οὔκ, εἰ τὸ ὁρᾶν γε ἐπίστασθαι θήσεις. τί

---

[1] πολλὰ om. T.   [2] εἷς om. T.   [3] σοὶ om. B.

THEAET. Evidently.

soc. It would not be so, I fancy, my friend, if the father of the first of the two tales were alive; he would have had a good deal to say in its defence. But he is dead, and we are abusing the orphan. Why, even the guardians whom Protagoras left—one of whom is Theodorus here—are unwilling to come to the child's assistance. So it seems that we shall have to do it ourselves, assisting him in the name of justice.

THEO. Do so, for it is not I, Socrates, but rather Callias the son of Hipponicus, who is the guardian of his children. As for me, I turned rather too soon from abstract speculations to geometry. However, I shall be grateful to you if you come to his assistance.

soc. Good, Theodorus! Now see how I shall help him; for a man might find himself involved in still worse inconsistencies than those in which we found ourselves just now, if he did not pay attention to the terms which we generally use in assent and denial. Shall I explain this to you, or only to Theaetetus?

THEO. To both of us, but let the younger answer; for he will be less disgraced if he is discomfited.

soc. Very well; now I am going to ask the most frightfully difficult question of all. It runs, I believe, something like this: Is it possible for a person, if he knows a thing, at the same time not to know that which he knows?

THEO. Now, then, what shall we answer, Theaetetus?

THEAET. It is impossible, I should think.

soc. Not if you make seeing and knowing identical.

165

γὰρ χρήσει ἀφύκτῳ ἐρωτήματι, τὸ λεγόμενον ἐν
φρέατι συνεχόμενος,[1] ὅταν ἐρωτᾷ ἀνέκπληκτος
ἀνήρ, καταλαβὼν τῇ χειρὶ σοῦ τὸν ἕτερον ὀφθαλμόν,
C εἰ ὁρᾷς τὸ ἱμάτιον τῷ κατειλημμένῳ;

ΘΕΑΙ. Οὐ φήσω, οἶμαι, τούτῳ γε, τῷ μέντοι
ἑτέρῳ.

ΣΩ. Οὐκοῦν ὁρᾷς τε καὶ οὐχ ὁρᾷς ἅμα ταὐτόν;

ΘΕΑΙ. Οὕτω γέ πως.

ΣΩ. Οὐδὲν ἐγώ, φήσει, τοῦτο οὔτε τάττω οὔτ᾽
ἠρόμην τὸ ὅπως, ἀλλ᾽ εἰ ὃ ἐπίστασαι, τοῦτο καὶ
οὐκ ἐπίστασαι. νῦν δ᾽ ὃ οὐχ ὁρᾷς ὁρῶν φαίνει.
ὡμολογηκὼς δὲ τυγχάνεις τὸ ὁρᾶν ἐπίστασθαι καὶ
τὸ μὴ ὁρᾶν μὴ ἐπίστασθαι. ἐξ οὖν τούτων λογίζου,
τί σοι συμβαίνει.

D ΘΕΑΙ. Ἀλλὰ λογίζομαι ὅτι τἀναντία οἷς ὑπε-
θέμην.

ΣΩ. Ἴσως δέ γ᾽, ὦ θαυμάσιε, πλείω ἂν τοιαῦτ᾽
ἔπαθες, εἴ τίς σε προσηρώτα, εἰ ἐπίστασθαι ἔστι
μὲν ὀξύ, ἔστι δὲ ἀμβλύ, καὶ ἐγγύθεν μὲν ἐπίστασθαι,
πόρρωθεν δὲ μή, καὶ σφόδρα καὶ ἠρέμα τὸ αὐτό,
καὶ ἄλλα μυρία, ἃ ἐλλοχῶν[2] ἂν πελταστικὸς ἀνὴρ
μισθοφόρος ἐν λόγοις ἐρόμενος, ἡνίκ᾽ ἐπιστήμην καὶ
αἴσθησιν ταὐτὸν ἔθου, ἐμβαλὼν ἂν εἰς τὸ ἀκούειν
καὶ ὀσφραίνεσθαι καὶ τὰς τοιαύτας αἰσθήσεις,
E ἤλεγχεν ἂν ἐπέχων καὶ οὐκ ἀνιεὶς πρὶν θαυμάσας
τὴν πολυάρατον σοφίαν συνεποδίσθης ὑπ᾽ αὐτοῦ,
οὗ δή σε χειρωσάμενός τε καὶ συνδήσας ἤδη ἂν

---

[1] συνεχόμενος B; συσχόμενος B²T.
[2] ἐλλοχῶν bt; ἐνλοχῶν BT.

For what will you do with a question from which there is no escape, by which you are, as the saying is, caught in a pit, when your adversary, unabashed, puts his hand over one of your eyes and asks if you see his cloak with the eye that is covered?

THEAET. I shall say, I think, "Not with that eye, but with the other."

soc. Then you see and do not see the same thing at the same time?

THEAET. After a fashion.

soc. "That," he will reply, "is not at all what I want, and I did not ask about the fashion, but whether you both know and do not know the same thing. Now manifestly you see that which you do not see. But you have agreed that seeing is knowing and not seeing is not knowing. Very well; from all this, reckon out what the result is."

THEAET. Well, I reckon out that the result is the contrary of my hypothesis.

soc. And perhaps, my fine fellow, more troubles of the same sort might have come upon you, if anyone asked you further questions—whether it is possible to know the same thing both sharply and dully, to know close at hand but not at a distance, to know both violently and gently, and countless other questions, such as a nimble fighter, fighting for pay in the war of words, might have lain in wait and asked you, when you said that knowledge and perception were the same thing; he would have charged down upon hearing and smelling and such senses, and would have argued persistently and unceasingly until you were filled with admiration of his greatly desired wisdom and were taken in his toils, and then, after subduing and binding you he would

91

τότε ἐλύτρου χρημάτων ὅσων σοί γε κἀκείνῳ
ἐδόκει. τίν' οὖν δὴ ὁ Πρωταγόρας, φαίης ἂν ἴσως,
λόγον ἐπίκουρον τοῖς αὐτοῦ ἐρεῖ; ἄλλο τι πειρώμεθα λέγειν;

ΘΕΑΙ. Πάνυ μὲν οὖν.

20. ΣΩ. Ταῦτά τε δὴ πάντα ὅσα ἡμεῖς ἐπα-
166 μύνοντες αὐτῷ λέγομεν, καὶ ὁμόσε, οἶμαι, χωρή-
σεται καταφρονῶν ἡμῶν καὶ λέγων· " οὗτος δὴ
ὁ Σωκράτης ὁ χρηστός, ἐπειδὴ αὐτῷ παιδίον τι
ἐρωτηθὲν ἔδεισεν εἰ οἷόν τε τὸν αὐτὸν τὸ αὐτὸ
μεμνῆσθαι ἅμα καὶ μὴ εἰδέναι, καὶ δεῖσαν ἀπέφησεν
διὰ τὸ μὴ δύνασθαι προορᾶν, γέλωτα δὴ τὸν ἐμὲ
ἐν τοῖς λόγοις ἀπέδειξεν. τὸ δέ, ὦ ῥᾳθυμότατε
Σώκρατες, τῇδ' ἔχει· ὅταν τι τῶν ἐμῶν δι' ἐρωτή-
σεως σκοπῇς, ἐὰν μὲν ὁ ἐρωτηθεὶς οἷάπερ ἂν ἐγὼ
ἀποκριναίμην ἀποκρινάμενος σφάλληται, ἐγὼ ἐλέγ-
B χομαι, εἰ δὲ ἀλλοῖα, αὐτὸς ὁ ἐρωτηθείς. αὐτίκα
γὰρ δοκεῖς τινά σοι συγχωρήσεσθαι μνήμην
παρεῖναί τῳ ὧν ἔπαθε, τοιοῦτόν τι οὖσαν πάθος
οἷον ὅτε ἔπασχε, μηκέτι πάσχοντι; πολλοῦ γε
δεῖ. ἢ αὖ ἀποκνήσειν ὁμολογεῖν οἷόν τ' εἶναι
εἰδέναι καὶ μὴ εἰδέναι τὸν αὐτὸν τὸ αὐτό; ἢ ἐάνπερ
τοῦτο δείσῃ, δώσειν ποτὲ τὸν αὐτὸν εἶναι τὸν
ἀνομοιούμενον τῷ πρὶν ἀνομοιοῦσθαι ὄντι; μᾶλλον
δὲ τὸν εἶναί τινα, ἀλλ' οὐχὶ τούς, καὶ τούτους
γιγνομένους ἀπείρους, ἐάνπερ ἀνομοίωσις γίγνηται,
C εἰ δὴ ὀνομάτων γε δεήσει θηρεύσεις διευλαβεῖσθαι

at once proceed to bargain with you for such ransom as might be agreed upon between you. What argument, then, you might ask, will Protagoras produce to strengthen his forces? Shall we try to carry on the discussion?

THEAET. By all means.

soc. He will, I fancy, say all that we have said in his defence and then will close with us, saying contemptuously, "Our estimable Socrates here frightened a little boy by asking if it was possible for one and the same person to remember and at the same time not to know one and the same thing, and when the child in his fright said 'no,' because he could not foresee what would result, Socrates made poor me a laughing-stock in his talk. But, you slovenly Socrates, the facts stand thus: when you examine any doctrine of mine by the method of questioning, if the person who is questioned makes such replies as I should make and comes to grief, then I am refuted, but if his replies are quite different, then the person questioned is refuted, not I. Take this example. Do you suppose you could get anybody to admit that the memory a man has of a past feeling he no longer feels is anything like the feeling at the time when he was feeling it? Far from it. Or that he would refuse to admit that it is possible for one and the same person to know and not to know one and the same thing? Or if he were afraid to admit this, would he ever admit that a person who has become unlike is the same as before he became unlike? In fact, if we are to be on our guard against such verbal entanglements, would he admit that a person is one at all, and not many, who become infinite in number, if the process of becoming

ἀλλήλων; ἀλλ᾽, ὦ μακάριε," φήσει, " γενναιοτέ-
ρως ἐπ᾽ αὐτὸ ἐλθὼν ὃ λέγω, εἰ δύνασαι, ἐξέλεγξον
ὡς οὐχὶ ἴδιαι αἰσθήσεις ἑκάστῳ ἡμῶν γίγνονται,
ἢ ὡς ἰδίων γιγνομένων οὐδέν τι ἂν μᾶλλον τὸ
φαινόμενον μόνῳ ἐκείνῳ γίγνοιτο, ἢ εἰ εἶναι δεῖ
ὀνομάζειν, εἴη ᾧπερ φαίνεται· ὗς δὲ δὴ καὶ κυνο-
κεφάλους λέγων οὐ μόνον αὐτὸς ὑηνεῖς, ἀλλὰ καὶ
τοὺς ἀκούοντας τοῦτο δρᾶν εἰς τὰ συγγράμματά

D μου ἀναπείθεις, οὐ καλῶς ποιῶν. ἐγὼ γάρ φημι
μὲν τὴν ἀλήθειαν ἔχειν ὡς γέγραφα· μέτρον γὰρ
ἕκαστον ἡμῶν εἶναι τῶν τε ὄντων καὶ μή· μυρίον
μέντοι διαφέρειν ἕτερον ἑτέρου αὐτῷ τούτῳ, ὅτι
τῷ μὲν ἄλλα ἔστι τε καὶ φαίνεται, τῷ δὲ ἄλλα.
καὶ σοφίαν καὶ σοφὸν ἄνδρα πολλοῦ δέω τὸ μὴ
φάναι εἶναι, ἀλλ᾽ αὐτὸν τοῦτον καὶ λέγω σοφόν,
ὃς ἄν τινι ἡμῶν, ᾧ φαίνεται καὶ ἔστι κακά, μετα-
βάλλων ποιήσῃ ἀγαθὰ φαίνεσθαί τε καὶ εἶναι.

E τὸν δὲ λόγον αὖ μὴ τῷ ῥήματί μου δίωκε, ἀλλ᾽
ὧδε ἔτι σαφέστερον μάθε τί λέγω. οἷον γὰρ ἐν
τοῖς πρόσθεν ἐλέγετο ἀναμνήσθητι, ὅτι τῷ μὲν
ἀσθενοῦντι πικρὰ φαίνεται ἃ ἐσθίει καὶ ἔστι, τῷ
δὲ ὑγιαίνοντι τἀναντία ἔστι καὶ φαίνεται. σοφώτερον μὲν οὖν τούτων οὐδέτερον δεῖ ποιῆσαι—οὐδὲ

167 γὰρ δυνατόν—οὐδὲ κατηγορητέον ὡς ὁ μὲν κάμνων
ἀμαθὴς ὅτι τοιαῦτα δοξάζει, ὁ δὲ ὑγιαίνων σοφὸς
ὅτι ἀλλοῖα· μεταβλητέον δ᾽ ἐπὶ θάτερα· ἀμείνων

THEAETETUS

different continues? But, my dear fellow," he will
say, "attack my real doctrines in a more generous
manner, and prove, if you can, that perceptions,
when they come, or become, to each of us, are
not individual, or that, if they are individual, what
appears to each one would not, for all that, become
to that one alone—or, if you prefer to say 'be,'
would not be—to whom it appears. But when you
talk of pigs and dog-faced baboons, you not only
act like a pig yourself, but you persuade your
hearers to act so toward my writings, and that
is not right. For I maintain that the truth is
as I have written; each one of us is the measure
of the things that are and those that are not;
but each person differs immeasurably from every
other in just this, that to one person some things
appear and are, and to another person other
things. And I do not by any means say that
wisdom and the wise man do not exist; on the
contrary, I say that if bad things appear and are to
any one of us, precisely that man is wise who causes
a change and makes good things appear and be to
him. And, moreover, do not lay too much stress
upon the words of my argument, but get a clearer
understanding of my meaning from what I am going
to say. Recall to your mind what was said before,
that his food appears and is bitter to the sick
man, but appears and is the opposite of bitter to the
man in health. Now neither of these two is to be
made wiser than he is—that is not possible—nor
should the claim be made that the sick man is
ignorant because his opinions are ignorant, or the
healthy man wise because his are different; but a
change must be made from the one condition to

95

γὰρ ἡ ἑτέρα ἕξις. οὕτω δὲ καὶ ἐν τῇ παιδείᾳ ἀπὸ
ἑτέρας ἕξεως ἐπὶ τὴν ἀμείνω μεταβλητέον· ἀλλ'
ὁ μὲν ἰατρὸς φαρμάκοις μεταβάλλει, ὁ δὲ σοφιστὴς
λόγοις. ἐπεὶ οὔ τί γε ψευδῆ δοξάζοντά τίς τινα
ὕστερον ἀληθῆ ἐποίησε δοξάζειν. οὔτε γὰρ τὰ
μὴ ὄντα δυνατὸν δοξάσαι, οὔτε ἄλλα παρ' ἃ ἂν
πάσχῃ· ταῦτα δὲ ἀεὶ ἀληθῆ. ἀλλ' οἶμαι, πονηρᾷ[1]
B ψυχῆς ἕξει δοξάζοντα[2] συγγενῆ ἑαυτῆς[3] χρηστὴ
ἐποίησε δοξάσαι ἕτερα τοιαῦτα, ἃ δή τινες τὰ
φαντάσματα ὑπὸ ἀπειρίας ἀληθῆ καλοῦσιν, ἐγὼ
δὲ βελτίω μὲν τὰ ἕτερα τῶν ἑτέρων, ἀληθέστερα
δὲ οὐδέν. καὶ τοὺς σοφούς, ὦ φίλε Σώκρατες,
πολλοῦ δέω βατράχους λέγειν, ἀλλὰ κατὰ μὲν
σώματα ἰατροὺς λέγω, κατὰ δὲ φυτὰ γεωργούς.
φημὶ γὰρ καὶ τούτους τοῖς φυτοῖς ἀντὶ πονηρῶν
αἰσθήσεων, ὅταν τι αὐτῶν ἀσθενῇ, χρηστὰς καὶ
C ὑγιεινὰς αἰσθήσεις τε καὶ ἀληθεῖς[4] ἐμποιεῖν, τοὺς
δέ γε σοφούς τε καὶ ἀγαθοὺς ῥήτορας ταῖς πόλεσι
τὰ χρηστὰ ἀντὶ τῶν πονηρῶν δίκαια δοκεῖν εἶναι
ποιεῖν. ἐπεὶ οἷά γ' ἂν ἑκάστῃ πόλει δίκαια καὶ
καλὰ δοκῇ, ταῦτα καὶ εἶναι αὐτῇ, ἕως ἂν αὐτὰ
νομίζῃ· ἀλλ' ὁ σοφὸς ἀντὶ πονηρῶν ὄντων αὐτοῖς
ἑκάστων χρηστὰ ἐποίησεν εἶναι καὶ δοκεῖν. κατὰ
δὲ τὸν αὐτὸν λόγον καὶ ὁ σοφιστὴς τοὺς παιδευομέ-
νους οὕτω δυνάμενος παιδαγωγεῖν σοφός τε καὶ
D ἄξιος πολλῶν χρημάτων τοῖς παιδευθεῖσιν· καὶ
οὕτω σοφώτεροί τέ εἰσιν ἕτεροι ἑτέρων καὶ οὐδεὶς

---

[1] πονηρᾷ Aldina ; πονηρᾶς BT.
[2] δοξάζοντα Tb ; δοξάζοντας B.
[3] ἑαυτῆς BT ; αὑτῆς some mss. and editors.
[4] ἀληθεῖς BT ; ἀληθείας Schleiermacher.

the other, for the other is better. So, too, in education a change has to be made from a worse to a
better condition ; but the physician causes the change
by means of drugs, and the teacher of wisdom by
means of words. And yet, in fact, no one ever
made anyone think truly who previously thought
falsely, since it is impossible to think that which
is not or to think any other things than those which
one feels ; and these are always true. But I believe
that a man who, on account of a bad condition
of soul, thinks thoughts akin to that condition,
is made by a good condition of soul to think corres-
pondingly good thoughts ; and some men, through
inexperience, call these appearances true, whereas I
call them better than the others, but in no wise
truer. And the wise, my dear Socrates, I do not by
any means call tadpoles ; when they have to do with
the human body, I call them physicians, and when
they have to do with plants, husbandmen ; for I
assert that these latter, when plants are sickly, instil
into them good and healthy sensations, and true ones
instead of bad sensations, and that the wise and
good orators make the good, instead of the evil,
seem to be right to their states. For I claim
that whatever seems right and honourable to a state
is really right and honourable to it, so long as it
believes it to be so ; but the wise man causes the
good, instead of that which is evil to them in each
instance, to be and seem right and honourable. And
on the same principle the teacher who is able to
train his pupils in this manner is not only wise but
is also entitled to receive high pay from them when
their education is finished. And in this sense it is
true that some men are wiser than others, and that

97

ψευδῆ δοξάζει, καὶ σοί, ἐάν τε βούλῃ ἐάν τε μή,
ἀνεκτέον ὄντι μέτρῳ· σῴζεται γὰρ ἐν τούτοις ὁ
λόγος οὗτος. ᾧ σὺ εἰ μὲν ἔχεις ἐξ ἀρχῆς ἀμφισ-
βητεῖν, ἀμφισβήτει λόγῳ ἀντιδιεξελθών· εἰ δὲ
δι' ἐρωτήσεων βούλει, δι' ἐρωτήσεων· οὐδὲ γὰρ
τοῦτο φευκτέον, ἀλλὰ πάντων μάλιστα διωκτέον
τῷ νοῦν ἔχοντι. ποίει μέντοι οὑτωσί· μὴ ἀδίκει
E ἐν τῷ ἐρωτᾶν· καὶ γὰρ πολλὴ ἀλογία ἀρετῆς
φάσκοντα ἐπιμελεῖσθαι μηδὲν ἀλλ' ἢ ἀδικοῦντα
ἐν λόγοις διατελεῖν. ἀδικεῖν δ' ἐστὶν ἐν τῷ τοιούτῳ,
ὅταν τις μὴ χωρὶς μὲν ὡς ἀγωνιζόμενος τὰς
διατριβὰς ποιῆται, χωρὶς δὲ διαλεγόμενος, καὶ ἐν
μὲν τῷ παίζῃ τε καὶ σφάλλῃ καθ' ὅσον ἂν δύνηται,
ἐν δὲ τῷ διαλέγεσθαι σπουδάζῃ τε καὶ ἐπανορθοῖ
τὸν προσδιαλεγόμενον, ἐκεῖνα μόνα αὐτῷ ἐνδεικνύμενος τὰ σφάλματα, ἃ αὐτὸς ὑφ' ἑαυτοῦ καὶ
168 τῶν προτέρων συνουσιῶν παρεκέκρουστο· ἂν μὲν
γὰρ οὕτω ποιῇς, ἑαυτοὺς αἰτιάσονται οἱ προσδια-
τρίβοντές σοι τῆς αὑτῶν ταραχῆς καὶ ἀπορίας,
ἀλλ' οὐ σέ, καὶ σὲ μὲν διώξονται καὶ φιλήσουσιν,
αὑτοὺς δὲ μισήσουσι καὶ φεύξονται ἀφ' ἑαυτῶν εἰς
φιλοσοφίαν, ἵν' ἄλλοι γενόμενοι ἀπαλλαγῶσι τῶν
οἳ πρότερον ἦσαν· ἐὰν δὲ τἀναντία τούτων δρᾷς
ὥσπερ οἱ πολλοί, τἀναντία ξυμβήσεταί σοι καὶ
τοὺς συνόντας ἀντὶ φιλοσόφων μισοῦντας τοῦτο
B τὸ πρᾶγμα ἀποφανεῖς, ἐπειδὰν πρεσβύτεροι γένων-
ται. ἐὰν οὖν ἐμοὶ πείθῃ, ὃ καὶ πρότερον ἐρρήθη,
οὐ δυσμενῶς οὐδὲ μαχητικῶς, ἀλλ' ἵλεῳ τῇ διανοίᾳ
συγκαθεὶς ὡς ἀληθῶς σκέψει τί ποτε λέγομεν,

no one thinks falsely, and that you, whether you will or no, must endure to be a measure. Upon these positions my doctrine stands firm; and if you can dispute it in principle, dispute it by bringing an opposing doctrine against it; or if you prefer the method of questions, ask questions; for an intelligent person ought not to reject this method, on the contrary, he should choose it before all others. However, let me make a suggestion: do not be unfair in your questioning; it is very inconsistent for a man who asserts that he cares for virtue to be constantly unfair in discussion; and it is unfair in discussion when a man makes no distinction between merely trying to make points and carrying on a real argument. In the former he may jest and try to trip up his opponent as much as he can, but in real argument he must be in earnest and must set his interlocutor on his feet, pointing out to him those slips only which are due to himself and his previous associations. For if you act in this way, those who debate with you will cast the blame for their confusion and perplexity upon themselves, not upon you; they will run after you and love you, and they will hate themselves and run away from themselves, taking refuge in philosophy, that they may escape from their former selves by becoming different. But if you act in the opposite way, as most teachers do, you will produce the opposite result, and instead of making your young associates philosophers, you will make them hate philosophy when they grow older. If, therefore, you will accept the suggestion which I made before, you will avoid a hostile and combative attitude and in a gracious spirit will enter the lists with me and inquire what we really mean

κινεῖσθαί τε ἀποφαινόμενοι τὰ πάντα, τό τε δοκοῦν
ἑκάστῳ τοῦτο καὶ εἶναι ἰδιώτῃ τε καὶ πόλει. καὶ
ἐκ τούτων ἐπισκέψει, εἴτε ταὐτὸν εἴτε καὶ ἄλλο
ἐπιστήμη καὶ αἴσθησις, ἀλλ' οὐχ, ὥσπερ ἄρτι, ἐκ
C συνηθείας ῥημάτων τε καὶ ὀνομάτων, ἃ οἱ πολλοὶ
ὅπῃ ἂν τύχωσιν ἕλκοντες ἀπορίας ἀλλήλοις παντο-
δαπὰς παρέχουσι.'' ταῦτα, ὦ Θεόδωρε, τῷ ἑταίρῳ
σου εἰς βοήθειαν προσηρξάμην κατ' ἐμὴν δύναμιν,
σμικρὰ ἀπὸ σμικρῶν· εἰ δ' αὐτὸς ἔζη, μεγαλειό-
τερον ἂν τοῖς αὑτοῦ ἐβοήθησεν.

21. ΘΕΟ. Παίζεις, ὦ Σώκρατες· πάνυ γὰρ
νεανικῶς τῷ ἀνδρὶ βεβοήθηκας.

ΣΩ. Εὖ λέγεις, ὦ ἑταῖρε. καί μοι εἰπέ· ἐνενόη-
σάς που λέγοντος ἄρτι τοῦ Πρωταγόρου καὶ ὀνειδί-
D ζοντος ἡμῖν ὅτι πρὸς παιδίον τοὺς λόγους ποιούμενοι τῷ τοῦ παιδὸς φόβῳ ἀγωνιζόμεθα[1] εἰς τὰ
ἑαυτοῦ, καὶ χαριεντισμόν τινα ἀποκαλῶν, ἀποσεμ-
νύνων δὲ τὸ πάντων μέτρον, σπουδάσαι ἡμᾶς
διεκελεύσατο περὶ τὸν αὑτοῦ λόγον;

ΘΕΟ. Πῶς γὰρ οὐκ ἐνενόησα, ὦ Σώκρατες;

ΣΩ. Τί οὖν; κελεύεις πείθεσθαι αὐτῷ;

ΘΕΟ. Σφόδρα γε.

ΣΩ. Ὁρᾷς οὖν ὅτι τάδε πάντα πλὴν σοῦ παιδία
ἐστίν. εἰ οὖν πεισόμεθα τῷ ἀνδρί, ἐμὲ καὶ σὲ

[1] ἀγωνιζόμεθα B; ἀγωνιζοίμεθα T.

when we declare that all things are in motion and that whatever seems is to each individual, whether man or state. And on the basis of that you will consider the question whether knowledge and perception are the same or different, instead of doing as you did a while ago, using as your basis the ordinary meaning of names and words, which most people pervert in haphazard ways and thereby cause all sorts of perplexity in one another." Such, Theodorus, is the help I have furnished your friend to the best of my ability—not much, for my resources are small; but if he were living himself he would have helped his offspring in a fashion more magnificent.

THEO. You are joking, Socrates, for you have come to the man's assistance with all the valour of youth.

SOC. Thank you, my friend. Tell me, did you observe just now that Protagoras reproached us for addressing our words to a boy, and said that we made the boy's timidity aid us in our argument against his doctrine, and that he called our procedure a mere display of wit, solemnly insisting upon the importance of "the measure of all things," and urging us to treat his doctrine seriously?

THEO. Of course I observed it, Socrates.

SOC. Well then, shall we do as he says?

THEO. By all means.

SOC. Now you see that all those present, except you and myself, are boys. So if we are to do as

101

168

Ε δεῖ ἐρωτῶντάς τε καὶ ἀποκρινομένους ἀλλήλοις σπουδάσαι αὐτοῦ περὶ τὸν λόγον, ἵνα μή τοι τοῦτό γε[1] ἔχῃ ἐγκαλεῖν, ὡς παίζοντες πρὸς μειράκια διεσκεψάμεθ' αὐτοῦ τὸν[2] λόγον.

ΘΕΟ. Τί δ'; οὐ πολλῶν τοι Θεαίτητος μεγάλους πώγωνας ἐχόντων ἄμεινον ἂν ἐπακολουθήσειε λόγῳ διερευνωμένῳ;

ΣΩ. Ἀλλ' οὔ τι σοῦ γε, ὦ Θεόδωρε, ἄμεινον. μὴ οὖν οἴου ἐμὲ μὲν τῷ σῷ ἑταίρῳ τετελευτηκότι
169 δεῖν παντὶ τρόπῳ ἐπαμύνειν, σὲ δὲ μηδενί, ἀλλ' ἴθι, ὦ ἄριστε, ὀλίγον ἐπίσπου, μέχρι τούτου αὐτοῦ ἕως ἂν εἰδῶμεν εἴτε ἄρα σὲ δεῖ διαγραμμάτων πέρι μέτρον εἶναι, εἴτε πάντες ὁμοίως σοὶ ἱκανοὶ ἑαυτοῖς εἴς τε ἀστρονομίαν καὶ τἆλλα ὧν δὴ σὺ πέρι αἰτίαν ἔχεις διαφέρειν.

ΘΕΟ. Οὐ ῥᾴδιον, ὦ Σώκρατες, σοὶ παρακαθήμενον μὴ διδόναι λόγον, ἀλλ' ἐγὼ ἄρτι παρελήρησα φάσκων σε ἐπιτρέψειν μοι μὴ ἀποδύεσθαι, καὶ οὐχὶ ἀναγκάσειν καθάπερ Λακεδαιμόνιοι· σὺ δέ μοι δοκεῖς πρὸς τὸν Σκίρωνα μᾶλλον τείνειν. Λακε-
Β δαιμόνιοι μὲν γὰρ ἀπιέναι ἢ ἀποδύεσθαι κελεύουσι, σὺ δὲ κατ' Ἀνταῖόν τί μοι μᾶλλον δοκεῖς τὸ δρᾶμα δρᾶν· τὸν γὰρ προσελθόντα οὐκ ἀνίης πρὶν ἂν[3] ἀναγκάσῃς ἀποδύσας ἐν τοῖς λόγοις προσπαλαῖσαι.

ΣΩ. Ἄριστά γε, ὦ Θεόδωρε, τὴν νόσον μου ἀπήκασας· ἰσχυρικώτερος μέντοι ἐγὼ ἐκείνων. μυρίοι

---

[1] τοι τοῦτό γε Β ; τοι τόγε Τ ; τοῦτό γε W.
[2] αὐτοῦ τὸν apogr. Coislinianum 155 ; αὖ τοῦ τὸν Β ; αὖ τοῦτον τὸν Τ.
[3] πρὶν ἂν Heindorf ; πρὶν ΒΤ.

the man asks, you and I must question each other and make reply in order to show our serious attitude towards his doctrine; then he cannot, at any rate, find fault with us on the ground that we examined his doctrine in a spirit of levity with mere boys.

THEO. Why is this? Would not Theaetetus follow an investigation better than many a man with a long beard?

SOC. Yes, but not better than you, Theodorus. So you must not imagine that I have to defend your deceased friend by any and every means, while you do nothing at all; but come, my good man, follow the discussion a little way, just until we can see whether, after all, you must be a measure in respect to diagrams, or whether all men are as sufficient unto themselves as you are in astronomy and the other sciences in which you are alleged to be superior.

THEO. It is not easy, Socrates, for anyone to sit beside you and not be forced to give an account of himself and it was foolish of me just now to say you would excuse me and would not oblige me, as the Lacedaemonians do, to strip; you seem to me to take rather after Sciron.[1] For the Lacedaemonians tell people to go away or else strip, but you seem to me to play rather the rôle of Antaeus; for you do not let anyone go who approaches you until you have forced him to strip and wrestle with you in argument.

SOC. Your comparison with Sciron and Antaeus pictures my complaint admirably; only I am a more

---

[1] Sciron was a mighty man who attacked all who came near him and threw them from a cliff. He was overcome by Theseus. Antaeus, a terrible giant, forced all passers-by to wrestle with him. He was invincible until Heracles crushed him in his arms.

γὰρ ἤδη μοι ‘Ηρακλέες τε καὶ Θησέες ἐντυχόντες[1]
καρτεροὶ[2] πρὸς τὸ λέγειν μάλ' εὖ ξυγκεκόφασιν,
ἀλλ' ἐγὼ οὐδέν τι μᾶλλον ἀφίσταμαι· οὕτω τις
C ἔρως δεινὸς ἐνδέδυκε τῆς περὶ ταῦτα γυμνασίας.
μὴ οὖν μηδὲ σὺ φθονήσῃς προσανατριψάμενος
σαυτόν τε ἅμα καὶ ἐμὲ ὀνῆσαι.

ΘΕΟ. Οὐδὲν ἔτι ἀντιλέγω, ἀλλ' ἄγε ὅπῃ θέλεις·
πάντως τὴν περὶ ταῦτα εἱμαρμένην ἣν ἂν[3] σὺ
ἐπικλώσῃς δεῖ ἀνατλῆναι ἐλεγχόμενον. οὐ μέντοι
περαιτέρω γε ὧν προτίθεσαι οἷός τ' ἔσομαι παρασχεῖν ἐμαυτόν σοι.

ΣΩ. 'Αλλ' ἀρκεῖ καὶ μέχρι τούτων. καί μοι
πάνυ τήρει τὸ τοιόνδε, μή που παιδικόν τι λάθωμεν
D εἶδος τῶν λόγων ποιούμενοι, καί τις πάλιν ἡμῖν
αὐτὸ ὀνειδίσῃ.

ΘΕΟ. 'Αλλὰ δὴ πειράσομαί γε καθ' ὅσον ἂν δύ-
νωμαι.

22. ΣΩ. Τοῦδε τοίνυν πρῶτον πάλιν ἀντιλα-
βώμεθα οὗπερ τὸ πρότερον, καὶ ἴδωμεν ὀρθῶς ἢ
οὐκ ὀρθῶς ἐδυσχεραίνομεν ἐπιτιμῶντες τῷ λόγῳ
ὅτι αὐτάρκη ἕκαστον εἰς φρόνησιν ἐποίει· καὶ
ἡμῖν συνεχώρησεν ὁ Πρωταγόρας περί τε τοῦ
ἀμείνονος καὶ χείρονος διαφέρειν τινάς, οὓς δὴ καὶ
εἶναι σοφούς. οὐχί;

ΘΕΟ. Ναί.

ΣΩ. Εἰ μὲν τοίνυν αὐτὸς παρὼν ὡμολόγει, ἀλλὰ
E μὴ ἡμεῖς βοηθοῦντες ὑπὲρ αὐτοῦ συνεχωρήσαμεν,
οὐδὲν ἂν πάλιν ἔδει ἐπαναλαβόντας βεβαιοῦσθαι·
νῦν δὲ τάχ' ἄν τις ἡμᾶς ἀκύρους τιθείη τῆς ὑπὲρ
ἐκείνου ὁμολογίας. διὸ καλλιόνως ἔχει σαφέ-

---

[1] ἐντυχόντες T ; ἐντυγχάνοντες B.
[2] καρτεροὶ B ; κρατεροὶ T.   [3] ἣν ἂν W ; ἣν BT.

stubborn combatant than they; for many a Heracles and many a Theseus, strong men of words, have fallen in with me and belaboured me mightily, but still I do not desist, such a terrible love of this kind of exercise has taken hold on me. So, now that it is your turn, do not refuse to try a bout with me; it will be good for both of us.

THEO. I say no more. Lead on as you like. Most assuredly I must endure whatsoever fate you spin for me, and submit to interrogation. However, I shall not be able to leave myself in your hands beyond the point you propose.

SOC. Even that is enough. And please be especially careful that we do not inadvertently give a playful turn to our argument and somebody reproach us again for it.

THEO. Rest assured that I will try so far as in me lies.

SOC. Let us, therefore, first take up the same question as before, and let us see whether we were right or wrong in being displeased and finding fault with the doctrine because it made each individual self-sufficient in wisdom. Protagoras granted that some persons excelled others in respect to the better and the worse, and these he said were wise, did he not?

THEO. Yes.

SOC. Now if he himself were present and could agree to this, instead of our making the concession for him in our effort to help him, there would be no need of taking up the question again or of reinforcing his argument. But, as it is, perhaps it might be said that we have no authority to make the agreement for him; therefore it is better to make the

105

PLATO

στερον περὶ τούτου αὐτοῦ διομολογήσασθαι· οὐ γάρ τι σμικρὸν παραλλάττει οὕτως ἔχον ἢ ἄλλως.

ΘΕΟ. Λέγεις ἀληθῆ.

ΣΩ. Μὴ τοίνυν δι’ ἄλλων ἀλλ’ ἐκ τοῦ ἐκείνου λόγου ὡς διὰ βραχυτάτων λάβωμεν τὴν ὁμολογίαν.

ΘΕΟ. Πῶς;

ΣΩ. Οὑτωσί· τὸ δοκοῦν ἑκάστῳ τοῦτο καὶ εἶναί φησί που ᾧ δοκεῖ;

ΘΕΟ. Φησὶ γὰρ οὖν.

ΣΩ. Οὐκοῦν, ὦ Πρωταγόρα, καὶ ἡμεῖς ἀνθρώπου, μᾶλλον δὲ πάντων ἀνθρώπων δόξας λέγομεν, καὶ φαμὲν οὐδένα ὅντινα οὐ τὰ μὲν αὐτὸν ἡγεῖσθαι τῶν ἄλλων σοφώτερον, τὰ δὲ ἄλλους ἑαυτοῦ, καὶ ἔν γε τοῖς μεγίστοις κινδύνοις, ὅταν ἐν στρατείαις ἢ νόσοις ἢ ἐν θαλάττῃ χειμάζωνται, ὥσπερ πρὸς θεοὺς ἔχειν τοὺς ἐν ἑκάστοις ἄρχοντας, σωτῆρας σφῶν προσδοκῶντας, οὐκ ἄλλῳ τῳ διαφέροντας ἢ τῷ εἰδέναι· καὶ πάντα που μεστὰ τἀνθρώπινα ζητούντων διδασκάλους τε καὶ ἄρχοντας ἑαυτῶν τε καὶ τῶν ἄλλων ζῴων τῶν τε ἐργασιῶν, οἰομένων τε αὖ ἱκανῶν μὲν διδάσκειν, ἱκανῶν δὲ ἄρχειν εἶναι. καὶ ἐν τούτοις ἅπασι τί ἄλλο φήσομεν ἢ αὐτοὺς τοὺς ἀνθρώπους ἡγεῖσθαι σοφίαν καὶ ἀμαθίαν εἶναι παρὰ σφίσιν;

ΘΕΟ. Οὐδὲν ἄλλο.

ΣΩ. Οὐκοῦν τὴν μὲν σοφίαν ἀληθῆ διάνοιαν ἡγοῦνται, τὴν δὲ ἀμαθίαν ψευδῆ δόξαν;

ΘΕΟ. Τί μήν;

ΣΩ. Τί οὖν, ὦ Πρωταγόρα, χρησόμεθα τῷ λόγῳ;

agreement still clearer on this particular point; for it makes a good deal of difference whether it is so or not.

THEO. That is true.

SOC. Let us then get the agreement in as concise a form as possible, not through others, but from his own statement.

THEO. How?

SOC. In this way: He says, does he not? "that which appears to each person really is to him to whom it appears."

THEO. Yes, that is what he says.

SOC. Well then, Protagoras, we also utter the opinions of a man, or rather, of all men, and we say that there is no one who does not think himself wiser than others in some respects and others wiser than himself in other respects; for instance, in times of greatest danger, when people are distressed in war or by diseases or at sea, they regard their commanders as gods and expect them to be their saviours, though they excel them in nothing except knowledge. And all the world of men is, I dare say, full of people seeking teachers and rulers for themselves and the animals and for human activities, and, on the other hand, of people who consider themselves qualified to teach and qualified to rule. And in all these instances we must say that men themselves believe that wisdom and ignorance exist in the world of men, must we not?

THEO. Yes, we must.

SOC. And therefore they think that wisdom is true thinking and ignorance false opinion, do they not?

THEO. Of course.

SOC. Well then, Protagoras, what shall we do

πότερον ἀληθῆ φῶμεν ἀεὶ τοὺς ἀνθρώπους δοξάζειν,
ἢ ποτὲ μὲν ἀληθῆ, ποτὲ δὲ ψευδῆ; ἐξ ἀμφοτέρων
γάρ που συμβαίνει μὴ ἀεὶ ἀληθῆ ἀλλ' ἀμφότερα
αὐτοὺς δοξάζειν. σκόπει γάρ, ὦ Θεόδωρε, εἰ
ἐθέλοι ἄν τις τῶν ἀμφὶ Πρωταγόραν ἢ σὺ αὐτὸς
διαμάχεσθαι ὡς οὐδεὶς ἡγεῖται ἕτερος ἕτερον
ἀμαθῆ τε εἶναι καὶ ψευδῆ δοξάζειν.

ΘΕΟ. Ἀλλ' ἄπιστον, ὦ Σώκρατες.

D   ΣΩ. Καὶ μὴν εἰς τοῦτό γε ἀνάγκης ὁ λόγος
ἥκει ὁ πάντων χρημάτων μέτρον ἄνθρωπον λέγων.

ΘΕΟ. Πῶς δή;

ΣΩ. Ὅταν σὺ κρίνας τι παρὰ σαυτῷ πρός με
ἀποφαίνῃ περί τινος δόξαν, σοὶ μὲν δὴ τοῦτο κατὰ
τὸν ἐκείνου λόγον ἀληθὲς ἔστω, ἡμῖν δὲ δὴ τοῖς
ἄλλοις περὶ τῆς σῆς κρίσεως πότερον οὐκ ἔστιν
κριταῖς γενέσθαι, ἢ ἀεὶ σὲ κρίνομεν ἀληθῆ δοξάζειν;
ἢ μυρίοι ἑκάστοτέ σοι μάχονται ἀντιδοξάζοντες,
ἡγούμενοι ψευδῆ κρίνειν τε καὶ οἴεσθαι;

E   ΘΕΟ. Νὴ τὸν Δία, ὦ Σώκρατες, μάλα μυρίοι
δῆτα, φησὶν Ὅμηρος, οἵ γέ μοι τὰ ἐξ ἀνθρώπων
πράγματα παρέχουσιν.

ΣΩ. Τί οὖν; βούλει λέγωμεν ὡς σὺ τότε σαυτῷ
μὲν ἀληθῆ δοξάζεις, τοῖς δὲ μυρίοις ψευδῆ;

ΘΕΟ. Ἔοικεν ἔκ γε τοῦ λόγου ἀνάγκη εἶναι.

ΣΩ. Τί δὲ αὐτῷ Πρωταγόρα; ἆρ' οὐχὶ ἀνάγκη,
εἰ μὲν μηδὲ αὐτὸς ᾤετο μέτρον εἶναι ἄνθρωπον
μηδὲ οἱ πολλοί, ὥσπερ οὐδὲ οἴονται, μηδενὶ δὴ
εἶναι ταύτην τὴν ἀλήθειαν ἣν ἐκεῖνος ἔγραψεν; εἰ

THEAETETUS

about the doctrine? Shall we say that the opinions
which men have are always true, or sometimes true
and sometimes false? For the result of either
statement is that their opinions are not always true,
but may be either true or false. Just think, Theodorus;
would any follower of Protagoras, or you yourself,
care to contend that no person thinks that another
is ignorant and has false opinions?

THEO. No, that is incredible, Socrates.

SOC. And yet this is the predicament to which
the doctrine that man is the measure of all things
inevitably leads.

THEO. How so?

SOC. When you have come to a decision in your
own mind about something, and declare your opinion
to me, this opinion is, according to his doctrine, true
to you; let us grant that; but may not the rest of
us sit in judgement on your decision, or do we always
judge that your opinion is true? Do not myriads of
men on each occasion oppose their opinions to yours,
believing that your judgement and belief are false?

THEO. Yes, by Zeus, Socrates, countless myriads
in truth, as Homer [1] says, and they give me all the
trouble in the world.

SOC. Well then, shall we say that in such a case
your opinion is true to you but false to the myriads?

THEO. That seems to be the inevitable deduction.

SOC. And what of Protagoras himself? If neither
he himself thought, nor people in general think, as
indeed they do not, that man is the measure of all
things, is it not inevitable that the "truth" which
he wrote is true to no one? But if he himself thought

---

[1] Homer, *Odyssey*, xvi. 121, xvii. 432, xix. 78.

171 δὲ αὐτὸς μὲν ᾤετο, τὸ δὲ πλῆθος μὴ συνοίεται, οἶσθ᾽ ὅτι πρῶτον μὲν ὅσῳ πλείους οἷς μὴ δοκεῖ ἢ οἷς δοκεῖ, τοσούτῳ μᾶλλον οὐκ ἔστιν ἢ ἔστιν.

ΘΕΟ. Ἀνάγκη, εἴπερ γε καθ᾽ ἑκάστην δόξαν ἔσται καὶ οὐκ ἔσται.

ΣΩ. Ἔπειτά γε τοῦτ᾽ ἔχει κομψότατον· ἐκεῖνος μὲν περὶ τῆς αὑτοῦ οἰήσεως τὴν τῶν ἀντιδοξαζόντων οἴησιν, ᾗ ἐκεῖνον ἡγοῦνται ψεύδεσθαι, ξυγχωρεῖ που ἀληθῆ εἶναι ὁμολογῶν τὰ ὄντα δοξάζειν ἅπαντας.

ΘΕΟ. Πάνυ μὲν οὖν.

B ΣΩ. Οὐκοῦν τὴν αὑτοῦ ἂν ψευδῆ συγχωροῖ, εἰ τὴν τῶν ἡγουμένων αὐτὸν ψεύδεσθαι ὁμολογεῖ ἀληθῆ εἶναι;

ΘΕΟ. Ἀνάγκη.

ΣΩ. Οἱ δέ γ᾽ ἄλλοι οὐ συγχωροῦσιν ἑαυτοῖς ψεύδεσθαι;

ΘΕΟ. Οὐ γὰρ οὖν.

ΣΩ. Ὁ δέ γ᾽ αὖ ὁμολογεῖ καὶ ταύτην ἀληθῆ τὴν δόξαν ἐξ ὧν γέγραφε.

ΘΕΟ. Φαίνεται.

ΣΩ. Ἐξ ἁπάντων ἄρα ἀπὸ Πρωταγόρου ἀρξαμένων ἀμφισβητήσεται, μᾶλλον δὲ ὑπό γε ἐκείνου ὁμολογήσεται, ὅταν τῷ τἀναντία λέγοντι συγχωρῇ ἀληθῆ αὐτὸν δοξάζειν, τότε καὶ ὁ Πρωταγόρας

C αὐτὸς συγχωρήσεται μήτε κύνα μήτε τὸν ἐπιτυχόντα ἄνθρωπον μέτρον εἶναι μηδὲ περὶ ἑνὸς οὗ ἂν μὴ μάθῃ. οὐχ οὕτως;

ΘΕΟ. Οὕτως.

ΣΩ. Οὐκοῦν ἐπειδὴ ἀμφισβητεῖται ὑπὸ πάντων, οὐδενὶ ἂν εἴη ἡ Πρωταγόρου "ἀλήθεια" ἀληθής, οὔτε τινὶ ἄλλῳ οὔτ᾽ αὐτῷ ἐκείνῳ.

it was true, and people in general do not agree with him, in the first place you know that it is just so much more false than true as the number of those who do not believe it is greater than the number of those who do.

THEO. Necessarily, if it is to be true or false according to each individual opinion.

SOC. Secondly, it involves this, which is a very pretty result; he concedes about his own opinion the truth of the opinion of those who disagree with him and think that his opinion is false, since he grants that the opinions of all men are true.

THEO. Certainly.

SOC. Then would he not be conceding that his own opinion is false, if he grants that the opinion of those who think he is in error is true?

THEO. Necessarily.

SOC. But the others do not concede that they are in error, do they?

THEO. No, they do not.

SOC. And he, in turn, according to his writings, grants that this opinion also is true.

THEO. Evidently.

SOC. Then all men, beginning with Protagoras, will dispute—or rather, he will grant, after he once concedes that the opinion of the man who holds the opposite view is true—even Protagoras himself, I say, will concede that neither a dog nor any casual man is a measure of anything whatsoever that he has not learned. Is not that the case?

THEO. Yes.

SOC. Then since the "truth" of Protagoras is disputed by all, it would be true to nobody, neither to anyone else nor to him.

ΘΕΟ. Ἄγαν, ὦ Σώκρατες, τὸν ἑταῖρόν μου καταθέομεν.

ΣΩ. Ἀλλά τοι, ὦ φίλε, ἄδηλον εἰ καὶ παραθέομεν τὸ ὀρθόν. εἰκός γε ἄρα ἐκεῖνον πρεσβύτερον D ὄντα σοφώτερον ἡμῶν εἶναι· καὶ εἰ αὐτίκα ἐντεῦθεν ἀνακύψειε μέχρι τοῦ αὐχένος, πολλὰ ἂν ἐμέ τε ἐλέγξας ληροῦντα, ὡς τὸ εἰκός, καὶ σὲ ὁμολογοῦντα, καταδὺς ἂν οἴχοιτο ἀποτρέχων. ἀλλ' ἡμῖν ἀνάγκη, οἶμαι, χρῆσθαι ἡμῖν αὐτοῖς, ὁποῖοί τινές ἐσμεν, καὶ τὰ δοκοῦντα ἀεὶ ταῦτα λέγειν. καὶ δῆτα καὶ νῦν ἄλλο τι φῶμεν ὁμολογεῖν ἂν τοῦτό γε ὁντινοῦν, τὸ εἶναι σοφώτερον ἕτερον ἑτέρου, εἶναι δὲ καὶ ἀμαθέστερον;

ΘΕΟ. Ἐμοὶ γοῦν δοκεῖ.

23. ΣΩ. Ἦ καὶ ταύτῃ ἂν μάλιστα ἵστασθαι τὸν λόγον, ᾗ ἡμεῖς ὑπεγράψαμεν βοηθοῦντες E Πρωταγόρᾳ, ὡς τὰ μὲν πολλὰ ᾗ δοκεῖ, ταύτῃ καὶ ἔστιν ἑκάστῳ, θερμά, ξηρά, γλυκέα, πάντα ὅσα τοῦ τύπου τούτου· εἰ δέ που ἔν τισι συγχωρήσεται διαφέρειν ἄλλον ἄλλου, περὶ τὰ ὑγιεινὰ καὶ νοσώδη ἐθελήσαι ἂν φάναι μὴ πᾶν γύναιον καὶ παιδίον, καὶ θηρίον δέ, ἱκανὸν εἶναι ἰᾶσθαι αὐτὸ γιγνῶσκον ἑαυτῷ τὸ ὑγιεινόν, ἀλλὰ ἐνταῦθα δὴ ἄλλον ἄλλου διαφέρειν, εἴπερ που;

ΘΕΟ. Ἔμοιγε δοκεῖ οὕτως.

172 ΣΩ. Οὐκοῦν καὶ περὶ πολιτικῶν, καλὰ μὲν καὶ αἰσχρὰ καὶ δίκαια καὶ ἄδικα καὶ ὅσια καὶ μή, οἷα ἂν ἑκάστη πόλις οἰηθεῖσα θῆται νόμιμα αὑτῇ, ταῦτα καὶ εἶναι τῇ ἀληθείᾳ ἑκάστῃ, καὶ ἐν τούτοις μὲν οὐδὲν σοφώτερον οὔτε ἰδιώτην ἰδιώτου οὔτε πόλιν πόλεως εἶναι· ἐν δὲ τῷ συμφέροντα ἑαυτῇ

THEO. I think, Socrates, we are running my friend too hard.

SOC. But, my dear man, I do not see that we are running beyond what is right. Most likely, though, he, being older, is wiser than we, and if, for example, he should emerge from the ground, here at our feet, if only as far as the neck, he would prove abundantly that I was making a fool of myself by my talk, in all probability, and you by agreeing with me; then he would sink down and be off at a run. But we, I suppose, must depend on ourselves, such as we are, and must say just what we think. And so now must we not say that everybody would agree that some men are wiser and some more ignorant than others?

THEO. Yes, I think at least we must.

SOC. And do you think his doctrine might stand most firmly in the form in which we sketched it when defending Protagoras, that most things—hot, dry, sweet, and everything of that sort—are to each person as they appear to him, and if Protagoras is to concede that there are cases in which one person excels another, he might be willing to say that in matters of health and disease not every woman or child—or beast, for that matter—knows what is wholesome for it and is able to cure itself, but in this point, if in any, one person excels another?

THEO. Yes, I think that is correct.

SOC. And likewise in affairs of state, the honourable and disgraceful, the just and unjust, the pious and its opposite, are in truth to each state such as it thinks they are and as it enacts into law for itself, and in these matters no citizen and no state is wiser than another; but in making laws that are advan-

ἢ μὴ συμφέροντα τίθεσθαι, ἐνταῦθ', εἴπερ που, αὖ
ὁμολογήσει σύμβουλόν τε συμβούλου διαφέρειν
καὶ πόλεως δόξαν ἑτέραν ἑτέρας πρὸς ἀλήθειαν,
B καὶ οὐκ ἂν πάνυ τολμήσειε φῆσαι, ἃ ἂν θῆται
πόλις συμφέροντα οἰηθεῖσα αὑτῇ, παντὸς μᾶλλον
ταῦτα καὶ συνοίσειν· ἀλλ' ἐκεῖ οὗ λέγω, ἐν τοῖς
δικαίοις καὶ ἀδίκοις¹ καὶ ὁσίοις καὶ ἀνοσίοις,
ἐθέλουσιν ἰσχυρίζεσθαι ὡς οὐκ ἔστι φύσει αὐτῶν
οὐδὲν οὐσίαν ἑαυτοῦ ἔχον ἀλλὰ τὸ κοινῇ δόξαν
τοῦτο γίγνεται ἀληθὲς τότε ὅταν δόξῃ καὶ ὅσον ἂν
δοκῇ χρόνον· καὶ ὅσοι γε δὴ² μὴ παντάπασι
τὸν Πρωταγόρου λόγον λέγουσιν,³ ὧδέ πως τὴν
σοφίαν ἄγουσι. λόγος δὲ ἡμᾶς, ὦ Θεόδωρε, ἐκ
C λόγου μείζων ἐξ ἐλάττονος καταλαμβάνει.

ΘΕΟ. Οὐκοῦν σχολὴν ἄγομεν, ὦ Σώκρατες;

ΣΩ. Φαινόμεθα. καὶ πολλάκις μέν γε δή, ὦ
δαιμόνιε, καὶ ἄλλοτε κατενόησα, ἀτὰρ καὶ νῦν, ὡς
εἰκότως οἱ ἐν ταῖς φιλοσοφίαις πολὺν χρόνον
διατρίψαντες εἰς τὰ δικαστήρια ἰόντες γελοῖοι
φαίνονται ῥήτορες.

ΘΕΟ. Πῶς δὴ οὖν λέγεις;

ΣΩ. Κινδυνεύουσιν οἱ ἐν δικαστηρίοις καὶ τοῖς
τοιούτοις ἐκ νέων κυλινδούμενοι πρὸς τοὺς ἐν
D φιλοσοφίᾳ καὶ τῇ τοιᾷδε διατριβῇ τεθραμμένους
ὡς οἰκέται πρὸς ἐλευθέρους τεθράφθαι.⁴

ΘΕΟ. Πῇ δή;

ΣΩ. Ἧι τοῖς μὲν τοῦτο ὃ σὺ εἶπες ἀεὶ πάρεστι,
σχολή, καὶ τοὺς λόγους ἐν εἰρήνῃ ἐπὶ σχολῆς
ποιοῦνται· ὥσπερ ἡμεῖς νυνὶ τρίτον ἤδη λόγον

---

¹ καὶ ἀδίκοις W; om. BT.   ² δὴ BT; ἂν Schanz.
³ λέγουσιν Naber, with inferior mss.; λέγωσιν BT.
⁴ τεθράφθαι W; τετράφθαι BT.

tageous to the state, or the reverse, Protagoras again will agree that one counsellor is better than another, and the opinion of one state better than that of another as regards the truth, and he would by no means dare to affirm that whatsoever laws a state makes in the belief that they will be advantageous to itself are perfectly sure to prove advantageous. But in the other class of things—I mean just and unjust, pious and impious—they are willing to say with confidence that no one of them possesses by nature an existence of its own; on the contrary, that the common opinion becomes true at the time when it is adopted and remains true as long as it is held; this is substantially the theory of those who do not altogether affirm the doctrine of Protagoras. But, Theodorus, argument after argument, a greater one after a lesser, is overtaking us.

THEO. Well, Socrates, we have plenty of leisure, have we not?

SOC. Apparently we have. And that makes me think, my friend, as I have often done before, how natural it is that those who have spent a long time in the study of philosophy appear ridiculous when they enter the courts of law as speakers.

THEO. What do you mean?

SOC. Those who have knocked about in courts and the like from their youth up seem to me, when compared with those who have been brought up in philosophy and similar pursuits, to be as slaves in breeding compared with freemen.

THEO. In what way is this the case?

SOC. In this way: the latter always have that which you just spoke of, leisure, and they talk at their leisure in peace; just as we are now taking up

ἐκ λόγου μεταλαμβάνομεν, οὕτω κἀκεῖνοι, ἐὰν
αὐτοὺς ὁ ἐπελθὼν τοῦ προκειμένου μᾶλλον καθάπερ
ἡμᾶς ἀρέσῃ· καὶ διὰ μακρῶν ἢ βραχέων μέλει
οὐδὲν λέγειν, ἂν μόνον τύχωσι τοῦ ὄντος· οἱ δὲ ἐν
ἀσχολίᾳ τε ἀεὶ λέγουσι—κατεπείγει γὰρ ὕδωρ ῥέον
E —καὶ οὐκ ἐγχωρεῖ περὶ οὗ ἂν ἐπιθυμήσωσι τοὺς
λόγους ποιεῖσθαι, ἀλλ' ἀνάγκην ἔχων ὁ ἀντίδικος
ἐφέστηκεν καὶ ὑπογραφὴν παραναγιγνωσκομένην,
ὧν ἐκτὸς οὐ ῥητέον· ἣν ἀντωμοσίαν καλοῦσιν·[1]
οἱ δὲ λόγοι ἀεὶ περὶ ὁμοδούλου πρὸς δεσπότην καθήμενον, ἐν χειρί τινα δίκην ἔχοντα, καὶ
οἱ ἀγῶνες οὐδέποτε τὴν ἄλλως ἀλλ' ἀεὶ τὴν περὶ
αὐτοῦ· πολλάκις δὲ καὶ περὶ ψυχῆς ὁ δρόμος·
173 ὥστ' ἐξ ἁπάντων τούτων ἔντονοι καὶ δριμεῖς
γίγνονται, ἐπιστάμενοι τὸν δεσπότην λόγῳ τε
θωπεῦσαι καὶ ἔργῳ χαρίσασθαι,[2] σμικροὶ δὲ καὶ
οὐκ ὀρθοὶ τὰς ψυχάς. τὴν γὰρ αὔξην καὶ τὸ εὐθύ
τε καὶ τὸ ἐλεύθερον [3] ἡ ἐκ νέων δουλεία ἀφῄρηται,
ἀναγκάζουσα πράττειν σκολιά, μεγάλους κινδύ-
νους καὶ φόβους ἔτι ἁπαλαῖς ψυχαῖς ἐπιβάλλουσα,
οὓς οὐ δυνάμενοι μετὰ τοῦ δικαίου καὶ ἀληθοῦς
ὑποφέρειν, εὐθὺς ἐπὶ τὸ ψεῦδός τε καὶ τὸ ἀλλήλους
ἀνταδικεῖν τρεπόμενοι πολλὰ κάμπτονται καὶ

[1] ἣν ἀντωμοσίαν καλοῦσιν mss.; om. Abresch et al.
[2] χαρίσασθαι BT; ὑπελθεῖν Cobet from Themistius.
[3] τὸ ἐλεύθερον BT; τὸ ἐλευθέριον Themistius.

argument after argument, already beginning a third, so can they, if, as in our case, the new one pleases them better than that in which they are engaged ; and they do not care at all whether their talk is long or short, if only they attain the truth. But the men of the other sort are always in a hurry—for the water flowing through the water-clock urges them on—and the other party in the suit does not permit them to talk about anything they please, but stands over them exercising the law's compulsion by reading the brief, from which no deviation is allowed (this is called the affidavit);[1] and their discourse is always about a fellow slave and is addressed to a master who sits there holding some case or other in his hands ; and the contests never run an indefinite course, but are always directed to the point at issue, and often the race is for the defendant's life. As a result of all this, the speakers become tense and shrewd ; they know how to wheedle their master with words and gain his favour by acts; but in their souls they become small and warped. For they have been deprived of growth and straightforwardness and independence by the slavery they have endured from their youth up, for this forces them to do crooked acts by putting a great burden of fears and dangers upon their souls while these are still tender; and since they cannot bear this burden with uprightness and truth, they turn forthwith to deceit and to requiting wrong with wrong, so that they become

[1] In Athenian legal procedure each party to a suit presented a written statement—the charge and the reply—at a preliminary hearing. These statements were subsequently confirmed by oath, and the sworn statement was called διωμοσία or ἀντωμοσία, which is rendered above by "affidavit" as the nearest English equivalent.

B συγκλῶνται, ὥσθ' ὑγιὲς οὐδὲν ἔχοντες τῆς διανοίας
εἰς ἄνδρας ἐκ μειρακίων τελευτῶσι, δεινοί τε καὶ
σοφοὶ γεγονότες, ὡς οἴονται. καὶ οὗτοι μὲν δὴ
τοιοῦτοι, ὦ Θεόδωρε· τοὺς δὲ τοῦ ἡμετέρου χοροῦ
πότερον βούλει διελθόντες ἢ ἐάσαντες πάλιν ἐπὶ
τὸν λόγον τρεπώμεθα, ἵνα μὴ καί, ὃ νῦν δὴ ἐλέγομεν,
λίαν πολὺ τῇ ἐλευθερίᾳ καὶ μεταλήψει τῶν λόγων
καταχρώμεθα;

ΘΕΟ. Μηδαμῶς, ὦ Σώκρατες, ἀλλὰ διελθόντες.
C πάνυ γὰρ εὖ τοῦτο εἴρηκας, ὅτι οὐχ ἡμεῖς οἱ ἐν
τῷ τοιῷδε χορεύοντες τῶν λόγων ὑπηρέται, ἀλλ'
οἱ λόγοι ἡμέτεροι[1] ὥσπερ οἰκέται, καὶ ἕκαστος
αὐτῶν περιμένει ἀποτελεσθῆναι ὅταν ἡμῖν δοκῇ·
οὔτε γὰρ δικαστὴς οὔτε θεατὴς ὥσπερ ποιηταῖς
ἐπιτιμήσων τε καὶ ἄρξων ἐπιστατεῖ παρ' ἡμῖν.

24. ΣΩ. Λέγωμεν δή, ὡς ἔοικεν, ἐπεὶ σοί γε
δοκεῖ, περὶ τῶν κορυφαίων· τί γὰρ ἄν τις τούς γε
φαύλως διατρίβοντας ἐν φιλοσοφίᾳ λέγοι; οὗτοι δέ
που ἐκ νέων πρῶτον μὲν εἰς ἀγορὰν οὐκ ἴσασι τὴν
D ὁδόν, οὐδὲ ὅπου δικαστήριον ἢ βουλευτήριον ἤ
τι κοινὸν ἄλλο τῆς πόλεως συνέδριον· νόμους δὲ
καὶ ψηφίσματα λεγόμενα ἢ γεγραμμένα οὔτε
ὁρῶσιν οὔτε ἀκούουσι· σπουδαὶ δὲ ἑταιριῶν ἐπ'
ἀρχὰς καὶ σύνοδοι καὶ δεῖπνα καὶ σὺν αὐλητρίσι
κῶμοι, οὐδὲ ὄναρ πράττειν προσίσταται αὐτοῖς.
εὖ δὲ ἢ κακῶς τις[2] γέγονεν ἐν πόλει, ἢ τί τῳ κακόν
ἐστιν ἐκ προγόνων γεγονὸς ἢ πρὸς ἀνδρῶν ἢ
γυναικῶν, μᾶλλον αὐτὸν λέληθεν ἢ οἱ τῆς θαλάττης
E λεγόμενοι χόες. καὶ ταῦτα πάντ' οὐδ' ὅτι οὐκ

---

[1] ἡμέτεροι W; οἱ ἡμέτεροι BT.
[2] τις W, Iambl., Clem. ; τι BT.

greatly bent and stunted. Consequently they pass from youth to manhood with no soundness of mind in them, but they think they have become clever and wise. So much for them, Theodorus. Shall we describe those who belong to our band, or shall we let that go and return to the argument, in order to avoid abuse of that freedom and variety of discourse, of which we were speaking just now?

THEO. By all means, Socrates, describe them; for I like your saying that we who belong to this band are not the servants of our arguments, but the arguments are, as it were, our servants, and each of them must await our pleasure to be finished; for we have neither judge, nor, as the poets have, any spectator set over us to censure and rule us.

SOC. Very well, that is quite appropriate, since it is your wish; and let us speak of the leaders; for why should anyone talk about the inferior philosophers? The leaders, in the first place, from their youth up, remain ignorant of the way to the agora, do not even know where the court-room is, or the senate-house, or any other public place of assembly; as for laws and decrees, they neither hear the debates upon them nor see them when they are published; and the strivings of political clubs after public offices, and meetings, and banquets, and revellings with chorus girls—it never occurs to them even in their dreams to indulge in such things. And whether anyone in the city is of high or low birth, or what evil has been inherited by anyone from his ancestors, male or female, are matters to which they pay no more attention than to the number of pints in the sea, as the saying is. And all these things the philosopher does not even know that he does not

119

οἶδεν, οἶδεν· οὐδὲ γὰρ αὐτῶν ἀπέχεται τοῦ εὐδο-
κιμεῖν χάριν, ἀλλὰ τῷ ὄντι τὸ σῶμα μόνον ἐν τῇ
πόλει κεῖται αὐτοῦ καὶ ἐπιδημεῖ, ἡ δὲ διάνοια,
ταῦτα πάντα ἡγησαμένη σμικρὰ καὶ οὐδέν, ἀτιμά-
σασα πανταχῇ φέρεται[1] κατὰ Πίνδαρον, " τᾶς[2]
τε γᾶς ὑπένερθε " καὶ τὰ ἐπίπεδα γεωμετροῦσα,
" οὐρανοῦ τε ὕπερ " ἀστρονομοῦσα, καὶ πᾶσαν
174 πάντῃ φύσιν ἐρευνωμένη τῶν ὄντων ἑκάστου
ὅλου, εἰς τῶν ἐγγὺς οὐδὲν αὐτὴν συγκαθιεῖσα.

ΘΕΟ. Πῶς τοῦτο λέγεις, ὦ Σώκρατες;

ΣΩ. Ὥσπερ καὶ Θαλῆν ἀστρονομοῦντα, ὦ Θεόδωρε, καὶ ἄνω βλέποντα, πεσόντα εἰς φρέαρ, Θρᾷττά
τις ἐμμελὴς καὶ χαρίεσσα θεραπαινὶς ἀποσκῶψαι
λέγεται, ὡς τὰ μὲν ἐν οὐρανῷ προθυμοῖτο εἰδέναι,
τὰ δ' ἔμπροσθεν αὐτοῦ καὶ παρὰ πόδας λανθάνοι
αὐτόν. ταὐτὸν δὲ ἀρκεῖ σκῶμμα ἐπὶ πάντας ὅσοι
B ἐν φιλοσοφίᾳ διάγουσι. τῷ γὰρ ὄντι τὸν τοιοῦτον
ὁ μὲν πλησίον καὶ ὁ γείτων λέληθεν, οὐ μόνον ὅ τι
πράττει, ἀλλ' ὀλίγου καὶ εἰ ἄνθρωπός ἐστιν ἤ τι
ἄλλο θρέμμα· τί δέ ποτ' ἐστὶν ἄνθρωπος καὶ τί
τῇ τοιαύτῃ φύσει προσήκει διάφορον τῶν ἄλλων
ποιεῖν ἢ πάσχειν ζητεῖ τε καὶ πράγματ' ἔχει
διερευνώμενος. μανθάνεις γάρ που, ὦ Θεόδωρε.
ἢ οὔ;

ΘΕΟ. Ἔγωγε· καὶ ἀληθῆ λέγεις.

ΣΩ. Τοιγάρτοι, ὦ φίλε, ἰδίᾳ τε συγγιγνόμενος ὁ

---

[1] φέρεται BT ; πέτεται B²W, Iambl., Clem., Euseb.
[2] τᾶς Campbell from Clement ; τᾶ C ; τά T.

know; for he does not keep aloof from them for the sake of gaining reputation, but really it is only his body that has its place and home in the city; his mind, considering all these things petty and of no account, disdains them and is borne in all directions, as Pindar[1] says, "both below the earth," and measuring the surface of the earth, and " above the sky," studying the stars, and investigating the universal nature of every thing that is, each in its entirety, never lowering itself to anything close at hand.

THEO. What do you mean by this, Socrates?

soc. Why, take the case of Thales, Theodorus. While he was studying the stars and looking upwards, he fell into a pit, and a neat, witty Thracian servant girl jeered at him, they say, because he was so eager to know the things in the sky that he could not see what was there before him at his very feet. The same jest applies to all who pass their lives in philosophy. For really such a man pays no attention to his next door neighbour; he is not only ignorant of what he is doing, but he hardly knows whether he is a human being or some other kind of a creature; but what a human being is and what is proper for such a nature to do or bear different from any other, this he inquires and exerts himself to find out. Do you understand, Theodorus, or not?

THEO. Yes, I do; you are right.

soc. Hence it is, my friend, such a man, both in

[1] This may refer to *Nem.* x. 87 f.—

ἥμισυ μέν κε πνέοις γαίας ὑπένερθεν ἐών,
ἥμισυ δ' οὐρανοῦ ἐν χρυσέοις δόμοσιν,

"Thou (Polydeuces) shalt live being half the time under the earth and half the time in the golden dwellings of heaven," but it may be a quotation from one of the lost poems of Pindar.

τοιοῦτος ἑκάστῳ καὶ δημοσίᾳ, ὅπερ ἀρχόμενος
C ἔλεγον, ὅταν ἐν δικαστηρίῳ ἤ που ἄλλοθι ἀναγκασθῇ περὶ τῶν παρὰ πόδας καὶ τῶν ἐν ὀφθαλμοῖς
διαλέγεσθαι, γέλωτα παρέχει οὐ μόνον Θρᾴτταις
ἀλλὰ καὶ τῷ ἄλλῳ ὄχλῳ, εἰς φρέατά τε καὶ πᾶσαν
ἀπορίαν ἐμπίπτων ὑπὸ ἀπειρίας, καὶ ἡ ἀσχημοσύνη
δεινή, δόξαν ἀβελτερίας παρεχομένη· ἔν τε γὰρ
ταῖς λοιδορίαις ἴδιον ἔχει οὐδὲν οὐδένα λοιδορεῖν,
ἅτ᾽ οὐκ εἰδὼς κακὸν οὐδὲν οὐδενὸς ἐκ τοῦ μὴ
μεμελετηκέναι. ἀπορῶν οὖν γελοῖος φαίνεται. ἔν
D τε τοῖς ἐπαίνοις καὶ ταῖς τῶν ἄλλων μεγαλαυχίαις,
οὐ προσποιήτως, ἀλλὰ τῷ ὄντι γελῶν ἔνδηλος
γιγνόμενος ληρώδης δοκεῖ εἶναι. τύραννόν τε
γὰρ ἢ βασιλέα ἐγκωμιαζόμενον ἕνα τῶν νομέων,
οἷον συβώτην ἢ ποιμένα ἤ τινα βουκόλον, ἡγεῖται
ἀκούειν εὐδαιμονιζόμενον πολὺ βδάλλοντα· δυσ-
κολώτερον δὲ ἐκείνων ζῷον καὶ ἐπιβουλότερον
ποιμαίνειν τε καὶ βδάλλειν νομίζει αὐτούς, ἄγροικον
δὲ καὶ ἀπαίδευτον ὑπὸ ἀσχολίας οὐδὲν ἧττον τῶν
E νομέων τὸν τοιοῦτον ἀναγκαῖον γίγνεσθαι, σηκὸν
ἐν ὄρει τὸ τεῖχος περιβεβλημένον. γῆς δὲ ὅταν
μυρία πλέθρα ἢ ἔτι πλείω ἀκούσῃ ὥς τις ἄρα
κεκτημένος θαυμαστὰ πλήθει κέκτηται, πάνσμικρα
δοκεῖ ἀκούειν εἰς ἅπασαν εἰωθὼς τὴν γῆν βλέπειν.
τὰ δὲ δὴ γένη ὑμνούντων, ὡς γενναῖός τις ἑπτὰ
πάππους πλουσίους ἔχων ἀποφῆναι, παντάπασιν
ἀμβλὺ καὶ ἐπὶ σμικρὸν ὁρώντων ἡγεῖται τὸν
175 ἔπαινον, ὑπὸ ἀπαιδευσίας οὐ δυναμένων εἰς τὸ

private, when he meets with individuals, and in public, as I said in the beginning, when he is obliged to speak in court or elsewhere about the things at his feet and before his eyes, is a laughing-stock not only to Thracian girls but to the multitude in general, for he falls into pits and all sorts of perplexities through inexperience, and his awkwardness is terrible, making him seem a fool; for when it comes to abusing people he has no personal abuse to offer against anyone, because he knows no evil of any man, never having cared for such things; so his perplexity makes him appear ridiculous; and as to laudatory speeches and the boastings of others, it becomes manifest that he is laughing at them—not pretending to laugh, but really laughing—and so he is thought to be a fool. When he hears a panegyric of a despot or a king he fancies he is listening to the praises of some herdsman—a swineherd, a shepherd, or a neatherd, for instance—who gets much milk from his beasts; but he thinks that the ruler tends and milks a more perverse and treacherous creature than the herdsmen, and that he must grow coarse and uncivilized, no less than they, for he has no leisure and lives surrounded by a wall, as the herdsmen live in their mountain pens. And when he hears that someone is amazingly rich, because he owns ten thousand acres of land or more, to him, accustomed as he is to think of the whole earth, this seems very little. And when people sing the praises of lineage and say someone is of noble birth, because he can show seven wealthy ancestors, he thinks that such praises betray an altogether dull and narrow vision on the part of those who utter them; because of lack of education they cannot keep their eyes fixed

123

πᾶν ἀεὶ βλέπειν οὐδὲ λογίζεσθαι ὅτι πάππων
καὶ προγόνων μυριάδες ἑκάστῳ γεγόνασιν ἀναρί-
θμητοι, ἐν αἷς πλούσιοι καὶ πτωχοὶ καὶ βασιλεῖς
καὶ δοῦλοι βάρβαροί τε καὶ Ἕλληνες πολλάκις
μυρίοι γεγόνασιν ὁτῳοῦν· ἀλλ᾽ ἐπὶ πέντε καὶ
εἴκοσι καταλόγῳ προγόνων σεμνυννομένων καὶ
ἀναφερόντων εἰς Ἡρακλέα τὸν Ἀμφιτρύωνος
ἄτοπα αὐτῷ καταφαίνεται τῆς σμικρολογίας, ὅτι
B δὲ ὁ ἀπ᾽ Ἀμφιτρύωνος εἰς τὸ ἄνω πεντεκαι-
εικοστὸς τοιοῦτος ἦν οἷα συνέβαινεν αὐτῷ τύχη, καὶ
ὁ πεντηκοστὸς ἀπ᾽ αὐτοῦ, γελᾷ οὐ δυναμένων λογί-
ζεσθαί τε καὶ χαυνότητα ἀνοήτου ψυχῆς ἀπαλλάττειν.
ἐν ἅπασι δὴ τούτοις ὁ τοιοῦτος ὑπὸ τῶν πολλῶν
καταγελᾶται, τὰ μὲν ὑπερηφάνως ἔχων, ὡς δοκεῖ,
τὰ δ᾽ ἐν ποσὶν ἀγνοῶν τε καὶ ἐν ἑκάστοις ἀπορῶν.

ΘΕΟ. Παντάπασι τὰ γιγνόμενα λέγεις, ὦ
Σώκρατες.

25. ΣΩ. Ὅταν δέ γέ τινα αὐτός, ὦ φίλε,
C ἑλκύσῃ ἄνω, καὶ ἐθελήσῃ τις αὐτῷ ἐκβῆναι ἐκ
τοῦ "τί ἐγὼ σὲ ἀδικῶ ἢ σὺ ἐμέ;" εἰς σκέψιν
αὐτῆς δικαιοσύνης τε καὶ ἀδικίας, τί τε ἑκάτερον
αὐτοῖν καὶ τί τῶν πάντων ἢ ἀλλήλων διαφέρετον,
ἢ ἐκ τοῦ "εἰ βασιλεὺς εὐδαίμων," "κεκτημένος
τ᾽ αὖ πολὺ[1] χρυσίον," βασιλείας πέρι καὶ ἀνθρω-
πίνης ὅλως εὐδαιμονίας καὶ ἀθλιότητος ἐπὶ
σκέψιν, ποίω τέ τινε ἐστὸν καὶ τίνα τρόπον
ἀνθρώπου φύσει προσήκει τὸ μὲν κτήσασθαι[2]
αὐτοῖν, τὸ δὲ ἀποφυγεῖν — περὶ τούτων ἁπάντων
D ὅταν αὖ δέῃ λόγον διδόναι τὸν σμικρὸν ἐκεῖνον
τὴν ψυχὴν καὶ δριμὺν καὶ δικανικόν, πάλιν αὖ τὰ

---

[1] πολὺ Euseb., Iamb.; om. BT.
[2] κτήσασθαι B², Iamb., Euseb.; κτήσεσθαι BT.

upon the whole and are unable to calculate that every man has had countless thousands of ancestors and progenitors, among whom have been in any instance rich and poor, kings and slaves, barbarians and Greeks. And when people pride themselves on a list of twenty-five ancestors and trace their pedigree back to Heracles, the son of Amphitryon, the pettiness of their ideas seems absurd to him; he laughs at them because they cannot free their silly minds of vanity by calculating that Amphitryon's twenty-fifth ancestor was such as fortune happened to make him, and the fiftieth for that matter. In all these cases the philosopher is derided by the common herd, partly because he seems to be contemptuous, partly because he is ignorant of common things and is always in perplexity.

THEO. That all happens just as you say, Socrates.

SOC. But when, my friend, he draws a man upwards and the other is willing to rise with him above the level of "What wrong have I done you or you me?" to the investigation of abstract right and wrong, to inquire what each of them is and wherein they differ from each other and from all other things, or above the level of "Is a king happy?" or, on the other hand, "Has he great wealth?" to the investigation of royalty and of human happiness and wretchedness in general, to see what the nature of each is and in what way man is naturally fitted to gain the one and escape the other—when that man of small and sharp and pettifogging mind is compelled in his turn to give an account of all these

ἀντίστροφα ἀποδίδωσιν· ἰλιγγιῶν τε ἀπὸ ὑψηλοῦ
κρεμασθεὶς καὶ βλέπων μετέωρος ἄνωθεν ὑπὸ
ἀηθείας ἀδημονῶν τε καὶ ἀπορῶν καὶ βατταρίζων [1]
γέλωτα Θρᾴτταις μὲν οὐ παρέχει οὐδ' ἄλλῳ ἀπαι-
δεύτῳ οὐδενί, οὐ γὰρ αἰσθάνονται, τοῖς δ' ἐναντίως
ἢ ὡς ἀνδραπόδοις τραφεῖσιν ἅπασιν. [2] οὗτος δὴ
ἑκατέρου τρόπος, ὦ Θεόδωρε, ὁ μὲν τῷ ὄντι ἐν
Ε ἐλευθερίᾳ τε καὶ σχολῇ τεθραμμένου, ὃν δὴ
φιλόσοφον καλεῖς, ᾧ ἀνεμέσητον εὐήθει δοκεῖν καὶ
οὐδενὶ εἶναι ὅταν εἰς δουλικὰ ἐμπέσῃ διακονήματα,
οἷον στρωματόδεσμον μὴ ἐπισταμένου συσκευά-
σασθαι μηδὲ ὄψον ἡδῦναι ἢ θῶπας λόγους· ὁ δ' [3]
αὖ τὰ μὲν τοιαῦτα πάντα δυναμένου τορῶς τε καὶ
ὀξέως διακονεῖν, ἀναβάλλεσθαι δὲ οὐκ ἐπισταμένου
ἐπιδέξια ἐλευθέρως [4] οὐδέ γ' ἁρμονίαν λόγων
176 λαβόντος ὀρθῶς ὑμνῆσαι θεῶν τε καὶ ἀνδρῶν
εὐδαιμόνων βίον ἀληθῆ. [5]

ΘΕΟ. Εἰ πάντας, ὦ Σώκρατες, πείθοις ἃ λέγεις
ὥσπερ ἐμέ, πλείων ἂν εἰρήνη καὶ κακὰ ἐλάττω
κατ' ἀνθρώπους εἴη.

ΣΩ. Ἀλλ' οὔτ' ἀπολέσθαι τὰ κακὰ δυνατόν, ὦ
Θεόδωρε· ὑπεναντίον γάρ τι τῷ ἀγαθῷ ἀεὶ εἶναι
ἀνάγκη· οὔτ' ἐν θεοῖς αὐτὰ ἱδρῦσθαι, τὴν δὲ
θνητὴν φύσιν καὶ τόνδε τὸν τόπον περιπολεῖ ἐξ

---

[1] βατταρίζων Themistius ; βαρβαρίζων ΒΤ.
[2] τραφεῖσιν ἅπασιν Β ; τραφεῖσι πᾶσιν Τ, Iamb., Euseb.
[3] ὁ δ' t, Iamb. ; οὐ δ' ΒΤ.
[4] ἐλευθέρως ΒΤ ; ἐλευθερίως Athenaeus.
[5] ἀληθῆ om. Athenaeus.

things, then the tables are turned; dizzied by the
new experience of hanging at such a height, he
gazes downward from the air in dismay and perplexity; he stammers and becomes ridiculous, not in
the eyes of Thracian girls or other uneducated
persons, for they have no perception of it, but in
those of all men who have been brought up as free
men, not as slaves. Such is the character of each
of the two classes, Theodorus, of the man who has
truly been brought up in freedom and leisure, whom
you call a philosopher—who may without censure
appear foolish and good for nothing when he is
involved in menial services, if, for instance, he does
not know how to pack up his bedding, much less
to put the proper sweetening into a sauce or a fawn-
ing speech—and of the other, who can perform all
such services smartly and quickly, but does not know
how to wear his cloak as a freeman should, properly
draped,[1] still less to acquire the true harmony of
speech and hymn aright the praises of the true life
of gods and blessed men.

THEO. If, Socrates, you could persuade all men
of the truth of what you say as you do me, there
would be more peace and fewer evils among mankind.

SOC. But it is impossible that evils should be done
away with, Theodorus, for there must always be
something opposed to the good; and they cannot
have their place among the gods, but must inevitably
hover about mortal nature and this earth. Therefore

---

[1] The Athenians regarded the proper draping of the
cloak as a sign of good breeding. The well-bred Athenian
first threw his cloak over the left shoulder, then passed it
round the back to the right side, then either above or below
the right arm, and finally over the left arm or shoulder.
See Aristophanes, *Birds*, 1567 f., with Blaydes's notes.

ἀνάγκης. διὸ καὶ πειρᾶσθαι χρὴ ἐνθένδε ἐκεῖσε
B φεύγειν ὅτι τάχιστα. φυγὴ δὲ ὁμοίωσις θεῷ
κατὰ τὸ δυνατόν· ὁμοίωσις δὲ δίκαιον καὶ ὅσιον
μετὰ φρονήσεως γενέσθαι. ἀλλὰ γάρ, ὦ ἄριστε,
οὐ πάνυ [1] ῥᾴδιον πεῖσαι ὡς ἄρα οὐχ ὧν ἕνεκα οἱ
πολλοί φασι δεῖν πονηρίαν μὲν φεύγειν, ἀρετὴν δὲ
διώκειν, τούτων χάριν τὸ μὲν ἐπιτηδευτέον, τὸ δ' οὔ,
ἵνα μὴ [2] κακὸς καὶ ἵνα ἀγαθὸς δοκῇ εἶναι· ταῦτα
γάρ ἐστιν ὁ λεγόμενος γραῶν ὕθλος, ὡς ἐμοὶ
C φαίνεται· τὸ δὲ ἀληθὲς ὧδε λέγωμεν. θεὸς
οὐδαμῇ οὐδαμῶς ἄδικος, ἀλλ' ὡς οἷόν τε δικαιότατος, καὶ οὐκ ἔστιν αὐτῷ ὁμοιότερον οὐδὲν ἢ ὃς
ἂν ἡμῶν αὖ γένηται ὅτι δικαιότατος. περὶ τοῦτο [3]
καὶ ἡ ὡς ἀληθῶς δεινότης ἀνδρὸς καὶ οὐδενία τε
καὶ ἀνανδρία. ἡ μὲν γὰρ τούτου γνῶσις σοφία καὶ
ἀρετὴ ἀληθινή, ἡ δὲ ἄγνοια ἀμαθία καὶ κακία
ἐναργής· αἱ δ' ἄλλαι δεινότητές τε δοκοῦσαι καὶ
σοφίαι ἐν μὲν πολιτικαῖς δυναστείαις γιγνόμεναι
φορτικαί, ἐν δὲ τέχναις βάναυσοι. τῷ οὖν ἀδι-
D κοῦντι καὶ ἀνόσια λέγοντι ἢ πράττοντι μακρῷ
ἄριστ' ἔχει τὸ μὴ συγχωρεῖν δεινῷ ὑπὸ πανουργίας
εἶναι· ἀγάλλονται γὰρ τῷ ὀνείδει καὶ οἴονται
ἀκούειν ὅτι οὐ ληροί εἰσι, γῆς ἄλλως ἄχθη, ἀλλ'
ἄνδρες οἵους δεῖ ἐν πόλει τοὺς σωθησομένους.
λεκτέον οὖν τἀληθές, ὅτι τοσούτῳ μᾶλλόν εἰσιν
οἷοι οὐκ οἴονται, ὅτι οὐχὶ οἴονται· ἀγνοοῦσι γὰρ
ζημίαν ἀδικίας, ὃ δεῖ ἥκιστα ἀγνοεῖν. οὐ γάρ

---

[1] πάνυ B; πάνυ τι T. [2] ἵνα μὴ B; ἵνα δὴ μὴ T.
[3] τοῦτο Euseb., Iamb., Stob.; τούτου BT.

we ought to try to escape from earth to the dwelling of the gods as quickly as we can; and to escape is to become like God, so far as this is possible; and to become like God is to become righteous and holy and wise. But, indeed, my good friend, it is not at all easy to persuade people that the reason generally advanced for the pursuit of virtue and the avoidance of vice—namely, in order that a man may not seem bad and may seem good—is not the reason why the one should be practised and the other not; that, I think, is merely old wives' chatter, as the saying is. Let us give the true reason. God is in no wise and in no manner unrighteous, but utterly and perfectly righteous, and there is nothing so like him as that one of us who in turn becomes most nearly perfect in righteousness. It is herein that the true cleverness of a man is found and also his worthlessness and cowardice; for the knowledge of this is wisdom or true virtue, and ignorance of it is folly or manifest wickedness; and all the other kinds of seeming cleverness and wisdom are paltry when they appear in public affairs and vulgar in the arts. Therefore by far the best thing for the unrighteous man and the man whose words or deeds are impious is not to grant that he is clever through knavery; for such men glory in that reproach, and think it means that they are not triflers, "useless burdens upon the earth,"[1] but such as men should be who are to live safely in a state. So we must tell them the truth—that just because they do not think they are such as they are, they are so all the more truly; for they do not know the penalty of unrighteousness, which is the thing they most ought to know. For

[1] Homer, *Iliad*, xviii. 104; *Odyssey*, xx. 379.

ἐστιν ἣν δοκοῦσι, πληγαί τε καὶ θάνατοι, ὧν ἐνίοτε
πάσχουσιν οὐδὲν ἀδικοῦντες, ἀλλὰ ἣν ἀδύνατον
E ἐκφυγεῖν.

ΘΕΟ. Τίνα δὴ λέγεις;

ΣΩ. Παραδειγμάτων, ὦ φίλε, ἐν τῷ ὄντι ἑστώ-
των, τοῦ μὲν θείου εὐδαιμονεστάτου, τοῦ δὲ ἀθέου
ἀθλιωτάτου, οὐχ ὁρῶντες ὅτι οὕτως ἔχει, ὑπὸ
ἠλιθιότητός τε καὶ τῆς ἐσχάτης ἀνοίας λανθάνουσι
177 τῷ μὲν ὁμοιούμενοι διὰ τὰς ἀδίκους πράξεις, τῷ
δὲ ἀνομοιούμενοι. οὗ δὴ τίνουσι δίκην ζῶντες τὸν
εἰκότα βίον ᾧ ὁμοιοῦνται· ἐὰν δ᾽ εἴπωμεν ὅτι, ἂν
μὴ ἀπαλλαγῶσι τῆς δεινότητος, καὶ τελευτήσαντας
αὐτοὺς ἐκεῖνος μὲν ὁ τῶν κακῶν καθαρὸς τόπος οὐ
δέξεται, ἐνθάδε δὲ τὴν αὐτοῖς ὁμοιότητα τῆς
διαγωγῆς ἀεὶ ἕξουσι, κακοὶ κακοῖς συνόντες,
ταῦτα δὴ καὶ παντάπασιν ὡς δεινοὶ καὶ πανοῦργοι
ἀνοήτων τινῶν ἀκούσονται.

ΘΕΟ. Καὶ μάλα δή, ὦ Σώκρατες.

B ΣΩ. Οἶδά τοι, ὦ ἑταῖρε. ἐν μέντοι τι αὐτοῖς
συμβέβηκεν· ὅταν[1] ἰδίᾳ λόγον δέῃ δοῦναί τε καὶ
δέξασθαι περὶ ὧν ψέγουσι, καὶ ἐθελήσωσιν ἀνδρικῶς πολὺν χρόνον ὑπομεῖναι καὶ μὴ ἀνάνδρως
φυγεῖν,[2] τότε ἀτόπως, ὦ δαιμόνιε, τελευτῶντες οὐκ
ἀρέσκουσιν αὐτοὶ αὐτοῖς περὶ ὧν λέγουσι, καὶ ἡ
ῥητορικὴ ἐκείνη πως ἀπομαραίνεται, ὥστε παίδων
μηδὲν δοκεῖν διαφέρειν. περὶ μὲν οὖν τούτων, ἐπειδὴ
καὶ πάρεργα τυγχάνει λεγόμενα, ἀποστῶμεν—εἰ δὲ
C μή, πλείω ἀεὶ ἐπιρρέοντα καταχώσει ἡμῶν τὸν

---

[1] ὅτ᾽ ἂν W, Iamb.; ὅτι ἂν BT.
[2] φυγεῖν W; φεύγειν BT, Iamb.

it is not what they think it is—scourgings and death, which they sometimes escape entirely when they have done wrong—but a penalty which it is impossible to escape.

THEO. What penalty do you mean?

SOC. Two patterns, my friend, are set up in the world, the divine, which is most blessed, and the godless, which is most wretched. But these men do not see that this is the case, and their silliness and extreme foolishness blind them to the fact that through their unrighteous acts they are made like the one and unlike the other. They therefore pay the penalty for this by living a life that conforms to the pattern they resemble; and if we tell them that, unless they depart from their "cleverness," the blessed place that is pure of all things evil will not receive them after death, and here on earth they will always live the life like themselves—evil men associating with evil—when they hear this, they will be so confident in their unscrupulous cleverness that they will think our words the talk of fools.

THEO. Very true, Socrates.

SOC. Yes, my friend, I know. However, there is one thing that has happened to them: whenever they have to carry on a personal argument about the doctrines to which they object, if they are willing to stand their ground for a while like men and do not run away like cowards, then, my friend, they at last become strangely dissatisfied with themselves and their arguments; their brilliant rhetoric withers away, so that they seem no better than children. But this is a digression. Let us turn away from these matters—if we do not, they will come on like

131

ἐξ ἀρχῆς λόγον—ἐπὶ δὲ τὰ ἔμπροσθεν ἴωμεν, εἰ καὶ σοὶ δοκεῖ.

ΘΕΟ. Ἐμοὶ μὲν τὰ τοιαῦτα, ὦ Σώκρατες, οὐκ ἀηδέστερα ἀκούειν· ῥᾴω γὰρ τηλικῷδε ὄντι ἐπακολουθεῖν· εἰ μέντοι δοκεῖ, πάλιν ἐπανίωμεν.

26. ΣΩ. Οὐκοῦν ἐνταῦθά που ἦμεν τοῦ λόγου, ἐν ᾧ ἔφαμεν τοὺς τὴν φερομένην οὐσίαν λέγοντας, καὶ τὸ ἀεὶ δοκοῦν ἑκάστῳ τοῦτο καὶ εἶναι τούτῳ ᾧ δοκεῖ, ἐν μὲν τοῖς ἄλλοις ἐθέλειν διισχυρί-
D ζεσθαι, καὶ οὐχ ἥκιστα περὶ τὰ δίκαια, ὡς παντὸς μᾶλλον ἃ ἂν θῆται πόλις δόξαντα αὐτῇ, ταῦτα καὶ ἔστι δίκαια τῇ θεμένῃ, ἔωσπερ ἂν κέηται· περὶ δὲ τἀγαθοῦ[1] οὐδένα ἀνδρεῖον ἔθ' οὕτως εἶναι, ὥστε τολμᾶν διαμάχεσθαι ὅτι καὶ ἃ ἂν ὠφέλιμα οἰηθεῖσα πόλις ἑαυτῇ θῆται, καὶ ἔστι τοσοῦτον χρόνον ὅσον ἂν κέηται ὠφέλιμα, πλὴν εἴ τις τὸ ὄνομα λέγοι· τοῦτο δέ που σκῶμμ' ἂν εἴη πρὸς ὃ λέγομεν. οὐχί;

ΘΕΟ. Πάνυ γε.

E ΣΩ. Μὴ γὰρ λεγέτω τὸ ὄνομα, ἀλλὰ τὸ πρᾶγμα τὸ ὀνομαζόμενον θεωρείτω.[2]

ΘΕΟ. Μὴ γάρ.

ΣΩ. Ἀλλ' ὃ ἂν τοῦτο ὀνομάζῃ, τούτου δήπου στοχάζεται νομοθετουμένη, καὶ πάντας τοὺς νόμους, καθ' ὅσον οἴεταί τε καὶ δύναται, ὡς ὠφελιμωτάτους ἑαυτῇ τίθεται· ἢ πρὸς ἄλλο τι βλέπουσα νομοθετεῖται;

[1] τἀγαθοῦ BW²; τἀγαθὰ TW.
[2] τὸ ὀνομαζόμενον θεωρείτω W; ὃ ὀνομαζόμενον θεωρεῖται B; λεγέτω . . . μὴ γάρ om. T.

an ever-rising flood and bury in silt our original
argument—and let us, if you please, proceed.

THEO. To me, Socrates, such digressions are quite
as agreeable as the argument; for they are easier for
a man of my age to follow. However, if you prefer,
let us return to our argument.

SOC. Very well. We were at about the point in
our argument where we said that those who declare
that only motion is reality, and that whatever seems
to each man really is to him to whom it seems, are
willing to maintain their position in regard to other
matters and to maintain especially in regard to
justice that whatever laws a state makes, because
they seem to it just, are just to the state that made
them, as long as they remain in force; but as regards
the good, that nobody has the courage to go on and
contend that whatever laws a state passes thinking
them advantageous to it are really advantageous as
long as they remain in force, unless what he means
is merely the name "advantageous"[1]; and that would
be making a joke of our argument. Am I right?

THEO. Certainly.

SOC. Yes; for he must not mean merely the name,
but the thing named must be the object of his
attention.

THEO. True.

SOC. But the state, in making laws, aims, of course,
at advantage, whatever the name it gives it, and
makes all its laws as advantageous as possible to
itself, to the extent of its belief and ability; or has
it in making laws anything else in view?

[1] The legislator may call his laws advantageous, and that
name, if it is given them when they are enacted, will belong
to them, whatever their character may be.

178 ΘΕΟ. Οὐδαμῶς.

ΣΩ. Ἡ οὖν καὶ τυγχάνει ἀεί, ἢ πολλὰ καὶ δια-
μαρτάνει ἑκάστη[1];

ΘΕΟ. Οἶμαι ἔγωγε καὶ ἁμαρτάνειν.

ΣΩ. Ἔτι τοίνυν ἐνθένδε ἂν μᾶλλον πᾶς τις
ὁμολογήσειεν ταὐτὰ ταῦτα, εἰ περὶ παντός τις τοῦ
εἴδους ἐρωτῴη, ἐν ᾧ καὶ τὸ ὠφέλιμον τυγχάνει
ὄν· ἔστι δέ που καὶ περὶ τὸν μέλλοντα χρόνον.
ὅταν γὰρ νομοθετώμεθα, ὡς ἐσομένους ὠφελίμους
τοὺς νόμους τιθέμεθα εἰς τὸν ἔπειτα χρόνον· τοῦτο
δὲ μέλλον[2] ὀρθῶς ἂν λέγοιμεν.

B   ΘΕΟ. Πάνυ γε.

ΣΩ. Ἴθι δή, οὑτωσὶ ἐρωτῶμεν Πρωταγόραν ἢ
ἄλλον τινὰ τῶν ἐκείνῳ τὰ αὐτὰ λεγόντων· πάντων
μέτρον ἄνθρωπός ἐστιν, ὡς φατέ, ὦ Πρωταγόρα,
λευκῶν, βαρέων, κούφων, οὐδενὸς ὅτου οὐ τῶν
τοιούτων· ἔχων γὰρ αὐτῶν τὸ κριτήριον ἐν αὑτῷ,
οἷα πάσχει τοιαῦτα οἰόμενος, ἀληθῆ τε οἴεται
αὑτῷ καὶ ὄντα. οὐχ οὕτω;

ΘΕΟ. Οὕτω.

ΣΩ. Ἡ καὶ τῶν μελλόντων ἔσεσθαι, φήσομεν, ὦ
Πρωταγόρα, ἔχει τὸ κριτήριον ἐν αὑτῷ, καὶ οἷα
C   ἂν οἰηθῇ ἔσεσθαι, ταῦτα καὶ γίγνεται ἐκείνῳ τῷ
οἰηθέντι; οἷον θερμά, ἆρ' ὅταν τις οἰηθῇ ἰδιώτης
αὑτὸν πυρετὸν λήψεσθαι καὶ ἔσεσθαι ταύτην τὴν
θερμότητα, καὶ ἕτερος, ἰατρὸς δέ, ἀντοιηθῇ, κατὰ
τὴν ποτέρου δόξαν φῶμεν τὸ μέλλον ἀποβήσεσθαι;
ἢ κατὰ τὴν ἀμφοτέρων, καὶ τῷ μὲν ἰατρῷ οὐ

---

[1] ἑκάστη W ; ἑκάστῃ BT.
[2] μέλλον W ; μᾶλλον BT.

THEO. Certainly not.

SOC. And does it always hit the mark, or does every state often miss it?

THEO. I should say they do often miss it!

SOC. Continuing, then, and proceeding from this point, every one would more readily agree to this assertion, if the question were asked concerning the whole class to which the advantageous belongs; and that whole class, it would seem, pertains to the future. For when we make laws, we make them with the idea that they will be advantageous in after time; and this is rightly called the future.

THEO. Certainly.

SOC. Come then, on this assumption, let us question Protagoras or someone of those who agree with him. Man is the measure of all things, as your school says, Protagoras, of the white, the heavy, the light, everything of that sort without exception; for he possesses within himself the standard by which to judge them, and when his thoughts about them coincide with his sensations, he thinks what to him is true and really is. Is not that what they say?

THEO. Yes.

SOC. Does he, then, also, Protagoras, we shall say, possess within himself the standard by which to judge of the things which are yet to be, and do those things which he thinks will be actually come to pass for him who thought them? Take, for instance, heat; if some ordinary man thinks he is going to take a fever, that is to say, that this particular heat will be, and some other man, who is a physician, thinks the contrary, whose opinion shall we expect the future to prove right? Or perhaps the opinion

θερμὸς οὐδὲ πυρέττων γενήσεται, ἑαυτῷ δὲ ἀμφότερα;

ΘΕΟ. Γελοῖον μέντ' ἂν εἴη.

ΣΩ. 'Αλλ', οἶμαι, περὶ οἴνου γλυκύτητος καὶ
D αὐστηρότητος μελλούσης ἔσεσθαι ἡ τοῦ γεωργοῦ
δόξα, ἀλλ' οὐχ ἡ τοῦ κιθαριστοῦ κυρία.

ΘΕΟ. Τί μήν;

ΣΩ. Οὐδ' ἂν αὖ περὶ ἀναρμόστου τε καὶ εὐαρ-
μόστου ἐσομένου παιδοτρίβης ἂν βέλτιον δοξάσειεν
μουσικοῦ, ὃ[1] καὶ ἔπειτα αὐτῷ παιδοτρίβῃ δόξει
εὐάρμοστον εἶναι.

ΘΕΟ. Οὐδαμῶς.

ΣΩ. Οὐκοῦν καὶ τοῦ μέλλοντος ἑστιάσεσθαι μὴ
μαγειρικοῦ ὄντος, σκευαζομένης θοίνης, ἀκυροτέρα
ἡ κρίσις τῆς τοῦ ὀψοποιοῦ περὶ τῆς ἐσομένης
E ἡδονῆς. περὶ μὲν γὰρ τοῦ ἤδη ὄντος ἑκάστῳ
ἡδέος ἢ γεγονότος μηδέν πω τῷ λόγῳ διαμαχώ-
μεθα, ἀλλὰ περὶ τοῦ μέλλοντος ἑκάστῳ καὶ δόξειν
καὶ ἔσεσθαι πότερον αὐτὸς αὑτῷ ἄριστος κριτής,
ἢ σύ, ὦ Πρωταγόρα, τό γε[2] περὶ λόγους πιθανὸν
ἑκάστῳ ἡμῶν ἐσόμενον εἰς δικαστήριον βέλτιον
ἂν προδοξάσαις ἢ τῶν ἰδιωτῶν ὁστισοῦν;

ΘΕΟ. Καὶ μάλα, ὦ Σώκρατες, τοῦτό γε
σφόδρα ὑπισχνεῖτο πάντων διαφέρειν αὐτός.

ΣΩ. Νὴ Δία, ὦ μέλε· ἢ οὐδείς γ' ἂν αὐτῷ διε-
179 λέγετο διδοὺς πολὺ ἀργύριον, εἰ μὴ τοὺς συνόντας
ἔπειθεν ὅτι καὶ τὸ μέλλον ἔσεσθαί τε καὶ δόξειν

_____
[1] δ om. T.   [2] τό γε W ; τότε BT.

of both, and the man will become, not hot or feverish to the physician, but to himself both ?

THEO. No, that would be ridiculous.

soc. But, I imagine, in regard to the sweetness or dryness which will be in a wine, the opinion of the husbandman, not that of the lyre-player, will be valid.

THEO. Of course.

soc. And again, in a matter of discord or tunefulness in music that has never been played, a gymnastic teacher could not judge better than a musician what will, when performed, seem tuneful even to a gymnastic teacher himself.

THEO. Certainly not.

soc. Then, too, when a banquet is in preparation the opinion of him who is to be a guest, unless he has training in cookery, is of less value concerning the pleasure that will be derived from the viands than that of the cook. For we need not yet argue about that which already is or has been pleasant to each one; but concerning that which will in the future seem and be pleasant to each one, is he himself the best judge for himself, or would you, Protagoras—at least as regards the arguments which will be persuasive in court to each of us—be able to give an opinion beforehand better than anyone whatsoever who has no especial training ?

THEO. Certainly, Socrates, in this, at any rate, he used to declare emphatically that he himself excelled everyone.

soc. Yes, my friend, he certainly did; otherwise nobody would have paid him a high fee for his conversations, if he had not made his pupils believe that neither a prophet nor anyone else could judge

οὔτε μάντις οὔτε τις ἄλλος ἄμεινον κρίνειεν ἂν ἢ αὐτός.[1]

ΘΕΟ. Ἀληθέστατα.

ΣΩ. Οὐκοῦν καὶ αἱ νομοθεσίαι καὶ τὸ ὠφέλιμον περὶ τὸ μέλλον ἐστί, καὶ πᾶς ἂν ὁμολογοῖ νομοθετουμένην πόλιν πολλάκις ἀνάγκην εἶναι τοῦ ὠφελιμωτάτου ἀποτυγχάνειν;

ΘΕΟ. Μάλα γε.

ΣΩ. Μετρίως ἄρα ἡμῖν πρὸς τὸν διδάσκαλόν B σου εἰρήσεται, ὅτι ἀνάγκη αὐτῷ ὁμολογεῖν σοφώτερόν τε ἄλλον ἄλλου εἶναι καὶ τὸν μὲν τοιοῦτον μέτρον εἶναι, ἐμοὶ δὲ τῷ ἀνεπιστήμονι μηδὲ ὁπωστιοῦν ἀνάγκην εἶναι μέτρῳ γίγνεσθαι, ὡς ἄρτι με ἠνάγκαζεν ὁ ὑπὲρ ἐκείνου λόγος, εἴτ' ἐβουλόμην εἴτε μή, τοιοῦτον εἶναι.

ΘΕΟ. Ἐκείνη μοι δοκεῖ, ὦ Σώκρατες, μάλιστα ἁλίσκεσθαι ὁ λόγος, ἁλισκόμενος καὶ ταύτῃ, ᾗ τὰς τῶν ἄλλων δόξας κυρίας ποιεῖ, αὗται δὲ ἐφάνησαν τοὺς ἐκείνου λόγους οὐδαμῇ ἀληθεῖς ἡγούμεναι.

C ΣΩ. Πολλαχῇ, ὦ Θεόδωρε, καὶ ἄλλῃ ἂν τό γε τοιοῦτον ἁλοίη μὴ πᾶσαν παντὸς ἀληθῆ δόξαν εἶναι· περὶ δὲ τὸ παρὸν ἑκάστῳ πάθος, ἐξ ὧν αἱ αἰσθήσεις καὶ αἱ κατὰ ταύτας δόξαι γίγνονται, χαλεπώτερον ἑλεῖν ὡς οὐκ ἀληθεῖς. ἴσως δὲ οὐδὲν λέγω· ἀνάλωτοι γάρ, εἰ ἔτυχον, εἰσίν, καὶ οἱ φάσκοντες αὐτὰς ἐναργεῖς τε εἶναι καὶ ἐπιστήμας τάχα ἂν ὄντα λέγοιεν, καὶ Θεαίτητος ὅδε οὐκ ἀπὸ σκοποῦ εἴρηκεν αἴσθησιν καὶ ἐπιστήμην ταὐτὸν D θέμενος. προσιτέον οὖν ἐγγυτέρω, ὡς ὁ ὑπὲρ

[1] αὑτὸς αὑτῷ MSS.; αὑτῷ om. Schleiermacher.

better than himself what was in the future to be
and seem.

THEO. Very true.

SOC. Both lawmaking, then, and the advantageous
are concerned with the future, and everyone would
agree that a state in making laws must often fail
to attain the greatest advantage?

THEO. Assuredly.

SOC. Then it will be a fair answer if we say to your
master that he is obliged to agree that one man is
wiser than another, and that such a wise man is a
measure, but that I, who am without knowledge, am
not in the least obliged to become a measure, as
the argument in his behalf just now tried to oblige
me to be, whether I would or no.

THEO. In that respect, Socrates, I think that the
argument is most clearly proved to be wrong, and
it is proved wrong in this also, in that it declares
the opinions of others to be valid, whereas it was
shown that they do not consider his arguments true
at all.

SOC. In many other respects, Theodorus, it could
be proved that not every opinion of every person is
true, at any rate in matters of that kind; but it is
more difficult to prove that opinions are not true in
regard to the momentary states of feeling of each
person, from which our perceptions and the opinions
concerning them arise. But perhaps I am quite
wrong; for it may be impossible to prove that they
are not true, and those who say that they are
manifest and are forms of knowledge may perhaps
be right, and Theaetetus here was not far from the
mark in saying that perception and knowledge are
identical. So we must, as the argument in behalf of

139

Πρωταγόρου λόγος ἐπέταττε, καὶ σκεπτέον τὴν
φερομένην ταύτην οὐσίαν διακρούοντα,[1] εἴτε ὑγιὲς
εἴτε σαθρὸν φθέγγεται· μάχη δ' οὖν περὶ αὐτῆς οὐ
φαύλη οὐδ' ὀλίγοις γέγονεν.

27. ΘΕΟ. Πολλοῦ καὶ δεῖ φαύλη εἶναι, ἀλλὰ
περὶ μὲν τὴν Ἰωνίαν καὶ ἐπιδίδωσι πάμπολυ. οἱ
γὰρ τοῦ Ἡρακλείτου ἑταῖροι χορηγοῦσι τούτου
τοῦ λόγου μάλα ἐρρωμένως.

ΣΩ. Τῷ τοι, ὦ φίλε Θεόδωρε, μᾶλλον σκεπτέον
Ε καὶ ἐξ ἀρχῆς, ὥσπερ αὐτοὶ ὑποτείνονται.

ΘΕΟ. Παντάπασι μὲν οὖν. καὶ γάρ, ὦ Σώκρατες,
περὶ τούτων τῶν Ἡρακλειτείων ἤ, ὥσπερ σὺ
λέγεις, Ὁμηρείων καὶ ἔτι παλαιοτέρων, αὐτοῖς
μὲν τοῖς περὶ τὴν Ἔφεσον, ὅσοι προσποιοῦνται
ἔμπειροι εἶναι,[2] οὐδὲν μᾶλλον οἷόν τε διαλεχθῆναι
ἢ τοῖς οἰστρῶσιν. ἀτεχνῶς γὰρ κατὰ τὰ συγγράμ-
ματα φέρονται, τὸ δ' ἐπιμεῖναι ἐπὶ λόγῳ καὶ
ἐρωτήματι καὶ ἡσυχίως ἐν μέρει ἀποκρίνασθαι
180 καὶ ἐρέσθαι ἧττον αὐτοῖς ἔνι ἢ τὸ μηδέν· μᾶλλον
δὲ ὑπερβάλλει τὸ οὐδ' οὐδὲν πρὸς τὸ μηδὲ σμικρὸν
ἐνεῖναι τοῖς ἀνδράσιν ἡσυχίας. ἀλλ' ἄν τινά τι
ἔρῃ, ὥσπερ ἐκ φαρέτρας ῥηματίσκια αἰνιγματώδη
ἀνασπῶντες ἀποτοξεύουσι, κἂν τούτου ζητῇς λόγον
λαβεῖν τί εἴρηκεν, ἑτέρῳ πεπλήξει καινῶς μετ-
ωνομασμένῳ. περανεῖς δὲ οὐδέποτε οὐδὲν πρὸς
οὐδένα αὐτῶν· οὐδέ γε ἐκεῖνοι αὐτοὶ πρὸς ἀλλή-
Β λους, ἀλλ' εὖ πάνυ φυλάττουσι τὸ μηδὲν βέβαιον

---

[1] διακρούοντα TW; ἀκούοντα Β.
[2] ἔμπειροι εἶναι Vindob. 21; ἔμπειροι ΒΤ, Euseb.

Protagoras[1] enjoined upon us, come up closer and examine this doctrine of motion as the fundamental essence, rapping on it to see whether it rings sound or unsound. As you know, a strife has arisen about it, no mean one, either, and waged by not a few combatants.

THEO. Yes, far from mean, and it is spreading far and wide all over Ionia; for the disciples of Heracleitus are supporting this doctrine very vigorously.

SOC. Therefore, my dear Theodorus, we must all the more examine it from the beginning as they themselves present it.

THEO. Certainly we must. For it is no more possible, Socrates, to discuss these doctrines of Heracleitus (or, as you say, of Homer or even earlier sages) with the Ephesians themselves—those, at least, who profess to be familiar with them—than with madmen. For they are, quite in accordance with their text-books, in perpetual motion; but as for keeping to an argument or a question and quietly answering and asking in turn, their power of doing that is less than nothing; or rather the words "nothing at all" fail to express the absence from these fellows of even the slightest particle of rest. But if you ask one of them a question, he pulls out puzzling little phrases, like arrows from a quiver, and shoots them off; and if you try to get hold of an explanation of what he has said, you will be struck with another phrase of novel and distorted wording, and you never make any progress whatsoever with any of them, nor do they themselves with one another, for that matter, but they take very good care to allow nothing to be settled either

[1] See 168 B.

ἐᾶν εἶναι μήτ᾽ ἐν λόγῳ μήτ᾽ ἐν ταῖς αὐτῶν ψυχαῖς,
ἡγούμενοι, ὡς ἐμοὶ δοκεῖ, αὐτὸ στάσιμον εἶναι·
τούτῳ δὲ πάνυ πολεμοῦσιν, καὶ καθ᾽ ὅσον δύνανται
πανταχόθεν ἐκβάλλουσιν.

ΣΩ. Ἴσως, ὦ Θεόδωρε, τοὺς ἄνδρας μαχομένους
ἑώρακας, εἰρηνεύουσιν δὲ οὐ συγγέγονας· οὐ γὰρ
σοὶ ἑταῖροί εἰσιν· ἀλλ᾽, οἶμαι, τὰ τοιαῦτα τοῖς
μαθηταῖς ἐπὶ σχολῆς φράζουσιν, οὓς ἂν βούλωνται
ὁμοίους αὑτοῖς ποιῆσαι.

ΘΕΟ. Ποίοις μαθηταῖς, ὦ δαιμόνιε; οὐδὲ γί-
C γνεται τῶν τοιούτων ἕτερος ἑτέρου μαθητής, ἀλλ᾽
αὐτόματοι ἀναφύονται, ὁπόθεν ἂν τύχῃ ἕκαστος
αὐτῶν ἐνθουσιάσας, καὶ τὸν ἕτερον ὁ ἕτερος οὐδὲν
ἡγεῖται εἰδέναι. παρὰ μὲν οὖν τούτων, ὅπερ ᾖα
ἐρῶν, οὐκ ἄν ποτε λάβοις λόγον οὔτε ἑκόντων οὔτ᾽
ἀκόντων· αὐτοὺς δὲ δεῖ παραλαβόντας ὥσπερ
πρόβλημα ἐπισκοπεῖσθαι.

ΣΩ. Καὶ μετρίως γε λέγεις. τό γε δὴ πρόβλημα
ἄλλο τι παρειλήφαμεν παρὰ μὲν τῶν ἀρχαίων μετὰ
D ποιήσεως ἐπικρυπτομένων τοὺς πολλούς, ὡς ἡ
γένεσις τῶν ἄλλων πάντων Ὠκεανός τε καὶ Τηθὺς
ῥεύματα τυγχάνει καὶ οὐδὲν ἕστηκε, παρὰ δὲ τῶν
ὑστέρων ἅτε σοφωτέρων ἀναφανδὸν ἀποδεικνυμέ-
νων, ἵνα καὶ οἱ σκυτοτόμοι αὐτῶν τὴν σοφίαν
μάθωσιν ἀκούσαντες καὶ παύσωνται ἠλιθίως οἰόμενοι τὰ μὲν ἑστάναι, τὰ δὲ κινεῖσθαι τῶν ὄντων,
μαθόντες δὲ ὅτι πάντα κινεῖται τιμῶσιν αὐτούς;
ὀλίγου δὲ ἐπελαθόμην, ὦ Θεόδωρε, ὅτι ἄλλοι αὖ
τἀναντία τούτοις ἀπεφήναντο,

in an argument or in their own minds, thinking, I suppose, that this is being stationary; but they wage bitter war against the stationary, and, so far as they can, they banish it altogether.

soc. Perhaps, Theodorus, you have seen the men when they are fighting, but have not been with them when they are at peace; for they are no friends of yours; but I fancy they utter such peaceful doctrines at leisure to those pupils whom they wish to make like themselves.

theo. What pupils, my good man? Such people do not become pupils of one another, but they grow up of themselves, each one getting his inspiration from any chance source, and each thinks the other knows nothing. From these people, then, as I was going to say, you would never get an argument either with their will or against it; but we must ourselves take over the question and investigate it as if it were a problem of mathematics.

soc. Yes, what you say is reasonable. Now as for the problem, have we not heard from the ancients, who concealed their meaning from the multitude by their poetry, that the origin of all things is Oceanus and Tethys, flowing streams, and that nothing is at rest; and likewise from the moderns, who, since they are wiser, declare their meaning openly, in order that even cobblers may hear and know their wisdom and may cease from the silly belief that some things are at rest and others in motion, and, after learning that everything is in motion, may honour their teachers? But, Theodorus, I almost forgot that others teach the opposite of this,

E   οἷον ἀκίνητον τελέθειν [1] ᾧ πάντ᾽ ὄνομ᾽ εἶναι,

καὶ ἄλλα ὅσα Μέλισσοί τε καὶ Παρμενίδαι ἐναν-
τιούμενοι πᾶσι τούτοις διισχυρίζονται, ὡς ἕν τε
πάντα ἐστὶ καὶ ἕστηκεν αὐτὸ ἐν αὑτῷ οὐκ ἔχον
χώραν ἐν ᾗ κινεῖται. τούτοις οὖν, ὦ ἑταῖρε, πᾶσι
τί χρησόμεθα; κατὰ σμικρὸν γὰρ προϊόντες λελήθαμεν ἀμφοτέρων εἰς τὸ μέσον πεπτωκότες, καὶ
181 ἂν μή πῃ ἀμυνόμενοι διαφύγωμεν, δίκην δώσομεν
ὥσπερ οἱ ἐν ταῖς παλαίστραις διὰ γραμμῆς
παίζοντες, ὅταν ὑπ᾽ ἀμφοτέρων ληφθέντες ἕλκωνται
εἰς τἀναντία. δοκεῖ οὖν μοι τοὺς ἑτέρους πρότερον
σκεπτέον, ἐφ᾽ οὕσπερ ὡρμήσαμεν, τοὺς ῥέοντας·
καὶ ἐὰν μέν τι φαίνωνται λέγοντες, συνέλξομεν μετ᾽
αὐτῶν ἡμᾶς αὐτούς, τοὺς ἑτέρους ἐκφυγεῖν πειρώ-
μενοι· ἐὰν δὲ οἱ τοῦ ὅλου στασιῶται ἀληθέστερα
λέγειν δοκῶσι, φευξόμεθα παρ᾽ αὐτοὺς ἀπ᾽ αὖ τῶν [2]
B τὰ ἀκίνητα κινούντων. ἀμφότεροι δ᾽ ἂν φανῶσι
μηδὲν μέτριον λέγοντες, γελοῖοι ἐσόμεθα ἡγούμενοι
ἡμᾶς μέν τι λέγειν φαύλους ὄντας, παμπαλαίους δὲ
καὶ πασσόφους ἄνδρας ἀποδεδοκιμακότες. ὅρα οὖν,
ὦ Θεόδωρε, εἰ λυσιτελεῖ εἰς τοσοῦτον προϊέναι
κίνδυνον.

ΘΕΟ. Οὐδὲν μὲν οὖν ἀνεκτόν, ὦ Σώκρατες, μὴ
οὐ διασκέψασθαι τί λέγουσιν ἑκάτεροι τῶν ἀνδρῶν.

---

[1] τελέθειν Stallbaum ; τελέθει BT.
[2] παρ᾽ αὐτοὺς ἀπ᾽ αὖ τῶν Schleiermacher ; παρ᾽ αὐτοὺς ἀπ᾽
αὐτῶν τῶν W ; ἀπ᾽ αὐτῶν τῶν παρ᾽ αὐτοὺς B ; τῶν παρ᾽ αὐτοὺς
ἀπ᾽ αὐτῶν T.

THEAETETUS

So that it is motionless, the name of which is the All,[1] and all the other doctrines maintained by Melissus and Parmenides and the rest, in opposition to all these; they maintain that everything is one and is stationary within itself, having no place in which to move. What shall we do with all these people, my friend? For, advancing little by little, we have unwittingly fallen between the two parties, and, unless we protect ourselves and escape somehow, we shall pay the penalty, like those in the palaestra, who in playing on the line are caught by both sides and dragged in opposite directions.[2] I think, then, we had better examine first the one party, those whom we originally set out to join, the flowing ones, and if we find their arguments sound, we will help them to pull us over, trying thus to escape the others; but if we find that the partisans of "the whole" seem to have truer doctrines, we will take refuge with them from those who would move what is motionless. But if we find that neither party has anything reasonable to say, we shall be ridiculous if we think that we, who are of no account, can say anything worth while after having rejected the doctrines of very ancient and very wise men. Therefore, Theodorus, see whether it is desirable to go forward into so great a danger.

THEO. Oh, it would be unendurable, Socrates, not to examine thoroughly the doctrines of both parties.

[1] Parmenides, line 98 (ed. Mullach). In its context the infinitive is necessary; but Plato may have quoted carelessly and may have used the indicative.

[2] In the game referred to (called διελκυστίνδα by Pollux, ix. 112) the players were divided into two parties, each of which tried to drag its opponents over a line drawn across the palaestra.

28. ΣΩ. Σκεπτέον ἂν εἴη σοῦ γε οὕτω προθυ-
μουμένου. δοκεῖ οὖν μοι ἀρχὴ εἶναι τῆς σκέψεως
C κινήσεως πέρι, ποῖόν τί ποτε ἄρα λέγοντές φασι
τὰ πάντα κινεῖσθαι. βούλομαι δὲ λέγειν τὸ τοιόνδε·
πότερον ἕν τι εἶδος αὐτῆς λέγουσιν ἤ, ὥσπερ ἐμοὶ
φαίνεται, δύο; μὴ μέντοι μόνον ἐμοὶ δοκείτω,
ἀλλὰ συμμέτεχε καὶ σύ, ἵνα κοινῇ πάσχωμεν, ἄν
τι καὶ δέῃ. καί μοι λέγε· ἆρα κινεῖσθαι καλεῖς,
ὅταν τι χώραν ἐκ χώρας μεταβάλλῃ ἢ καὶ ἐν τῷ
αὐτῷ στρέφηται;

ΘΕΟ. Ἔγωγε.

ΣΩ. Τοῦτο μὲν τοίνυν ἓν ἔστω εἶδος. ὅταν δὲ
D ᾖ μὲν ἐν τῷ αὐτῷ, γηράσκῃ δέ, ἢ μέλαν ἐκ λευκοῦ
ἢ σκληρὸν ἐκ μαλακοῦ γίγνηται, ἤ τινα ἄλλην
ἀλλοίωσιν ἀλλοιῶται, ἆρα οὐκ ἄξιον ἕτερον εἶδος
φάναι κινήσεως;

ΘΕΟ. Ἔμοιγε δοκεῖ.[1]

ΣΩ. Ἀναγκαῖον μὲν οὖν.[2] δύο δὴ λέγω τούτω
εἴδη κινήσεως, ἀλλοίωσιν, τὴν δὲ φοράν.[3]

ΘΕΟ. Ὀρθῶς γε λέγων.

ΣΩ. Τοῦτο τοίνυν οὕτω διελόμενοι διαλεγώμεθα
ἤδη τοῖς τὰ πάντα φάσκουσιν κινεῖσθαι καὶ ἐρω-
τῶμεν· πότερον πᾶν φατε ἀμφοτέρως κινεῖσθαι,
E φερόμενόν τε καὶ ἀλλοιούμενον, ἢ τὸ μέν τι ἀμφοτέρως, τὸ δ' ἑτέρως;

ΘΕΟ. Ἀλλὰ μὰ Δί' ἔγωγε οὐκ ἔχω εἰπεῖν·
οἶμαι δ' ἂν φάναι ἀμφοτέρως.

ΣΩ. Εἰ δέ γε μή, ὦ ἑταῖρε, κινούμενά τε αὐτοῖς[4]

---

[1] ἔμοιγε δοκεῖ om. Stobaeus.
[2] ἀναγκαῖον μὲν οὖν given to Theodorus by B.
[3] φοράν W ; περιφοράν BT, Stobaeus.
[4] αὐτοῖς W ; ἑαυτοῖς BT.

soc. Then they must be examined, since you are so urgent. Now I think the starting-point of our examination of the doctrine of motion is this: Exactly what do they mean, after all, when they say that all things are in motion? What I wish to ask is this: Do they mean to say that there is only one kind of motion or, as I believe, two? But it must not be my belief alone; you must share it also, that if anything happens to us we may suffer it in common. Tell me, do you call it motion when a thing changes its place or turns round in the same place?

THEO. Yes.

soc. Let this, then, be one kind of motion. Now when a thing remains in the same place, but grows old, or becomes black instead of white, or hard instead of soft, or undergoes any other kind of alteration, is it not proper to say that this is another kind of motion?

THEO. I think so.

soc. Nay, it must be true. So I say that there are these two kinds of motion: "alteration," and "motion in space."

THEO. And you are right.

soc. Now that we have made this distinction, let us at once converse with those who say that all things are in motion, and let us ask them, "Do you mean that everything moves in both ways, moving in space and undergoing alteration, or one thing in both ways and another in one of the two ways only?"

THEO. By Zeus, I cannot tell! But I think they would say that everything moves in both ways.

soc. Yes; otherwise, my friend, they will find that things in motion are also things at rest, and it will

147

181

καὶ ἑστῶτα φανεῖται, καὶ οὐδὲν μᾶλλον ὀρθῶς ἕξει
εἰπεῖν ὅτι κινεῖται τὰ πάντα ἢ ὅτι ἕστηκεν.

ΘΕΟ. Ἀληθέστατα λέγεις.

ΣΩ. Οὐκοῦν ἐπειδὴ κινεῖσθαι αὐτὰ δεῖ, τὸ δὲ
μὴ κινεῖσθαι μὴ ἐνεῖναι [1] μηδενί, πάντα δὴ πᾶσαν
182 κίνησιν ἀεὶ κινεῖται.

ΘΕΟ. Ἀνάγκη.

ΣΩ. Σκόπει δή μοι τόδε αὐτῶν· τῆς θερμότητος
ἢ λευκότητος ἢ ὁτουοῦν γένεσιν οὐχ οὕτω πως ἐλέγομεν φάναι αὐτούς, φέρεσθαι ἕκαστον τούτων ἅμα
αἰσθήσει μεταξὺ τοῦ ποιοῦντός τε καὶ πάσχοντος,
καὶ τὸ μὲν πάσχον αἰσθητικὸν [2] ἀλλ' οὐκ αἴσθησιν [3]
γίγνεσθαι, τὸ δὲ ποιοῦν ποιόν τι ἀλλ' οὐ ποιότητα;
ἴσως οὖν ἡ ποιότης ἅμα ἀλλόκοτόν τε φαίνεται
ὄνομα καὶ οὐ μανθάνεις ἀθρόον λεγόμενον· κατὰ
B μέρη οὖν ἄκουε. τὸ γὰρ ποιοῦν οὔτε θερμότης
οὔτε λευκότης, θερμὸν δὲ καὶ λευκὸν γίγνεται, καὶ
τἆλλα οὕτω· μέμνησαι γάρ που καὶ ἐν τοῖς
πρόσθεν ὅτι οὕτως ἐλέγομεν, ἓν μηδὲν αὐτὸ καθ'
αὑτὸ εἶναι, μηδ' αὖ τὸ ποιοῦν ἢ πάσχον, ἀλλ'
ἐξ ἀμφοτέρων πρὸς ἄλληλα συγγιγνομένων τὰς
αἰσθήσεις καὶ τὰ αἰσθητὰ ἀποτίκτοντα τὰ μὲν
ποιὰ [4] ἄττα γίγνεσθαι, τὰ δὲ αἰσθανόμενα.

ΘΕΟ. Μέμνημαι· πῶς δ' οὔ;

ΣΩ. Τὰ μὲν τοίνυν ἄλλα χαίρειν ἐάσωμεν, εἴτε
C ἄλλως εἴτε οὕτως λέγουσιν· οὗ δ' ἕνεκα λέγομεν,
τοῦτο μόνον φυλάττωμεν, ἐρωτῶντες· κινεῖται
καὶ ῥεῖ, ὥς φατε, τὰ πάντα; ἢ γάρ;

---

[1] ἐνεῖναι W ; ἐν εἶναι BT.
[2] αἰσθητικὸν Burnet ; αἰσθητὸν BT ; αἰσθητὴν Buttmann ;
αἰσθανόμενον Heindorf.
[3] αἴσθησιν W ; αἴσθησιν ἔτι BT.   [4] ποιὰ bt ; ποι BT.

be no more correct to say that all things are in motion than that all things are at rest.

THEO. What you say is very true.

soc. Then since they must be in motion, and since absence of motion must be impossible for anything, all things are always in all kinds of motion.

THEO. Necessarily.

soc. Then just examine this point of their doctrine. Did we not find that they say that heat or whiteness or anything you please arises in some such way as this, namely that each of these moves simultaneously with perception between the active and the passive element, and the passive becomes percipient, but not perception, and the active becomes, not a quality, but endowed with a quality? Now perhaps quality seems an extraordinary word, and you do not understand it when used with general application, so let me give particular examples. For the active element becomes neither heat nor whiteness, but hot or white, and other things in the same way; you probably remember that this was what we said earlier in our discourse, that nothing is in itself unvaryingly one, neither the active nor the passive, but from the union of the two with one another the perceptions and the perceived give birth and the latter become things endowed with some quality while the former become percipient.

THEO. I remember, of course.

soc. Let us then pay no attention to other matters, whether they teach one thing or another; but let us attend strictly to this only, which is the object of our discussion. Let us ask them, "Are all things, according to your doctrine, in motion and flux?" Is that so?

ΘΕΟ. Ναί.

ΣΩ. Οὐκοῦν ἀμφοτέρας ἃς διειλόμεθα κινήσεις, φερόμενά τε καὶ ἀλλοιούμενα;

ΘΕΟ. Πῶς δ' οὔ; εἴπερ γε δὴ τελέως κινήσεται.

ΣΩ. Εἰ μὲν τοίνυν ἐφέρετο μόνον, ἠλλοιοῦτο δὲ μή, εἴχομεν ἄν που εἰπεῖν οἷα ἄττα ῥεῖ τὰ φερόμενα· ἢ πῶς λέγωμεν[1];

ΘΕΟ. Οὕτως.

D ΣΩ. Ἐπειδὴ δὲ οὐδὲ τοῦτο μένει, τὸ λευκὸν ῥεῖν τὸ ῥέον, ἀλλὰ μεταβάλλει, ὥστε καὶ αὐτοῦ τούτου εἶναι ῥοήν, τῆς λευκότητος, καὶ μεταβολὴν εἰς ἄλλην χρόαν, ἵνα μὴ ἁλῷ ταύτῃ μένον, ἆρά ποτε οἷόν τέ τι προσειπεῖν χρῶμα, ὥστε καὶ ὀρθῶς προσαγορεύειν;

ΘΕΟ. Καὶ τίς μηχανή, ὦ Σώκρατες; ἢ ἄλλο γέ τι τῶν τοιούτων, εἴπερ ἀεὶ λέγοντος ὑπεξέρχεται, ἅτε δὴ ῥέον;

ΣΩ. Τί δὲ περὶ αἰσθήσεως ἐροῦμεν ὁποιασοῦν, οἷον τῆς τοῦ ὁρᾶν ἢ ἀκούειν; μένειν ποτὲ ἐν αὐτῷ E τῷ ὁρᾶν ἢ ἀκούειν;

ΘΕΟ. Οὔκουν δεῖ γε, εἴπερ πάντα κινεῖται.

ΣΩ. Οὔτε ἄρα ὁρᾶν προσρητέον τι μᾶλλον ἢ μὴ ὁρᾶν, οὐδέ τιν' ἄλλην αἴσθησιν μᾶλλον ἢ μή, πάντων γε πάντως κινουμένων.

ΘΕΟ. Οὐ γὰρ οὖν.

ΣΩ. Καὶ μὴν αἴσθησίς γε ἐπιστήμη, ὡς ἔφαμεν ἐγώ τε καὶ Θεαίτητος.

ΘΕΟ. Ἦν ταῦτα.

---

[1] λέγωμεν B; λέγομεν T.

THEAETETUS

THEO. Yes.

soc. Have they then both kinds of motion which we distinguished? Are they moving in space and also undergoing alteration?

THEO. Of course; that is, if they are to be in perfect motion.

soc. Then if they moved only in space, but did not undergo alteration, we could perhaps say what qualities belong to those moving things which are in flux, could we not?

THEO. That is right.

soc. But since not even this remains fixed—that the thing in flux flows white, but changes, so that there is a flux of the very whiteness, and a change of colour, that it may not in that way be convicted of remaining fixed, is it possible to give any name to a colour, and yet to speak accurately?

THEO. How can it be possible, Socrates, or to give a name to anything else of this sort, if while we are speaking it always evades us, being, as it is, in flux?

soc. But what shall we say of any of the perceptions, such as seeing or hearing? Does it perhaps remain fixed in the condition of seeing or hearing?

THEO. It must be impossible, if all things are in motion.

soc. Then we must not speak of seeing more than not-seeing, or of any other perception more than of non-perception, if all things are in all kinds of motion.

THEO. No, we must not.

soc. And yet perception is knowledge, as Theaetetus and I said.

THEO. Yes, you did say that.

151

ΣΩ. Οὐδὲν ἄρα ἐπιστήμην μᾶλλον ἢ μὴ ἐπιστήμην ἀπεκρινάμεθα ἐρωτώμενοι ὅ τί ἐστιν ἐπιστήμη.

183   ΘΕΟ. Ἐοίκατε.

ΣΩ. Καλὸν ἂν ἡμῖν συμβαίνοι τὸ ἐπανόρθωμα
τῆς ἀποκρίσεως, προθυμηθεῖσιν ἀποδεῖξαι ὅτι
πάντα κινεῖται, ἵνα δὴ ἐκείνη ἡ ἀπόκρισις ὀρθὴ
φανῇ. τὸ δ᾽, ὡς ἔοικεν, ἐφάνη, εἰ πάντα κινεῖται,
πᾶσα ἀπόκρισις, περὶ ὅτου ἄν τις ἀποκρίνηται,
ὁμοίως ὀρθὴ εἶναι, οὕτω τ᾽ ἔχειν φάναι καὶ μὴ
οὕτω, εἰ δὲ βούλει, γίγνεσθαι, ἵνα μὴ στήσωμεν
αὐτοὺς τῷ λόγῳ.

ΘΕΟ. Ὀρθῶς λέγεις.

ΣΩ. Πλήν γε, ὦ Θεόδωρε, ὅτι " οὕτω " τε εἶπον
καὶ " οὐχ οὕτω." δεῖ δὲ οὐδὲ τοῦτο " οὕτω "
B λέγειν· οὐδὲ γὰρ ἂν ἔτι κινοῖτο " οὕτω "· οὐδ᾽
αὖ " μὴ οὕτω "· οὐδὲ γὰρ " τοῦτο " κινησις·
ἀλλά τιν᾽ ἄλλην φωνὴν θετέον τοῖς τὸν λόγον τοῦτον
λέγουσιν, ὡς νῦν γε πρὸς τὴν αὐτῶν ὑπόθεσιν οὐκ
ἔχουσι ῥήματα, εἰ μὴ ἄρα τὸ " οὐδ᾽ ὅπως.[1] "
μάλιστα δ᾽ οὕτως[2] ἂν αὐτοῖς ἁρμόττοι, ἄπειρον
λεγόμενον.

ΘΕΟ. Οἰκειοτάτη γοῦν διάλεκτος αὕτη αὐτοῖς.

ΣΩ. Οὐκοῦν, ὦ Θεόδωρε, τοῦ τε σοῦ ἑταίρου
ἀπηλλάγμεθα, καὶ οὔπω συγχωροῦμεν αὐτῷ πάντ᾽
ἄνδρα πάντων χρημάτων μέτρον εἶναι, ἂν μὴ
C φρόνιμός τις ᾖ· ἐπιστήμην τε αἴσθησιν οὐ συγχωρησόμεθα κατά γε τὴν τοῦ πάντα κινεῖσθαι μέθοδον,
εἰ μή[3] τί πως ἄλλως Θεαίτητος ὅδε λέγει.

ΘΕΟ. Ἄριστ᾽ εἴρηκας, ὦ Σώκρατες· τούτων
γὰρ περανθέντων καὶ ἐμὲ δεῖ ἀπηλλάχθαι σοι

---

[1] ὅπως BT; οὕτως W.
[2] δ᾽ οὕτως om. W.   [3] εἰ μὴ W; ἢ εἰ μὴ BT.

soc. Then when we were asked "what is knowledge?" we answered no more what knowledge is than what not-knowledge is.

THEO. So it seems.

soc. This would be a fine result of the correction of our answer, when we were so eager to show that all things are in motion, just for the purpose of making that answer prove to be correct. But this, I think, did prove to be true, that if all things are in motion, every answer to any question whatsoever is equally correct, and we may say it is thus or not thus—or, if you prefer, "becomes thus," to avoid giving them fixity by using the word "is."

THEO. You are right.

soc. Except, Theodorus, that I said "thus," and "not thus"; but we ought not even to say "thus"; for "thus" would no longer be in motion; nor, again, "not thus." For there is no motion in "this" either; but some other expression must be supplied for those who maintain this doctrine, since now they have, according to their own hypothesis, no words, unless it be perhaps the word "nohow." That might be most fitting for them, since it is indefinite.

THEO. At any rate that is the most appropriate form of speech for them.

soc. So, Theodorus, we have got rid of your friend, and we do not yet concede to him that every man is a measure of all things, unless he be a sensible man; and we are not going to concede that knowledge is perception, at least not by the theory of universal motion, unless Theaetetus here has something different to say.

THEO. An excellent idea, Socrates; for now that this matter is settled, I too should be rid of the duty

ἀποκρινόμενον κατὰ τὰς συνθήκας, ἐπειδὴ τὸ περὶ
τοῦ Πρωταγόρου λόγου τέλος σχοίη.

29. ΘΕΑΙ. Μή, πρίν γ᾽ ἂν, ὦ Θεόδωρε, Σω-
D κράτης τε καὶ σὺ τοὺς φάσκοντας αὖ τὸ πᾶν ἑστάναι διέλθητε, ὥσπερ ἄρτι προύθεσθε.

ΘΕΟ. Νέος ὤν, ὦ Θεαίτητε, τοὺς πρεσβυτέρους
ἀδικεῖν διδάσκεις ὁμολογίας παραβαίνοντας; ἀλλὰ
παρασκευάζου ὅπως τῶν ἐπιλοίπων Σωκράτει
δώσεις λόγον.

ΘΕΑΙ. Ἐάνπερ γε βούληται. ἥδιστα μέντ᾽ ἂν
ἤκουσα περὶ ὧν λέγω.

ΘΕΟ. Ἱππέας εἰς πεδίον προκαλεῖ Σωκράτη εἰς
λόγους προκαλούμενος· ἐρώτα οὖν καὶ ἀκούσει.

ΣΩ. Ἀλλά μοι δοκῶ, ὦ Θεόδωρε, περί γε ὧν
E κελεύει Θεαίτητος οὐ πείσεσθαι αὐτῷ.

ΘΕΟ. Τί δὴ οὖν οὐ πείσεσθαι;

ΣΩ. Μέλισσον μὲν καὶ τοὺς ἄλλους, οἳ ἓν ἑστὸς
λέγουσι τὸ πᾶν, αἰσχυνόμενος μὴ φορτικῶς σκοπῶμεν, ἧττον αἰσχύνομαι ἢ ἕνα ὄντα Παρμενίδην.
Παρμενίδης δέ μοι φαίνεται, τὸ τοῦ Ὁμήρου,
" αἰδοῖός τέ μοι " εἶναι ἅμα " δεινός τε." συμπροσ-
έμιξα γὰρ δὴ τῷ ἀνδρὶ πάνυ νέος πάνυ πρεσβύτῃ,
καί μοι ἐφάνη βάθος τι ἔχειν παντάπασι γενναῖον.
184 φοβοῦμαι οὖν μὴ οὔτε τὰ λεγόμενα ξυνιῶμεν, τί
τε διανοούμενος εἶπε πολὺ πλέον λειπώμεθα, καὶ
τὸ μέγιστον, οὗ ἕνεκα ὁ λόγος ὥρμηται, ἐπιστήμης
πέρι, τί ποτ᾽ ἐστίν, ἄσκεπτον γένηται ὑπὸ τῶν

THEAETETUS

of answering your questions according to our agreement, since the argument about Protagoras is ended.

THEAET. No, Theodorus, not until you and Socrates have discussed those who say all things are at rest, as you proposed just now.

THEO. A young man like you, Theaetetus, teaching your elders to do wrong by breaking their agreements! No; prepare to answer Socrates yourself for the rest of the argument.

THEAET. I will if he wishes it. But I should have liked best to hear about the doctrine I mentioned.

THEO. Calling Socrates to an argument is calling cavalry into an open plain.[1] Just ask him a question and you shall hear.

SOC. Still I think, Theodorus, I shall not comply with the request of Theaetetus.

THEO. Why will you not comply with it?

SOC. Because I have a reverential fear of examining in a flippant manner Melissus and the others who teach that the universe is one and motionless, and because I reverence still more one man, Parmenides. Parmenides seems to me to be, in Homer's words, "one to be venerated" and also "awful."[2] For I met him when I was very young and he was very old, and he appeared to me to possess an absolutely noble depth of mind. So I am afraid we may not understand his words and may be still farther from understanding what he meant by them; but my chief fear is that the question with which we started, about the nature of knowledge, may fail to be investigated, because of the disorderly crowd of

[1] A proverbial expression. An open plain is just what cavalry desires.
[2] *Iliad*, iii. 172; *Odyssey*, viii. 22; xiv. 234.

ἐπεισκωμαζόντων λόγων, εἴ τις αὐτοῖς πείσεται·
ἄλλως τε καὶ ὃν νῦν ἐγείρομεν πλήθει ἀμήχανον,
εἴτε τις ἐν παρέργῳ σκέψεται, ἀνάξι᾽ ἂν πάθοι,
εἴτε ἱκανῶς, μηκυνόμενος τὸ τῆς ἐπιστήμης
ἀφανιεῖ· δεῖ δὲ οὐδέτερα, ἀλλὰ Θεαίτητον ὧν
B κυεῖ περὶ ἐπιστήμης πειρᾶσθαι ἡμᾶς τῇ μαιευτικῇ
τέχνῃ ἀπολῦσαι.

ΘΕΟ. Ἀλλὰ χρή, εἰ δοκεῖ, οὕτω ποιεῖν.

ΣΩ. Ἔτι τοίνυν, ὦ Θεαίτητε, τοσόνδε περὶ τῶν
εἰρημένων ἐπίσκεψαι. αἴσθησιν γὰρ δὴ ἐπιστήμην
ἀπεκρίνω· ἢ γάρ;

ΘΕΑΙ. Ναί.

ΣΩ. Εἰ οὖν τίς σε ὧδ᾽ ἐρωτῴη· " τῷ τὰ λευκὰ
καὶ μέλανα ὁρᾷ ἄνθρωπος καὶ τῷ τὰ ὀξέα καὶ
βαρέα ἀκούει;" εἴποις ἄν, οἶμαι, "ὄμμασί τε
καὶ ὠσίν."

ΘΕΑΙ. Ἔγωγε.

C ΣΩ. Τὸ δὲ εὐχερὲς τῶν ὀνομάτων τε καὶ ῥημάτων καὶ μὴ δι᾽ ἀκριβείας ἐξεταζόμενον τὰ μὲν
πολλὰ οὐκ ἀγεννές, ἀλλὰ μᾶλλον τὸ τούτου ἐναντίον
ἀνελεύθερον, ἔστι δὲ ὅτε ἀναγκαῖον, οἷον καὶ νῦν
ἀνάγκη ἐπιλαβέσθαι τῆς ἀποκρίσεως ἣν ἀποκρίνει,
ᾗ οὐκ ὀρθή. σκόπει γάρ, ἀπόκρισις ποτέρα
ὀρθοτέρα, ᾧ ὁρῶμεν, τοῦτο εἶναι ὀφθαλμούς, ἢ
δι᾽ οὗ ὁρῶμεν, καὶ ᾧ ἀκούομεν, ὦτα, ἢ δι᾽ οὗ
ἀκούομεν;

ΘΕΑΙ. Δι᾽ ὧν ἕκαστα αἰσθανόμεθα, ἔμοιγε δοκεῖ,
ὦ Σώκρατες, μᾶλλον ἢ οἷς.

D ΣΩ. Δεινὸν γάρ που, ὦ παῖ, εἰ πολλαί τινες
ἐν ἡμῖν, ὥσπερ ἐν δουρείοις ἵπποις, αἰσθήσεις

arguments which will burst in upon us if we let them in; especially as the argument we are now proposing is of vast extent, and would not receive its deserts if we treated it as a side issue, and if we treat it as it deserves, it will take so long as to do away with the discussion about knowledge. Neither of these things ought to happen, but we ought to try by the science of midwifery to deliver Theaetetus of the thoughts about knowledge with which he is pregnant.

THEO. Yes, if that is your opinion, we ought to do so.

soc. Consider, then, Theaetetus, this further point about what has been said. Now you answered that perception is knowledge, did you not?

THEAET. Yes.

soc. If, then, anyone should ask you, " By what does a man see white and black colours and by what does he hear high and low tones?" you would, I fancy, say, " By his eyes and ears."

THEAET. Yes, I should.

soc. The easy use of words and phrases and the avoidance of strict precision is in general a sign of good breeding; indeed, the opposite is hardly worthy of a gentleman, but sometimes it is necessary, as now it is necessary to object to your answer, in so far as it is incorrect. Just consider; which answer is more correct, that our eyes are that by which we see or that through which we see, and our ears that by which or that through which we hear?

THEAET. I think, Socrates, we perceive through, rather than by them, in each case.

soc. Yes, for it would be strange indeed, my boy, if there are many senses ensconced within us, as if

157

ἐγκάθηνται, ἀλλὰ μὴ εἰς μίαν τινὰ ἰδέαν, εἴτε
ψυχὴν εἴτε ὅ τι δεῖ καλεῖν, πάντα ταῦτα ξυντείνει,
ᾗ διὰ τούτων οἷον ὀργάνων αἰσθανόμεθα ὅσα
αἰσθητά.

ΘΕΑΙ. Ἀλλά μοι δοκεῖ οὕτω μᾶλλον ἢ ἐκείνως.

ΣΩ. Τοῦδέ τοι ἕνεκα αὐτά σοι διακριβοῦμαι,
εἴ τινι ἡμῶν αὐτῶν τῷ αὐτῷ διὰ μὲν ὀφθαλμῶν
ἐφικνούμεθα λευκῶν τε καὶ μελάνων, διὰ δὲ τῶν
Ε ἄλλων ἑτέρων αὖ τινῶν, καὶ ἕξεις ἐρωτώμενος
πάντα τὰ τοιαῦτα εἰς τὸ σῶμα ἀναφέρειν. ἴσως
δὲ βέλτιον σὲ λέγειν αὐτὰ ἀποκρινόμενον μᾶλλον
ἢ ἐμὲ ὑπὲρ σοῦ πολυπραγμονεῖν. καί μοι λέγε·
θερμὰ καὶ σκληρὰ καὶ κοῦφα καὶ γλυκέα δι' ὧν
αἰσθάνει, ἆρα οὐ τοῦ σώματος ἕκαστα τίθης; ἢ
ἄλλου τινός;

ΘΕΑΙ. Οὐδενὸς ἄλλου.

ΣΩ. Ἦ καὶ ἐθελήσεις ὁμολογεῖν, ἃ δι'· ἑτέρας
185 δυνάμεως αἰσθάνει, ἀδύνατον εἶναι δι' ἄλλης
ταῦτ' αἰσθέσθαι, οἷον ἃ δι' ἀκοῆς, δι' ὄψεως, ἢ ἃ
δι' ὄψεως, δι' ἀκοῆς;

ΘΕΑΙ. Πῶς γὰρ οὐκ ἐθελήσω;

ΣΩ. Εἴ τι ἄρα περὶ ἀμφοτέρων διανοεῖ, οὐκ ἂν
διά γε τοῦ ἑτέρου ὀργάνου, οὐδ' αὖ διὰ τοῦ ἑτέρου
περὶ ἀμφοτέρων αἰσθάνοι' ἄν.

ΘΕΑΙ. Οὐ γὰρ οὖν.

ΣΩ. Περὶ δὴ φωνῆς καὶ περὶ χρόας πρῶτον μὲν

we were so many wooden horses of Troy, and they do not all unite in one power, whether we should call it soul or something else, by which we perceive through these as instruments the objects of perception.

THEAET. I think what you suggest is more likely than the other way.

soc. Now the reason why I am so precise about the matter is this: I want to know whether there is some one and the same power within ourselves by which we perceive black and white through the eyes, and again other qualities through the other organs, and whether you will be able, if asked, to refer all such activities to the body. But perhaps it is better that you make the statement in answer to a question than that I should take all the trouble for you. So tell me: do you not think that all the organs through which you perceive hot and hard and light and sweet are parts of the body? Or are they parts of something else?

THEAET. Of nothing else.

soc. And will you also be ready to agree that it is impossible to perceive through one sense what you perceive through another; for instance, to perceive through sight what you perceive through hearing, or through hearing what you perceive through sight?

THEAET. Of course I shall.

soc. Then if you have any thought about both of these together, you would not have perception about both together either through one organ or through the other.

THEAET. No.

soc. Now in regard to sound and colour, you have,

185

αὐτὸ τοῦτο περὶ ἀμφοτέρων ἢ διανοεῖ, ὅτι ἀμφοτέρω ἐστόν;

ΘΕΑΙ. Ἔγωγε.

ΣΩ. Οὐκοῦν καὶ ὅτι ἑκάτερον ἑκατέρου μὲν ἕτερον, ἑαυτῷ δὲ ταὐτόν;

B   ΘΕΑΙ. Τί μήν;

ΣΩ. Καὶ ὅτι ἀμφοτέρω δύο, ἑκάτερον δὲ ἕν;

ΘΕΑΙ. Καὶ τοῦτο.

ΣΩ. Οὐκοῦν καὶ εἴτε ἀνομοίω εἴτε ὁμοίω ἀλλήλοιν, δυνατὸς εἶ ἐπισκέψασθαι;

ΘΕΑΙ. Ἴσως.

ΣΩ. Ταῦτα δὴ πάντα διὰ τίνος περὶ αὐτοῖν διανοεῖ; οὔτε γὰρ δι᾽ ἀκοῆς οὔτε δι᾽ ὄψεως οἷόν τε τὸ κοινὸν λαμβάνειν περὶ αὐτῶν. ἔτι δὲ καὶ τόδε τεκμήριον περὶ οὗ λέγομεν· εἰ γὰρ δυνατὸν εἴη ἀμφοτέρω σκέψασθαι, ἆρ᾽ ἐστὸν ἁλμυρὼ ἢ οὔ, οἶσθ᾽ ὅτι ἕξεις εἰπεῖν ᾧ ἐπισκέψει, καὶ τοῦτο οὔτε
C ὄψις οὔτε ἀκοὴ φαίνεται, ἀλλά τι ἄλλο.

ΘΕΑΙ. Τί δ᾽ οὐ μέλλει; ἥ γε διὰ τῆς γλώττης δύναμις.

ΣΩ. Καλῶς λέγεις. ἡ δὲ δὴ διὰ τίνος δύναμις τό τ᾽ ἐπὶ πᾶσι κοινὸν καὶ τὸ ἐπὶ τούτοις δηλοῖ σοι, ᾧ τὸ "ἔστιν" ἐπονομάζεις καὶ τὸ "οὐκ ἔστι," καὶ ἃ νῦν δὴ ἠρωτῶμεν περὶ αὐτῶν; τούτοις πᾶσι ποῖα ἀποδώσεις ὄργανα δι᾽ ὧν αἰσθάνεται ἡμῶν τὸ αἰσθανόμενον ἕκαστα;

ΘΕΑΙ. Οὐσίαν λέγεις καὶ τὸ μὴ εἶναι, καὶ ὁμοιό-

in the first place, this thought about both of them, that they both exist?

THEAET. Certainly.

soc. And that each is different from the other and the same as itself?

THEAET. Of course.

soc. And that both together are two and each separately is one?

THEAET. Yes, that also.

soc. And are you able also to observe whether they are like or unlike each other?

THEAET. May be.

soc. Now through what organ do you think all this about them? For it is impossible to grasp that which is common to them both either through hearing or through sight. Here is further evidence for the point I am trying to make: if it were possible to investigate the question whether the two, sound and colour, are bitter or not, you know that you will be able to tell by what faculty you will investigate it, and that is clearly neither hearing nor sight, but something else.

THEAET. Of course it is,—the faculty exerted through the tongue.

soc. Very good. But through what organ is the faculty exerted which makes known to you that which is common to all things, as well as to these of which we are speaking—that which you call being and not-being, and the other attributes of things, about which we were asking just now? What organs will you assign for all these, through which that part of us which perceives gains perception of each and all of them?

THEAET. You mean being and not-being, and like-

161

τητα καὶ ἀνομοιότητα, καὶ τὸ ταὐτόν τε καὶ τὸ
D ἕτερον, ἔτι δὲ ἕν τε καὶ τὸν ἄλλον ἀριθμὸν περὶ
αὐτῶν. δῆλον δὲ ὅτι καὶ ἄρτιόν τε καὶ περιττὸν
ἐρωτᾷς, καὶ τἆλλα ὅσα τούτοις ἕπεται, διὰ τίνος
ποτὲ τῶν τοῦ σώματος τῇ ψυχῇ αἰσθανόμεθα.

ΣΩ. Ὑπέρευ, ὦ Θεαίτητε, ἀκολουθεῖς, καὶ ἔστιν
ἃ ἐρωτῶ αὐτὰ ταῦτα.

ΘΕΑΙ. Ἀλλὰ μὰ Δία, ὦ Σώκρατες, ἔγωγε οὐκ
ἂν ἔχοιμι εἰπεῖν, πλήν γ' ὅτι μοι δοκεῖ τὴν ἀρχὴν
οὐδ' εἶναι τοιοῦτον οὐδὲν τούτοις ὄργανον ἴδιον
ὥσπερ ἐκείνοις, ἀλλ' αὐτὴ δι' αὑτῆς ἡ ψυχὴ τὰ
E κοινά μοι φαίνεται περὶ πάντων ἐπισκοπεῖν.

ΣΩ. Καλὸς γὰρ εἶ, ὦ Θεαίτητε, καὶ οὐχ, ὡς
ἔλεγε Θεόδωρος, αἰσχρός· ὁ γὰρ καλῶς λέγων
καλός τε καὶ ἀγαθός. πρὸς δὲ τῷ καλῷ εὖ ἐποίησάς
με μάλα συχνοῦ λόγου ἀπαλλάξας, εἰ φαίνεταί σοι
τὰ μὲν αὐτὴ δι' αὑτῆς ἡ ψυχὴ ἐπισκοπεῖν, τὰ δὲ
διὰ τῶν τοῦ σώματος δυνάμεων. τοῦτο γὰρ ἦν
ὃ καὶ αὐτῷ μοι ἐδόκει, ἐβουλόμην δὲ καὶ σοὶ
δόξαι.

186 ΘΕΑΙ. Ἀλλὰ μὴν φαίνεταί γε.

30. ΣΩ. Ποτέρων οὖν τίθης τὴν οὐσίαν; τοῦτο
γὰρ μάλιστα ἐπὶ πάντων παρέπεται.

ΘΕΑΙ. Ἐγὼ μὲν ὧν αὐτὴ ἡ ψυχὴ καθ' αὑτὴν
ἐπορέγεται.

ΣΩ. Ἦ καὶ τὸ ὅμοιον καὶ τὸ ἀνόμοιον καὶ τὸ
ταὐτὸν καὶ ἕτερον;

ΘΕΑΙ. Ναί.

ΣΩ. Τί δέ; καλὸν καὶ αἰσχρὸν καὶ ἀγαθὸν καὶ
κακόν;

ΘΕΑΙ. Καὶ τούτων μοι δοκεῖ ἐν τοῖς μάλιστα
πρὸς ἄλληλα σκοπεῖσθαι τὴν οὐσίαν, ἀναλογι-

ness and unlikeness, and identity and difference, and also unity and plurality as applied to them. And you are evidently asking also through what bodily organs we perceive by our soul the odd and the even and everything else that is in the same category.

soc. Bravo, Theaetetus! you follow me exactly; that is just what I mean by my question.

THEAET. By Zeus, Socrates, I cannot answer, except that I think there is no special organ at all for these notions, as there are for those others; but it appears to me that the soul views by itself directly what all things have in common.

soc. Why, you are beautiful, Theaetetus, and not, as Theodorus said, ugly; for he who speaks beautifully is beautiful and good. But besides being beautiful, you have done me a favour by relieving me from a long discussion, if you think that the soul views some things by itself directly and others through the bodily faculties; for that was my own opinion, and I wanted you to agree.

THEAET. Well, I do think so.

soc. To which class, then, do you assign being; for this, more than anything else, belongs to all things?

THEAET. I assign them to the class of notions which the soul grasps by itself directly.

soc. And also likeness and unlikeness and identity and difference?

THEAET. Yes.

soc. And how about beautiful and ugly, and good and bad?

THEAET. I think that these also are among the things the essence of which the soul most certainly

163

ζομένη ἐν ἑαυτῇ τὰ γεγονότα καὶ τὰ παρόντα
B πρὸς τὰ μέλλοντα.

ΣΩ. Ἔχε δή· ἄλλο τι τοῦ μὲν σκληροῦ τὴν
σκληρότητα διὰ τῆς ἐπαφῆς αἰσθήσεται, καὶ τοῦ
μαλακοῦ τὴν μαλακότητα ὡσαύτως;

ΘΕΑΙ. Ναί.

ΣΩ. Τὴν δέ γε οὐσίαν καὶ ὅ τι ἐστὸν καὶ τὴν
ἐναντιότητα πρὸς ἀλλήλω καὶ τὴν οὐσίαν αὖ τῆς
ἐναντιότητος αὐτὴ ἡ ψυχὴ ἐπανιοῦσα καὶ συμβάλ-
λουσα πρὸς ἄλληλα κρίνειν πειρᾶται ἡμῖν.

ΘΕΑΙ. Πάνυ μὲν οὖν.

ΣΩ. Οὐκοῦν τὰ μὲν εὐθὺς γενομένοις πάρεστι
C φύσει αἰσθάνεσθαι ἀνθρώποις τε καὶ θηρίοις, ὅσα
διὰ τοῦ σώματος παθήματα ἐπὶ τὴν ψυχὴν τείνει·
τὰ δὲ περὶ τούτων ἀναλογίσματα πρός τε οὐσίαν
καὶ ὠφέλειαν μόγις καὶ ἐν χρόνῳ διὰ πολλῶν πραγμάτων καὶ παιδείας παραγίγνεται οἷς ἂν καὶ
παραγίγνηται;

ΘΕΑΙ. Παντάπασι μὲν οὖν.

ΣΩ. Οἷόν τε οὖν ἀληθείας τυχεῖν, ᾧ μηδὲ οὐσίας;

ΘΕΑΙ. Ἀδύνατον.

ΣΩ. Οὗ δὲ ἀληθείας τις ἀτυχήσει, ποτὲ τούτου
ἐπιστήμων ἔσται;

D ΘΕΑΙ. Καὶ πῶς ἄν, ὦ Σώκρατες;

ΣΩ. Ἐν μὲν ἄρα τοῖς παθήμασιν οὐκ ἔνι ἐπιστήμη, ἐν δὲ τῷ περὶ ἐκείνων συλλογισμῷ·
οὐσίας γὰρ καὶ ἀληθείας ἐνταῦθα μέν, ὡς ἔοικε,
δυνατὸν ἅψασθαι, ἐκεῖ δὲ ἀδύνατον.

ΘΕΑΙ. Φαίνεται.

ΣΩ. Ἦ οὖν ταὐτὸν ἐκεῖνό τε καὶ τοῦτο [1] καλεῖς,
τοσαύτας διαφορὰς ἔχοντε;

[1] τοῦτο] ταὐτὸ T; ταὐτὸν B.

views in their relations to one another, reflecting within itself upon the past and present in relation to the future.

soc. Stop there. Does it not perceive the hardness of the hard through touch, and likewise the softness of the soft?

THEAET. Yes.

soc. But their essential nature and the fact that they exist, and their opposition to one another, and, in turn, the essential nature of this opposition, the soul itself tries to determine for us by reverting to them and comparing them with one another.

THEAET. Certainly.

soc. Is it not true, then, that all sensations which reach the soul through the body, can be perceived by human beings, and also by animals, from the moment of birth; whereas reflections about these, with reference to their being and usefulness, are acquired, if at all, with difficulty and slowly, through many troubles, in other words, through education?

THEAET. Assuredly.

soc. Is it, then, possible for one to attain "truth" who cannot even get as far as "being"?

THEAET. No.

soc. And will a man ever have knowledge of anything the truth of which he fails to attain?

THEAET. How can he, Socrates?

soc. Then knowledge is not in the sensations, but in the process of reasoning about them; for it is possible, apparently, to apprehend being and truth by reasoning, but not by sensation.

THEAET. So it seems.

soc. Then will you call the two by the same name, when there are so great differences between them?

165

ΘΕΑΙ. Οὔκουν δὴ δίκαιόν γε.

ΣΩ. Τί οὖν δὴ ἐκείνῳ ἀποδίδως ὄνομα, τῷ ὁρᾶν, ἀκούειν, ὀσφραίνεσθαι, ψύχεσθαι, θερμαίνεσθαι;

E   ΘΕΑΙ. Αἰσθάνεσθαι ἔγωγε· τί γὰρ ἄλλο;

ΣΩ. Ξύμπαν ἄρ᾽ αὐτὸ καλεῖς αἴσθησιν;

ΘΕΑΙ. Ἀνάγκη.

ΣΩ. Ὧι γε, φαμέν, οὐ μέτεστιν ἀληθείας ἅψασθαι· οὐδὲ γὰρ οὐσίας.

ΘΕΑΙ. Οὐ γὰρ οὖν.

ΣΩ. Οὐδ᾽ ἄρ᾽ ἐπιστήμης.

ΘΕΑΙ. Οὐ γάρ.

ΣΩ. Οὐκ ἄρ᾽ ἂν εἴη ποτέ, ὦ Θεαίτητε, αἴσθησίς τε καὶ ἐπιστήμη ταὐτόν.

ΘΕΑΙ. Οὐ φαίνεται, ὦ Σώκρατες. καὶ μάλιστά γε νῦν καταφανέστατον γέγονεν ἄλλο ὂν αἰσθήσεως ἐπιστήμη.

187   ΣΩ. Ἀλλ᾽ οὔ τι μὲν δὴ τούτου γε ἕνεκα ἠρχόμεθα διαλεγόμενοι, ἵνα εὕρωμεν τί ποτ᾽ οὐκ ἔστ᾽ ἐπιστήμη, ἀλλὰ τί ἔστιν. ὅμως δὲ τοσοῦτόν γε προβεβήκαμεν, ὥστε μὴ ζητεῖν αὐτὴν ἐν αἰσθήσει τὸ παράπαν, ἀλλ᾽ ἐν ἐκείνῳ τῷ ὀνόματι, ὅ τί ποτ᾽ ἔχει ἡ ψυχή, ὅταν αὐτὴ καθ᾽ αὑτὴν πραγματεύηται περὶ τὰ ὄντα.

ΘΕΑΙ. Ἀλλὰ μὴν τοῦτό γε καλεῖται, ὦ Σώκρατες, ὡς ἐγῷμαι, δοξάζειν.

ΣΩ. Ὀρθῶς γὰρ οἴει, ὦ φίλε. καὶ ὅρα δὴ νῦν
B πάλιν ἐξ ἀρχῆς, πάντα τὰ πρόσθεν ἐξαλείψας, εἴ τι μᾶλλον καθορᾷς, ἐπειδὴ ἐνταῦθα προελήλυθας. καὶ λέγε αὖθις τί ποτ᾽ ἐστὶν ἐπιστήμη.

31. ΘΕΑΙ. Δόξαν μὲν πᾶσαν εἰπεῖν, ὦ Σώ-

THEAET. No, that would certainly not be right.

SOC. What name will you give, then, to the one which includes seeing, hearing, smelling, being cold, and being hot?

THEAET. Perceiving. What other name can I give it?

SOC. Collectively you call it, then, perception?

THEAET. Of course.

SOC. By which, we say, we are quite unable to apprehend truth, since we cannot apprehend being, either.

THEAET. No; certainly not.

SOC. Nor knowledge either, then.

THEAET. No.

SOC. Then, Theaetetus, perception and knowledge could never be the same.

THEAET. Evidently not, Socrates; and indeed now at last it has been made perfectly clear that knowledge is something different from perception.

SOC. But surely we did not begin our conversation in order to find out what knowledge is not, but what it is. However, we have progressed so far, at least, as not to seek for knowledge in perception at all, but in some function of the soul, whatever name is given to it when it alone and by itself is engaged directly with realities.

THEAET. That, Socrates, is, I suppose, called having opinion.

SOC. You suppose rightly, my friend. Now begin again at the beginning. Wipe out all we said before, and see if you have any clearer vision, now that you have advanced to this point. Say once more what knowledge is.

THEAET. To say that all opinion is knowledge is

κρατες, ἀδύνατον, ἐπειδὴ καὶ ψευδής ἐστι δόξα·
κινδυνεύει δὲ ἡ ἀληθὴς δόξα ἐπιστήμη εἶναι, καί
μοι τοῦτο ἀποκεκρίσθω. ἐὰν γὰρ μὴ φανῇ προ-
ϊοῦσιν, ὥσπερ τὸ νῦν, ἄλλο τι πειρασόμεθα λέγειν.

ΣΩ. Οὕτω μέντοι χρή, ὦ Θεαίτητε, λέγειν προθύμως μᾶλλον, ἢ ὡς τὸ πρῶτον ὤκνεις ἀποκρίνεσθαι.
ἐὰν γὰρ οὕτω δρῶμεν, δυοῖν θάτερα, ἢ εὑρήσομεν
C ἐφ' ὃ ἐρχόμεθα, ἢ ἧττον οἰησόμεθα εἰδέναι ὃ μηδαμῇ
ἴσμεν· καίτοι οὐκ ἂν εἴη μεμπτὸς μισθὸς ὁ τοιοῦτος. καὶ δὴ καὶ νῦν τί φής; δυοῖν ὄντοιν εἰδέοιν
δόξης, τοῦ μὲν ἀληθινοῦ, ψευδοῦς δὲ τοῦ ἑτέρου,
τὴν ἀληθῆ δόξαν ἐπιστήμην ὁρίζει;

ΘΕΑΙ. Ἔγωγε· τοῦτο γὰρ αὖ νῦν μοι φαίνεται.

ΣΩ. Ἆρ' οὖν ἔτ' ἄξιον περὶ δόξης ἀναλαβεῖν
πάλιν—;

ΘΕΑΙ. Τὸ ποῖον δὴ λέγεις;

ΣΩ. Θράττει μέ πως νῦν τε καὶ ἄλλοτε δὴ πολ-
D λάκις, ὥστ' ἐν ἀπορίᾳ πολλῇ πρὸς ἐμαυτὸν καὶ
πρὸς ἄλλον γεγονέναι, οὐκ ἔχοντα εἰπεῖν τί ποτ'
ἐστὶ τοῦτο τὸ πάθος παρ' ἡμῖν καὶ τίνα τρόπον
ἐγγιγνόμενον.

ΘΕΑΙ. Τὸ ποῖον δή;

ΣΩ. Τὸ δοξάζειν τινὰ ψευδῆ. σκοπῶ δὴ καὶ
νῦν ἔτι διστάζων, πότερον ἐάσωμεν αὐτὸ ἢ ἐπισκεψώμεθα ἄλλον τρόπον ἢ ὀλίγον πρότερον.

ΘΕΑΙ. Τί μήν, ὦ Σώκρατες, εἴπερ γε καὶ ὁπητιοῦν[1] φαίνεται δεῖν; ἄρτι γὰρ οὐ κακῶς γε σὺ

[1] ὁπητιοῦν Burnet; ὁπηγοῦν B; ὅπη γοῦν W; ὁπηοῦν T.

impossible, Socrates, for there is also false opinion; but true opinion probably is knowledge. Let that be my answer. For if it is proved to be wrong as we proceed, I will try to give another, just as I have given this.

soc. That is the right way, Theaetetus. It is better to speak up boldly than to hesitate about answering, as you did at first. For if we act in this way, one of two things will happen: either we shall find what we are after, or we shall be less inclined to think we know what we do not know at all; and surely even that would be a recompense not to be despised. Well, then, what do you say now? Assuming that there are two kinds of opinion, one true and the other false, do you define knowledge as the true opinion?

theaet. Yes. That now seems to me to be correct.

soc. Is it, then, still worth while, in regard to opinion, to take up again—?

theaet. What point do you refer to?

soc. Somehow I am troubled now and have often been troubled before, so that I have been much perplexed in my own reflections and in talking with others, because I cannot tell what this experience is which we human beings have, and how it comes about.

theaet. What experience?

soc. That anyone has false opinions. And so I am considering and am still in doubt whether we had better let it go or examine it by another method than the one we followed a while ago.

theaet. Why not, Socrates, if there seems to be the least need of it? For just now, in talking about

καὶ Θεόδωρος ἐλέγετε σχολῆς πέρι, ὡς οὐδὲν ἐν
τοῖς τοιοῖσδε κατεπείγει.

Ε   ΣΩ. Ὀρθῶς ὑπέμνησας. ἴσως γὰρ οὐκ ἀπὸ
καιροῦ πάλιν ὥσπερ ἴχνος μετελθεῖν. κρεῖττον
γάρ που σμικρὸν εὖ ἢ πολὺ μὴ ἱκανῶς περᾶναι.

ΘΕΑΙ. Τί μήν;

ΣΩ. Πῶς οὖν; τί δὴ καὶ λέγομεν; ψευδῆ φαμεν
ἑκάστοτε εἶναι δόξαν, καί τινα ἡμῶν δοξάζειν
ψευδῆ, τὸν δ' αὖ ἀληθῆ, ὡς φύσει οὕτως ἐχόντων;

ΘΕΑΙ. Φαμὲν γὰρ δή.

188   ΣΩ. Οὐκοῦν τόδε γ' ἔσθ' ἡμῖν περὶ πάντα καὶ
καθ' ἕκαστον, ἤτοι εἰδέναι ἢ μὴ εἰδέναι; μανθάνειν
γὰρ καὶ ἐπιλανθάνεσθαι μεταξὺ τούτων ὡς ὄντα
χαίρειν λέγω ἐν τῷ παρόντι· νῦν γὰρ ἡμῖν πρὸς
λόγον ἐστὶν οὐδέν.

ΘΕΑΙ. Ἀλλὰ μήν, ὦ Σώκρατες, ἄλλο γ' οὐδὲν
λείπεται περὶ ἕκαστον πλὴν εἰδέναι ἢ μὴ εἰδέναι.

ΣΩ. Οὐκοῦν ἤδη ἀνάγκη τὸν δοξάζοντα δοξάζειν
ἢ ὧν τι οἶδεν ἢ μὴ οἶδεν;

ΘΕΑΙ. Ἀνάγκη.

ΣΩ. Καὶ μὴν εἰδότα γε μὴ εἰδέναι τὸ αὐτὸ ἢ μὴ
Β εἰδότα εἰδέναι ἀδύνατον.

ΘΕΑΙ. Πῶς δ' οὔ;

ΣΩ. Ἆρ' οὖν ὁ τὰ ψευδῆ δοξάζων, ἃ οἶδε, ταῦτα
οἴεται οὐ ταῦτα εἶναι ἀλλὰ ἕτερα ἄττα ὧν οἶδε,
καὶ ἀμφότερα εἰδὼς ἀγνοεῖ ἀμφότερα;

leisure, you and Theodorus said very truly that there is no hurry in discussions of this sort.

soc. You are right in reminding me. For perhaps this is a good time to retrace our steps. For it is better to finish a little task well than a great deal imperfectly.

THEAET. Of course.

soc. How, then, shall we set about it? What is it that we do say? Do we say that in every case of opinion there is a false opinion, and one of us has a false, and another a true opinion, because, as we believe, it is in the nature of things that this should be so?

THEAET. Yes, we do.

soc. Then this, at any rate, is possible for us, is it not, regarding all things collectively and each thing separately, either to know or not to know them? For learning and forgetting, as intermediate stages, I leave out of account for the present, for just now they have no bearing upon our argument.

THEAET. Certainly, Socrates, nothing is left in any particular case except knowing or not knowing it.

soc. Then he who forms opinion must form opinion either about what he knows or about what he does not know?

THEAET. Necessarily.

soc. And it is surely impossible that one who knows a thing does not know it, or that one who does not know it knows it.

THEAET. Certainly.

soc. Then does he who forms false opinions think that the things which he knows are not these things, but some others of the things he knows, and so, knowing both, is he ignorant of both?

ΘΕΑΙ. 'Αλλ' ἀδύνατον, ὦ Σώκρατες.

ΣΩ. 'Αλλ' ἄρα, ἃ μὴ οἶδεν, ἡγεῖται αὐτὰ εἶναι ἕτερα ἄττα ὧν μὴ οἶδε, καὶ τοῦτ' ἔστι τῷ μήτε Θεαίτητον μήτε Σωκράτη εἰδότι εἰς τὴν διάνοιαν λαβεῖν ὡς ὁ Σωκράτης Θεαίτητος ἢ ὁ Θεαίτητος Σωκράτης;

C   ΘΕΑΙ. Καὶ πῶς ἄν;

ΣΩ. 'Αλλ' οὐ μήν, ἅ γέ τις οἶδεν, οἴεταί που ἃ μὴ οἶδεν αὐτὰ εἶναι, οὐδ' αὖ ἃ μὴ οἶδεν, ἃ οἶδεν.

ΘΕΑΙ. Τέρας γὰρ ἔσται.

ΣΩ. Πῶς οὖν ἂν ἔτι ψευδῆ δοξάσειεν; ἐκτὸς γὰρ τούτων ἀδύνατόν που δοξάζειν, ἐπείπερ πάντ' ἢ ἴσμεν ἢ οὐκ ἴσμεν, ἐν δὲ τούτοις οὐδαμοῦ φαίνεται δυνατὸν ψευδῆ δοξάσαι.

ΘΕΑΙ. 'Αληθέστατα.

ΣΩ. *Αρ' οὖν οὐ ταύτῃ σκεπτέον ὃ ζητοῦμεν, κατὰ τὸ εἰδέναι καὶ μὴ εἰδέναι ἰόντας, ἀλλὰ κατὰ D τὸ εἶναι καὶ μή;

ΘΕΑΙ. Πῶς λέγεις;

ΣΩ. Μὴ ἁπλοῦν ᾖ ὅτι ὁ τὰ μὴ ὄντα περὶ ὁτουοῦν δοξάζων οὐκ ἔσθ' ὡς οὐ ψευδῆ δοξάσει, κἂν ὁπωσοῦν ἄλλως τὰ τῆς διανοίας ἔχῃ.

ΘΕΑΙ. Εἰκός γ' αὖ, ὦ Σώκρατες.

ΣΩ. Πῶς οὖν; τί ἐροῦμεν, ὦ Θεαίτητε, ἐάν τις ἡμᾶς ἀνακρίνῃ· " δυνατὸν δὲ ὁτῳοῦν ὃ λέγεται, καί τις ἀνθρώπων τὸ μὴ ὂν δοξάσει, εἴτε περὶ τῶν ὄντων του εἴτε αὐτὸ καθ' αὑτό "; καὶ ἡμεῖς

THEAET. That is impossible, Socrates.

soc. Well then, does he think that the things he does not know are other things which he does not know—which is as if a man who knows neither Theaetetus nor Socrates should conceive the idea that Socrates is Theaetetus or Theaetetus Socrates?

THEAET. That is impossible.

soc. But surely a man does not think that the things he knows are the things he does not know, or again that the things he does not know are the things he knows.

THEAET. That would be a monstrous absurdity.

soc. Then how could he still form false opinions? For inasmuch as all things are either known or unknown to us, it is impossible, I imagine, to form opinions outside of these alternatives, and within them it is clear that there is no place for false opinion.

THEAET. Very true.

soc. Had we, then, better look for what we are seeking, not by this method of knowing and not knowing, but by that of being and not being?

THEAET. What do you mean?

soc. We may simply assert that he who on any subject holds opinions which are not, will certainly think falsely, no matter what the condition of his mind may be in other respects.

THEAET. That, again, is likely, Socrates.

soc. Well then, what shall we say, Theaetetus, if anyone asks us, "Is that which is assumed in common speech possible at all, and can any human being hold an opinion which is not, whether it be concerned with any of the things which are, or be entirely independent of them?" We, I fancy, shall

173

188

Ε δή, ὡς ἔοικεν, πρὸς ταῦτα φήσομεν· ὅταν γε
μὴ ἀληθῆ οἴηται οἰόμενος·" ἢ πῶς ἐροῦμεν;

ΘΕΑΙ. Οὕτως.

ΣΩ. Ἦ οὖν καὶ ἄλλοθί που τὸ τοιοῦτόν ἐστιν;

ΘΕΑΙ. Τὸ ποῖον;

ΣΩ. Εἴ τις ὁρᾷ μέν τι, ὁρᾷ δὲ οὐδέν.

ΘΕΑΙ. Καὶ πῶς;

ΣΩ. Ἀλλὰ μὴν εἰ ἕν γέ τι ὁρᾷ, τῶν ὄντων τι
ὁρᾷ. ἢ σὺ οἴει ποτὲ τὸ ἓν ἐν τοῖς μὴ οὖσιν εἶναι;

ΘΕΑΙ. Οὐκ ἔγωγε.

ΣΩ. Ὁ ἄρα ἕν γέ τι ὁρῶν ὄν τι ὁρᾷ.

ΘΕΑΙ. Φαίνεται.

189   ΣΩ. Καὶ ὁ ἄρα τι ἀκούων ἕν γέ τι ἀκούει καὶ ὃν
ἀκούει.

ΘΕΑΙ. Ναί.

ΣΩ. Καὶ ὁ ἁπτόμενος δή του, ἑνός γέ του ἅπτεται καὶ ὄντος, εἴπερ ἑνός;

ΘΕΑΙ. Καὶ τοῦτο.

ΣΩ. Ὁ δὲ δὴ δοξάζων οὐχ ἕν τι [1] δοξάζει;

ΘΕΑΙ. Ἀνάγκη.

ΣΩ. Ὁ δ' ἕν τι δοξάζων οὐκ ὄν τι;

ΘΕΑΙ. Συγχωρῶ.

ΣΩ. Ὁ ἄρα μὴ ὂν δοξάζων οὐδὲν δοξάζει.

ΘΕΑΙ. Οὐ φαίνεται.

ΣΩ. Ἀλλὰ μὴν ὅ γε μηδὲν δοξάζων τὸ παράπαν
οὐδὲ δοξάζει.

ΘΕΑΙ. Δῆλον, ὡς ἔοικεν.

[1] ἕν τι BT; ἕν γέ τι W.

reply, "Yes, when, in thinking, he thinks what is not true," shall we not?

THEAET. Yes.

soc. And is the same sort of thing possible in any other field?

THEAET. What sort of thing?

soc. For instance, that a man sees something, but sees nothing.

THEAET. How can he?

soc. Yet surely if a man sees any one thing, he sees something that is. Or do you, perhaps, think "one" is among the things that are not?

THEAET. No, I do not.

soc. Then he who sees any one thing, sees something that is.

THEAET. That is clear.

soc. And therefore he who hears anything, hears some one thing and therefore hears what is.

THEAET. Yes.

soc. And he who touches anything, touches some one thing, which is, since it is one?

THEAET. That also is true.

soc. So, then, does not he who holds an opinion hold an opinion of some one thing?

THEAET. He must do so.

soc. And does not he who holds an opinion of some one thing hold an opinion of something that is?

THEAET. I agree.

soc. Then he who holds an opinion of what is not holds an opinion of nothing.

THEAET. Evidently.

soc. Well then, he who holds an opinion of nothing, holds no opinion at all.

THEAET. That is plain, apparently.

B   ΣΩ. Οὐκ ἄρα οἷόν τε τὸ μὴ ὂν δοξάζειν, οὔτε
περὶ τῶν ὄντων οὔτε αὐτὸ καθ᾽ αὑτό.

ΘΕΑΙ. Οὐ φαίνεται.

ΣΩ. Ἄλλο τι ἄρ᾽ ἐστὶ τὸ ψευδῆ δοξάζειν τοῦ
τὰ μὴ ὄντα δοξάζειν.

ΘΕΑΙ. Ἄλλο ἔοικεν.

ΣΩ. Οὐ γὰρ οὕτως οὔτε ὡς ὀλίγον πρότερον
ἐσκοπούμεν, ψευδής ἐστι δόξα ἐν ἡμῖν.

ΘΕΑΙ. Οὐ γὰρ οὖν δή.

32. ΣΩ. Ἀλλ᾽ ἆρα ὧδε γιγνόμενον τοῦτο
προσαγορεύομεν;

ΘΕΑΙ. Πῶς;

ΣΩ. Ἀλλοδοξίαν τινὰ οὖσαν ψευδῆ φαμεν εἶναι
C δόξαν, ὅταν τίς τι [1] τῶν ὄντων ἄλλο αὖ τῶν ὄντων
ἀνταλλαξάμενος τῇ διανοίᾳ φῇ εἶναι. οὕτω γὰρ
ὂν μὲν ἀεὶ δοξάζει, ἕτερον δὲ ἀνθ᾽ ἑτέρου, καὶ
ἁμαρτάνων οὗ ἐσκόπει δικαίως ἂν καλοῖτο ψευδῆ
δοξάζων.

ΘΕΑΙ. Ὀρθότατά μοι νῦν δοκεῖς εἰρηκέναι. ὅταν
γάρ τις ἀντὶ καλοῦ αἰσχρὸν ἢ ἀντὶ αἰσχροῦ καλὸν
δοξάζῃ, τότε ὡς ἀληθῶς δοξάζει ψευδῆ.

ΣΩ. Δῆλος εἶ, ὦ Θεαίτητε, καταφρονῶν μου
καὶ οὐ δεδιώς.

ΘΕΑΙ. Τί μάλιστα;

ΣΩ. Οὐκ ἄν, οἶμαι, σοὶ δοκῶ τοῦ ἀληθῶς ψεύ-
D δους ἀντιλαβέσθαι, ἐρόμενος εἰ οἷόν τε ταχὺ
βραδέως ἢ κοῦφον βαρέως ἢ ἄλλο τι ἐναντίον μὴ
κατὰ τὴν αὑτοῦ φύσιν ἀλλὰ κατὰ τὴν τοῦ ἐναντίου

[1] τι om. BT.

soc. Then it is impossible to hold an opinion of that which is not, either in relation to things that are, or independently of them.

THEAET. Evidently.

soc. Then holding false opinion is something different from holding an opinion of that which is not.

THEAET. So it seems.

soc. Then false opinion is not found to exist in us either by this method or by that which we followed a little while ago.

THEAET. No, it certainly is not.

soc. But does not that which we call by that name arise after the following manner?

THEAET. After what manner?

soc. We say that false opinion is a kind of interchanged opinion, when a person makes an exchange in his mind and says that one thing which exists is another thing which exists. For in this way he always holds an opinion of what exists, but of one thing instead of another; so he misses the object he was aiming at in his thought and might fairly be said to hold a false opinion.

THEAET. Now you seem to me to have said what is perfectly right. For when a man, in forming an opinion, puts ugly instead of beautiful, or beautiful instead of ugly, he does truly hold a false opinion.

soc. Evidently, Theaetetus, you feel contempt of me, and not fear.

THEAET. Why in the world do you say that?

soc. You think, I fancy, that I would not attack your "truly false" by asking whether it is possible for a thing to become slowly quick or heavily light, or any other opposite, by a process opposite to itself, in accordance, not with its own nature, but with that

γίγνεσθαι ἑαυτῷ ἐναντίως. τοῦτο μὲν οὖν, ἵνα
μὴ μάτην θαρρήσῃς, ἀφίημι. ἀρέσκει δέ, ὡς φῄς,
τὸ τὰ ψευδῆ δοξάζειν ἀλλοδοξεῖν εἶναι;

ΘΕΑΙ. Ἔμοιγε.

ΣΩ. Ἔστιν ἄρα κατὰ τὴν σὴν δόξαν ἕτερόν τι
ὡς ἕτερον καὶ μὴ ὡς ἐκεῖνο τῇ διανοίᾳ τίθεσθαι.

ΘΕΑΙ. Ἔστι μέντοι.

ΣΩ. Ὅταν οὖν τοῦθ' ἡ διάνοιά του δρᾷ, οὐ καὶ
Ε ἀνάγκη αὐτὴν ἤτοι ἀμφότερα ἢ τὸ ἕτερον διανοεῖσθαι;

ΘΕΑΙ. Ἀνάγκη μὲν οὖν· ἤτοι ἅμα γε ἢ ἐν μέρει.

ΣΩ. Κάλλιστα. τὸ δὲ διανοεῖσθαι ἆρ' ὅπερ
ἐγὼ καλεῖς;

ΘΕΑΙ. Τί καλῶν;

ΣΩ. Λόγον ὃν αὐτὴ πρὸς αὑτὴν ἡ ψυχὴ διεξέρχεται περὶ ὧν ἂν σκοπῇ. ὥς γε μὴ εἰδώς σοι ἀπο-
φαίνομαι. τοῦτο γάρ μοι ἰνδάλλεται διανοουμένη
οὐκ ἄλλο τι ἢ διαλέγεσθαι, αὐτὴ ἑαυτὴν ἐρωτῶσα
190 καὶ ἀποκρινομένη, καὶ φάσκουσα καὶ οὐ φάσκουσα.
ὅταν δὲ ὁρίσασα, εἴτε βραδύτερον εἴτε καὶ ὀξύτερον
ἐπᾴξασα, τὸ αὐτὸ ἤδη φῇ καὶ μὴ διστάζῃ, δόξαν
ταύτην τίθεμεν αὐτῆς. ὥστ' ἔγωγε τὸ δοξάζειν
λέγειν καλῶ καὶ τὴν δόξαν λόγον εἰρημένον, οὐ
μέντοι πρὸς ἄλλον οὐδὲ φωνῇ, ἀλλὰ σιγῇ πρὸς
αὑτόν· σὺ δὲ τί;

ΘΕΑΙ. Κἀγώ.

ΣΩ. Ὅταν ἄρα τις τὸ ἕτερον ἕτερον δοξάζῃ, καὶ
φησίν, ὡς ἔοικε, τὸ ἕτερον ἕτερον εἶναι πρὸς ἑαυτόν.

Β ΘΕΑΙ. Τί μήν;

of its opposite. But I let this pass, that your courage may not fail. You are satisfied, you say, that false opinion is interchanged opinion?

THEAET. I am.

soc. It is, then, in your opinion, possible for the mind to regard one thing as another and not as what it is.

THEAET. Yes, it is.

soc. Now when one's mind does this, does it not necessarily have a thought either of both things together or of one or the other of them?

THEAET. Yes, it must; either of both at the same time or in succession.

soc. Excellent. And do you define thought as I do?

THEAET. How do you define it?

soc. As the talk which the soul has with itself about any subjects which it considers. You must not suppose that I know this that I am declaring to you. But the soul, as the image presents itself to me, when it thinks, is merely conversing with itself, asking itself questions and answering, affirming and denying. When it has arrived at a decision, whether slowly or with a sudden bound, and is at last agreed, and is not in doubt, we call that its opinion; and so I define forming opinion as talking and opinion as talk which has been held, not with someone else, nor yet aloud, but in silence with oneself. How do you define it?

THEAET. In the same way.

soc. Then whenever a man has an opinion that one thing is another, he says to himself, we believe, that the one thing is the other.

THEAET. Certainly.

ΣΩ. Ἀναμιμνήσκου δὴ εἰ πώποτ' εἶπες πρὸς
σεαυτὸν ὅτι παντὸς μᾶλλον τό τοι καλὸν αἰσχρόν
ἐστιν ἢ τὸ ἄδικον δίκαιον, ἢ καί, τὸ πάντων κεφά-
λαιον, σκόπει εἴ ποτ' ἐπεχείρησας σεαυτὸν πείθειν
ὡς παντὸς μᾶλλον τὸ ἕτερον ἕτερόν ἐστιν, ἢ πᾶν
τοὐναντίον οὐδ' ἐν ὕπνῳ πώποτε ἐτόλμησας εἰπεῖν
πρὸς σεαυτὸν ὡς παντάπασιν ἄρα τὰ περιττὰ ἄρτιά
ἐστιν ἤ τι ἄλλο τοιοῦτον.

ΘΕΑΙ. Ἀληθῆ λέγεις.

C ΣΩ. Ἄλλον δέ τινα οἴει ὑγιαίνοντα ἢ μαινό-
μενον τολμῆσαι σπουδῇ πρὸς ἑαυτὸν εἰπεῖν ἀνα-
πείθοντα αὑτόν, ὡς ἀνάγκη τὸν βοῦν ἵππον εἶναι
ἢ τὰ δύο ἕν;

ΘΕΑΙ. Μὰ Δί' οὐκ ἔγωγε.

ΣΩ. Οὐκοῦν εἰ τὸ λέγειν πρὸς ἑαυτὸν δοξάζειν
ἐστίν, οὐδεὶς ἀμφότερά γε λέγων καὶ δοξάζων καὶ [1]
ἐφαπτόμενος ἀμφοῖν τῇ ψυχῇ εἴποι ἂν καὶ δοξάσειεν ὡς τὸ ἕτερον ἕτερόν ἐστιν. ἐατέον δὲ καὶ
σοὶ τὸ ῥῆμα [2] περὶ τοῦ ἑτέρου. λέγω γὰρ αὐτὸ
τῇδε, μηδένα δοξάζειν ὡς τὸ αἰσχρὸν καλὸν ἢ
D ἄλλο τι τῶν τοιούτων.

ΘΕΑΙ. Ἀλλ', ὦ Σώκρατες, ἐῶ τε καί μοι δοκεῖ
ὡς λέγεις.

ΣΩ. Ἄμφω μὲν ἄρα δοξάζοντα ἀδύνατον τό
γε [3] ἕτερον ἕτερον δοξάζειν.

ΘΕΑΙ. Ἔοικεν.

ΣΩ. Ἀλλὰ μὴν τὸ ἕτερόν γε μόνον δοξάζων, τὸ

[1] καί om. T.
[2] After ῥῆμα B adds ἐπὶ τῶν ἐν μέρει, ἐπειδὴ τὸ ῥῆμα ἕτερον τῷ
ἑτέρῳ κατὰ ῥῆμα ταὐτόν ἐστιν, applied to things in succession,
since the word " one " is, as a word, the same as " other "
(i.e. the Greek uses ἕτερον for " one " and " other ").
[3] τό γε Heindorf; τότε B; τό ** T.

soc. Now call to mind whether you have ever said to yourself that the beautiful is most assuredly ugly, or the wrong right, or—and this is the sum of the whole matter—consider whether you have ever tried to persuade yourself that one thing is most assuredly another, or whether quite the contrary is the case, and you have never ventured, even in sleep, to say to yourself that the odd is, after all, certainly even, or anything of that sort.

THEAET. You are right.

soc. Do you imagine that anyone else, sane or insane, ever ventured to say to himself seriously and try to persuade himself that the ox must necessarily be a horse, or two one?

THEAET. No, by Zeus, I do not.

soc. Then if forming opinion is talking to oneself, no one who talks and forms opinion of two objects and apprehends them both with his soul, could say and have the opinion that one is the other. But you will also have to give up the expression " one and other." This is what I mean, that nobody holds the opinion that the ugly is beautiful, or anything of that sort.

THEAET. Well, Socrates, I do give it up; and I agree with you in what you say.

soc. You agree, therefore, that he who holds an opinion of both things cannot hold the opinion that one is the other.

THEAET. So it seems.

soc. But surely he who holds an opinion of one

δὲ ἕτερον μηδαμῇ, οὐδέποτε δοξάσει τὸ ἕτερον ἕτερον εἶναι.

ΘΕΑΙ. Ἀληθῆ λέγεις· ἀναγκάζοιτο γὰρ ἂν ἐφάπτεσθαι καὶ οὗ μὴ δοξάζει.

ΣΩ. Οὔτ' ἄρ' ἀμφότερα οὔτε τὸ ἕτερον δοξάζοντι Ε ἐγχωρεῖ ἀλλοδοξεῖν. ὥστ' εἴ τις ὁριεῖται δόξαν εἶναι ψευδῆ τὸ ἑτεροδοξεῖν, οὐδὲν ἂν λέγοι· οὔτ' ἄρα ταύτῃ οὔτε κατὰ τὰ πρότερα φαίνεται ψευδὴς ἐν ἡμῖν οὖσα δόξα.

ΘΕΑΙ. Οὐκ ἔοικεν.

33. ΣΩ. Ἀλλὰ μέντοι, ὦ Θεαίτητε, εἰ τοῦτο μὴ φανήσεται ὄν, πολλὰ ἀναγκασθησόμεθα ὁμολογεῖν καὶ ἄτοπα.

ΘΕΑΙ. Τὰ ποῖα δή;

ΣΩ. Οὐκ ἐρῶ σοι πρὶν ἂν πανταχῇ πειραθῶ σκοπῶν. αἰσχυνοίμην γὰρ ἂν ὑπὲρ ἡμῶν, ἐν ᾧ ἀποροῦμεν, ἀναγκαζομένων ὁμολογεῖν οἷα λέγω. ἀλλ' 191 ἐὰν εὕρωμεν καὶ ἐλεύθεροι γενώμεθα, τότ' ἤδη περὶ τῶν ἄλλων ἐροῦμεν ὡς πασχόντων αὐτὰ ἐκτὸς τοῦ γελοίου ἑστῶτες· ἐὰν δὲ πάντῃ ἀπορήσωμεν, ταπεινωθέντες, οἶμαι, τῷ λόγῳ παρέξομεν ὡς ναυτιῶντες πατεῖν τε καὶ χρῆσθαι ὅ τι ἂν βούληται. ᾗ οὖν ἔτι πόρον τινὰ εὑρίσκω τοῦ ζητήματος ἡμῖν, ἄκουε.

ΘΕΑΙ. Λέγε μόνον.

ΣΩ. Οὐ φήσω ἡμᾶς ὀρθῶς ὁμολογῆσαι, ἡνίκα ὡμολογήσαμεν ἅ τις οἶδεν, ἀδύνατον δοξάσαι ἃ μὴ Β οἶδεν εἶναι αὐτὰ καὶ ψευσθῆναι· ἀλλά πῃ δυνατόν.

only, and not of the other at all, will never hold the opinion that one is the other.

THEAET. You are right; for he would be forced to apprehend also that of which he holds no opinion.

SOC. Then neither he who holds opinion of both nor he who holds it of one can hold the opinion that a thing is something else. And so anyone who sets out to define false opinion as interchanged opinion would be talking nonsense. Then neither by this method nor by our previous methods is false opinion found to exist in us.

THEAET. Apparently not.

SOC. But yet, Theaetetus, if this is found not to exist, we shall be forced to admit many absurdities.

THEAET. What absurdities?

SOC. I will not tell you until I have tried to consider the matter in every way. For I should be ashamed of us, if, in our perplexity, we were forced to make such admissions as those to which I refer. But if we find the object of our quest, and are set free from perplexity, then, and not before, we will speak of others as involved in those absurdities, and we ourselves shall stand free from ridicule. But if we find no escape from our perplexity, we shall, I fancy, become low-spirited, like seasick people, and shall allow the argument to trample on us and do to us anything it pleases. Hear, then, by what means I still see a prospect of success for our quest.

THEAET. Do speak.

SOC. I shall deny that we were right when we agreed that it is impossible for a man to have opinion that the things he does not know are the things which he knows, and thus to be deceived. But there is a way in which it is possible.

ΘΕΑΙ. Ἆρα λέγεις ὃ καὶ ἐγὼ τότε ὑπώπτευσα, ἡνίκ᾽ αὐτὸ ἔφαμεν τοιοῦτον εἶναι, ὅτι ἐνίοτ᾽ ἐγὼ γιγνώσκων Σωκράτη, πόρρωθεν δὲ ὁρῶν ἄλλον ὃν οὐ γιγνώσκω, ᾠήθην εἶναι Σωκράτη ὃν οἶδα; γίγνεται γὰρ δὴ ἐν τῷ τοιούτῳ οἷον λέγεις.

ΣΩ. Οὐκοῦν ἀπέστημεν αὐτοῦ, ὅτι ἃ ἴσμεν ἐποίει ἡμᾶς εἰδότας μὴ εἰδέναι;

ΘΕΑΙ. Πάνυ μὲν οὖν.

ΣΩ. Μὴ γὰρ οὕτω τιθῶμεν, ἀλλ᾽ ὧδε· ἴσως C πῃ ἡμῖν συγχωρήσεται, ἴσως δὲ ἀντιτενεῖ. ἀλλὰ γὰρ ἐν τοιούτῳ ἐχόμεθα, ἐν ᾧ ἀνάγκη πάντα μεταστρέφοντα λόγον βασανίζειν. σκόπει οὖν εἴ τι λέγω. ἆρα ἔστιν μὴ εἰδότα τι πρότερον ὕστερον μαθεῖν;

ΘΕΑΙ. Ἔστι μέντοι.

ΣΩ. Οὐκοῦν καὶ αὖθις ἕτερον καὶ ἕτερον;

ΘΕΑΙ. Τί δ᾽ οὔ;

ΣΩ. Θὲς δή μοι λόγου ἕνεκα ἐν ταῖς ψυχαῖς ἡμῶν ἐνὸν κήρινον ἐκμαγεῖον, τῷ μὲν μεῖζον, τῷ δ᾽ ἔλαττον, καὶ τῷ μὲν καθαρωτέρου κηροῦ, τῷ δὲ κοπρωδεστέρου, καὶ σκληροτέρου, ἐνίοις δὲ D ὑγροτέρου, ἔστι δ᾽ οἷς μετρίως ἔχοντος.

ΘΕΑΙ. Τίθημι.

ΣΩ. Δῶρον τοίνυν αὐτὸ φῶμεν εἶναι τῆς τῶν Μουσῶν μητρὸς Μνημοσύνης, καὶ ἐς τοῦτο, ὅ τι ἂν βουληθῶμεν μνημονεῦσαι ὧν ἂν ἴδωμεν[1] ἢ ἀκούσωμεν[2] ἢ αὐτοὶ ἐννοήσωμεν, ὑπέχοντας αὐτὸ ταῖς αἰσθήσεσι καὶ ἐννοίαις, ἀποτυποῦσθαι, ὥσπερ δακτυλίων σημεῖα ἐνσημαινομένους· καὶ ὃ μὲν

[1] εἰδῶμεν B.   [2] ἀκούωμεν BT.

THEAET. Do you mean what I myself suspected when we made the statement to which you refer, that sometimes I, though I know Socrates, saw at a distance someone whom I did not know, and thought it was Socrates whom I do know? In such a case false opinion does arise.

soc. But did not we reject that, because it resulted in our knowing and not knowing the things which we know?

THEAET. Certainly we did.

soc. Let us, then, not make that assumption, but another; perhaps it will turn out well for us, perhaps the opposite. But we are in such straits that we must turn every argument round and test it from all sides. Now see if this is sensible: Can a man who did not know a thing at one time learn it later?

THEAET. To be sure he can.

soc. Again, then, can he learn one thing after another?

THEAET. Why not?

soc. Please assume, then, for the sake of argument, that there is in our souls a block of wax, in one case larger, in another smaller, in one case the wax is purer, in another more impure and harder, in some cases softer, and in some of proper quality.

THEAET. I assume all that.

soc. Let us, then, say that this is the gift of Memory, the mother of the Muses, and that whenever we wish to remember anything we see or hear or think of in our own minds, we hold this wax under the perceptions and thoughts and imprint them upon it, just as we make impressions from seal rings;

191

ἂν ἐκμαγῇ, μνημονεύειν τε καὶ ἐπίστασθαι ἕως
ἂν ἐνῇ τὸ εἴδωλον αὐτοῦ· ὃ δ' ἂν [1] ἐξαλειφθῇ ἢ
E μὴ οἷόν τε γένηται ἐκμαγῆναι, ἐπιλελῆσθαί τε
καὶ μὴ ἐπίστασθαι.

ΘΕΑΙ. Ἔστω οὕτως.

ΣΩ. Ὁ τοίνυν ἐπιστάμενος μὲν αὐτά, σκοπῶν
δέ τι ὧν ὁρᾷ ἢ ἀκούει, ἄθρει εἰ ἄρα τοιῷδε τρόπῳ
ψευδῆ ἂν δοξάσαι.

ΘΕΑΙ. Ποίῳ δή τινι;

ΣΩ. Ἃ οἶδεν, οἰηθεὶς εἶναι τοτὲ μὲν ἃ οἶδε,
τοτὲ δὲ ἃ μή. ταῦτα γὰρ ἐν τοῖς πρόσθεν οὐ καλῶς
ὡμολογήσαμεν ὁμολογοῦντες ἀδύνατα.

ΘΕΑΙ. Νῦν δὲ πῶς λέγεις;

192 ΣΩ. Δεῖ ὧδε λέγεσθαι περὶ αὐτῶν ἐξ ἀρχῆς
διοριζομένους, ὅτι ὃ μέν τις οἶδεν σχὼν [2] αὐτοῦ
μνημεῖον ἐν τῇ ψυχῇ, αἰσθάνεται δὲ αὐτὸ μή,
τοῦτο [3] οἰηθῆναι ἕτερόν τι ὧν οἶδεν, ἔχοντα καὶ
ἐκείνου τύπον, αἰσθανόμενον δὲ μή, ἀδύνατον.
καὶ ὅ γε οἶδεν αὖ, οἰηθῆναι εἶναι ὃ μὴ οἶδε μηδ'
ἔχει αὐτοῦ σφραγῖδα· καὶ ὃ μὴ οἶδεν, ὃ μὴ οἶδεν
αὖ· καὶ ὃ μὴ οἶδεν, ὃ οἶδε· καὶ ὃ αἰσθάνεταί γε,
ἕτερόν τι ὧν αἰσθάνεται οἰηθῆναι εἶναι· καὶ ὃ
αἰσθάνεται, ὧν τι μὴ αἰσθάνεται· καὶ ὃ μὴ
αἰσθάνεται, ὧν μὴ αἰσθάνεται· καὶ ὃ μὴ
B αἰσθάνεται, ὧν αἰσθάνεται.[4] καὶ ἔτι γε αὖ ὧν
οἶδε καὶ αἰσθάνεται καὶ ἔχει τὸ σημεῖον κατὰ τὴν

[1] ὃ δ' ἂν B²W; ὅταν B; ὅταν δὲ T.
[2] σχὼν BT; ἔχων W.   [3] τοῦτο B; om. al.
[4] καὶ . . . ὧν αἰσθάνεται om. B.

and whatever is imprinted we remember and know as long as its image lasts, but whatever is rubbed out or cannot be imprinted we forget and do not know.

THEAET. Let us assume that.

soc. Now take a man who knows the things which he sees and hears, and is considering some one of them; observe whether he may not gain a false opinion in the following manner.

THEAET. In what manner?

soc. By thinking that the things which he knows are sometimes things which he knows and sometimes things which he does not know. For we were wrong before in agreeing that this is impossible.

THEAET. What do you say about it now?

soc. We must begin our discussion of the matter by making the following distinctions: It is impossible for anyone to think that one thing which he knows and of which he has received a memorial imprint in his soul, but which he does not perceive, is another thing which he knows and of which also he has an imprint, and which he does not perceive. And, again, he cannot think that what he knows is that which he does not know and of which he has no seal; nor that what he does not know is another thing which he does not know; nor that what he does not know is what he knows; nor can he think that what he perceives is something else which he perceives; nor that what he perceives is something which he does not perceive; nor that what he does not perceive is something else which he does not perceive; nor that what he does not perceive is something which he perceives. And, again, it is still more impossible, if that can be, to think that a thing which he knows and perceives and of which he has an imprint which accords

αἴσθησιν, οἰηθῆναι αὖ ἕτερόν τι ὧν οἶδε καὶ
αἰσθάνεται καὶ ἔχει αὖ καὶ ἐκείνου τὸ σημεῖον
κατὰ τὴν αἴσθησιν, ἀδυνατώτερον ἔτι ἐκείνων, εἰ
οἶόν τε. καὶ ὃ οἶδε καὶ¹ αἰσθάνεται ἔχων τὸ
μνημεῖον ὀρθῶς, ὃ οἶδεν οἰηθῆναι ἀδύνατον·
καὶ ὃ οἶδε καὶ αἰσθάνεται ἔχων² κατὰ ταὐτά, ὃ
C αἰσθάνεται· καὶ ὃ αὖ μὴ οἶδε μηδὲ αἰσθάνεται,
ὃ μὴ οἶδε μηδὲ αἰσθάνεται· καὶ ὃ μὴ οἶδε μηδὲ
αἰσθάνεται, ὃ μὴ οἶδε· καὶ ὃ μὴ οἶδε μηδὲ αἰσθάνεται, ὃ μὴ αἰσθάνεται³· πάντα ταῦτα ὑπερβάλλει
ἀδυναμίᾳ τοῦ ἐν αὐτοῖς ψευδῆ τινα δοξάσαι. λείπεται δὴ ἐν τοῖς τοιοῖσδε, εἴπερ που ἄλλοθι, τὸ
τοιοῦτον γενέσθαι.

ΘΕΑΙ. Ἐν τίσι δή; ἐὰν ἄρα ἐξ αὐτῶν τι μᾶλλον
μάθω· νῦν μὲν γὰρ οὐχ ἕπομαι.

ΣΩ. Ἐν οἷς οἶδεν, οἰηθῆναι αὐτὰ ἕτερ' ἄττα
εἶναι ὧν οἶδε καὶ αἰσθάνεται· ἢ ὧν μὴ οἶδεν,
αἰσθάνεται δέ· ἢ ὧν οἶδε καὶ αἰσθάνεται, ὧν
D οἶδεν αὖ καὶ αἰσθάνεται.

ΘΕΑΙ. Νῦν πολὺ πλέον ἀπελείφθην ἢ τότε.

34. ΣΩ. Ὧδε δὴ ἀνάπαλιν ἄκουε. ἐγὼ εἰδὼς
Θεόδωρον καὶ ἐν ἐμαυτῷ μεμνημένος οἷός ἐστι,
καὶ Θεαίτητον κατὰ ταὐτά, ἄλλο τι ἐνίοτε μὲν ὁρῶ
αὐτούς, ἐνίοτε δὲ οὔ, καὶ ἅπτομαί ποτ' αὐτῶν,

---

¹ After καὶ the mss. read ὅ, expunged by Bonitz.
² τὸ μνημεῖον . . . ἔχων om. BT; add. B²T in marg.
³ ὃ μὴ οἶδε . . . μὴ αἰσθάνεται om. B.

with the perception is another thing which he knows and perceives and of which he has an imprint which accords with the perception. And he cannot think that what he knows and perceives and of which he has a correct memorial imprint is another thing which he knows; nor that a thing which he knows and perceives and of which he has such an imprint is another thing which he perceives; nor again that a thing which he neither knows nor perceives is another thing which he neither knows nor perceives; nor that a thing which he neither knows nor perceives is another thing which he does not know; nor that a thing which he neither knows nor perceives is another thing which he does not perceive. In all these cases it is impossible beyond everything for false opinion to arise in the mind of anyone. The possibility that it may arise remains, if anywhere, in the following cases.

THEAET. What cases are they? I hope they may help me to understand better; for now I cannot follow you.

soc. The cases in which he may think that things which he knows are some other things which he knows and perceives; or which he does not know, but perceives; or that things which he knows and perceives are other things which he knows and perceives.

THEAET. Now I am even more out of the running than before.

soc. Then let me repeat it in a different way. I know Theodorus and remember within myself what sort of a person he is, and just so I know Theaetetus, but sometimes I see them, and sometimes I do not,

τοτὲ δ' οὔ, καὶ ἀκούω ἤ τινα ἄλλην αἴσθησιν
αἰσθάνομαι, τοτὲ δ' αἴσθησιν μὲν οὐδεμίαν ἔχω
περὶ ὑμῶν, μέμνημαι δὲ ὑμᾶς οὐδὲν ἧττον καὶ
ἐπίσταμαι αὐτὸς ἐν ἐμαυτῷ;

E   ΘΕΑΙ. Πάνυ μὲν οὖν.

ΣΩ. Τοῦτο τοίνυν πρῶτον μάθε ὧν βούλομαι
δηλῶσαι, ὡς ἔστι μὲν ἃ οἶδε μὴ αἰσθάνεσθαι, ἔστι [1]
δὲ αἰσθάνεσθαι.

ΘΕΑΙ. Ἀληθῆ.

ΣΩ. Οὐκοῦν καὶ ἃ μὴ οἶδε, πολλάκις μὲν ἔστι
μηδὲ αἰσθάνεσθαι, πολλάκις δὲ αἰσθάνεσθαι μόνον;

ΘΕΑΙ. Ἔστι καὶ τοῦτο.

ΣΩ. Ἰδὲ δὴ ἐάν τι μᾶλλον νῦν ἐπίσπῃ. Σωκρά-
193 της εἰ γιγνώσκει [2] Θεόδωρον καὶ Θεαίτητον, ὁρᾷ
δὲ μηδέτερον, μηδὲ ἄλλη αἴσθησις αὐτῷ πάρεστι
περὶ αὐτῶν, οὐκ ἄν ποτε ἐν ἑαυτῷ δοξάσειεν ὡς
ὁ Θεαίτητός ἐστι Θεόδωρος. λέγω τὶ ἢ οὐδέν;

ΘΕΑΙ. Ναί, ἀληθῆ γε.

ΣΩ. Τοῦτο μὲν τοίνυν ἐκείνων πρῶτον ἦν ὧν
ἔλεγον.

ΘΕΑΙ. Ἦν γάρ.

ΣΩ. Δεύτερον τοίνυν, ὅτι τὸν μὲν γιγνώσκων
ὑμῶν, τὸν δὲ μὴ γιγνώσκων, αἰσθανόμενος δὲ
μηδέτερον, οὐκ ἄν ποτε αὖ οἰηθείην ὃν οἶδα εἶναι
ὃν μὴ οἶδα.

ΘΕΑΙ. Ὀρθῶς.

ΣΩ. Τρίτον δέ, μηδέτερον γιγνώσκων μηδὲ
B αἰσθανόμενος οὐκ ἄν οἰηθείην ὃν μὴ οἶδα ἕτερόν
τιν' εἶναι ὧν μὴ οἶδα. καὶ τἆλλα τὰ πρότερα
πάνθ' ἑξῆς νόμιζε πάλιν ἀκηκοέναι, ἐν οἷς οὐδέποτ'

---

[1] ἔστι . . . μηδὲ αἰσθάνεσθαι below om. B.
[2] εἰ γιγνώσκει W ; ἐπιγιγνώσκει BT.

sometimes I touch them, sometimes not, sometimes I hear them or perceive them through some other sense, and sometimes I have no perception of you at all, but I remember you none the less and know you in my own mind. Is it not so?

THEAET. Certainly.

soc. This, then, is the first of the points which I wish to make clear. Note that one may perceive or not perceive that which one knows.

THEAET. That is true.

soc. So, too, with that which he does not know—he may often not even perceive it, and often he may merely perceive it?

THEAET. That too is possible.

soc. See if you follow me better now. If Socrates knows Theodorus and Theaetetus, but sees neither of them and has no other perception of them, he never could have the opinion within himself that Theaetetus is Theodorus. Am I right or wrong?

THEAET. You are right.

soc. Now that was the first of the cases of which I spoke.

THEAET. Yes, it was.

soc. The second is this: knowing one of you and not knowing the other, and not perceiving either of you, I never could think that the one whom I know is the one whom I do not know.

THEAET. Right.

soc. And this is the third case: not knowing and not perceiving either of you, I could not think that he whom I do not know is someone else whom I do not know. And imagine that you have heard all the other cases again in succession, in which I

191

ἐγὼ περὶ σοῦ καὶ Θεοδώρου τὰ ψευδῆ δοξάσω,
οὔτε γιγνώσκων οὔτε ἀγνοῶν ἄμφω, οὔτε τὸν μέν,
τὸν δ᾽ οὐ γιγνώσκων· καὶ περὶ αἰσθήσεων κατὰ
ταὐτά, εἰ ἄρα ἔπει.

ΘΕΑΙ. Ἕπομαι.

ΣΩ. Λείπεται τοίνυν τὰ ψευδῆ δοξάσαι ἐν τῷδε,
ὅταν γιγνώσκων σὲ καὶ Θεόδωρον, καὶ ἔχων ἐν
C ἐκείνῳ τῷ κηρίνῳ ὥσπερ δακτυλίων σφῷν ἀμφοῖν
τὰ σημεῖα, διὰ μακροῦ καὶ μὴ ἱκανῶς ὁρῶν ἄμφω
προθυμηθῶ, τὸ οἰκεῖον ἑκατέρου σημεῖον ἀποδοὺς
τῇ οἰκείᾳ ὄψει, ἐμβιβάσας προσαρμόσαι εἰς τὸ
ἑαυτῆς ἴχνος, ἵνα γένηται ἀναγνώρισις, εἶτα τούτων ἀποτυχὼν καὶ ὥσπερ οἱ ἔμπαλιν ὑποδούμενοι
παραλλάξας προσβάλω τὴν ἑκατέρου ὄψιν πρὸς τὸ
ἀλλότριον σημεῖον, ἢ καὶ οἷα τὰ ἐν τοῖς κατόπτροις
τῆς ὄψεως πάθη, δεξιὰ εἰς ἀριστερὰ μεταρρεούσης,
D ταὐτὸν παθὼν διαμάρτω· τότε δὴ συμβαίνει
ἡ ἑτεροδοξία καὶ τὸ ψευδῆ δοξάζειν.

ΘΕΑΙ. Ἔοικε γάρ, ὦ Σώκρατες· θαυμασίως
ὡς λέγεις τὸ τῆς δόξης πάθος.

ΣΩ. Ἔτι τοίνυν καὶ ὅταν ἀμφοτέρους γιγνώσκων τὸν μὲν πρὸς τῷ γιγνώσκειν αἰσθάνωμαι,
τὸν δὲ μή, τὴν δὲ γνῶσιν τοῦ ἑτέρου μὴ κατὰ τὴν
αἴσθησιν ἔχω, ὃ ἐν τοῖς πρόσθεν οὕτως ἔλεγον καὶ
μου τότε οὐκ ἐμάνθανες.

could never form false opinions about you and
Theodorus, either when I know or do not know both
of you, or when I know one and not the other; and
the same is true if we say "perceive" instead of
"know." Do you follow me?

THEAET. I follow you.

soc. Then the possibility of forming false opinion
remains in the following case: when, for example,
knowing you and Theodorus, and having on that
block of wax the imprint of both of you, as if you
were signet-rings, but seeing you both at a distance
and indistinctly, I hasten to assign the proper imprint of each of you to the proper vision, and to
make it fit, as it were, its own footprint, with the
purpose of causing recognition;[1] but I may fail in
this by interchanging them, and put the vision of
one upon the imprint of the other, as people put a
shoe on the wrong foot; or, again, I may be affected
as the sight is affected when we use a mirror and the
sight as it flows makes a change from right to left,
and thus make a mistake; it is in such cases, then,
that interchanged opinion occurs and the forming of
false opinion arises.

THEAET. I think it does, Socrates. You describe
what happens to opinion marvellously well.

soc. There is still the further case, when, knowing
both of you, I perceive one in addition to knowing
him, but do not perceive the other, and the knowledge
which I have of that other is not in accord with my
perception. This is the case I described in this way
before, and at that time you did not understand me.

---

[1] Aeschylus, *Choeph.* 197 ff., makes Electra recognize the
presence of her brother Orestes by the likeness of his foot-
prints to her own.

ΘΕΑΙ. Οὐ γὰρ οὖν.

ΣΩ. Τοῦτο μὴν ἔλεγον, ὅτι γιγνώσκων τὸν
Ε ἕτερον καὶ αἰσθανόμενος, καὶ τὴν γνῶσιν κατὰ
τὴν αἴσθησιν αὐτοῦ ἔχων, οὐδέποτε οἰήσεται εἶναι
αὐτὸν ἕτερόν τινα ὃν γιγνώσκει τε καὶ αἰσθάνεται
καὶ τὴν γνῶσιν αὖ καὶ ἐκείνου ἔχει κατὰ τὴν
αἴσθησιν. ἦν γὰρ τοῦτο;

ΘΕΑΙ. Ναί.

ΣΩ. Παρελείπετο δέ γέ που τὸ νῦν λεγόμενον,
ἐν ᾧ δή φαμεν τὴν ψευδῆ δόξαν γίγνεσθαι τὸ ἄμφω
γιγνώσκοντα καὶ ἄμφω ὁρῶντα ἤ τινα ἄλλην
194 αἴσθησιν ἔχοντα ἀμφοῖν τὼ σημείω [1] μὴ κατὰ
τὴν αὑτοῦ αἴσθησιν ἑκάτερον ἔχειν, ἀλλ' οἷον
τοξότην φαῦλον ἱέντα παραλλάξαι τοῦ σκοποῦ
καὶ ἁμαρτεῖν, ὃ δὴ καὶ ψεῦδος ἄρα ὠνόμασται.

ΘΕΑΙ. Εἰκότως γε.

ΣΩ. Καὶ ὅταν τοίνυν τῷ μὲν παρῇ αἴσθησις τῶν
σημείων, τῷ δὲ μή, τὸ δὲ τῆς ἀπούσης αἰσθήσεως
τῇ παρούσῃ προσαρμόσῃ, πάντῃ ταύτῃ ψεύδεται
ἡ διάνοια. καὶ ἑνὶ λόγῳ, περὶ ὧν μὲν μὴ οἶδέ τις
Β μηδὲ ᾔσθετο [2] πώποτε, οὐκ ἔστιν, ὡς ἔοικεν,
οὔτε ψεύδεσθαι οὔτε ψευδὴς δόξα, εἴ τι νῦν ἡμεῖς
ὑγιὲς λέγομεν· περὶ δὲ ὧν ἴσμεν τε καὶ αἰσθανόμεθα, ἐν αὐτοῖς τούτοις στρέφεται καὶ ἑλίττεται
ἡ δόξα ψευδὴς καὶ ἀληθὴς γιγνομένη, καταντικρὺ
μὲν καὶ κατὰ τὸ εὐθὺ τὰ οἰκεῖα συνάγουσα ἀπο-
τυπώματα καὶ τύπους ἀληθής, εἰς πλάγια δὲ καὶ
σκολιὰ ψευδής.

ΘΕΑΙ. Οὐκοῦν καλῶς, ὦ Σώκρατες, λέγεται;

[1] τὼ σημείω al. Heusde ; τῷ σημείῳ TW² ; τὸ σημεῖον BW.
[2] μηδὲ ᾔσθετο TW ; μηδὲ ἐπείθετο ἐπῇσθετο B ; μηδ' ἐπῇσθετο
B².

THEAET. No, I did not.

soc. This is what I meant, that if anyone knows and perceives one of you, and has knowledge of him which accords with the perception, he will never think that he is someone else whom he knows and perceives and his knowledge of whom accords with the perception. That was the case, was it not ?

THEAET. Yes.

soc. But we omitted, I believe, the case of which I am speaking now—the case in which we say the false opinion arises : when a man knows both and sees both (or has some other perception of them), but fails to hold the two imprints each under its proper perception ; like a bad archer he shoots beside the mark and misses it; and it is just this which is called error or deception.

THEAET. And properly so.

soc. Now when perception is present to one of the imprints but not to the other, and the mind applies the imprint of the absent perception to the perception which is present, the mind is deceived in every such instance. In a word, if our present view is sound, false opinion or deception seems to be impossible in relation to things which one does not know and has never perceived ; but it is precisely in relation to things which we know and perceive that opinion turns and twists, becoming false and true— true when it puts the proper imprints and seals fairly and squarely upon one another, and false when it applies them sideways and aslant.

THEAET. Well, then, Socrates, is that view not a good one ?

Ο ΣΩ. Ἔτι τοίνυν καὶ τάδε ἀκούσας μᾶλλον αὐτὸ
ἐρεῖς. τὸ μὲν γὰρ τἀληθὲς δοξάζειν καλόν, τὸ δὲ
ψεύδεσθαι αἰσχρόν.

ΘΕΑΙ. Πῶς δ' οὔ;

ΣΩ. Ταῦτα τοίνυν φασὶν ἐνθένδε γίγνεσθαι.
ὅταν μὲν ὁ κηρός του ἐν τῇ ψυχῇ βαθύς τε καὶ
πολὺς καὶ λεῖος καὶ μετρίως ὠργασμένος¹ ᾖ, τὰ
ἰόντα διὰ τῶν αἰσθήσεων, ἐνσημαινόμενα εἰς τοῦτο
τὸ τῆς ψυχῆς κέαρ, ὃ ἔφη Ὅμηρος αἰνιττόμενος
τὴν τοῦ κηροῦ ὁμοιότητα, τότε μὲν καὶ τούτοις
Δ καθαρὰ τὰ σημεῖα ἐγγιγνόμενα καὶ ἱκανῶς τοῦ
βάθους ἔχοντα πολυχρόνιά τε γίγνεται καὶ εἰσὶν
οἱ τοιοῦτοι πρῶτον μὲν εὐμαθεῖς, ἔπειτα μνήμονες,
εἶτα οὐ παραλλάττουσι τῶν αἰσθήσεων τὰ σημεῖα
ἀλλὰ δοξάζουσιν ἀληθῆ. σαφῆ γὰρ καὶ ἐν εὐρυ-
χωρίᾳ ὄντα ταχὺ διανέμουσιν ἐπὶ τὰ αὑτῶν ἕκαστα
ἐκμαγεῖα, ἃ δὴ ὄντα καλεῖται, καὶ σοφοὶ δὴ οὗτοι
καλοῦνται. ἢ οὐ δοκεῖ σοι;

ΘΕΑΙ. Ὑπερφυῶς μὲν οὖν.

Ε ΣΩ. Ὅταν τοίνυν λάσιόν του τὸ² κέαρ ᾖ, ὃ δὴ
ἐπῄνεσεν ὁ πάντα σοφὸς ποιητής, ἢ ὅταν κοπρῶδες
καὶ μὴ καθαροῦ τοῦ κηροῦ, ἢ ὑγρὸν σφόδρα ἢ
σκληρόν, ὧν μὲν ὑγρόν, εὐμαθεῖς μέν, ἐπιλήσμονες
δὲ γίγνονται, ὧν δὲ σκληρόν, τἀναντία. οἱ δὲ δὴ
λάσιον καὶ τραχὺ λιθῶδές τι ἢ γῆς ἢ κόπρου συμ-

---

¹ ὠργασμένος Suidas, Timaeus ; εἰργασμένος ΒΤ.
² του τὸ] τοῦτο τὸ Β.

soc. After you have heard the rest, you will be still more inclined to say so. For to hold a true opinion is a good thing, but to be deceived is a disgrace.

THEAET. Certainly.

soc. They say the cause of these variations is as follows: When the wax in the soul of a man is deep and abundant and smooth and properly kneaded, the images that come through the perceptions are imprinted upon this heart of the soul—as Homer calls it in allusion to its similarity to wax [1]—; when this is the case, and in such men, the imprints, being clear and of sufficient depth, are also lasting. And men of this kind are in the first place quick to learn, and secondly they have retentive memories, and moreover they do not interchange the imprints of their perceptions, but they have true opinions. For the imprints are clear and have plenty of room, so that such men quickly assign them to their several moulds, which are called realities; and these men, then, are called wise. Or do you not agree?

THEAET. Most emphatically.

soc. Now when the heart of anyone is shaggy (a condition which the all-wise poet commends), or when it is unclean or of impure wax, or very soft or hard, those whose wax is soft are quick to learn, but forgetful, and those in whom it is hard are the reverse. But those in whom it is shaggy and rough and stony, infected with earth or dung which is mixed

---

[1] The similarity is in the Greek words κέαρ or κῆρ, *heart*, and κηρός, *wax*. The shaggy heart is mentioned in the *Iliad*, ii. 851; xvi. 554. The citation of Homer, here and below, is probably sarcastic—in reference to the practice of some of the sophists who used and perverted his words in support of their doctrines.

μιγείσης ἔμπλεων ἔχοντες ἀσαφῆ τὰ ἐκμαγεῖα
ἴσχουσιν. ἀσαφῆ δὲ καὶ οἱ τὰ σκληρά· βάθος
γὰρ οὐκ ἔνι. ἀσαφῆ δὲ καὶ οἱ τὰ ὑγρά· ὑπὸ γὰρ
195 τοῦ συγχεῖσθαι ταχὺ γίγνεται ἀμυδρά. ἐὰν δὲ
πρὸς πᾶσι τούτοις ἐπ' ἀλλήλων συμπεπτωκότα ᾖ
ὑπὸ στενοχωρίας, ἐάν του σμικρὸν ᾖ τὸ ψυχάριον,
ἔτι ἀσαφέστερα ἐκείνων. πάντες οὖν οὗτοι γίγνονται οἷοι δοξάζειν ψευδῆ. ὅταν γάρ τι ὁρῶσιν ἢ
ἀκούωσιν ἢ ἐπινοῶσιν, ἕκαστα¹ ἀπονέμειν ταχὺ
ἑκάστοις οὐ δυνάμενοι βραδεῖς τέ εἰσι καὶ ἀλλο-
τριονομοῦντες παρορῶσί τε καὶ παρακούουσι καὶ
παρανοοῦσι πλεῖστα, καὶ καλοῦνται αὖ οὗτοι
ἐψευσμένοι τε δὴ τῶν ὄντων καὶ ἀμαθεῖς.

Β ΘΕΑΙ. Ὀρθότατα ἀνθρώπων λέγεις, ὦ Σώκρατες.

ΣΩ. Φῶμεν ἄρα ἐν ἡμῖν ψευδεῖς δόξας εἶναι;

ΘΕΑΙ. Σφόδρα γε.

ΣΩ. Καὶ ἀληθεῖς δή;

ΘΕΑΙ. Καὶ ἀληθεῖς.

ΣΩ. Ἤδη οὖν οἰόμεθα ἱκανῶς ὡμολογῆσθαι ὅτι
παντὸς μᾶλλον ἐστὸν ἀμφότερα τούτω τὼ δόξα;

ΘΕΑΙ. Ὑπερφυῶς μὲν οὖν.

35. ΣΩ. Δεινόν τε, ὦ Θεαίτητε, ὡς ἀληθῶς
κινδυνεύει καὶ ἀηδὲς εἶναι ἀνὴρ ἀδολέσχης.

ΘΕΑΙ. Τί δέ; πρὸς τί τοῦτ' εἶπες;

C ΣΩ. Τὴν ἐμαυτοῦ δυσμαθίαν δυσχεράνας καὶ
ὡς ἀληθῶς ἀδολεσχίαν. τί γὰρ ἄν τις ἄλλο θεῖτο
ὄνομα, ὅταν ἄνω κάτω τοὺς λόγους ἕλκῃ τις ὑπὸ
νωθείας οὐ δυνάμενος πεισθῆναι, καὶ ᾖ δυσαπάλ-
λακτος ἀφ' ἑκάστου λόγου;

ΘΕΑΙ. Σὺ δὲ δὴ τί δυσχεραίνεις;

¹ ἕκαστα] ἕκαστοι BT.

in it, receive indistinct imprints from the moulds. So also do those whose wax is hard; for the imprints lack depth. And imprints in soft wax are also indistinct, because they melt together and quickly become blurred; but if besides all this they are crowded upon one another through lack of room, in some mean little soul, they are still more indistinct. So all these men are likely to have false opinions. For when they see or hear or think of anything, they cannot quickly assign things to the right imprints, but are slow about it, and because they assign them wrongly they usually see and hear and think amiss. These men, in turn, are accordingly said to be deceived about realities and ignorant.

THEAET. You are right as right could be, Socrates.

SOC. Shall we, then, say that false opinions exist in us?

THEAET. Assuredly.

SOC. And true opinions, no doubt?

THEAET. And true ones also.

SOC. Then now at last we think we have reached a valid agreement, that these two kinds of opinion incontestably exist?

THEAET. Most emphatically.

SOC. Truly, Theaetetus, a garrulous man is a strange and unpleasant creature!

THEAET. Eh? What makes you say that?

SOC. Vexation at my own stupidity and genuine garrulity. For what else could you call it when a man drags his arguments up and down because he is so stupid that he cannot be convinced, and is hardly to be induced to give up any one of them?

THEAET. But you, why are you vexed?

ΣΩ. Οὐ δυσχεραίνω μόνον, ἀλλὰ καὶ δέδοικα,
ὅ τι ἀποκρινοῦμαι, ἄν τις ἔρηταί με· " ὦ Σώκρατες, ηὕρηκας δὴ ψευδῆ δόξαν, ὅτι οὔτε ἐν ταῖς
αἰσθήσεσίν ἐστι πρὸς ἀλλήλας οὔτ᾽ ἐν ταῖς διανοίαις,
D ἀλλ᾽ ἐν τῇ συνάψει αἰσθήσεως πρὸς διάνοιαν ; "
φήσω δὲ ἐγώ, οἶμαι, καλλωπιζόμενος ὥς τι ηὑρηκό-
των ἡμῶν καλόν.

ΘΕΑΙ. Ἔμοιγε δοκεῖ, ὦ Σώκρατες, οὐκ αἰσχρὸν
εἶναι τὸ νῦν ἀποδεδειγμένον.

ΣΩ. " Οὐκοῦν," φήσει, " λέγεις ὅτι αὖ τὸν
ἄνθρωπον, ὃν διανοούμεθα μόνον, ὁρῶμεν δ᾽ οὔ,
ἵππον οὐκ ἄν ποτε οἰηθείημεν εἶναι, ὃν αὖ οὔτε
ὁρῶμεν οὔτε ἁπτόμεθα, διανοούμεθα δὲ μόνον καὶ
ἀλλ᾽ οὐδὲν αἰσθανόμεθα περὶ αὐτοῦ ; " ταῦτα,
οἶμαι, φήσω λέγειν.

ΘΕΑΙ. Καὶ ὀρθῶς γε.

E ΣΩ. " Τί οὖν," φήσει,[1] " τὰ ἕνδεκα, ἃ μηδὲν
ἄλλο ἢ διανοεῖταί τις, ἄλλο τι ἐκ τούτου τοῦ λόγου
οὐκ ἄν ποτε οἰηθείη δώδεκα εἶναι, ἃ μόνον αὖ
διανοεῖται ; " ἴθι οὖν δή, σὺ ἀποκρίνου.

ΘΕΑΙ. Ἀλλ᾽ ἀποκρινοῦμαι, ὅτι ὁρῶν μὲν ἄν τις
ἢ ἐφαπτόμενος οἰηθείη τὰ ἕνδεκα δώδεκα εἶναι, ἃ
μέντοι ἐν τῇ διανοίᾳ ἔχει, οὐκ ἄν ποτε περὶ αὐτῶν
ταῦτα δοξάσειεν οὕτως.

ΣΩ. Τί οὖν; οἴει τινὰ πώποτε αὐτὸν ἐν αὑτῷ
196 πέντε καὶ ἑπτά, λέγω δὲ μὴ ἀνθρώπους ἑπτὰ καὶ
πέντε προθέμενον σκοπεῖν μηδ᾽ ἄλλο τοιοῦτον,
ἀλλ᾽ αὐτὰ πέντε καὶ ἑπτά, ἅ φαμεν ἐκεῖ μνημεῖα
ἐν τῷ ἐκμαγείῳ εἶναι καὶ ψευδῆ ἐν αὐτοῖς οὐκ
εἶναι δοξάσαι, ταῦτα αὐτὰ εἴ τις ἀνθρώπων ἤδη

---

[1] φήσει Stephanus ; φής B ; φησί Burnet.

THEAETETUS

soc. I am not merely vexed, I am actually afraid; for I do not know what answer to make if anyone asks me: "Socrates, have you found out, I wonder, that false opinion exists neither in the relations of the perceptions to one another nor in the thoughts, but in the combination of perception with thought?" I shall say "yes," I suppose, and put on airs, as if we had made a fine discovery.

THEAET. It seems to me, Socrates, that the result we have now brought out is not half bad.

soc. "Do you go on and assert, then," he will say, "that we never could imagine that the man whom we merely think of, but do not see, is a horse which also we do not see or touch or perceive by any other sense, but merely think of?" I suppose I shall say that I do make that assertion.

THEAET. Yes, and you will be right.

soc. "Then," he will say, "according to that, could we ever imagine that the number eleven which is merely thought of, is the number twelve which also is merely thought of?" Come now, it is for you to answer.

THEAET. Well, my answer will be that a man might imagine the eleven that he sees or touches to be twelve, but that he could never have that opinion concerning the eleven that he has in his mind.

soc. Well, then, do you think that anyone ever considered in his own mind five and seven,—I do not mean by setting before his eyes seven men and five men and considering them, or anything of that sort, but seven and five in the abstract, which we say are imprints in the block of wax, and in regard to which we deny the possibility of forming false opinions—taking these by themselves, do you imagine

πώποτε ἐσκέψατο λέγων πρὸς αὑτὸν καὶ ἐρωτῶν
πόσα ποτ᾽ ἐστίν, καὶ ὁ μέν τις εἶπεν οἰηθεὶς ἕνδεκα
αὐτὰ εἶναι, ὁ δὲ δώδεκα, ἢ πάντες λέγουσί τε καὶ
οἴονται δώδεκα αὐτὰ εἶναι;

ΘΕΑΙ. Οὐ μὰ τὸν Δία, ἀλλὰ πολλοὶ δὴ καὶ ἕν-
B δεκα· ἐὰν δέ γε ἐν πλείονι ἀριθμῷ τις σκοπῆται,
μᾶλλον σφάλλεται. οἶμαι γάρ σε περὶ παντὸς
μᾶλλον [1] ἀριθμοῦ λέγειν.

ΣΩ. Ὀρθῶς γὰρ οἴει· καὶ ἐνθυμοῦ μή τι τότε [2]
γίγνεται ἄλλο ἢ αὐτὰ τὰ δώδεκα τὰ ἐν τῷ ἐκμαγείῳ
ἕνδεκα οἰηθῆναι.

ΘΕΑΙ. Ἔοικέ γε.

ΣΩ. Οὐκοῦν εἰς τοὺς πρώτους πάλιν ἀνήκει
λόγους; ὁ γὰρ τοῦτο παθών, ὃ οἶδεν, ἕτερον αὐτὸ
οἴεται εἶναι ὧν αὖ οἶδεν· ὃ ἔφαμεν ἀδύνατον, καὶ
C τούτῳ αὐτῷ ἠναγκάζομεν μὴ εἶναι ψευδῆ δόξαν,
ἵνα μὴ τὰ αὐτὰ ὁ αὐτὸς ἀναγκάζοιτο εἰδὼς μὴ
εἰδέναι ἅμα.

ΘΕΑΙ. Ἀληθέστατα.

ΣΩ. Οὐκοῦν ἄλλ᾽ ὁτιοῦν δεῖ ἀποφαίνειν τὸ τὰ
ψευδῆ δοξάζειν ἢ διανοίας πρὸς αἴσθησιν παραλλα-
γήν. εἰ γὰρ τοῦτ᾽ ἦν, οὐκ ἄν ποτε ἐν αὐτοῖς
τοῖς διανοήμασιν ἐψευδόμεθα. νῦν δὲ ἤτοι οὐκ
ἔστι ψευδὴς δόξα, ἢ ἅ τις οἶδεν, οἷόν τε μὴ εἰδέναι.
καὶ τούτων πότερα [3] αἱρεῖ;

ΘΕΑΙ. Ἄπορον αἵρεσιν προτίθης, ὦ Σώκρατες.

D ΣΩ. Ἀλλὰ μέντοι ἀμφότερά γε κινδυνεύει ὁ
λόγος οὐκ ἐάσειν. ὅμως δέ, πάντα γὰρ τολμητέον,
τί εἰ ἐπιχειρήσαιμεν ἀναισχυντεῖν;

ΘΕΑΙ. Πῶς;

[1] μᾶλλον om. W.   [2] τότε W; ποτε BT.
[3] πότερα W; ποτέραν BT.

that anybody in the world has ever considered them, talking to himself and asking himself what their sum is, and that one person has said and thought eleven, and another twelve, or do all say and think that it is twelve?

THEAET. No, by Zeus; many say eleven, and if you take a larger number for consideration, there is greater likelihood of error. For I suppose you are speaking of any number rather than of these only.

SOC. You are right in supposing so; and consider whether in that instance the abstract twelve in the block of wax is not itself imagined to be eleven.

THEAET. It seems so.

SOC. Have we not, then, come back again to the beginning of our talk? For the man who is affected in this way imagines that one thing which he knows is another thing which he knows. This we said was impossible, and by this very argument we were forcing false opinion out of existence, that the same man might not be forced to know and not know the same things at the same time.

THEAET. Very true.

SOC. Then we must show that forming false opinion is something or other different from the interchange of thought and perception. For if it were that, we should never be deceived in abstract thoughts. But as the case now stands, either there is no false opinion or it is possible for a man not to know that which he knows. Which alternative will you choose?

THEAET. There is no possible choice, Socrates.

SOC. And yet the argument is not likely to admit both. But still, since we must not shrink from any risk, what if we should try to do a shameless deed?

THEAET. What is it?

ΣΩ. Ἐθελήσαντες εἰπεῖν ποῖόν τί ποτ' ἐστὶ τὸ
ἐπίστασθαι.

ΘΕΑΙ. Καὶ τί τοῦτο ἀναίσχυντον;

ΣΩ. Ἔοικας οὐκ ἐννοεῖν ὅτι πᾶς ἡμῖν ἐξ ἀρχῆς
ὁ λόγος ζήτησις γέγονεν ἐπιστήμης, ὡς οὐκ εἰδόσι
τί ποτ' ἐστίν.

ΘΕΑΙ. Ἐννοῶ μὲν οὖν.

ΣΩ. Ἔπειτ' οὐκ ἀναιδὲς δοκεῖ, μὴ εἰδότας ἐπιστήμην ἀποφαίνεσθαι τὸ ἐπίστασθαι οἷόν ἐστιν;
Ε ἀλλὰ γάρ, ὦ Θεαίτητε, πάλαι ἐσμὲν ἀνάπλεω
τοῦ μὴ καθαρῶς διαλέγεσθαι. μυριάκις γὰρ εἰρήκαμεν τὸ " γιγνώσκομεν " καὶ " οὐ γιγνώσκομεν,"
καὶ " ἐπιστάμεθα " καὶ " οὐκ ἐπιστάμεθα," ὡς
τι συνιέντες ἀλλήλων ἐν ᾧ ἔτι ἐπιστήμην ἀγνοοῦμεν·
εἰ δὲ βούλει, καὶ νῦν ἐν τῷ παρόντι κεχρήμεθ'
αὖ τῷ " ἀγνοεῖν " τε καὶ " συνιέναι," ὡς προσῆκον
αὐτοῖς χρῆσθαι, εἴπερ στερόμεθα ἐπιστήμης.

ΘΕΑΙ. Ἀλλὰ τίνα τρόπον διαλέξει, ὦ Σώκρατες,
τούτων ἀπεχόμενος;

197 ΣΩ. Οὐδένα ὤν γε ὃς εἰμί· εἰ μέντοι ἦν ἀντι-
λογικός, οἷος ἀνὴρ εἰ καὶ νῦν παρῆν, τούτων τ' ἂν
ἔφη ἀπέχεσθαι καὶ ἡμῖν σφόδρ' ἂν ἃ ἐγὼ λέγω
ἐπέπληττεν. ἐπειδὴ οὖν ἐσμεν φαῦλοι, βούλει
τολμήσω εἰπεῖν οἷόν ἐστι τὸ ἐπίστασθαι; φαίνεται
γάρ μοι προὔργου τι ἂν γενέσθαι.

ΘΕΑΙ. Τόλμα τοίνυν νὴ Δία. τούτων δὲ μὴ
ἀπεχομένῳ σοι ἔσται πολλὴ συγγνώμη.

36. ΣΩ. Ἀκήκοας οὖν ὃ νῦν λέγουσιν τὸ
ἐπίστασθαι;

ΘΕΑΙ. Ἴσως· οὐ μέντοι ἔν γε τῷ παρόντι μνημονεύω.

Β ΣΩ. Ἐπιστήμης που ἕξιν φασὶν αὐτὸ εἶναι.

THEAETETUS

soc. To undertake to tell what it really is to know.

THEAET. And why is that shameless?

soc. You seem not to remember that our whole talk from the beginning has been a search for knowledge, because we did not know what it is.

THEAET. Oh yes, I remember.

soc. Then is it not shameless to proclaim what it is to know, when we are ignorant of knowledge? But really, Theaetetus, our talk has been badly tainted with unclearness all along; for we have said over and over again " we know" and "we do not know" and "we have knowledge" and "we have no knowledge," as if we could understand each other, while we were still ignorant of knowledge; and at this very moment, if you please, we have again used the terms "be ignorant" and "understand," as though we had any right to use them if we are deprived of knowledge.

THEAET. But how will you converse, Socrates, if you refrain from these words?

soc. Not at all, being the man I am; but I might if I were a real reasoner; if such a man were present at this moment he would tell us to refrain from these terms, and would criticize my talk scathingly. But since we are poor creatures, shall I venture to say what the nature of knowing is? For it seems to me that would be of some advantage.

THEAET. Venture it then, by Zeus. You shall have full pardon for not refraining from those terms.

soc. Have you heard what they say nowadays that knowing is?

THEAET. Perhaps; however, I don't remember just at this moment.

soc. They say it is having knowledge.

ΘΕΑΙ. Ἀληθῆ.

ΣΩ. Ἡμεῖς τοίνυν σμικρὸν μεταθώμεθα καὶ εἴπωμεν ἐπιστήμης κτῆσιν.

ΘΕΑΙ. Τί οὖν δὴ φήσεις τοῦτο ἐκείνου διαφέρειν;

ΣΩ. Ἴσως μὲν οὐδέν· ὃ δ' οὖν δοκεῖ, ἀκούσας συνδοκίμαζε.

ΘΕΑΙ. Ἐάνπερ γε οἷός τ' ὦ.

ΣΩ. Οὐ τοίνυν μοι ταὐτὸν φαίνεται τῷ κεκτῆσθαι τὸ ἔχειν. οἷον εἰ¹ ἱμάτιον πριάμενός τις καὶ ἐγκρατὴς ὢν μὴ φοροῖ,² ἔχειν μὲν οὐκ ἂν αὐτὸν αὐτό, κεκτῆσθαί γε μὴν³ φαῖμεν.

ΘΕΑΙ. Ὀρθῶς γε.

C ΣΩ. Ὅρα δὴ καὶ ἐπιστήμην εἰ δυνατὸν οὕτω κεκτημένον μὴ ἔχειν, ἀλλ' ὥσπερ εἴ τις ὄρνιθας ἀγρίας, περιστερὰς ἤ τι ἄλλο, θηρεύσας οἴκοι κατασκευασάμενος περιστερεῶνα τρέφοι. τρόπον μὲν γὰρ ἄν πού τινα φαῖμεν αὐτὸν αὐτὰς ἀεὶ ἔχειν, ὅτι δὴ κέκτηται. ἦ γάρ;

ΘΕΑΙ. Ναί.

ΣΩ. Τρόπον δέ γ' ἄλλον οὐδεμίαν ἔχειν, ἀλλὰ δύναμιν μὲν αὐτῷ περὶ αὐτὰς παραγεγονέναι, ἐπειδὴ ἐν οἰκείῳ περιβόλῳ ὑποχειρίους ἐποιή-D σατο, λαβεῖν καὶ σχεῖν, ἐπειδὰν βούληται, θηρευσαμένῳ ἣν ἂν ἀεὶ ἐθέλῃ, καὶ πάλιν ἀφιέναι· καὶ τοῦτο ἐξεῖναι ποιεῖν, ὁποσάκις ἂν δοκῇ αὐτῷ.

ΘΕΑΙ. Ἔστι ταῦτα.

ΣΩ. Πάλιν δή, ὥσπερ ἐν τοῖς πρόσθεν κήρινόν τι ἐν ταῖς ψυχαῖς κατεσκευάζομεν οὐκ οἶδ' ὅ τι πλάσμα, νῦν αὖ ἐν ἑκάστῃ ψυχῇ ποιήσωμεν

---

¹ εἰ vulg. ex emend. apogr. P ; om. BTW.
² φοροῖ vulg.; φορῶν b ; φορῶ B ; φορῷ TW.
³ γε μὴν W ; γε δὴ B ; γε T ; δέ γε vulg.

THEAET. True.

SOC. Let us make a slight change and say possessing knowledge.

THEAET. Why, how will you claim that the one differs from the other?

SOC. Perhaps it doesn't; but first hear how it seems to me to differ, and then help me to test my view.

THEAET. I will if I can.

SOC. Well, then, having does not seem to me the same as possessing. For instance, if a man bought a cloak and had it under his control, but did not wear it, we should certainly say, not that he had it, but that he possessed it.

THEAET. And rightly.

SOC. Now see whether it is possible in the same way for one who possesses knowledge not to have it, as, for instance, if a man should catch wild birds —pigeons or the like—and should arrange an aviary at home and keep them in it, we might in a way assert that he always has them because he possesses them, might we not?

THEAET. Yes.

SOC. And yet in another way that he has none of them, but that he has acquired power over them, since he has brought them under his control in his own enclosure, to take them and hold them whenever he likes, by catching whichever bird he pleases, and to let them go again; and he can do this as often as he sees fit.

THEAET. That is true.

SOC. Once more, then, just as a while ago we contrived some sort of a waxen figment in the soul, so now let us make in each soul an aviary stocked

περιστερεῶνά τινα παντοδαπῶν ὀρνίθων, τὰς μὲν
κατ᾽ ἀγέλας οὔσας χωρὶς τῶν ἄλλων, τὰς δὲ κατ᾽
ὀλίγας, ἐνίας δὲ μόνας διὰ πασῶν ὅπη ἂν τύχωσι
πετομένας.

E   ΘΕΑΙ. Πεποιήσθω δή. ἀλλὰ τί τοὐντεῦθεν;

ΣΩ. Παιδίων μὲν ὄντων φάναι χρὴ εἶναι τοῦτο
τὸ ἀγγεῖον κενόν, ἀντὶ δὲ τῶν ὀρνίθων ἐπιστήμας
νοῆσαι· ἣν δ᾽ ἂν ἐπιστήμην κτησάμενος καθείρξῃ
εἰς τὸν περίβολον, φάναι αὐτὸν μεμαθηκέναι ἢ
ηὑρηκέναι τὸ πρᾶγμα οὗ ἦν αὕτη ἡ ἐπιστήμη, καὶ
τὸ ἐπίστασθαι τοῦτ᾽ εἶναι.

ΘΕΑΙ. Ἔστω.

198   ΣΩ. Τὸ τοίνυν πάλιν ἣν ἂν βούληται τῶν ἐπιστημῶν θηρεύειν καὶ λαβόντα ἴσχειν καὶ αὖθις
ἀφιέναι, σκόπει τίνων δεῖται ὀνομάτων, εἴτε τῶν
αὐτῶν ὧν τὸ πρῶτον ὅτε ἐκτᾶτο εἴτε ἑτέρων.
μαθήσει δ᾽ ἐνθένδε [1] σαφέστερον τί λέγω. ἀριθμη-
τικὴν μὲν γὰρ λέγεις τέχνην;

ΘΕΑΙ. Ναί.

ΣΩ. Ταύτην δὴ ὑπόλαβε θήραν ἐπιστημῶν ἀρ-
τίου τε καὶ περιττοῦ παντός.

ΘΕΑΙ. Ὑπολαμβάνω.

ΣΩ. Ταύτῃ δή, οἶμαι, τῇ τέχνῃ αὐτός τε ὑπο-
B χειρίους τὰς ἐπιστήμας τῶν ἀριθμῶν ἔχει καὶ
ἄλλῳ παραδίδωσιν ὁ παραδιδούς.

ΘΕΑΙ. Ναί.

ΣΩ. Καὶ καλοῦμέν γε παραδιδόντα μὲν διδάσκειν, παραλαμβάνοντα δὲ μανθάνειν, ἔχοντα δὲ
δὴ τῷ κεκτῆσθαι ἐν τῷ περιστερεῶνι ἐκείνῳ
ἐπίστασθαι.

---

[1] ἐνθένδε] ἐντεῦθεν B.

with all sorts of birds, some in flocks apart from the rest, others in small groups, and some solitary, flying hither and thither among them all.

THEAET. Consider it done. What next?

soc. We must assume that while we are children this receptacle is empty, and we must understand that the birds represent the varieties of knowledge. And whatsoever kind of knowledge a person acquires and shuts up in the enclosure, we must say that he has learned or discovered the thing of which this is the knowledge, and that just this is knowing.

THEAET. So be it.

soc. Consider then what expressions are needed for the process of recapturing and taking and holding and letting go again whichever he please of the kinds of knowledge, whether they are the same expressions as those needed for the original acquisition, or others. But you will understand better by an illustration. You admit that there is an art of arithmetic?

THEAET. Yes.

soc. Now suppose this to be a hunt after the kinds of knowledge, or sciences, of all odd and even numbers.

THEAET. I do so.

soc. Now it is by this art, I imagine, that a man has the sciences of numbers under his own control and also that any man who transmits them to another does this.

THEAET. Yes.

soc. And we say that when anyone transmits them he teaches, and when anyone receives them he learns, and when anyone, by having acquired them, has them in that aviary of ours, he knows them.

ΘΕΑΙ. Πάνυ μὲν οὖν.

ΣΩ. Τῷ δὲ δὴ ἐντεῦθεν ἤδη πρόσσχες τὸν νοῦν. ἀριθμητικὸς γὰρ ὢν τελέως ἄλλο τι πάντας ἀριθμοὺς ἐπίσταται; πάντων γὰρ ἀριθμῶν εἰσιν αὐτῷ ἐν τῇ ψυχῇ ἐπιστῆμαι.

ΘΕΑΙ. Τί μήν;

C ΣΩ. Ἦ οὖν ὁ τοιοῦτος ἀριθμοῖ ἄν ποτέ τι ἢ αὐτὸς πρὸς αὑτὸν αὐτὰ ἢ ἄλλο τι τῶν ἔξω ὅσα ἔχει ἀριθμόν;

ΘΕΑΙ. Πῶς γὰρ οὔ;

ΣΩ. Τὸ δὲ ἀριθμεῖν γε οὐκ ἄλλο τι θήσομεν τοῦ σκοπεῖσθαι πόσος τις ἀριθμὸς τυγχάνει ὤν.

ΘΕΑΙ. Οὕτως.

ΣΩ. Ὃ ἄρα ἐπίσταται, σκοπούμενος φαίνεται ὡς οὐκ εἰδώς, ὃν ὡμολογήκαμεν ἅπαντα ἀριθμὸν εἰδέναι. ἀκούεις γάρ που τὰς τοιαύτας ἀμφισβητήσεις.

ΘΕΑΙ. Ἔγωγε.

37. ΣΩ. Οὐκοῦν ἡμεῖς ἀπεικάζοντες τῇ τῶν
D περιστερῶν κτήσει τε καὶ θήρᾳ ἐροῦμεν ὅτι διττὴ ἦν ἡ θήρα, ἡ μὲν πρὶν ἐκτῆσθαι τοῦ κεκτῆσθαι ἕνεκα· ἡ δὲ κεκτημένῳ τοῦ λαβεῖν καὶ ἔχειν ἐν ταῖς χερσὶν ἃ πάλαι ἐκέκτητο. οὕτως δὲ καὶ ὧν πάλαι ἐπιστῆμαι ἦσαν αὐτῷ μαθόντι καὶ [1] ἠπίστατο αὐτά, πάλιν ἔστι καταμανθάνειν ταὐτὰ ταῦτα ἀναλαμβάνοντα τὴν ἐπιστήμην ἑκάστου καὶ ἴσχοντα, ἣν ἐκέκτητο μὲν πάλαι, πρόχειρον δ' οὐκ εἶχε τῇ διανοίᾳ;

ΘΕΑΙ. Ἀληθῆ.

E ΣΩ. Τοῦτο δὴ ἄρτι ἠρώτων, ὅπως χρὴ τοῖς

[1] μαθόντι καὶ W ; μαθόντι ΒΤ.

THEAET. Certainly.

soc. Now pay attention to what follows from this. Does not the perfect arithmetician understand all numbers; for he has the sciences of all numbers in his mind?

THEAET. To be sure.

soc. Then would such a man ever count anything —either any abstract numbers in his head, or any such external objects as possess number?

THEAET. Of course.

soc. But we shall affirm that counting is the same thing as considering how great any number in question is.

THEAET. We shall.

soc. Then he who by our previous admission knows all number is found to be considering that which he knows as if he did not know it. You have doubtless heard of such ambiguities.

THEAET. Yes, I have.

soc. Continuing, then, our comparison with the acquisition and hunting of the pigeons, we shall say that the hunting is of two kinds, one before the acquisition for the sake of possessing, the other carried on by the possessor for the sake of taking and holding in his hands what he had acquired long before. And just so when a man long since by learning came to possess knowledge of certain things, and knew them, he may have these very things afresh by taking up again the knowledge of each of them separately and holding it—the knowlege which he had acquired long before, but had not at hand in his mind?

THEAET. That is true.

soc. This, then, was my question just now: How

ὀνόμασι χρώμενον λέγειν περὶ αὐτῶν, ὅταν ἀριθμή-
σων ἴῃ ὁ ἀριθμητικὸς ἢ τι ἀναγνωσόμενος ὁ γραμμα-
τικός, ὡς ἐπιστάμενος ἄρα ἐν τῷ τοιούτῳ πάλιν
ἔρχεται μαθησόμενος παρ' ἑαυτοῦ ἃ ἐπίσταται;

ΘΕΑΙ. Ἀλλ' ἄτοπον, ὦ Σώκρατες.

ΣΩ. Ἀλλ' ἃ οὐκ ἐπίσταται φῶμεν αὐτὸν ἀνα-
γνώσεσθαι καὶ ἀριθμήσειν, δεδωκότες αὐτῷ πάντα
μὲν γράμματα, πάντα δὲ ἀριθμὸν ἐπίστασθαι;

199 ΘΕΑΙ. Ἀλλὰ καὶ τοῦτ' ἄλογον.

ΣΩ. Βούλει οὖν λέγωμεν ὅτι τῶν μὲν ὀνομάτων
οὐδὲν ἡμῖν μέλει, ὅπῃ τις χαίρει ἕλκων τὸ ἐπίστασθαι καὶ μανθάνειν, ἐπειδὴ δὲ ὡρισάμεθα ἕτερον
μέν τι τὸ κεκτῆσθαι τὴν ἐπιστήμην, ἕτερον δὲ τὸ
ἔχειν, ὃ μέν τις ἔκτηται μὴ κεκτῆσθαι ἀδύνατόν
φαμεν εἶναι, ὥστε οὐδέποτε συμβαίνει ὅ τις οἶδεν
μὴ εἰδέναι, ψευδῆ μέντοι δόξαν οἷόν τ' εἶναι περὶ
B αὐτοῦ λαβεῖν; μὴ γὰρ ἔχειν τὴν ἐπιστήμην τούτου
οἷόν τε, ἀλλ' ἑτέραν ἀντ' ἐκείνης, ὅταν θηρεύων
τινὰ πού ποτ' [1] ἐπιστήμην διαπετομένων ἀνθ'
ἑτέρας ἑτέραν ἁμαρτὼν λάβῃ, τότε [2] ἄρα τὰ ἕνδεκα
δώδεκα ᾠήθη εἶναι, τὴν τῶν ἕνδεκα ἐπιστήμην
ἀντὶ τῆς τῶν δώδεκα λαβὼν τὴν ἐν ἑαυτῷ οἷον
φάτταν ἀντὶ περιστερᾶς.

ΘΕΑΙ. Ἔχει γὰρ οὖν λόγον.

ΣΩ. Ὅταν δέ γε ἣν ἐπιχειρεῖ λαβεῖν λάβῃ,
ἀψευδεῖν τε καὶ τὰ ὄντα δοξάζειν τότε, καὶ οὕτω
δὴ εἶναι ἀληθῆ τε καὶ ψευδῆ δόξαν, καὶ ὧν ἐν τοῖς
C πρόσθεν ἐδυσχεραίνομεν οὐδὲν ἐμποδὼν γίγνεσθαι; ἴσως οὖν μοι συμφήσεις· ἢ πῶς ποιήσεις;

---

[1] πού ποτ' W ; ἀπ' αὐτοῦ BT.
[2] τότε W ; ὅτε BT.

should we express ourselves in speaking about them
when an arithmetician undertakes to count or a man
of letters to read something? In such a case shall
we say that although he knows he sets himself to
learn again from himself that which he knows?

THEAET. But that is extraordinary, Socrates.

soc. But shall we say that he is going to read or
count that which he does not know, when we have
granted that he knows all letters and all numbers?

THEAET. But that too is absurd.

soc. Shall we then say that words are nothing to
us, if it amuses anyone to drag the expressions
"know" and "learn" one way and another, but
since we set up the distinction that it is one thing
to possess knowledge and another thing to have it,
we affirm that it is impossible not to possess what
one possesses, so that it never happens that a man
does not know that which he knows, but that it is
possible to conceive a false opinion about it? For
it is possible to have not the knowledge of this thing,
but some other knowledge instead, when in hunting
for some one kind of knowledge, as the various
kinds fly about, he makes a mistake and catches one
instead of another; so in one example he thought
eleven was twelve, because he caught the knowledge
of twelve, which was within him, instead of that of
eleven, caught a ringdove, as it were, instead of a
pigeon.

THEAET. Yes, that is reasonable.

soc. But when he catches the knowledge he
intends to catch, he is not deceived and has true
opinion, and so true and false opinion exist and none
of the things which formerly annoyed us interferes?
Perhaps you will agree to this; or what will you do?

PLATO

ΘΕΑΙ. Οὕτως.

ΣΩ. Καὶ γὰρ τοῦ μὲν ἃ ἐπίστανται μὴ ἐπίστασθαι ἀπηλλάγμεθα· ἃ γὰρ κεκτήμεθα μὴ
κεκτῆσθαι οὐδαμοῦ ἔτι συμβαίνει, οὔτε ψευσθεῖσί
τινος οὔτε μή. δεινότερον μέντοι πάθος ἄλλο
παραφαίνεσθαί μοι δοκεῖ.

ΘΕΑΙ. Τὸ ποῖον;

ΣΩ. Εἰ ἡ τῶν ἐπιστημῶν μεταλλαγὴ ψευδὴς
γενήσεταί ποτε δόξα.

ΘΕΑΙ. Πῶς δή;

D ΣΩ. Πρῶτον μὲν τό τινος ἔχοντα ἐπιστήμην
τοῦτο αὐτὸ ἀγνοεῖν, μὴ ἀγνωμοσύνῃ ἀλλὰ τῇ
ἑαυτοῦ ἐπιστήμῃ· ἔπειτα ἕτερον αὖ τοῦτο δοξάζειν, τὸ δ' ἕτερον τοῦτο, πῶς οὐ πολλὴ ἀλογία,
ἐπιστήμης παραγενομένης γνῶναι μὲν τὴν ψυχὴν
μηδέν, ἀγνοῆσαι δὲ πάντα; ἐκ γὰρ τούτου τοῦ
λόγου κωλύει οὐδὲν καὶ ἄγνοιαν παραγενομένην
γνῶναί τι ποιῆσαι καὶ τυφλότητα ἰδεῖν, εἴπερ
καὶ ἐπιστήμη ἀγνοῆσαί ποτέ τινα ποιήσει.

E ΘΕΑΙ. Ἴσως γάρ, ὦ Σώκρατες, οὐ καλῶς τὰς
ὄρνιθας ἐτίθεμεν ἐπιστήμας μόνον τιθέντες, ἔδει
δὲ καὶ ἀνεπιστημοσύνας τιθέναι ὁμοῦ συνδιαπε-
τομένας ἐν τῇ ψυχῇ, καὶ τὸν θηρεύοντα τοτὲ μὲν
ἐπιστήμην λαμβάνοντα, τοτὲ δ' ἀνεπιστημοσύνην
τοῦ αὐτοῦ πέρι ψευδῆ μὲν δοξάζειν τῇ ἀνεπιστημο-
σύνῃ, ἀληθῆ δὲ τῇ ἐπιστήμῃ.

ΣΩ. Οὐ ῥᾴδιόν γε, ὦ Θεαίτητε, μὴ ἐπαινεῖν σε·
ὃ μέντοι εἶπες πάλιν ἐπίσκεψαι. ἔστω μὲν γὰρ

THEAET. I will agree.

soc. Yes, for we have got rid of our difficulty about men not knowing that which they know; for we no longer find ourselves not possessing that which we possess, whether we are deceived about anything or not. However, another more dreadful disaster seems to be coming in sight.

THEAET. What disaster?

soc. If the interchange of kinds of knowledge should ever turn out to be false opinion.

THEAET. How so?

soc. Is it not the height of absurdity, in the first place for one who has knowledge of something to be ignorant of this very thing, not through ignorance but through his knowledge; secondly, for him to be of opinion that this thing is something else and something else is this thing — for the soul, when knowledge has come to it, to know nothing and be ignorant of all things? For by this argument there is nothing to prevent ignorance from coming to us and making us know something and blindness from making us see, if knowledge is ever to make us ignorant.

THEAET. Perhaps, Socrates, we were not right in making the birds represent kinds of knowledge only, but we ought to have imagined kinds of ignorance also flying about in the soul with the others; then the hunter would catch sometimes knowledge and sometimes ignorance of the same thing, and through the ignorance he would have false, but through the knowledge true opinion.

soc. It is not easy, Theaetetus, to refrain from praising you. However, examine your suggestion once more. Let it be as you say: the man who

215

200 ὡς λέγεις· ὁ δὲ δὴ τὴν ἀνεπιστημοσύνην λαβὼν
ψευδῆ μέν, φῄς, δοξάσει. ἢ γάρ;

ΘΕΑΙ. Ναί.

ΣΩ. Οὐ δήπου καὶ ἡγήσεταί γε ψευδῆ δοξάζειν.

ΘΕΑΙ. Πῶς γάρ;

ΣΩ. Ἀλλ' ἀληθῆ γε, καὶ ὡς εἰδὼς διακείσεται
περὶ ὧν ἔψευσται.

ΘΕΑΙ. Τί μήν;

ΣΩ. Ἐπιστήμην ἄρα οἰήσεται τεθηρευκὼς ἔχειν,
ἀλλ' οὐκ ἀνεπιστημοσύνην.

ΘΕΑΙ. Δῆλον.

ΣΩ. Οὐκοῦν μακρὰν περιελθόντες πάλιν ἐπὶ
τὴν πρώτην πάρεσμεν ἀπορίαν. ὁ γὰρ ἐλεγκτικὸς
B ἐκεῖνος γελάσας φήσει· ''πότερον, ὦ βέλτιστοι,
ἀμφοτέρας τις εἰδώς, ἐπιστήμην τε καὶ ἀνεπιστημοσύνην, ἣν οἶδεν, ἑτέραν αὐτὴν οἴεταί τινα εἶναι
ὧν οἶδεν; ἢ οὐδετέραν αὐτοῖν [1] εἰδώς, ἣν μὴ οἶδε,
δοξάζει ἑτέραν ὧν οὐκ οἶδεν; ἢ τὴν μὲν εἰδώς,
τὴν δ' οὔ, ἣν οἶδεν, ἣν μὴ οἶδεν; ἢ ἣν μὴ οἶδεν,
ἣν οἶδεν ἡγεῖται; ἢ πάλιν αὖ μοι ἐρεῖτε ὅτι τῶν
ἐπιστημῶν καὶ ἀνεπιστημοσυνῶν εἰσὶν αὖ ἐπιστῆμαι,
ἃς ὁ κεκτημένος ἐν ἑτέροις τισὶ γελοίοις περιστε-
C ρεῶσιν ἢ κηρίνοις πλάσμασι καθείρξας, ἕωσπερ
ἂν κεκτῆται ἐπίσταται, καὶ ἐὰν μὴ προχείρους
ἔχῃ ἐν τῇ ψυχῇ; καὶ οὕτω δὴ ἀναγκασθή-
σεσθε εἰς ταὐτὸν περιτρέχειν μυριάκις οὐδὲν πλέον
ποιοῦντες;'' τί πρὸς ταῦτα, ὦ Θεαίτητε, ἀποκρινούμεθα;

---

[1] αὐτοῖν] αὐτὴν BT ; om. W

catches the ignorance will, you say, have false opinion. Is that it?

THEAET. Yes.

soc. But surely he will not also think that he has false opinion.

THEAET. Certainly not.

soc. No, but true opinion, and will have the attitude of knowing that about which he is deceived.

THEAET. Of course.

soc. Hence he will fancy that he has caught, and has, knowledge, not ignorance.

THEAET. Evidently.

soc. Then, after our long wanderings, we have come round again to our first difficulty. For the real reasoner will laugh and say, "Most excellent Sirs, does a man who knows both knowledge and ignorance think that one of them, which he knows, is another thing which he knows; or, knowing neither of them, is he of opinion that one, which he does not know, is another thing which he does not know; or, knowing one and not the other, does he think that the one he does not know is the one he knows; or that the one he knows is the one he does not know? Or will you go on and tell me that there are kinds of knowledge of the kinds of knowledge and of ignorance, and that he who possesses these kinds of knowledge and has enclosed them in some sort of other ridiculous aviaries or waxen figments, knows them, so long as he possesses them, even if he has them not at hand in his soul? And in this fashion are you going to be compelled to trot about endlessly in the same circle without making any progress?" What shall we reply to this, Theaetetus?

ΘΕΑΙ. Ἀλλὰ μὰ Δί᾽, ὦ Σώκρατες, ἔγωγε οὐκ ἔχω τί χρὴ λέγειν.

ΣΩ. Ἆρ᾽ οὖν ἡμῖν, ὦ παῖ, καλῶς ὁ λόγος ἐπιπλήττει, καὶ ἐνδείκνυται ὅτι οὐκ ὀρθῶς ψευδῆ δόξαν προτέραν ζητοῦμεν ἐπιστήμης, ἐκείνην ἀφ-
D έντες; τὸ δ᾽ ἐστὶν ἀδύνατον γνῶναι, πρὶν ἄν τις ἐπιστήμην ἱκανῶς λάβῃ τί ποτ᾽ ἐστίν.

ΘΕΑΙ. Ἀνάγκη, ὦ Σώκρατες, ἐν τῷ παρόντι ὡς λέγεις οἴεσθαι.

38. ΣΩ. Τί οὖν τις ἐρεῖ πάλιν ἐξ ἀρχῆς ἐπιστήμην; οὐ γάρ που ἀπεροῦμέν γέ πω;

ΘΕΑΙ. Ἥκιστα, ἐάνπερ μὴ σύ γε ἀπαγορεύῃς.

ΣΩ. Λέγε δή, τί ἂν αὐτὸ μάλιστα εἰπόντες ἥκιστ᾽ ἂν ἡμῖν αὐτοῖς ἐναντιωθεῖμεν;

E ΘΕΑΙ. Ὅπερ ἐπεχειροῦμεν, ὦ Σώκρατες, ἐν τῷ πρόσθεν· οὐ γὰρ ἔχω ἔγωγε ἄλλο οὐδέν.

ΣΩ. Τὸ ποῖον;

ΘΕΑΙ. Τὴν ἀληθῆ δόξαν ἐπιστήμην εἶναι. ἀναμάρτητόν γέ πού ἐστιν τὸ δοξάζειν ἀληθῆ, καὶ τὰ ὑπ᾽ αὐτοῦ γιγνόμενα πάντα καλὰ καὶ ἀγαθὰ γίγνεται.

ΣΩ. Ὁ τὸν ποταμὸν καθηγούμενος, ὦ Θεαίτητε, ἔφη ἄρα δείξειν αὐτό· καὶ τοῦτο ἐὰν ἰόντες ἐρευνῶμεν, τάχ᾽ ἂν ἐμπόδιον γενόμενον αὐτὸ
201 φήνειεν τὸ ζητούμενον, μένουσι δὲ δῆλον οὐδέν.

ΘΕΑΙ. Ὀρθῶς λέγεις· ἀλλ᾽ ἴωμέν γε καὶ σκοπῶμεν.

THEAETETUS

THEAET. By Zeus, Socrates, I don't know what to say.

soc. Then, my boy, is the argument right in rebuking us and in pointing out that we were wrong to abandon knowledge and seek first for false opinion? It is impossible to know the latter until we have adequately comprehended the nature of knowledge.

THEAET. As the case now stands, Socrates, we cannot help thinking as you say.

soc. To begin, then, at the beginning once more, what shall we say knowledge is? For surely we are not going to give it up yet, are we?

THEAET. Not by any means, unless, that is, you give it up.

soc. Tell us, then, what definition will make us contradict ourselves least.

THEAET. The one we tried before, Socrates; at any rate, I have nothing else to offer.

soc. What one?

THEAET. That knowledge is true opinion; for true opinion is surely free from error and all its results are fine and good.

soc. The man who was leading the way through the river,[1] Theaetetus, said: "The result itself will show;" and so in this matter, if we go on with our search, perhaps the thing will turn up in our path and of itself reveal the object of our search; but if we stay still, we shall discover nothing.

THEAET. You are right; let us go on with our investigation.

[1] A man who was leading the way through a river was asked if the water was deep. He replied αὐτὸ δείξει, "the event itself will show" (i.e. you can find out by trying). The expression became proverbial.

ΣΩ. Οὐκοῦν τοῦτό γε βραχείας σκέψεως· τέχνη
γάρ σοι ὅλη σημαίνει μὴ εἶναι ἐπιστήμην αὐτό.

ΘΕΑΙ. Πῶς δή; καὶ τίς αὕτη;

ΣΩ. Ἡ τῶν μεγίστων εἰς σοφίαν, οὓς δὴ καλοῦσιν ῥήτοράς τε καὶ δικανικούς. οὗτοι γάρ που τῇ
ἑαυτῶν τέχνῃ πείθουσιν οὐ διδάσκοντες, ἀλλὰ
δοξάζειν ποιοῦντες ἃ ἂν βούλωνται. ἢ σὺ οἴει
δεινούς τινας οὕτω διδασκάλους εἶναι, ὥστε οἷς
B μὴ παρεγένοντό τινες ἀποστερουμένοις χρήματα
ἢ τι ἄλλο βιαζομένοις, τούτοις [1] δύνασθαι πρὸς
ὕδωρ σμικρὸν διδάξαι ἱκανῶς τῶν γενομένων τὴν
ἀλήθειαν;

ΘΕΑΙ. Οὐδαμῶς ἔγωγε οἶμαι, ἀλλὰ πεῖσαι μέν.

ΣΩ. Τὸ πεῖσαι δ' οὐχὶ δοξάσαι λέγεις ποιῆσαι;

ΘΕΑΙ. Τί μήν;

ΣΩ. Οὐκοῦν ὅταν δικαίως πεισθῶσιν δικασταὶ
περὶ ὧν ἰδόντι [2] μόνον ἔστιν εἰδέναι, ἄλλως δὲ μή,
ταῦτα τότε ἐξ ἀκοῆς κρίνοντες, ἀληθῆ δόξαν
C λαβόντες, ἄνευ ἐπιστήμης ἔκριναν, ὀρθὰ πεισθέντες,
εἴπερ εὖ ἐδίκασαν;

ΘΕΑΙ. Παντάπασι μὲν οὖν.

ΣΩ. Οὐκ ἄν, ὦ φίλε, εἴ γε ταὐτὸν ἦν δόξα τε
ἀληθὴς κατὰ [3] δικαστήρια [4] καὶ ἐπιστήμη, ὀρθά
ποτ' ἂν δικαστὴς ἄκρος ἐδόξαζεν ἄνευ ἐπιστήμης·
νῦν δὲ ἔοικεν ἄλλο τι ἑκάτερον εἶναι.

---

[1] τούτοις] τούτους T.
[2] ἰδόντι] εἶδον τί B ; εἰδότι W.
[3] κατὰ Jowett ; καὶ mss. ; om. Heindorf.
[4] δικαστήρια] δικαστήριον T ; om. Heindorf.

soc. Well, then, this at least calls for slight investigation; for you have a whole profession which declares that true opinion is not knowledge.

THEAET. How so? What profession is it?

soc. The profession of those who are greatest in wisdom, who are called orators and lawyers; for they persuade men by the art which they possess, not teaching them, but making them have whatever opinion they like. Or do you think there are any teachers so clever as to be able, in the short time allowed by the water-clock,[1] satisfactorily to teach the judges the truth about what happened to people who have been robbed of their money or have suffered other acts of violence, when there were no eyewitnesses?

THEAET. I certainly do not think so; but I think they can persuade them.

soc. And persuading them is making them have an opinion, is it not?

THEAET. Of course.

soc. Then when judges are justly persuaded about matters which one can know only by having seen them and in no other way, in such a case, judging of them from hearsay, having acquired a true opinion of them, they have judged without knowledge, though they are rightly persuaded, if the judgement they have passed is correct, have they not?

THEAET. Certainly.

soc. But, my friend, if true opinion and knowledge were the same thing in law courts, the best of judges could never have true opinion without knowledge; in fact, however, it appears that the two are different.

[1] The length of speeches in the Athenian law courts was limited by a water-clock.

ΘΕΑΙ. Ὁ γε ἐγώ, ὦ Σώκρατες, εἰπόντος του
ἀκούσας ἐπελελήσμην, νῦν δ' ἐννοῶ· ἔφη δὲ τὴν
μὲν μετὰ λόγου ἀληθῆ δόξαν ἐπιστήμην εἶναι,
D τὴν δὲ ἄλογον ἐκτὸς ἐπιστήμης· καὶ ὧν μὲν μή
ἐστι λόγος, οὐκ ἐπιστητὰ εἶναι, οὑτωσὶ καὶ ὀνομά-
ζων, ἃ δ' ἔχει, ἐπιστητά.

ΣΩ. Ἦ καλῶς λέγεις. τὰ δὲ δὴ ἐπιστητὰ
ταῦτα καὶ μὴ πῇ διῄρει, λέγε, εἰ ἄρα κατὰ ταὐτὰ
σύ τε κἀγὼ ἀκηκόαμεν.

ΘΕΑΙ. Ἀλλ' οὐκ οἶδα εἰ ἐξευρήσω· λέγοντος
μέντ' ἂν ἑτέρου, ὡς ἐγᾦμαι, ἀκολουθήσαιμ' ἄν.[1]

39. ΣΩ. Ἄκουε δὴ ὄναρ ἀντὶ ὀνείρατος. ἐγὼ
E γὰρ αὖ ἐδόκουν ἀκούειν τινῶν ὅτι τὰ μὲν πρῶτα
οἱονπερεὶ στοιχεῖα, ἐξ ὧν ἡμεῖς τε συγκείμεθα καὶ
τἆλλα, λόγον οὐκ ἔχοι. αὐτὸ γὰρ καθ' αὑτὸ ἕκαστον ὀνομάσαι μόνον εἴη, προσειπεῖν δὲ οὐδὲν
ἄλλο δυνατόν, οὔθ' ὡς ἔστιν, οὔθ' ὡς οὐκ ἔστιν·
202 ἤδη γὰρ ἂν οὐσίαν ἢ μὴ οὐσίαν αὐτῷ προστίθεσθαι,
δεῖν δὲ οὐδὲν προσφέρειν, εἴπερ αὐτὸ ἐκεῖνο μόνον
τις ἐρεῖ. ἐπεὶ οὐδὲ τὸ "αὐτὸ" οὐδὲ τὸ "ἐκεῖνο"
οὐδὲ τὸ "ἕκαστον" οὐδὲ τὸ "μόνον" οὐδὲ
"τοῦτο" προσοιστέον οὐδ' ἄλλα πολλὰ τοιαῦτα·
ταῦτα μὲν γὰρ περιτρέχοντα πᾶσι προσφέρεσθαι,
ἕτερα ὄντα ἐκείνων οἷς προστίθεται, δεῖν δέ,
εἴπερ ἦν δυνατὸν αὐτὸ λέγεσθαι καὶ εἶχεν οἰκεῖον
αὐτοῦ λόγον, ἄνευ τῶν ἄλλων ἁπάντων λέγεσθαι.
νῦν δὲ ἀδύνατον εἶναι ὁτιοῦν τῶν πρώτων ῥηθῆναι

---

[1] ἀκολουθήσαιμ' ἄν Schanz ; ἀκολουθησαίμην BT ; ἀκολουθή-
σαιμι al.

THEAETETUS

THEAET. Oh yes, I remember now, Socrates, having heard someone make the distinction, but I had forgotten it. He said that knowledge was true opinion accompanied by reason, but that unreasoning true opinion was outside of the sphere of knowledge; and matters of which there is not a rational explanation are unknowable—yes, that is what he called them—and those of which there is are knowable.

soc. I am glad you mentioned that. But tell us how he distinguished between the knowable and the unknowable, that we may see whether the accounts that you and I have heard agree.

THEAET. But I do not know whether I can think it out; but if someone else were to make the statement of it, I think I could follow.

soc. Listen then, while I relate it to you—"a dream for a dream." I in turn used to imagine that I heard certain persons say that the primary elements of which we and all else are composed admit of no rational explanation; for each alone by itself can only be named, and no qualification can be added, neither that it is nor that it is not, for that would at once be adding to it existence or non-existence, whereas we must add nothing to it, if we are to speak of that itself alone. Indeed, not even "itself" or "that" or "each" or "alone" or "this" or anything else of the sort, of which there are many, must be added; for these are prevalent terms which are added to all things indiscriminately and are different from the things to which they are added; but if it were possible to explain an element, and it admitted of a rational explanation of its own, it would have to be explained apart from everything else. But in fact none of the primal elements can be ex-

B λόγῳ· οὐ γὰρ εἶναι αὐτῷ ἀλλ' ἢ ὀνομάζεσθαι
μόνον· ὄνομα γὰρ μόνον ἔχειν· τὰ δὲ ἐκ τούτων
ἤδη συγκείμενα, ὥσπερ αὐτὰ πέπλεκται, οὕτω
καὶ τὰ ὀνόματα αὐτῶν συμπλακέντα λόγον γεγο-
νέναι· ὀνομάτων γὰρ συμπλοκὴν εἶναι λόγου
οὐσίαν. οὕτω δὴ τὰ μὲν στοιχεῖα ἄλογα καὶ
ἄγνωστα εἶναι, αἰσθητὰ δέ· τὰς δὲ συλλαβὰς
γνωστάς τε καὶ ῥητὰς καὶ ἀληθεῖ δόξῃ δοξαστάς.
ὅταν μὲν οὖν ἄνευ λόγου τὴν ἀληθῆ δόξαν τινός
C τις λάβῃ, ἀληθεύειν μὲν αὐτοῦ τὴν ψυχὴν περὶ
αὐτό, γιγνώσκειν δ' οὔ· τὸν γὰρ μὴ δυνάμενον
δοῦναί τε καὶ δέξασθαι λόγον ἀνεπιστήμονα εἶναι
περὶ τούτου· προσλαβόντα δὲ λόγον δυνατόν τε
ταῦτα πάντα γεγονέναι καὶ τελείως πρὸς ἐπιστήμην
ἔχειν. οὕτως σὺ τὸ ἐνύπνιον ἢ ἄλλως ἀκήκοας;

ΘΕΑΙ. Οὕτω μὲν οὖν παντάπασιν.

ΣΩ. Ἀρέσκει οὖν σε καὶ τίθεσαι ταύτῃ, δόξαν
ἀληθῆ μετὰ λόγου ἐπιστήμην εἶναι;

ΘΕΑΙ. Κομιδῇ μὲν οὖν.

D ΣΩ. Ἆρ', ὦ Θεαίτητε, νῦν οὕτω τῇδε τῇ
ἡμέρᾳ εἰλήφαμεν ὃ πάλαι καὶ πολλοὶ τῶν σοφῶν
ζητοῦντες πρὶν εὑρεῖν κατεγήρασαν;

ΘΕΑΙ. Ἐμοὶ γοῦν δοκεῖ, ὦ Σώκρατες, καλῶς
λέγεσθαι τὸ νῦν ῥηθέν.

ΣΩ. Καὶ εἰκός γε αὐτὸ τοῦτο οὕτως ἔχειν· τίς
γὰρ ἂν καὶ ἔτι ἐπιστήμη εἴη χωρὶς τοῦ λόγου τε
καὶ ὀρθῆς δόξης; ἓν μέντοι τί με τῶν ῥηθέντων
ἀπαρέσκει.

ΘΕΑΙ. Τὸ ποῖον δή;

pressed by reason; they can only be named, for they have only a name; but the things composed of these are themselves complex, and so their names are complex and form a rational explanation; for the combination of names is the essence of reasoning. Thus the elements are not objects of reason or of knowledge, but only of perception, whereas the combinations of them are objects of knowledge and expression and true opinion. When therefore a man acquires without reasoning the true opinion about anything, his mind has the truth about it, but has no knowledge; for he who cannot give and receive a rational explanation of a thing is without knowledge of it; but when he has acquired also a rational explanation he may possibly have become all that I have said and may now be perfect in knowledge. Is that the version of the dream you have heard, or is it different?

THEAET. That was it exactly.

soc. Are you satisfied, then, and do you state it in this way, that true opinion accompanied by reason is knowledge?

THEAET. Precisely.

soc. Can it be, Theaetetus, that we now, in this casual manner, have found out on this day what many wise men have long been seeking and have grown grey in the search?

THEAET. I, at any rate, Socrates, think our present statement is good.

soc. Probably this particular statement is so; for what knowledge could there still be apart from reason and right opinion? One point, however, in what has been said is unsatisfactory to me.

THEAET. What point?

PLATO

ΣΩ. Ὁ καὶ δοκεῖ λέγεσθαι κομψότατα, ὡς τὰ μὲν στοιχεῖα ἄγνωστα, τὸ δὲ τῶν συλλαβῶν γένος E γνωστόν.

ΘΕΑΙ. Οὐκοῦν ὀρθῶς;

ΣΩ. Ἰστέον δή· ὥσπερ γὰρ ὁμήρους ἔχομεν τοῦ λόγου τὰ παραδείγματα, οἷς χρώμενος εἶπε πάντα ταῦτα.

ΘΕΑΙ. Ποῖα δή;

ΣΩ. Τὰ τῶν γραμμάτων στοιχεῖά τε καὶ συλλαβάς. ἢ οἴει ἄλλοσέ ποι βλέποντα ταῦτα εἰπεῖν τὸν εἰπόντα ἃ λέγομεν;

ΘΕΑΙ. Οὔκ, ἀλλ' εἰς ταῦτα.

203   40. ΣΩ. Βασανίζωμεν δὴ αὐτὰ ἀναλαμβάνοντες, μᾶλλον δὲ ἡμᾶς αὐτούς, οὕτως ἢ οὐχ οὕτως γράμματα ἐμάθομεν. φέρε πρῶτον· ἆρ' αἱ μὲν συλλαβαὶ λόγον ἔχουσι, τὰ δὲ στοιχεῖα ἄλογα;

ΘΕΑΙ. Ἴσως.

ΣΩ. Πάνυ μὲν οὖν καὶ ἐμοὶ φαίνεται. Σωκράτους γοῦν εἴ τις ἔροιτο τὴν πρώτην συλλαβὴν οὑτωσί· "ὦ Θεαίτητε, λέγε τί ἐστι σω;" τί ἀποκρινεῖ;

ΘΕΑΙ. Ὅτι σῖγμα καὶ ὦ.

ΣΩ. Οὐκοῦν τοῦτον ἔχεις λόγον τῆς συλλαβῆς;

ΘΕΑΙ. Ἔγωγε.

B   ΣΩ. Ἴθι δή, οὕτως εἰπὲ καὶ τὸν τοῦ σῖγμα λόγον.

ΘΕΑΙ. Καὶ πῶς τοῦ στοιχείου τις ἐρεῖ στοιχεῖα; καὶ γὰρ δή, ὦ Σώκρατες, τό τε σῖγμα τῶν ἀφώνων

THEAETETUS

soc. Just that which seems to be the cleverest; the assertion that the elements are unknowable and the class of combinations is knowable.

THEAET. Is that not right?

soc. We are sure to find out, for we have as hostages the examples which he who said all this used in his argument.

THEAET. What examples?

soc. The elements in writing, the letters of the alphabet, and their combinations, the syllables[1]; or do you think the author of the statements we are discussing had something else in view?

THEAET. No; those are what he had in view.

soc. Let us, then, take them up and examine them, or rather, let us examine ourselves and see whether it was in accordance with this theory, or not, that we learned letters. First then, the syllables have a rational explanation, but the letters have not?

THEAET. I suppose so.

soc. I think so, too, decidedly. Now if anyone should ask about the first syllable of Socrates; "Theaetetus, tell me, what is SO?" What would you reply?

THEAET. I should say "S and O."

soc. This, then, is your explanation of the syllable?

THEAET. Yes.

soc. Come now, in the same manner give me the explanation of the S.

THEAET. How can one give any elements of an element? For really, Socrates, the S is a voiceless

---

[1] Στοιχεῖον and συλλαβή, originally general terms for element and combination, became the common words for letter and syllable.

ἐστί, ψόφος τις μόνον, οἷον συριττούσης τῆς γλώτ-
της· τοῦ δ' αὖ βῆτα οὔτε φωνὴ οὔτε ψόφος, οὐδὲ
τῶν πλείστων στοιχείων· ὥστε πάνυ εὖ ἔχει τὸ
λέγεσθαι αὐτὰ ἄλογα, ὧν γε τὰ ἐναργέστατα αὐτὰ
τὰ ἑπτὰ φωνὴν μόνον ἔχει, λόγον δὲ οὐδ' ὁντινοῦν.

ΣΩ. Τουτὶ μὲν ἄρα, ὦ ἑταῖρε, κατωρθώκαμεν
περὶ ἐπιστήμης.

ΘΕΑΙ. Φαινόμεθα.

C   ΣΩ. Τί δέ; τὸ μὴ γνωστὸν εἶναι τὸ στοιχεῖον,
ἀλλὰ τὴν συλλαβὴν ἆρ' ὀρθῶς ἀποδεδείγμεθα;

ΘΕΑΙ. Εἰκός γε.

ΣΩ. Φέρε δή, τὴν συλλαβὴν πότερον λέγωμεν[1]
τὰ ἀμφότερα στοιχεῖα, καὶ ἐὰν πλείω ᾖ ἢ δύο, τὰ
πάντα, ἢ μίαν τινὰ ἰδέαν γεγονυῖαν συντεθέντων
αὐτῶν;

ΘΕΑΙ. Τὰ ἅπαντα ἔμοιγε δοκοῦμεν.

ΣΩ. Ὅρα δὴ ἐπὶ δυοῖν, σίγμα καὶ ὦ. ἀμφότερά
ἐστιν ἡ πρώτη συλλαβὴ τοῦ ἐμοῦ ὀνόματος. ἄλλο
τι ὁ γιγνώσκων αὐτὴν τὰ ἀμφότερα γιγνώσκει;

D   ΘΕΑΙ. Τί μήν;

ΣΩ. Τὸ σίγμα καὶ τὸ ὦ ἄρα γιγνώσκει.

ΘΕΑΙ. Ναί.

ΣΩ. Τί δ'; ἑκάτερον ἆρ' ἀγνοεῖ, καὶ οὐδέτερον
εἰδὼς ἀμφότερα γιγνώσκει;

ΘΕΑΙ. Ἀλλὰ δεινὸν καὶ ἄλογον, ὦ Σώκρατες.

ΣΩ. Ἀλλὰ μέντοι εἴ γε ἀνάγκη ἑκάτερον γιγνώσκειν, εἴπερ ἀμφότερά τις γνώσεται, προγιγνώσκειν

[1] λέγωμεν B ; λέγομεν T et al.

THEAETETUS

letter,[1] a mere noise, as of the tongue hissing; B again has neither voice nor noise, nor have most of the other letters; and so it is quite right to say that they have no explanation, seeing that the most distinct of them, the seven vowels, have only voice, but no explanation whatsoever.

soc. In this point, then, my friend, it would seem that we have reached a right conclusion about knowledge.

THEAET. I think we have.

soc. But have we been right in laying down the principle that whereas the letter is unknowable, yet the syllable is knowable?

THEAET. Probably.

soc. Well then, shall we say that the syllable is the two letters, or, if there be more than two, all of them, or is it a single concept that has arisen from their combination?

THEAET. I think we mean all the letters it contains.

soc. Now take the case of two, S and O. The two together are the first syllable of my name. He who knows it knows the two letters, does he not?

THEAET. Of course.

soc. He knows, that is, the S and the O.

THEAET. Yes.

soc. How is that? He is ignorant of each, and knowing neither of them he knows them both?

THEAET. That is monstrous and absurd, Socrates.

soc. And yet if a knowledge of each letter is necessary before one can know both, he who is

[1] The distinction here made is that which we make between vowels and consonants. The seven Greek vowels are α, ε, η, ι, ο, υ, ω, called φωνήεντα.

229

τὰ στοιχεῖα ἅπασα ἀνάγκη τῷ μέλλοντί ποτε
γνώσεσθαι συλλαβήν, καὶ οὕτως ἡμῖν ὁ καλὸς
λόγος ἀποδεδρακὼς οἰχήσεται.

E ΘΕΑΙ. Καὶ μάλα γε ἐξαίφνης.

ΣΩ. Οὐ γὰρ καλῶς αὐτὸν φυλάττομεν. χρῆν
γὰρ ἴσως τὴν συλλαβὴν τίθεσθαι μὴ τὰ στοιχεῖα,
ἀλλ' ἐξ ἐκείνων ἕν τι γεγονὸς εἶδος, ἰδέαν μίαν
αὐτὸ αὑτοῦ ἔχον, ἕτερον δὲ τῶν στοιχείων.

ΘΕΑΙ. Πάνυ μὲν οὖν· καὶ τάχα γ' ἂν μᾶλλον
οὕτως ἢ 'κείνως ἔχοι.

ΣΩ. Σκεπτέον καὶ οὐ προδοτέον οὕτως ἀνάνδρως μέγαν τε καὶ σεμνὸν λόγον.

ΘΕΑΙ. Οὐ γὰρ οὖν.

204 ΣΩ. Ἐχέτω δὴ ὡς νῦν φαμεν, μία ἰδέα ἐξ
ἑκάστων τῶν συναρμοττόντων στοιχείων γιγνομένη ἡ συλλαβή, ὁμοίως ἔν τε γράμμασι καὶ ἐν
τοῖς ἄλλοις ἅπασι.

ΘΕΑΙ. Πάνυ μὲν οὖν.

ΣΩ. Οὐκοῦν μέρη αὐτῆς οὐ δεῖ εἶναι.

ΘΕΑΙ. Τί δή;

ΣΩ. Ὅτι οὗ ἂν ᾖ μέρη, τὸ ὅλον ἀνάγκη τὰ
πάντα μέρη εἶναι. ἢ καὶ τὸ ὅλον ἐκ τῶν μερῶν
λέγεις γεγονὸς ἕν τι εἶδος ἕτερον τῶν πάντων
μερῶν;

ΘΕΑΙ. Ἔγωγε.

ΣΩ. Τὸ δὲ δὴ πᾶν καὶ τὸ ὅλον πότερον ταὐτὸν
B καλεῖς ἢ ἕτερον ἑκάτερον;

ΘΕΑΙ. Ἔχω μὲν οὐδὲν σαφές, ὅτι δὲ κελεύεις
προθύμως ἀποκρίνασθαι, παρακινδυνεύων λέγω
ὅτι ἕτερον.

ΣΩ. Ἡ μὲν προθυμία, ὦ Θεαίτητε, ὀρθή· εἰ
δὲ καὶ ἡ ἀπόκρισις, σκεπτέον.

ever to know a syllable must certainly know the letters first, and so our fine theory will have run away and vanished!

THEAET. And very suddenly, too.

SOC. Yes, for we are not watching it carefully. Perhaps we ought to have said that the syllable is not the letters, but a single concept that has arisen from them, having a single form of its own, different from the letters.

THEAET. Certainly; and perhaps that will be better than the other way.

SOC. Let us look into that; we must not give up in such unmanly fashion a great and impressive theory.

THEAET. No, we must not.

SOC. Let it be, then, as we say now, that the syllable or combination is a single form arising out of the several conjoined elements, and that it is the same in words and in all other things.

THEAET. Certainly.

SOC. Therefore there must be no parts of it.

THEAET. How so?

SOC. Because if there are parts of anything, the whole must inevitably be all the parts; or do you assert also that the whole that has arisen out of the parts is a single concept different from all the parts?

THEAET. Yes, I do.

SOC. Do you then say that all and the whole are the same, or that each of the two is different from the other?

THEAET. I am not sure; but you tell me to answer boldly, so I take the risk and say that they are different.

SOC. Your boldness, Theaetetus, is right; but whether your answer is so remains to be seen.

ΘΕΑΙ. Δεῖ δέ γε δή.¹

41. ΣΩ. Οὐκοῦν διαφέροι ἂν τὸ ὅλον τοῦ παντός, ὡς ὁ νῦν λόγος;

ΘΕΑΙ. Ναί.

ΣΩ. Τί δὲ δή; τὰ πάντα καὶ τὸ πᾶν ἔσθ' ὅ τι διαφέρει; οἷον ἐπειδὰν λέγωμεν ἕν, δύο, τρία, C τέτταρα, πέντε, ἕξ, καὶ ἐὰν δὶς τρία ἢ τρὶς δύο ἢ τέτταρά τε καὶ δύο ἢ τρία καὶ δύο καὶ ἕν, πότερον ἐν πᾶσι τούτοις τὸ αὐτὸ ἢ ἕτερον λέγομεν;

ΘΕΑΙ. Τὸ αὐτό.

ΣΩ. Ἆρ' ἄλλο τι ἢ ἕξ;

ΘΕΑΙ. Οὐδέν.

ΣΩ. Οὐκοῦν ἐφ' ἑκάστης λέξεως πάντα τὰ² ἓξ εἰρήκαμεν;

ΘΕΑΙ. Ναί.

ΣΩ. Πάλιν δ' οὐχ ἕν³ λέγομεν τὰ πάντα λέγοντες;

ΘΕΑΙ. Ἀνάγκη.

ΣΩ. Ἦ ἄλλο τι ἢ τὰ ἕξ;

ΘΕΑΙ. Οὐδέν.

D ΣΩ. Ταὐτὸν ἄρα ἔν γε τοῖς ὅσα ἐξ ἀριθμοῦ ἐστι, τό τε πᾶν προσαγορεύομεν καὶ τὰ ἅπαντα;

ΘΕΑΙ. Φαίνεται.

ΣΩ. Ὧδε δὴ περὶ αὐτῶν λέγωμεν. ὁ τοῦ πλέθρου ἀριθμὸς καὶ τὸ πλέθρον ταὐτόν· ἦ γάρ;

ΘΕΑΙ. Ναί.

ΣΩ. Καὶ ὁ τοῦ σταδίου δὴ ὡσαύτως.

ΘΕΑΙ. Ναί.

ΣΩ. Καὶ μὴν καὶ ὁ τοῦ στρατοπέδου γε καὶ τὸ

---

¹ δέ γε δή BT ; γε δή W.
² πάντα τὰ BT ; πάντα W.
³ πάλιν δ οὐχ ἕν Hermann ; πάλιν δ' οὐδὲν BT ; πᾶν δ' οὐδὲν Burnet, after Campbell.

THEAET. Yes, certainly, we must see about that.

soc. The whole, then, according to our present view, would differ from all?

THEAET. Yes.

soc. How about this? Is there any difference between all in the plural and all in the singular? For instance, if we say one, two, three, four, five, six, or twice three, or three times two, or four and two, or three and two and one, are we in all these forms speaking of the same or of different numbers?

THEAET. Of the same.

soc. That is, of six?

THEAET. Yes.

soc. Then in each form of speech we have spoken of all the six?

THEAET. Yes.

soc. And again do we not speak of one thing when we speak of them all?

THEAET. Assuredly.

soc. That is, of six?

THEAET. Yes.

soc. Then in all things that are made up of number, we apply the same term to all in the plural and all in the singular?

THEAET. Apparently.

soc. Here is another way of approaching the matter. The number of the fathom and the fathom are the same, are they not?

THEAET. Yes.

soc. And of the furlong likewise.

THEAET. Yes.

soc. And the number of the army is the same

στρατόπεδον, καὶ πάντα τὰ τοιαῦτα ὁμοίως; ὁ γὰρ ἀριθμὸς πᾶς τὸ ὂν πᾶν ἕκαστον αὐτῶν ἐστιν.

ΘΕΑΙ. Ναί.

ΣΩ. Ὁ δὲ ἑκάστων ἀριθμὸς μῶν ἄλλο τι ἢ E μέρη ἐστίν;

ΘΕΑΙ. Οὐδέν.

ΣΩ. Ὅσα ἄρα ἔχει μέρη, ἐκ μερῶν ἂν εἴη;

ΘΕΑΙ. Φαίνεται.

ΣΩ. Τὰ δέ γε πάντα μέρη τὸ πᾶν εἶναι ὡμολόγηται,[1] εἴπερ καὶ ὁ πᾶς ἀριθμὸς τὸ πᾶν ἔσται.

ΘΕΑΙ. Οὕτως.

ΣΩ. Τὸ ὅλον ἄρ' οὐκ ἔστιν ἐκ μερῶν. πᾶν γὰρ ἂν εἴη τὰ πάντα ὂν μέρη.

ΘΕΑΙ. Οὐκ ἔοικεν.

ΣΩ. Μέρος δ' ἔσθ' ὅτου ἄλλου ἐστὶν ὅπερ ἐστὶν ἢ τοῦ ὅλου;

ΘΕΑΙ. Τοῦ παντός γε.

205 ΣΩ. Ἀνδρικῶς γε, ὦ Θεαίτητε, μάχει. τὸ πᾶν δὲ οὐχ ὅταν μηδὲν ἀπῇ, αὐτὸ τοῦτο πᾶν ἐστιν;

ΘΕΑΙ. Ἀνάγκη.

ΣΩ. Ὅλον δὲ οὐ ταὐτὸν τοῦτο ἔσται, οὗ ἂν μηδαμῇ μηδὲν ἀποστατῇ; οὗ δ' ἂν ἀποστατῇ, οὔτε ὅλον οὔτε πᾶν, ἅμα γενόμενον ἐκ τοῦ αὐτοῦ τὸ αὐτό;

ΘΕΑΙ. Δοκεῖ μοι νῦν οὐδὲν διαφέρειν πᾶν τε καὶ ὅλον.

ΣΩ. Οὐκοῦν ἐλέγομεν ὅτι οὗ ἂν μέρη ᾖ, τὸ ὅλον τε καὶ πᾶν τὰ πάντα μέρη ἔσται;

ΘΕΑΙ. Πάνυ γε.

---

[1] ὡμολόγηται T; ὁμολογεῖται B.

as the army, and all such cases are alike? In each of them all the number is all the thing.

THEAET. Yes.

soc. And is the number of each anything but the parts of each?

THEAET. No.

soc. Everything that has parts, accordingly, consists of parts, does it not?

THEAET. Evidently.

soc. But we are agreed that the all must be all the parts if all the number is to be the all.[1]

THEAET. Yes.

soc. Then the whole does not consist of parts, for if it consisted of all the parts it would be the all.

THEAET. That seems to be true.

soc. But is a part a part of anything in the world but the whole?

THEAET. Yes, of the all.

soc. You are putting up a brave fight, Theaetetus. But is not the all precisely that of which nothing is wanting?

THEAET. Necessarily.

soc. And is not just this same thing, from which nothing whatsoever is lacking, a whole? For that from which anything is lacking is neither a whole nor all, which have become identical simultaneously and for the same reason.

THEAET. I think now that there is no difference between all and whole.

soc. We were saying, were we not, that if there are parts of anything, the whole and all of it will be all the parts?

THEAET. Certainly.

[1] *Cf.* 204 B.

ΣΩ. Πάλιν δή, ὅπερ ἄρτι ἐπεχείρουν, οὐκ, εἴπερ
ἡ συλλαβὴ μὴ τὰ στοιχεῖά ἐστιν, ἀνάγκη αὐτὴν
Β μὴ ὡς μέρη ἔχειν ἑαυτῆς τὰ στοιχεῖα, ἢ ταὐτὸν
οὖσαν αὐτοῖς ὁμοίως ἐκείνοις γνωστὴν εἶναι;

ΘΕΑΙ. Οὕτως.

ΣΩ. Οὐκοῦν τοῦτο ἵνα μὴ γένηται, ἕτερον αὐτῶν αὐτὴν ἐθέμεθα;

ΘΕΑΙ. Ναί.

ΣΩ. Τί δ'; εἰ μὴ τὰ στοιχεῖα συλλαβῆς μέρη
ἐστίν, ἔχεις ἄλλ' ἄττα εἰπεῖν ἃ μέρη μέν ἐστι
συλλαβῆς, οὐ μέντοι στοιχεῖά γ' ἐκείνης;

ΘΕΑΙ. Οὐδαμῶς. εἰ γάρ, ὦ Σώκρατες, μόρι'
ἄττα αὐτῆς [1] συγχωροίην, γελοῖόν που τὰ στοιχεῖα
ἀφέντα ἐπ' ἄλλα ἰέναι.

C ΣΩ. Παντάπασι δή, ὦ Θεαίτητε, κατὰ τὸν
νῦν λόγον μία τις ἰδέα ἀμέριστος συλλαβὴ ἂν εἴη.

ΘΕΑΙ. Ἔοικεν.

ΣΩ. Μέμνησαι οὖν, ὦ φίλε, ὅτι ὀλίγον ἐν τῷ
πρόσθεν ἀπεδεχόμεθα ἡγούμενοι εὖ λέγεσθαι ὅτι
τῶν πρώτων οὐκ εἴη λόγος ἐξ ὧν τἆλλα σύγκειται,
διότι αὐτὸ καθ' αὑτὸ ἕκαστον εἴη ἀσύνθετον, καὶ
οὐδὲ τὸ " εἶναι " περὶ αὐτοῦ ὀρθῶς ἔχοι προσφέ-
ροντα εἰπεῖν, οὐδὲ " τοῦτο," ὡς ἕτερα καὶ ἀλλότρια
λεγόμενα, καὶ αὕτη δὴ ἡ αἰτία ἄλογόν τε καὶ
ἄγνωστον αὐτὸ ποιοῖ;

ΘΕΑΙ. Μέμνημαι.

D ΣΩ. Ἦ οὖν ἄλλη τις ἢ αὕτη ἡ αἰτία τοῦ μονο-
ειδές τε [2] καὶ ἀμέριστον αὐτὸ εἶναι; ἐγὼ μὲν γὰρ
οὐχ ὁρῶ ἄλλην.

---

[1] μόρι' ἄττα αὐτῆς W ; μόρια ταύτης BT.
[2] τε W in ras. B ; τι T.

soc. Once more, then, as I was trying to say just now, if the syllable is not the letters, does it not follow necessarily that it contains the letters, not as parts of it, or else that being the same as the letters, it is equally knowable with them?

THEAET. It does.

soc. And it was in order to avoid this that we assumed that it was different from them?

THEAET. Yes.

soc. Well then, if the letters are not parts of the syllable, can you mention any other things which are parts of it, but are not the letters [1] of it?

THEAET. Certainly not. For if I grant that there are parts of the syllable, it would be ridiculous to give up the letters and look for other things as parts.

soc. Without question, then, Theaetetus, the syllable would be, according to our present view, some indivisible concept.

THEAET. I agree.

soc. Do you remember, then, my friend, that we admitted a little while ago, on what we considered good grounds, that there can be no rational explanation of the primary elements of which other things are composed, because each of them, when taken by itself, is not composite, and we could not properly apply to such an element even the expression " be " or " this," because these terms are different and alien, and for this reason it is irrational and unknowable?

THEAET. I remember.

soc. And is not this the sole reason why it is single in form and indivisible? I can see no other.

---

[1] The reader is reminded that the words στοιχεῖον and συλλαβή have the meanings " element " and " combination " as well as " letter " and " syllable."

ΘΕΑΙ. Οὐ γὰρ οὖν δὴ φαίνεται.

ΣΩ. Οὐκοῦν εἰς ταὐτὸν ἐμπέπτωκεν ἡ συλλαβὴ εἶδος ἐκείνῳ, εἴπερ μέρη τε μὴ ἔχει καὶ μία ἐστὶν ἰδέα;

ΘΕΑΙ. Παντάπασι μὲν οὖν.

ΣΩ. Εἰ μὲν ἄρα πολλὰ στοιχεῖα ἡ συλλαβή ἐστιν καὶ ὅλον τι, μέρη δ' αὐτῆς ταῦτα, ὁμοίως αἵ τε συλλαβαὶ γνωσταὶ καὶ ῥηταὶ καὶ τὰ στοιχεῖα, ἐπείπερ τὰ πάντα μέρη τῷ ὅλῳ ταὐτὸν ἐφάνη.

E ΘΕΑΙ. Καὶ μάλα.

ΣΩ. Εἰ δέ γε ἕν τε καὶ ἀμερές, ὁμοίως μὲν συλλαβή, ὡσαύτως δὲ στοιχεῖον ἄλογόν τε καὶ ἄγνωστον· ἡ γὰρ αὐτὴ αἰτία ποιήσει αὐτὰ τοιαῦτα.

ΘΕΑΙ. Οὐκ ἔχω ἄλλως εἰπεῖν.

ΣΩ. Τοῦτο μὲν ἄρα μὴ ἀποδεχώμεθα, ὃς ἂν λέγῃ συλλαβὴν μὲν γνωστὸν[1] καὶ ῥητόν, στοιχεῖον δὲ τοὐναντίον.

ΘΕΑΙ. Μὴ γάρ, εἴπερ τῷ λόγῳ πειθόμεθα.

206 ΣΩ. Τί δ' αὖ; τοὐναντίον λέγοντος ἆρ' οὐ μᾶλλον ἂν ἀποδέξαιο ἐξ ὧν αὐτὸς σύνοισθα σαυτῷ ἐν τῇ τῶν γραμμάτων μαθήσει;

ΘΕΑΙ. Τὸ ποῖον;

ΣΩ. Ὡς οὐδὲν ἄλλο μανθάνων διετέλεσας ἢ τὰ στοιχεῖα ἕν τε[2] τῇ ὄψει διαγιγνώσκειν πειρώμενος καὶ ἐν τῇ ἀκοῇ αὐτὸ καθ' αὑτὸ ἕκαστον, ἵνα μὴ ἡ θέσις σε ταράττοι λεγομένων τε καὶ γραφομένων.

ΘΕΑΙ. Ἀληθέστατα λέγεις.

ΣΩ. Ἐν δὲ κιθαριστοῦ τελέως μεμαθηκέναι μῶν
B ἄλλο τι ἦν ἢ τὸ τῷ φθόγγῳ ἑκάστῳ δύνασθαι

---

[1] γνωστὸν W; ἄγνωστον pr. BT.
[2] τε W; om. BT.

THEAET. There is no other to be seen.

soc. Then the syllable falls into the same class with the letter, if it has no parts and is a single form?

THEAET. Yes, unquestionably.

soc. If, then, the syllable is a plurality of letters and is a whole of which the letters are parts, the syllables and the letters are equally knowable and expressible, if all the parts were found to be the same as the whole.

THEAET. Certainly.

soc. But if one and indivisible, then syllable and likewise letter are equally irrational and unknowable; for the same cause will make them so.

THEAET. I cannot dispute it.

soc. Then we must not accept the statement of any one who says that the syllable is knowable and expressible, but the letter is not.

THEAET. No, not if we are convinced by our argument.

soc. But would you not rather accept the opposite belief, judging by your own experience when you were learning to read?

THEAET. What experience?

soc. In learning, you were merely constantly trying to distinguish between the letters both by sight and by hearing, keeping each of them distinct from the rest, that you might not be disturbed by their sequence when they were spoken or written.

THEAET. That is very true.

soc. And in the music school was not perfect attainment the ability to follow each note and tell

ἐπακολουθεῖν, ποίας χορδῆς εἴη· ἃ δὴ στοιχεῖα πᾶς ἂν ὁμολογήσειε μουσικῆς λέγεσθαι;

ΘΕΑΙ. Οὐδὲν ἄλλο.

ΣΩ. Ὧν μὲν ἄρ' αὐτοὶ ἔμπειροί ἐσμεν στοιχείων καὶ συλλαβῶν, εἰ δεῖ ἀπὸ τούτων τεκμαίρεσθαι καὶ εἰς τὰ ἄλλα, πολὺ τὸ τῶν στοιχείων γένος ἐναργεστέραν τε τὴν γνῶσιν ἔχειν φήσομεν καὶ κυριωτέραν τῆς συλλαβῆς πρὸς τὸ λαβεῖν τελέως ἕκαστον μάθημα, καὶ ἐάν τις φῇ συλλαβὴν μὲν γνωστόν, ἄγνωστον δὲ πεφυκέναι στοιχεῖον, ἑκόντα ἢ ἄκοντα παίζειν ἡγησόμεθ' αὐτόν.

ΘΕΑΙ. Κομιδῇ μὲν οὖν.

C   42. ΣΩ. Ἀλλὰ δὴ τούτου μὲν ἔτι κἂν ἄλλαι φανεῖεν ἀποδείξεις, ὡς ἐμοὶ δοκεῖ· τὸ δὲ προκείμενον μὴ ἐπιλαθώμεθα δι' αὐτὰ ἰδεῖν, ὅ τι δή ποτε καὶ λέγεται τὸ μετὰ δόξης ἀληθοῦς λόγον προσγενόμενον τὴν τελεωτάτην ἐπιστήμην γεγονέναι.

ΘΕΑΙ. Οὐκοῦν χρὴ ὁρᾶν.

ΣΩ. Φέρε δή, τί ποτε βούλεται τὸν λόγον ἡμῖν σημαίνειν; τριῶν γὰρ ἕν τί μοι δοκεῖ λέγειν.

ΘΕΑΙ. Τίνων δή;

D   ΣΩ. Τὸ μὲν πρῶτον εἴη ἂν τὸ τὴν αὑτοῦ διάνοιαν ἐμφανῆ ποιεῖν διὰ φωνῆς μετὰ ῥημάτων τε καὶ ὀνομάτων, ὥσπερ εἰς κάτοπτρον ἢ ὕδωρ τὴν δόξαν ἐκτυπούμενον εἰς τὴν διὰ τοῦ στόματος ῥοήν. ἢ οὐ δοκεῖ σοι τὸ τοιοῦτον λόγος εἶναι;

ΘΕΑΙ. Ἔμοιγε. τὸν γοῦν[1] αὐτὸ δρῶντα λέγειν φαμέν.

ΣΩ. Οὐκοῦν τοῦτό γε πᾶς ποιεῖν δυνατὸς θᾶττον ἢ σχολαίτερον, τὸ ἐνδείξασθαι τί δοκεῖ περὶ ἑκάστου

---

[1] γοῦν W ; οὖν BT.

which string produced it; and everyone would agree that the notes are the elements of music?

THEAET. Yes, that is all true.

soc. Then if we are to argue from the elements and combinations in which we ourselves have experience to other things in general, we shall say that the elements as a class admit of a much clearer knowledge than the compounds and of a knowledge that is much more important for the complete attainment of each branch of learning, and if anyone says that the compound is by its nature knowable and the element unknowable, we shall consider that he is, intentionally or unintentionally, joking.

THEAET. Certainly.

soc. Still other proofs of this might be brought out, I think; but let us not on that account lose sight of the question before us, which is: What is meant by the doctrine that the most perfect knowledge arises from the addition of rational explanation to true opinion?

THEAET. No, we must not.

soc. Now what are we intended to understand by "rational explanation"? I think it means one of three things.

THEAET. What are they?

soc. The first would be making one's own thought clear through speech by means of verbs and nouns, imaging the opinion in the stream that flows through the lips, as in a mirror or water. Do you not think the rational explanation is something of that sort?

THEAET. Yes, I do. At any rate, we say that he who does that speaks or explains.

soc. Well, that is a thing that anyone can do sooner or later; he can show what he thinks about

αὐτῷ, ὁ μὴ ἐνεὸς ἢ κωφὸς ἀπ' ἀρχῆς· καὶ οὕτως
Ε ὅσοι τι ὀρθὸν δοξάζουσι, πάντες αὐτὸ μετὰ λόγου
φανοῦνται ἔχοντες, καὶ οὐδαμοῦ ἔτι ὀρθὴ δόξα
χωρὶς ἐπιστήμης γενήσεται.

ΘΕΑΙ. Ἀληθῆ.

ΣΩ. Μὴ τοίνυν ῥᾳδίως καταγιγνώσκωμεν τὸ
μηδὲν εἰρηκέναι τὸν ἀποφηνάμενον ἐπιστήμην ὃ
νῦν σκοποῦμεν. ἴσως γὰρ ὁ λέγων οὐ τοῦτο ἔλεγεν,
ἀλλὰ τὸ ἐρωτηθέντα τί ἕκαστον δυνατὸν εἶναι τὴν
207 ἀπόκρισιν διὰ τῶν στοιχείων ἀποδοῦναι τῷ ἐρο-
μένῳ.

ΘΕΑΙ. Οἷον τί λέγεις, ὦ Σώκρατες;

ΣΩ. Οἷον καὶ Ἡσίοδος περὶ ἁμάξης λέγει τὸ
" ἑκατὸν δέ τε δούραθ' ἁμάξης." ἃ ἐγὼ μὲν οὐκ
ἂν δυναίμην εἰπεῖν, οἶμαι δὲ οὐδὲ σύ· ἀλλ' ἀγα-
πῷμεν ἂν ἐρωτηθέντες ὅ τί ἐστιν ἅμαξα, εἰ ἔχοιμεν
εἰπεῖν τροχοί, ἄξων, ὑπερτερία,[1] ἄντυγες, ζυγόν.

ΘΕΑΙ. Πάνυ μὲν οὖν.

ΣΩ. Ὁ δέ γε ἴσως οἴοιτ' ἂν ἡμᾶς, ὥσπερ ἂν τὸ
σὸν ὄνομα ἐρωτηθέντας καὶ ἀποκρινομένους κατὰ
Β συλλαβήν, γελοίους εἶναι, ὀρθῶς μὲν δοξάζοντας
καὶ λέγοντας ἃ λέγομεν, οἰομένους δὲ γραμματικοὺς
εἶναι καὶ ἔχειν τε καὶ λέγειν γραμματικῶς τὸν
τοῦ Θεαιτήτου ὀνόματος λόγον· τὸ δ' οὐκ εἶναι
ἐπιστημόνως οὐδὲν λέγειν, πρὶν ἂν διὰ τῶν στοιχείων μετὰ τῆς ἀληθοῦς δόξης ἕκαστον περαίνῃ
τις, ὅπερ καὶ ἐν τοῖς πρόσθε που ἐρρήθη.

---

[1] ὑπερτερία Kuhn ; ὑπερτηρία Β ; ὑπερτήρια Τ.

anything, unless he is deaf or dumb from the first; and so all who have any right opinion will be found to have it with the addition of rational explanation, and there will henceforth be no possibility of right opinion apart from knowledge.

THEAET. True.

SOC. Let us not, therefore, carelessly accuse him of talking nonsense who gave the definition of knowledge which we are now considering; for perhaps that is not what he meant. He may have meant that each person if asked about anything must be able in reply to give his questioner an account of it in terms of its elements.

THEAET. As for example, Socrates?

SOC. As, for example, Hesiod, speaking of a wagon, says, "a hundred pieces of wood in a wagon." [1] Now I could not name the pieces, nor, I fancy, could you; but if we were asked what a wagon is, we should be satisfied if we could say "wheels, axle, body, rims, yoke."

THEAET. Certainly.

SOC. But he, perhaps, would think we were ridiculous, just as he would if, on being asked about your name, we should reply by telling the syllables, holding a right opinion and expressing correctly what we have to say, but should think we were grammarians and as such both possessed and were expressing as grammarians would the rational explanation of the name Theaetetus. He would say that it is impossible for anyone to give a rational explanation of anything with knowledge, until he gives a complete enumeration of the elements, combined with true opinion. That, I believe, is what was said before.

[1] *Works and Days,* 456 (454).

ΘΕΑΙ. Ἐρρήθη γάρ.

ΣΩ. Οὕτω τοίνυν καὶ περὶ ἁμάξης ἡμᾶς μὲν ὀρθὴν ἔχειν δόξαν, τὸν δὲ διὰ τῶν ἑκατὸν ἐκείνων C δυνάμενον διελθεῖν αὐτῆς τὴν οὐσίαν, προσλαβόντα τοῦτο, λόγον τε προσειληφέναι τῇ ἀληθεῖ δόξῃ καὶ ἀντὶ δοξαστικοῦ τεχνικόν τε καὶ ἐπιστήμονα περὶ ἁμάξης οὐσίας γεγονέναι, διὰ στοιχείων τὸ ὅλον περάναντα.

ΘΕΑΙ. Οὐκοῦν εὖ δοκεῖ σοι, ὦ Σώκρατες;

ΣΩ. Εἰ σοί, ὦ ἑταῖρε, δοκεῖ, καὶ ἀποδέχει τὴν διὰ στοιχείου διέξοδον περὶ ἑκάστου λόγον εἶναι, τὴν δὲ κατὰ συλλαβὰς ἢ καὶ κατὰ μεῖζον ἔτι D ἀλογίαν, τοῦτό μοι λέγε, ἵν᾽ αὐτὸ ἐπισκοπῶμεν.

ΘΕΑΙ. Ἀλλὰ πάνυ ἀποδέχομαι.

ΣΩ. Πότερον ἡγούμενος ἐπιστήμονα εἶναι ὁντινοῦν ὁτουοῦν, ὅταν τὸ αὐτὸ τοτὲ[1] μὲν τοῦ αὐτοῦ δοκῇ αὐτῷ εἶναι, τοτὲ δὲ ἑτέρου, ἢ καὶ ὅταν τοῦ αὐτοῦ τοτὲ μὲν ἕτερον, τοτὲ δὲ ἕτερον δοξάζῃ;

ΘΕΑΙ. Μὰ Δί᾽ οὐκ ἔγωγε.

ΣΩ. Εἶτα ἀμνημονεῖς ἐν τῇ τῶν γραμμάτων μαθήσει κατ᾽ ἀρχὰς σαυτόν τε καὶ τοὺς ἄλλους δρῶντας αὐτά;

ΘΕΑΙ. Ἆρα λέγεις τῆς αὐτῆς συλλαβῆς τοτὲ μὲν E ἕτερον, τοτὲ δὲ ἕτερον ἡγουμένους γράμμα, καὶ τὸ αὐτὸ τοτὲ μὲν εἰς τὴν προσήκουσαν, τοτὲ δὲ εἰς ἄλλην τιθέντας συλλαβήν;

ΣΩ. Ταῦτα λέγω.

ΘΕΑΙ. Μὰ Δί᾽ οὐ τοίνυν ἀμνημονῶ, οὐδέ γέ πω ἡγοῦμαι ἐπίστασθαι τοὺς οὕτως ἔχοντας.

---

[1] τοτὲ] τότε W; ὅτε BT.

THEAETETUS

THEAET. Yes, it was.

SOC. So, too, he would say that we have right opinion about a wagon, but that he who can give an account of its essential nature in terms of those one hundred parts has by this addition added rational explanation and has acquired technical knowledge of the essential nature of a wagon, in place of mere opinion, by describing the whole in terms of its elements.

THEAET. Do you agree to that, Socrates?

SOC. If you, my friend, agree to it and accept the view that orderly description in terms of its elements is a rational account of anything, but that description in terms of syllables or still larger units is irrational, tell me so, that we may examine the question.

THEAET. Certainly I accept it.

SOC. Do you accept it in the belief that anyone has knowledge of anything when he thinks that the same element is a part sometimes of one thing and sometimes of another or when he is of opinion that the same thing has as a part of it sometimes one thing and sometimes another?

THEAET. Not at all, by Zeus.

SOC. Then do you forget that when you began to learn to read you and the others did just that?

THEAET. Do you mean when we thought that sometimes one letter and sometimes another belonged to the same syllable, and when we put the same letter sometimes into the proper syllable and sometimes into another?

SOC. That is what I mean.

THEAET. By Zeus, I do not forget, nor do I think that those have knowledge who are in that condition.

ΣΩ. Τί οὖν; ὅταν ἐν τῷ τοιούτῳ καιρῷ " Θεαίτητον " γράφων τις θῆτα καὶ εἶ οἴηταί[1] τε δεῖν
208 γράφειν καὶ γράψῃ, καὶ αὖ " Θεόδωρον " ἐπιχειρῶν γράφειν ταῦ καὶ εἶ οἴηταί[1] τε δεῖν γράφειν
καὶ γράψῃ, ἆρ᾽ ἐπίστασθαι φήσομεν αὐτὸν τὴν
πρώτην τῶν ὑμετέρων ὀνομάτων συλλαβήν;

ΘΕΑΙ. Ἀλλ᾽ ἄρτι ὡμολογήσαμεν τὸν οὕτως
ἔχοντα μήπω εἰδέναι.

ΣΩ. Κωλύει οὖν τι καὶ περὶ τὴν δευτέραν συλλαβὴν καὶ τρίτην καὶ τετάρτην οὕτως ἔχειν τὸν
αὐτόν;

ΘΕΑΙ. Οὐδέν γε.

ΣΩ. Ἆρ᾽ οὖν τότε τὴν διὰ στοιχείου διέξοδον
ἔχων γράψει " Θεαίτητον " μετὰ ὀρθῆς δόξης,
ὅταν ἑξῆς γράφῃ;

ΘΕΑΙ. Δῆλον δή.

B ΣΩ. Οὐκοῦν ἔτι ἀνεπιστήμων ὤν, ὀρθὰ δὲ
δοξάζων, ὥς φαμεν;

ΘΕΑΙ. Ναί.

ΣΩ. Λόγον γε ἔχων μετὰ ὀρθῆς δόξης· τὴν
γὰρ διὰ τοῦ στοιχείου ὁδὸν ἔχων ἔγραφεν, ἣν δὴ
λόγον ὡμολογήσαμεν.

ΘΕΑΙ. Ἀληθῆ.

ΣΩ. Ἔστιν ἄρα, ὦ ἑταῖρε, μετὰ λόγου ὀρθὴ
δόξα, ἣν οὔπω δεῖ ἐπιστήμην καλεῖν.

ΘΕΑΙ. Κινδυνεύει.

43. ΣΩ. Ὄναρ δή, ὡς ἔοικεν, ἐπλουτήσαμεν
οἰηθέντες ἔχειν τὸν ἀληθέστατον ἐπιστήμης λόγον.
ἢ μήπω κατηγορῶμεν; ἴσως γὰρ οὐ τοῦτό τις

[1] οἴηται] οἴεται ΒΤ.

246

soc. Take an example: When at such a stage in his progress a person in writing "Theaetetus" thinks he ought to write, and actually does write, TH and E, and again in trying to write "Theodorus" thinks he ought to write, and does write, T and E, shall we say that he knows the first syllable of your names?

THEAET. No, we just now agreed that a person in such a condition has not yet gained knowledge.

soc. Then there is nothing to prevent the same person from being in that condition with respect to the second and third and fourth syllables?

THEAET. No, nothing.

soc. Then, in that case, he has in mind the orderly description in terms of letters, and will write "Theaetetus" with right opinion, when he writes the letters in order?

THEAET. Evidently.

soc. But he is still, as we say, without knowledge, though he has right opinion?

THEAET. Yes.

soc. Yes, but with his opinion he has rational explanation; for he wrote with the method in terms of letters in his mind, and we agreed that that was rational explanation.

THEAET. True.

soc. There is, then, my friend, a combination of right opinion with rational explanation, which cannot as yet properly be called knowledge?

THEAET. There is not much doubt about it.

soc. So it seems that the perfectly true definition of knowledge, which we thought we had, was but a golden dream. Or shall we wait a bit before we condemn it? Perhaps the definition to be adopted

C αὐτὸν ὁριεῖται, ἀλλὰ τὸ λοιπὸν εἶδος τῶν τριῶν,
ὧν ἕν γέ τι ἔφαμεν λόγον θήσεσθαι τὸν ἐπιστήμην
ὁριζόμενον δόξαν εἶναι ὀρθὴν μετὰ λόγου.

ΘΕΑΙ. Ὀρθῶς ὑπέμνησας· ἔτι γὰρ ἓν λοιπόν.
τὸ μὲν γὰρ ἦν διανοίας ἐν φωνῇ ὥσπερ εἴδωλον,
τὸ δ' ἄρτι λεχθὲν διὰ στοιχείου ὁδὸς ἐπὶ τὸ ὅλον·
τὸ δὲ δὴ τρίτον τί λέγεις;

ΣΩ. Ὅπερ ἂν οἱ πολλοὶ εἴποιεν, τὸ ἔχειν τι σημεῖον εἰπεῖν ᾧ τῶν ἁπάντων διαφέρει τὸ ἐρωτηθέν.

ΘΕΑΙ. Οἷον τίνα τίνος ἔχεις μοι λόγον εἰπεῖν;

D ΣΩ. Οἷον, εἰ βούλει, ἡλίου πέρι ἱκανὸν οἶμαί
σοι εἶναι ἀποδέξασθαι, ὅτι τὸ λαμπρότατόν ἐστι
τῶν κατὰ τὸν οὐρανὸν ἰόντων περὶ γῆν.

ΘΕΑΙ. Πάνυ μὲν οὖν.

ΣΩ. Λαβὲ δὴ οὗ χάριν εἴρηται. ἔστι δὲ ὅπερ
ἄρτι ἐλέγομεν, ὡς ἄρα τὴν διαφορὰν ἑκάστου ἂν
λαμβάνῃς ᾗ τῶν ἄλλων διαφέρει, λόγον, ὥς φασί
τινες, λήψει· ἕως δ' ἂν κοινοῦ τινος ἐφάπτῃ,
ἐκείνων πέρι σοι ἔσται ὁ λόγος ὧν ἂν ἡ κοινότης ᾖ.

E ΘΕΑΙ. Μανθάνω· καί μοι δοκεῖ καλῶς ἔχειν
λόγον τὸ τοιοῦτον καλεῖν.

ΣΩ. Ὃς δ' ἂν μετ' ὀρθῆς δόξης περὶ ὁτουοῦν
τῶν ὄντων τὴν διαφορὰν τῶν ἄλλων προσλάβῃ,

is not this, but the remaining one of the three possibilities one of which we said must be affirmed by anyone who asserts that knowledge is right opinion combined with rational explanation.

THEAET. I am glad you called that to mind. For there is still one left. The first was a kind of vocal image of the thought, the second the orderly approach to the whole through the elements, which we have just been discussing, and what is the third?

soc. It is just the definition which most people would give, that knowledge is the ability to tell some characteristic by which the object in question differs from all others.

THEAET. As an example of the method, what explanation can you give me, and of what thing?

soc. As an example, if you like, take the sun: I think it is enough for you to be told that it is the brightest of the heavenly bodies that revolve about the earth.

THEAET. Certainly.

soc. Understand why I say this. It is because, as we were just saying, if you get hold of the distinguishing characteristic by which a given thing differs from the rest, you will, as some say, get hold of the definition or explanation of it; but so long as you cling to some common quality, your explanation will pertain to all those objects to which the common quality belongs.

THEAET. I understand; and it seems to me that it is quite right to call that kind a rational explanation or definition.

soc. Then he who possesses right opinion about anything and adds thereto a comprehension of the difference which distinguishes it from other things

249

αὐτοῦ ἐπιστήμων γεγονὼς ἔσται, οὗ πρότερον ἦν
δοξαστής.

ΘΕΑΙ. Φαμέν γε μὴν οὕτω.

ΣΩ. Νῦν δῆτα, ὦ Θεαίτητε, παντάπασιν ἔγωγε,[1]
ἐπειδὴ ἐγγὺς ὥσπερ σκιαγραφήματος γέγονα τοῦ
λεγομένου, ξυνίημι οὐδὲ σμικρόν· ἕως δὲ ἀφεστήκη
πόρρωθεν, ἐφαίνετό τί μοι λέγεσθαι.

ΘΕΑΙ. Πῶς τί τοῦτο;

209 ΣΩ. Φράσω, ἐὰν οἷός τε γένωμαι. ὀρθὴν
ἔγωγε[2] ἔχων δόξαν περὶ σοῦ, ἐὰν μὲν προσλάβω
τὸν σὸν λόγον, γιγνώσκω δή σε, εἰ δὲ μή, δοξάζω
μόνον.

ΘΕΑΙ. Ναί.

ΣΩ. Λόγος δέ γε ἦν ἡ τῆς σῆς διαφορότητος
ἑρμηνεία.

ΘΕΑΙ. Οὕτως.

ΣΩ. 'Ηνίκ' οὖν ἐδόξαζον μόνον, ἄλλο τι ᾧ τῶν
ἄλλων διαφέρεις, τούτων οὐδενὸς ἡπτόμην τῇ
διανοίᾳ;

ΘΕΑΙ. Οὐκ ἔοικεν.

ΣΩ. Τῶν κοινῶν τι ἄρα διενοούμην, ὧν οὐδὲν
σὺ μᾶλλον ἤ τις ἄλλος ἔχει.

B ΘΕΑΙ. 'Ανάγκη.

ΣΩ. Φέρε δὴ πρὸς Διός· πῶς ποτε ἐν τῷ
τοιούτῳ σὲ μᾶλλον ἐδόξαζον ἢ ἄλλον ὁντινοῦν;
θὲς γάρ με διανοούμενον ὡς ἔστιν οὗτος Θεαίτητος,
ὃς ἂν ᾖ τε ἄνθρωπος καὶ ἔχῃ ῥῖνα καὶ ὀφθαλμοὺς
καὶ στόμα καὶ οὕτω δὴ ἓν ἕκαστον τῶν μελῶν.
αὕτη οὖν ἡ διάνοια ἔσθ' ὅ τι μᾶλλον ποιήσει με

---

[1] παντάπασιν ἔγωγε W ; παντάπασί γε ἐγώ T.
[2] ἔγωγε W ; ἐγὼ T.

will have acquired knowledge of that thing of which he previously had only opinion.

THEAET. That is what we affirm.

soc. Theaetetus, now that I have come closer to our statement, I do not understand it at all. It is like coming close to a scene-painting.[1] While I stood off at a distance, I thought there was something in it.

THEAET. What do you mean?

soc. I will tell you if I can. Assume that I have right opinion about you; if I add the explanation or definition of you, then I have knowledge of you, otherwise I have merely opinion.

THEAET. Yes.

soc. But explanation was, we agreed, the interpretation of your difference.

THEAET. It was.

soc. Then so long as I had merely opinion, I did not grasp in my thought any of the points in which you differ from others?

THEAET. Apparently not.

soc. Therefore I was thinking of some one of the common traits which you possess no more than other men.

THEAET. You must have been.

soc. For heaven's sake! How in the world could I in that case have any opinion about you more than about anyone else? Suppose that I thought "That is Theaetetus which is a man and has nose and eyes and mouth" and so forth, mentioning all the parts. Can this thought make me think of Theaetetus any

---

[1] In which perspective is the main thing.

Θεαίτητον ἢ Θεόδωρον διανοεῖσθαι, ἢ τῶν λεγομένων Μυσῶν τὸν ἔσχατον;

ΘΕΑΙ. Τί γάρ;

ΣΩ. 'Αλλ' ἐὰν δὴ μὴ μόνον τὸν ἔχοντα ῥῖνα καὶ
C ὀφθαλμοὺς διανοηθῶ, ἀλλὰ καὶ τὸν σιμόν τε καὶ
ἐξόφθαλμον, μή τι σὲ αὖ μᾶλλον δοξάσω ἢ ἐμαυτὸν
ἢ ὅσοι τοιοῦτοι;

ΘΕΑΙ. Οὐδέν.

ΣΩ. 'Αλλ' οὐ πρότερόν γε, οἶμαι, Θεαίτητος ἐν
ἐμοὶ δοξασθήσεται, πρὶν ἂν ἡ σιμότης αὕτη τῶν
ἄλλων σιμοτήτων ὧν ἐγὼ ἑώρακα διάφορόν τι
μνημεῖον παρ' ἐμοὶ ἐνσημηναμένη κατάθηται, καὶ
τἆλλα οὕτω ἐξ ὧν εἶ σύ· ἢ ἐμέ,[1] καὶ ἐὰν αὔριον
ἀπαντήσω, ἀναμνήσει καὶ ποιήσει ὀρθὰ δοξάζειν
περὶ σοῦ.

ΘΕΑΙ. 'Αληθέστατα.

D ΣΩ. Περὶ τὴν διαφορότητα ἄρα καὶ ἡ ὀρθὴ
δόξα ἂν εἴη ἑκάστου πέρι.

ΘΕΑΙ. Φαίνεταί γε.

ΣΩ. Τὸ οὖν προσλαβεῖν λόγον τῇ ὀρθῇ δόξῃ τί
ἂν ἔτι εἴη; εἰ μὲν γὰρ προσδοξάσαι λέγει ᾗ διαφέρει
τι τῶν ἄλλων, πάνυ γελοία γίγνεται ἡ ἐπίταξις.

ΘΕΑΙ. Πῶς;

ΣΩ. Ὧν ὀρθὴν δόξαν ἔχομεν ᾗ τῶν ἄλλων διαφέρει, τούτων προσλαβεῖν κελεύει ἡμᾶς ὀρθὴν
δόξαν ᾗ τῶν ἄλλων διαφέρει. καὶ οὕτως ἡ μὲν

[1] εἰ σύ· ἢ ἐμέ Wohlrab; εἰ σύ· ἢ με W (but ἢ added later);
εἰ σὺ ἐμέ B; εἴσει ἐμὲ T.

more than of Theodorus or of the meanest of the
Mysians,[1] as the saying is?

THEAET. Of course not.

SOC. But if I think not only of a man with nose
and eyes, but of one with snub nose and protruding
eyes, shall I then have an opinion of you any more
than of myself and all others like me?

THEAET. Not at all.

SOC. No; I fancy Theaetetus will not be the
object of opinion in me until this snubnosedness of
yours has stamped and deposited in my mind a
memorial different from those of the other examples of snubnosedness that I have seen, and
the other traits that make up your personality
have done the like. Then that memorial, if I
meet you again tomorrow, will awaken my
memory and make me have right opinion about
you.

THEAET. Very true.

SOC. Then right opinion also would have to do
with differences in any given instance?

THEAET. At any rate, it seems so.

SOC. Then what becomes of the addition of reason
or explanation to right opinion? For if it is defined
as the addition of an opinion of the way in which a
given thing differs from the rest, it is an utterly
absurd injunction.

THEAET. How so?

SOC. When we have a right opinion of the way in
which certain things differ from other things, we are
told to acquire a right opinion of the way in which
those same things differ from other things! On this

[1] The Mysians were despised as especially effeminate and
worthless.

σκυτάλης ἢ ὑπέρου ἢ ὅτου δὴ λέγεται περιτροπὴ
Ε πρὸς ταύτην τὴν ἐπίταξιν οὐδὲν ἂν λέγοι, τυφλοῦ
δὲ παρακέλευσις ἂν καλοῖτο δικαιότερον· τὸ
γάρ, ἃ ἔχομεν, ταῦτα προσλαβεῖν κελεύειν, ἵνα
μάθωμεν ἃ δοξάζομεν, πάνυ γενναίως ἔοικεν ἐσκο-
τωμένῳ.

ΘΕΑΙ. Εἰπὲ δὴ ¹ τί νῦν δὴ ὡς ἐρῶν ἐπύθου;

ΣΩ. Εἰ τὸ λόγον, ὦ παῖ, προσλαβεῖν γνῶναι
κελεύει, ἀλλὰ μὴ δοξάσαι τὴν διαφορότητα, ἡδὺ
χρῆμ᾽ ἂν εἴη τοῦ καλλίστου τῶν περὶ ἐπιστήμης
λόγου. τὸ γὰρ γνῶναι ἐπιστήμην **που** λαβεῖν
210 ἐστιν· ἦ γάρ;

ΘΕΑΙ. Ναί.

ΣΩ. Οὐκοῦν ἐρωτηθείς, ὡς ἔοικε, τί ἐστιν ἐπιστήμη, ἀποκρινεῖται ὅτι δόξα ὀρθὴ μετὰ ἐπιστήμης
διαφορότητος. λόγου γὰρ πρόσληψις τοῦτ᾽ ἂν
εἴη κατ᾽ ἐκεῖνον.

ΘΕΑΙ. Ἔοικεν.

ΣΩ. Καὶ παντάπασί γε εὔηθες, ζητούντων ἡμῶν
ἐπιστήμην, δόξαν φάναι ὀρθὴν εἶναι μετ᾽ ἐπιστήμης
εἴτε διαφορότητος εἴτε ὁτουοῦν. οὔτε ἄρα αἴσθησις, ὦ Θεαίτητε, οὔτε δόξα ἀληθὴς οὔτε μετ᾽
Β ἀληθοῦς δόξης λόγος προσγιγνόμενος ἐπιστήμη
ἂν εἴη.

ΘΕΑΙ. Οὐκ ἔοικεν.

---

¹ εἰπὲ δη T (and W in marg.); εἰ γε δη B; εἴ γε δὴ B²W.

THEAETETUS

plan the twirling of a scytale [1] or a pestle or anything of the sort would be as nothing compared with this injunction. It might more justly be called a blind man's giving directions; for to command us to acquire that which we already have, in order to learn that of which we already have opinion, is very like a man whose sight is mightily darkened.

THEAET. Tell me now, what did you intend to say when you asked the question a while ago?

SOC. If, my boy, the command to add reason or explanation means learning to know and not merely getting an opinion about the difference, our splendid definition of knowledge would be a fine affair! For learning to know is acquiring knowledge, is it not?

THEAET. Yes.

SOC. Then, it seems, if asked, "What is knowledge?" our leader will reply that it is right opinion with the addition of a knowledge of difference; for that would, according to him, be the addition of reason or explanation.

THEAET. So it seems.

SOC. And it is utterly silly, when we are looking for a definition of knowledge, to say that it is right opinion with knowledge, whether of difference or of anything else whatsoever. So neither perception, Theaetetus, nor true opinion, nor reason or explanation combined with true opinion could be knowledge.

THEAET. Apparently not.

[1] A σκυτάλη was a staff, especially a staff about which a strip of leather was rolled, on which dispatches were so written that when unrolled they were illegible until rolled again upon another staff of the same size and shape.

PLATO

ΣΩ. Ἦ οὖν ἔτι κυοῦμέν τι καὶ ὠδίνομεν, ὦ φίλε, περὶ ἐπιστήμης, ἢ πάντα ἐκτετόκαμεν;

ΘΕΑΙ. Καὶ ναὶ μὰ Δί᾽ ἔγωγε πλείω ἢ ὅσα εἶχον ἐν ἐμαυτῷ διὰ σὲ εἴρηκα.

ΣΩ. Οὐκοῦν ταῦτα μὲν πάντα ἡ μαιευτικὴ ἡμῖν τέχνη ἀνεμιαῖά φησι γεγενῆσθαι καὶ οὐκ ἄξια τροφῆς;

ΘΕΑΙ. Παντάπασι μὲν οὖν.

44. ΣΩ. Ἐὰν τοίνυν ἄλλων μετὰ ταῦτα ἐγκύμων ἐπιχειρῇς γίγνεσθαι, ὦ Θεαίτητε, ἐάντε
C γίγνῃ, βελτιόνων ἔσει πλήρης διὰ τὴν νῦν ἐξέτασιν, ἐάντε κενὸς ᾖς, ἧττον ἔσει βαρὺς τοῖς συνοῦσι καὶ ἡμερώτερος, σωφρόνως οὐκ οἰόμενος εἰδέναι ἃ μὴ οἶσθα. τοσοῦτον γὰρ μόνον ἡ ἐμὴ τέχνη δύναται, πλέον δὲ οὐδέν, οὐδέ τι οἶδα ὧν οἱ ἄλλοι, ὅσοι μεγάλοι καὶ θαυμάσιοι ἄνδρες εἰσί τε καὶ γεγόνασι. τὴν δὲ μαιείαν ταύτην ἐγώ τε καὶ ἡ μήτηρ ἐκ θεοῦ ἐλάχομεν, ἡ μὲν τῶν γυναικῶν, ἐγὼ δὲ τῶν νέων τε καὶ γενναίων καὶ ὅσοι καλοί.
D Νῦν μὲν οὖν ἀπαντητέον μοι εἰς τὴν τοῦ βασιλέως στοὰν ἐπὶ τὴν Μελήτου γραφήν, ἥν με γέγραπται· ἕωθεν δέ, ὦ Θεόδωρε, δεῦρο πάλιν ἀπαντῶμεν.

soc. Are we then, my friend, still pregnant and in travail with knowledge, or have we brought forth everything?

THEAET. Yes, we have, and, by Zeus, Socrates, with your help I have already said more than there was in me.

soc. Then does our art of midwifery declare to us that all the offspring that have been born are mere wind-eggs and not worth rearing?

THEAET. It does, decidedly.

soc. If after this you ever undertake to conceive other thoughts, Theaetetus, and do conceive, you will be pregnant with better thoughts than these by reason of the present search, and if you remain barren, you will be less harsh and gentler to your associates, for you will have the wisdom not to think you know that which you do not know. So much and no more my art can accomplish; nor do I know aught of the things that are known by others, the great and wonderful men who are to-day and have been in the past. This art, however, both my mother and I received from God, she for women and I for young and noble men and for all who are fair.

And now I must go to the Porch of the King, to answer to the suit which Meletus[1] has brought against me. But in the morning, Theodorus, let us meet here again.

---

[1] Meletus was one of those who brought the suit which led to the condemnation and death of Socrates.

THE SOPHIST

THE KALILE

INTRODUCTION TO *THE SOPHIST*

In *The Sophist* Theodorus and Theaetetus meet Socrates in accordance with the agreement made in the final paragraph of the *Theaetetus*. They bring with them an Eleatic Stranger, who presently agrees to undertake, with the aid of Theaetetus, the definition of the Philosopher, the Statesman, and the Sophist. Thereupon, after selecting the Sophist as the first of the three to be defined, he proceeds to illustrate his method by defining the angler, on the ground that the Sophist is a difficult subject and that practice on an easier and slighter matter is desirable. The method employed in defining first the angler and then the Sophist is that of comparison and division successively into two parts. This method was probably, at the time when this dialogue was written, something of a novelty, and is employed also in *The Statesman*, which is closely connected with *The Sophist* both in form and substance. It must be admitted that the process of dichotomy becomes very tedious, which may possibly be one of Plato's reasons for making the Stranger, not Socrates, the chief speaker in these two dialogues. The definition of the Sophist—the avowed purpose of the dialogue—is

carried on in a satirical and polemic spirit which is abundantly evident even when it is no longer possible to name the particular persons against whom the attack is directed.

But all this occupies only the opening and concluding passages. It is interrupted by what is in form a long digression, but is really the most serious and important part of the whole. In this (236 D— 264 B) the method of dichotomy is given up and abstract questions are treated in a quite different manner. The Sophist has been found to be a juggler and deceiver, and the question arises whether deception or falsehood does not involve the assumption of Not-Being, which was persistently opposed by Parmenides and the Eleatic philosophers in general. Plato refutes the doctrine that Not-Being cannot exist by showing that it has a relative existence— that in each particular instance it denotes a difference or condition of being other than that in connexion with which it is said to exist. It is not mere negation—the opposite of Being—but becomes the positive notion of Difference. This is the most important doctrine promulgated in this dialogue.

Hereupon follows the discussion of the nature of Being, and the conclusion is reached that everything which possesses any power, either to produce a change or to be affected by a cause, has existence (247 D), *i.e.*, that power—whether active or passive— is Being.

The problem of predication—of the possibility of assertion—is solved by making the distinction between verbs and nouns and defining the sentence as a combination of those two. If that combination corresponds to reality, the assertion is true, if not, it

is false. How far this is original with Plato is difficult to determine. Other subjects discussed in this dialogue are the theory of knowledge, the relation between reality and appearance, and that between the one and the many. The introduction of the five "forms" or categories—Being, Motion, Rest, Same and Other—is an interesting feature which may be interpreted as marking a stage in the development of the theory of ideas. This dialogue is important in content, though not especially attractive in form.

The date of *The Sophist* cannot be earlier, and may be considerably later, than that of the *Theaetetus.*

There is an edition of *The Sophist and Politicus,* with English notes, by Lewis Campbell (Oxford, 1864).

ΣΟΦΙΣΤΗΣ

[Η ΠΕΡΙ ΤΟΥ ΟΝΤΟΣ · ΛΟΓΙΚΟΣ]

ΤΑ ΤΟΥ ΔΙΑΛΟΓΟΥ ΠΡΟΣΩΠΑ

ΘΕΟΔΩΡΟΣ, ΣΩΚΡΑΤΗΣ, ΞΕΝΟΣ ΕΛΕΑΤΗΣ, ΘΕΑΙΤΗΤΟΣ

1. ΘΕΟ. Κατὰ τὴν χθὲς ὁμολογίαν, ὦ Σώκρατες, ἥκομεν αὐτοί τε κοσμίως καὶ τόνδε τινὰ ξένον ἄγομεν, τὸ μὲν γένος ἐξ Ἐλέας, ἑταῖρον δὲ τῶν ἀμφὶ Παρμενίδην καὶ Ζήνωνα,[1] μάλα δὲ ἄνδρα φιλόσοφον.

ΣΩ. Ἆρ' οὖν, ὦ Θεόδωρε, οὐ ξένον ἀλλά τινα θεὸν ἄγων κατὰ τὸν Ὁμήρου λόγον λέληθας; ὅς
B φησιν ἄλλους τε θεοὺς τοῖς ἀνθρώποις ὁπόσοι μετέχουσιν αἰδοῦς δικαίας, καὶ δὴ καὶ τὸν ξένιον οὐχ ἥκιστα θεὸν συνοπαδὸν γιγνόμενον ὕβρεις τε καὶ εὐνομίας τῶν ἀνθρώπων καθορᾶν. τάχ' οὖν ἂν καὶ σοί τις οὗτος τῶν κρειττόνων συνέποιτο, φαύλους ἡμᾶς ὄντας ἐν τοῖς λόγοις ἐποψόμενός τε καὶ ἐλέγξων, θεὸς ὤν τις ἐλεγκτικός.

ΘΕΟ. Οὐχ οὗτος ὁ τρόπος, ὦ Σώκρατες, τοῦ

---

[1] Ζήνωνα ἑταίρων mss. ; ἑταίρων om. Upton.

264

THE SOPHIST

[OR ON BEING: LOGICAL]

CHARACTERS

THEODORUS, SOCRATES, AN ELEAN STRANGER, THEAETETUS

THEO. According to our yesterday's agreement, Socrates, we have come ourselves, as we were bound to do, and we bring also this man with us; he is a stranger from Elea, one of the followers of Parmenides and Zeno, and a real philosopher.

SOC. Are you not unwittingly bringing, as Homer says, some god, and no mere stranger, Theodorus? He says that the gods, and especially the god of strangers, enter into companionship with men who have a share of due reverence [1] and that they behold the deeds, both violent and righteous,[1] of mankind. So perhaps this companion of yours may be one of the higher powers, who comes to watch over and refute us because we are worthless in argument—a kind of god of refutation.

THEO. No, Socrates, that is not the stranger's

---

[1] A modified quotation from *Odyssey*, ix. 271; xvii. 485-7.

ξένου, ἀλλὰ μετριώτερος τῶν περὶ τὰς ἔριδας
ἐσπουδακότων. καί μοι δοκεῖ θεὸς μὲν ἀνὴρ [1]
C οὐδαμῶς εἶναι, θεῖος μήν· πάντας γὰρ ἐγὼ τοὺς
φιλοσόφους τοιούτους προσαγορεύω.

ΣΩ. Καλῶς γε, ὦ φίλε. τοῦτο μέντοι κινδυνεύει
τὸ γένος οὐ πολύ τι ῥᾶον, ὡς ἔπος εἰπεῖν, εἶναι
διακρίνειν ἢ τὸ τοῦ θεοῦ· πάνυ γὰρ ἄνδρες [2] οὗτοι
παντοῖοι φανταζόμενοι διὰ τὴν τῶν ἄλλων ἄγνοιαν
ἐπιστρωφῶσι πόληας, οἱ μὴ πλαστῶς ἀλλ' ὄντως
φιλόσοφοι, καθορῶντες ὑψόθεν τὸν τῶν κάτω βίον,
καὶ τοῖς μὲν δοκοῦσιν εἶναι τοῦ μηδενὸς τίμιοι,
τοῖς δ' ἄξιοι τοῦ παντός· καὶ τοτὲ μὲν πολιτικοὶ
D φαντάζονται, τοτὲ δὲ σοφισταί, τοτὲ δ' ἔστιν
οἷς δόξαν παράσχοιντο ἂν ὡς παντάπασιν ἔχοντες
μανικῶς. τοῦ μέντοι ξένου ἡμῖν ἡδέως ἂν πυνθα-
νοίμην, εἰ φίλον αὐτῷ, τί ταῦθ' οἱ περὶ τὸν ἐκεῖ
217 τόπον ἡγοῦντο καὶ ὠνόμαζον.

ΘΕΟ. Τὰ ποῖα δή;

ΣΩ. Σοφιστήν, πολιτικόν, φιλόσοφον.

ΘΕΟ. Τί δὲ μάλιστα καὶ τὸ ποῖόν τι περὶ αὐτῶν
διαπορηθεὶς ἐρέσθαι διενοήθης;

ΣΩ. Τόδε· πότερον ἓν πάντα ταῦτα ἐνόμιζον
ἢ δύο, ἢ καθάπερ τὰ ὀνόματα τρία, τρία καὶ γένη
διαιρούμενοι καθ' ἓν ὄνομα γένος ἑκάστῳ προσ-
ῆπτον;

ΘΕΟ. Ἀλλ' οὐδείς, ὡς ἐγῷμαι, φθόνος αὐτῷ
διελθεῖν αὐτά· ἢ πῶς, ὦ ξένε, λέγωμεν;

B ΞΕ. Οὕτως, ὦ Θεόδωρε. φθόνος μὲν γὰρ
οὐδεὶς οὐδὲ χαλεπὸν εἰπεῖν ὅτι γε τρί' ἡγοῦντο·

---

[1] ἀνὴρ Bekker; ἀνήρ BT.
[2] ἄνδρες Bekker; ἄνδρες BT.

THE SOPHIST

character; he is more reasonable than those who devote themselves to disputation. And though I do not think he is a god at all, I certainly do think he is divine, for I give that epithet to all philosophers.

soc. And rightly, my friend. However, I fancy it is not much easier, if I may say so, to recognize this class, than that of the gods. For these men—I mean those who are not feignedly but really philosophers—appear disguised in all sorts of shapes,[1] thanks to the ignorance of the rest of mankind, and visit the cities,[1] beholding from above the life of those below, and they seem to some to be of no worth and to others to be worth everything. And sometimes they appear disguised as statesmen and sometimes as sophists, and sometimes they may give some people the impression that they are altogether mad. But I should like to ask our stranger here, if agreeable to him, what people in his country thought about these matters, and what names they used.

theo. What matters do you mean?

soc. Sophist, statesman, philosopher.

theo. What particular difficulty and what kind of difficulty in regard to them is it about which you had in mind to ask?

soc. It is this: Did they consider all these one, or two, or, as there are three names, did they divide them into three classes and ascribe to each a class, corresponding to a single name?

theo. I think he has no objection to talking about them. What do you say, stranger?

str. Just what you did, Theodorus; for I have no objection, and it is not difficult to say that they

[1] *Cf. Od.* xvii. 485-7.

καθ' ἕκαστον μὴν διορίσασθαι σαφῶς τί ποτ'
ἔστιν, οὐ σμικρὸν οὐδὲ ῥάδιον ἔργον.

ΘΕΟ. Καὶ μὲν δὴ κατὰ τύχην γε, ὦ Σώκρατες,
λόγων ἐπελάβου παραπλησίων ὧν καὶ πρὶν ἡμᾶς
δεῦρ' ἐλθεῖν διερωτῶντες αὐτὸν ἐτυγχάνομεν· ὁ
δὲ ταῦτα ἅπερ πρὸς σὲ νῦν, καὶ τότε ἐσκήπτετο
πρὸς ἡμᾶς· ἐπεὶ διακηκοέναι γέ φησιν ἱκανῶς
καὶ οὐκ ἀμνημονεῖν.

C 2. ΣΩ. Μὴ τοίνυν, ὦ ξένε, ἡμῶν τήν γε πρώτην αἰτησάντων χάριν ἀπαρνηθεὶς γένῃ, τοσόνδε
δ' ἡμῖν φράζε· πότερον εἴωθας ἥδιον αὐτὸς ἐπὶ
σαυτοῦ μακρῷ λόγῳ διεξιέναι λέγων τοῦτο ὃ ἂν
ἐνδείξασθαί τῳ βουληθῇς, ἢ δι' ἐρωτήσεων, οἷόν
ποτε καὶ Παρμενίδῃ χρωμένῳ καὶ διεξιόντι λόγους
παγκάλους παρεγενόμην ἐγὼ νέος ὤν, ἐκείνου
μάλα δὴ τότε ὄντος πρεσβύτου;

ΞΕ. Τῷ μέν, ὦ Σώκρατες, ἀλύπως τε καὶ
D εὐηνίως προσδιαλεγομένῳ ῥᾷον οὕτω, τὸ πρὸς
ἄλλον· εἰ δὲ μή, τὸ καθ' αὑτόν.

ΣΩ. Ἔξεστι τοίνυν τῶν παρόντων ὃν ἂν βουληθῇς ἐκλέξασθαι· πάντες γὰρ ὑπακούσονταί σοι
πράῳς· συμβούλῳ μὴν ἐμοὶ χρώμενος τῶν νέων
τινὰ αἱρήσει, Θεαίτητον τόνδε, ἢ καὶ τῶν ἄλλων
εἴ τίς σοι κατὰ νοῦν.

ΞΕ. Ὦ Σώκρατες, αἰδώς τίς μ' ἔχει τὸ νῦν
πρῶτον συγγενόμενον ὑμῖν μὴ κατὰ σμικρὸν ἔπος
πρὸς ἔπος ποιεῖσθαι τὴν συνουσίαν, ἀλλ' ἐκτεί-
ναντα ἀπομηκύνειν λόγον συχνὸν κατ' ἐμαυτόν,
E εἴτε καὶ πρὸς ἕτερον, οἷον [1] ἐπίδειξιν ποιούμενον·
τῷ γὰρ ὄντι τὸ νῦν ῥηθὲν οὐχ ὅσον ὧδε ἐρωτηθὲν
ἐλπίσειεν ἂν αὐτὸ εἶναί τις, ἀλλὰ τυγχάνει λόγου

[1] οἷον Ast; ὅσον BT.

THE SOPHIST

considered them three. But it is no small or easy task to define clearly the nature of each.

THEO. The fact is, Socrates, that by chance you have hit upon a question very like what we happened to be asking him before we came here; and he made excuses to us then, as he does now to you; though he admits that he has heard it thoroughly discussed and remembers what he heard.

soc. In that case, stranger, do not refuse us the first favour we have asked; but just tell us this: Do you generally prefer to expound in a long uninterrupted speech of your own whatever you wish to explain to anyone, or do you prefer the method of questions? I was present once when Parmenides employed the latter method and carried on a splendid discussion. I was a young man then, and he was very old.

STR. The method of dialogue, Socrates, is easier with an interlocutor who is tractable and gives no trouble; but otherwise I prefer the continuous speech by one person.

soc. Well, you may choose whomever you please of those present; they will all respond pleasantly to you; but if you take my advice you will choose one of the young fellows, Theaetetus here, or any of the others who suits you.

STR. Socrates, this is the first time I have come among you, and I am somewhat ashamed, instead of carrying on the discussion by merely giving brief replies to your questions, to deliver an extended, long drawn out speech, either as an address of my own or in reply to another, as if I were giving an exhibition; but I must, for really the present subject is not what one might expect from the form of the question, but is a matter for very long speech. On

παμμήκους ὄν. τὸ δὲ αὖ σοὶ μὴ χαρίζεσθαι καὶ
τοῖσδε, ἄλλως τε καὶ σοῦ λέξαντος ὡς εἶπες,
ἄξενόν τι καταφαίνεταί μοι καὶ ἄγριον. ἐπεὶ
218 Θεαίτητόν γε τὸν προσδιαλεγόμενον εἶναι δέχομαι
παντάπασιν ἐξ ὧν αὐτός τε πρότερον διείλεγμαι
καὶ σὺ τὰ νῦν μοι διακελεύει.

ΘΕΑΙ. Ἆρα τοίνυν, ὦ ξένε, οὕτω καὶ καθάπερ
εἶπε Σωκράτης πᾶσι κεχαρισμένος ἔσει;

ΞΕ. Κινδυνεύει πρὸς μὲν ταῦτα οὐδὲν ἔτι λεκτέον
εἶναι, Θεαίτητε· πρὸς δὲ σὲ ἤδη τὸ μετὰ τοῦτο,
ὡς ἔοικε, γίγνοιτο ἂν ὁ λόγος. ἂν δ' ἄρα τι τῷ
μήκει πονῶν ἄχθῃ, μὴ ἐμὲ αἰτιᾶσθαι τούτων, ἀλλὰ
τούσδε τοὺς σοὺς ἑταίρους.

Β ΘΕΑΙ. Ἀλλ' οἶμαι μὲν δὴ νῦν οὕτως οὐκ ἀπ-
ερεῖν· ἂν δ' ἄρα τι τοιοῦτον γίγνηται, καὶ τόνδε
παραληψόμεθα Σωκράτη, τὸν Σωκράτους μὲν
ὁμώνυμον, ἐμὸν δὲ ἡλικιώτην καὶ συγγυμναστήν,
ᾧ συνδιαπονεῖν μετ' ἐμοῦ τὰ πολλὰ οὐκ ἄηθες.

3. ΞΕ. Εὖ λέγεις, καὶ ταῦτα μὲν ἰδίᾳ βουλεύσει
προϊόντος τοῦ λόγου· κοινῇ δὲ μετ' ἐμοῦ σοι
συσκεπτέον ἀρχομένῳ πρῶτον, ὡς ἐμοὶ φαίνεται,
νῦν ἀπὸ τοῦ σοφιστοῦ, ζητοῦντι καὶ ἐμφανίζοντι
C λόγῳ τί ποτ' ἔστι. νῦν γὰρ δὴ σὺ κἀγὼ τούτου
πέρι τοὔνομα μόνον ἔχομεν κοινῇ· τὸ δὲ ἔργον
ἐφ' ᾧ καλοῦμεν ἑκάτερος τάχ' ἂν ἰδίᾳ παρ' ἡμῖν
αὐτοῖς ἔχοιμεν· δεῖ δὲ ἀεὶ παντὸς πέρι τὸ πρᾶγμα
αὐτὸ μᾶλλον διὰ λόγων ἢ τοὔνομα μόνον συνομο-
λογήσασθαι χωρὶς λόγου. τὸ δὲ φῦλον ὃ νῦν ἐπι-
νοοῦμεν ζητεῖν οὐ πάντων ῥᾷστον συλλαβεῖν τί

THE SOPHIST

the other hand it seems unfriendly and discourteous to refuse a favour to you and these gentlemen, especially when you have spoken as you did. As for Theaetetus I accept him most willingly as interlocutor in view of my previous conversation with him and of your present recommendation.

THEAET. But, stranger, by taking this course and following Socrates's suggestion will you please the others too?

STR. I am afraid there is nothing more to be said about that, Theaetetus; but from now on, my talk will, I fancy, be addressed to you. And if you get tired and are bored by the length of the talk, do not blame me, but these friends of yours.

THEAET. Oh, no, I do not think I shall get tired of it so easily, but if such a thing does happen, we will call in this Socrates, the namesake of the other Socrates; he is of my own age and my companion in the gymnasium, and is in the habit of working with me in almost everything.

STR. Very well; you will follow your own devices about that as the discussion proceeds; but now you and I must investigate in common, beginning first, as it seems to me, with the sophist, and must search out and make plain by argument what he is. For as yet you and I have nothing in common about him but the name; but as to the thing to which we give the name, we may perhaps each have a conception of it in our own minds; however, we ought always in every instance to come to agreement about the thing itself by argument rather than about the mere name without argument. But the tribe which we now intend to search for, the sophist, is not the easiest thing in the world to catch and define, and

271

ποτ᾽ ἔστιν, ὁ σοφιστής· ὅσα δ᾽ αὖ τῶν μεγάλων
δεῖ διαπονεῖσθαι καλῶς, περὶ τῶν τοιούτων δέδοκται πᾶσιν καὶ πάλαι τὸ πρότερον ἐν σμικροῖς
D καὶ ῥάοσιν αὐτὰ δεῖν μελετᾶν, πρὶν ἐν αὐτοῖς τοῖς
μεγίστοις. νῦν οὖν, ὦ Θεαίτητε, ἔγωγε καὶ νῷν
οὕτω συμβουλεύω, χαλεπὸν καὶ δυσθήρευτον ἡγη-
σαμένοις εἶναι τὸ τοῦ σοφιστοῦ γένος πρότερον ἐν
ἄλλῳ ῥάονι τὴν μέθοδον αὐτοῦ προμελετᾶν, εἰ
μὴ σύ ποθεν εὐπετεστέραν ἔχεις εἰπεῖν ἄλλην ὁδόν.

ΘΕΑΙ. Ἀλλ᾽ οὐκ ἔχω.

ΞΕ. Βούλει δῆτα περί τινος τῶν φαύλων μετιόντες
πειραθῶμεν παράδειγμα αὐτὸ θέσθαι τοῦ μείζονος;

E ΘΕΑΙ. Ναί.

ΞΕ. Τί δῆτα προταξαίμεθ᾽ ἂν εὔγνωστον μὲν καὶ
σμικρόν, λόγον δὲ μηδενὸς ἐλάττονα ἔχον τῶν
μειζόνων; οἷον ἀσπαλιευτής· ἆρ᾽ οὐ πᾶσί τε
γνώριμον καὶ σπουδῆς οὐ πάνυ τι πολλῆς τινος
ἐπάξιον;

ΘΕΑΙ. Οὕτως.

219 ΞΕ. Μέθοδον μὴν αὐτὸν ἐλπίζω καὶ λόγον οὐκ
ἀνεπιτήδειον ἡμῖν ἔχειν πρὸς ὃ βουλόμεθα.

ΘΕΑΙ. Καλῶς ἂν ἔχοι.

4. ΞΕ. Φέρε δή, τῇδε ἀρχώμεθα αὐτοῦ. καί
μοι λέγε· πότερον ὡς τεχνίτην αὐτὸν ἤ τινα ἄτεχνον, ἄλλην δὲ δύναμιν ἔχοντα θήσομεν;

ΘΕΑΙ. Ἥκιστά γε ἄτεχνον.

ΞΕ. Ἀλλὰ μὴν τῶν γε τεχνῶν πασῶν σχεδὸν
εἴδη δύο.

ΘΕΑΙ. Πῶς;

ΞΕ. Γεωργία μὲν καὶ ὅση περὶ τὸ θνητὸν πᾶν
σῶμα θεραπεία, τό τε αὖ περὶ τὸ σύνθετον καὶ
B πλαστόν, ὃ δὴ σκεῦος ὠνομάκαμεν, ἥ τε μιμητική,

272

everyone has agreed long ago that if investigations of great matters are to be properly worked out we ought to practise them on small and easier matters before attacking the very greatest. So now, Theaetetus, this is my advice to ourselves, since we think the family of sophists is troublesome and hard to catch, that we first practise the method of hunting in something easier, unless you perhaps have some simpler way to suggest.

THEAET. I have not.

STR. Then shall we take some lesser thing and try to use it as a pattern for the greater?

THEAET. Yes.

STR. Well, then, what example can we set before us which is well known and small, but no less capable of definition than any of the greater things? Say an angler; is he not known to all and unworthy of any great interest?

THEAET. Yes.

STR. But I hope he offers us a method and is capable of a definition not unsuitable to our purpose.

THEAET. That would be good.

STR. Come now; let us begin with him in this way: Tell me, shall we say that he is a man with an art, or one without an art, but having some other power?

THEAET. Certainly not one without an art.

STR. But of all arts there are, speaking generally, two kinds?

THEAET. How so?

STR. Agriculture and all kinds of care of any living beings, and that which has to do with things which are put together or moulded (utensils we call

ξύμπαντα ταῦτα δικαιότατ' ἂν[1] ἑνὶ προσαγο-
ρεύοιτ' ἂν ὀνόματι.

ΘΕΑΙ. Πῶς καὶ τίνι;

ΞΕ. Πᾶν ὅπερ ἂν μὴ πρότερόν τις ὂν ὕστερον
εἰς οὐσίαν ἄγῃ, τὸν μὲν ἄγοντα ποιεῖν, τὸ δὲ ἀγό-
μενον ποιεῖσθαί πού φαμεν.

ΘΕΑΙ. Ὀρθῶς.

ΞΕ. Τὰ δέ γε νῦν δὴ ἃ[2] διήλθομεν ἅπαντα εἶχεν
εἰς τοῦτο τὴν αὐτῶν δύναμιν.

ΘΕΑΙ. Εἶχε γὰρ οὖν.

ΞΕ. Ποιητικὴν τοίνυν αὐτὰ συγκεφαλαιωσάμενοι
προσείπωμεν.

C ΘΕΑΙ. Ἔστω.

ΞΕ. Τὸ δὲ μαθηματικὸν αὖ μετὰ τοῦτο εἶδος
ὅλον καὶ τὸ τῆς γνωρίσεως τό τε χρηματιστικὸν
καὶ ἀγωνιστικὸν καὶ θηρευτικόν, ἐπειδὴ δημιουργεῖ
μὲν οὐδὲν τούτων, τὰ δὲ ὄντα καὶ γεγονότα τὰ
μὲν χειροῦται λόγοις καὶ πράξεσι, τὰ δὲ τοῖς
χειρουμένοις οὐκ ἐπιτρέπει, μάλιστ' ἂν που διὰ
ταῦτα ξυνάπαντα τὰ μέρη τέχνῃ τις κτητικὴ
λεχθεῖσα ἂν διαπρέψειεν.

ΘΕΑΙ. Ναί· πρέποι γὰρ ἄν.

5. ΞΕ. Κτητικῆς δὴ καὶ ποιητικῆς ξυμπασῶν
D οὐσῶν τῶν τεχνῶν ἐν ποτέρᾳ τὴν ἀσπαλιευτικήν,
ὦ Θεαίτητε, τιθῶμεν;

ΘΕΑΙ. Ἐν κτητικῇ που δῆλον.

ΞΕ. Κτητικῆς δὲ ἆρ' οὐ δύο εἴδη; τὸ μὲν ἑκόντων πρὸς ἑκόντας μεταβλητικὸν ὂν διά τε δωρεῶν
καὶ μισθώσεων καὶ ἀγοράσεων, τὸ δὲ λοιπὸν ἢ

---

[1] δικαιότατ' ἂν BT ; δικαιότατα W, Stobaeus.
[2] ἃ om. BTW.

them), and the art of imitation—all these might properly be called by one name.

THEAET. How so, and what is the name?

STR. When anyone brings into being something which did not previously exist, we say that he who brings it into being produces it and that which is brought into being is produced.

THEAET. Certainly.

STR. Now all the arts which we have just mentioned direct their energy to production.

THEAET. Yes, they do.

STR. Let us, then, call these collectively the productive art.

THEAET. Agreed.

STR. And after this comes the whole class of learning and that of acquiring knowledge, and money making, and fighting, and hunting. None of these is creative, but they are all engaged in coercing, by deeds or words, things which already exist and have been produced, or in preventing others from coercing them; therefore all these divisions together might very properly be called acquisitive art.

THEAET. Yes, that would be proper.

STR. Then since acquisitive and productive art comprise all the arts, in which, Theaetetus, shall we place the art of angling?

THEAET. In acquisitive art, clearly.

STR. And are there not two classes of acquisitive art—one the class of exchange between voluntary agents by means of gifts and wages and purchases, and the other, which comprises all the rest of

κατ' ἔργα ἢ κατὰ λόγους χειρούμενον ξύμπαν χειρωτικὸν ἂν εἴη;

ΘΕΑΙ. Φαίνεται γοῦν ἐκ τῶν εἰρημένων.

ΞΕ. Τί δέ; τὴν χειρωτικὴν ἆρ' οὐ διχῇ τμητέον;

ΘΕΑΙ. Πῇ;

ΞΕ. Τὸ μὲν ἀναφανδὸν ὅλον ἀγωνιστικὸν θέντας,[1]
E τὸ δὲ κρυφαῖον αὐτῆς πᾶν θηρευτικόν.

ΘΕΑΙ. Ναί.

ΞΕ. Τὴν δέ γε μὴν θηρευτικὴν ἄλογον τὸ μὴ οὐ τέμνειν διχῇ.

ΘΕΑΙ. Λέγε ὅπῃ.

ΞΕ. Τὸ μὲν ἀψύχου γένους διελομένους, τὸ δ' ἐμψύχου.

ΘΕΑΙ. Τί μήν; εἴπερ ἔστον γε ἄμφω.

220 ΞΕ. Πῶς δὲ οὐκ ἔστον; καὶ δεῖ γε ἡμᾶς τὸ μὲν τῶν ἀψύχων, ἀνώνυμον ὂν[2] πλὴν κατ' ἔνια τῆς κολυμβητικῆς ἄττα μέρη καὶ τοιαῦτ' ἄλλα βραχέα, χαίρειν ἐᾶσαι, τὸ δέ, τῶν ἐμψύχων ζῴων οὖσαν θήραν, προσειπεῖν ζωοθηρικήν.

ΘΕΑΙ. Ἔστω.

ΞΕ. Ζωοθηρικῆς δὲ ἆρ' οὐ διπλοῦν εἶδος ἂν λέγοιτο ἐν δίκῃ, τὸ μὲν πεζοῦ γένους, πολλοῖς εἴδεσι καὶ ὀνόμασι διῃρημένον, πεζοθηρικόν, τὸ δ' ἕτερον νευστικοῦ ζῴου πᾶν ἐνυγροθηρικόν;

ΘΕΑΙ. Πάνυ γε.

B ΞΕ. Νευστικοῦ μὴν τὸ μὲν πτηνὸν φῦλον ὁρῶμεν, τὸ δὲ ἔνυδρον;

ΘΕΑΙ. Πῶς δ' οὔ;

ΞΕ. Καὶ τοῦ πτηνοῦ μὴν γένους πᾶσα ἡμῖν ἡ θήρα λέγεταί πού τις ὀρνιθευτική.

[1] θέντας Stobaeus; θέντες BT.
[2] ὂν Heindorf; ἐᾶν BTW.

acquisitive art, and, since it coerces either by word or deed, might be called coercive?

THEAET. It appears so, at any rate, from what you have said.

STR. Well then, shall we not divide coercive art into two parts?

THEAET. In what way?

STR. By calling all the open part of it fighting and all the secret part hunting.

THEAET. Yes.

STR. But it would be unreasonable not to divide hunting into two parts.

THEAET. Say how it can be done.

STR. By dividing it into the hunting of the lifeless and of the living.

THEAET. Certainly, if both exist.

STR. Of course they exist. And we must pass over the hunting of lifeless things, which has no name, with the exception of some kinds of diving and the like, which are of little importance; but the hunting of living things we will call animal-hunting.

THEAET. Very well.

STR. And two classes of animal-hunting might properly be made, one (and this is divided under many classes and names) the hunting of creatures that go on their feet, land-animal hunting, and the other that of swimming creatures, to be called, as a whole, water-animal hunting?

THEAET. Certainly.

STR. And of swimming creatures we see that one tribe is winged and the other is in the water?

THEAET. Of course.

STR. And the hunting of winged creatures is called, as a whole, fowling.

ΘΕΑΙ. Λέγεται γὰρ οὖν.

ΞΕ. Τοῦ δὲ ἐνύδρου σχεδὸν τὸ σύνολον ἁλιευτική.

ΘΕΑΙ. Ναί.

ΞΕ. Τί δέ; ταύτην αὖ τὴν θήραν ἆρ' οὐκ ἂν κατὰ μέγιστα μέρη δύο διελοίμην;

ΘΕΑΙ. Κατὰ ποῖα;

ΞΕ. Καθ' ἃ τὸ μὲν ἕρκεσιν αὐτόθεν[1] ποιεῖται τὴν θήραν, τὸ δὲ πληγῇ.

ΘΕΑΙ. Πῶς λέγεις, καὶ πῇ διαιρούμενος ἑκάτερον;

ΞΕ. Τὸ μέν, ὅτι πᾶν ὅσον ἂν ἕνεκα κωλύσεως C εἴργῃ τι περιέχον, ἕρκος εἰκὸς ὀνομάζειν.

ΘΕΑΙ. Πάνυ μὲν οὖν.

ΞΕ. Κύρτους δὴ καὶ δίκτυα καὶ βρόχους καὶ πόρκους καὶ τὰ τοιαῦτα μῶν ἄλλο τι πλὴν ἕρκη χρὴ προσαγορεύειν;

ΘΕΑΙ. Οὐδέν.

ΞΕ. Τοῦτο μὲν ἄρα ἑρκοθηρικὸν τῆς ἄγρας τὸ μέρος φήσομεν ἤ τι τοιοῦτον.

ΘΕΑΙ. Ναί.

ΞΕ. Τὸ δὲ ἀγκίστροις καὶ τριόδουσι πληγῇ γιγνόμενον ἕτερον μὲν ἐκείνου, πληκτικὴν δέ τινα D θήραν ἡμᾶς προσειπεῖν ἑνὶ λόγῳ νῦν χρεών· ἢ τί τις ἄν, Θεαίτητε, εἴποι κάλλιον;

ΘΕΑΙ. Ἀμελῶμεν τοῦ ὀνόματος· ἀρκεῖ γὰρ καὶ τοῦτο.

ΞΕ. Τῆς τοίνυν πληκτικῆς τὸ μὲν νυκτερινόν, οἶμαι, πρὸς πυρὸς φῶς γιγνόμενον ὑπ' αὐτῶν τῶν περὶ τὴν θήραν πυρευτικὴν ῥηθῆναι συμβέβηκεν.

ΘΕΑΙ. Πάνυ γε.

ΞΕ. Τὸ δέ γε μεθημερινόν, ὡς ἐχόντων ἐν ἄκροις ἄγκιστρα καὶ τῶν τριοδόντων, πᾶν ἀγκιστρευτικόν.

---

[1] αὐτόθεν al. ; αὐτόθι BT.

THE SOPHIST

THEAET. It is.

STR. And the hunting of water creatures goes by the general name of fishing.

THEAET. Yes.

STR. And might I not divide this kind of hunting into two principal divisions?

THEAET. What divisions?

STR. The one carries on the hunt by means of enclosures merely, the other by a blow.

THEAET. What do you mean, and how do you distinguish the two?

STR. As regards the first, because whatever surrounds anything and encloses it so as to constrain it is properly called an enclosure.

THEAET. Certainly.

STR. May not, then, wicker baskets and seines and snares and nets and the like be called enclosures?

THEAET. Assuredly.

STR. Then we will call this division hunting by enclosures, or something of that sort.

THEAET. Yes.

STR. And the other, which is done with a blow, by means of hooks and three pronged spears, we must now—to name it with a single word—call striking; or could a better name be found, Theaetetus?

THEAET. Never mind the name; that will do well enough.

STR. Then the kind of striking which takes place at night by the light of a fire is, I suppose, called by the hunters themselves fire-hunting.

THEAET. To be sure.

STR. And that which belongs to the daytime is, as a whole, barb-hunting, since the spears, as well as the hooks, are tipped with barbs.

Ε   ΘΕΑΙ. Λέγεται γὰρ οὖν.

6. ΞΕ. Τοῦ τοίνυν ἀγκιστρευτικοῦ τῆς πληκτικῆς τὸ μὲν ἄνωθεν εἰς τὸ κάτω γιγνόμενον διὰ τὸ
τοῖς τριόδουσιν οὕτω μάλιστα χρῆσθαι τριοδοντία
τις, οἶμαι, κέκληται.

ΘΕΑΙ. Φασὶ γοῦν τινές.

ΞΕ. Τὸ δέ γε λοιπόν ἐστιν ἓν ἔτι μόνον ὡς εἰπεῖν
εἶδος.

ΘΕΑΙ. Τὸ ποῖον;

ΞΕ. Τὸ τῆς ἐναντίας ταύτῃ πληγῆς, ἀγκίστρῳ
τε γιγνόμενον καὶ τῶν ἰχθύων οὐχ ᾗ τις ἂν τύχῃ
221 τοῦ σώματος, ὥσπερ τοῖς τριόδουσιν, ἀλλὰ περὶ
τὴν κεφαλὴν καὶ τὸ στόμα τοῦ θηρευθέντος ἑκάστοτε, καὶ κάτωθεν εἰς τοὐναντίον ἄνω ῥάβδοις
καὶ καλάμοις ἀνασπώμενον· οὗ τί φήσομεν, ὦ
Θεαίτητε, δεῖν τοὔνομα λέγεσθαι;

ΘΕΑΙ. Δοκῶ μέν, ὅπερ ἄρτι προὐθέμεθα δεῖν
ἐξευρεῖν, τοῦτ' αὐτὸ νῦν ἀποτετελέσθαι.

7. ΞΕ. Νῦν ἄρα τῆς ἀσπαλιευτικῆς πέρι σύ [1]
Β τε κἀγὼ συνωμολογήκαμεν οὐ μόνον τοὔνομα,
ἀλλὰ καὶ τὸν λόγον περὶ αὐτὸ τοὖργον εἰλήφαμεν
ἱκανῶς. ξυμπάσης γὰρ τέχνης τὸ μὲν ἥμισυ
μέρος κτητικὸν ἦν, κτητικοῦ δὲ χειρωτικόν, χειρω-
τικοῦ δὲ θηρευτικόν, τοῦ δὲ θηρευτικοῦ ζωοθηρικόν,
ζωοθηρικοῦ δὲ ἐνυγροθηρικόν, ἐνυγροθηρικοῦ δὲ
τὸ κάτωθεν τμῆμα ὅλον ἁλιευτικόν, ἁλιευτικῆς δὲ
πληκτικόν, πληκτικῆς δὲ ἀγκιστρευτικόν· τούτου
δὲ τὸ περὶ τὴν κάτωθεν ἄνω πληγὴν ἀνασπωμένην,

[1] σύ Heindorf; οὖ σύ BT.

[1] Plato's etymology—ἀσπαλιευτική from ἀνασπᾶσθαι—is
hardly less absurd than that suggested in the translation.

THEAET. Yes, it is so called.

STR. Then of striking which belongs to barb-hunting, that part which proceeds downward from above, is called, because tridents are chiefly used in it, tridentry, I suppose.

THEAET. Yes, some people, at any rate, call it so.

STR. Then there still remains, I may say, only one further kind.

THEAET. What is that?

STR. The kind that is characterized by the opposite sort of blow, which is practised with a hook and strikes, not any chance part of the body of the fishes, as tridents do, but only the head and mouth of the fish caught, and proceeds from below upwards, being pulled up by twigs and rods. By what name, Theaetetus, shall we say this ought to be called?

THEAET. I think our search is now ended and we have found the very thing we set before us a while ago as necessary to find.

STR. Now, then, you and I are not only agreed about the name of angling, but we have acquired also a satisfactory definition of the thing itself. For of art as a whole, half was acquisitive, and of the acquisitive, half was coercive, and of the coercive, half was hunting, and of hunting, half was animal hunting, and of animal hunting, half was water hunting, and, taken as a whole, of water hunting the lower part was fishing, and of fishing, half was striking, and of striking, half was barb-hunting, and of this the part in which the blow is pulled from below upwards at an angle [1] has a name in the very

The words *at an angle* are inserted merely to give a reason in English for the words which follow them.

C ἀπ' αὐτῆς τῆς πράξεως ἀφομοιωθὲν τοὔνομα, ἡ
νῦν ἀσπαλιευτικὴ ζητηθεῖσα ἐπίκλην γέγονεν.

ΘΕΑΙ. Παντάπασι μὲν οὖν τοῦτό γε ἱκανῶς δε-
δήλωται.

8. ΞΕ. Φέρε δή, κατὰ τοῦτο τὸ παράδειγμα
καὶ τὸν σοφιστὴν ἐπιχειρῶμεν εὑρεῖν, ὅ τί ποτ'
ἔστιν.

ΘΕΑΙ. Κομιδῇ μὲν οὖν.

ΞΕ. Καὶ μὴν ἐκεῖνό γ' ἦν τὸ ζήτημα πρῶτον,
πότερον ἰδιώτην ἤ τινα τέχνην ἔχοντα θετέον εἶναι
τὸν ἀσπαλιευτήν.

ΘΕΑΙ. Ναί.

ΞΕ. Καὶ νῦν δὴ τοῦτον ἰδιώτην θήσομεν, ὦ
D Θεαίτητε, ἢ παντάπασιν ὡς ἀληθῶς σοφιστήν;

ΘΕΑΙ. Οὐδαμῶς ἰδιώτην· μανθάνω γὰρ ὃ λέγεις,
ὡς παντὸς δεῖ τοιοῦτος[1] εἶναι τό γε ὄνομα τοῦτο
ἔχων.

ΞΕ. Ἀλλά τινα τέχνην αὐτὸν ἡμῖν ἔχοντα, ὡς
ἔοικε, θετέον.

ΘΕΑΙ. Τίνα ποτ' οὖν δὴ ταύτην;

ΞΕ. Ἆρ' ὦ πρὸς θεῶν ἠγνοήκαμεν τἀνδρὸς τὸν
ἄνδρα ὄντα ξυγγενῆ;

ΘΕΑΙ. Τίνα τοῦ;

ΞΕ. Τὸν ἀσπαλιευτὴν τοῦ σοφιστοῦ.

ΘΕΑΙ. Πῇ;

ΞΕ. Θηρευτά τινε καταφαίνεσθον ἄμφω μοι.

E ΘΕΑΙ. Τίνος θήρας ἅτερος; τὸν μὲν γὰρ ἕτερον
εἴπομεν.

ΞΕ. Δίχα που νῦν δὴ[2] διείλομεν τὴν ἄγραν
πᾶσαν, νευστικοῦ μέρους, τὸ δὲ πεζοῦ τέμνοντες.

---

[1] παντὸς δεῖ τοιοῦτος Winckelmann; πάντως δεῖ τοιοῦτος B;
πάντως δεῖ τοιοῦτον T.   [2] νῦν δὴ T; νῦν B.

THE SOPHIST

likeness of the act and is called angling, which was the object of our present search.

THEAET. That at all events has been made perfectly clear.

STR. Come, then, let us use this as a pattern and try to find out what a sophist is.

THEAET. By all means.

STR. Well, then, the first question we asked was whether we must assume that the angler was just a man or was a man with an art.

THEAET. Yes.

STR. Now take this man of ours, Theaetetus. Shall we assume that he is just a man, or by all means really a man of wisdom?

THEAET. Certainly not just a man; for I catch your meaning that he is very far from being wise, although his name implies wisdom.

STR. But we must, it seems, assume that he has an art of some kind.

THEAET. Well, then, what in the world is this art that he has?

STR. Good gracious! Have we failed to notice that the man is akin to the other man?

THEAET. Who is akin to whom?

STR. The angler to the sophist.

THEAET. How so?

STR. They both seem clearly to me to be a sort of hunters.

THEAET. What is the hunting of the second? We have spoken about the first.

STR. We just now divided hunting as a whole into two classes, and made one division that of swimming creatures and the other that of land-hunting.

283

221

ΘΕΑΙ. Ναί.

ΞΕ. Καὶ τὸ μὲν διήλθομεν, ὅσον περὶ τὰ νευ-
στικὰ τῶν ἐνύδρων· τὸ δὲ πεζὸν εἰάσαμεν ἄσχιστον,
εἰπόντες ὅτι πολυειδὲς εἴη.

222 ΘΕΑΙ. Πάνυ γε.

ΞΕ. Μέχρι μὲν τοίνυν ἐνταῦθα ὁ σοφιστής τε
καὶ ὁ ἀσπαλιευτὴς ἅμα ἀπὸ τῆς κτητικῆς τέχνης
πορεύεσθον.

ΘΕΑΙ. Ἐοίκατον γοῦν.

ΞΕ. Ἐκτρέπεσθον δέ γε ἀπὸ τῆς ζωοθηρικῆς,
ὁ μὲν ἐπὶ θάλατταν που καὶ ποταμοὺς καὶ λίμνας,
τἀν τούτοις ζῷα θηρευσόμενος.

ΘΕΑΙ. Τί μήν;

ΞΕ. Ὁ δέ γε ἐπὶ τὴν γῆν καὶ ποταμοὺς ἑτέρους
αὖ τινας, πλούτου καὶ νεότητος οἷον λειμῶνας
ἀφθόνους, τἀν τούτοις θρέμματα χειρωσόμενος.

B ΘΕΑΙ. Πῶς λέγεις;

ΞΕ. Τῆς πεζῆς θήρας γίγνεσθον δύο μεγίστω
τινὲ μέρη.

ΘΕΑΙ. Ποῖον ἑκάτερον;

ΞΕ. Τὸ μὲν τῶν ἡμέρων, τὸ δὲ τῶν ἀγρίων.

9. ΘΕΑΙ. Εἶτ' ἔστι τις θήρα τῶν ἡμέρων;

ΞΕ. Εἴπερ γέ ἐστιν ἄνθρωπος ἥμερον ζῷον.
θὲς δὲ ὅπῃ χαίρεις, εἴτε μηδὲν τιθεὶς ἥμερον, εἴτε
ἄλλο μὲν ἥμερόν τι, τὸν δὲ ἄνθρωπον ἄγριον, εἴτε
ἥμερον μὲν λέγεις αὖ τὸν ἄνθρωπον, ἀνθρώπων
δὲ μηδεμίαν ἡγεῖ θήραν· τούτων ὁπότερ' ἂν ἡγῇ
φίλον εἰρῆσθαί σοι, τοῦτο ἡμῖν διόρισον.

C ΘΕΑΙ. Ἀλλ' ἡμᾶς τε ἥμερον, ὦ ξένε, ἡγοῦμαι
ζῷον, θήραν τε ἀνθρώπων εἶναι λέγω.

THE SOPHIST

THEAET. Yes.

STR. And the one we discussed, so far as the swimming creatures that live in the water are concerned; but we left the land-hunting undivided, merely remarking that it has many forms.

THEAET. Certainly.

STR. Now up to that point the sophist and the angler proceed together from the starting-point of acquisitive art.

THEAET. I think they do.

STR. But they separate at the point of animal-hunting, where the one turns to the sea and rivers and lakes to hunt the animals in those.

THEAET. To be sure.

STR. But the other turns toward the land and to rivers of a different kind—rivers of wealth and youth, bounteous meadows, as it were—and he intends to coerce the creatures in them.

THEAET. What do you mean?

STR. Of land-hunting there are two chief divisions.

THEAET. What are they?

STR. One is the hunting of tame, the other of wild creatures.

THEAET. Is there, then, a hunting of tame creatures?

STR. Yes, if man is a tame animal; but make any assumption you like, that there is no tame animal, or that some other tame animal exists but man is a wild one or that man is tame but there is no hunting of man. For the purpose of our definition choose whichever of these statements you think is satisfactory to you.

THEAET. Why, Stranger, I think we are a tame animal, and I agree that there is a hunting of man.

ΞΕ. Διττὴν τοίνυν καὶ τὴν ἡμεροθηρικὴν εἴπωμεν.

ΘΕΑΙ. Κατὰ τί λέγοντες;

ΞΕ. Τὴν μὲν ληστικὴν καὶ ἀνδραποδιστικὴν καὶ τυραννικὴν καὶ ξύμπασαν τὴν πολεμικήν, ἓν πάντα βίαιον θήραν ὁρισάμενοι.

ΘΕΑΙ. Καλῶς.

ΞΕ. Τὴν δέ γε δικανικὴν καὶ δημηγορικὴν καὶ προσομιλητικήν, ἓν αὖ τὸ ξύνολον, πιθανουργικήν D τινα μίαν τέχνην προσειπόντες.

ΘΕΑΙ. Ὀρθῶς.

ΞΕ. Τῆς δὴ πιθανουργικῆς διττὰ λέγωμεν γένη.

ΘΕΑΙ. Ποῖα;

ΞΕ. Τὸ μὲν ἕτερον ἰδίᾳ, τὸ δὲ δημοσίᾳ γιγνόμενον.

ΘΕΑΙ. Γίγνεσθον γὰρ οὖν εἶδος ἑκάτερον.

ΞΕ. Οὐκοῦν αὖ τῆς ἰδιοθηρευτικῆς τὸ μὲν μισθαρνητικόν [1] ἐστι, τὸ δὲ δωροφορικόν;

ΘΕΑΙ. Οὐ μανθάνω.

ΞΕ. Τῇ τῶν ἐρώντων θήρᾳ τὸν νοῦν, ὡς ἔοικας, οὔπω προσέσχες.

ΘΕΑΙ. Τοῦ πέρι;

E   ΞΕ. Ὅτι τοῖς θηρευθεῖσι δῶρα προσεπιδιδόασιν.

ΘΕΑΙ. Ἀληθέστατα λέγεις.

ΞΕ. Τοῦτο μὲν τοίνυν ἐρωτικῆς τέχνης ἔστω εἶδος.

ΘΕΑΙ. Πάνυ γε.

ΞΕ. Τοῦ δέ γε μισθαρνητικοῦ τὸ μὲν προσομι-λοῦν διὰ χάριτος καὶ παντάπασι δι' ἡδονῆς τὸ δέλεαρ πεποιημένον καὶ τὸν μισθὸν πραττόμενον τροφὴν ἑαυτῷ μόνον κολακικήν, ὡς ἐγῷμαι,

[1] μισθαρνητικόν Heindorf; μισθαρνευτικόν BTW (so also below).

286

STR. Let us, then, say that the hunting of tame animals is also of two kinds.

THEAET. How do we justify that assertion?

STR. By defining piracy, man-stealing, tyranny, and the whole art of war all collectively as hunting by force.

THEAET. Excellent.

STR. And by giving the art of the law courts, of the public platform, and of conversation also a single name and calling them all collectively an art of persuasion.

THEAET. Correct.

STR. Now let us say that there are two kinds of persuasion.

THEAET. What kinds?

STR. The one has to do with private persons, the other with the community.

THEAET. Granted; each of them does form a class.

STR. Then again of the hunting of private persons one kind receives pay, and the other brings gifts, does it not?

THEAET. I do not understand.

STR. Apparently you have never yet paid attention to the lovers' method of hunting.

THEAET. In what respect?

STR. That in addition to their other efforts they give presents to those whom they hunt.

THEAET. You are quite right.

STR. Let us, then, call this the amatory art.

THEAET. Agreed.

STR. But that part of the paid kind which converses to furnish gratification and makes pleasure exclusively its bait and demands as its pay only maintenance, we might all agree, if I am not mis-

223 πάντες φαῖμεν ἂν ἢ[1] ἡδυντικήν τινα τέχνην εἶναι.

ΘΕΑΙ. Πῶς γὰρ οὔ;

ΞΕ. Τὸ δὲ ἐπαγγελλόμενον μὲν ὡς ἀρετῆς ἕνεκα τὰς ὁμιλίας ποιούμενον, μισθὸν δὲ νόμισμα πραττόμενον, ἆρα οὐ τοῦτο τὸ γένος ἑτέρῳ προσειπεῖν ἄξιον ὀνόματι;

ΘΕΑΙ. Πῶς γὰρ οὔ;

ΞΕ. Τίνι δὴ τούτῳ; πειρῶ λέγειν.

ΘΕΑΙ. Δῆλον δή· τὸν γὰρ σοφιστὴν μοι δοκοῦμεν ἀνηυρηκέναι. τοῦτ᾽ οὖν ἔγωγε εἰπὼν τὸ προσῆκον ὄνομ᾽ ἂν ἡγοῦμαι καλεῖν αὐτόν.

B 10. ΞΕ. Κατὰ δὴ τὸν νῦν, ὦ Θεαίτητε, λόγον, ὡς ἔοικεν, ἡ τέχνης οἰκειωτικῆς, χειρωτικῆς,[2] θηρευτικῆς, ζῳοθηρίας,[3] χερσαίας, ἡμεροθηρικῆς, ἀνθρωποθηρίας, ἰδιοθηρίας, μισθαρνικῆς, νομισματοπωλικῆς, δοξοπαιδευτικῆς, νέων πλουσίων καὶ ἐνδόξων γιγνομένη θήρα προσρητέον, **ὡς ὁ** νῦν λόγος ἡμῖν συμβαίνει, σοφιστική.

ΘΕΑΙ. Παντάπασι μὲν οὖν.

ΞΕ. Ἔτι δὲ καὶ τῇδε ἴδωμεν[4]· οὐ γάρ τι φαύλης
C μέτοχόν ἐστι τέχνης τὸ νῦν ζητούμενον, ἀλλ᾽ εὖ μάλα ποικίλης. καὶ γὰρ οὖν ἐν τοῖς πρόσθεν εἰρημένοις φάντασμα παρέχεται, μὴ τοῦτο ὃ νῦν αὐτὸ ἡμεῖς φαμεν ἀλλ᾽ ἕτερον εἶναί τι γένος.

ΘΕΑΙ. Πῇ δή;

ΞΕ. Τὸ τῆς κτητικῆς τέχνης διπλοῦν ἦν **εἶδός που**, τὸ μὲν θηρευτικὸν μέρος ἔχον, τὸ δὲ ἀλλακτικόν.

---

[1] ἢ Heindorf; ἦ om. mss.
[2] χειρωτικῆς add. Aldina; κτητικῆς mss.; secl. Schleiermacher.
[3] ζῳοθηρίας πεζοθηρίας mss.; πεζοθηρίας secl. Schleiermacher.
[4] ἴδωμεν W; εἰδῶμεν BT.

taken, to call the art of flattery or of making things pleasant.

THEAET. Certainly.

STR. But the class which proposes to carry on its conversations for the sake of virtue and demands its pay in cash—does not this deserve to be called by another name?

THEAET. Of course.

STR. And what is that name? Try to tell

THEAET. It is obvious; for I think we have discovered the sophist. And therefore by uttering that word I think I should give him the right name.

STR. Then, as it seems, according to our present reasoning, Theaetetus, the part of appropriative, coercive, hunting art which hunts animals, land animals, tame animals, man, privately, for pay, is paid in cash, claims to give education, and is a hunt after rich and promising youths, must—so our present argument concludes—be called sophistry.

THEAET. Most assuredly.

STR. But let us look at it in still another way; for the class we are now examining partakes of no mean art, but of a very many-sided one. And we must indeed do so, for in our previous talk it presents an appearance of being, not what we now say it is, but another class.

THEAET. How so?

STR. The acquisitive art was of two sorts, the one the division of hunting, the other that of exchange.

ΘΕΑΙ. Ἦν γὰρ οὖν.

ΞΕ. Τῆς τοίνυν ἀλλακτικῆς δύο εἴδη λέγωμεν, τὸ μὲν δωρητικόν, τὸ δὲ ἕτερον ἀγοραστικόν;

ΘΕΑΙ. Εἰρήσθω.

ΞΕ. Καὶ μὴν αὖ φήσομεν ἀγοραστικὴν διχῇ τέμνεσθαι.

D   ΘΕΑΙ. Πῇ;

ΞΕ. Τὴν μὲν τῶν αὐτουργῶν αὐτοπωλικὴν διαιρούμενοι, τὴν δὲ τὰ ἀλλότρια ἔργα μεταβαλλομένην μεταβλητικήν.

ΘΕΑΙ. Πάνυ γε.

ΞΕ. Τί δέ; τῆς μεταβλητικῆς οὐχ ἡ μὲν κατὰ πόλιν ἀλλαγή, σχεδὸν αὐτῆς ἥμισυ μέρος ὄν, καπηλικὴ [1] προσαγορεύεται;

ΘΕΑΙ. Ναί.

ΞΕ. Τὸ δέ γε ἐξ ἄλλης εἰς ἄλλην πόλιν διαλλαττόμενον [2] ὠνῇ καὶ πράσει ἐμπορική;

ΘΕΑΙ. Τί δ᾽ οὔ;

ΞΕ. Τῆς δ᾽ ἐμπορικῆς ἆρ᾽ οὐκ ᾐσθήμεθα ὅτι τὸ

E μὲν ὅσοις τὸ σῶμα τρέφεται καὶ χρῆται,[3] τὸ δὲ ὅσοις ἡ ψυχὴ πωλοῦν διὰ νομίσματος ἀλλάττεται;

ΘΕΑΙ. Πῶς τοῦτο λέγεις;

ΞΕ. Τὸ περὶ τὴν ψυχὴν ἴσως ἀγνοοῦμεν, ἐπεὶ τό γε ἕτερόν που ξυνίεμεν.

ΘΕΑΙ. Ναί.

224   ΞΕ. Μουσικήν τε τοίνυν ξυνάπασαν λέγωμεν,

---

[1] καπηλικὴ bt; καὶ πηλίκη BT.
[2] διαλαττόμενον] διαλαττομένων BT; διαλάττον W.
[3] καὶ χρῆται Heindorf; κέχρηται BT.

THEAET. Yes, it was.

STR. Now shall we say that there are two sorts of exchange, the one by gift, the other by sale?

THEAET. So be it.

STR. And we shall say further that exchange by sale is divided into two parts.

THEAET. How so?

STR. We make this distinction—calling the part which sells a man's own productions the selling of one's own, and the other, which exchanges the works of others, exchange.

THEAET. Certainly.

STR. Well, then, that part of exchange which is carried on in the city, amounting to about half of it, is called retailing, is it not?

THEAET. Yes.

STR. And that which exchanges goods from city to city by purchase and sale is called merchandising?

THEAET. Certainly.

STR. And have we not observed that one part of merchandising sells and exchanges for cash whatever serves the body for its support and needs, and the other whatever serves the soul?

THEAET. What do you mean by that?

STR. Perhaps we do not know about the part that has to do with the soul; though I fancy we do understand the other division.

THEAET. Yes.

STR. Take, therefore, the liberal arts [1] in general

[1] The word μουσική, here rendered "liberal arts," is much more inclusive than the English word "music," designating, as it does, nearly all education and culture except the purely physical. In the Athens of Socrates' day many, possibly most, of the teachers of music in this larger sense were foreigners, Greeks, of course, but not Athenians.

ἐκ πόλεως ἑκάστοτε εἰς πόλιν ἔνθεν μὲν ὠνηθεῖσαν,
ἑτέρωσε δὲ ἀγομένην καὶ πιπρασκομένην, καὶ
γραφικὴν καὶ θαυματοποιικὴν καὶ πολλὰ ἕτερα
τῆς ψυχῆς, τὰ μὲν παραμυθίας, τὰ δὲ καὶ σπουδῆς
χάριν ἀχθέντα καὶ πωλούμενα, τὸν ἄγοντα καὶ
πωλοῦντα μηδὲν ἧττον τῆς τῶν σιτίων καὶ ποτῶν
πράσεως ἔμπορον ὀρθῶς ἂν λεγόμενον παρασχεῖν.

ΘΕΑΙ. Ἀληθέστατα λέγεις.

Β   ΞΕ. Οὐκοῦν καὶ τὸν μαθήματα ξυνωνούμενον
πόλιν τε ἐκ πόλεως νομίσματος ἀμείβοντα ταὐτὸν
προσερεῖς ὄνομα;

ΘΕΑΙ. Σφόδρα γε.

II.   ΞΕ. Τῆς δὴ ψυχεμπορικῆς ταύτης ἆρ' οὐ
τὸ μὲν ἐπιδεικτικὴ δικαιότατα λέγοιτ' ἄν, τὸ δὲ
γελοῖον μὲν οὐχ ἧττον τοῦ πρόσθεν, ὅμως δὲ μαθημάτων οὖσαν πρᾶσιν αὐτὴν ἀδελφῷ τινι τῆς πράξεως ὀνόματι προσειπεῖν ἀνάγκη;

ΘΕΑΙ. Πάνυ μὲν οὖν.

ΞΕ. Ταύτης τοίνυν τῆς μαθηματοπωλικῆς τὸ
C μὲν περὶ τὰ τῶν ἄλλων τεχνῶν μαθήματα ἑτέρῳ,
τὸ δὲ περὶ τὸ τῆς ἀρετῆς ἄλλῳ προσρητέον.

ΘΕΑΙ. Πῶς γὰρ οὔ;

ΞΕ. Τεχνοπωλικὸν μὴν τό γε περὶ τἆλλα ἂν
ἁρμόττοι· τὸ δὲ περὶ ταῦτα σὺ προθυμήθητι
λέγειν ὄνομα.

ΘΕΑΙ. Καὶ τί τις ἂν ἄλλο ὄνομα εἰπὼν οὐκ ἂν
πλημμελοίη πλὴν τὸ νῦν ζητούμενον αὐτὸ εἶναι
τὸ σοφιστικὸν γένος;

ΞΕ. Οὐδὲν ἄλλο. ἴθι δὴ νῦν [1] συναγάγωμεν
αὐτὸ λέγοντες ὡς τὸ κτητικῆς, μεταβλητικῆς,[2]

[1] ἴθι νῦν BT (δὴ above the line T); ἴθι δὴ W.
[2] μεταβλητικῆς] μεταβλητικὸν BT.

that constantly go about from city to city, bought in one place and carried to another and sold—painting, and conjuring, and the many other things that affect the soul, which are imported and sold partly for its entertainment and partly for its serious needs; we cannot deny that he who carries these about and sells them constitutes a merchant properly so called, no less than he whose business is the sale of food and drink.

THEAET. Very true.

STR. Then will you give the same name to him who buys up knowledge and goes about from city to city exchanging his wares for money?

THEAET. Certainly.

STR. One part of this soul-merchandising might very properly be called the art of display, might it not? But since the other part, though no less ridiculous than the first, is nevertheless a traffic in knowledge, must we not call it by some name akin to its business?

THEAET. Certainly.

STR. Now of this merchandising in knowledge the part which has to do with the knowledge of the other arts should be called by one name, and that which has to do with virtue by another.

THEAET. Of course.

STR. The name of art-merchant would fit the one who trades in the other arts, and now do you be so good as to tell the name of him who trades in virtue.

THEAET. And what other name could one give, without making a mistake, than that which is the object of our present investigation—the sophist?

STR. No other. Come then, let us now summarize the matter by saying that sophistry has appeared a

D ἀγοραστικῆς, ἐμπορικῆς,[1] ψυχεμπορικῆς περὶ λόγους καὶ μαθήματα, ἀρετῆς πωλητικὸν δεύτερον
ἀνεφάνη σοφιστική.

ΘΕΑΙ. Μάλα γε.

ΞΕ. Τρίτον δέ γ᾽ οἶμαί σε, κἂν εἴ τις αὐτοῦ
καθιδρυμένος ἐν πόλει, τὰ μὲν ὠνούμενος, τὰ δὲ
καὶ τεκταινόμενος αὐτὸς μαθήματα περὶ τὰ αὐτὰ
ταῦτα καὶ πωλῶν ἐκ τούτου τὸ ζῆν προὐτάξατο,
καλεῖν οὐδὲν ἄλλο πλὴν ὅπερ νῦν δή.

ΘΕΑΙ. Τί δ᾽ οὐ μέλλω;

ΞΕ. Καὶ τὸ κτητικῆς ἄρα μεταβλητικόν, ἀγορα-
E στικόν, καπηλικὸν εἴτε αὐτοπωλικόν, ἀμφοτέρως,
ὅτιπερ ἂν ᾖ περὶ τὰ τοιαῦτα μαθηματοπωλικὸν
γένος, ἀεὶ σὺ προσερεῖς, ὡς φαίνει, σοφιστικόν.

ΘΕΑΙ. Ἀνάγκη· τῷ γὰρ λόγῳ δεῖ συνακολου-
θεῖν.

12. ΞΕ. Ἔτι δὴ σκοπῶμεν, εἴ τινι τοιῷδε
προσέοικεν ἄρα τὸ νῦν μεταδιωκόμενον γένος.

225 ΘΕΑΙ. Ποίῳ δή;

ΞΕ. Τῆς κτητικῆς ἀγωνιστική τι μέρος ἡμῖν ἦν.

ΘΕΑΙ. Ἦν γὰρ οὖν.

ΞΕ. Οὐκ ἀπὸ τρόπου τοίνυν ἐστὶ διαιρεῖν αὐτὴν
δίχα.

ΘΕΑΙ. Καθ᾽ ὁποῖα λέγε.

ΞΕ. Τὸ μὲν ἁμιλλητικὸν αὐτῆς τιθέντας, τὸ δὲ
μαχητικόν.

ΘΕΑΙ. Ἔστιν.

ΞΕ. Τῆς τοίνυν μαχητικῆς τῷ μὲν σώματι

[1] ἐμπορικῆς] ἐμπορικοῦ BT.

second time as that part of acquisitive art, art of exchange, of trafficking, of merchandising, of soul-merchandising which deals in words and knowledge, and trades in virtue.

THEAET. Very well.

STR. But there is a third case: If a man settled down here in town and proposed to make his living by selling these same wares of knowledge, buying some of them and making others himself, you would, I fancy, not call him by any other name than that which you used a moment ago.

THEAET. Certainly not.

STR. Then also that part of acquisitive art which proceeds by exchange, and by sale, whether as mere retail trade or the sale of one's own productions, no matter which, so long as it is of the class of merchandising in knowledge, you will always, apparently, call sophistry.

THEAET. I must do so, for I have to follow where the argument leads.

STR. Let us examine further and see if the class we are now pursuing has still another aspect, of similar nature.

THEAET. Of what nature?

STR. We agreed that fighting was a division of acquisitive art.

THEAET. Yes, we did.

STR. Then it is quite fitting to divide it into two parts.

THEAET. Tell what the parts are.

STR. Let us call one part of it the competitive and the other the pugnacious.

THEAET. Agreed.

STR. Then it is reasonable and fitting to give to

πρὸς σώματα γιγνομένῳ σχεδὸν εἰκὸς καὶ πρέπον
ὄνομα λέγειν τι τοιοῦτον τιθεμένους οἷον βιαστικόν.

ΘΕΑΙ. Ναί.

ΞΕ. Τῷ δὲ λόγοις πρὸς λόγους τί τις, ὦ Θεαί-
B τητε, ἄλλο εἴπῃ πλὴν ἀμφισβητητικόν[1];

ΘΕΑΙ. Οὐδέν.

ΞΕ. Τὸ δέ γε περὶ τὰς ἀμφισβητήσεις θετέον
διττόν.

ΘΕΑΙ. Πῇ;

ΞΕ. Καθ᾽ ὅσον μὲν γὰρ γίγνεται μήκεσί τε πρὸς
ἐναντία μήκη λόγων καὶ περὶ τὰ[2] δίκαια καὶ
ἄδικα δημοσίᾳ, δικανικόν.

ΘΕΑΙ. Ναί.

ΞΕ. Τὸ δ᾽ ἐν ἰδίοις αὖ καὶ κατακεκερματισμένον
ἐρωτήσεσι πρὸς ἀποκρίσεις μῶν εἰθίσμεθα καλεῖν
ἄλλο πλὴν ἀντιλογικόν;

ΘΕΑΙ. Οὐδέν.

ΞΕ. Τοῦ δὲ ἀντιλογικοῦ τὸ μὲν ὅσον περὶ τὰ
C ξυμβόλαια ἀμφισβητεῖται μέν, εἰκῇ δὲ καὶ ἀτέ-
χνως περὶ αὐτὸ πράττεται, ταῦτα[3] θετέον μὲν
εἶδος, ἐπείπερ αὐτὸ διέγνωκεν ὡς ἕτερον ὂν ὁ λόγος,
ἀτὰρ ἐπωνυμίας οὔθ᾽ ὑπὸ τῶν ἔμπροσθεν ἔτυχεν
οὔτε νῦν ὑφ᾽ ἡμῶν τυχεῖν ἄξιον.

ΘΕΑΙ. Ἀληθῆ· κατὰ σμικρὰ γὰρ λίαν καὶ
παντοδαπὰ διῄρηται.

ΞΕ. Τὸ δέ γε ἔντεχνον, καὶ περὶ δικαίων αὐτῶν
καὶ ἀδίκων καὶ περὶ τῶν ἄλλων ὅλως ἀμφισβητοῦν,
ἆρ᾽ οὐκ ἐριστικὸν αὖ λέγειν εἰθίσμεθα;

ΘΕΑΙ. Πῶς γὰρ οὔ;

---

[1] ἀμφισβητητικόν Stephanus ; ἀμφισβητικόν BTW.
[2] τὰ om. TW.   [3] ταῦτα BT ; τοῦτο al.

that part of the pugnacious which consists of bodily contests some such name as violent.

THEAET. Yes.

STR. And what other name than controversy shall we give to the contests of words?

THEAET. No other.

STR. But controversy must be divided into two kinds.

THEAET. How?

STR. Whenever long speeches are opposed by long speeches on questions of justice and injustice in public, that is forensic controversy.

THEAET. Yes.

STR. But that which is carried on among private persons and is cut up into little bits by means of questions and their answers, we are accustomed to call argumentation, are we not?

THEAET. We are.

STR. And that part of argumentation which deals with business contracts, in which there is controversy, to be sure, but it is carried on informally and without rules of art—all that must be considered a distinct class, now that our argument has recognized it as different from the rest, but it received no name from our predecessors, nor does it now deserve to receive one from us.

THEAET. True; for the divisions into which it falls are too small and too miscellaneous.

STR. But that which possesses rules of art and carries on controversy about abstract justice and injustice and the rest in general terms, we are accustomed to call disputation, are we not?

THEAET. Certainly.

D   ΞΕ. Τοῦ μὴν ἐριστικοῦ τὸ μὲν χρηματοφθο-
ρικόν, τὸ δὲ χρηματιστικὸν ὂν τυγχάνει.

ΘΕΑΙ. Παντάπασί γε.

ΞΕ. Τὴν ἐπωνυμίαν τοίνυν, ἣν ἑκάτερον δεῖ
καλεῖν αὐτῶν, πειραθῶμεν εἰπεῖν.

ΘΕΑΙ. Οὐκοῦν χρή.

ΞΕ. Δοκῶ μὴν τό γε[1] δι' ἡδονὴν τῆς περὶ ταῦτα
διατριβῆς ἀμελὲς τῶν οἰκείων γιγνόμενον, περὶ
δὲ τὴν λέξιν τοῖς πολλοῖς τῶν ἀκουόντων οὐ μεθ'
ἡδονῆς ἀκουόμενον καλεῖσθαι κατὰ γνώμην τὴν
ἐμὴν οὐχ ἕτερον ἀδολεσχικοῦ.

ΘΕΑΙ. Λέγεται γὰρ οὖν οὕτω πως.

E   ΞΕ. Τούτου τοίνυν τοὐναντίον, ἀπὸ τῶν ἰδιωτι-
κῶν ἐρίδων χρηματιζόμενον, ἐν τῷ μέρει σὺ πειρῶ
νῦν εἰπεῖν.

ΘΕΑΙ. Καὶ τί[2] τις ἂν αὖ εἰπὼν ἕτερον οὐκ ἐξ-
αμάρτοι πλήν γε τὸν θαυμαστὸν πάλιν ἐκεῖνον
ἥκειν αὖ νῦν τέταρτον τὸν μεταδιωκόμενον ὑφ'
ἡμῶν σοφιστήν;

226   ΞΕ. Οὐδὲν ἀλλ' ἢ τὸ χρηματιστικὸν γένος, ὡς
ἔοικεν, ἐριστικῆς ὂν τέχνης, τῆς ἀντιλογικῆς, τῆς
ἀμφισβητητικῆς,[3] τῆς μαχητικῆς, τῆς ἀγωνιστικῆς, τῆς κτητικῆς ἔστιν, ὡς ὁ λόγος αὖ μεμήνυκε
νῦν, ὁ σοφιστής.

ΘΕΑΙ. Κομιδῇ μὲν οὖν.

13. ΞΕ. Ὁρᾷς οὖν ὡς ἀληθῆ λέγεται τὸ ποι-
κίλον εἶναι τοῦτο τὸ θηρίον καὶ τὸ λεγόμενον οὐ
τῇ ἑτέρᾳ ληπτόν[4];

ΘΕΑΙ. Οὐκοῦν ἀμφοῖν χρή.

[1] τό γε vulg. ; τόδε BT ; τὸ δε W.   [2] τί add. Heindorf.
[3] ἀμφισβητητικῆς] ἀμφισβητικῆς BTW.
[4] ληπτόν W ; ληπτέον BT.

THE SOPHIST

STR. Well, of disputation, one sort wastes money, the other makes money.

THEAET. Certainly.

STR. Then let us try to tell the name by which we must call each of these.

THEAET. Yes, we must do so.

STR. Presumably the kind which causes a man to neglect his own affairs for the pleasure of engaging in it, but the style of which causes no pleasure to most of his hearers, is, in my opinion, called by no other name than garrulity.

THEAET. Yes, that is about what it is called.

STR. Then the opposite of this, the kind which makes money from private disputes—try now, for it is your turn, to give its name.

THEAET. What other answer could one give without making a mistake, than that now again for the fourth time that wonderful being whom we have so long been pursuing has turned up—the sophist!

STR. Yes, and the sophist is nothing else, apparently, than the money-making class of the disputatious, argumentative, controversial, pugnacious, combative, acquisitive art, as our argument has now again stated.

THEAET. Certainly.

STR. Do you see the truth of the statement that this creature is many-sided and, as the saying is, not to be caught with one hand?

THEAET. Then we must catch him with both.

299

ΞΕ. Χρὴ γὰρ οὖν, καὶ κατὰ δύναμίν γε οὕτω
Β ποιητέον, τοιόνδε τι μεταθέοντας ἴχνος αὐτοῦ.
καί μοι λέγε· τῶν οἰκετικῶν ὀνομάτων καλοῦμεν
ἄττα που;

ΘΕΑΙ. Καὶ πολλά· ἀτὰρ ποῖα δὴ τῶν πολλῶν
πυνθάνει;

ΞΕ. Τὰ τοιάδε, οἷον διηθεῖν τε λέγομεν καὶ
διαττᾶν καὶ βράττειν καὶ διακρίνειν.[1]

ΘΕΑΙ. Τί μήν;

ΞΕ. Καὶ πρός γε τούτοις ἔτι ξαίνειν, κατάγειν,
κερκίζειν, καὶ μυρία ἐν ταῖς τέχναις ἄλλα τοιαῦτα
ἐνόντα ἐπιστάμεθα. ἢ γάρ;

ΘΕΑΙ. Τὸ ποῖον αὐτῶν πέρι βουληθεὶς δηλῶσαι
C παραδείγματα προθεὶς ταῦτα κατὰ πάντων ἤρου;

ΞΕ. Διαιρετικά που τὰ λεχθέντα εἴρηται ξύμπαντα.

ΘΕΑΙ. Ναί.

ΞΕ. Κατὰ τὸν ἐμὸν τοίνυν λόγον ὡς περὶ ταῦτα
μίαν οὖσαν ἐν ἅπασι τέχνην ἑνὸς ὀνόματος ἀξιώ-
σομεν αὐτήν.

ΘΕΑΙ. Τίνα προσειπόντες;

ΞΕ. Διακριτικήν.

ΘΕΑΙ. Ἔστω.

ΞΕ. Σκόπει δὴ ταύτης αὖ δύο ἄν πῃ δυνώμεθα
κατιδεῖν εἴδη.

ΘΕΑΙ. Ταχεῖαν ὡς ἐμοὶ σκέψιν ἐπιτάττεις.

D ΞΕ. Καὶ μὴν ἔν γε ταῖς εἰρημέναις διακρίσεσι
τὸ μὲν χεῖρον ἀπὸ βελτίονος ἀποχωρίζειν ἦν, τὸ
δ᾽ ὅμοιον ἀφ᾽ ὁμοίου.

---

[1] διακρινειν] many emendations have been suggested, none
entirely satisfactory, and all probably unnecessary.

STR. Yes, we must, and must go at it with all our might, by following another track of his—in this way. Tell me; of the expressions connected with menial occupations some are in common use, are they not?

THEAET. Yes, many. But to which of the many does your question refer?

STR. To such as these: we say "sift" and "strain" and "winnow" and "separate."[1]

THEAET. Certainly.

STR. And besides these there are "card" and "comb" and "beat the web" and countless other technical terms which we know. Is it not so?

THEAET. Why do you use these as examples and ask about them all? What do you wish to show in regard to them?

STR. All those that I have mentioned imply a notion of division.

THEAET. Yes.

STR. Then since there is, according to my reckoning, one art involved in all of these operations, let us give it one name.

THEAET. What shall we call it?

STR. The art of discrimination.

THEAET. Very well.

STR. Now see if we can discover two divisions of this.

THEAET. You demand quick thinking, for a boy like me.

STR. And yet, in the instance of discrimination just mentioned there was, first, the separation of worse from better, and, secondly, of like from like.

[1] Apparently a term descriptive of some part of the process of weaving; cf. *Cratylus*, 338 B.

ΘΕΑΙ. Σχεδὸν οὕτω νῦν λεχθὲν φαίνεται.

ΞΕ. Τῆς μὲν τοίνυν ὄνομα οὐκ ἔχω λεγόμενον· τῆς δὲ καταλειπούσης μὲν τὸ βέλτιον διακρίσεως, τὸ δὲ χεῖρον ἀποβαλλούσης ἔχω.

ΘΕΑΙ. Λέγε τί.

ΞΕ. Πᾶσα ἡ τοιαύτη διάκρισις, ὡς ἐγὼ ξυννοῶ, λέγεται παρὰ πάντων καθαρμός τις.

ΘΕΑΙ. Λέγεται γὰρ οὖν.

E ΞΕ. Οὐκοῦν τό γε καθαρτικὸν εἶδος αὖ διπλοῦν ὂν πᾶς ἂν ἴδοι;

ΘΕΑΙ. Ναί, κατὰ σχολήν γε ἴσως· οὐ μὴν ἔγωγε καθορῶ νῦν.

14. ΞΕ. Καὶ μὴν τὰ περὶ τὰ σώματα πολλὰ εἴδη καθάρσεων ἑνὶ περιλαβεῖν ὀνόματι προσήκει.

ΘΕΑΙ. Ποῖα καὶ τίνι;

ΞΕ. Τά τε τῶν ζῴων, ὅσα ἐντὸς σωμάτων ὑπὸ γυμναστικῆς ἰατρικῆς τε ὀρθῶς διακρινόμενα 227 καθαίρεται καὶ περὶ τἀκτός,[1] εἰπεῖν μὲν φαῦλα, ὅσα βαλανευτικὴ παρέχεται· καὶ τῶν ἀψύχων σωμάτων, ὧν γναφευτικὴ καὶ ξύμπασα κοσμητικὴ τὴν ἐπιμέλειαν παρεχομένη κατὰ σμικρὰ πολλὰ καὶ γελοῖα δοκοῦντα ὀνόματα ἔσχεν.

ΘΕΑΙ. Μάλα γε.

ΞΕ. Παντάπασι μὲν οὖν, ὦ Θεαίτητε. ἀλλὰ γὰρ τῇ τῶν λόγων μεθόδῳ σπογγιστικῆς ἢ φαρμακοποσίας οὐδὲν ἧττον οὐδέ τι μᾶλλον τυγχάνει μέλον, εἰ τὸ μὲν σμικρά, τὸ δὲ μεγάλα ἡμᾶς ὠφελεῖ καθαί-

[1] περὶ τἀκτός] περιτακτός B; τὰ περὶ τὰ ἐκτὸς ᾱ T.

THEAET. Yes, as you now express it, that is pretty clear.

STR. Now I know no common name for the second kind of discrimination; but I do know the name of the kind which retains the better and throws away the worse.

THEAET. What is it?

STR. Every such discrimination, as I think, is universally called a sort of purification.

THEAET. Yes, so it is.

STR. And could not anyone see that purification. is of two kinds?

THEAET. Yes, perhaps, in time; but still I do not see it now.

STR. Still there are many kinds of purifications of bodies, and they may all properly be included under one name.

THEAET. What are they and what is the name?

STR. The purification of living creatures, having to do with impurities within the body, such as are successfully discriminated by gymnastics and medicine, and with those outside of the body, not nice to speak of, such as are attended to by the bath-keeper's art; and the purification of inanimate bodies, which is the special care of the fuller's art and in general of the art of exterior decoration; this, with its petty subdivisions, has taken on many names which seem ridiculous.

THEAET. Very.

STR. Certainly they do, Theaetetus. However, the method of argument is neither more nor less concerned with the art of medicine than with that of sponging, but is indifferent if the one benefits us little, the other greatly by its purifying. It en-

B ρον. τοῦ κτήσασθαι γὰρ ἕνεκα νοῦν πασῶν τεχνῶν
τὸ ξυγγενὲς καὶ τὸ μὴ ξυγγενὲς κατανοεῖν πει-
ρωμένη τιμᾷ πρὸς τοῦτο ἐξ ἴσου πάσας, καὶ θάτερα
τῶν ἑτέρων κατὰ τὴν ὁμοιότητα οὐδὲν ἡγεῖται
γελοιότερα, σεμνότερον δέ τι τὸν διὰ στρατηγικῆς
ἢ φθειριστικῆς δηλοῦντα θηρευτικὴν οὐδὲν νενόμικεν,
ἀλλ' ὡς τὸ πολὺ χαυνότερον. καὶ δὴ καὶ νῦν,
ὅπερ ἤρου, τί προσεροῦμεν ὄνομα ξυμπάσας
δυνάμεις, ὅσαι σῶμα εἴτε ἔμψυχον εἴτε ἄψυχον
εἰλήχασι[1] καθαίρειν, οὐδὲν αὐτῇ διοίσει, ποῖόν τι
C λεχθὲν εὐπρεπέστατον εἶναι δόξει· μόνον ἐχέτω
χωρὶς τῶν τῆς ψυχῆς καθάρσεων πάντα ξυνδῆσαν,
ὅσα ἄλλο τι καθαίρει. τὸν γὰρ περὶ τὴν διάνοιαν
καθαρμὸν ἀπὸ τῶν ἄλλων ἐπικεχείρηκεν ἀφορίσα-
σθαι τὰ νῦν, εἴ γε ὅπερ βούλεται μανθάνομεν.

ΘΕΑΙ. Ἀλλὰ μεμάθηκα, καὶ συγχωρῶ δύο μὲν
εἴδη καθάρσεως, ἓν δὲ τὸ περὶ τὴν ψυχὴν εἶδος εἶναι,
τοῦ περὶ τὸ σῶμα χωρὶς ὄν.

ΞΕ. Πάντων κάλλιστα. καί μοι τὸ μετὰ τοῦτο
D ἐπάκουε πειρώμενος αὖ τὸ λεχθὲν διχῇ τέμνειν.

ΘΕΑΙ. Καθ' ὁποῖ' ἂν ὑφηγῇ πειράσομαί σοι συν-
τέμνειν.

15. ΞΕ. Πονηρίαν ἕτερον ἀρετῆς ἐν ψυχῇ λέγο-
μέν τι;

ΘΕΑΙ. Πῶς γὰρ οὔ;

ΞΕ. Καὶ μὴν καθαρμὸς ἦν τὸ λείπειν[2] μὲν
θάτερον, ἐκβάλλειν δὲ ὅσον ἂν ᾖ πού τι φλαῦρον.

ΘΕΑΙ. Ἦν γὰρ οὖν.

ΞΕ. Καὶ ψυχῆς ἄρα, καθ' ὅσον ἂν εὑρίσκωμεν

---

[1] εἰλήχασι W ; εἰλήφασι BT.
[2] λείπειν Heindorf ; λιπεῖν BT.

deavours to understand what is related and what is not related in all arts, for the purpose of acquiring intelligence; and therefore it honours them all equally and does not in making comparisons think one more ridiculous than another, and does not consider him who employs, as his example of hunting, the art of generalship, any more dignified than him who employs the art of louse-catching, but only, for the most part, as more pretentious. And now as to your question, what name we shall give to all the activities whose function it is to purify the body, whether animate or inanimate, it will not matter at all to our method what name sounds finest; it cares only to unite under one name all purifications of everything else and to keep them separate from the purification of the soul. For it has in our present discussion been trying to separate this purification definitely from the rest, if we understand its desire.

THEAET. But I do understand and I agree that there are two kinds of purification and that one kind is the purification of the soul, which is separate from that of the body.

STR. Most excellent. Now pay attention to the next point and try again to divide the term.

THEAET. In whatever way you suggest, I will try to help you in making the division.

STR. Do we say that wickedness is distinct from virtue in the soul?

THEAET. Of course.

STR. And purification was retaining the one and throwing out whatever is bad anywhere?

THEAET. Yes, it was.

STR. Hence whenever we find any removal of evil

κακίας ἀφαίρεσίν τινα, καθαρμὸν αὐτὸν λέγοντες ἐν
μέλει φθεγξόμεθα.

ΘΕΑΙ. Καὶ μάλα γε.

ΞΕ. Δύο μὲν εἴδη κακίας περὶ ψυχὴν ῥητέον.

ΘΕΑΙ. Ποῖα;

228 ΞΕ. Τὸ μὲν οἷον νόσον ἐν σώματι, τὸ δ' οἷον
αἶσχος ἐγγιγνόμενον.

ΘΕΑΙ. Οὐκ ἔμαθον.

ΞΕ. Νόσον ἴσως καὶ στάσιν οὐ ταὐτὸν νενόμικας;

ΘΕΑΙ. Οὐδ' αὖ πρὸς τοῦτο ἔχω τί χρή με ἀποκρίνασθαι.

ΞΕ. Πότερον ἄλλο τι στάσιν ἡγούμενος ἢ τὴν τοῦ
φύσει ξυγγενοῦς ἔκ τινος διαφθορᾶς διαφοράν¹;

ΘΕΑΙ. Οὐδέν.

ΞΕ. Ἀλλ' αἶσχος ἄλλο τι πλὴν τὸ τῆς ἀμετρίας
πανταχοῦ δυσειδὲς ἐνὸν² γένος;

Β ΘΕΑΙ. Οὐδαμῶς ἄλλο.

ΞΕ. Τί δέ; ἐν ψυχῇ δόξας ἐπιθυμίαις καὶ θυμὸν
ἡδοναῖς καὶ λόγον λύπαις καὶ πάντα ἀλλήλοις ταῦτα
τῶν φλαύρως ἐχόντων οὐκ ᾐσθήμεθα διαφερόμενα;

ΘΕΑΙ. Καὶ σφόδρα γε.

ΞΕ. Ξυγγενῆ γε μὴν ἐξ ἀνάγκης ξύμπαντα
γέγονεν.

ΘΕΑΙ. Πῶς γὰρ οὔ;

ΞΕ. Στάσιν ἄρα καὶ νόσον τῆς ψυχῆς πονηρίαν
λέγοντες ὀρθῶς ἐροῦμεν.

ΘΕΑΙ. Ὀρθότατα μὲν οὖν.

C ΞΕ. Τί δ'; ὅσ' ἂν³ κινήσεως μετασχόντα καὶ
σκοπόν τινα θέμενα πειρώμενα⁴ τούτου τυγχάνειν

---

¹ διαφθορᾶς διαφοράν Galen; διαφορᾶς διαφθοράν BT, Stobaeus.
² ἐνὸν Schleiermacher; ἐν ὂν Stobaeus; ἐν ὂν t; ὂν BT.
³ ὅσ' ἂν Cobet; ὅσα BT.

THE SOPHIST

from the soul, we shall be speaking properly if we call that a purification.

THEAET. Very properly.

STR. We must say that there are two kinds of evil in the soul.

THEAET. What kinds?

STR. The one is comparable to a disease in the body, the other to a deformity.

THEAET. I do not understand.

STR. Perhaps you have not considered that disease and discord are the same thing?

THEAET. I do not know what reply I ought to make to this, either.

STR. Is that because you think discord is anything else than the disagreement of the naturally related, brought about by some corruption?

THEAET. No; I think it is nothing else.

STR. But is deformity anything else than the presence of the quality of disproportion, which is always ugly?

THEAET. Nothing else at all.

STR. Well then; do we not see that in the souls of worthless men opinions are opposed to desires, anger to pleasures, reason to pain, and all such things to one another?

THEAET. Yes, they are, decidedly.

STR. Yet they must all be naturally related.

THEAET. Of course.

STR. Then we shall be right if we say that wickedness is a discord and disease of the soul.

THEAET. Yes, quite right.

STR. But if things which partake of motion and aim at some particular mark pass beside the mark

―――――――――
⁴ πειρώμενα T, Galen, Stobaeus; πειρώμεθα W; om. B.

228

καθ' ἑκάστην ὁρμὴν παράφορα αὐτοῦ γίγνηται[1] καὶ
ἀποτυγχάνῃ,[2] πότερον αὐτὰ φήσομεν ὑπὸ συμμετρίας
τῆς πρὸς ἄλληλα ἢ τοὐναντίον ὑπὸ ἀμετρίας αὐτὰ
πάσχειν;

ΘΕΑΙ. Δῆλον ὡς ὑπὸ ἀμετρίας.

ΞΕ. Ἀλλὰ μὴν ψυχήν γε ἴσμεν ἄκουσαν πᾶσαν πᾶν
ἀγνοοῦσαν.

ΘΕΑΙ. Σφόδρα γε.

ΞΕ. Τό γε μὴν ἀγνοεῖν ἐστιν ἐπ' ἀλήθειαν ὁρμω-
D μένης ψυχῆς, παραφόρου συνέσεως γιγνομένης,
οὐδὲν ἄλλο πλὴν παραφροσύνη.

ΘΕΑΙ. Πάνυ μὲν οὖν.

ΞΕ. Ψυχὴν ἄρα ἀνόητον αἰσχρὰν καὶ ἄμετρον
θετέον.

ΘΕΑΙ. Ἔοικεν.

ΞΕ. Ἔστι δὴ δύο ταῦτα, ὡς φαίνεται, κακῶν ἐν
αὐτῇ γένη, τὸ μὲν πονηρία καλούμενον ὑπὸ τῶν
πολλῶν, νόσος αὐτῆς σαφέστατα ὄν.

ΘΕΑΙ. Ναί.

ΞΕ. Τὸ δέ γε ἄγνοιαν μὲν καλοῦσι, κακίαν δὲ
αὐτὸ ἐν ψυχῇ μόνον γιγνόμενον οὐκ ἐθέλουσιν
ὁμολογεῖν.

E   ΘΕΑΙ. Κομιδῇ συγχωρητέον, ὃ νῦν δὴ λέξαντος
ἠμφεγνόησά σου, τὸ δύο εἶναι γένη κακίας ἐν ψυχῇ,
καὶ δειλίαν μὲν καὶ ἀκολασίαν καὶ ἀδικίαν ξύμπαντα
ἡγητέον νόσον ἐν ἡμῖν, τὸ δὲ τῆς πολλῆς καὶ παντο-
δαπῆς ἀγνοίας πάθος αἶσχος θετέον.

---

[1] γίγνηται BT ; γίγνεται al.
[2] ἀποτυγχάνῃ T ; ἀποτυγχάνει B et al.

and miss it on every occasion when they try to hit it, shall we say that this happens to them through right proportion to one another or, on the contrary, through disproportion?[1]

THEAET. Evidently through disproportion.

STR. But yet we know that every soul, if ignorant of anything, is ignorant against its will.

THEAET. Very much so.

STR. Now being ignorant is nothing else than the aberration of a soul that aims at truth, when the understanding passes beside the mark.

THEAET. Very true.

STR. Then we must regard a foolish soul as deformed and ill-proportioned.

THEAET. So it seems.

STR. Then there are, it appears, these two kinds of evils in the soul, one, which people call wickedness, which is very clearly a disease.

THEAET. Yes.

STR. And the other they call ignorance, but they are not willing to acknowledge that it is vice, when it arises only in the soul.

THEAET. It must certainly be admitted, though I disputed it when you said it just now, that there are two kinds of vice in the soul, and that cowardice, intemperance, and injustice must all alike be considered a disease in us, and the widespread and various condition of ignorance must be regarded as a deformity.

---

[1] The connexion between disproportion and missing the mark is not obvious. The explanation that a missile (*e.g.* an arrow) which is not evenly balanced will not fly straight, fails to take account of the words πρὸς ἄλληλα. The idea seems rather to be that moving objects of various sizes, shapes, and rates of speed must interfere with each other.

228

16. ΞΕ. Οὐκοῦν ἐν σώματί γε περὶ δύο παθήματε τούτω δύο τέχνα τινὲ ἐγενέσθην;

ΘΕΑΙ. Τίνε τούτω;

229 ΞΕ. Περὶ μὲν αἶσχος γυμναστική, περὶ δὲ νόσον ἰατρική.

ΘΕΑΙ. Φαίνεσθον.

ΞΕ. Οὐκοῦν καὶ περὶ μὲν ὕβριν καὶ ἀδικίαν καὶ δειλίαν ἡ κολαστικὴ πέφυκε τεχνῶν μάλιστα δὴ πασῶν προσήκουσα Δίκῃ[1];

ΘΕΑΙ. Τὸ γοῦν εἰκός, ὡς εἰπεῖν κατὰ τὴν ἀνθρωπίνην δόξαν.

ΞΕ. Τί δέ; περὶ ξύμπασαν ἄγνοιαν μῶν ἄλλην τινὰ ἢ διδασκαλικὴν ὀρθότερον εἴποι τις ἄν;

ΘΕΑΙ. Οὐδεμίαν.

ΞΕ. Φέρε δή· διδασκαλικῆς δὲ ἆρα ἓν μόνον
B γένος φατέον εἶναι ἢ πλείω, δύο δέ τινε αὐτῆς εἶναι μεγίστω, σκόπει.

ΘΕΑΙ. Σκοπῶ.

ΞΕ. Καί μοι δοκοῦμεν τῇδε ἄν πῃ τάχιστα εὑρεῖν.

ΘΕΑΙ. Πῇ;

ΞΕ. Τὴν ἄγνοιαν ἰδόντες εἴ πῃ κατὰ μέσον αὐτῆς[2] τομὴν ἔχει τινά. διπλῆ γὰρ αὕτη γιγνομένη δῆλον ὅτι καὶ τὴν διδασκαλικὴν δύο ἀναγκάζει μόρια ἔχειν, ἓν ἐφ᾽ ἑνὶ γένει τῶν αὐτῆς ἑκατέρῳ.

ΘΕΑΙ. Τί οὖν; καταφανές πῇ σοι τὸ νῦν ζητούμενον;

C ΞΕ. Ἀγνοίας γοῦν[3] μέγα τί μοι δοκῶ καὶ χαλεπὸν ἀφωρισμένον ὁρᾶν εἶδος, πᾶσι τοῖς ἄλλοις αὐτῆς ἀντίσταθμον μέρεσιν.

ΘΕΑΙ. Ποῖον δή;

ΞΕ. Τὸ μὴ κατειδότα τι δοκεῖν εἰδέναι· δι᾽ οὗ

---

[1] Δίκῃ Cobet; δίκῃ BT, Stobaeus.
[2] αὐτῆς W; αὑτῆς BT. [3] γοῦν W; δ᾽ οὖν BT.

THE SOPHIST

STR. In the case of the body there are two arts which have to do with these two evil conditions, are there not?

THEAET. What are they?

STR. For deformity there is gymnastics, and for disease medicine.

THEAET. That is clear.

STR. Hence for insolence and injustice and cowardice is not the corrective art the one of all arts most closely related to Justice?

THEAET. Probably it is, at least according to the judgement of mankind.

STR. And for all sorts of ignorance is there any art it would be more correct to suggest than that of instruction?

THEAET. No, none.

STR. Come now, think. Shall we say that there is only one kind of instruction, or that there are more and that two are the most important?

THEAET. I am thinking.

STR. I think we can find out most quickly in this way.

THEAET. In what way?

STR. By seeing whether ignorance admits of being cut in two in the middle; for if ignorance turns out to be twofold, it is clear that instruction must also consist of two parts, one for each part of ignorance.

THEAET. Well, can you see what you are now looking for?

STR. I at any rate think I do see one large and grievous kind of ignorance, separate from the rest, and as weighty as all the other parts put together.

THEAET. What is it?

STR. Thinking that one knows a thing when one

311

κινδυνεύει πάντα ὅσα διανοίᾳ σφαλλόμεθα γίγνεσθαι πᾶσιν.

ΘΕΑΙ. Ἀληθῆ.

ΞΕ. Καὶ δὴ καὶ τούτῳ γε οἶμαι μόνῳ τῆς ἀγνοίας ἀμαθίαν τοὔνομα προσρηθῆναι.

ΘΕΑΙ. Πάνυ γε.

ΞΕ. Τί δὲ δὴ τῷ τῆς διδασκαλικῆς ἄρα μέρει τῷ τοῦτο ἀπαλλάττοντι λεκτέον;

D ΘΕΑΙ. Οἶμαι μὲν οὖν, ὦ ξένε, τὸ μὲν ἄλλο δημιουργικὰς διδασκαλίας, τοῦτο δὲ ἐνθάδε γε παιδείαν δι' ἡμῶν κεκλῆσθαι.

ΞΕ. Καὶ γὰρ σχεδόν, ὦ Θεαίτητε, ἐν πᾶσιν Ἕλλησιν. ἀλλὰ γὰρ ἡμῖν ἔτι καὶ τοῦτο σκεπτέον, εἰ ἄτομον ἤδη ἐστὶ πᾶν ἤ τινα ἔχον διαίρεσιν ἀξίαν ἐπωνυμίας.

ΘΕΑΙ. Οὐκοῦν χρὴ σκοπεῖν.

17. ΞΕ. Δοκεῖ τοίνυν μοι καὶ τοῦτο ἔτι πῃ σχίζεσθαι.

ΘΕΑΙ. Κατὰ τί;

ΞΕ. Τῆς ἐν τοῖς λόγοις διδασκαλικῆς ἡ μὲν
E τραχυτέρα τις ἔοικεν ὁδὸς εἶναι, τὸ δ' ἕτερον αὐτῆς μόριον λειότερον.

ΘΕΑΙ. Τὸ ποῖον δὴ τούτων ἑκάτερον λέγωμεν;

ΞΕ. Τὸ μὲν ἀρχαιοπρεπές τι πάτριον, ᾧ πρὸς τοὺς υἱεῖς μάλιστ' ἐχρῶντό τε καὶ ἔτι πολλοὶ χρῶν-
ται τὰ νῦν, ὅταν αὐτοῖς ἐξαμαρτάνωσί τι, τὰ μὲν
230 χαλεπαίνοντες, τὰ δὲ μαλθακωτέρως παραμυθού-
μενοι· τὸ δ' οὖν ξύμπαν αὐτὸ ὀρθότατα εἴποι τις ἂν νουθετητικήν.

ΘΕΑΙ. Ἔστιν οὕτως.

ΞΕ. Τὸ δέ γε, εἴξασί [1] τινες αὖ λόγον ἑαυτοῖς

1 εἴξασί ΒΤ, Stobaeus; ὡς εἴξασί vulg.

does not know it. Through this, I believe, all the mistakes of the mind are caused in all of us.

THEAET. True.

STR. And furthermore to this kind of ignorance alone the name of stupidity is given.

THEAET. Certainly.

STR. Now what name is to be given to that part of instruction which gets rid of this?

THEAET. I think, Stranger, that the other part is called instruction in handicraft, and that this part is here at Athens through our influence called education.

STR. And so it is, Theaetetus, among nearly all the Hellenes. But we must examine further and see whether it is one and indivisible or still admits of division important enough to have a name.

THEAET. Yes, we must see about that.

STR. I think there is still a way in which this also may be divided.

THEAET. On what principle?

STR. Of instruction in arguments one method seems to be rougher, and the other section smoother.

THEAET. What shall we call each of these?

STR. The venerable method of our fathers, which they generally employed towards their sons, and which many still employ, of sometimes showing anger at their errors and sometimes more gently exhorting them—that would most properly be called as a whole admonition.

THEAET. That is true.

STR. On the other hand, some appear to have con-

δόντες ἡγήσασθαι πᾶσαν ἀκούσιον ἀμαθίαν εἶναι, καὶ μαθεῖν οὐδέν ποτ' ἂν ἐθέλειν τὸν οἰόμενον εἶναι σοφὸν τούτων ὧν οἴοιτο πέρι δεινὸς εἶναι, μετὰ δὲ πολλοῦ πόνου τὸ νουθετητικὸν εἶδος τῆς παιδείας σμικρὸν ἀνύτειν.

ΘΕΑΙ. Ὀρθῶς γε νομίζοντες.

B   ΞΕ. Τῷ τοι ταύτης τῆς δόξης ἐπὶ ἐκβολὴν ἄλλῳ τρόπῳ στέλλονται.

ΘΕΑΙ. Τίνι δή;

ΞΕ. Διερωτῶσιν ὧν ἂν οἴηταί τίς τι πέρι λέγειν λέγων μηδέν· εἶθ' ἅτε πλανωμένων τὰς δόξας ῥᾳδίως ἐξετάζουσι, καὶ συνάγοντες δὴ τοῖς λόγοις εἰς ταὐτὸν τιθέασι παρ' ἀλλήλας, τιθέντες δὲ ἐπιδεικνύουσιν αὐτὰς αὑταῖς[1] ἅμα περὶ τῶν αὐτῶν πρὸς τὰ αὐτὰ κατὰ ταὐτὰ ἐναντίας· οἱ δ' ὁρῶντες ἑαυτοῖς μὲν χαλεπαίνουσι, πρὸς δὲ τοὺς ἄλλους ἡμεροῦνται, καὶ τούτῳ δὴ τῷ τρόπῳ τῶν περὶ

C αὑτοὺς μεγάλων καὶ σκληρῶν δοξῶν ἀπαλλάττονται πασῶν[2] ἀπαλλαγῶν ἀκούειν τε ἡδίστην καὶ τῷ πάσχοντι βεβαιότατα γιγνομένην. νομίζοντες γάρ, ὦ παῖ φίλε, οἱ καθαίροντες αὐτούς, ὥσπερ οἱ περὶ τὰ σώματα ἰατροὶ νενομίκασι μὴ πρότερον ἂν τῆς προσφερομένης τροφῆς ἀπολαύειν δύνασθαι σῶμα, πρὶν ἂν τὰ ἐμποδίζοντα ἐν αὐτῷ τις ἐκβάλῃ, ταὐτὸν καὶ περὶ ψυχῆς διενοήθησαν ἐκεῖνοι, μὴ πρότερον αὐτὴν ἕξειν τῶν προσφερομένων μαθημάτων ὄνησιν,

D πρὶν ἂν ἐλέγχων τις τὸν ἐλεγχόμενον εἰς αἰσχύνην καταστήσας, τὰς τοῖς μαθήμασιν ἐμποδίους δόξας ἐξελών, καθαρὸν ἀποφήνῃ καὶ ταῦτα ἡγούμενον, ἅπερ οἶδεν, εἰδέναι μόνα, πλείω δὲ μή.

¹ αὑταῖς] αὐταῖς BT.
² πασῶν Stobaeus; πασῶν τε BT.

THE SOPHIST

vinced themselves that all ignorance is involuntary, and that he who thinks himself wise would never be willing to learn any of those things in which he believes he is clever, and that the admonitory kind of education takes a deal of trouble and accomplishes little.

THEAET. They are quite right.

STR. So they set themselves to cast out the conceit of cleverness in another way.

THEAET. In what way?

STR. They question a man about the things about which he thinks he is talking sense when he is talking nonsense; then they easily discover that his opinions are like those of men who wander, and in their discussions they collect those opinions and compare them with one another, and by the comparison they show that they contradict one another about the same things, in relation to the same things and in respect to the same things. But those who see this grow angry with themselves and gentle towards others, and this is the way in which they are freed from their high and obstinate opinions about themselves. The process of freeing them, moreover, affords the greatest pleasure to the listeners and the most lasting benefit to him who is subjected to it. For just as physicians who care for the body believe that the body cannot get benefit from any food offered to it until all obstructions are removed, so, my boy, those who purge the soul believe that the soul can receive no benefit from any teachings offered to it until someone by cross-questioning reduces him who is cross-questioned to an attitude of modesty, by removing the opinions that obstruct the teachings, and thus purges him and makes him think that he knows only what he knows, and no more.

PLATO

230

ΘΕΑΙ. Βελτίστη γοῦν καὶ σωφρονεστάτη τῶν ἕξεων αὕτη.

ΞΕ. Διὰ ταῦτα δὴ πάντα ἡμῖν, ὦ Θεαίτητε, καὶ τὸν ἔλεγχον λεκτέον ὡς ἄρα μεγίστη καὶ κυριωτάτη τῶν καθάρσεών ἐστι, καὶ τὸν ἀνέλεγκτον αὖ νομιστέον, ἂν καὶ τυγχάνῃ βασιλεὺς ὁ μέγας ὤν,
E τὰ μέγιστα ἀκάθαρτον ὄντα, ἀπαίδευτόν τε καὶ αἰσχρὸν γεγονέναι ταῦτα, ἃ καθαρώτατον καὶ κάλλιστον ἔπρεπε τὸν ὄντως ἐσόμενον εὐδαίμονα εἶναι.

ΘΕΑΙ. Παντάπασι μὲν οὖν.

18. ΞΕ. Τί δέ; τοὺς ταύτῃ χρωμένους τῇ τέχνῃ
231 τίνας φήσομεν; ἐγὼ μὲν γὰρ φοβοῦμαι σοφιστὰς φάναι.

ΘΕΑΙ. Τί δή;

ΞΕ. Μὴ μεῖζον αὐτοῖς προσάπτωμεν γέρας.

ΘΕΑΙ. Ἀλλὰ μὴν προσέοικε τοιούτῳ τινὶ τὰ νῦν εἰρημένα.

ΞΕ. Καὶ γὰρ κυνὶ λύκος, ἀγριώτατον ἡμερωτάτῳ. τὸν δὲ ἀσφαλῆ δεῖ πάντων μάλιστα περὶ τὰς ὁμοιότητας ἀεὶ ποιεῖσθαι τὴν φυλακήν· ὀλισθηρότατον γὰρ τὸ γένος. ὅμως δὲ ἔστωσαν· οὐ γὰρ περὶ σμικρῶν ὅρων τὴν ἀμφισβήτησιν οἴομαι γενήσεσθαι
B τότε ὁπόταν ἱκανῶς φυλάττωσιν.

ΘΕΑΙ. Οὔκουν τό γε εἰκός.

ΞΕ. Ἔστω δὴ διακριτικῆς τέχνης καθαρτική, καθαρτικῆς δὲ τὸ περὶ ψυχὴν μέρος ἀφωρίσθω, τούτου δὲ διδασκαλική, διδασκαλικῆς δὲ παιδευτική· τῆς δὲ παιδευτικῆς ὁ περὶ τὴν μάταιον δοξοσοφίαν γιγνόμενος ἔλεγχος ἐν τῷ νῦν λόγῳ παραφανέντι μηδὲν ἄλλ' ἡμῖν εἶναι λεγέσθω πλὴν ἡ γένει γενναία σοφιστική.

316

THE SOPHIST

THEAET. That is surely the best and most reasonable state of mind.

STR. For all these reasons, Theaetetus, we must assert that cross-questioning is the greatest and most efficacious of all purifications, and that he who is not cross-questioned, even though he be the Great King, has not been purified of the greatest taints, and is therefore uneducated and deformed in those things in which he who is to be truly happy ought to be most pure and beautiful.

THEAET. Perfectly true.

STR. Well then, who are those who practise this art? I am afraid to say the sophists.

THEAET. Why so?

STR. Lest we grant them too high a meed of honour.

THEAET. But the description you have just given is very like someone of that sort.

STR. Yes, and a wolf is very like a dog, the wildest like the tamest of animals. But the cautious man must be especially on his guard in the matter of resemblances, for they are very slippery things. However, let us agree that they are the sophists; for I think the strife will not be about petty discriminations when people are sufficiently on their guard.

THEAET. No, probably not.

STR. Then let it be agreed that part of the discriminating art is purification, and as part of purification let that which is concerned with the soul be separated off, and as part of this, instruction, and as part of instruction, education; and let us agree that the cross-questioning of empty conceit of wisdom, which has come to light in our present discussion, is nothing else than the true-born art of sophistry.

317

ΘΕΑΙ. Λεγέσθω μέν· ἀπορῶ δὲ ἔγωγε ἤδη διὰ
C τὸ πολλὰ πεφάνθαι, τί χρή ποτε ὡς ἀληθῆ λέγοντα
καὶ διισχυριζόμενον εἰπεῖν ὄντως εἶναι τὸν σοφιστήν.

ΞΕ. Εἰκότως γε σὺ ἀπορῶν. ἀλλά τοι κἀκεῖνον
ἡγεῖσθαι χρὴ νῦν ἤδη σφόδρα ἀπορεῖν ὅπη ποτὲ ἔτι
διαδύσεται τὸν λόγον· ὀρθὴ γὰρ ἡ παροιμία, τὸ τὰς
ἁπάσας μὴ ῥάδιον εἶναι διαφεύγειν. νῦν οὖν καὶ
μάλιστα ἐπιθετέον αὐτῷ.

ΘΕΑΙ. Καλῶς λέγεις.

19. ΞΕ. Πρῶτον δὴ στάντες οἷον ἐξαναπνεύσω-
μεν, καὶ πρὸς ἡμᾶς αὐτοὺς διαλογισώμεθα ἅμα ἀνα-
D παυόμενοι, φέρε, ὁπόσα ἡμῖν ὁ σοφιστὴς πέφανται.
δοκῶ μὲν γάρ,[1] τὸ πρῶτον ηὑρέθη νέων καὶ
πλουσίων ἔμμισθος θηρευτής.

ΘΕΑΙ. Ναί.

ΞΕ. Τὸ δέ γε δεύτερον ἔμπορός τις περὶ τὰ τῆς
ψυχῆς μαθήματα.

ΘΕΑΙ. Πάνυ γε.

ΞΕ. Τρίτον δὲ ἆρα οὐ περὶ ταὐτὰ ταῦτα κάπηλος
ἀνεφάνη;

ΘΕΑΙ. Ναί, καὶ τέταρτόν γε αὐτοπώλης περὶ τὰ
μαθήματα ἡμῖν ἦν.[2]

ΞΕ. Ὀρθῶς ἐμνημόνευσας. πέμπτον δ' ἐγὼ
πειράσομαι μνημονεύειν· τῆς γὰρ ἀγωνιστικῆς
E περὶ λόγους ἦν τις ἀθλητής, τὴν ἐριστικὴν τέχνην
ἀφωρισμένος.

ΘΕΑΙ. Ἦν γὰρ οὖν.

ΞΕ. Τό γε μὴν ἕκτον ἀμφισβητήσιμον μέν, ὅμως
δ' ἔθεμεν αὐτῷ συγχωρήσαντες δοξῶν ἐμποδίων
μαθήμασι περὶ ψυχὴν καθαρτὴν αὐτὸν εἶναι.

ΘΕΑΙ. Παντάπασι μὲν οὖν.

[1] γάρ W; γὰρ ἂν BT.   [2] ἦν add. Heindorf.

THE SOPHIST

THEAET. Let us agree to all that; but the sophist has by this time appeared to be so many things that I am at a loss to know what in the world to say he really is, with any assurance that I am speaking the truth.

STR. No wonder you are at a loss. But it is fair to suppose that by this time he is still more at a loss to know how he can any longer elude our argument; for the proverb is right which says it is not easy to escape all the wrestler's grips. So now we must attack him with redoubled vigour.

THEAET. You are right.

STR. First, then, let us stop to take breath and while we are resting let us count up the number of forms in which the sophist has appeared to us. First, I believe, he was found to be a paid hunter after the young and wealthy.

THEAET. Yes.

STR. And secondly a kind of merchant in articles of knowledge for the soul.

THEAET. Certainly.

STR. And thirdly did he not turn up as a retailer of these same articles of knowledge?

THEAET. Yes, and fourthly we found he was a seller of his own productions of knowledge.

STR. Your memory is good; but I will try to recall the fifth case myself. He was an athlete in contests of words, who had taken for his own the art of disputation.

THEAET. Yes, he was.

STR. The sixth case was doubtful, but nevertheless we agreed to consider him a purger of souls, who removes opinions that obstruct learning.

THEAET. Very true.

232 ΞΕ. Ἆρ' οὖν ἐννοεῖς, ὅταν ἐπιστήμων τις πολλῶν φαίνηται, μιᾶς δὲ τέχνης ὀνόματι προσαγορεύηται, τὸ φάντασμα τοῦτο ὡς οὐκ ἔσθ' ὑγιές, ἀλλὰ δῆλον ὡς ὁ πάσχων αὐτὸ πρός τινα τέχνην οὐ δύναται κατιδεῖν ἐκεῖνο αὐτῆς εἰς ὃ πάντα τὰ μαθήματα ταῦτα βλέπει, διὸ καὶ πολλοῖς ὀνόμασιν ἀνθ' ἑνὸς τὸν ἔχοντα αὐτὰ προσαγορεύει;

ΘΕΑΙ. Κινδυνεύει τοῦτο ταύτῃ πῃ μάλιστα πεφυκέναι.

B 20. ΞΕ. Μὴ τοίνυν ἡμεῖς γε αὐτὸ ἐν τῇ ζητήσει δι' ἀργίαν πάσχωμεν, ἀλλ' ἀναλάβωμεν πρῶτόν τι τῶν περὶ τὸν σοφιστὴν εἰρημένων. ἓν γάρ τί μοι μάλιστα κατεφάνη αὐτὸν μηνῦον.

ΘΕΑΙ. Τὸ ποῖον;

ΞΕ. Ἀντιλογικὸν αὐτὸν ἔφαμεν εἶναί που.

ΘΕΑΙ. Ναί.

ΞΕ. Τί δ'; οὐ καὶ τῶν ἄλλων αὐτοῦ τούτου διδάσκαλον γίγνεσθαι;

ΘΕΑΙ. Τί μήν;

ΞΕ. Σκοπῶμεν δή, περὶ τίνος ἄρα καὶ φασὶν οἱ τοιοῦτοι ποιεῖν ἀντιλογικούς. ἡ δὲ σκέψις ἡμῖν ἐξ
C ἀρχῆς ἔστω τῇδέ πῃ. φέρε, περὶ τῶν θείων, ὅσ' ἀφανῆ τοῖς πολλοῖς, ἆρ' ἱκανοὺς ποιοῦσι τοῦτο δρᾶν;

ΘΕΑΙ. Λέγεται γοῦν [1] δὴ περὶ αὐτῶν ταῦτα.

ΞΕ. Τί δ' ὅσα φανερὰ γῆς τε καὶ οὐρανοῦ καὶ τῶν περὶ τὰ τοιαῦτα;

ΘΕΑΙ. Τί γάρ;

ΞΕ. Ἀλλὰ μὴν ἔν γε ταῖς ἰδίαις συνουσίαις, ὁπόταν γενέσεώς τε καὶ οὐσίας πέρι κατὰ πάντων

---

[1] γοῦν W ; οὖν BT.

THE SOPHIST

STR. Then do you see that when a man appears to know many things, but is called by the name of a single art, there is something wrong about this impression, and that, in fact, the person who labours under this impression in connexion with any art is clearly unable to see the common principle of the art, to which all these kinds of knowledge pertain, so that he calls him who possesses them by many names instead of one?

THEAET. Something like that is very likely to be the case.

STR. We must not let that happen to us in our search through lack of diligence. So let us first take up again one of our statements about the sophist. For there is one of them which seemed to me to designate him most plainly.

THEAET. Which was it?

STR. I think we said he was a disputer.

THEAET. Yes.

STR. And did we not also say that he taught this same art of disputing to others?

THEAET. Certainly.

STR. Now let us examine and see what the subjects are about which such men say they make their pupils able to dispute. Let us begin our examination at the beginning with this question: Is it about divine things which are invisible to others that they make people able to dispute?

THEAET. That is their reputation, at any rate.

STR. And how about the visible things of earth and heaven and the like?

THEAET. Those are included, of course.

STR. And furthermore in private conversations, when the talk is about generation and being in

λέγηταί τι, ξύνισμεν ὡς αὐτοί τε ἀντειπεῖν δεινοὶ
τούς τε ἄλλους ὅτι ποιοῦσιν ἅπερ αὐτοὶ δυνατούς;

ΘΕΑΙ. Παντάπασί γε.

D ΞΕ. Τί δ' αὖ περὶ νόμων καὶ ξυμπάντων τῶν
πολιτικῶν, ἆρ' οὐχ ὑπισχνοῦνται ποιεῖν ἀμφισβη-
τητικούς[1];

ΘΕΑΙ. Οὐδεὶς γὰρ ἂν αὐτοῖς, ὡς ἔπος εἰπεῖν,
διελέγετο μὴ τοῦτο ὑπισχνουμένοις.

ΞΕ. Τά γε μὴν περὶ πασῶν τε καὶ κατὰ μίαν
ἑκάστην τέχνην, ἃ δεῖ πρὸς ἕκαστον αὐτὸν τὸν
δημιουργὸν ἀντειπεῖν, δεδημοσιωμένα που καταβέ-
βληται γεγραμμένα τῷ βουλομένῳ μαθεῖν.

ΘΕΑΙ. Τὰ Πρωταγόρειά μοι φαίνει περί τε πάλης
E καὶ τῶν ἄλλων τεχνῶν εἰρηκέναι.

ΞΕ. Καὶ πολλῶν γε, ὦ μακάριε, ἑτέρων. ἀτὰρ
δὴ τὸ τῆς ἀντιλογικῆς τέχνης ἆρ' οὐκ ἐν κεφαλαίῳ
περὶ πάντων πρὸς ἀμφισβήτησιν ἱκανή τις δύναμις
ἔοικ' εἶναι;

ΘΕΑΙ. Φαίνεται γοῦν σχεδὸν οὐδὲν ὑπολιπεῖν.

ΞΕ. Σὺ δὴ πρὸς θεῶν, ὦ παῖ, δυνατὸν ἡγεῖ τοῦτο;
τάχα γὰρ ἂν ὑμεῖς μὲν ὀξύτερον οἱ νέοι πρὸς αὐτὸ
βλέποιτε, ἡμεῖς δὲ ἀμβλύτερον.

233 ΘΕΑΙ. Τὸ ποῖον, καὶ πρὸς τί μάλιστα λέγεις; οὐ
γάρ πω κατανοῶ τὸ νῦν ἐρωτώμενον.

ΞΕ. Εἰ πάντα ἐπίστασθαί τινα ἀνθρώπων ἐστὶ
δυνατόν.

ΘΕΑΙ. Μακάριον μέντ' ἂν ἡμῶν, ὦ ξένε, ἦν τὸ
γένος.

ΞΕ. Πῶς οὖν ἄν ποτέ τις πρός γε τὸν ἐπιστά-
μενον αὐτὸς ἀνεπιστήμων ὢν δύναιτ' ἂν ὑγιές τι
λέγων ἀντειπεῖν;

[1] ἀμφισβητητικούς] ἀμφισβητικούς T.

THE SOPHIST

general, we know (do we not?) that they are clever disputants themselves and impart equal ability to others.

THEAET. Certainly.

STR. And how about laws and public affairs in general? Do they not promise to make men able to argue about those?

THEAET. Yes, for nobody, to speak broadly, would attend their classes if they did not make that promise.

STR. However in all arts jointly and severally what the professional ought to answer to every opponent is written down somewhere and published that he who will may learn.

THEAET. You seem to refer to the text-books of Protagoras on wrestling and the other arts.

STR. Yes, my friend, and to those of many other authors. But is not the art of disputation, in a word, a trained ability for arguing about all things?

THEAET. Well, at any rate, it does not seem to leave much out.

STR. For heaven's sake, my boy, do you think that is possible? For perhaps you young people may look at the matter with sharper vision than our duller sight.

THEAET. What do you mean and just what do you refer to? I do not yet understand your question.

STR. I ask whether it is possible for a man to know all things.

THEAET. If that were possible, Stranger, ours would indeed be a blessed race.

STR. How, then, can one who is himself ignorant say anything worth while in arguing with one who knows?

PLATO

233

ΘΕΑΙ. Οὐδαμῶς.

ΞΕ. Τί ποτ' οὖν ἂν εἴη τὸ τῆς σοφιστικῆς δυνάμεως θαῦμα;

ΘΕΑΙ. Τοῦ δὴ πέρι;

B ΞΕ. Καθ' ὅν τινα τρόπον ποτὲ δυνατοὶ τοῖς
νέοις δόξαν παρασκευάζειν, ὡς εἰσὶ πάντα πάντων
αὐτοὶ σοφώτατοι. δῆλον γὰρ ὡς εἰ μήτε ἀντέλεγον
ὀρθῶς μήτε ἐκείνοις ἐφαίνοντο, φαινόμενοί τε εἰ
μηδὲν αὖ μᾶλλον ἐδόκουν διὰ τὴν ἀμφισβήτησιν
εἶναι φρόνιμοι, τὸ σὸν [1] δὴ τοῦτο, σχολῇ ποτ' ἂν
αὐτοῖς τις χρήματα διδοὺς ἤθελεν ἂν τούτων αὐτῶν
μαθητὴς γίγνεσθαι.

ΘΕΑΙ. Σχολῇ μέντ' ἄν.

ΞΕ. Νῦν δέ γ' ἐθέλουσιν;

ΘΕΑΙ. Καὶ μάλα.

C ΞΕ. Δοκοῦσι γάρ, οἶμαι, πρὸς ταῦτα ἐπιστημόνως ἔχειν αὐτοὶ πρὸς ἅπερ ἀντιλέγουσιν.

ΘΕΑΙ. Πῶς γὰρ οὔ;

ΞΕ. Δρῶσι δέ γε τοῦτο πρὸς ἅπαντα, φαμέν;

ΘΕΑΙ. Ναί.

ΞΕ. Πάντα ἄρα σοφοὶ τοῖς μαθηταῖς φαίνονται.

ΘΕΑΙ. Τί μήν;

ΞΕ. Οὐκ ὄντες γε· ἀδύνατον γὰρ τοῦτό γε ἐφάνη.

ΘΕΑΙ. Πῶς γὰρ οὐκ ἀδύνατον;

21. ΞΕ. Δοξαστικὴν ἄρα τινὰ περὶ πάντων
ἐπιστήμην ὁ σοφιστὴς ἡμῖν, ἀλλ' οὐκ ἀλήθειαν
ἔχων ἀναπέφανται.

_____
[1] τὸ σὸν] τόσον BTW.

THEAET. He cannot at all.

STR. Then what in the world can the magical power of the sophistical art be?

THEAET. Magical power in what respect?

STR. In the way in which they are able to make young men think that they themselves are in all matters the wisest of men. For it is clear that if they neither disputed correctly nor seemed to the young men to do so, or again if they did seem to dispute rightly but were not considered wiser on that account, nobody, to quote from you,[1] would care to pay them money to become their pupil in these subjects.

THEAET. Certainly not.

STR. But now people do care to do so?

THEAET. Very much.

STR. Yes, for they are supposed, I fancy, to have knowledge themselves of the things about which they dispute.

THEAET. Of course.

STR. And they do that about all things, do they not?

THEAET. Yes.

STR. Then they appear to their pupils to be wise in all things.

THEAET. To be sure.

STR. Though they are not; for that was shown to be impossible.

THEAET. Of course it is impossible.

STR. Then it is a sort of knowledge based upon mere opinion that the sophist has been shown to possess about all things, not true knowledge.

---

[1] *Cf.* 232 D.

D ΘΕΑΙ. Παντάπασι μὲν οὖν, καὶ κινδυνεύει γε τὸ νῦν εἰρημένον ὀρθότατα περὶ αὐτῶν εἰρῆσθαι.

ΞΕ. Λάβωμεν τοίνυν σαφέστερόν τι παράδειγμα περὶ τούτων.

ΘΕΑΙ. Τὸ ποῖον δή;

ΞΕ. Τόδε. καί μοι πειρῶ προσέχων τὸν νοῦν εὖ μάλα ἀποκρίνασθαι.

ΘΕΑΙ. Τὸ ποῖον;

ΞΕ. Εἴ τις φαίη μὴ λέγειν μηδ᾽ ἀντιλέγειν, ἀλλὰ ποιεῖν καὶ δρᾶν μιᾷ τέχνῃ ξυνάπαντα ἐπίστασθαι πράγματα.

E ΘΕΑΙ. Πῶς πάντα εἶπες;

ΞΕ. Τὴν ἀρχὴν τοῦ ῥηθέντος σύ γ᾽ ἡμῖν εὐθὺς ἀγνοεῖς· τὰ γὰρ ξύμπαντα, ὡς ἔοικας, οὐ μανθάνεις.

ΘΕΑΙ. Οὐ γὰρ οὖν.

ΞΕ. Λέγω τοίνυν σὲ καὶ ἐμὲ τῶν πάντων καὶ πρὸς ἡμῖν τἆλλα ζῷα καὶ δένδρα.

ΘΕΑΙ. Πῶς λέγεις;

ΞΕ. Εἴ τις ἐμὲ καὶ σὲ καὶ τἆλλα φυτὰ πάντα ποιήσειν [1] φαίη.

ΘΕΑΙ. Τίνα δὴ λέγων τὴν ποίησιν; οὐ γὰρ δὴ 234 γεωργόν γε ἐρεῖς τινα· καὶ γὰρ ζῴων αὐτὸν εἶπες ποιητήν.

ΞΕ. Φημί, καὶ πρός γε θαλάττης καὶ γῆς [2] καὶ οὐρανοῦ καὶ θεῶν καὶ τῶν ἄλλων ξυμπάντων· καὶ τοίνυν καὶ ταχὺ ποιήσας αὐτῶν ἕκαστα πάνυ σμικροῦ νομίσματος ἀποδίδοται.

ΘΕΑΙ. Παιδιὰν λέγεις τινά.

ΞΕ. Τί δέ; τὴν τοῦ λέγοντος ὅτι πάντα οἶδε καὶ

---

[1] ποιήσειν W ; ποιησιν BT.   [2] καὶ γῆς W ; om. BT.

THEAET. Certainly; and I shouldn't be surprised if that were the most accurate statement we have made about him so far.

STR. Let us then take a clearer example to explain this.

THEAET. What sort of an example?

STR. This one; and try to pay attention and to give a very careful answer to my question.

THEAET. What is the question?

STR. If anyone should say that by virtue of a single art he knew how, not to assert or dispute, but to do and make all things—

THEAET. What do you mean by all things?

STR. You fail to grasp the very beginning of what I said; for apparently you do not understand the word "all."

THEAET. No, I do not.

STR. I mean you and me among the "all," and the other animals besides, and the trees.

THEAET. What do you mean?

STR. If one should say that he would make you and me and all other created beings.

THEAET. What would he mean by "making"? Evidently you will not say that he means a husband-man; for you said he was a maker of animals also.

STR. Yes, and of sea and earth and heaven and gods and everything else besides; and, moreover, he makes them all quickly and sells them for very little.

THEAET. This is some joke of yours.

STR. Yes? And when a man says that he knows all things and can teach them to another for a small

ταῦτα ἕτερον ἂν διδάξειεν ὀλίγου καὶ ἐν ὀλίγῳ
χρόνῳ, μῶν οὐ παιδιὰν νομιστέον;

ΘΕΑΙ. Πάντως που.

B ΞΕ. Παιδιᾶς δὲ ἔχεις ἤ τι τεχνικώτερον ἢ καὶ
χαριέστερον εἶδος ἢ τὸ μιμητικόν;

ΘΕΑΙ. Οὐδαμῶς· πάμπολυ γὰρ εἴρηκας εἶδος
εἰς ἓν πάντα ξυλλαβὼν καὶ σχεδὸν ποικιλώτατον.

22. ΞΕ. Οὐκοῦν τόν γ' ὑπισχνούμενον δυνατὸν
εἶναι μιᾷ τέχνῃ πάντα ποιεῖν γιγνώσκομέν που
τοῦτο, ὅτι μιμήματα καὶ ὁμώνυμα τῶν ὄντων
ἀπεργαζόμενος τῇ γραφικῇ τέχνῃ δυνατὸς ἔσται
τοὺς ἀνοήτους τῶν νέων παίδων, πόρρωθεν τὰ
γεγραμμένα ἐπιδεικνύς, λανθάνειν ὡς ὅτιπερ ἂν
βουληθῇ δρᾶν, τοῦτο ἱκανώτατος ὢν ἀποτελεῖν
ἔργῳ.

C ΘΕΑΙ. Πῶς γὰρ οὔ;

ΞΕ. Τί δὲ δή; περὶ τοὺς λόγους ἆρ' οὐ προσ-
δοκῶμεν εἶναί τινα ἄλλην τέχνην, ᾗ αὖ δυνατὸν ὂν
τυγχάνει [1] τοὺς νέους καὶ ἔτι πόρρω τῶν πραγμάτων
τῆς ἀληθείας ἀφεστῶτας διὰ τῶν ὤτων τοῖς λόγοις
γοητεύειν, δεικνύντας εἴδωλα λεγόμενα περὶ πάντων,
ὥστε ποιεῖν ἀληθῆ δοκεῖν λέγεσθαι καὶ τὸν λέγοντα
δὴ σοφώτατον πάντων ἅπαντ' εἶναι;

D ΘΕΑΙ. Τί γὰρ οὐκ ἂν εἴη ἄλλη τις τοιαύτη
τέχνη;

ΞΕ. Τοὺς πολλοὺς οὖν, ὦ Θεαίτητε, τῶν τότε
ἀκουόντων ἆρ' οὐκ ἀνάγκη χρόνου τε ἐπελθόντος
αὐτοῖς ἱκανοῦ καὶ προϊούσης ἡλικίας τοῖς τε οὖσι
προσπίπτοντας ἐγγύθεν καὶ διὰ παθημάτων ἀναγκα-
ζομένους ἐναργῶς ἐφάπτεσθαι τῶν ὄντων, μετα-

[1] ᾗ αὖ δυνατὸν ὂν τυγχάνει Burnet; ἡ (ᾗ T) οὐ δυνατὸν αὖ
τυγχάνειν BT; ᾗ ὂν δυνατὸν αὖ τυγχάνει Madvig.

price in a little time, must we not consider that a joke?

THEAET. Surely we must.

STR. And is there any more artistic or charming kind of joke than the imitative kind?

THEAET. Certainly not; for it is of very frequent occurrence and, if I may say so, most diverse. Your expression is very comprehensive.

STR. And so we recognize that he who professes to be able by virtue of a single art to make all things will be able by virtue of the painter's art, to make imitations which have the same names as the real things, and by showing the pictures at a distance will be able to deceive the duller ones among young children into the belief that he is perfectly able to accomplish in fact whatever he wishes to do.

THEAET. Certainly.

STR. Well then, may we not expect to find that there is another art which has to do with words, by virtue of which it is possible to bewitch the young through their ears with words while they are still standing at a distance from the realities of truth, by exhibiting to them spoken images of all things, so as to make it seem that they are true and that the speaker is the wisest of all men in all things?

THEAET. Why should there not be such another art?

STR. Now most of the hearers, Theaetetus, when they have lived longer and grown older, will perforce come closer to realities and will be forced by sad experience [1] openly to lay hold on realities; they

---

[1] Apparently a reference to a proverbial expression. *Cf.* Hesiod, *Works*, 216 ἔγνω παθών; Herodotus, i. 207 τὰ παθήματα μαθήματα.

234

βάλλειν τὰς τότε γενομένας δόξας, ὥστε σμικρὰ
μὲν φαίνεσθαι τὰ μεγάλα, χαλεπὰ δὲ τὰ ῥᾴδια, καὶ
E πάντα πάντῃ ἀνατετράφθαι τὰ ἐν τοῖς λόγοις
φαντάσματα ὑπὸ τῶν ἐν ταῖς πράξεσιν ἔργων
παραγενομένων;

ΘΕΑΙ. Ὡς γοῦν ἐμοὶ τηλικῷδε ὄντι κρῖναι. οἶμαι
δὲ καὶ ἐμὲ τῶν ἔτι πόρρωθεν ἀφεστηκότων εἶναι.

ΞΕ. Τοιγαροῦν ἡμεῖς σε οἵδε πάντες πειρασόμεθα
καὶ νῦν πειρώμεθα ὡς ἐγγύτατα ἄνευ τῶν παθημάτων
προσάγειν. περὶ δ' οὖν τοῦ σοφιστοῦ τόδε μοι
235 λέγε· πότερον ἤδη τοῦτο σαφές, ὅτι τῶν γοήτων
ἐστί τις, μιμητὴς ὢν τῶν ὄντων, ἢ διστάζομεν ἔτι
μὴ περὶ ὅσωνπερ ἀντιλέγειν δοκεῖ δυνατὸς εἶναι,
περὶ τοσούτων καὶ τὰς ἐπιστήμας ἀληθῶς ἔχων
τυγχάνει;

ΘΕΑΙ. Καὶ πῶς ἄν, ὦ ξένε; ἀλλὰ σχεδὸν ἤδη
σαφὲς ἐκ τῶν εἰρημένων, ὅτι τῶν τῆς παιδιᾶς μετεχόντων ἐστί τις εἷς.[1]

ΞΕ. Γόητα μὲν δὴ καὶ μιμητὴν ἄρα θετέον
αὐτόν τινα.

ΘΕΑΙ. Πῶς γὰρ οὐ θετέον;

23. ΞΕ. Ἄγε δή, ·νῦν ἡμέτερον ἔργον ἤδη τὸν
B θῆρα μηκέτ' ἀνεῖναι· σχεδὸν γὰρ αὐτὸν περιειλή-
φαμεν ἐν ἀμφιβληστρικῷ τινι τῶν ἐν τοῖς λόγοις
περὶ τὰ τοιαῦτα ὀργάνων, ὥστε οὐκέτ'[2] ἐκφεύξεται
τόδε γε.

ΘΕΑΙ. Τὸ[3] ποῖον;

[1] τις εἷς Heusde; τις μερῶν εἷς BT (giving εἷς to the stranger);
τις μερῶν εἷς W.
[2] οὐκέτ' W ; οὐκ ἔτι B ; οὐκ T.
[3] τὸ W; om. BT.

will have to change the opinions which they had at first accepted, so that what was great will appear small and what was easy, difficult, and all the apparent truths in arguments will be turned topsy-turvy by the facts that have come upon them in real life. Is not this true?

THEAET. Yes, at least so far as one of my age can judge. But I imagine I am one of those who are still standing at a distance.

STR. Therefore all of us elders here will try, and are now trying, to bring you as near as possible without the sad experience. So answer this question about the sophist: Is this now clear, that he is a kind of a juggler, an imitator of realities, or are we still uncertain whether he may not truly possess the knowledge of all the things about which he seems to be able to argue?

THEAET. How could that be, my dear sir? Surely it is pretty clear by this time from what has been said that he is one of those whose business is entertainment.

STR. That is to say, he must be classed as a juggler and imitator.

THEAET. Of course he must.

STR. Look sharp, then; it is now our business not to let the beast get away again, for we have almost got him into a kind of encircling net of the devices we employ in arguments about such subjects, so that he will not now escape the next thing.

THEAET. What next thing?

ΞΕ. Τὸ μὴ οὐ τοῦ γένους εἶναι τοῦ τῶν θαυματο-
ποιῶν τις εἷς.

ΘΕΑΙ. Κἀμοὶ τοῦτό γε οὕτω περὶ αὐτοῦ ξυνδοκεῖ.

ΞΕ. Δέδοκται[1] τοίνυν ὅτι τάχιστα διαιρεῖν τὴν
εἰδωλοποιικὴν τέχνην, καὶ καταβάντας εἰς αὐτήν,
ἐὰν μὲν ἡμᾶς εὐθὺς ὁ σοφιστὴς ὑπομείνῃ, συλλαβεῖν
αὐτὸν κατὰ τὰ ἐπεσταλμένα ὑπὸ τοῦ βασιλικοῦ
C λόγου, κἀκείνῳ παραδόντας ἀποφῆναι τὴν ἄγραν·
ἐὰν δ' ἄρα κατὰ μέρη τῆς μιμητικῆς δύηταί πῃ,
ξυνακολουθεῖν αὐτῷ διαιροῦντας ἀεὶ τὴν ὑποδεχο-
μένην αὐτὸν μοῖραν, ἔωσπερ ἂν ληφθῇ. πάντως
οὔτε οὗτος οὔτε ἄλλο γένος οὐδὲν μή ποτε ἐκφυγὸν
ἐπεύξηται τὴν τῶν οὕτω δυναμένων μετιέναι καθ'
ἕκαστά τε καὶ ἐπὶ πάντα μέθοδον.

ΘΕΑΙ. Λέγεις εὖ, καὶ ταῦτα ταύτῃ ποιητέον.

ΞΕ. Κατὰ δὴ τὸν παρεληλυθότα τρόπον τῆς
D διαιρέσεως ἔγωγέ μοι καὶ νῦν φαίνομαι δύο
καθορᾶν εἴδη τῆς μιμητικῆς· τὴν δὲ ζητουμένην
ἰδέαν, ἐν ὁποτέρῳ ποθ' ἡμῖν οὖσα τυγχάνει, κατα-
μαθεῖν οὐδέπω μοι δοκῶ νῦν δυνατὸς εἶναι.

ΘΕΑΙ. Σὺ δ' ἀλλ' εἰπὲ πρῶτον καὶ δίελε ἡμῖν,
τίνε τὼ δύο λέγεις.

ΞΕ. Μίαν μὲν τὴν εἰκαστικὴν ὁρῶν ἐν αὐτῇ
τέχνην. ἔστι δ' αὕτη μάλιστα, ὁπόταν κατὰ τὰς
τοῦ παραδείγματος συμμετρίας τις ἐν μήκει καὶ
πλάτει καὶ βάθει, καὶ πρὸς τούτοις ἔτι χρώματα
E ἀποδιδοὺς τὰ προσήκοντα ἑκάστοις,[2] τὴν τοῦ
μιμήματος γένεσιν ἀπεργάζηται.

ΘΕΑΙ. Τί δ'; οὐ πάντες οἱ μιμούμενοί τι τοῦτ'
ἐπιχειροῦσι δρᾶν;

---

[1] δέδοκται] δέδεικται BT ; δεδείκται W.
[2] ἑκάστοις Stobaeus, W ; ἑκάσταις BT.

STR. The conclusion that he belongs to the class of conjurers.

THEAET. I agree to that opinion of him, too.

STR. It is decided, then, that we will as quickly as possible divide the image-making art and go down into it, and if the sophist stands his ground against us at first, we will seize him by the orders of reason, our king, then deliver him up to the king and display his capture. But if he tries to take cover in any of the various sections of the imitative art, we must follow him, always dividing the section into which he has retreated, until he is caught. For assuredly neither he nor any other creature will ever boast of having escaped from pursuers who are able to follow up the pursuit in detail and everywhere in this methodical way.

THEAET. You are right. That is what we must do.

STR. To return, then, to our previous method of division, I think I see this time also two classes of imitation, but I do not yet seem to be able to make out in which of them the form we are seeking is to be found.

THEAET. Please first make the division and tell us what two classes you mean.

STR. I see the likeness-making art as one part of imitation. This is met with, as a rule, whenever anyone produces the imitation by following the proportions of the original in length, breadth, and depth, and giving, besides, the appropriate colours to each part.

THEAET. Yes, but do not all imitators try to do this?

ΞΕ. Οὔκουν ὅσοι γε τῶν μεγάλων πού τι πλάττου-
σιν ἔργων ἢ γράφουσιν. εἰ γὰρ ἀποδιδοῖεν τὴν τῶν
καλῶν ἀληθινὴν συμμετρίαν, οἶσθ᾽ ὅτι σμικρότερα
236 μὲν τοῦ δέοντος τὰ ἄνω, μείζω δὲ τὰ κάτω
φαίνοιτ᾽ ἂν διὰ τὸ τὰ μὲν πόρρωθεν, τὰ δ᾽ ἐγγύθεν
ὑφ᾽ ἡμῶν ὁρᾶσθαι.

ΘΕΑΙ. Πάνυ μὲν οὖν.[1]

ΞΕ. Ἆρ᾽ οὖν οὐ χαίρειν τὸ ἀληθὲς ἐάσαντες οἱ
δημιουργοὶ νῦν οὐ τὰς οὔσας συμμετρίας, ἀλλὰ τὰς
δοξούσας εἶναι καλὰς τοῖς εἰδώλοις ἐναπεργάζονται;

ΘΕΑΙ. Πάνυ μὲν οὖν.[2]

ΞΕ. Τὸ μὲν ἄρα ἕτερον οὐ δίκαιον, εἰκός γε ὄν,
εἰκόνα καλεῖν;

ΘΕΑΙ. Ναί.

B ΞΕ. Καὶ τῆς γε μιμητικῆς τὸ ἐπὶ τούτῳ μέρος
κλητέον, ὅπερ εἴπομεν ἐν τῷ πρόσθεν, εἰκαστικήν;

ΘΕΑΙ. Κλητέον.

ΞΕ. Τί δέ; τὸ φαινόμενον μὲν διὰ τὴν οὐκ ἐκ
καλοῦ θέαν ἐοικέναι τῷ καλῷ, δύναμιν δὲ εἴ τις
λάβοι τὰ τηλικαῦτα ἱκανῶς ὁρᾶν, μηδ᾽ εἰκὸς ᾧ
φησιν ἐοικέναι, τί καλοῦμεν; ἆρ᾽ οὐκ, ἐπείπερ
φαίνεται μέν, ἔοικε δὲ οὔ, φάντασμα;

ΘΕΑΙ. Τί μήν;

ΞΕ. Οὐκοῦν πάμπολυ καὶ κατὰ τὴν ζωγραφίαν
C τοῦτο τὸ μέρος ἐστὶ καὶ κατὰ ξύμπασαν μιμητικήν;

ΘΕΑΙ. Πῶς δ᾽ οὔ;

ΞΕ. Τὴν δὴ φάντασμα[3] ἀλλ᾽ οὐκ εἰκόνα ἀπεργα-
ζομένην τέχνην ἆρ᾽ οὐ φανταστικὴν ὀρθότατ᾽ ἂν
προσαγορεύοιμεν;

___
[1] πάνυ μὲν οὖν T, Stobaeus; om. B.
[2] πάνυ μὲν οὖν BT; παντάπασί γε W.
[3] φάντασμα W; φαντάσματα BT.

THE SOPHIST

STR. Not those who produce some large work of sculpture or painting. For if they reproduced the true proportions of beautiful forms, the upper parts, you know, would seem smaller and the lower parts larger than they ought, because we see the former from a distance, the latter from near at hand.

THEAET. Certainly.

STR. So the artists abandon the truth and give their figures not the actual proportions but those which seem to be beautiful, do they not?

THEAET. Certainly.

STR. That, then, which is other, but like, we may fairly call a likeness, may we not?

THEAET. Yes.

STR. And the part of imitation which is concerned with such things, is to be called, as we called it before, likeness-making?

THEAET. It is to be so called.

STR. Now then, what shall we call that which appears, because it is seen from an unfavourable position, to be like the beautiful, but which would not even be likely to resemble that which it claims to be like, if a person were able to see such large works adequately? Shall we not call it, since it appears, but is not like, an appearance?

THEAET. Certainly.

STR. And this is very common in painting and in all imitation?

THEAET. Of course.

STR. And to the art which produces appearance, but not likeness, the most correct name we could give would be "fantastic art," would it not?

ΘΕΑΙ. Πολύ γε.

ΞΕ. Τούτω τοίνυν τὼ δύο ἔλεγον εἴδη τῆς εἰδωλοποιικῆς, εἰκαστικὴν καὶ φανταστικήν.

ΘΕΑΙ. Ὀρθῶς.

ΞΕ. Ὁ δέ γε καὶ τότ᾿ ἠμφεγνόουν, ἐν [1] ποτέρᾳ [2]
τὸν σοφιστὴν θετέον, οὐδὲ νῦν πω δύναμαι θεάσα-
D σθαι σαφῶς, ἀλλ᾿ ὄντως θαυμαστὸς ἀνὴρ [3] καὶ
κατιδεῖν παγχάλεπος, ἐπεὶ καὶ νῦν μάλα εὖ καὶ
κομψῶς εἰς ἄπορον εἶδος διερευνήσασθαι κατα-
πέφευγεν.

ΘΕΑΙ. Ἔοικεν.

ΞΕ. Ἆρ᾿ οὖν αὐτὸ γιγνώσκων ξύμφης, ἤ σε
οἷον ῥύμη τις ὑπὸ τοῦ λόγου συνειθισμένον συνεπεσπάσατο [4] πρὸς τὸ ταχὺ ξυμφῆσαι;

ΘΕΑΙ. Πῶς καὶ πρὸς τί [5] τοῦτο εἴρηκας;

24. ΞΕ. Ὄντως, ὦ μακάριε, ἐσμὲν ἐν παντά-
E πασι χαλεπῇ σκέψει. τὸ γὰρ φαίνεσθαι τοῦτο καὶ
τὸ δοκεῖν, εἶναι δὲ μή, καὶ τὸ λέγειν μὲν ἄττα,
ἀληθῆ δὲ μή, πάντα ταῦτά ἐστι μεστὰ ἀπορίας ἀεὶ
ἐν τῷ πρόσθεν χρόνῳ καὶ νῦν. ὅπως γὰρ εἰπόντα
χρὴ ψευδῆ λέγειν ἢ δοξάζειν ὄντως εἶναι, καὶ τοῦτο
φθεγξάμενον ἐναντιολογίᾳ μὴ συνέχεσθαι, παντά-
237 πασιν, ὦ Θεαίτητε, χαλεπόν.

ΘΕΑΙ. Τί δή;

ΞΕ. Τετόλμηκεν ὁ λόγος οὗτος ὑποθέσθαι τὸ μὴ
ὂν εἶναι· ψεῦδος γὰρ οὐκ ἂν ἄλλως ἐγίγνετο ὄν.
Παρμενίδης δὲ ὁ μέγας, ὦ παῖ, παισὶν ἡμῖν οὖσιν

---

[1] ἐν add. Bessarionis liber.
[2] ποτέρα B ; πότερα TW.
[3] ἀνὴρ Bekker ; ἀνήρ BT.
[4] συνεπεσπάσατο W ; νῦν ἐπεσπάσατο BT.
[5] τί W ; ὅτι BT.

THEAET. By all means.

STR. These, then, are the two forms of the image-making art that I meant, the likeness-making and the fantastic.

THEAET. You are right.

STR. But I was uncertain before in which of the two the sophist should be placed, and even now I cannot see clearly. The fellow is really wonderful and very difficult to keep in sight, for once more, in the very cleverest manner he has withdrawn into a baffling classification where it is hard to track him.

THEAET. So it seems.

STR. Do you assent because you recognize the fact, or did the force of habit hurry you along to a speedy assent?

THEAET. What do you mean, and why did you say that?

STR. We are really, my dear friend, engaged in a very difficult investigation; for the matter of appearing and seeming, but not being, and of saying things, but not true ones—all this is now and always has been very perplexing. You see, Theaetetus, it is extremely difficult to understand how a man is to say or think that falsehood really exists and in saying this not be involved in contradiction.

THEAET. Why?

STR. This statement involves the bold assumption that not-being exists, for otherwise falsehood could not come into existence. But the great Parmenides, my boy, from the time when we were children to

ἀρχόμενός τε καὶ διὰ τέλους τοῦτο ἀπεμαρτύρατο,
πεζῇ τε ὧδε ἑκάστοτε λέγων καὶ μετὰ μέτρων·

οὐ γὰρ μή ποτε τοῦτο δαμῇ,[1] φησίν, εἶναι μὴ ἐόντα·
ἀλλὰ σὺ τῆσδ᾽ ἀφ᾽ ὁδοῦ διζήμενος[2] εἶργε νόημα.

B παρ᾽ ἐκείνου τε οὖν μαρτυρεῖται, καὶ μάλιστά γε
δὴ πάντων ὁ λόγος αὐτός[3] ἂν δηλώσειε μέτρια
βασανισθείς. τοῦτο οὖν αὐτὸ πρῶτον θεασώμεθα,
εἰ μή τί σοι διαφέρει.

ΘΕΑΙ. Τὸ μὲν ἐμὸν ὅπῃ βούλει τίθεσο, τὸν δὲ
λόγον ᾗ βέλτιστα διέξεισι σκοπῶν αὐτός τε ἴθι
κἀμὲ κατὰ ταύτην τὴν ὁδὸν ἄγε.

25. ΞΕ. Ἀλλὰ χρὴ δρᾶν ταῦτα. καί μοι λέγε·
τὸ μηδαμῶς ὂν τολμῶμέν που φθέγγεσθαι;

ΘΕΑΙ. Πῶς γὰρ οὔ;

ΞΕ. Μὴ τοίνυν ἔριδος ἕνεκα μηδὲ παιδιᾶς, ἀλλ᾽
C εἰ σπουδῇ[4] δέοι συννοήσαντά τινα ἀποκρίνασθαι
τῶν ἀκροατῶν ποῖ χρὴ τοὔνομ᾽ ἐπιφέρειν τοῦτο τὸ
μὴ ὄν· τί[5] δοκοῦμεν ἂν εἰς τί καὶ ἐπὶ ποῖον αὐτόν
τε καταχρήσασθαι καὶ τῷ πυνθανομένῳ δεικνύναι;

ΘΕΑΙ. Χαλεπὸν ἤρου καὶ σχεδὸν εἰπεῖν οἵῳ γε
ἐμοὶ παντάπασιν ἄπορον.

ΞΕ. Ἀλλ᾽ οὖν τοῦτό γε δῆλον, ὅτι τῶν ὄντων
ἐπί τι[6] τὸ μὴ ὂν οὐκ οἰστέον.

ΘΕΑΙ. Πῶς γὰρ ἄν;

ΞΕ. Οὐκοῦν ἐπείπερ οὐκ ἐπὶ τὸ ὄν, οὐδ᾽ ἐπὶ τὸ
τὶ φέρων ὀρθῶς ἄν τις φέροι.

---

[1] τοῦτο δαμῇ Simplicius ; τοῦτ᾽ οὐδαμῇ ΒΤ.
[2] διζήμενος ΒΤW (διζήσιος 258 D).
[3] αὐτὸς W ; οὗτος ΒΤ.
[4] ἀλλ᾽ εἰ σπουδῇ Bekker; ἄλλης ποῦ δὴ Β ; ἀλλὴ σπουδῇ Τ.
[5] τί] ὅτι ΤW.   [6] τι om. ΒΤ.

the end of his life, always protested against this and constantly repeated both in prose and in verse:

Never let this thought prevail, saith he, that not-being is;
But keep your mind from this way of investigation.

So that is his testimony, and a reasonable examination of the statement itself would make it most absolutely clear. Let us then consider this matter first, if it's all the same to you.

THEAET. Assume my consent to anything you wish. Consider only the argument, how it may best be pursued; follow your own course, and take me along with you.

STR. Very well, then. Now tell me; do we venture to use the phrase absolute not-being?

THEAET. Of course.

STR. If, then, not merely for the sake of discussion or as a joke, but seriously, one of his pupils were asked to consider and answer the question "To what is the designation 'not-being' to be applied?" how do we think he would reply to his questioner, and how would he apply the term, for what purpose, and to what object?

THEAET. That is a difficult question; I may say that for a fellow like me it is unanswerable.

STR. But this is clear, anyhow, that the term "not-being" cannot be applied to any being.

THEAET. Of course not.

STR. And if not to being, then it could not properly be applied to something, either.

339

ΘΕΑΙ. Πῶς δή;

D ΞΕ. Καὶ τοῦτο ἡμῖν που φανερόν, ὡς καὶ τὸ
"τὶ" τοῦτο ῥῆμα ἐπ᾽ ὄντι λέγομεν ἑκάστοτε·
μόνον γὰρ αὐτὸ λέγειν, ὥσπερ γυμνὸν καὶ ἀπηρημω-
μένον ἀπὸ τῶν ὄντων ἁπάντων, ἀδύνατον· ἦ γάρ;

ΘΕΑΙ. Ἀδύνατον.

ΞΕ. Ἆρα τῇδε σκοπῶν ξύμφῃς ὡς ἀνάγκη τόν τι
λέγοντα ἕν γέ τι λέγειν;

ΘΕΑΙ. Οὕτως.

ΞΕ. Ἑνὸς γὰρ δὴ τό γε "τὶ" φήσεις σημεῖον
εἶναι, τὸ δὲ "τινὲ" δυοῖν, τὸ δὲ "τινὲς" πολλῶν.

ΘΕΑΙ. Πῶς γὰρ οὔ;

E ΞΕ. Τὸν δὲ δὴ μὴ τὶ λέγοντα ἀναγκαιότατον,
ὡς ἔοικε, παντάπασι μηδὲν λέγειν.

ΘΕΑΙ. Ἀναγκαιότατον μὲν οὖν.

ΞΕ. Ἆρ᾽ οὖν οὐδὲ τοῦτο συγχωρητέον, τὸ τὸν
τοιοῦτον λέγειν μέν,[1] λέγειν μέντοι μηδέν, ἀλλ᾽
οὐδὲ λέγειν φατέον, ὅς γ᾽ ἂν ἐπιχειρῇ μὴ ὂν φθέγγεσθαι;

ΘΕΑΙ. Τέλος γοῦν ἂν ἀπορίας ὁ λόγος ἔχοι.

238   26. ΞΕ. Μήπω μέγ᾽ εἴπῃς· ἔτι γάρ, ὦ μακάριε, ἔστι, καὶ ταῦτά γε τῶν ἀποριῶν ἡ μεγίστη
καὶ πρώτη. περὶ γὰρ αὐτὴν αὐτοῦ τὴν ἀρχὴν οὖσα
τυγχάνει.

ΘΕΑΙ. Πῶς φής; λέγε καὶ μηδὲν ἀποκνήσῃς.

ΞΕ. Τῷ μὲν ὄντι που προσγένοιτ᾽ ἄν τι τῶν
ὄντων ἕτερον;

ΘΕΑΙ. Πῶς γὰρ οὔ;

ΞΕ. Μὴ ὄντι δέ τι[2] τῶν ὄντων ἆρα προσγίγνεσθαι
φήσομεν δυνατὸν εἶναι;

---

[1] μέν τι ΒΤ ; τι om. Schleiermacher.
[2] ὄντι δέ τι] ὂν δέ τι Β ; ὄντι δὲ Τ.

THEAET. How could it?

STR. And this is plain to us, that we always use the word "something" of some being, for to speak of "something" in the abstract, naked, as it were, and disconnected from all beings is impossible, is it not?

THEAET. Yes, it is.

STR. You assent because you recognize that he who says something must say some one thing?

THEAET. Yes.

STR. And you will agree that "something" or "some" in the singular is the sign of one, in the dual of two, and in the plural of many.

THEAET. Of course.

STR. And he who says not something, must quite necessarily say absolutely nothing.

THEAET. Quite necessarily.

STR. Then we cannot even concede that such a person speaks, but says nothing? We must even declare that he who undertakes to say "not-being" does not speak at all?

THEAET. The argument could go no further in perplexity.

STR. Boast not too soon! For there still remains, my friend, the first and greatest of perplexities. It affects the very beginning of the matter.

THEAET. What do you mean? Do not hesitate to speak.

STR. To that which is may be added or attributed some other thing which is?

THEAET. Of course.

STR. But shall we assert that to that which is not anything which is can be attributed?

ΘΕΑΙ. Καὶ πῶς;

ΞΕ. Ἀριθμὸν δὴ τὸν ξύμπαντα τῶν ὄντων τίθεμεν.

B ΘΕΑΙ. Εἴπερ γε καὶ ἄλλο τι θετέον ὡς ὄν.

ΞΕ. Μὴ τοίνυν μηδ' ἐπιχειρῶμεν ἀριθμοῦ μήτε πλῆθος μήτε τὸ ἓν πρὸς τὸ μὴ ὂν προσφέρειν.

ΘΕΑΙ. Οὔκουν ἂν ὀρθῶς γε, ὡς ἔοικεν, ἐπιχειροῖμεν, ὥς φησιν ὁ λόγος.

ΞΕ. Πῶς οὖν ἂν ἢ διὰ τοῦ στόματος φθέγξαιτο ἄν τις ἢ καὶ τῇ διανοίᾳ τὸ παράπαν λάβοι τὰ μὴ ὄντα ἢ τὸ μὴ ὂν χωρὶς ἀριθμοῦ;

ΘΕΑΙ. Λέγε πῇ;

ΞΕ. Μὴ ὄντα μὲν ἐπειδὰν λέγωμεν, ἆρα οὐ πλῆθος

C ἐπιχειροῦμεν ἀριθμοῦ προστιθέναι;

ΘΕΑΙ. Τί μήν;

ΞΕ. Μὴ ὂν δέ, ἆρα οὐ τὸ ἓν αὖ;

ΘΕΑΙ. Σαφέστατά γε.

ΞΕ. Καὶ μὴν οὔτε δίκαιόν γε οὔτε ὀρθόν φαμεν ὂν ἐπιχειρεῖν μὴ ὄντι προσαρμόττειν.

ΘΕΑΙ. Λέγεις ἀληθέστατα.

ΞΕ. Συννοεῖς οὖν ὡς οὔτε φθέγξασθαι δυνατὸν ὀρθῶς οὔτ' εἰπεῖν οὔτε διανοηθῆναι τὸ μὴ ὂν αὐτὸ καθ' αὑτό, ἀλλ' ἔστιν ἀδιανόητόν τε καὶ ἄρρητον καὶ ἄφθεγκτον καὶ ἄλογον;

ΘΕΑΙ. Παντάπασι μὲν οὖν.

D ΞΕ. Ἆρ' οὖν ἐψευσάμην ἄρτι λέγων τὴν μεγίστην ἀπορίαν ἐρεῖν αὐτοῦ πέρι;

ΘΕΑΙ. Τοῦ δὲ [1] ἔτι μείζω τινὰ λέγειν ἄλλην ἔχομεν;

ΞΕ. Τί δέ,[2] ὦ θαυμάσιε; οὐκ ἐννοεῖς αὐτοῖς τοῖς

---

[1] τοῦ δὲ in marg. T; τόδε BT; τὸ δὲ W; τί δὲ in marg. al.; τὸ δὲ (τί δέ) . . . ἔχομεν attributed to the Stranger by Winckelmann and others.

[2] τί δέ B; τί δαί T; τίνα δή Winckelmann and others.

THEAET. Certainly not.

STR. Now we assume that all number is among the things which are.

THEAET. Yes, if anything can be assumed to be.

STR. Then let us not even undertake to attribute either the singular or the plural of number to not-being.

THEAET. We should, apparently, not be right in undertaking that, as our argument shows.

STR. How then could a man either utter in speech or even so much as conceive in his mind things which are not, or not-being, apart from number?

THEAET. Tell me how number is involved in such conceptions.

STR. When we say " things which are not," do we not attribute plurality to them?

THEAET. Certainly.

STR. And in saying " a thing which is not," do we not equally attribute the singular number?

THEAET. Obviously.

STR. And yet we assert that it is neither right nor fair to undertake to attribute being to not-being.

THEAET. Very true.

STR. Do you see, then, that it is impossible rightly to utter or to say or to think of not-being without any attribute, but it is a thing inconceivable, inexpressible, unspeakable, irrational?

THEAET. Absolutely.

STR. Then was I mistaken just now in saying that the difficulty I was going to speak of was the greatest in our subject?

THEAET. But is there a still greater one that we can mention?

STR. Why, my dear fellow, don't you see, by the

λεχθεῖσιν ὅτι καὶ τὸν ἐλέγχοντα εἰς ἀπορίαν καθίστησι τὸ μὴ ὂν οὕτως, ὥστε, ὁπόταν αὐτὸ ἐπιχειρῇ τις ἐλέγχειν, ἐναντία αὐτὸν αὑτῷ περὶ ἐκεῖνο ἀναγκάζεσθαι λέγειν;

ΘΕΑΙ. Πῶς φής; εἰπὲ ἔτι σαφέστερον.

ΞΕ. Οὐδὲν δεῖ τὸ σαφέστερον ἐν ἐμοὶ σκοπεῖν.
E ἐγὼ μὲν γὰρ ὑποθέμενος οὔτε ἑνὸς οὔτε τῶν πολλῶν τὸ μὴ ὂν δεῖν μετέχειν, ἄρτι τε καὶ νῦν οὕτως ἓν αὐτὸ εἴρηκα· τὸ μὴ ὂν γὰρ φημί. ξυνίης τοι·

ΘΕΑΙ. Ναί.

ΞΕ. Καὶ μὴν αὖ καὶ σμικρὸν ἔμπροσθεν ἄφθεγκτόν τε αὐτὸ καὶ ἄρρητον καὶ ἄλογον ἔφην εἶναι. ξυνέπει;

ΘΕΑΙ. Ξυνέπομαι. πῶς γὰρ οὔ;

ΞΕ. Οὐκοῦν τό γε εἶναι προσάπτειν πειρώμενος
239 ἐναντία τοῖς πρόσθεν ἔλεγον;

ΘΕΑΙ. Φαίνει.

ΞΕ. Τί δέ; τοῦτο προσάπτων οὐχ ὡς ἑνὶ διελεγόμην;

ΘΕΑΙ. Ναί.

ΞΕ. Καὶ μὴν ἄλογόν τε λέγων καὶ ἄρρητον καὶ ἄφθεγκτον ὥς γε πρὸς ἓν τὸν λόγον ἐποιούμην.

ΘΕΑΙ. Πῶς δ' οὔ;

ΞΕ. Φαμὲν δέ γε δεῖν, εἴπερ ὀρθῶς τις λέξει, μήτε ὡς ἓν μήτε ὡς πολλὰ διορίζειν αὐτό, μηδὲ τὸ παράπαν αὐτὸ καλεῖν· ἑνὸς γὰρ εἴδει καὶ κατὰ ταύτην ἂν τὴν πρόσρησιν προσαγορεύοιτο.

ΘΕΑΙ. Παντάπασί γε.

very arguments we have used, that not-being reduces him who would refute it to such difficulties that when he attempts to refute it he is forced to contradict himself?

THEAET. What do you mean? Speak still more clearly.

STR. You must not look for more clearness in me; for although I maintained that not-being could have nothing to do with either the singular or the plural number, I spoke of it just now, and am still speaking of it, as one; for I say "that which is not." You understand surely?

THEAET. Yes.

STR. And again a little while ago I said it was inexpressible, unspeakable, irrational. Do you follow me?

THEAET. Yes, of course.

STR. Then when I undertook to attach the verb "to be" to not-being I was contradicting what I said before.

THEAET. Evidently.

STR. Well, then; when I attached this verb to it, did I not address it in the singular?

THEAET. Yes.

STR. And when I called it irrational, inexpressible, and unspeakable, I addressed my speech to it as singular.

THEAET. Of course you did.

STR. But we say that, if one is to speak correctly, one must not define it as either singular or plural, and must not even call it "it" at all; for even by this manner of referring to it one would be giving it the form of the singular.

THEAET. Certainly.

B   **27.** ΞΕ. Τὸν μὲν τοίνυν ἐμέ γ᾽ ἔτι τί τις[1] ἂν λέγοι; καὶ γὰρ πάλαι καὶ τὰ νῦν ἡττημένον ἂν εὕροι περὶ τὸν τοῦ μὴ ὄντος ἔλεγχον. ὥστε ἐν ἔμοιγε λέγοντι, καθάπερ εἶπον, μὴ σκοπῶμεν τὴν ὀρθολογίαν περὶ τὸ μὴ ὄν, ἀλλ᾽ εἶα[2] δὴ νῦν ἐν σοὶ σκεψώμεθα.

ΘΕΑΙ. Πῶς φής;

ΞΕ. Ἴθι ἡμῖν εὖ καὶ γενναίως, ἅτε νέος ὤν, ὅτι μάλιστα δύνασαι συντείνας πειράθητι, μήτε οὐσίαν μήτε τὸ ἓν μήτε πλῆθος ἀριθμοῦ προστιθεὶς τῷ μὴ ὄντι, κατὰ τὸ ὀρθὸν[3] φθέγξασθαί τι περὶ αὐτοῦ.

C   ΘΕΑΙ. Πολλή μέντ᾽ ἄν με καὶ ἄτοπος ἔχοι προθυμία τῆς ἐπιχειρήσεως, εἰ σὲ τοιαῦθ᾽ ὁρῶν πάσχοντα αὐτὸς ἐπιχειροίην.

ΞΕ. Ἀλλ᾽ εἰ δοκεῖ, σὲ μὲν καὶ ἐμὲ χαίρειν ἐῶμεν· ἕως δ᾽ ἄν τινι δυναμένῳ δρᾶν τοῦτο ἐντυγχάνωμεν, μέχρι τούτου λέγωμεν ὡς παντὸς μᾶλλον πανούργως εἰς ἄπορον ὁ σοφιστὴς τόπον καταδέδυκεν.

ΘΕΑΙ. Καὶ μάλα δὴ φαίνεται.

ΞΕ. Τοιγαροῦν εἴ τινα φήσομεν αὐτὸν ἔχειν φαν-
D   ταστικὴν τέχνην, ῥᾳδίως ἐκ ταύτης τῆς χρείας τῶν λόγων ἀντιλαμβανόμενος ἡμῶν εἰς τοὐναντίον ἀποστρέψει[4] τοὺς λόγους, ὅταν εἰδωλοποιὸν αὐτὸν καλῶμεν, ἀνερωτῶν τί ποτε τὸ παράπαν εἴδωλον λέγομεν. σκοπεῖν οὖν, ὦ Θεαίτητε, χρή, τί τις τῷ νεανίᾳ πρὸς τὸ ἐρωτώμενον ἀποκρινεῖται.

ΘΕΑΙ. Δῆλον ὅτι φήσομεν τά τε ἐν τοῖς ὕδασι καὶ κατόπτροις εἴδωλα, ἔτι καὶ τὰ γεγραμμένα καὶ τὰ τετυπωμένα καὶ τἆλλα ὅσα που τοιαῦτ᾽ ἔσθ᾽ ἕτερα.

---

[1] ἐμέ γ᾽ ἔτι τί τις] ἐμέ τε τι τίς B ; ἐμέ γε ἔτι τις T ; ἐμὲ ἔτι τί τις W.   [2] εἶα Bessarion's copy ; ἔα BT.

STR. But poor me, what can anyone say of me any longer? For you would find me now, as always before, defeated in the refutation of not-being. So, as I said before, we must not look to me for correctness of speech about not-being. But come now, let us look to you for it.

THEAET. What do you mean?

STR. Come, I beg of you, make a sturdy effort, young man as you are, and try with might and main to say something correctly about not-being, without attributing to it either existence or unity or plurality.

THEAET. But I should be possessed of great and absurd eagerness for the attempt, if I were to undertake it with your experience before my eyes.

STR. Well, if you like, let us say no more of you and me; but until we find someone who can accomplish this, let us confess that the sophist has in most rascally fashion hidden himself in a place we cannot explore.

THEAET. That seems to be decidedly the case.

STR. And so, if we say he has an art, as it were, of making appearances, he will easily take advantage of our poverty of terms to make a counter attack, twisting our words to the opposite meaning; when we call him an image-maker, he will ask us what we mean by "image," exactly. So, Theaetetus, we must see what reply is to be made to the young man's question.

THEAET. Obviously we shall reply that we mean the images in water and in mirrors, and those in paintings, too, and sculptures, and all the other things of the same sort.

---

³ τὸ ὀρθὸν B ; τὸν ὀρθὸν λόγον T.
⁴ ἀποστρέψει corr. T ; ἀποτρέψει BTW.

Ε 28. ΞΕ. Φανερός, ὦ Θεαίτητε, εἰ σοφιστὴν οὐχ ἑωρακώς.

ΘΕΑΙ. Τί δή;

ΞΕ. Δόξει σοι μύειν ἢ παντάπασιν οὐκ ἔχειν ὄμματα.

ΘΕΑΙ. Πῶς;

ΞΕ. Τὴν ἀπόκρισιν ὅταν οὕτως αὐτῷ διδῷς ἐὰν ἐν κατόπτροις ἢ πλάσμασι λέγῃς τι, καταγελάσεταί σου τῶν λόγων, ὅταν ὡς βλέποντι λέγῃς αὐτῷ, 240 προσποιούμενος οὔτε κάτοπτρα οὔτε ὕδατα γιγνώσκειν οὔτε τὸ παράπαν ὄψιν, τὸ δ᾽ ἐκ τῶν λόγων ἐρωτήσει σε μόνον.

ΘΕΑΙ. Ποῖον;

ΞΕ. Τὸ διὰ πάντων τούτων ἃ πολλὰ εἰπὼν ἠξίωσας ἑνὶ προσειπεῖν ὀνόματι φθεγξάμενος εἴδωλον ἐπὶ πᾶσιν ὡς ἓν ὄν. λέγε οὖν καὶ ἀμύνου μηδὲν ὑποχωρῶν τὸν ἄνδρα.

ΘΕΑΙ. Τί δῆτα, ὦ ξένε, εἴδωλον ἂν φαῖμεν εἶναι πλήν γε τὸ πρὸς τἀληθινὸν ἀφωμοιωμένον ἕτερον τοιοῦτον;

ΞΕ. Ἕτερον δὲ λέγεις τοιοῦτον ἀληθινόν, ἢ ἐπὶ Β τίνι τὸ τοιοῦτον εἶπες;

ΘΕΑΙ. Οὐδαμῶς ἀληθινόν γε, ἀλλ᾽ ἐοικὸς μέν.

ΞΕ. Ἆρα τὸ ἀληθινὸν ὄντως ὂν λέγων;

ΘΕΑΙ. Οὕτως.

ΞΕ. Τί δέ; τὸ μὴ ἀληθινὸν ἆρ᾽ ἐναντίον ἀληθοῦς;

ΘΕΑΙ. Τί μήν;

ΞΕ. Οὐκ ὄντως [1] ὂν [2] ἄρα λέγεις τὸ ἐοικός, εἴπερ αὐτό γε μὴ ἀληθινὸν ἐρεῖς.

---

[1] ὄντως W; ὄντων B; om. T.
[2] ὂν T; οὐκὸν B; οὐκ ὂν W.

THE SOPHIST

STR. It is evident, Theaetetus, that you never saw a sophist.

THEAET. Why?

STR. He will make you think his eyes are shut or he has none at all.

THEAET. How so?

STR. When you give this answer, if you speak of something in mirrors or works of art, he will laugh at your words, when you talk to him as if he could see. He will feign ignorance of mirrors and water and of sight altogether, and will question you only about that which is deduced from your words.

THEAET. What is that?

STR. That which exists throughout all these things which you say are many but which you saw fit to call by one name, when you said "image" of them all, as if they were all one thing. So speak and defend yourself. Do not give way to the man at all.

THEAET. Why, Stranger, what can we say an image is, except another such thing fashioned in the likeness of the true one?

STR. Do you mean another such true one, or in what sense did you say "such"?

THEAET. Not a true one by any means, but only one like the true.

STR. And by the true you mean that which really is?

THEAET. Exactly.

STR. And the not true is the opposite of the true?

THEAET. Of course.

STR. That which is like, then, you say does not really exist, if you say it is not true.

ΘΕΑΙ. Ἀλλ᾽ ἔστι γε μήν πως.[1]

ΞΕ. Οὔκουν[2] ἀληθῶς γε, φῄς.

ΘΕΑΙ. Οὐ γὰρ οὖν· πλήν γ᾽ εἰκὼν ὄντως.

ΞΕ. Οὐκ ὂν[3] ἄρα[4] ὄντως ἐστὶν ὄντως ἣν λέγομεν εἰκόνα;

C ΘΕΑΙ. Κινδυνεύει τοιαύτην τινὰ πεπλέχθαι συμπλοκὴν τὸ μὴ ὂν τῷ ὄντι, καὶ μάλα ἄτοπον.

ΞΕ. Πῶς γὰρ οὐκ ἄτοπον; ὁρᾷς γοῦν ὅτι καὶ νῦν διὰ τῆς ἐπαλλάξεως ταύτης ὁ πολυκέφαλος σοφιστὴς ἠνάγκακεν ἡμᾶς τὸ μὴ ὂν οὐχ ἑκόντας ὁμολογεῖν εἶναί πως.

ΘΕΑΙ. Ὁρῶ καὶ μάλα.

ΞΕ. Τί δὲ δή; τὴν τέχνην αὐτοῦ τίνα ἀφορίσαντες ἡμῖν αὐτοῖς συμφωνεῖν οἷοί τε ἐσόμεθα;

ΘΕΑΙ. Πῇ καὶ τὸ ποῖόν τι φοβούμενος οὕτω λέγεις;

D ΞΕ. Ὅταν περὶ τὸ φάντασμα αὐτὸν ἀπατᾶν φῶμεν καὶ τὴν τέχνην εἶναί τινα ἀπατητικὴν αὐτοῦ, τότε πότερον ψευδῆ δοξάζειν τὴν ψυχὴν ἡμῶν φήσομεν ὑπὸ τῆς ἐκείνου τέχνης, ἢ τί ποτ᾽ ἐροῦμεν;

ΘΕΑΙ. Τοῦτο· τί γὰρ ἂν ἄλλο εἴπαιμεν;

ΞΕ. Ψευδὴς δ᾽ αὖ δόξα ἔσται τἀναντία τοῖς οὖσι δοξάζουσα, ἢ πῶς;

ΘΕΑΙ. Τἀναντία.

ΞΕ. Λέγεις ἄρα τὰ μὴ ὄντα δοξάζειν τὴν ψευδῆ δόξαν;

ΘΕΑΙ. Ἀνάγκη.

E ΞΕ. Πότερον μὴ εἶναι τὰ μὴ ὄντα δοξάζουσαν, ἤ πως εἶναι τὰ μηδαμῶς ὄντα;

[1] πως Hermann ; πῶς; BT (the previous words being given to the stranger).
[2] οὔκουν W ; οὐκοῦν T ; οὐκὸν B.

THE SOPHIST

THEAET. But it does exist, in a way.

STR. But not truly, you mean.

THEAET. No, except that it is really a likeness.

STR. Then what we call a likeness, though not really existing, really does exist?

THEAET. Not-being does seem to have got into some such entanglement with being, and it is very absurd.

STR. Of course it is absurd. You see, at any rate, how by this interchange of words the many-headed sophist has once more forced us against our will to admit that not-being exists in a way.

THEAET. Yes, I see that very well.

STR. Well then, how can we define his art without contradicting ourselves?

THEAET. Why do you say that? What are you afraid of?

STR. When, in talking about appearance, we say that he deceives and that his art is an art of deception, shall we say that our mind is misled by his art to hold a false opinion, or what shall we say?

THEAET. We shall say that. What else could we say?

STR. But, again, false opinion will be that which thinks the opposite of reality, will it not?

THEAET. Yes.

STR. You mean, then, that false opinion thinks things which are not?

THEAET. Necessarily.

STR. Does it think that things which are not, are not, or that things which are not at all, in some sense are?

---

³ οὐκ ὄν] οὐκὸν B ; οὐκ οὖν T.
⁴ ἆρα Badham ; ἆρα οὐκ BT.

ΘΕΑΙ. Εἶναί πως τὰ μὴ ὄντα δεῖ γε, εἴπερ ψεύσεταί ποτέ τίς τι καὶ κατὰ βραχύ.

ΞΕ. Τί δ'; οὐ καὶ μηδαμῶς εἶναι τὰ πάντως ὄντα δοξάζεται;

ΘΕΑΙ. Ναί.

ΞΕ. Καὶ τοῦτο δὴ ψεῦδος;

ΘΕΑΙ. Καὶ τοῦτο.

ΞΕ. Καὶ λόγος, οἶμαι, ψευδὴς οὕτω κατὰ ταὐτὰ [1] 241 νομισθήσεται τά τε ὄντα λέγων μὴ εἶναι καὶ τὰ μὴ ὄντα εἶναι.

ΘΕΑΙ. Πῶς γὰρ ἂν ἄλλως [2] τοιοῦτος γένοιτο;

ΞΕ. Σχεδὸν οὐδαμῶς· ἀλλὰ ταῦτα ὁ σοφιστὴς οὐ φήσει. ἢ τίς μηχανὴ συγχωρεῖν τινα τῶν εὖ φρονούντων, ὅταν ἄφθεγκτα καὶ ἄρρητα καὶ ἄλογα καὶ ἀδιανόητα προδιωμολογημένα [3] ᾖ τὰ πρὸ τούτων ὁμολογηθέντα; μανθάνομεν, ὦ Θεαίτητε, ἃ λέγει [4];

ΘΕΑΙ. Πῶς γὰρ οὐ μανθάνομεν ὅτι τἀναντία φήσει λέγειν ἡμᾶς τοῖς νῦν δή, ψευδῆ τολμήσαντας εἰπεῖν ὡς ἔστιν ἐν δόξαις τε καὶ κατὰ λόγους; τῷ B γὰρ μὴ ὄντι τὸ ὂν προσάπτειν ἡμᾶς πολλάκις ἀναγκάζεσθαι, διομολογησαμένους νῦν δή που τοῦτο εἶναι πάντων ἀδυνατώτατον.

29. ΞΕ. Ὀρθῶς ἀπεμνημόνευσας. ἀλλ' ὥρα [5] δὴ βουλεύσασθαι [6] τί χρὴ δρᾶν τοῦ σοφιστοῦ πέρι· τὰς γὰρ ἀντιλήψεις καὶ ἀπορίας, ἐὰν αὐτὸν διερευνῶμεν ἐν τῇ τῶν ψευδουργῶν καὶ γοήτων τέχνῃ τιθέντες, ὁρᾷς ὡς εὔποροι καὶ πολλαί.

---

[1] ταὐτὰ Stobaeus; ταῦτα ταῦτα B; ταῦτα T; ταὐτὰ ταῦτα W.
[2] ἄλλως W, Stobaeus; ἄλλος BT.
[3] προδιωμολογημένα T; προσδιωμολογημένα B; ἄφθεγκτα . . . ἀδιανόητα om. Madvig, Schanz, Burnet.

THEAET. It must think that things which are not in some sense are—that is, if anyone is ever to think falsely at all, even in a slight degree.

STR. And does it not also think that things which certainly are, are not at all?

THEAET. Yes.

STR. And this too is falsehood?

THEAET. Yes, it is.

STR. And therefore a statement will likewise be considered false, if it declares that things which are, are not, or that things which are not, are.

THEAET. In what other way could a statement be made false?

STR. Virtually in no other way; but the sophist will not assent to this. Or how can any reasonable man assent to it, when the expressions we just agreed upon were previously agreed to be inexpressible, unspeakable, irrational, and inconceivable? Do we understand his meaning, Theaetetus?

THEAET. Of course we understand that he will say we are contradicting our recent statements, since we dare to say that falsehood exists in opinions and words; for he will say that we are thus forced repeatedly to attribute being to not-being, although we agreed a while ago that nothing could be more impossible than that.

STR. You are quite right to remind me. But I think it is high time to consider what ought to be done about the sophist; for you see how easily and repeatedly he can raise objections and difficulties, if we conduct our search by putting him in the guild of false-workers and jugglers.

---

⁴ λέγει] λέγεις BT.   ⁵ ὥρα] ὅρα BT.
⁶ βουλεύσασθαι T ; βουλεύεσθαι B ; om. Burnet.

ΘΕΑΙ. Καὶ μάλα.

ΞΕ. Μικρὸν μέρος τοίνυν αὐτῶν διεληλύθαμεν,
C οὐσῶν ὡς ἔπος εἰπεῖν ἀπεράντων.

ΘΕΑΙ. Ἀδύνατόν γ' ἄν,[1] ὡς ἔοικεν, εἴη τὸν
σοφιστὴν ἑλεῖν, εἰ ταῦτα οὕτως ἔχει.

ΞΕ. Τί οὖν; ἀποστησόμεθα νῦν μαλθακισθέντες;

ΘΕΑΙ. Οὔκουν ἔγωγέ φημι δεῖν, εἰ καὶ κατὰ σμικρὸν οἷοί τ' ἐπιλαβέσθαι πῃ τἀνδρός ἐσμεν.

ΞΕ. Ἕξεις οὖν συγγνώμην καὶ καθάπερ νῦν εἶπες
ἀγαπήσεις ἐάν πῃ καὶ κατὰ βραχὺ παρασπασώμεθα
οὕτως ἰσχυροῦ λόγου;

ΘΕΑΙ. Πῶς γὰρ οὐχ ἕξω;

D ΞΕ. Τόδε τοίνυν ἔτι μᾶλλον παραιτοῦμαί σε.

ΘΕΑΙ. Τὸ ποῖον;

ΞΕ. Μή με οἷον πατραλοίαν ὑπολάβῃς γίγνε-
σθαί τινα.

ΘΕΑΙ. Τί δή;

ΞΕ. Τὸν τοῦ πατρὸς Παρμενίδου λόγον ἀναγκαῖον ἡμῖν ἀμυνομένοις ἔσται βασανίζειν, καὶ
βιάζεσθαι τό τε μὴ ὂν ὡς ἔστι κατά τι καὶ τὸ ὂν
αὖ πάλιν ὡς οὐκ ἔστι πῃ.

ΘΕΑΙ. Φαίνεται τὸ τοιοῦτον διαμαχητέον ἐν τοῖς
λόγοις.

ΞΕ. Πῶς γὰρ οὐ φαίνεται καὶ τὸ λεγόμενον
δὴ τοῦτο τυφλῷ; τούτων γὰρ μήτε ἐλεγχθέντων
E μήτε ὁμολογηθέντων σχολῇ ποτέ τις οἷός τε ἔσται
περὶ λόγων ψευδῶν λέγων ἢ δόξης, εἴτε εἰδώλων
εἴτε εἰκόνων εἴτε μιμημάτων εἴτε φαντασμάτων
αὐτῶν, ἢ καὶ περὶ τεχνῶν τῶν ὅσαι περὶ ταῦτά εἰσι,
μὴ καταγέλαστος εἶναι τὰ ἐναντία ἀναγκαζόμενος
αὐτῷ λέγειν.

[1] γ' ἄν Burnet; γάρ BT; ἀρ' W; γὰρ ἄν al.

THE SOPHIST

THEAET. Very true.

STR. Yes, we have gone through only a small part of them, and they are, if I may say so, infinite.

THEAET. It would, apparently, be impossible to catch the sophist, if that is the case.

STR. Well, then, shall we weaken and give up the struggle now?

THEAET. No, I say; we must not do that, if we can in any way get the slightest hold of the fellow.

STR. Will you then pardon me, and, as your words imply, be content if I somehow withdraw just for a short distance from this strong argument of his?

THEAET. Of course I will.

STR. I have another still more urgent request to make of you.

THEAET. What is it?

STR. Do not assume that I am becoming a sort of parricide.

THEAET. What do you mean?

STR. In defending myself I shall have to test the theory of my father Parmenides, and contend forcibly that after a fashion not-being is and on the other hand in a sense being is not.

THEAET. It is plain that some such contention is necessary.

STR. Yes, plain even to a blind man, as they say; for unless these statements are either disproved or accepted, no one who speaks about false words, or false opinion—whether images or likenesses or imitations or appearances—or about the arts which have to do with them, can ever help being forced to contradict himself and make himself ridiculous.

241 ΘΕΑΙ. Ἀληθέστατα.

242 ΞΕ. Διὰ ταῦτα μέντοι τολμητέον ἐπιτίθεσθαι τῷ πατρικῷ λόγῳ νῦν, ἢ τὸ παράπαν ἐατέον, εἰ τοῦτό τις εἴργει δρᾶν ὄκνος.

ΘΕΑΙ. Ἀλλ' ἡμᾶς τοῦτό γε μηδὲν μηδαμῇ εἴρξῃ.

ΞΕ. Τρίτον τοίνυν ἔτι σε σμικρόν τι παραιτήσομαι.

ΘΕΑΙ. Λέγε μόνον.

ΞΕ. Εἶπόν που νῦν δὴ λέγων ὡς πρὸς τὸν περὶ ταῦτ' ἔλεγχον ἀεί τε ἀπειρηκὼς ἐγὼ τυγχάνω καὶ δὴ καὶ τὰ νῦν.

ΘΕΑΙ. Εἶπες.

ΞΕ. Φοβοῦμαι δὴ τὰ εἰρημένα, μή ποτε διὰ ταῦτά σοι μανικὸς εἶναι δόξω παρὰ πόδα μεταβαλὼν
B ἐμαυτὸν ἄνω καὶ κάτω. σὴν γὰρ δὴ χάριν ἐλέγχειν τὸν λόγον ἐπιθησόμεθα, ἐάνπερ ἐλέγχωμεν.

ΘΕΑΙ. Ὡς τοίνυν ἔμοιγε μηδαμῇ δόξων μηδὲν πλημμελεῖν, ἂν ἐπὶ τὸν ἔλεγχον τοῦτον καὶ τὴν ἀπόδειξιν ἴῃς, θαρρῶν ἴθι τούτου γε ἕνεκα.

30. ΞΕ. Φέρε δή, τίνα ἀρχήν τις ἂν ἄρξαιτο παρακινδυνευτικοῦ λόγου; δοκῶ μὲν γὰρ τήνδ', ὦ παῖ, τὴν ὁδὸν ἀναγκαιοτάτην ἡμῖν εἶναι τρέπεσθαι.

ΘΕΑΙ. Ποίαν δή;

ΞΕ. Τὰ δοκοῦντα νῦν ἐναργῶς ἔχειν ἐπισκέψασθαι
C πρῶτον, μή πῃ τεταραγμένοι μὲν ὦμεν [1] περὶ ταῦτα, ῥᾳδίως δ' ἀλλήλοις ὁμολογῶμεν ὡς εὐκρινῶς ἔχοντες.

ΘΕΑΙ. Λέγε σαφέστερον ὃ λέγεις.

ΞΕ. Εὐκόλως μοι δοκεῖ Παρμενίδης ἡμῖν διειλέχθαι καὶ πᾶς ὅστις πώποτε ἐπὶ κρίσιν ὥρμησε

---

[1] μὲν ὦμεν W ; μένωμεν BT.

THE SOPHIST

THEAET. Very true.

STR. And so we must take courage and attack our father's theory here and now, or else, if any scruples prevent us from doing this, we must give the whole thing up.

THEAET. But nothing in the world must prevent us.

STR. Then I have a third little request to make of you.

THEAET. You have only to utter it.

STR. I said a while ago that I always have been too faint-hearted for the refutation of this theory, and so I am now.

THEAET. Yes, so you did.

STR. I am afraid that on account of what I have said you will think I am mad because I have at once reversed my position. You see it is for your sake that I am going to undertake the refutation, if I succeed in it.

THEAET. I certainly shall not think you are doing anything improper if you proceed to your refutation and proof; so go ahead boldly, so far as that is concerned.

STR. Well, what would be a good beginning of a perilous argument? Ah, my boy, I believe the way we certainly must take is this.

THEAET. What way?

STR. We must first examine the points which now seem clear, lest we may have fallen into some confusion about them and may therefore carelessly agree with one another, thinking that we are judging correctly.

THEAET. Express your meaning more clearly.

STR. It seems to me that Parmenides and all who ever undertook a critical definition of the number

τοῦ τὰ ὄντα διορίσασθαι πόσα τε καὶ ποῖά
ἐστιν.

ΘΕΑΙ. Πῇ;

ΞΕ. Μῦθόν τινα ἕκαστος φαίνεταί μοι διηγεῖσθαι
παισὶν ὡς οὖσιν ἡμῖν, ὁ μὲν ὡς τρία τὰ ὄντα,
πολεμεῖ δὲ ἀλλήλοις ἐνίοτε αὐτῶν ἄττα πῃ, τοτὲ δὲ
D καὶ φίλα γιγνόμενα γάμους τε καὶ τόκους καὶ
τροφὰς τῶν ἐκγόνων παρέχεται· δύο δὲ ἕτερος
εἰπών, ὑγρὸν καὶ ξηρὸν ἢ θερμὸν καὶ ψυχρόν, συν-
οικίζει τε αὐτὰ καὶ ἐκδίδωσι· τὸ δὲ παρ' ἡμῖν [1]
'Ελεατικὸν ἔθνος, ἀπὸ Ξενοφάνους τε καὶ ἔτι
πρόσθεν ἀρξάμενον, ὡς ἑνὸς ὄντος τῶν πάντων
καλουμένων οὕτω διεξέρχεται τοῖς μύθοις. 'Ιάδες
δὲ καὶ Σικελαί τινες ὕστερον Μοῦσαι ξυνενόησαν [2]
E ὅτι συμπλέκειν ἀσφαλέστατον ἀμφότερα καὶ λέγειν
ὡς τὸ ὂν πολλά τε καὶ ἕν ἐστιν, ἔχθρᾳ δὲ καὶ φιλίᾳ
συνέχεται. διαφερόμενον γὰρ ἀεὶ ξυμφέρεται, φασὶν
αἱ συντονώτεραι τῶν Μουσῶν· αἱ δὲ μαλακώτεραι
τὸ μὲν ἀεὶ ταῦτα οὕτως ἔχειν ἐχάλασαν, ἐν μέρει δὲ
τοτὲ μὲν ἕν εἶναί φασι τὸ πᾶν καὶ φίλον ὑπ' 'Αφρο-
243 δίτης, τοτὲ δὲ πολλὰ καὶ πολέμιον αὐτὸ αὑτῷ διὰ
νεῖκός τι. ταῦτα δὲ πάντα εἰ μὲν ἀληθῶς τις ἢ
μὴ τούτων εἴρηκε, χαλεπὸν καὶ πλημμελὲς οὕτω
μεγάλα κλεινοῖς καὶ παλαιοῖς ἀνδράσιν ἐπιτιμᾶν·
ἐκεῖνο δὲ ἀνεπίφθονον ἀποφήνασθαι.

ΘΕΑΙ. Τὸ ποῖον;

ΞΕ. "Ότι λίαν τῶν πολλῶν ἡμῶν ὑπεριδόντες

---

[1] ἡμῖν al. Eusebius ; ἡμῶν BTW.
[2] ξυνενόησαν T, Eusebius, Simplicius ; ξυννενοήκασιν B.

and nature of realities have talked to us rather carelessly.

THEAET. How so?

STR. Every one of them seems to tell us a story, as if we were children. One says there are three principles, that some of them are sometimes waging a sort of war with each other, and sometimes become friends and marry and have children and bring them up; and another says there are two, wet and dry or hot and cold, which he settles together and unites in marriage.[1] And the Eleatic sect in our region, beginning with Xenophanes and even earlier, have their story that all things, as they are called, are really one. Then some Ionian[2] and later some Sicilian[3] Muses reflected that it was safest to combine the two tales and to say that being is many and one, and is (or are) held together by enmity and friendship. For the more strenuous Muses say it is always simultaneously coming together and separating; but the gentler ones relaxed the strictness of the doctrine of perpetual strife; they say that the all is sometimes one and friendly, under the influence of Aphrodite, and sometimes many and at variance with itself by reason of some sort of strife. Now whether any of them spoke the truth in all this, or not, it is harsh and improper to impute to famous men of old such a great wrong as falsehood. But one assertion can be made without offence.

THEAET. What is that?

STR. That they paid too little attention and con-

---

[1] This refers apparently to Pherecydes and the early Ionians.
[2] Heracleitus and his followers.
[3] Empedocles and his disciples.

ὠλιγώρησαν· οὐδὲν γὰρ φροντίσαντες εἴτ᾽ ἐπ-
ακολουθοῦμεν αὐτοῖς λέγουσιν εἴτε ἀπολειπόμεθα,
B περαίνουσι τὸ σφέτερον αὐτῶν ἕκαστοι.

ΘΕΑΙ. Πῶς λέγεις;

ΞΕ. Ὅταν τις αὐτῶν φθέγξηται λέγων ὡς ἔστιν
ἢ γέγονεν ἢ γίγνεται πολλὰ ἢ ἓν ἢ δύο, καὶ θερμὸν
αὖ ψυχρῷ συγκεραννύμενον, ἄλλοθί πῃ διακρίσεις
καὶ συγκρίσεις ὑποτιθείς, τούτων, ὦ Θεαίτητε,
ἑκάστοτε σύ τι πρὸς θεῶν ξυνίης ὅ τι λέγουσιν; ἐγὼ
μὲν γὰρ ὅτε μὲν ἦν νεώτερος, τοῦτό τε τὸ νῦν
ἀπορούμενον ὁπότε τις εἴποι, τὸ μὴ ὄν, ἀκριβῶς
ᾤμην ξυνιέναι. νῦν δὲ ὁρᾷς ἵν᾽ ἐσμὲν αὐτοῦ πέρι
τῆς ἀπορίας.

C ΘΕΑΙ. Ὁρῶ.

ΞΕ. Τάχα τοίνυν ἴσως οὐχ ἧττον κατὰ τὸ ὂν
ταὐτὸν τοῦτο πάθος εἰληφότες ἐν τῇ ψυχῇ περὶ
μὲν τοῦτο εὐπορεῖν φαμεν καὶ μανθάνειν ὁπόταν τις
αὐτὸ φθέγξηται, περὶ δὲ θάτερον οὔ, πρὸς ἀμφότερα
ὁμοίως ἔχοντες.

ΘΕΑΙ. Ἴσως.

ΞΕ. Καὶ περὶ τῶν ἄλλων δὴ τῶν προειρημένων
ἡμῖν ταὐτὸν τοῦτο εἰρήσθω.

ΘΕΑΙ. Πάνυ γε.

31. ΞΕ. Τῶν μὲν τοίνυν πολλῶν πέρι καὶ
D μετὰ τοῦτο σκεψόμεθ᾽, ἂν δόξῃ, περὶ δὲ τοῦ
μεγίστου τε καὶ ἀρχηγοῦ πρώτου νῦν σκεπτέον.

ΘΕΑΙ. Τίνος δὴ λέγεις; ἢ δῆλον ὅτι τὸ ὂν φῂς
πρῶτον δεῖν διερευνήσασθαι τί ποθ᾽ οἱ λέγοντες
αὐτὸ δηλοῦν ἡγοῦνται;

THE SOPHIST

sideration to the mass of people like ourselves. For they go on to the end, each in his own way, without caring whether their arguments carry us along with them, or whether we are left behind.

THEAET. What do you mean?

STR. When one of them says in his talk that many, or one, or two are, or have become, or are becoming, and again speaks of hot mingling with cold, and in some other part of his discourse suggests separations and combinations, for heaven's sake, Theaetetus, do you ever understand what they mean by any of these things? I used to think, when I was younger, that I understood perfectly whenever anyone used this term "not-being," which now perplexes us. But you see what a slough of perplexity we are in about it now.

THEAET. Yes, I see.

STR. And perhaps our minds are in this same condition as regards being also; we may think that it is plain sailing and that we understand when the word is used, though we are in difficulties about not-being, whereas really we understand equally little of both.

THEAET. Perhaps.

STR. And we may say the same of all the subjects about which we have been speaking.

THEAET. Certainly.

STR. We will consider most of them later, if you please, but now the greatest and foremost chief of them must be considered.

THEAET. What do you mean? Or, obviously, do you mean that we must first investigate the term "being," and see what those who use it think it signifies?

ΞΕ. Κατὰ πόδα¹ γε, ὦ Θεαίτητε, ὑπέλαβες. λέγω γὰρ δὴ ταύτῃ δεῖν ποιεῖσθαι τὴν μέθοδον ἡμᾶς, οἷον αὐτῶν παρόντων ἀναπυνθανομένους ὧδε· φέρε, ὁπόσοι θερμὸν καὶ ψυχρὸν ἤ τινε δύο τοιούτω τὰ πάντ᾽ εἶναί φατε, τί ποτε ἄρα τοῦτ᾽ ἐπ᾽

Ε ἀμφοῖν φθέγγεσθε, λέγοντες ἄμφω καὶ ἑκάτερον εἶναι; τί τὸ εἶναι τοῦτο ὑπολάβωμεν ὑμῶν; πότερον τρίτον παρὰ τὰ δύο ἐκεῖνα, καὶ τρία τὸ πᾶν ἀλλὰ μὴ δύο ἔτι καθ᾽ ὑμᾶς τιθῶμεν; οὐ γάρ που τοῖν γε δυοῖν καλοῦντες θάτερον ὂν ἀμφότερα ὁμοίως εἶναι λέγετε· σχεδὸν γὰρ ἂν ἀμφοτέρως ἕν, ἀλλ᾽ οὐ δύο εἴτην.²

ΘΕΑΙ. Ἀληθῆ λέγεις.

ΞΕ. Ἀλλ᾽ ἄρα τὰ ἄμφω βούλεσθε καλεῖν ὄν;

ΘΕΑΙ. Ἴσως.

244 ΞΕ. Ἀλλ᾽, ὦ φίλοι, φήσομεν, κἂν οὕτω τὰ δύο λέγοιτ᾽³ ἂν σαφέστατα ἕν.

ΘΕΑΙ. Ὀρθότατα εἴρηκας.

ΞΕ. Ἐπειδὴ τοίνυν ἡμεῖς ἠπορήκαμεν, ὑμεῖς αὐτὰ ἡμῖν ἐμφανίζετε ἱκανῶς τί ποτε βούλεσθε σημαίνειν ὁπόταν ὂν φθέγγησθε. δῆλον γὰρ ὡς ὑμεῖς μὲν ταῦτα πάλαι γιγνώσκετε, ἡμεῖς δὲ πρὸ τοῦ μὲν ᾠόμεθα, νῦν δ᾽ ἠπορήκαμεν. διδάσκετε οὖν πρῶτον τοῦτ᾽ αὐτὸ ἡμᾶς, ἵνα μὴ δοξάζωμεν μανθάνειν μὲν τὰ λεγόμενα παρ᾽ ὑμῶν, τὸ δὲ τούτου γίγνηται πᾶν

Β τοὐναντίον. ταῦτα δὴ λέγοντές τε καὶ ἀξιοῦντες παρά τε τούτων καὶ παρὰ τῶν ἄλλων, ὅσοι πλεῖον ἑνὸς λέγουσι τὸ πᾶν εἶναι, μῶν, ὦ παῖ, τι πλημμελήσομεν;

¹ πόδα Τ (emend.) W ; πολλά Β pr. Τ.
² εἴτην W ; εἰ τὴν ΒΤ.
³ λέγοιτ᾽] λέγοιτο Β ; λέγετε Τ ; λέγετ᾽ W.

STR. You have caught my meaning at once, Theaetetus. For I certainly do mean that this is the best method for us to use, by questioning them directly, as if they were present in person; so here goes: Come now, all you who say that hot and cold or any two such principles are the universe, what is this that you attribute to both of them when you say that both and each are? What are we to understand by this "being" (or "are") of yours? Is this a third principle besides those two others, and shall we suppose that the universe is three, and not two any longer, according to your doctrine? For surely when you call one only of the two "being" you do not mean that both of them equally are; for in both cases[1] they would pretty certainly be one and not two.

THEAET. True.

STR. Well, then, do you wish to call both of them together being?

THEAET. Perhaps.

STR. But, friends, we will say, even in that way you would very clearly be saying that the two are one.

THEAET. You are perfectly right.

STR. Then since we are in perplexity, do you tell us plainly what you wish to designate when you say "being." For it is clear that you have known this all along, whereas we formerly thought we knew, but are now perplexed. So first give us this information, that we may not think we understand what you say, when the exact opposite is the case.—If we speak in this way and make this request of them and of all who say that the universe is more than one, shall we, my boy, be doing anything improper?

---

[1] "In both cases," *i.e.* whether you say that one only is or that both are, they would both be one, namely being.

ΘΕΑΙ. Ἥκιστά γε.

32. ΞΕ. Τί δέ; παρὰ τῶν ἓν τὸ πᾶν λεγόντων ἆρ' οὐ πευστέον εἰς δύναμιν τί ποτε λέγουσι τὸ
ὄν;

ΘΕΑΙ. Πῶς γὰρ οὔ;

ΞΕ. Τόδε τοίνυν ἀποκρινέσθων.¹ ἓν πού φατε
μόνον εἶναι; φαμὲν γάρ, φήσουσιν. ἢ γάρ;

ΘΕΑΙ. Ναί.

ΞΕ. Τί δέ; ὂν καλεῖτέ τι;

ΘΕΑΙ. Ναί.

C ΞΕ. Πότερον ὅπερ ἕν, ἐπὶ τῷ αὐτῷ προσχρώ-
μενοι δυοῖν ὀνόμασιν, ἢ πῶς;

ΘΕΑΙ. Τίς οὖν αὐτοῖς ἡ μετὰ τοῦτ', ὦ ξένε, ἀπόκρισις;

ΞΕ. Δῆλον, ὦ Θεαίτητε, ὅτι τῷ ταύτην τὴν ὑπόθεσιν ὑποθεμένῳ πρὸς τὸ νῦν ἐρωτηθὲν καὶ πρὸς
ἄλλο δὲ ὁτιοῦν οὐ πάντων ῥᾷστον ἀποκρίνασθαι.

ΘΕΑΙ. Πῶς;

ΞΕ. Τό τε δύο ὀνόματα ὁμολογεῖν εἶναι μηδὲν
θέμενον πλὴν ἓν καταγέλαστόν που.

ΘΕΑΙ. Πῶς δ' οὔ;

ΞΕ. Καὶ τὸ παράπαν γε ἀποδέχεσθαί του²
D λέγοντος ὡς ἔστιν ὄνομά τι, λόγον οὐκ ἂν ἔχον.

ΘΕΑΙ. Πῇ;

ΞΕ. Τιθείς τε τοὔνομα τοῦ πράγματος ἕτερον δύο
λέγει πού τινε.

ΘΕΑΙ. Ναί.

ΞΕ. Καὶ μὴν ἂν ταὐτόν γε αὐτῷ τιθῇ τοὔνομα,

¹ ἀποκρινέσθων Simplicius; ἀποκρινέσθωσαν BTW.
² του Hermann; τοῦ BT.

THE SOPHIST

THEAET. Not in the least.

STR. Well then, must we not, so far as we can, try to learn from those who say that the universe is one [1] what they mean when they say "being"?

THEAET. Of course we must.

STR. Then let them answer this question: Do you say that one only is? We do, they will say; will they not?

THEAET. Yes.

STR. Well then, do you give the name of being to anything?

THEAET. Yes.

STR. Is it what you call "one," using two names for the same thing, or how is this?

THEAET. What is their next answer, Stranger?

STR. It is plain, Theaetetus, that he who maintains their theory will not find it the easiest thing in the world to reply to our present question or to any other.

THEAET. Why not?

STR. It is rather ridiculous to assert that two names exist when you assert that nothing exists but unity.

THEAET. Of course it is.

STR. And in general there would be no sense in accepting the statement that a name has any existence.

THEAET. Why?

STR. Because he who asserts that the name is other than the thing, says that there are two entities.

THEAET. Yes.

STR. And further, if he asserts that the name is

[1] The Eleatic Zeno and his school.

ἢ μηδενὸς ὄνομα ἀναγκασθήσεται λέγειν, εἰ δέ τινος
αὐτὸ φήσει, συμβήσεται τὸ ὄνομα ὀνόματος ὄνομα
μόνον, ἄλλου δὲ οὐδενὸς ὄν.

ΘΕΑΙ. Οὕτως.

ΞΕ. Καὶ τὸ ἕν γε, ἑνὸς ὄνομα ὂν [1] καὶ τοῦ [2]
ὀνόματος αὖ τὸ [3] ἓν ὄν.

ΘΕΑΙ. Ἀνάγκη.

ΞΕ. Τί δέ; τὸ ὅλον ἕτερον τοῦ ὄντος ἑνὸς ἢ ταὐτὸν φήσουσι τούτῳ;

Ε ΘΕΑΙ. Πῶς γὰρ οὐ φήσουσί τε καὶ φασίν;

ΞΕ. Εἰ τοίνυν ὅλον ἐστίν, ὥσπερ καὶ Παρμενίδης
λέγει,

πάντοθεν εὐκύκλου σφαίρης [4] ἐναλίγκιον ὄγκῳ,
μεσσόθεν ἰσοπαλὲς πάντῃ· τὸ γὰρ οὔτε τι μεῖζον
οὔτε τι βαιότερον πελέναι χρεόν ἐστι τῇ ἢ τῇ,

τοιοῦτόν γε ὂν τὸ ὂν μέσον τε καὶ ἔσχατα ἔχει, [5]
ταῦτα δὲ ἔχον πᾶσα ἀνάγκη μέρη ἔχειν· ἢ πῶς;

ΘΕΑΙ. Οὕτως.

245 ΞΕ. Ἀλλὰ μὴν τό γε μεμερισμένον πάθος μὲν
τοῦ ἑνὸς ἔχειν ἐπὶ τοῖς μέρεσι πᾶσιν οὐδὲν ἀποκωλύει, καὶ ταύτῃ δὴ πᾶν τε ὂν καὶ ὅλον ἓν εἶναι.

ΘΕΑΙ. Τί δ' οὔ;

ΞΕ. Τὸ δὲ πεπονθὸς ταῦτα ἆρ' οὐκ ἀδύνατον
αὐτό γε τὸ ἓν αὐτὸ εἶναι;

ΘΕΑΙ. Πῶς;

---

[1] ὄνομα ὂν Apelt ; ἓν ὂν μόνον B ; ὂν μόνον T.
[2] τοῦ BW ; τοῦτο T.
[3] αὖ τὸ Schleiermacher ; αὐτὸ BTW.
[4] σφαίρης Simplicius ; σφαίρας BT.
[5] ἔχει] ἔχειν al.

the same as the thing, he will be obliged to say that it is the name of nothing, or if he says it is the name of something, the name will turn out to be the name of a name merely and of nothing else.

THEAET. True.

STR. And the one will turn out to be the name of one and also the one of the name.[1]

THEAET. Necessarily.

STR. And will they say that the whole is other than the one which exists or the same with it?

THEAET. Of course they will and do say it is the same.

STR. If then the whole is, as Parmenides says,

On all sides like the mass of a well-rounded sphere, equally weighted in every direction from the middle; for neither greater nor less must needs be on this or that,

then being, being such as he describes it, has a centre and extremes, and, having these, must certainly have parts, must it not?

THEAET. Certainly.

STR. But yet nothing hinders that which has parts from possessing the attribute of unity in all its parts and being in this way one, since it is all and whole.

THEAET. Very true.

STR. But is it not impossible for that which is in this condition to be itself absolute unity?

THEAET. Why?

[1] In other words, "one," considered as a word, will be the name of unity, but considered as a reality, it will be the unity of which the word "one" is the name. The sentence is made somewhat difficult of comprehension, doubtless for the purpose of indicating the confusion caused by the identification of the name with the thing.

ΞΕ. Ἀμερὲς δήπου δεῖ παντελῶς τό γε ἀληθῶς
ἓν κατὰ τὸν ὀρθὸν λόγον εἰρῆσθαι.

ΘΕΑΙ. Δεῖ γὰρ οὖν.

B ΞΕ. Τὸ δέ γε τοιοῦτον ἐκ πολλῶν μερῶν ὂν οὐ
συμφωνήσει τῷ λόγῳ.[1]

ΘΕΑΙ. Μανθάνω.

ΞΕ. Πότερον δὴ πάθος ἔχον τὸ ὂν τοῦ ἑνὸς οὕτως ἕν τε ἔσται καὶ ὅλον, ἢ παντάπασι μὴ λέγωμεν
ὅλον εἶναι τὸ ὄν[2];

ΘΕΑΙ. Χαλεπὴν προβέβληκας αἵρεσιν.

ΞΕ. Ἀληθέστατα μέντοι λέγεις. πεπονθός τε γὰρ
τὸ ὂν ἓν εἶναί πως, οὐ ταὐτὸν ὂν τῷ ἑνὶ φανεῖται[3]
καὶ πλέονα δὴ τὰ πάντα ἑνὸς ἔσται.

ΘΕΑΙ. Ναί.

ΞΕ. Καὶ μὴν ἐάν γε τὸ ὂν ᾖ μὴ ὅλον διὰ τὸ
C πεπονθέναι τὸ ὑπ᾽ ἐκείνου πάθος, ᾖ δὲ αὐτὸ τὸ ὅλον,
ἐνδεὲς τὸ ὂν ἑαυτοῦ ξυμβαίνει.

ΘΕΑΙ. Πάνυ γε.

ΞΕ. Καὶ κατὰ τοῦτον δὴ τὸν λόγον ἑαυτοῦ στερό-
μενον οὐκ ὂν ἔσται τὸ ὄν.

ΘΕΑΙ. Οὕτως.

ΞΕ. Καὶ ἑνός γε αὖ πλείω τὰ πάντα γίγνεται, τοῦ
τε ὄντος καὶ τοῦ ὅλου χωρὶς ἰδίαν ἑκατέρου φύσιν
εἰληφότος.

ΘΕΑΙ. Ναί.

ΞΕ. Μὴ ὄντος δέ γε τὸ παράπαν τοῦ ὅλου, ταὐτά
τε ταῦτα ὑπάρχει τῷ ὄντι καὶ πρὸς τῷ μὴ εἶναι
D μηδ᾽ ἂν γενέσθαι ποτὲ ὄν.

---

[1] τῷ λόγῳ Simplicius (codd. EF); τῷ ὅλῳ λόγῳ B; τῷ
λόγῳ ὅλῳ T, Simpl. (cod. D).
[2] ὂν Schleiermacher; ὅλον BT.
[3] φανεῖται Simplicius; φαίνεται BT.

STR. Why surely that which is really one must, according to right reason, be affirmed to be absolutely without parts.

THEAET. Yes, it must.

STR. But such a unity consisting of many parts will not harmonize with reason.

THEAET. I understand.

STR. Then shall we agree that being is one and a whole because it has the attribute of unity, or shall we deny that being is a whole at all?

THEAET. It is a hard choice that you offer me.

STR. That is very true; for being, having in a way had unity imposed upon it, will evidently not be the same as unity, and the all will be more than one.

THEAET. Yes.

STR. And further, if being is not a whole through having had the attribute of unity imposed upon it, and the absolute whole exists, then it turns out that being lacks something of being.

THEAET. Certainly.

STR. And so, by this reasoning, since being is deprived of being, it will be not-being.

THEAET. So it will.

STR. And again the all becomes more than the one, since being and the whole have acquired each its own nature.

THEAET. Yes.

STR. But if the whole does not exist at all, being is involved in the same difficulties as before, and besides not existing it could not even have ever come into existence.

ΘΕΑΙ. Τί δή;

ΞΕ. Τὸ γενόμενον ἀεὶ γέγονεν ὅλον· ὥστε οὔτε οὐσίαν οὔτε γένεσιν ὡς οὖσαν δεῖ προσαγορεύειν τὸ ὅλον [1] ἐν τοῖς οὖσι μὴ τιθέντα.

ΘΕΑΙ. Παντάπασιν ἔοικε ταῦθ᾽ οὕτως ἔχειν.

ΞΕ. Καὶ μὴν οὐδ᾽ ὁποσονοῦν τι δεῖ τὸ μὴ ὅλον εἶναι· ποσόν τι γὰρ ὄν, ὁπόσον ἂν ᾖ, τοσοῦτον ὅλον ἀναγκαῖον αὐτὸ [2] εἶναι.

ΘΕΑΙ. Κομιδῇ γε.

ΞΕ. Καὶ τοίνυν ἄλλα μυρία ἀπεράντους ἀπορίας
Ε ἕκαστον εἰληφὸς φανεῖται τῷ τὸ ὂν εἴτε δύο τινὲ εἴτε ἓν μόνον εἶναι λέγοντι.

ΘΕΑΙ. Δηλοῖ σχεδὸν καὶ τὰ νῦν ὑποφαίνοντα· συνάπτεται γὰρ ἕτερον ἐξ ἄλλου, μείζω καὶ χαλεπωτέραν φέρον περὶ τῶν ἔμπροσθεν ἀεὶ ῥηθέντων πλάνην.

33. ΞΕ. Τοὺς μὲν τοίνυν διακριβολογουμένους ὄντος τε πέρι καὶ μὴ πάντας [3] μὲν οὐ διεληλύθαμεν, ὅμως δὲ ἱκανῶς ἐχέτω· τοὺς δὲ ἄλλως λέγοντας αὖ θεατέον, ἵν᾽ ἐκ πάντων εἰδῶμεν ὅτι τὸ ὂν τοῦ μὴ
246 ὄντος οὐδὲν εὐπορώτερον εἰπεῖν ὅ τι ποτ᾽ ἔστιν.

ΘΕΑΙ. Οὐκοῦν πορεύεσθαι χρὴ καὶ ἐπὶ τούτους.

ΞΕ. Καὶ μὴν ἔοικέ γε ἐν αὐτοῖς οἷον γιγαντομαχία τις εἶναι διὰ τὴν ἀμφισβήτησιν περὶ τῆς οὐσίας πρὸς ἀλλήλους.

ΘΕΑΙ. Πῶς;

---

[1] τὸ ὅλον Bekker; τὸ ἓν ἢ τὸ ὅλον BT.
[2] αὐτὸ W, Simplicius; om. BT.
[3] πάντας Eusebius; πάνυ BT.

THE SOPHIST

THEAET. What do you mean?

STR. That which comes into existence always comes into existence as a whole. Therefore no one who does not reckon the whole among things that are can speak of existence or generation as being.

THEAET. That certainly seems to be true.

STR. And moreover, that which is not a whole cannot have any quantity at all; for if it has any quantity, whatever that quantity may be, it must necessarily be of that quantity as a whole.

THEAET. Precisely.

STR. And so countless other problems, each one involving infinite difficulties, will confront him who says that being is, whether it be two or only one.

THEAET. The problems now in sight make that pretty clear; for each leads up to another which brings greater and more grievous wandering in connexion with whatever has previously been said.

STR. Now we have not discussed all those who treat accurately of being and not-being[1]; however, let this suffice. But we must turn our eyes to those whose doctrines are less precise, that we may know from all sources that it is no easier to define the nature of being than that of not-being.

THEAET. Very well, then, we must proceed towards those others also.

STR. And indeed there seems to be a battle like that of the gods and the giants going on among them, because of their disagreement about existence.

THEAET. How so?

[1] The Ionic philosophers, the Eleatics, Heracleitus, Empedocles, the Megarians, Gorgias, Protagoras, and Antisthenes all discussed the problem of being and not-being.

371

ΞΕ. Οἱ μὲν εἰς γῆν ἐξ οὐρανοῦ καὶ τοῦ ἀοράτου πάντα ἕλκουσι, ταῖς χερσὶν ἀτεχνῶς πέτρας καὶ δρῦς περιλαμβάνοντες. τῶν γὰρ τοιούτων ἐφαπτόμενοι πάντων διισχυρίζονται τοῦτο εἶναι μόνον ὃ παρέχει προσβολὴν καὶ ἐπαφήν τινα, ταὐτὸν σῶμα

B καὶ οὐσίαν ὁριζόμενοι, τῶν δὲ ἄλλων εἴ τίς τί¹ φήσει² μὴ σῶμα ἔχον εἶναι, καταφρονοῦντες τὸ παράπαν καὶ οὐδὲν ἐθέλοντες ἄλλο ἀκούειν.

ΘΕΑΙ. Ἦ δεινοὺς εἴρηκας ἄνδρας· ἤδη γὰρ καὶ ἐγὼ τούτων συχνοῖς προσέτυχον.

ΞΕ. Τοιγαροῦν οἱ πρὸς αὐτοὺς ἀμφισβητοῦντες μάλα εὐλαβῶς ἄνωθεν ἐξ ἀοράτου ποθὲν ἀμύνονται, νοητὰ ἄττα καὶ ἀσώματα εἴδη βιαζόμενοι τὴν ἀληθινὴν οὐσίαν εἶναι· τὰ δὲ ἐκείνων σώματα καὶ τὴν λεγομένην ὑπ' αὐτῶν ἀλήθειαν κατὰ σμικρὰ

C διαθραύοντες ἐν τοῖς λόγοις γένεσιν ἀντ' οὐσίας φερομένην τινὰ προσαγορεύουσιν. ἐν μέσῳ δὲ περὶ ταῦτα ἄπλετος ἀμφοτέρων μάχη τις, ὦ Θεαίτητε, ἀεὶ ξυνέστηκεν.

ΘΕΑΙ. Ἀληθῆ.

ΞΕ. Παρ' ἀμφοῖν τοίνυν τοῖν γενοῖν κατὰ μέρος λάβωμεν λόγον ὑπὲρ ἧς τίθενται τῆς οὐσίας.

ΘΕΑΙ. Πῶς οὖν δὴ ληψόμεθα;

ΞΕ. Παρὰ μὲν τῶν ἐν εἴδεσιν αὐτὴν τιθεμένων

---

¹ τι al. ; om. BT.
² φήσει B, Eusebius ; φησι T.

THE SOPHIST

STR. Some of them[1] drag down everything from heaven and the invisible to earth, actually grasping rocks and trees with their hands; for they lay their hands on all such things and maintain stoutly that that alone exists which can be touched and handled; for they define existence and body, or matter, as identical, and if anyone says that anything else, which has no body, exists, they despise him utterly, and will not listen to any other theory than their own.

THEAET. Terrible men they are of whom you speak. I myself have met with many of them.

STR. Therefore those who contend against them defend themselves very cautiously with weapons derived from the invisible world above, maintaining forcibly that real existence consists of certain ideas which are only conceived by the mind and have no body. But the bodies of their opponents, and that which is called by them truth, they break up into small fragments in their arguments, calling them, not existence, but a kind of generation combined with motion. There is always, Theaetetus, a tremendous battle being fought about these questions between the two parties.

THEAET. True.

STR. Let us, therefore, get from each party in turn a statement in defence of that which they regard as being.

THEAET. How shall we get it?

STR. It is comparatively easy to get it from those

---

[1] The atomists (Leucippus, Democritus, and their followers), who taught that nothing exists except atoms and the void. Possibly there is a covert reference to Aristippus who was, like Plato, a pupil of Socrates.

246

ῥᾷον· ἡμερώτεροι γάρ· παρὰ δὲ τῶν εἰς σῶμα
D πάντα ἑλκόντων βίᾳ χαλεπώτερον, ἴσως δὲ καὶ
σχεδὸν ἀδύνατον. ἀλλ' ὧδέ μοι δεῖν δοκεῖ περὶ
αὐτῶν δρᾶν.

ΘΕΑΙ. Πῶς;

ΞΕ. Μάλιστα μέν, εἴ πῃ δυνατὸν ἦν, ἔργῳ βελτίους αὐτοὺς ποιεῖν· εἰ δὲ τοῦτο μὴ ἐγχωρεῖ,
λόγῳ ποιῶμεν, ὑποτιθέμενοι νομιμώτερον αὐτοὺς
ἢ νῦν ἐθέλοντας ἂν ἀποκρίνασθαι. τὸ γὰρ ὁμολο-
γηθὲν παρὰ βελτιόνων που κυριώτερον ἢ τὸ παρὰ
χειρόνων· ἡμεῖς δὲ οὐ τούτων φροντίζομεν, ἀλλὰ
τἀληθὲς ζητοῦμεν.

E   ΘΕΑΙ. Ὀρθότατα.

34. ΞΕ. Κέλευε δὴ τοὺς βελτίους γεγονότας
ἀποκρίνασθαί σοι, καὶ τὸ λεχθὲν παρ' αὐτῶν ἀφερμήνευε.

ΘΕΑΙ. Ταῦτ' ἔσται.

ΞΕ. Λεγόντων δὴ θνητὸν ζῷον εἴ φασιν εἶναί τι.

ΘΕΑΙ. Πῶς δ' οὔ;

ΞΕ. Τοῦτο δὲ οὐ σῶμα ἔμψυχον ὁμολογοῦσιν;

ΘΕΑΙ. Πάνυ γε.

ΞΕ. Τιθέντες τι τῶν ὄντων ψυχήν;

247   ΘΕΑΙ. Ναί.

ΞΕ. Τί δέ; ψυχὴν οὐ τὴν μὲν δικαίαν, τὴν δὲ
ἄδικόν φασιν εἶναι, καὶ τὴν μὲν φρόνιμον, τὴν δὲ
ἄφρονα;

ΘΕΑΙ. Τί μήν;

ΞΕ. Ἀλλ' οὐ δικαιοσύνης ἕξει καὶ παρουσίᾳ τοι-

374

who say that it consists in ideas, for they are peaceful folk; but from those who violently drag down everything into matter, it is more difficult, perhaps even almost impossible, to get it. However, this is the way I think we must deal with them.

THEAET. What way?

STR. Our first duty would be to make them really better, if it were in any way possible; but if this cannot be done, let us pretend that they are better, by assuming that they would be willing to answer more in accordance with the rules of dialectic than they actually are. For the acknowledgement of anything by better men is more valid than if made by worse men. But it is not these men that we care about; we merely seek the truth.

THEAET. Quite right.

STR. Now tell them, assuming that they have become better, to answer you, and do you interpret what they say.

THEAET. I will do so.

STR. Let them tell whether they say there is such a thing as a mortal animal.

THEAET. Of course they do.

STR. And they agree that this is a body with a soul in it, do they not?

THEAET. Certainly.

STR. Giving to soul a place among things which exist?

THEAET. Yes.

STR. Well then, do they not say that one soul is just and another unjust, one wise and another foolish?

THEAET. Of course.

STR. And do they not say that each soul becomes just by the possession and presence of justice, and

αὐτὴν αὐτῶν ἑκάστην γίγνεσθαι, καὶ τῶν ἐναντίων
τὴν ἐναντίαν;

ΘΕΑΙ. Ναί, καὶ ταῦτα ξύμφασιν.

ΞΕ. Ἀλλὰ μὴν τό γε δυνατόν τῳ[1] παραγίγνεσθαι
καὶ ἀπογίγνεσθαι πάντως εἶναί τι φήσουσιν.

ΘΕΑΙ. Φασὶ μὲν οὖν.

B ΞΕ. Οὔσης οὖν δικαιοσύνης καὶ φρονήσεως καὶ
τῆς ἄλλης ἀρετῆς καὶ τῶν ἐναντίων, καὶ δὴ καὶ
ψυχῆς ἐν ᾗ ταῦτα ἐγγίγνεται, πότερον ὁρατὸν καὶ
ἁπτὸν εἶναί φασί τι αὐτῶν ἢ πάντα ἀόρατα;

ΘΕΑΙ. Σχεδὸν οὐδὲν τούτων γε ὁρατόν.

ΞΕ. Τί δὲ τῶν τοιούτων; μῶν σῶμά τι λέγουσιν
ἴσχειν;

ΘΕΑΙ. Τοῦτο οὐκέτι κατὰ ταὐτὰ[2] ἀποκρίνονται
πᾶν, ἀλλὰ τὴν μὲν ψυχὴν αὐτὴν δοκεῖν σφίσι σῶμά
τι κεκτῆσθαι, φρόνησιν δὲ καὶ τῶν ἄλλων ἕκαστον
ὧν ἠρώτηκας, αἰσχύνονται τὸ τολμᾶν ἢ μηδὲν τῶν
C ὄντων αὐτὰ ὁμολογεῖν ἢ πάντ' εἶναι σώματα
διισχυρίζεσθαι.

ΞΕ. Σαφῶς γὰρ ἡμῖν, ὦ Θεαίτητε, βελτίους
γεγόνασιν ἄνδρες[3]· ἐπεὶ τούτων οὐδ' ἂν ἐν
ἐπαισχυνθεῖεν οἵ γε αὐτῶν σπαρτοί τε καὶ αὐτό-
χθονες, ἀλλὰ διατείνοιντ' ἂν πᾶν ὃ μὴ δυνατοὶ ταῖς
χερσὶ ξυμπιέζειν εἰσίν, ὡς ἄρα τοῦτο οὐδὲν τὸ παράπαν ἐστίν.

ΘΕΑΙ. Σχεδὸν οἷα διανοοῦνται λέγεις.

ΞΕ. Πάλιν τοίνυν ἀνερωτῶμεν αὐτούς· εἰ γάρ
τι καὶ σμικρὸν ἐθέλουσι τῶν ὄντων συγχωρεῖν ἀσώ-

---

[1] τῳ] τῷ BT ; τὸ W.
[2] ταὐτὰ] τὰ αὐτὰ W ; ταῦτα BT.
[3] ἄνδρες Bekker ; ἄνδρες BT.

the opposite by the possession and presence of the opposite?

THEAET. Yes, they agree to this also.

STR. But surely they will say that that which is capable of becoming present or absent exists.

THEAET. Yes, they say that.

STR. Granting, then, that justice and wisdom and virtue in general and their opposites exist, and also, of course, the soul in which they become present, do they say that any of these is visible and tangible, or that they are all invisible?

THEAET. That none of them is visible, or pretty nearly that.

STR. Now here are some other questions. Do they say they possess any body?

THEAET. They no longer answer the whole of that question in the same way. They say they believe the soul itself has a sort of body, but as to wisdom and the other several qualities about which you ask, they have not the face either to confess that they have no existence or to assert that they are all bodies.

STR. It is clear, Theaetetus, that our men have grown better; for the aboriginal sons of the dragon's teeth [1] among them would not shrink from any such utterance; they would maintain that nothing which they cannot squeeze with their hands has any existence at all.

THEAET. That is pretty nearly what they believe.

STR. Then let us question them further; for if they are willing to admit that any existence, no

---

[1] This refers to the story of Cadmus, who killed a dragon and then sowed its teeth, from which sprang fierce warriors to be his companions. Born of the dragon's teeth and of earth, they would naturally be of the earth, earthy.

D ματον, ἐξαρκεῖ. τὸ γὰρ ἐπί τε τούτοις ἅμα καὶ
ἐπ᾽ ἐκείνοις ὅσα ἔχει σῶμα ξυμφυὲς γεγονός, εἰς ὃ
βλέποντες ἀμφότερα εἶναι λέγουσι, τοῦτο αὐτοῖς
ῥητέον. τάχ᾽ οὖν ἴσως ἂν ἀποροῖεν· εἰ δή τι
τοιοῦτον πεπόνθασι, σκόπει, προτεινομένων ἡμῶν,
ἆρ᾽ ἐθέλοιεν ἂν δέχεσθαι καὶ ὁμολογεῖν τοιόνδ᾽
εἶναι τὸ ὄν.

ΘΕΑΙ. Τὸ ποῖον δή; λέγε, καὶ τάχα εἰσόμεθα.

ΞΕ. Λέγω δὴ τὸ καὶ ὁποιανοῦν τινα κεκτημένον
δύναμιν εἴτ᾽ εἰς [1] τὸ ποιεῖν ἕτερον ὁτιοῦν πεφυκὸς
E εἴτ᾽ εἰς τὸ παθεῖν καὶ σμικρότατον ὑπὸ τοῦ φαυ-
λοτάτου, κἂν εἰ μόνον εἰς ἅπαξ, πᾶν τοῦτο ὄντως
εἶναι· τίθεμαι γὰρ ὅρον ὁρίζειν τὰ ὄντα, ὡς ἔστιν
οὐκ ἄλλο τι πλὴν δύναμις.

ΘΕΑΙ. Ἀλλ᾽ ἐπείπερ αὐτοί γε οὐκ ἔχουσιν ἐν τῷ
παρόντι τούτου βέλτιον λέγειν, δέχονται τοῦτο.

ΞΕ. Καλῶς· ἴσως γὰρ ἂν εἰς ὕστερον ἡμῖν τε
καὶ τούτοις ἕτερον ἂν φανείη. πρὸς μὲν οὖν τούτους
248 τοῦτο ἡμῖν ἐνταῦθα μενέτω ξυνομολογηθέν.

ΘΕΑΙ. Μένει.

35. ΞΕ. Πρὸς δὴ τοὺς ἑτέρους ἴωμεν, τοὺς
τῶν εἰδῶν φίλους· σὺ δ᾽ ἡμῖν καὶ τὰ παρὰ τούτων
ἀφερμήνευε.

ΘΕΑΙ. Ταῦτ᾽ ἔσται.

ΞΕ. Γένεσιν, τὴν δὲ οὐσίαν χωρίς που διελόμενοι
λέγετε; ἦ γάρ;

_____
[1] εἴτ᾽ εἰς W; εἴ τις BT.

_____
[1] i.e., between the process of coming into existence and
existence itself. It is difficult to determine exactly who the
idealists are whose doctrines are here discussed. Possibly

matter how small, is incorporeal, that is enough. They will then have to tell what that is which is inherent in the incorporeal and the corporeal alike, and which they have in mind when they say that both exist. Perhaps they would be at a loss for an answer; and if they are in that condition, consider whether they might not accept a suggestion if we offered it, and might not agree that the nature of being is as follows.

THEAET. What is it? Speak, and we shall soon know.

STR. I suggest that everything which possesses any power of any kind, either to produce a change in anything of any nature or to be affected even in the least degree by the slightest cause, though it be only on one occasion, has real existence. For I set up as a definition which defines being, that it is nothing else than power.

THEAET. Well, since they have at the moment nothing better of their own to offer, they accept this.

STR. Good; for perhaps later something else may occur both to them and to us. As between them and us, then, let us assume that this is for the present agreed upon and settled.

THEAET. It is settled.

STR. Then let us go to the others, the friends of ideas; and do you interpret for us their doctrines also.

THEAET. I will.

STR. You distinguish in your speech between generation and being, do you not?[1]

Plato is restating or amending some of his own earlier beliefs.

ΘΕΑΙ. Ναί.

ΞΕ. Καὶ σώματι μὲν ἡμᾶς γενέσει δι᾽ αἰσθήσεως κοινωνεῖν, διὰ λογισμοῦ δὲ ψυχῇ πρὸς τὴν ὄντως οὐσίαν, ἣν ἀεὶ κατὰ ταὐτὰ ὡσαύτως ἔχειν φατέ, γένεσιν δὲ ἄλλοτε ἄλλως.

B ΘΕΑΙ. Φαμὲν γὰρ οὖν.

ΞΕ. Τὸ δὲ δὴ κοινωνεῖν, ὦ πάντων ἄριστοι, τί τοῦθ᾽ ὑμᾶς ἐπ᾽ ἀμφοῖν λέγειν φῶμεν; ἆρ᾽ οὐ τὸ νῦν δὴ παρ᾽ ἡμῶν ῥηθέν;

ΘΕΑΙ. Τὸ ποῖον;

ΞΕ. Πάθημα ἢ ποίημα ἐκ δυνάμεώς τινος ἀπὸ τῶν πρὸς ἄλληλα ξυνιόντων γιγνόμενον. τάχ᾽ οὖν, ὦ Θεαίτητε, αὐτῶν τὴν πρὸς ταῦτα ἀπόκρισιν σὺ μὲν οὐ κατακούεις, ἐγὼ δὲ ἴσως διὰ συνήθειαν.

ΘΕΑΙ. Τίν᾽ οὖν δὴ λέγουσι λόγον;

C ΞΕ. Οὐ συγχωροῦσιν ἡμῖν τὸ νῦν δὴ ῥηθὲν πρὸς τοὺς γηγενεῖς οὐσίας πέρι.

ΘΕΑΙ. Τὸ ποῖον;

ΞΕ. Ἱκανὸν ἔθεμεν ὅρον που τῶν ὄντων, ὅταν τῳ παρῇ ἡ τοῦ πάσχειν ἢ δρᾶν καὶ πρὸς τὸ σμικρότατον δύναμις;

ΘΕΑΙ. Ναί.

ΞΕ. Πρὸς δὴ ταῦτα τόδε λέγουσιν, ὅτι γενέσει μὲν μέτεστι τοῦ πάσχειν καὶ ποιεῖν δυνάμεως, πρὸς δὲ οὐσίαν τούτων οὐδετέρου τὴν δύναμιν ἁρμόττειν φασίν.

ΘΕΑΙ. Οὐκοῦν λέγουσί τι;

ΞΕ. Πρὸς ὅ γε λεκτέον ἡμῖν ὅτι δεόμεθα παρ᾽
D αὐτῶν ἔτι πυθέσθαι σαφέστερον εἰ προσομολογοῦσι τὴν μὲν ψυχὴν γιγνώσκειν, τὴν δ᾽ οὐσίαν γιγνώσκεσθαι.

THE SOPHIST

THEAET. Yes, we do.

STR. And you say that with the body, by means of perception, we participate in generation, and with the soul, by means of thought, we participate in real being, which last is always unchanged and the same, whereas generation is different at different times.

THEAET. Yes, that is what we say.

STR. But, most excellent men, how shall we define this participation which you attribute to both? Is it not that of which we were just speaking?

THEAET. What is that?

STR. A passive or active condition arising out of some power which is derived from a combination of elements. Possibly, Theaetetus, you do not hear their reply to this, but I hear it, perhaps, because I am used to them.

THEAET. What is it, then, that they say?

STR. They do not concede to us what we said just now to the aboriginal giants about being.

THEAET. What was it?

STR. We set up as a satisfactory sort of definition of being, the presence of the power to act or be acted upon in even the slightest degree.

THEAET. Yes.

STR. It is in reply to this that they say generation participates in the power of acting and of being acted upon, but that neither power is connected with being.

THEAET. And is there not something in that?

STR. Yes, something to which we must reply that we still need to learn more clearly from them whether they agree that the soul knows and that being is known.

ΘΕΑΙ. Φασὶ μὴν τοῦτό γε.

ΞΕ. Τί δέ; τὸ γιγνώσκειν ἢ τὸ γιγνώσκεσθαί φατε ποίημα ἢ πάθος ἢ ἀμφότερον; ἢ τὸ μὲν πάθημα, τὸ δὲ θάτερον; ἢ παντάπασιν οὐδέτερον οὐδετέρου τούτων μεταλαμβάνειν;

ΘΕΑΙ. Δῆλον ὡς οὐδέτερον οὐδετέρου· τἀναντία γὰρ ἂν τοῖς ἔμπροσθεν λέγοιεν.[1]

ΞΕ. Μανθάνω· τόδε γε,[2] ὡς τὸ γιγνώσκειν E εἴπερ ἔσται ποιεῖν τι, τὸ γιγνωσκόμενον ἀναγκαῖον αὖ ξυμβαίνει πάσχειν. τὴν οὐσίαν δὴ κατὰ τὸν λόγον τοῦτον γιγνωσκομένην ὑπὸ τῆς γνώσεως, καθ' ὅσον γιγνώσκεται, κατὰ τοσοῦτον κινεῖσθαι διὰ τὸ πάσχειν, ὃ δή φαμεν οὐκ ἂν γενέσθαι περὶ τὸ ἠρεμοῦν.

ΘΕΑΙ. Ὀρθῶς.

ΞΕ. Τί δὲ πρὸς Διός; ὡς ἀληθῶς κίνησιν καὶ ζωὴν καὶ ψυχὴν καὶ φρόνησιν ἢ ῥᾳδίως πεισθησόμεθα τῷ παντελῶς ὄντι μὴ παρεῖναι, μηδὲ ζῆν αὐτὸ μηδὲ 249 φρονεῖν, ἀλλὰ σεμνὸν καὶ ἅγιον, νοῦν οὐκ ἔχον, ἀκίνητον ἑστὸς εἶναι;

ΘΕΑΙ. Δεινὸν μέντ' ἄν, ὦ ξένε, λόγον συγχωροῖμεν.

ΞΕ. Ἀλλὰ νοῦν μὲν ἔχειν, ζωὴν δὲ μὴ φῶμεν;

ΘΕΑΙ. Καὶ πῶς;

ΞΕ. Ἀλλὰ ταῦτα μὲν ἀμφότερα ἐνόντ' αὐτῷ λέγομεν, οὐ μὴν ἐν ψυχῇ γε φήσομεν αὐτὸ ἔχειν αὐτά;

ΘΕΑΙ. Καὶ τίν' ἂν ἕτερον ἔχοι τρόπον;

ΞΕ. Ἀλλὰ δῆτα νοῦν μὲν καὶ ζωὴν καὶ ψυχὴν

[1] δῆλον . . . λέγοιεν first attributed to Theaetetus by Heindorf.

[2] τόδε γε] τὸ δέ γε T; τὸ δὲ B.

THEAET. They certainly assent to that.

STR. Well then, do you say that knowing or being known is an active or passive condition, or both? Or that one is passive and the other active? Or that neither has any share at all in either of the two?

THEAET. Clearly they would say that neither has any share in either; for otherwise they would be contradicting themselves.

STR. I understand; this at least is true, that if to know is active, to be known must in turn be passive. Now being, since it is, according to this theory, known by the intelligence, in so far as it is known, is moved, since it is acted upon, which we say cannot be the case with that which is in a state of rest.

THEAET. Right.

STR. But for heaven's sake, shall we let ourselves easily be persuaded that motion and life and soul and mind are really not present to absolute being, that it neither lives nor thinks, but awful and holy, devoid of mind, is fixed and immovable?

THEAET. That would be a shocking admission to make, Stranger.

STR. But shall we say that it has mind, but not life?

THEAET. How can we?

STR. But do we say that both of these exist in it, and yet go on to say that it does not possess them in a soul?

THEAET. But how else can it possess them?

STR. Then shall we say that it has mind and

ἔχειν,[1] ἀκίνητον μέντοι τὸ παράπαν ἔμψυχον ὂν
ἑστάναι;

B   ΘΕΑΙ. Πάντα ἔμοιγε ἄλογα ταῦτ᾽ εἶναι φαίνεται.

ΞΕ. Καὶ τὸ κινούμενον δὴ καὶ κίνησιν συγχωρητέον ὡς ὄντα.

ΘΕΑΙ. Πῶς δ᾽ οὔ;

ΞΕ. Ξυμβαίνει δ᾽ οὖν, ὦ Θεαίτητε, ἀκινήτων τε
ὄντων νοῦν μηδενὶ περὶ μηδενὸς εἶναι μηδαμοῦ.

ΘΕΑΙ. Κομιδῇ μὲν οὖν.

ΞΕ. Καὶ μὴν ἐὰν αὖ φερόμενα καὶ κινούμενα
πάντ᾽ εἶναι συγχωρῶμεν, καὶ τούτῳ τῷ λόγῳ
ταὐτὸν τοῦτο ἐκ τῶν ὄντων ἐξαιρήσομεν.

ΘΕΑΙ. Πῶς;

ΞΕ. Τὸ κατὰ ταὐτὰ καὶ ὡσαύτως καὶ περὶ τὸ
C αὐτὸ δοκεῖ σοι χωρὶς στάσεως γενέσθαι ποτ᾽ ἄν;

ΘΕΑΙ. Οὐδαμῶς.

ΞΕ. Τί δ᾽; ἄνευ τούτων νοῦν καθορᾷς ὄντα ἢ
γενόμενον ἂν καὶ ὁπουοῦν;

ΘΕΑΙ. Ἥκιστα.

ΞΕ. Καὶ μὴν πρός γε τοῦτον παντὶ λόγῳ μαχετέον,
ὃς ἂν ἐπιστήμην ἢ φρόνησιν ἢ νοῦν ἀφανίζων
ἰσχυρίζηται περί τινος ὁπῃοῦν.

ΘΕΑΙ. Σφόδρα γε.

ΞΕ. Τῷ δὴ φιλοσόφῳ καὶ ταῦτα μάλιστα τιμῶντι
πᾶσα, ὡς ἔοικεν, ἀνάγκη διὰ ταῦτα μήτε τῶν ἓν
ἢ καὶ τὰ πολλὰ εἴδη λεγόντων τὸ πᾶν ἑστηκὸς
D ἀποδέχεσθαι, τῶν τε αὖ πανταχῇ τὸ ὂν κινούντων

[1] ἔχειν add. Schleiermacher.

life and soul, but, although endowed with soul, is absolutely immovable?

THEAET. All those things seem to me absurd.

STR. And it must be conceded that motion and that which is moved exist.

THEAET. Of course.

STR. Then the result is, Theaetetus, that if there is no motion, there is no mind in anyone about anything anywhere.

THEAET. Exactly.

STR. And on the other hand, if we admit that all things are in flux and motion, we shall remove mind itself from the number of existing things by this theory also.

THEAET. How so?

STR. Do you think that sameness of quality or nature or relations could ever come into existence without the state of rest?

THEAET. Not at all.

STR. What then? Without these can you see how mind could exist or come into existence anywhere?

THEAET. By no means.

STR. And yet we certainly must contend by every argument against him who does away with knowledge or reason or mind and then makes any dogmatic assertion about anything.

THEAET. Certainly.

STR. Then the philosopher, who pays the highest honour to these things, must necessarily, as it seems, because of them refuse to accept the theory of those who say the universe is at rest, whether as a unity or in many forms, and must also refuse utterly to listen to those who say that being is universal

μηδὲ τὸ παράπαν ἀκούειν, ἀλλὰ κατὰ τὴν τῶν
παίδων εὐχήν, ὅσα ἀκίνητα καὶ κεκινημένα, τὸ ὄν
τε καὶ τὸ πᾶν ξυναμφότερα λέγειν.

ΘΕΑΙ. Ἀληθέστατα.

36. ΞΕ. Τί οὖν; ἆρ᾽ οὐκ ἐπιεικῶς ἤδη φαινόμεθα περιειληφέναι τῷ λόγῳ τὸ ὄν;

ΘΕΑΙ. Πάνυ μὲν οὖν.

ΞΕ. Βαβαὶ μέντ᾽ ἂν ἄρα, ὦ Θεαίτητε, ὥς μοι
δοκοῦμεν νῦν αὐτοῦ γνώσεσθαι περὶ τὴν ἀπορίαν
τῆς σκέψεως.

E   ΘΕΑΙ. Πῶς αὖ καὶ τί τοῦτ᾽ εἴρηκας;

ΞΕ. Ὦ μακάριε, οὐκ ἐννοεῖς ὅτι νῦν ἐσμεν ἐν
ἀγνοίᾳ τῇ πλείστῃ περὶ αὐτοῦ, φαινόμεθα δέ τι
λέγειν ἡμῖν αὐτοῖς;

ΘΕΑΙ. Ἐμοὶ γοῦν· ὅπῃ δ᾽ αὖ λελήθαμεν οὕτως
ἔχοντες, οὐ πάνυ ξυνίημι.

ΞΕ. Σκόπει δὴ σαφέστερον, εἰ ταῦτα νῦν ξυν-
250 ομολογοῦντες δικαίως ἂν ἐπερωτηθεῖμεν ἅπερ
αὐτοὶ τότε ἠρωτῶμεν τοὺς λέγοντας εἶναι τὸ πᾶν
θερμὸν καὶ ψυχρόν.

ΘΕΑΙ. Ποῖα; ὑπόμνησόν με.

ΞΕ. Πάνυ μὲν οὖν· καὶ πειράσομαί γε δρᾶν
τοῦτο, ἐρωτῶν σὲ καθάπερ ἐκείνους τότε, ἵνα ἅμα
τι καὶ προΐωμεν.

ΘΕΑΙ. Ὀρθῶς.

ΞΕ. Εἶεν δή, κίνησιν καὶ στάσιν ἆρ᾽ οὐκ ἐναν-
τιώτατα λέγεις ἀλλήλοις;

ΘΕΑΙ. Πῶς γὰρ οὔ;

motion; he must quote the children's prayer,[1] "all things immovable and in motion," and must say that being and the universe consist of both.

THEAET. Very true.

STR. Do we not, then, seem to have attained at last a pretty good definition of being?

THEAET. Certainly.

STR. But dear me, Theaetetus! I think we are now going to discover the difficulty of the inquiry about being.

THEAET. What is this again? What do you mean?

STR. My dear fellow, don't you see that we are now densely ignorant about it, but think that we are saying something worth while?

THEAET. I think so, at any rate, and I do not at all understand what hidden error we have fallen into.

STR. Then watch more closely and see whether, if we make these admissions, we may not justly be asked the same questions we asked a while ago of those who said the universe was hot and cold.[2]

THEAET. What questions? Remind me.

STR. Certainly; and I will try to do this by questioning you, as we questioned them at the time. I hope we shall at the same time make a little progress.

THEAET. That is right.

STR. Very well, then; you say that motion and rest are most directly opposed to each other, do you not?

THEAET. Of course.

---

[1] Nothing further seems to be known about this prayer. Stallbaum thought the reference was to a game in which the children said ὅσα ἀκίνητα καὶ κεκινημένα εἴη, "may all unmoved things be moved."

[2] *Cf.* 242 D above.

ΞΕ. Καὶ μὴν εἶναί γε ὁμοίως φῂς ἀμφότερα αὐτὰ καὶ ἑκάτερον;

B ΘΕΑΙ. Φημὶ γὰρ οὖν.

ΞΕ. ᾿Αρα κινεῖσθαι λέγων ἀμφότερα καὶ ἑκάτερον, ὅταν εἶναι συγχωρῇς;

ΘΕΑΙ. Οὐδαμῶς.

ΞΕ. ᾿Αλλ᾿ ἑστάναι σημαίνεις λέγων αὐτὰ ἀμφότερα εἶναι;

ΘΕΑΙ. Καὶ πῶς;

ΞΕ. Τρίτον ἄρα τι παρὰ ταῦτα τὸ ὂν ἐν τῇ ψυχῇ τιθείς, ὡς ὑπ᾿ ἐκείνου τήν τε στάσιν καὶ τὴν κίνησιν περιεχομένην, συλλαβὼν καὶ ἀπιδὼν αὐτῶν πρὸς τὴν τῆς οὐσίας κοινωνίαν, οὕτως εἶναι προσεῖπες ἀμφότερα;

C ΘΕΑΙ. Κινδυνεύομεν ὡς ἀληθῶς τρίτον ἀπομαντεύεσθαί τι τὸ ὄν, ὅταν κίνησιν καὶ στάσιν εἶναι λέγωμεν.

ΞΕ. Οὐκ ἄρα κίνησις καὶ στάσις ἐστὶ ξυναμφότερον τὸ ὄν, ἀλλ᾿ ἕτερον δή τι τούτων.

ΘΕΑΙ. Ἔοικεν.

ΞΕ. Κατὰ τὴν αὑτοῦ φύσιν ἄρα τὸ ὂν οὔτε ἕστηκεν οὔτε κινεῖται.

ΘΕΑΙ. Σχεδόν.

ΞΕ. Ποῖ δὴ χρὴ τὴν διάνοιαν ἔτι τρέπειν τὸν βουλόμενον ἐναργές τι περὶ αὐτοῦ παρ᾿ ἑαυτῷ βεβαιώσασθαι;

ΘΕΑΙ. Ποῖ γάρ;

ΞΕ. Οἶμαι μὲν οὐδαμόσε ἔτι ῥᾴδιον. εἰ γάρ τι D μὴ κινεῖται, πῶς οὐχ ἕστηκεν; ἢ τὸ μηδαμῶς ἑστὸς πῶς οὐκ αὖ κινεῖται; τὸ δὲ ὂν ἡμῖν νῦν ἐκτὸς τούτων ἀμφοτέρων ἀναπέφανται. ἦ δυνατὸν οὖν τοῦτο;

STR. And yet you say that both and each of them equally exist?

THEAET. Yes, I do.

STR. And in granting that they exist, do you mean to say that both and each are in motion?

THEAET. By no means.

STR. But do you mean that they are at rest, when you say that both exist?

THEAET. Of course not.

STR. Being, then, you consider to be something else in the soul, a third in addition to these two, inasmuch as you think rest and motion are embraced by it; and since you comprehend and observe that they participate in existence, you therefore said that they are. Eh?

THEAET. We really do seem to have a vague vision of being as some third thing, when we say that motion and rest are.

STR. Then being is not motion and rest in combination, but something else, different from them.

THEAET. Apparently.

STR. According to its own nature, then, being is neither at rest nor in motion.

THEAET. You are about right.

STR. What is there left, then, to which a man can still turn his mind who wishes to establish within himself any clear conception of being?

THEAET. What indeed?

STR. There is nothing left, I think, to which he can turn easily. For if a thing is not in motion, it must surely be at rest; and again, what is not at rest, must surely be in motion. But now we find that being has emerged outside of both these classes. Is that possible, then?

389

ΘΕΑΙ. Πάντων μὲν οὖν ἀδυνατώτατον.

ΞΕ. Τόδε τοίνυν μνησθῆναι δίκαιον ἐπὶ τούτοις.

ΘΕΑΙ. Τὸ ποῖον;

ΞΕ. Ὅτι τοῦ μὴ ὄντος ἐρωτηθέντες τοὔνομα ἐφ᾽ ὅ τί ποτε δεῖ φέρειν, πάσῃ συνεσχόμεθα ἀπορίᾳ. μέμνησαι;

ΘΕΑΙ. Πῶς γὰρ οὔ;

ΞΕ. Μῶν οὖν ἐν ἐλάττονί τινι νῦν ἐσμεν ἀπορίᾳ
E περὶ τὸ ὄν;

ΘΕΑΙ. Ἐμοὶ μέν, ὦ ξένε, εἰ δυνατὸν εἰπεῖν, ἐν πλείονι φαινόμεθα.

ΞΕ. Τοῦτο μὲν τοίνυν ἐνταῦθα κείσθω διηπορη-μένον· ἐπειδὴ δὲ ἐξ ἴσου τό τε ὂν καὶ τὸ μὴ ὂν ἀπο-ρίας μετειλήφατον, νῦν ἐλπὶς ἤδη καθ᾽ ἅπερ ἂν αὐτῶν θάτερον εἴτε ἀμυδρότερον εἴτε σαφέστερον ἀναφαίνηται, καὶ θάτερον οὕτως ἀναφαίνεσθαι· καὶ
251 ἐὰν αὖ μηδέτερον ἰδεῖν δυνώμεθα, τὸν γοῦν λόγον ὅπηπερ ἂν οἷοί τε ὦμεν εὐπρεπέστατα διωσόμεθα οὕτως ἀμφοῖν ἅμα.

ΘΕΑΙ. Καλῶς.

ΞΕ. Λέγωμεν δὴ καθ᾽ ὅντινά ποτε τρόπον πολλοῖς ὀνόμασι ταὐτὸν τοῦτο ἑκάστοτε προσαγορεύομεν.

ΘΕΑΙ. Οἷον δὴ τί; παράδειγμα εἰπέ.

37. ΞΕ. Λέγομεν ἄνθρωπον δή που πόλλ᾽ ἄττα ἐπονομάζοντες, τά τε χρώματα ἐπιφέροντες αὐτῷ καὶ τὰ σχήματα καὶ μεγέθη καὶ κακίας καὶ ἀρετάς,
B ἐν οἷς πᾶσι καὶ ἑτέροις μυρίοις οὐ μόνον ἄνθρωπον αὐτὸν εἶναί φαμεν, ἀλλὰ καὶ ἀγαθὸν καὶ ἕτερα ἄπειρα, καὶ τἆλλα δὴ κατὰ τὸν αὐτὸν λόγον οὕτως ἓν ἕκαστον ὑποθέμενοι πάλιν αὐτὸ πολλὰ καὶ πολλοῖς ὀνόμασι λέγομεν.

THEAET. No, nothing could be more impossible.

STR. Then there is this further thing which we ought to remember.

THEAET. What is it?

STR. That when we were asked to what the appellation of not-being should be applied, we were in the greatest perplexity. Do you remember?

THEAET. Of course I do.

STR. Well, then, are we now in any less perplexity about being?

THEAET. It seems to me, stranger, that we are, if possible, in even greater.

STR. This point, then, let us put down definitely as one of complete perplexity. But since being and not-being participate equally in the perplexity, there is now at last some hope that as either of them emerges more dimly or more clearly, so also will the other emerge. If, however, we are able to see neither of them, we will at any rate push our discussion through between both of them at once as creditably as we can.

THEAET. Good.

STR. Let us, then, explain how we come to be constantly calling this same thing by many names.

THEAET. What, for instance? Please give an example.

STR. We speak of man, you know, and give him many additional designations; we attribute to him colours and forms and sizes and vices and virtues, and in all these cases and countless others we say not only that he is man, but we say he is good and numberless other things. So in the same way every single thing which we supposed to be one, we treat as many and call by many names.

ΘΕΑΙ. Ἀληθῆ λέγεις.

ΞΕ. Ὅθεν γε, οἶμαι, τοῖς τε νέοις καὶ τῶν γερόντων τοῖς ὀψιμαθέσι θοίνην παρεσκευάκαμεν· εὐθὺς γὰρ ἀντιλαβέσθαι παντὶ πρόχειρον ὡς ἀδύνατον τά τε πολλὰ ἓν καὶ τὸ ἓν πολλὰ εἶναι, καὶ δή που χαίρουσιν οὐκ ἐῶντες ἀγαθὸν λέγειν ἄνθρωπον, ἀλλὰ τὸ μὲν ἀγαθὸν ἀγαθόν, τὸν δὲ ἄνθρωπον ἄνθρωπον. ἐντυγχάνεις γάρ, ὦ Θεαίτητε, ὡς ἐγᾦμαι, πολλάκις τὰ τοιαῦτα ἐσπουδακόσιν, ἐνίοτε πρεσβυτέροις ἀνθρώποις, καὶ ὑπὸ πενίας τῆς περὶ φρόνησιν κτήσεως τὰ τοιαῦτα τεθαυμακόσι, καὶ δή τι καὶ πάσσοφον οἰομένοις τοῦτο αὐτὸ ἀνηυρηκέναι.

ΘΕΑΙ. Πάνυ μὲν οὖν.

ΞΕ. Ἵνα τοίνυν πρὸς ἅπαντας ἡμῖν ὁ λόγος ᾖ τοὺς πώποτε περὶ οὐσίας καὶ ὁτιοῦν διαλεχθέντας, ἔστω καὶ πρὸς τούτους καὶ πρὸς τοὺς ἄλλους, ὅσοις ἔμπροσθεν διειλέγμεθα, τὰ νῦν ὡς ἐν ἐρωτήσει λεχθησόμενα.

ΘΕΑΙ. Τὰ ποῖα δή;

ΞΕ. Πότερον μήτε τὴν οὐσίαν κινήσει καὶ στάσει προσάπτωμεν μήτε ἄλλο ἄλλῳ μηδὲν μηδενί, ἀλλ᾽ ὡς ἄμικτα ὄντα καὶ ἀδύνατον μεταλαμβάνειν ἀλλήλων οὕτως αὐτὰ ἐν τοῖς παρ᾽ ἡμῖν λόγοις τιθῶμεν; ἢ πάντα εἰς ταὐτὸν ξυνάγωμεν ὡς δυνατὰ ἐπικοινωνεῖν ἀλλήλοις; ἢ τὰ μέν, τὰ δὲ μή; τούτων, ὦ

THE SOPHIST

THEAET. True.

STR. And it is in this way, I fancy, that we have provided a fine feast for youngsters and for old men whose learning has come to them late in life; for example, it is easy enough for anyone to grasp the notion that the many cannot possibly be one, nor the one many, and so, apparently, they take pleasure in saying that we must not call a man good, but must call the good good, and a man man. I fancy, Theaetetus, you often run across people who take such matters seriously; sometimes they are elderly men whose poverty of intellect makes them admire such quibbles, and who think this is a perfect mine of wisdom they have discovered.[1]

THEAET. Certainly.

STR. Then, to include in our discussion all those who have ever engaged in any talk whatsoever about being, let us address our present arguments to these men as well as to all those with whom we were conversing before, and let us employ the form of questions.

THEAET. What are the arguments?

STR. Shall we attribute neither being to rest and motion, nor any attribute to anything, but shall we in our discussions assume that they do not mingle and cannot participate in one another? Or shall we gather all things together, believing that they are capable of combining with one another? Or are some capable of it and others not? Which of these

[1] Those are here satirized who deny the possibility of all except identical predication. Such were Antisthenes, Euthydemus, and Dionysodorus. The two last are probably those referred to as old men whose learning came late in life.

251

E Θεαίτητε, τί ποτ' ἂν αὐτοὺς προαιρεῖσθαι φήσαιμεν;

ΘΕΑΙ. Ἐγὼ μὲν ὑπὲρ αὐτῶν οὐδὲν ἔχω πρὸς ταῦτα ἀποκρίνασθαι.

ΞΕ. Τί οὖν οὐ καθ' ἓν ἀποκρινόμενος ἐφ' ἑκάστου τὰ ξυμβαίνοντα ἐσκέψω;[1]

ΘΕΑΙ. Καλῶς λέγεις.[2]

ΞΕ. Καὶ τιθῶμέν γε αὐτοὺς λέγειν, εἰ βούλει, πρῶτον μηδενὶ μηδὲν μηδεμίαν δύναμιν ἔχειν κοινωνίας εἰς μηδέν. οὐκοῦν κίνησίς τε καὶ στάσις οὐδαμῇ μεθέξετον οὐσίας;

252 ΘΕΑΙ. Οὐ γὰρ οὖν.

ΞΕ. Τί δέ; ἔσται πότερον αὐτῶν οὐσίας μὴ προσκοινωνοῦν[3];

ΘΕΑΙ. Οὐκ ἔσται.

ΞΕ. Ταχὺ δὴ ταύτῃ γε τῇ συνομολογίᾳ πάντα ἀνάστατα γέγονεν, ὡς ἔοικεν, ἅμα τε τῶν τὸ πᾶν κινούντων καὶ τῶν ὡς ἓν ἱστάντων καὶ ὅσοι κατ' εἴδη τὰ ὄντα κατὰ ταὐτὰ ὡσαύτως ἔχοντα εἶναί φασιν ἀεί· πάντες γὰρ οὗτοι τό γε εἶναι προσάπτουσιν, οἱ μὲν ὄντως κινεῖσθαι λέγοντες, οἱ δὲ ὄντως ἑστηκότ' εἶναι.

ΘΕΑΙ. Κομιδῇ μὲν οὖν.

B ΞΕ. Καὶ μὴν καὶ ὅσοι τοτὲ μὲν ξυντιθέασι τὰ πάντα, τοτὲ δὲ διαιροῦσιν, εἴτε εἰς ἓν καὶ ἐξ ἑνὸς ἄπειρα εἴτε εἰς πέρας ἔχοντα στοιχεῖα διαιρούμενοι καὶ ἐκ τούτων συντιθέντες, ὁμοίως μὲν ἐὰν ἐν μέρει τοῦτο τιθῶσι γιγνόμενον, ὁμοίως δὲ καὶ ἐὰν ἀεί,

---

[1] τί οὖν . . . ἐσκέψω; attributed to the Stranger by Badham.
[2] καλῶς λέγεις attributed to Theaetetus by Badham.
[3] προσκοινωνοῦν W; προσκοινωνεῖν BT.

alternatives, Theaetetus, should we say is their choice?

THEAET. I cannot answer these questions for them.

STR. Then why did you not answer each separately and see what the result was in each case?

THEAET. A good suggestion.

STR. And let us, if you please, assume that they say first that nothing has any power to combine with anything else. Then motion and rest will have no share in being, will they?

THEAET. No.

STR. Well, then, will either of them be, if it has no share in being?

THEAET. It will not.

STR. See how by this admission everything is overturned at once, as it seems—the doctrine of those who advocate universal motion, that of the partisans of unity and rest, and that of the men who teach that all existing things are distributed into invariable and everlasting kinds. For all of these make use of being as an attribute. One party says that the universe "is" in motion, another that it "is" at rest.

THEAET. Exactly.

STR. And further, all who teach that things combine at one time and separate at another, whether infinite elements combine in unity and are derived from unity or finite elements separate and then unite, regardless of whether they say that these changes take place successively or without interrup-

κατὰ πάντα ταῦτα λέγοιεν ἂν οὐδέν, εἴπερ μηδεμία
ἔστι ξύμμιξις.

ΘΕΑΙ. Ὀρθῶς.

ΞΕ. Ἔτι τοίνυν ἂν αὐτοὶ πάντων καταγελαστό-
τατα μετίοιεν [1] τὸν λόγον οἱ μηδὲν ἐῶντες κοινωνίᾳ
παθήματος ἑτέρου θάτερον προσαγορεύειν.

C   ΘΕΑΙ. Πῶς;

ΞΕ. Τῷ τε " εἶναί " που περὶ πάντα ἀναγκάζονται
χρῆσθαι καὶ τῷ " χωρὶς " καὶ τῷ " τῶν ἄλλων " [2]
καὶ τῷ " καθ' αὑτὸ " καὶ μυρίοις ἑτέροις, ὧν
ἀκρατεῖς ὄντες εἴργεσθαι καὶ μὴ συνάπτειν ἐν τοῖς
λόγοις οὐκ ἄλλων δέονται τῶν ἐξελεγξόντων, ἀλλὰ
τὸ λεγόμενον οἴκοθεν τὸν πολέμιον καὶ ἐναντιω-
σόμενον ἔχοντες, ἐντὸς ὑποφθεγγόμενον ὥσπερ τὸν
ἄτοπον Εὐρυκλέα περιφέροντες ἀεὶ πορεύονται.

D   ΘΕΑΙ. Κομιδῇ λέγεις ὅμοιόν τε καὶ ἀληθές.

ΞΕ. Τί δ', ἂν πάντα ἀλλήλοις ἐῶμεν δύναμιν
ἔχειν ἐπικοινωνίας;

ΘΕΑΙ. Τοῦτο μὲν οἷός τε κἀγὼ διαλύειν.

ΞΕ. Πῶς;

ΘΕΑΙ. Ὅτι κίνησίς τε [3] αὐτὴ παντάπασιν ἵσταιτ'
ἂν καὶ στάσις αὖ πάλιν αὐτὴ κινοῖτο, εἴπερ ἐπιγι-
γνοίσθην ἐπ' ἀλλήλοιν.

ΞΕ. Ἀλλὰ μὴν τοῦτό γέ που ταῖς μεγίσταις ἀνάγ-
καις ἀδύνατον, κίνησίν τε ἵστασθαι καὶ στάσιν
κινεῖσθαι;

ΘΕΑΙ. Πῶς γὰρ οὔ;

ΞΕ. Τὸ τρίτον δὴ μόνον λοιπόν.

ΘΕΑΙ. Ναί.

[1] μετίοιεν] μετίοιμεν BTW.
[2] τῶν ἄλλων B; ἄλλων T.
[3] τε] γε BTW.

THE SOPHIST

tion, would be talking nonsense in all these doctrines, if there is no intermingling.

THEAET. Quite right.

STR. Then, too, the very men who forbid us to call anything by another name because it participates in the effect produced by another, would be made most especially ridiculous by this doctrine.

THEAET. How so?

STR. Because they are obliged in speaking of anything to use the expressions "to be," "apart," "from the rest," "by itself," and countless others; they are powerless to keep away from them or avoid working them into their discourse; and therefore there is no need of others to refute them, but, as the saying goes, their enemy and future opponent is of their own household whom they always carry about with them as they go, giving forth speech from within them, like the wonderful Eurycles.[1]

THEAET. That is a remarkably accurate illustration.

STR. But what if we ascribe to all things the power of participation in one another?

THEAET. Even I can dispose of that assumption.

STR. How?

THEAET. Because motion itself would be wholly at rest, and rest in turn would itself be in motion, if these two could be joined with one another.

STR. But surely this at least is most absolutely impossible, that motion be at rest and rest be in motion?

THEAET. Of course.

STR. Then only the third possibility is left.

THEAET. Yes.

[1] Eurycles was a ventriloquist and soothsayer of the fifth century, cf. Aristophanes, *Wasps*, 1019.

Ε   38. ΞΕ. Καὶ μὴν ἕν γέ τι τούτων ἀναγκαῖον, ἢ πάντα ἢ μηδὲν ἢ τὰ μὲν ἐθέλειν, τὰ δὲ μὴ
συμμίγνυσθαι.

ΘΕΑΙ. Πῶς γὰρ οὔ;

ΞΕ. Καὶ μὴν τά γε δύο ἀδύνατον εὑρέθη.

ΘΕΑΙ. Ναί.[1]

ΞΕ. Πᾶς ἄρα ὁ βουλόμενος ὀρθῶς ἀποκρίνεσθαι
τὸ λοιπὸν τῶν τριῶν θήσει.

ΘΕΑΙ. Κομιδῇ μὲν οὖν.

ΞΕ. Ὅτε δὴ τὰ μὲν ἐθέλει τοῦτο δρᾶν, τὰ δ᾽ οὔ,
253 σχεδὸν οἷον τὰ γράμματα πεπονθότ᾽ ἂν εἴη. καὶ
γὰρ ἐκείνων τὰ μὲν ἀναρμοστεῖ που πρὸς ἄλληλα,
τὰ δὲ ξυναρμόττει.

ΘΕΑΙ. Πῶς δ᾽ οὔ;

ΞΕ. Τὰ δέ γε φωνήεντα διαφερόντως τῶν ἄλλων
οἷον δεσμὸς διὰ πάντων κεχώρηκεν, ὥστε ἄνευ τινὸς
αὐτῶν ἀδύνατον ἁρμόττειν καὶ τῶν ἄλλων ἕτερον
ἑτέρῳ.

ΘΕΑΙ. Καὶ μάλα γε.

ΞΕ. Πᾶς οὖν οἶδεν ὁποῖα ὁποίοις δυνατὰ κοινωνεῖν, ἢ τέχνης δεῖ τῷ μέλλοντι δρᾶν ἱκανῶς αὐτά;

ΘΕΑΙ. Τέχνης.

ΞΕ. Ποίας;

ΘΕΑΙ. Τῆς γραμματικῆς.

ΞΕ. Τί δέ; περὶ τοὺς τῶν ὀξέων καὶ βαρέων
Β φθόγγους ἆρ᾽ οὐχ οὕτως; ὁ μὲν τοὺς συγκεραννυ-
μένους τε καὶ μὴ τέχνην ἔχων γιγνώσκειν μουσικός,
ὁ δὲ μὴ ξυνιεὶς ἄμουσος;

ΘΕΑΙ. Οὕτως.

---

[1] εὑρέθη. ναί Heindorf; εὑρεθῆναι ΒΤ; εὑρεθῆναι· ναί W.

STR. And certainly one of these three must be true ; either all things will mingle with one another, or none will do so, or some will and others will not.

THEAET. Of course.

STR. And certainly the first two were found to be impossible.

THEAET. Yes.

STR. Then everybody who wishes to answer correctly will adopt the remaining one of the three possibilities.

THEAET. Precisely.

STR. Now since some things will commingle and others will not, they are in much the same condition as the letters of the alphabet ; for some of these do not fit each other, and others do.

THEAET. Of course.

STR. And the vowels, to a greater degree than the others, run through them all as a bond, so that without one of the vowels the other letters cannot be joined one to another.

THEAET. Certainly.

STR. Now does everybody know which letters can join with which others ? Or does he who is to join them properly have need of art ?

THEAET. He has need of art.

STR. What art ?

THEAET. The art of grammar.

STR. And is not the same true in connexion with high and low sounds ? Is not he who has the art to know the sounds which mingle and those which do not, musical, and he who does not know unmusical ?

THEAET. Yes.

ΞΕ. Καὶ κατὰ τῶν ἄλλων δὴ τεχνῶν καὶ ἀτεχνιῶν τοιαῦτα εὑρήσομεν ἕτερα.

ΘΕΑΙ. Πῶς δ' οὔ;

ΞΕ. Τί δ'; ἐπειδὴ καὶ τὰ γένη πρὸς ἄλληλα κατὰ ταὐτὰ μίξεως ἔχειν ὡμολογήκαμεν, ἆρ' οὐ μετ' ἐπιστήμης τινὸς ἀναγκαῖον διὰ τῶν λόγων πορεύεσθαι τὸν ὀρθῶς μέλλοντα δείξειν ποῖα ποίοις συμφωνεῖ τῶν γενῶν καὶ ποῖα ἄλληλα οὐ δέχεται; C καὶ δὴ καὶ διὰ πάντων εἰ συνέχοντ' ἄττ' αὔτ'[1] ἐστιν, ὥστε συμμίγνυσθαι δυνατὰ εἶναι, καὶ πάλιν ἐν ταῖς διαιρέσεσιν, εἰ δι' ὅλων ἕτερα τῆς διαιρέσεως αἴτια;

ΘΕΑΙ. Πῶς γὰρ οὐκ ἐπιστήμης δεῖ, καὶ σχεδόν γε ἴσως τῆς μεγίστης;

39. ΞΕ. Τίν' οὖν αὖ προσεροῦμεν, ὦ Θεαίτητε, ταύτην; ἢ πρὸς Διὸς ἐλάθομεν εἰς τὴν τῶν ἐλευθέρων ἐμπεσόντες ἐπιστήμην, καὶ κινδυνεύομεν ζητοῦντες τὸν σοφιστὴν πρότερον ἀνηυρηκέναι τὸν φιλόσοφον;

ΘΕΑΙ. Πῶς λέγεις;

D ΞΕ. Τὸ κατὰ γένη διαιρεῖσθαι καὶ μήτε ταὐτὸν εἶδος ἕτερον ἡγήσασθαι μήτε ἕτερον ὂν ταὐτὸν μῶν οὐ τῆς διαλεκτικῆς φήσομεν ἐπιστήμης εἶναι;

ΘΕΑΙ. Ναί, φήσομεν.

ΞΕ. Οὐκοῦν ὅ γε τοῦτο δυνατὸς δρᾶν μίαν ἰδέαν διὰ πολλῶν, ἑνὸς ἑκάστου κειμένου χωρίς, πάντη διατεταμένην ἱκανῶς διαισθάνεται, καὶ πολλὰς ἑτέρας ἀλλήλων ὑπὸ μιᾶς ἔξωθεν περιεχομένας, καὶ μίαν αὖ δι' ὅλων πολλῶν ἐν ἑνὶ ξυνημμένην, καὶ

[1] συνέχοντ' ἄττ' αὔτ' Wagner; συνέχοντα ταῦτ' BTW.

THE SOPHIST

STR. And we shall find similar conditions, then, in all the other arts and processes which are devoid of art?

THEAET. Of course.

STR. Now since we have agreed that the classes or genera also commingle with one another, or do not commingle, in the same way, must not he possess some science and proceed by the processes of reason who is to show correctly which of the classes harmonize with which, and which reject one another, and also if he is to show whether there are some elements extending through all and holding them together so that they can mingle, and again, when they separate, whether there are other universal causes of separation?

THEAET. Certainly he needs science, and perhaps even the greatest of sciences.

STR. Then, Theaetetus, what name shall we give to this science? Or, by Zeus, have we unwittingly stumbled upon the science that belongs to free men and perhaps found the philosopher while we were looking for the sophist?

THEAET. What do you mean?

STR. Shall we not say that the division of things by classes and the avoidance of the belief that the same class is another, or another the same, belongs to the science of dialectic?

THEAET. Yes, we shall.

STR. Then he who is able to do this has a clear perception of one form or idea extending entirely through many individuals each of which lies apart, and of many forms differing from one another but included in one greater form, and again of one form evolved by the union of many wholes, and of many

253

Ε πολλὰς χωρὶς πάντῃ διωρισμένας· τοῦτο δ' ἔστιν, ᾗ τε κοινωνεῖν ἕκαστα δύναται καὶ ὅπῃ μή, διακρίνειν κατὰ γένος ἐπίστασθαι.

ΘΕΑΙ. Παντάπασι μὲν οὖν.

ΞΕ. Ἀλλὰ μὴν τό γε διαλεκτικὸν οὐκ ἄλλῳ δώσεις, ὡς ἐγῷμαι, πλὴν τῷ καθαρῶς τε καὶ δικαίως φιλοσοφοῦντι.

ΘΕΑΙ. Πῶς γὰρ ἂν ἄλλῳ δοίη τις;

ΞΕ. Τὸν μὲν δὴ φιλόσοφον ἐν τοιούτῳ τινὶ τόπῳ καὶ νῦν καὶ ἔπειτα ἀνευρήσομεν, ἐὰν ζητῶμεν, ἰδεῖν 254 μὲν χαλεπὸν ἐναργῶς καὶ τοῦτον, ἕτερον μὴν τρόπον ἥ τε τοῦ σοφιστοῦ χαλεπότης ἥ τε τούτου.

ΘΕΑΙ. Πῶς;

ΞΕ. Ὁ μὲν ἀποδιδράσκων εἰς τὴν τοῦ μὴ ὄντος σκοτεινότητα, τριβῇ προσαπτόμενος αὐτῆς, διὰ τὸ σκοτεινὸν τοῦ τόπου κατανοῆσαι χαλεπός· ἦ γάρ;

ΘΕΑΙ. Ἔοικεν.

ΞΕ. Ὁ δέ γε φιλόσοφος, τῇ τοῦ ὄντος ἀεὶ διὰ λογισμῶν προσκείμενος ἰδέᾳ, διὰ τὸ λαμπρὸν αὖ τῆς χώρας οὐδαμῶς εὐπετὴς ὀφθῆναι· τὰ γὰρ τῆς τῶν Β πολλῶν ψυχῆς ὄμματα καρτερεῖν πρὸς τὸ θεῖον ἀφορῶντα ἀδύνατα.

ΘΕΑΙ. Καὶ ταῦτα εἰκὸς οὐχ ἧττον ἐκείνων οὕτως ἔχειν.

ΞΕ. Οὐκοῦν περὶ μὲν τούτου καὶ τάχα ἐπισκεψόμεθα σαφέστερον, ἂν ἔτι βουλομένοις ἡμῖν ᾖ· περὶ δὲ τοῦ σοφιστοῦ που δῆλον ὡς οὐκ ἀνετέον, πρὶν ἂν ἱκανῶς αὐτὸν θεασώμεθα.

forms entirely apart and separate. This is the knowledge and ability to distinguish by classes how individual things can or cannot be associated with one another.

THEAET. Certainly it is.

STR. But you surely, I suppose, will not grant the art of dialectic to any but the man who pursues philosophy in purity and righteousness.

THEAET. How could it be granted to anyone else?

STR. Then it is in some region like this that we shall always, both now and hereafter, discover the philosopher, if we look for him; he also is hard to see clearly, but the difficulty is not the same in his case and that of the sophist.

THEAET. How do they differ?

STR. The sophist runs away into the darkness of not-being, feeling his way in it by practice,[1] and is hard to discern on account of the darkness of the place. Don't you think so?

THEAET. It seems likely.

STR. But the philosopher, always devoting himself through reason to the idea of being, is also very difficult to see on account of the brilliant light of the place; for the eyes of the soul of the multitude are not strong enough to endure the sight of the divine.

THEAET. This also seems no less true than what you said about the sophist.

STR. Now we will make more accurate investigations about the philosopher hereafter, if we still care to do so; but as to the sophist, it is clear that we must not relax our efforts until we have a satisfactory view of him.

[1] By practice, *i.e.*, by empirical knowledge as opposed to reason.

ΘΕΑΙ. Καλῶς εἶπες.

40. ΞΕ. Ὅτ' οὖν δὴ τὰ μὲν ἡμῖν τῶν γενῶν ὡμολόγηται κοινωνεῖν ἐθέλειν ἀλλήλοις, τὰ δὲ μή, καὶ
τὰ μὲν ἐπ' ὀλίγον, τὰ δ' ἐπὶ πολλά, τὰ δὲ καὶ διὰ
C πάντων οὐδὲν κωλύειν τοῖς πᾶσι κεκοινωνηκέναι,
τὸ δὴ μετὰ τοῦτο ξυνεπισπώμεθα τῷ λόγῳ τῇδε
σκοποῦντες, μὴ περὶ πάντων τῶν εἰδῶν, ἵνα μὴ
ταραττώμεθα ἐν πολλοῖς, ἀλλὰ προελόμενοι τῶν
μεγίστων λεγομένων ἄττα, πρῶτον μὲν ποῖα
ἕκαστά ἐστιν, ἔπειτα κοινωνίας ἀλλήλων πῶς ἔχει
δυνάμεως, ἵνα τό τε ὂν καὶ μὴ ὂν εἰ μὴ πάσῃ
σαφηνείᾳ δυνάμεθα λαβεῖν, ἀλλ' οὖν λόγου γε
ἐνδεεῖς μηδὲν γιγνώμεθα περὶ αὐτῶν, καθ' ὅσον ὁ
τρόπος ἐνδέχεται τῆς νῦν σκέψεως, ἐὰν ἄρα ἡμῖν πῃ
D παρεικάθῃ [1] τὸ μὴ ὂν λέγουσιν ὡς ἔστιν ὄντως μὴ
ὂν ἀθῴοις ἀπαλλάττειν.

ΘΕΑΙ. Οὐκοῦν χρή.

ΞΕ. Μέγιστα μὴν τῶν γενῶν, ἃ νῦν δὴ διῆμεν,
τό τε ὂν αὐτὸ καὶ στάσις καὶ κίνησις.

ΘΕΑΙ. Πολύ γε.

ΞΕ. Καὶ μὴν τώ γε δύο φαμὲν αὐτοῖν ἀμίκτω
πρὸς ἀλλήλω.

ΘΕΑΙ. Σφόδρα γε.

ΞΕ. Τὸ δέ γε ὂν μικτὸν ἀμφοῖν· ἐστὸν γὰρ
ἄμφω που.

ΘΕΑΙ. Πῶς δ' οὔ;

ΞΕ. Τρία δὴ γίγνεται ταῦτα.

ΘΕΑΙ. Τί μήν;

ΞΕ. Οὐκοῦν αὐτῶν ἕκαστον τοῖν μὲν δυοῖν ἕτερόν
ἐστιν, αὐτὸ δ' ἑαυτῷ ταὐτόν.

---

[1] παρεικάθῃ Boeckh; παρεικασθῇ ΒΤ.

THEAET. You are right.

STR. Since, therefore, we are agreed that some of the classes will mingle with one another, and others will not, and some will mingle with few and others with many, and that there is nothing to hinder some from mingling universally with all, let us next proceed with our discussion by investigating, not all the forms or ideas, lest we become confused among so many, but some only, selecting them from those that are considered the most important; let us first consider their several natures, then what their power of mingling with one another is, and so, if we cannot grasp being and not-being with perfect clearness, we shall at any rate not fail to reason fully about them, so far as the method of our present inquiry permits. Let us in this way see whether it is, after all, permitted us to say that not-being really is, although not being, and yet come off unscathed.

THEAET. Yes; that is the proper thing for us to do.

STR. The most important, surely, of the classes or genera are those which we just mentioned; being itself and rest and motion.

THEAET. Yes, by far.

STR. And further, two of them, we say, cannot mingle with each other.

THEAET. Decidedly not.

STR. But being can mingle with both of them, for they both are.

THEAET. Of course.

STR. Then these prove to be three.

THEAET. To be sure.

STR. Each of them is, then, other than the remaining two, but the same as itself.

E ΘΕΑΙ. Οὕτως.

ΞΕ. Τί ποτ᾽ αὖ νῦν οὕτως εἰρήκαμεν τό τε ταὐτὸν καὶ θάτερον; πότερα δύο γένη τινὲ αὐτώ,[1] τῶν μὲν τριῶν ἄλλω, ξυμμιγνυμένω μὴν ἐκείνοις ἐξ ἀνάγκης ἀεί, καὶ περὶ πέντε ἀλλ᾽ οὐ περὶ τριῶν ὡς ὄντων αὐτῶν σκεπτέον, ἢ τό τε ταὐτὸν τοῦτο καὶ θάτερον 255 ὡς ἐκείνων τι προσαγορεύοντες λανθάνομεν ἡμᾶς αὐτούς;

ΘΕΑΙ. Ἴσως.

ΞΕ. Ἀλλ᾽ οὔ τι μὴν κίνησίς γε καὶ στάσις οὔθ᾽ ἕτερον οὔτε ταὐτόν ἐστι.

ΘΕΑΙ. Πῶς;

ΞΕ. Ὅτιπερ ἂν κοινῇ προσείπωμεν κίνησιν καὶ στάσιν, τοῦτο οὐδέτερον αὐτοῖν οἷόν τε εἶναι.

ΘΕΑΙ. Τί δή;

ΞΕ. Κίνησίς τε στήσεται καὶ στάσις αὖ κινηθήσεται· περὶ γὰρ ἀμφότερα θάτερον ὁποτερονοῦν γιγνόμενον αὐτοῖν ἀναγκάσει μεταβάλλειν αὖ θάτερον ἐπὶ τοὐναντίον τῆς αὑτοῦ φύσεως, ἅτε B μετασχὸν τοῦ ἐναντίου.

ΘΕΑΙ. Κομιδῇ γε.

ΞΕ. Μετέχετον μὴν ἄμφω ταὐτοῦ καὶ θατέρου.

ΘΕΑΙ. Ναί.

ΞΕ. Μὴ τοίνυν λέγωμεν κίνησίν γ᾽ εἶναι ταὐτὸν ἢ θάτερον, μηδ᾽ αὖ στάσιν.

ΘΕΑΙ. Μὴ γάρ.

ΞΕ. Ἀλλ᾽ ἆρα τὸ ὂν καὶ τὸ ταὐτὸν ὡς ἕν τι διανοητέον ἡμῖν;

ΘΕΑΙ. Ἴσως.

ΞΕ. Ἀλλ᾽ εἰ τὸ ὂν καὶ τὸ ταὐτὸν μηδὲν διάφορον σημαίνετον, κίνησιν αὖ πάλιν καὶ στάσιν ἀμφότερα

[1] αὐτώ] αυτοῦ B; αὑτοῦ T.

THE SOPHIST

THEAET. Yes.

STR. But what do we mean by these words, "the same" and "other," which we have just used? Are they two new classes, different from the other three, but always of necessity mingled with them, and must we conduct our inquiry on the assumption that there are five classes, not three, or are we unconsciously speaking of one of those three when we say "the same" or "other"?

THEAET. Perhaps.

STR. But certainly motion and rest are neither other nor the same.

THEAET. How so?

STR. Whatever term we apply to rest and motion in common cannot be either of those two.

THEAET. Why not?

STR. Because motion would be at rest and rest would be in motion; in respect of both, for whichever of the two became "other" would force the other to change its nature into that of its opposite, since it would participate in its opposite.

THEAET. Exactly so.

STR. Both certainly partake of the same and the other.[1]

THEAET. Yes.

STR. Then we must not say that motion, or rest either, is the same or other.

THEAET. No.

STR. But should we conceive of "being" and "the same" as one?

THEAET. Perhaps.

STR. But if "being" and "the same" have no difference of meaning, then when we go on and say

[1] *i.e.*, sameness and difference can be predicated of both.

407

εἶναι λέγοντες ἀμφότερα οὕτως αὐτὰ ταὐτὸν ὡς
C ὄντα προσεροῦμεν.

ΘΕΑΙ. Ἀλλὰ μὴν τοῦτό γε ἀδύνατον.

ΞΕ. Ἀδύνατον ἄρα ταὐτὸν καὶ τὸ ὂν ἓν εἶναι.

ΘΕΑΙ. Σχεδόν.

ΞΕ. Τέταρτον δὴ πρὸς τοῖς τρισὶν εἴδεσι [1] τὸ
ταὐτὸν τιθῶμεν;

ΘΕΑΙ. Πάνυ μὲν οὖν.

ΞΕ. Τί δέ; τὸ θάτερον ἆρα ἡμῖν λεκτέον πέμπτον;
ἢ τοῦτο καὶ τὸ ὂν ὡς δύ' ἄττα ὀνόματα ἐφ' ἑνὶ γένει
διανοεῖσθαι δεῖ;

ΘΕΑΙ. Τάχ' ἄν.

ΞΕ. Ἀλλ' οἶμαί σε συγχωρεῖν τῶν ὄντων τὰ μὲν
αὐτὰ καθ' αὑτά, τὰ δὲ πρὸς ἄλλα [2] ἀεὶ λέγεσθαι.

ΘΕΑΙ. Τί δ' οὔ;

D ΞΕ. Τὸ δ' ἕτερον ἀεὶ πρὸς ἕτερον· ἦ γάρ;

ΘΕΑΙ. Οὕτως.

ΞΕ. Οὐκ ἄν, εἴ γε τὸ ὂν καὶ τὸ θάτερον μὴ
πάμπολυ διεφερέτην· ἀλλ' εἴπερ θάτερον ἀμφοῖν
μετεῖχε τοῖν εἰδοῖν ὥσπερ τὸ ὄν, ἦν ἄν ποτέ τι καὶ
τῶν ἑτέρων ἕτερον οὐ πρὸς ἕτερον· νῦν δὲ ἀτεχνῶς
ἡμῖν, ὅτιπερ ἂν ἕτερον ᾖ, συμβέβηκεν ἐξ ἀνάγκης
ἑτέρου τοῦτο ὅπερ ἐστὶν εἶναι.

ΘΕΑΙ. Λέγεις καθάπερ ἔχει.

ΞΕ. Πέμπτον δὴ τὴν θατέρου φύσιν λεκτέον ἐν
E τοῖς εἴδεσιν οὖσαν, ἐν οἷς προαιρούμεθα.

ΘΕΑΙ. Ναί.

ΞΕ. Καὶ διὰ πάντων γε αὐτὴν αὐτῶν φήσομεν
εἶναι διεληλυθυῖαν· ἓν ἕκαστον γὰρ ἕτερον εἶναι

---

[1] εἴδεσι ΒΤ; εἴδεσιν εἶδος W.
[2] ἄλλα TW; ἄλληλα Β.

that both rest and motion are, we shall be saying that they are both the same, since they are.

THEAET. But surely that is impossible.

STR. Then it is impossible for being and the same to be one.

THEAET. Pretty nearly.

STR. So we shall consider "the same" a fourth class in addition to the other three?

THEAET. Certainly.

STR. Then shall we call "the other" a fifth class? Or must we conceive of this and "being" as two names for one class?

THEAET. May be.

STR. But I fancy you admit that among the entities some are always conceived as absolute, and some as relative.

THEAET. Of course.

STR. And other is always relative to other, is it not?

THEAET. Yes.

STR. It would not be so, if being and the other were not utterly different. If the other, like being, partook of both absolute and relative existence, there would be also among the others that exist another not in relation to any other; but as it is, we find that whatever is other is just what it is through compulsion of some other.

THEAET. The facts are as you say.

STR. Then we must place the nature of "the other" as a fifth among the classes in which we select our examples.

THEAET. Yes.

STR. And we shall say that it permeates them all; for each of them is other than the rest, not by reason

τῶν ἄλλων οὐ διὰ τὴν αὑτοῦ φύσιν, ἀλλὰ διὰ τὸ
μετέχειν τῆς ἰδέας τῆς θατέρου.

ΘΕΑΙ. Κομιδῇ μὲν οὖν.

41. ΞΕ. Ὧδε δὴ λέγωμεν ἐπὶ τῶν πέντε καθ᾽
ἓν ἀναλαμβάνοντες.

ΘΕΑΙ. Πῶς;

ΞΕ. Πρῶτον μὲν κίνησιν, ὡς ἔστι παντάπασιν
ἕτερον στάσεως. ἢ πῶς λέγωμεν;

ΘΕΑΙ. Οὕτως.

ΞΕ. Οὐ στάσις ἄρ᾽ ἐστίν.

ΘΕΑΙ. Οὐδαμῶς.

256 ΞΕ. Ἔστι δέ γε διὰ τὸ μετέχειν τοῦ ὄντος.

ΘΕΑΙ. Ἔστιν.

ΞΕ. Αὖθις δὴ πάλιν ἡ κίνησις ἕτερον ταὐτοῦ ἐστιν.

ΘΕΑΙ. Σχεδόν.

ΞΕ. Οὐ ταὐτὸν ἄρα ἐστίν.

ΘΕΑΙ. Οὐ γὰρ οὖν.

ΞΕ. Ἀλλὰ μὴν αὕτη γ᾽ ἦν ταὐτὸν διὰ τὸ μετέχειν
αὖ πάντ᾽ αὐτοῦ.

ΘΕΑΙ. Καὶ μάλα.

ΞΕ. Τὴν κίνησιν δὴ ταὐτόν τε εἶναι καὶ μὴ ταὐτὸν
ὁμολογητέον καὶ οὐ δυσχεραντέον. οὐ γὰρ ὅταν
εἴπωμεν αὐτὴν ταὐτὸν καὶ μὴ ταὐτόν, ὁμοίως
εἰρήκαμεν, ἀλλ᾽ ὁπόταν μὲν ταὐτόν, διὰ τὴν μέθεξιν
B ταὐτοῦ πρὸς ἑαυτὴν οὕτω λέγομεν,[1] ὅταν δὲ μὴ
ταὐτόν, διὰ τὴν κοινωνίαν αὖ θατέρου, δι᾽ ἣν
ἀποχωριζομένη ταὐτοῦ γέγονεν οὐκ ἐκεῖνο ἀλλ᾽
ἕτερον, ὥστε ὀρθῶς αὖ λέγεται πάλιν οὐ ταὐτόν.

ΘΕΑΙ. Πάνυ μὲν οὖν.

ΞΕ. Οὐκοῦν κἂν εἴ πῃ μεταλάμβανεν αὐτὴ

---

[1] λέγομεν W ; λέγωμεν BT.

410

of its own nature, but because it partakes of the idea of the other.

THEAET. Exactly.

STR. Let us now state our conclusions, taking up the five classes one at a time.

THEAET. How?

STR. Take motion first; we say that it is entirely other than rest, do we not?

THEAET. We do.

STR. Then it is not rest.

THEAET. Not at all.

STR. But it exists, by reason of its participation in being.

THEAET. Yes, it exists.

STR. Now motion again is other than the same.

THEAET. You're about right.

STR. Therefore it is not the same.

THEAET. No, it is not.

STR. But yet we found it was the same, because all things partake of the same.

THEAET. Certainly.

STR. Then we must admit that motion is the same and is not the same, and we must not be disturbed thereby; for when we say it is the same and not the same, we do not use the words alike. When we call it the same, we do so because it partakes of the same in relation to itself, and when we call it not the same, we do so on account of its participation in the other, by which it is separated from the same and becomes not that but other, so that it is correctly spoken of in turn as not the same.

THEAET. Yes, certainly.

STR. Then even if absolute motion partook in

κίνησις στάσεως, οὐδὲν ἂν ἄτοπον ἦν στάσιμον
αὐτὴν προσαγορεύειν;

ΘΕΑΙ. Ὀρθότατά γε, εἴπερ τῶν γενῶν συγχωρησόμεθα τὰ μὲν ἀλλήλοις ἐθέλειν μίγνυσθαι, τὰ
δὲ μή.

C ΞΕ. Καὶ μὴν ἐπί γε τὴν τούτου πρότερον ἀπόδειξιν ἢ τῶν νῦν ἀφικόμεθα, ἐλέγχοντες ὡς ἔστι
κατὰ φύσιν ταύτῃ.

ΘΕΑΙ. Πῶς γὰρ οὔ;

ΞΕ. Λέγωμεν δὴ πάλιν· ἡ κίνησίς ἐστιν ἕτερον
τοῦ ἑτέρου, καθάπερ ταὐτοῦ τε ἦν ἄλλο καὶ τῆς
στάσεως;

ΘΕΑΙ. Ἀναγκαῖον.

ΞΕ. Οὐχ ἕτερον ἄρ' ἐστί πῃ καὶ ἕτερον κατὰ τὸν
νῦν δὴ λόγον.

ΘΕΑΙ. Ἀληθῆ.

ΞΕ. Τί οὖν δὴ τὸ μετὰ τοῦτο; ἆρ' αὖ [1] τῶν μὲν
τριῶν ἕτερον αὐτὴν φήσομεν εἶναι, τοῦ δὲ τετάρτου
μὴ φῶμεν, ὁμολογήσαντες αὐτὰ εἶναι πέντε, περὶ
D ὧν καὶ ἐν οἷς προυθέμεθα σκοπεῖν;

ΘΕΑΙ. Καὶ πῶς; ἀδύνατον γὰρ συγχωρεῖν ἐλάττω
τὸν ἀριθμὸν τοῦ νῦν δὴ φανέντος.

ΞΕ. Ἀδεῶς ἄρα τὴν κίνησιν ἕτερον εἶναι τοῦ
ὄντος διαμαχόμενοι λέγωμεν;

ΘΕΑΙ. Ἀδεέστατα μὲν οὖν.

ΞΕ. Οὐκοῦν δὴ σαφῶς ἡ κίνησις ὄντως οὐκ ὄν
ἐστι καὶ ὄν, ἐπείπερ τοῦ ὄντος μετέχει;

ΘΕΑΙ. Σαφέστατά γε.

ΞΕ. Ἔστιν ἄρα ἐξ ἀνάγκης τὸ μὴ ὂν ἐπί τε κινήσεως εἶναι καὶ κατὰ πάντα τὰ γένη. κατὰ πάντα
E γὰρ ἡ θατέρου φύσις ἕτερον ἀπεργαζομένη τοῦ

[1] αὖ Heindorf; οὐ ΒΤ.

any way of rest, it would not be absurd to say it was at rest?

THEAET. It would be perfectly right, if we are to admit that some of the classes will mingle with one another, and others will not.

STR. And surely we demonstrated that before we took up our present points; we proved that it was according to nature.[1]

THEAET. Yes, of course.

STR. Then let us recapitulate: Motion is other than the other, just as we found it to be other than the same and than rest. Is that true?

THEAET. Inevitably.

STR. Then it is in a sense not other and also other, according to our present reasoning.

THEAET. True.

STR. Now how about the next point? Shall we say next that motion is other than the three, but not other than the fourth,—that is, if we have agreed that the classes about which and within which we undertook to carry on our inquiry are five in number?

THEAET. How can we say that? For we cannot admit that the number is less than was shown just now.

STR. Then we may fearlessly persist in contending that motion is other than being?

THEAET. Yes, most fearlessly.

STR. It is clear, then, that motion really is not, and also that it is, since it partakes of being?

THEAET. That is perfectly clear.

STR. In relation to motion, then, not-being is That is inevitable. And this extends to all the classes; for in all of them the nature of other so operates as to make each one other than being, and

[1] See 251 E ff.

ὄντος ἕκαστον οὐκ ὂν ποιεῖ, καὶ ξύμπαντα δὴ κατὰ
ταὐτὰ οὕτως οὐκ ὄντα ὀρθῶς ἐροῦμεν, καὶ πάλιν,
ὅτι μετέχει τοῦ ὄντος, εἶναί τε καὶ ὄντα.

ΘΕΑΙ. Κινδυνεύει.

ΞΕ. Περὶ ἕκαστον ἄρα τῶν εἰδῶν πολὺ μέν ἐστι
τὸ ὄν, ἄπειρον δὲ πλήθει τὸ μὴ ὄν.

ΘΕΑΙ. Ἔοικεν.

257   ΞΕ. Οὐκοῦν καὶ τὸ ὂν αὐτὸ τῶν ἄλλων ἕτερον
εἶναι λεκτέον.

ΘΕΑΙ. Ἀνάγκη.

ΞΕ. Καὶ τὸ ὂν ἄρ' ἡμῖν, ὅσαπέρ ἐστι τὰ ἄλλα,
κατὰ τοσαῦτα οὐκ ἔστιν· ἐκεῖνα γὰρ οὐκ ὂν ἓν
μὲν αὐτό ἐστιν, ἀπέραντα δὲ τὸν ἀριθμὸν τἆλλα
οὐκ ἔστιν αὖ.

ΘΕΑΙ. Σχεδὸν οὕτως.

ΞΕ. Οὐκοῦν δὴ καὶ ταῦτα οὐ δυσχεραντέον, ἐπείπερ ἔχει κοινωνίαν ἀλλήλοις ἡ τῶν γενῶν φύσις. εἰ
δέ τις ταῦτα μὴ συγχωρεῖ, πείσας ἡμῶν τοὺς
ἔμπροσθεν λόγους οὕτω πειθέτω τὰ μετὰ ταῦτα.

ΘΕΑΙ. Δικαιότατα εἴρηκας.

B   ΞΕ. Ἴδωμεν[1] δὴ καὶ τόδε.

ΘΕΑΙ. Τὸ ποῖον;

ΞΕ. Ὁπόταν τὸ μὴ ὂν λέγωμεν, ὡς ἔοικεν, οὐκ
ἐναντίον τι λέγομεν τοῦ ὄντος, ἀλλ' ἕτερον μόνον.

ΘΕΑΙ. Πῶς;

---

[1] ἴδωμεν W ; εἰδῶμεν B ; εἴδωμεν T.

---

[1] Being is many, for each and every thing in all the
classes is ; but not-being is infinite, for not only is it true
that every thing in each of the classes is not, but not-being
extends also to all conceptions which do not and cannot
have any reality.

therefore not-being. So we may, from this point of view, rightly say of all of them alike that they are not; and again, since they partake of being, that they are and have being.

THEAET. Yes, I suppose so.

STR. And so, in relation to each of the classes, being is many, and not-being is infinite in number.[1]

THEAET. So it seems.

STR. Then being itself must also be said to be other than all other things.

THEAET. Yes, it must.

STR. And we conclude that whatever the number of other things is, just that is the number of the things in relation to which being is not; for not being those things, it is itself one, and again, those other things are not unlimited in number.

THEAET. That is not far from the truth.

STR. Then we must not be disturbed by this either, since by their nature the classes have participation in one another. But if anyone refuses to accept our present results, let him reckon with our previous arguments and then proceed to reckon with the next step.[2]

THEAET. That is very fair.

STR. Then here is a point to consider.

THEAET. What is it?

STR. When we say not-being, we speak, I think, not of something that is the opposite of being, but only of something different.

THEAET. What do you mean?

---

[2] *i.e.*, if he will not accept our proof that being is not, etc., he must disprove our arguments respecting the participation of ideas in one another, and then proceed to draw his inference.

ΞΕ. Οἷον ὅταν εἴπωμέν τι μὴ μέγα, τότε μᾶλλόν τί σοι φαινόμεθα τὸ σμικρὸν ἢ τὸ ἴσον δηλοῦν τῷ ῥήματι;

ΘΕΑΙ. Καὶ πῶς;

ΞΕ. Οὐκ ἄρ', ἐναντίον ὅταν ἀπόφασις λέγηται σημαίνειν, συγχωρησόμεθα, τοσοῦτον δὲ μόνον, ὅτι τῶν ἄλλων τὶ μηνύει τὸ μὴ καὶ τὸ οὗ προτιθέμενα C τῶν ἐπιόντων ὀνομάτων, μᾶλλον δὲ τῶν πραγμάτων περὶ ἅττ' ἂν κέηται τὰ ἐπιφθεγγόμενα ὕστερον τῆς ἀποφάσεως ὀνόματα.

ΘΕΑΙ. Παντάπασι μὲν οὖν.

42. ΞΕ. Τόδε δὲ διανοηθῶμεν, εἰ καὶ σοὶ ξυνδοκεῖ.

ΘΕΑΙ. Τὸ ποῖον;

ΞΕ. Ἡ θατέρου μοι φύσις φαίνεται κατακεκερματίσθαι καθάπερ ἐπιστήμη.

ΘΕΑΙ. Πῶς;

ΞΕ. Μία μέν ἐστί που καὶ ἐκείνη,[1] τὸ δ' ἐπί τῳ γιγνόμενον μέρος αὐτῆς ἕκαστον ἀφορισθὲν ἐπω- D νυμίαν ἴσχει τινὰ ἑαυτῆς ἰδίαν· διὸ πολλαὶ τέχναι τ' εἰσὶ[2] λεγόμεναι καὶ ἐπιστῆμαι.

ΘΕΑΙ. Πάνυ μὲν οὖν.

ΞΕ. Οὐκοῦν καὶ τὰ τῆς θατέρου φύσεως μόρια μιᾶς οὔσης ταὐτὸν πέπονθε τοῦτο.

ΘΕΑΙ. Τάχ' ἄν· ἀλλ' ὅπῃ δὴ[3] λέγωμεν.

ΞΕ. Ἔστι τῷ καλῷ τι θατέρου μόριον ἀντιτιθέμενον;

ΘΕΑΙ. Ἔστιν.

ΞΕ. Τοῦτ' οὖν ἀνώνυμον ἐροῦμεν ἤ τιν' ἔχον ἐπωνυμίαν;

---

[1] ἐκείνη W ; ἐκείνῃ ΒΤ.   [2] τέ εἰσι W ; τεῖσι Τ ; τισιν Β.
[3] ἀλλ' ὅπῃ δὴ W ; ἄλλό πῃ Τ ; ἄλλο πῆ Β.

THE SOPHIST

STR. For instance, when we speak of a thing as not great, do we seem to you to mean by the expression what is small any more than what is of middle size?

THEAET. No, of course not.

STR. Then when we are told that the negative signifies the opposite, we shall not admit it; we shall admit only that the particle "not"[1] indicates something different from the words to which it is prefixed, or rather from the things denoted by the words that follow the negative.

THEAET. Certainly.

STR. Let us consider another point and see if you agree with me.

THEAET. What is it?

STR. It seems to me that the nature of the other is all cut up into little bits, like knowledge.

THEAET. What do you mean?

STR. Knowledge, like other, is one, but each separate part of it which applies to some particular subject has a name of its own; hence there are many arts, as they are called, and kinds of knowledge, or sciences.

THEAET. Yes, certainly.

STR. And the same is true, by their nature, of the parts of the other, though it also is one concept.

THEAET. Perhaps; but let us discuss the matter and see how it comes about.

STR. Is there a part of the other which is opposed to the beautiful?

THEAET. There is.

STR. Shall we say that this is nameless or that it has a name?

[1] The two particles οὐ and μή in Greek.

417

ΘΕΑΙ. Ἔχον· ὃ γὰρ μὴ καλὸν ἑκάστοτε φθεγγόμεθα, τοῦτο οὐκ ἄλλου τινὸς ἕτερόν ἐστιν ἢ τῆς τοῦ καλοῦ φύσεως.

ΞΕ. Ἴθι νῦν τόδε μοι λέγε.

E ΘΕΑΙ. Τὸ ποῖον;

ΞΕ. Ἄλλο τι τῶν ὄντων τινὸς ἑνὸς γένους [1] ἀφορισθὲν καὶ πρός τι τῶν ὄντων αὖ πάλιν ἀντιτεθὲν οὕτω ξυμβέβηκεν εἶναι [2] τὸ μὴ καλόν;

ΘΕΑΙ. Οὕτως.

ΞΕ. Ὄντος δὴ πρὸς ὂν [3] ἀντίθεσις, ὡς ἔοικ', εἶναί τις [4] συμβαίνει τὸ μὴ καλόν.

ΘΕΑΙ. Ὀρθότατα.

ΞΕ. Τί οὖν; κατὰ τοῦτον τὸν λόγον ἆρα μᾶλλον μὲν τὸ καλὸν ἡμῖν ἐστι τῶν ὄντων, ἧττον δὲ τὸ μὴ καλόν;

ΘΕΑΙ. Οὐδέν.

258 ΞΕ. Ὁμοίως ἄρα τὸ μὴ μέγα καὶ τὸ μέγα αὐτὸ εἶναι λεκτέον;

ΘΕΑΙ. Ὁμοίως.

ΞΕ. Οὐκοῦν καὶ τὸ μὴ δίκαιον τῷ δικαίῳ κατὰ ταὐτὰ θετέον πρὸς τὸ μηδέν τι μᾶλλον εἶναι θάτερον θατέρου;

ΘΕΑΙ. Τί μήν;

ΞΕ. Καὶ τἆλλα δὴ ταύτῃ λέξομεν, ἐπείπερ ἡ θατέρου φύσις ἐφάνη τῶν ὄντων οὖσα, ἐκείνης δὲ οὔσης ἀνάγκη δὴ καὶ τὰ μόρια αὐτῆς μηδενὸς ἧττον ὄντα τιθέναι.

ΘΕΑΙ. Πῶς γὰρ οὔ;

B ΞΕ. Οὐκοῦν, ὡς ἔοικεν, ἡ τῆς θατέρου μορίου φύσεως καὶ τῆς τοῦ ὄντος πρὸς ἄλληλα ἀντι-

---

[1] ἑνὸς γένους T; γένους B.
[2] ξυμβέβηκεν εἶναι Stephanus; ξυμβεβηκέναι BT.

THEAET. That it has one; for that which in each case we call not-beautiful is surely the other of the nature of the beautiful and of nothing else.

STR. Now, then, tell me something more.

THEAET. What?

STR. Does it not result from this that the not-beautiful is a distinct part of some one class of being and also, again, opposed to some class of being?

THEAET. Yes.

STR. Then, apparently, it follows that the not-beautiful is a contrast of being with being.

THEAET. Quite right.

STR. Can we, then, in that case, say that the beautiful is more and the not-beautiful less a part of being?

THEAET. Not at all.

STR. Hence the not-great must be said to be no less truly than the great?

THEAET. No less truly.

STR. And so we must recognize the same relation between the just and the not-just, in so far as neither has any more being than the other?

THEAET. Of course.

STR. And we shall, then, say the same of other things, since the nature of the other is proved to possess real being; and if it has being, we must necessarily ascribe being in no less degree to its parts also.

THEAET. Of course.

STR. Then, as it seems, the opposition of the nature of a part of the other, and of the nature of being, when they are opposed to one another, is no

---

κειμένων ἀντίθεσις οὐδὲν ἧττον, εἰ θέμις εἰπεῖν,
αὐτοῦ τοῦ ὄντος οὐσία ἐστίν, οὐκ ἐναντίον ἐκείνῳ
σημαίνουσα, ἀλλὰ τοσοῦτον μόνον, ἕτερον ἐκείνου.

ΘΕΑΙ. Σαφέστατά γε.

ΞΕ. Τίν' οὖν αὐτὴν προσείπωμεν;

ΘΕΑΙ. Δῆλον ὅτι τὸ μὴ ὄν, ὃ διὰ τὸν σοφιστὴν
ἐζητοῦμεν, αὐτό ἐστι τοῦτο.

ΞΕ. Πότερον οὖν, ὥσπερ εἶπες, ἔστιν οὐδενὸς
τῶν ἄλλων οὐσίας ἐλλειπόμενον, καὶ δεῖ θαρροῦντα
ἤδη λέγειν ὅτι τὸ μὴ ὂν βεβαίως ἐστὶ τὴν αὑτοῦ
C φύσιν ἔχον, ὥσπερ τὸ μέγα ἦν μέγα καὶ τὸ καλὸν
ἦν καλὸν καὶ τὸ μὴ μέγα μὴ μέγα [1] καὶ τὸ μὴ καλὸν
μὴ καλόν,[2] οὕτω δὲ καὶ τὸ μὴ ὂν κατὰ ταὐτὸν ἦν
τε καὶ ἔστι μὴ ὄν, ἐνάριθμον τῶν πολλῶν ὄντων
εἶδος ἕν; ἤ τινα ἔτι πρὸς αὐτό, ὦ Θεαίτητε, ἀ-
πιστίαν ἔχομεν;

ΘΕΑΙ. Οὐδεμίαν.

43. ΞΕ. Οἶσθ' οὖν ὅτι Παρμενίδῃ μακροτέρως
τῆς ἀπορρήσεως ἠπιστήκαμεν;

ΘΕΑΙ. Τί δή;

ΞΕ. Πλεῖον ἢ 'κεῖνος ἀπεῖπε σκοπεῖν, ἡμεῖς εἰς
τὸ πρόσθεν ἔτι ζητήσαντες ἀπεδείξαμεν αὐτῷ.

ΘΕΑΙ. Πῶς;

D ΞΕ. Ὅτι ὁ μέν πού φησιν,

οὐ γὰρ μή ποτε τοῦτο δαμῇ,[3] εἶναι μὴ ἐόντα,[4]
ἀλλὰ σὺ τῆσδ' ἀφ' ὁδοῦ διζήσιος [5] εἶργε νόημα.

ΘΕΑΙ. Λέγει γὰρ οὖν οὕτως.

---

[1] μὴ μέγα add. Boeckh.
[2] μὴ καλόν add. Boeckh.
[3] τοῦτο δαμῇ Simplicius ; τοῦτ' οὐδαμῇ BT.
[4] ἐόντα Aristot. ; ὄντα BT.
[5] διζήσιος BT (cf. 237 Α).

less truly existence than is being itself, if it is not wrong for me to say so, for it signifies not the opposite of being, but only the other of being, and nothing more.

THEAET. That is perfectly clear.

STR. Then what shall we call this?

THEAET. Evidently this is precisely not-being, which we were looking for because of the sophist.

STR. And is this, as you were saying, as fully endowed with being as anything else, and shall we henceforth say with confidence that not-being has an assured existence and a nature of its own? Just as we found that the great was great and the beautiful was beautiful, the not-great was not-great and the not-beautiful was not-beautiful, shall we in the same way say that not-being was and is not-being, to be counted as one class among the many classes of being? Or have we, Theaetetus, any remaining distrust about the matter?

THEAET. None whatever.

STR. Do you observe, then, that we have gone farther in our distrust of Parmenides than the limit set by his prohibition?

THEAET. What do you mean?

STR. We have proceeded farther in our investigation and have shown him more than that which he forbade us to examine.

THEAET. How so?

STR. Because he says somewhere [1]:

Never shall this thought prevail, that not-being is;
Nay, keep your mind from this path of investigation.

THEAET. Yes, that is what he says.

[1] Parmenides, 52 f., ed. Mullach.

PLATO

ΞΕ. Ἡμεῖς δέ γε οὐ μόνον ὡς ἔστι τὰ μὴ ὄντα ἀπεδείξαμεν, ἀλλὰ καὶ τὸ εἶδος ὃ τυγχάνει ὂν τοῦ μὴ ὄντος ἀπεφηνάμεθα· τὴν γὰρ θατέρου φύσιν ἀποδείξαντες οὐσάν τε καὶ κατακεκερματισμένην Ε ἐπὶ πάντα τὰ ὄντα πρὸς ἄλληλα, τὸ πρὸς τὸ ὂν ἕκαστον¹ μόριον αὐτῆς ἀντιτιθέμενον ἐτολμήσαμεν εἰπεῖν ὡς αὐτὸ τοῦτό ἐστιν ὄντως τὸ μὴ ὄν.

ΘΕΑΙ. Καὶ παντάπασί γε, ὦ ξένε, ἀληθέστατά μοι δοκοῦμεν εἰρηκέναι.

ΞΕ. Μὴ τοίνυν ἡμᾶς εἴπῃ τις ὅτι τοὐναντίον τοῦ ὄντος τὸ μὴ ὂν ἀποφαινόμενοι τολμῶμεν λέγειν ὡς ἔστιν. ἡμεῖς γὰρ περὶ μὲν ἐναντίου τινὸς αὐτῷ χαίρειν πάλαι λέγομεν, εἴτ' ἔστιν εἴτε μή, λόγον 259 ἔχον ἢ καὶ παντάπασιν ἄλογον· ὃ δὲ νῦν εἰρήκαμεν εἶναι τὸ μὴ ὄν, ἢ πεισάτω τις ὡς οὐ καλῶς λέγομεν ἐλέγξας, ἢ μέχριπερ ἂν ἀδυνατῇ, λεκτέον καὶ ἐκείνῳ καθάπερ ἡμεῖς λέγομεν, ὅτι συμμίγνυταί τε ἀλλήλοις τὰ γένη καὶ τό τε ὂν καὶ θάτερον διὰ πάντων καὶ δι' ἀλλήλων διεληλυθότα τὸ μὲν ἕτερον μετασχὸν τοῦ ὄντος ἔστι μὲν διὰ ταύτην τὴν μέθεξιν, οὐ μὴν ἐκεῖνό γε οὗ μετέσχεν ἀλλ' ἕτερον, ἕτερον δὲ τοῦ ὄντος ὂν ἔστι σαφέστατα ἐξ ἀνάγκης εἶναι μὴ ὄν· Β τὸ δὲ ὂν αὖ θατέρου μετειληφὸς ἕτερον τῶν ἄλλων ἂν εἴη γενῶν, ἕτερον δ' ἐκείνων ἁπάντων ὂν οὐκ ἔστιν ἕκαστον αὐτῶν οὐδὲ ξύμπαντα τὰ ἄλλα πλὴν αὑτό, ὥστε τὸ ὂν ἀναμφισβητήτως αὖ μυρία ἐπὶ μυρίοις οὐκ ἔστι, καὶ τἆλλα δὴ καθ' ἕκαστον οὕτω καὶ ξύμπαντα πολλαχῇ μὲν ἔστι, πολλαχῇ δ' οὐκ ἔστιν.

ΘΕΑΙ. Ἀληθῆ.

¹ ἕκαστον Simplicius ; ἑκάστου ΒΤ.

THE SOPHIST

STR. But we have not only pointed out that things which are not exist, but we have even shown what the form or class of not-being is; for we have pointed out that the nature of the other exists and is distributed in small bits throughout all existing things in their relations to one another, and we have ventured to say that each part of the other which is contrasted with being, really is exactly not-being.

THEAET. And certainly, Stranger, I think that what we have said is perfectly true.

STR. Then let not anyone assert that we declare that not-being is the opposite of being, and hence are so rash as to say that not-being exists. For we long ago gave up speaking of any opposite of being, whether it exists or not and is capable or totally incapable of definition. But as for our present definition of not-being, a man must either refute us and show that we are wrong, or, so long as he cannot do that, he too must say, as we do, that the classes mingle with one another, and being and the other permeate all things, including each other, and the other, since it participates in being, is, by reason of this participation, yet is not that in which it participates, but other, and since it is other than being, must inevitably be not-being. But being, in turn, participates in the other and is therefore other than the rest of the classes, and since it is other than all of them, it is not each one of them or all the rest, but only itself; there is therefore no doubt that there are thousands and thousands of things which being is not, and just so all other things, both individually and collectively, in many relations are, and in many are not.

THEAET. True.

ΞΕ. Καὶ ταύταις δὴ ταῖς ἐναντιώσεσιν εἴτε ἀπιστεῖ τις, σκεπτέον αὐτῷ καὶ λεκτέον βέλτιόν τι τῶν C νῦν εἰρημένων· εἴτε ὥς τι χαλεπὸν κατανενοηκὼς χαίρει τοτὲ μὲν ἐπὶ θάτερα τοτὲ δ' ἐπὶ θάτερα τοὺς λόγους ἕλκων, οὐκ ἄξια πολλῆς σπουδῆς ἐσπούδακεν, ὡς οἱ νῦν λόγοι φασί. τοῦτο μὲν γὰρ οὔτε τι κομψὸν οὔτε χαλεπὸν εὑρεῖν, ἐκεῖνο δ' ἤδη καὶ χαλεπὸν ἅμα καὶ καλόν.

ΘΕΑΙ. Τὸ ποῖον;

ΞΕ. Ὃ καὶ πρόσθεν εἴρηται, τὸ ταῦτα ἐάσαντα ὡς δυνατὰ[1] τοῖς λεγομένοις οἷόν τ' εἶναι καθ' ἕκαστον ἐλέγχοντα ἐπακολουθεῖν, ὅταν τέ τις ἕτερον ὄν πῃ ταὐτὸν εἶναι φῇ καὶ ὅταν ταὐτὸν ὂν D ἕτερον, ἐκείνῃ καὶ κατ' ἐκεῖνο ὅ φησι τούτων πεπονθέναι πότερον. τὸ δὲ ταὐτὸν ἕτερον ἀποφαίνειν ἁμῇ γέ πῃ καὶ τὸ θάτερον ταὐτὸν καὶ τὸ μέγα σμικρὸν καὶ τὸ ὅμοιον ἀνόμοιον, καὶ χαίρειν οὕτω τἀναντία ἀεὶ προφέροντα ἐν τοῖς λόγοις, οὔτε τις ἔλεγχος οὗτος ἀληθινὸς ἄρτι τε τῶν ὄντων τινὸς ἐφαπτομένου δῆλος νεογενὴς ὤν.

ΘΕΑΙ. Κομιδῇ μὲν οὖν.

44. ΞΕ. Καὶ γάρ, ὠγαθέ, τό γε πᾶν ἀπὸ παντὸς ἐπιχειρεῖν ἀποχωρίζειν ἄλλως τε οὐκ ἐμμελὲς E καὶ δὴ καὶ παντάπασιν ἀμούσου τινὸς καὶ ἀφιλοσόφου.

ΘΕΑΙ. Τί δή;

ΞΕ. Τελεωτάτη πάντων λόγων ἐστὶν ἀφάνισις τὸ διαλύειν ἕκαστον ἀπὸ πάντων· διὰ γὰρ τὴν

---

[1] δυνατὰ BTW; δυνατώτατα Schanz; ἀνήνυτα Badham; δυνατὸν μάλιστα Campbell; δέον αὐτὰ? Apelt.; δυνατὰ is certainly wrong. Possibly οὐκ ὄντα or οὐκ ἄξια (the interpretation adopted in the translation).

STR. And if any man has doubts about these oppositions, he must make investigations and advance better doctrines than these of ours; or if he finds pleasure in dragging words about and applying them to different things at different times, with the notion that he has invented something difficult to explain, our present argument asserts that he has taken up seriously matters which are not worth serious attention; for this process is neither clever nor difficult, whereas here now is something both difficult and beautiful.

THEAET. What is it?

STR. What I have spoken of before—the ability to let those quibbles go as of no account and to follow and refute in detail the arguments of a man who says that other is in a sense the same, or that the same is other, and to do this from that point of view and with regard for those relations which he presupposes for either of these conditions. But to show that in some sort of fashion the same is the other, and the other the same, and the great small, and the like unlike, and to take pleasure in thus always bringing forward opposites in the argument,—all that is no true refutation, but is plainly the newborn offspring of some brain that has just begun to lay hold upon the problem of realities.

THEAET. Exactly so.

STR. For certainly, my friend, the attempt to separate everything from everything else is not only not in good taste but also shows that a man is utterly uncultivated and unphilosophical.

THEAET. Why so?

STR. The complete separation of each thing from all is the utterly final obliteration of all discourse.

ἀλλήλων τῶν εἰδῶν συμπλοκὴν ὁ λόγος γέγονεν
ἡμῖν.

ΘΕΑΙ. Ἀληθῆ.

260 ΞΕ. Σκόπει τοίνυν ὡς ἐν καιρῷ νῦν δὴ τοῖς
τοιούτοις διεμαχόμεθα καὶ προσηναγκάζομεν ἐὰν
ἕτερον ἑτέρῳ μίγνυσθαι.

ΘΕΑΙ. Πρὸς δὴ τί;

ΞΕ. Πρὸς τὸ τὸν ¹ λόγον ἡμῖν τῶν ὄντων ἕν τι
γενῶν εἶναι. τούτου γὰρ στερηθέντες, τὸ μὲν
μέγιστον, φιλοσοφίας ἂν στερηθεῖμεν, ἔτι δ' ἐν τῷ
παρόντι δεῖ λόγον ἡμᾶς διομολογήσασθαι τί ποτ'
ἔστιν, εἰ δὲ ἀφῃρέθημεν αὐτὸ μηδ' εἶναι τὸ παράπαν,
οὐδὲν ἂν ἔτι που λέγειν οἷοί τ' ἦμεν· ἀφῃρέθημεν
B δ' ἄν, εἰ συνεχωρήσαμεν μηδεμίαν εἶναι μῖξιν
μηδενὶ πρὸς μηδέν.

ΘΕΑΙ. Ὀρθῶς τοῦτό γε· λόγον δὲ δι' ὅ τι νῦν
διομολογητέον οὐκ ἔμαθον.

ΞΕ. Ἀλλ' ἴσως τῇδ' ἑπόμενος ῥᾷστ' ἂν μάθοις.

ΘΕΑΙ. Πῆ;

ΞΕ. Τὸ μὲν δὴ μὴ ὂν ἡμῖν ἕν τι τῶν ἄλλων
γένος ὂν ἀνεφάνη, κατὰ πάντα τὰ ὄντα διεσπαρμένον.

ΘΕΑΙ. Οὕτως.

ΞΕ. Οὐκοῦν τὸ μετὰ τοῦτο σκεπτέον εἰ δόξῃ τε
καὶ λόγῳ μίγνυται.

ΘΕΑΙ. Τί δή;

¹ τὸν W; om. BT.

---

¹ The denial, that is to say, of all interrelations of ideas
leads to purely negative results.   Examples of this are the
exclusive antithesis of being and not-being and the mutual
exclusion of rest and motion.   The difficulty is solved at

For our power of discourse is derived from the interweaving of the classes or ideas with one another.[1]

THEAET. True.

STR. Observe, then, that we have now been just in time in carrying our point against the supporters of such doctrine, and in forcing them to admit that one thing mingles with another.

THEAET. What was our object?

STR. Our object was to establish discourse as one of our classes of being. For if we were deprived of this, we should be deprived of philosophy, which would be the greatest calamity; moreover, we must at the present moment come to an agreement about the nature of discourse, and if we were robbed of it by its absolute non-existence, we could no longer discourse; and we should be robbed of it if we agreed that there is no mixture of anything with anything.

THEAET. That is true enough; but I do not understand why we must come to an agreement about discourse just now.

STR. Perhaps the easiest way for you to understand is by following this line of argument.

THEAET. What line?

STR. We found that not-being was one of the classes of being, permeating all being.

THEAET. Yes.

STR. So the next thing is to inquire whether it mingles with opinion and speech.

THEAET. Why?

once when we recognize that positive and negative are necessarily interwoven in the nature of things, that the negative has only a relative existence and is not the opposite of the positive, but only different from it.

427

ΞΕ. Μὴ μιγνυμένου μὲν αὐτοῦ τούτοις ἀναγ-
C καῖον ἀληθῆ πάντ᾽ εἶναι, μιγνυμένου δὲ δόξα τε
ψευδὴς γίγνεται καὶ λόγος· τὸ γὰρ τὰ μὴ ὄντα
δοξάζειν ἢ λέγειν, τοῦτ᾽ ἔστι που τὸ ψεῦδος ἐν
διανοίᾳ τε καὶ λόγοις γιγνόμενον.

ΘΕΑΙ. Οὕτως.

ΞΕ. Ὄντος δέ γε ψεύδους ἔστιν ἀπάτη.

ΘΕΑΙ. Ναί.

ΞΕ. Καὶ μὴν ἀπάτης οὔσης εἰδώλων τε καὶ εἰκόνων ἤδη καὶ φαντασίας πάντα ἀνάγκη μεστὰ εἶναι.

ΘΕΑΙ. Πῶς γὰρ οὔ;

ΞΕ. Τὸν δέ γε[1] σοφιστὴν ἔφαμεν ἐν τούτῳ που
D τῷ τόπῳ καταπεφευγέναι μέν, ἔξαρνον δὲ γεγονέναι τὸ παράπαν μηδ᾽ εἶναι ψεῦδος· τὸ γὰρ μὴ
ὂν οὔτε διανοεῖσθαί τινα οὔτε λέγειν· οὐσίας γὰρ
οὐδὲν οὐδαμῇ τὸ μὴ ὂν μετέχειν.

ΘΕΑΙ. Ἦν ταῦτα.

ΞΕ. Νῦν δέ γε τοῦτο μὲν ἐφάνη μετέχον τοῦ
ὄντος, ὥστε ταύτῃ μὲν ἴσως οὐκ ἂν μάχοιτο ἔτι·
τάχα δ᾽ ἂν φαίη τῶν εἰδῶν τὰ μὲν μετέχειν τοῦ μὴ
ὄντος, τὰ δ᾽ οὔ, καὶ λόγον δὴ καὶ δόξαν εἶναι τῶν
οὐ μετεχόντων, ὥστε τὴν εἰδωλοποιικὴν καὶ φαν-
E ταστικήν, ἐν ᾗ φαμεν αὐτὸν εἶναι, διαμάχοιτ᾽ ἂν
πάλιν ὡς παντάπασιν οὐκ ἔστι, ἐπειδὴ δόξα καὶ
λόγος οὐ κοινωνεῖ τοῦ μὴ ὄντος· ψεῦδος γὰρ τὸ
παράπαν οὐκ εἶναι ταύτης μὴ συνισταμένης τῆς
κοινωνίας. διὰ ταῦτ᾽ οὖν λόγον πρῶτον καὶ δόξαν
καὶ φαντασίαν διερευνητέον ὅ τί ποτ᾽ ἔστιν, ἵνα

[1] δέ γε W; δὲ ΒΤ.

---

[1] The English word "fancy," though etymologically
identical with the Greek φαντασία, has lost the close con-

STR. If it does not mingle with them, the necessary result is that all things are true, but if it does, then false opinion and false discourse come into being; for to think or say what is not—that is, I suppose, falsehood arising in mind or in words.

THEAET. So it is.

STR. But if falsehood exists, deceit exists.

THEAET. Yes.

STR. And if deceit exists, all things must be henceforth full of images and likenesses and fancies.

THEAET. Of course.

STR. But we said that the sophist had taken refuge in this region and had absolutely denied the existence of falsehood: for he said that not-being could be neither conceived nor uttered, since not-being did not in any way participate in being.

THEAET. Yes, so it was.

STR. But now not-being has been found to partake of being, and so, perhaps, he would no longer keep up the fight in this direction; but he might say that some ideas partake of not-being and some do not, and that speech and opinion are among those which do not; and he would therefore again contend that the image-making and fantastic art, in which we placed him, has absolutely no existence, since opinion and speech have no participation in not-being; for falsehood cannot possibly exist unless such participation takes place. For this reason we must first inquire into the nature of speech and opinion and fancy,[1] in order that when they are made clear we may perceive

nexion with " seeming " ($\phi\alpha\iota\nu\epsilon\sigma\theta\alpha\iota$) which the Greek retains. The Greek word is therefore more comprehensive than the English, denoting that which appears to be, whether as the result of imagination or of sensation. *Cf.* 235 D ff.

φανέντων καὶ τὴν κοινωνίαν αὐτῶν τῷ μὴ ὄντι
261 κατίδωμεν, κατιδόντες δὲ τὸ ψεῦδος ὂν ἀποδεί-
ξωμεν, ἀποδείξαντες δὲ τὸν σοφιστὴν εἰς αὐτὸ [1]
ἐνδήσωμεν, εἴπερ ἔνοχός ἐστιν, ἢ καὶ ἀπολύσαντες
ἐν ἄλλῳ γένει ζητῶμεν.

ΘΕΑΙ. Κομιδῇ γε,[2] ὦ ξένε, ἔοικεν ἀληθὲς εἶναι
τὸ περὶ τὸν σοφιστὴν κατ᾽ ἀρχὰς λεχθέν, ὅτι δυσθήρευτον εἴη τὸ γένος. φαίνεται γὰρ οὖν προβλημάτων
γέμειν, ὧν ἐπειδάν τι προβάλῃ, τοῦτο πρότερον
ἀναγκαῖον διαμάχεσθαι πρὶν ἐπ᾽ αὐτὸν ἐκεῖνον
ἀφικέσθαι. νῦν γὰρ μόγις μὲν τὸ μὴ ὂν ὡς οὐκ
B ἔστι προβληθὲν διεπεράσαμεν, ἕτερον δὲ προβέ-
βληται, καὶ δεῖ δὴ ψεῦδος ὡς ἔστι καὶ περὶ λόγον
καὶ περὶ δόξαν ἀποδεῖξαι, καὶ μετὰ τοῦτο ἴσως
ἕτερον, καὶ ἔτ᾽ ἄλλο μετ᾽ ἐκεῖνο· καὶ πέρας, ὡς
ἔοικεν, οὐδὲν φανήσεται ποτε.

ΞΕ. Θαρρεῖν, ὦ Θεαίτητε, χρὴ τὸν καὶ σμικρόν
τι δυνάμενον εἰς τὸ πρόσθεν ἀεὶ προϊέναι. τί γὰρ ὃ
γ᾽ ἀθυμῶν ἐν τούτοις δράσειεν ἂν ἐν ἄλλοις, ἢ μηδὲν
ἐν ἐκείνοις ἀνύτων ἢ καὶ πάλιν εἰς τοὔπισθεν ἀπ-
ωσθείς; σχολῇ που, τὸ κατὰ τὴν παροιμίαν λεγό-
C μενον, ὅ γε τοιοῦτος ἄν ποτε ἕλοι πόλιν. νῦν δ᾽
ἐπεί, ὦγαθέ, τοῦτο ὃ λέγεις διαπεπέρανται, τό τοι
μέγιστον ἡμῖν τεῖχος ᾑρημένον ἂν εἴη, τὰ δ᾽ ἄλλα
ἤδη ῥᾴω καὶ σμικρότερα.

ΘΕΑΙ. Καλῶς εἶπες.

45. ΞΕ. Λόγον δὴ πρῶτον καὶ δόξαν, καθάπερ
ἐρρήθη νῦν δή, λάβωμεν, ἵνα ἐναργέστερον ἀπολογισώμεθα [3] πότερον αὐτῶν ἅπτεται τὸ μὴ ὂν ἢ

---

[1] αὐτὸ W ; αὐτὸν BT.
[2] γε TW ; δέ γε B.
[3] ἀπολογισώμεθα Heindorf ; ἀπολογησώμεθα BT.

that they participate in not-being, and when we have perceived that, may prove the existence of falsehood, and after proving that, may imprison the sophist therein, if he can be held on that charge, and if not, may set him free and seek him in another class.

THEAET. It certainly seems, Stranger, that what you said at first about the sophist—that he was a hard kind of creature to catch—is true ; for he seems to have no end of defences,[1] and when he throws one of them up, his opponent has first to fight through it before he can reach the man himself; for now, you see, we have barely passed through the non-existence of being, which was his first prepared line of defence, when we find another line ready ; and so we must prove that falsehood exists in relation to opinion and to speech ; and after this, perhaps, there will be another line, and still another after that ; and it seems no end will ever appear.

STR. No one should be discouraged, Theaetetus, who can make constant progress, even though it be slow.   For if a man is discouraged under these conditions, what would he do under others—if he did not get ahead at all or were even pressed back ? It would be a long time, as the saying is, before such a man would ever take a city.   But now, my friend, since we have passed the line you speak of, the main defences would surely be in our hands, and the rest will now be smaller and easier to take.

THEAET. Good.

STR. First, then, let us take up speech and opinion, as I said just now, in order to come to a clearer understanding whether not-being touches

---

[1] Perhaps a sort of pun is intended, for πρόβλημα was already beginning to have the meaning of " problem."

παντάπασιν ἀληθῆ μέν ἐστιν ἀμφότερα ταῦτα
ψεῦδος δὲ οὐδέποτε οὐδέτερον.

ΘΕΑΙ. Ὀρθῶς.

D ΞΕ. Φέρε δή, καθάπερ περὶ τῶν εἰδῶν καὶ τῶν
γραμμάτων ἐλέγομεν, περὶ τῶν ὀνομάτων πάλιν
ὡσαύτως ἐπισκεψώμεθα. φαίνεται γάρ πῃ ταύτῃ
τὸ νῦν ζητούμενον.

ΘΕΑΙ. Τὸ ποῖον οὖν δὴ περὶ τῶν ὀνομάτων ὑπ-
ακουστέον;

ΞΕ. Εἴτε πάντα ἀλλήλοις ξυναρμόττει [1] εἴτε
μηδέν, εἴτε τὰ μὲν ἐθέλει, τὰ δὲ μή.

ΘΕΑΙ. Δῆλον τοῦτό γε, ὅτι τὰ μὲν ἐθέλει, τὰ
δ' οὔ.

ΞΕ. Τὸ τοιόνδε λέγεις ἴσως, ὅτι τὰ μὲν ἐφεξῆς
E λεγόμενα καὶ δηλοῦντά τι ξυναρμόττει, τὰ δὲ τῇ
συνεχείᾳ μηδὲν σημαίνοντα ἀναρμοστεῖ.

ΘΕΑΙ. Πῶς τί τοῦτ' εἶπες;

ΞΕ. Ὅπερ ᾠήθην ὑπολαβόντα σε προσομολογεῖν.
ἔστι γὰρ ἡμῖν που τῶν τῇ φωνῇ περὶ τὴν οὐσίαν
δηλωμάτων διττὸν γένος.

ΘΕΑΙ. Πῶς;

262 ΞΕ. Τὸ μὲν ὀνόματα, τὸ δὲ ῥήματα κληθέν.

ΘΕΑΙ. Εἰπὲ ἑκάτερον.

ΞΕ. Τὸ μὲν ἐπὶ ταῖς πράξεσιν ὂν δήλωμα ῥῆμά
που λέγομεν.

ΘΕΑΙ. Ναί.

---

[1] ξυναρμόττει W ; ξυναρμόττειν BT.

---

[1] The science of language, in all its branches, was young
in the time of Plato. Words of general meaning were
necessarily used in a technical sense. So here ὄνομα and
ῥῆμα are used as parts of grammatical terminology in the

them, or they are both entirely true, and neither is ever false.

THEAET. Very well.

STR. Then let us now investigate names, just as we spoke a while ago about ideas and letters ; for in that direction the object of our present search is coming in sight.

THEAET. What do we need to understand about names ?

STR. Whether they all unite with one another, or none of them, or some will and some will not.

THEAET. Evidently the last ; some will and some will not.

STR. This, perhaps, is what you mean, that those which are spoken in order and mean something do unite, but those that mean nothing in their sequence do not unite.

THEAET. How so, and what do you mean by that ?

STR. What I supposed you had in mind when you assented ; for we have two kinds of vocal indications of being.

THEAET. How so ?

STR. One called nouns, the other verbs.[1]

THEAET. Define each of them.

STR. The indication which relates to action we may call a verb.

THEAET. Yes.

sense of "verb" and "noun," though Plato elsewhere employs them with their ordinary meanings. Similarly the distinction between vowels and consonants (*Theaetetus*, 203 ; *cf. The Sophist*, 253) was at least relatively new, as was that between the active and the passive voice. How important Plato's part was in the development of linguistic study can no longer be accurately determined.

ΞΕ. Τὸ δέ γ' ἐπ' αὐτοῖς τοῖς [1] ἐκεῖνα πράττουσι σημεῖον τῆς φωνῆς ἐπιτεθὲν ὄνομα.

ΘΕΑΙ. Κομιδῇ μὲν οὖν.

ΞΕ. Οὐκοῦν ἐξ ὀνομάτων μὲν μόνων συνεχῶς λεγομένων οὐκ ἔστι ποτὲ λόγος, οὐδ' αὖ ῥημάτων χωρὶς ὀνομάτων λεχθέντων.

ΘΕΑΙ. Ταῦτ' οὐκ ἔμαθον.

B ΞΕ. Δῆλον γὰρ ὡς πρὸς ἕτερόν τι βλέπων ἄρτι ξυνωμολόγεις· ἐπεὶ τοῦτ' αὐτὸ ἐβουλόμην εἰπεῖν, ὅτι συνεχῶς ὧδε λεγόμενα ταῦτα οὐκ ἔστι λόγος.

ΘΕΑΙ. Πῶς;

ΞΕ. Οἷον "βαδίζει," "τρέχει," "καθεύδει," καὶ τἆλλα ὅσα πράξεις σημαίνει ῥήματα, κἂν πάντα τις ἐφεξῆς αὔτ' εἴπῃ, λόγον οὐδέν τι μᾶλλον ἀπεργάζεται.

ΘΕΑΙ. Πῶς γάρ;

ΞΕ. Οὐκοῦν καὶ πάλιν ὅταν λέγηται "λέων," "ἔλαφος," "ἵππος," ὅσα τε ὀνόματα τῶν τὰς πράξεις αὖ πραττόντων ὠνομάσθη, καὶ κατὰ C ταύτην δὴ τὴν συνέχειαν οὐδείς πω ξυνέστη λόγος· οὐδεμίαν γὰρ οὔτε οὕτως οὔτ' ἐκείνως πρᾶξιν οὐδ' ἀπραξίαν οὐδὲ οὐσίαν ὄντος οὐδὲ μὴ ὄντος δηλοῖ τὰ φωνηθέντα, πρὶν ἄν τις τοῖς ὀνόμασι τὰ ῥήματα κεράσῃ· τότε δ' ἥρμοσέν τε καὶ λόγος ἐγένετο εὐθὺς ἡ πρώτη συμπλοκή, σχεδὸν τῶν λόγων ὁ πρῶτός τε καὶ [2] σμικρότατος.

ΘΕΑΙ. Πῶς ἄρ' ὧδε λέγεις;

ΞΕ. Ὅταν εἴπῃ τις· "ἄνθρωπος μανθάνει," λόγον εἶναι φῂς τοῦτον ἐλάχιστόν τε καὶ πρῶτον;

D ΘΕΑΙ. Ἔγωγε.

---

[1] αὐτοῖς τοῖς B, Stobaeus; αὐτοῖς T.
[2] τε καὶ W, Stobaeus; εἰ καὶ T; καὶ B.

THE SOPHIST

STR. And the vocal sign applied to those who perform the actions in question we call a noun.

THEAET. Exactly.

STR. Hence discourse is never composed of nouns alone spoken in succession, nor of verbs spoken without nouns.

THEAET. I do not understand that.

STR. I see; you evidently had something else in mind when you assented just now; for what I wished to say was just this, that verbs and nouns do not make discourse if spoken successively in this way.

THEAET. In what way?

STR. For instance, "walks," "runs," "sleeps" and the other verbs which denote actions, even if you utter all there are of them in succession, do not make discourse for all that.

THEAET. No, of course not.

STR. And again, when "lion," "stag," "horse," and all other names of those who perform these actions are uttered, such a succession of words does not yet make discourse; for in neither case do the words uttered indicate action or inaction or existence of anything that exists or does not exist, until the verbs are mingled with the nouns; then the words fit, and their first combination is a sentence, about the first and shortest form of discourse.

THEAET. What do you mean by that?

STR. When one says "a man learns," you agree that this is the least and first of sentences, do you not?

THEAET. Yes.

ΞΕ. Δηλοῖ γὰρ ἤδη που τότε περὶ τῶν ὄντων ἢ γιγνομένων ἢ γεγονότων ἢ μελλόντων, καὶ οὐκ ὀνομάζει μόνον, ἀλλά τι περαίνει, συμπλέκων τὰ ῥήματα τοῖς ὀνόμασι. διὸ λέγειν τε αὐτὸν ἀλλ' οὐ μόνον ὀνομάζειν εἴπομεν,[1] καὶ δὴ καὶ τῷ πλέγματι τούτῳ τὸ ὄνομα ἐφθεγξάμεθα λόγον.

ΘΕΑΙ. Ὀρθῶς.

46. ΞΕ. Οὕτω δὴ καθάπερ τὰ πράγματα[2] τὰ μὲν ἀλλήλοις ἥρμοττε, τὰ δ' οὔ, καὶ περὶ τὰ τῆς φωνῆς αὖ σημεῖα τὰ μὲν οὐχ ἁρμόττει, τὰ δὲ
E ἁρμόττοντα αὐτῶν λόγον ἀπειργάσατο.

ΘΕΑΙ. Παντάπασι μὲν οὖν.

ΞΕ. Ἔτι δὴ σμικρὸν τόδε.

ΘΕΑΙ. Τὸ ποῖον;

ΞΕ. Λόγον ἀναγκαῖον, ὅτανπερ ᾖ, τινὸς εἶναι λόγον, μὴ δέ τινος ἀδύνατον.

ΘΕΑΙ. Οὕτως.

ΞΕ. Οὐκοῦν καὶ ποιόν τινα αὐτὸν εἶναι δεῖ;

ΘΕΑΙ. Πῶς δ' οὔ;

ΞΕ. Προσέχωμεν δὴ τὸν νοῦν ἡμῖν αὐτοῖς.

ΘΕΑΙ. Δεῖ γοῦν.

ΞΕ. Λέξω τοίνυν σοι λόγον συνθεὶς πρᾶγμα πράξει δι' ὀνόματος καὶ ῥήματος· ὅτου δ' ἂν ὁ λόγος ᾖ, σύ μοι φράζειν.

263 ΘΕΑΙ. Ταῦτ' ἔσται κατὰ δύναμιν.

ΞΕ. Θεαίτητος κάθηται. μῶν μὴ μακρὸς ὁ λόγος;

ΘΕΑΙ. Οὔκ, ἀλλὰ μέτριος.

ΞΕ. Σὸν ἔργον δὴ φράζειν περὶ οὗ τ' ἐστὶ καὶ ὅτου.

ΘΕΑΙ. Δῆλον ὅτι περὶ ἐμοῦ τε καὶ ἐμός.

---

[1] εἴπομεν Stobaeus; εἴποιμεν BT.

THE SOPHIST

STR. For when he says that, he makes a statement about that which is or is becoming or has become or is to be; he does not merely give names, but he reaches a conclusion by combining verbs with nouns. That is why we said that he discourses and does not merely give names, and therefore we gave to this combination the name of discourse.

THEAET. That was right.

STR. So, then, just as of things some fit each other and some do not, so too some vocal signs do not fit, but some of them do fit and form discourse.

THEAET. Certainly.

STR. Now there is another little point.

THEAET. What is it?

STR. A sentence, if it is to be a sentence, must have a subject; without a subject it is impossible.

THEAET. True.

STR. And it must also be of some quality, must it not?

THEAET. Of course.

STR. Now let us pay attention to each other.

THEAET. Yes, at any rate we ought to do so.

STR. Now, then, I will speak a sentence to you in which an action and the result of action are combined by means of a noun and a verb, and whatever the subject of the sentence is do you tell me.

THEAET. I will, to the best of my ability.

STR. "Theaetetus sits." It isn't a long sentence, is it?

THEAET. No, it is fairly short.

STR. Now it is for you to say what it is about and what its subject is.

THEAET. Clearly it is about me, and I am its subject.

---

[1] πράγματα BTW; γράμματα, letters, Bury (cf. 253).

437

ΞΕ. Τί δὲ ὅδ' αὖ;

ΘΕΑΙ. Ποῖος;

ΞΕ. Θεαίτητος, ᾧ νῦν ἐγὼ διαλέγομαι, πέτεται.

ΘΕΑΙ. Καὶ τοῦτον οὐδ' ἂν εἷς ἄλλως εἴποι πλὴν ἐμόν τε καὶ περὶ ἐμοῦ.

ΞΕ. Ποιὸν δέ γέ τινά φαμεν ἀναγκαῖον ἕκαστον εἶναι τῶν λόγων.

B ΘΕΑΙ. Ναί.

ΞΕ. Τούτων δὴ ποῖόν τινα ἑκάτερον φατέον εἶναι;

ΘΕΑΙ. Τὸν μὲν ψευδῆ που, τὸν δὲ ἀληθῆ.

ΞΕ. Λέγει δὲ αὐτῶν ὁ μὲν ἀληθὴς τὰ ὄντα ὡς ἔστι περὶ σοῦ.

ΘΕΑΙ. Τί μήν;

ΞΕ. Ὁ δὲ δὴ ψευδὴς ἕτερα τῶν ὄντων.

ΘΕΑΙ. Ναί.

ΞΕ. Τὰ μὴ ὄντ' ἄρα ὡς ὄντα λέγει.

ΘΕΑΙ. Σχεδόν.

ΞΕ. Ὄντων[1] δέ γε ὄντα ἕτερα περὶ σοῦ. πολλὰ μὲν γὰρ ἔφαμεν ὄντα περὶ ἕκαστον εἶναί που, πολλὰ δὲ οὐκ ὄντα.

ΘΕΑΙ. Κομιδῇ μὲν οὖν.

C ΞΕ. Ὃν ὕστερον δὴ λόγον εἴρηκα περὶ σοῦ, πρῶτον μέν, ἐξ ὧν ὡρισάμεθα τί ποτ' ἔστι λόγος, ἀναγκαιότατον αὐτὸν ἕνα τῶν βραχυτάτων εἶναι.

ΘΕΑΙ. Νῦν δὴ γοῦν ταύτῃ ξυνωμολογήσαμεν.

ΞΕ. Ἔπειτα δέ γε τινός.

ΘΕΑΙ. Οὕτως.

ΞΕ. Εἰ δὲ μὴ ἔστι σός, οὐκ ἄλλου γε οὐδενός.

[1] ὄντων Cornarius ; ὄντως BT.

STR. And how about this sentence?

THEAET. What one?

STR. "Theaetetus, with whom I am now talking, flies."

THEAET. Every one would agree that this also is about me and I am its subject.

STR. But we agree that every sentence must have some quality.

THEAET. Yes.

STR. Now what quality shall be ascribed to each of these sentences?

THEAET. One is false, I suppose, the other true.

STR. The true one states facts as they are about you.

THEAET. Certainly.

STR. And the false one states things that are other than the facts.

THEAET. Yes.

STR. In other words, it speaks of things that are not as if they were.

THEAET. Yes, that is pretty much what it does.

STR. And states with reference to you that things are which are other than things which actually are; for we said, you know, that in respect to everything there are many things that are and many that are not.

THEAET. To be sure.

STR. Now the second of my sentences about you is in the first place by sheer necessity one of the shortest which conform to our definition of sentence.

THEAET. At any rate we just now agreed on that point.

STR. And secondly it has a subject.

THEAET. Yes.

STR. And if you are not the subject, there is none.

ΘΕΑΙ. Πῶς γάρ;

ΞΕ. Μηδενὸς δὲ [1] ὢν οὐδ' ἂν λόγος εἴη τὸ παράπαν· ἀπεφήναμεν γὰρ ὅτι τῶν ἀδυνάτων ἦν λόγον ὄντα μηδενὸς εἶναι λόγον.

ΘΕΑΙ. Ὀρθότατα.

D ΞΕ. Περὶ δὴ σοῦ λεγόμενα, λεγόμενα [2] μέντοι θάτερα ὡς τὰ αὐτὰ καὶ μὴ ὄντα ὡς ὄντα, παντάπασιν ἔοικεν [3] ἡ τοιαύτη σύνθεσις ἔκ τε ῥημάτων γιγνομένη καὶ ὀνομάτων ὄντως τε καὶ ἀληθῶς γίγνεσθαι λόγος ψευδής.

ΘΕΑΙ. Ἀληθέστατα μὲν οὖν.

47. ΞΕ. Τί δὲ δή; διάνοιά τε καὶ δόξα καὶ φαντασία, μῶν οὐκ ἤδη δῆλον ὅτι ταῦτα τὰ γένη ψευδῆ τε καὶ ἀληθῆ πάνθ' ἡμῶν ἐν ταῖς ψυχαῖς ἐγγίγνεται;

ΘΕΑΙ. Πῶς;

ΞΕ. Ὧδ' εἴσει ῥᾷον, ἂν πρῶτον λάβῃς αὐτά, [4] τί E ποτ' ἔστι καὶ τί διαφέρουσιν ἕκαστα ἀλλήλων.

ΘΕΑΙ. Δίδου μόνον.

ΞΕ. Οὐκοῦν διάνοια μὲν καὶ λόγος ταὐτόν· πλὴν ὁ μὲν ἐντὸς τῆς ψυχῆς πρὸς αὑτὴν διάλογος ἄνευ φωνῆς γιγνόμενος τοῦτ' αὐτὸ ἡμῖν ἐπωνομάσθη, διάνοια;

ΘΕΑΙ. Πάνυ μὲν οὖν.

ΞΕ. Τὸ δέ γ' ἀπ' ἐκείνης ῥεῦμα διὰ τοῦ στόματος ἰὸν μετὰ φθόγγου κέκληται λόγος;

ΘΕΑΙ. Ἀληθῆ.

ΞΕ. Καὶ μὴν ἐν λόγοις αὐτὸ ἴσμεν ὄν—

ΘΕΑΙ. Τὸ ποῖον;

ΞΕ. Φάσιν τε καὶ ἀπόφασιν.

---

[1] δὲ emend. apogr. Parisinum 1811; γε BT; δὲ or δέ γε Heindorf.

THE SOPHIST

THEAET. Certainly not.

STR. And if there is no subject, it would not be a sentence at all; for we showed that a sentence without a subject is impossible.

THEAET. Quite right.

STR. Now when things are said about you, but things other are said as the same and things that are not as things that are, it appears that when such a combination is formed of verbs and nouns we have really and truly false discourse.

THEAET. Yes, very truly.

STR. Is it, then, not already plain that the three classes, thought, opinion, and fancy, all arise in our minds as both false and true?

THEAET. How is it plain?

STR. You will understand more easily if you first grasp their natures and the several differences between them.

THEAET. Give me an opportunity.

STR. Well, then, thought and speech are the same; only the former, which is a silent inner conversation of the soul with itself, has been given the special name of thought. Is not that true?

THEAET. Certainly.

STR. But the stream that flows from the soul in vocal utterance through the mouth has the name of speech?

THEAET. True.

STR. And in speech we know there is just—

THEAET. What?

STR. Affirmation and negation.

² λεγόμενα add. Badham.
³ ἔοικεν W ; ὡς ἔοικεν BT.
⁴ αὐτά W, Stobaeus ; om. BT.

ΘΕΑΙ. Ἴσμεν.

264 ΞΕ. Ὅταν οὖν τοῦτο ἐν ψυχῇ κατὰ διάνοιαν ἐγγίγνηται μετὰ σιγῆς, πλὴν δόξης ἔχεις ὅ τι προσείπῃς αὐτό;

ΘΕΑΙ. Καὶ πῶς;

ΞΕ. Τί δ' ὅταν μὴ καθ' αὑτὸ[1] ἀλλὰ δι' αἰσθήσεως παρῇ τινι τὸ τοιοῦτον αὖ πάθος, ἆρ' οἷόν τε ὀρθῶς εἰπεῖν ἕτερόν τι πλὴν φαντασίαν;

ΘΕΑΙ. Οὐδέν.

ΞΕ. Οὐκοῦν ἐπείπερ λόγος ἀληθὴς ἦν καὶ ψευδής, τούτων δ' ἐφάνη διάνοια μὲν αὐτῆς πρὸς ἑαυτὴν ψυχῆς διάλογος, δόξα δὲ διανοίας ἀποτελεύτησις, B "φαίνεται" δὲ ὃ λέγομεν σύμμιξις αἰσθήσεως καὶ δόξης, ἀνάγκη δὴ καὶ τούτων τῷ λόγῳ ξυγγενῶν ὄντων ψευδῆ τε αὐτῶν ἔνια καὶ ἐνίοτε εἶναι.

ΘΕΑΙ. Πῶς δ' οὔ;

ΞΕ. Κατανοεῖς οὖν ὅτι πρότερον ηὑρέθη ψευδὴς δόξα καὶ λόγος ἢ κατὰ τὴν προσδοκίαν ἣν ἐφοβήθημεν ἄρτι, μὴ παντάπασιν ἀνήνυτον ἔργον ἐπιβαλλοίμεθα ζητοῦντες αὐτό;

ΘΕΑΙ. Κατανοῶ.

48. ΞΕ. Μὴ τοίνυν μηδ' εἰς τὰ λοιπὰ ἀθυ-
C μῶμεν. ἐπειδὴ γὰρ πέφανται ταῦτα, τῶν ἔμπροσθεν ἀναμνησθῶμεν κατ' εἴδη διαιρέσεων.

ΘΕΑΙ. Ποίων δή;

ΞΕ. Διειλόμεθα τῆς εἰδωλοποιικῆς εἴδη δύο, τὴν μὲν εἰκαστικήν, τὴν δὲ φανταστικήν.

ΘΕΑΙ. Ναί.

ΞΕ. Καὶ τὸν σοφιστὴν εἴπομεν ὡς ἀποροῖμεν εἰς ὁποτέραν θήσομεν.

---

[1] αὐτὸ Stobaeus; αὑτὴν BT.

THEAET. Yes, we know that.

STR. Now when this arises in the soul silently by way of thought, can you give it any other name than opinion?

THEAET. Certainly not.

STR. And when such a condition is brought about in anyone, not independently, but through sensation, can it properly be called anything but seeming, or fancy?

THEAET. No.

STR. Then since speech, as we found, is true and false, and we saw that thought is conversation of the soul with itself, and opinion is the final result of thought, and what we mean when we say "it seems" is a mixture of sensation and opinion, it is inevitable that, since these are all akin to speech, some of them must sometimes be false.

THEAET. Certainly.

STR. Do you see, then, that false opinion and false discourse were found sooner than we expected when we feared a few moments ago that in looking for them we were undertaking an endless task?

THEAET. Yes, I see.

STR. Then let us not be discouraged about the rest of our search, either; for now that these points are settled, we have only to revert to our previous divisions into classes.

THEAET. What divisions?

STR. We made two classes of image-making, the likeness-making and the fantastic.[1]

THEAET. Yes.

STR. And we said that we did not know to which of the two the sophist should be assigned.

[1] See 235 D ff.

ΘΕΑΙ. Ἦν ταῦτα.

ΞΕ. Καὶ τοῦθ' ἡμῶν ἀπορουμένων ἔτι μείζων κατεχύθη σκοτοδινία, φανέντος τοῦ λόγου τοῦ πᾶσιν ἀμφισβητοῦντος, ὡς οὔτε εἰκὼν οὔτε εἴδωλον D οὔτε φάντασμα εἴη τὸ παράπαν οὐδὲν διὰ τὸ μηδαμῶς μηδέποτε μηδαμοῦ ψεῦδος εἶναι.

ΘΕΑΙ. Λέγεις ἀληθῆ.

ΞΕ. Νῦν δέ γ' ἐπειδὴ πέφανται μὲν λόγος, πέφανται δ' οὖσα δόξα ψευδής, ἐγχωρεῖ δὴ μιμήματα τῶν ὄντων εἶναι καὶ τέχνην ἐκ ταύτης γίγνεσθαι τῆς διαθέσεως ἀπατητικήν.

ΘΕΑΙ. Ἐγχωρεῖ.

ΞΕ. Καὶ μὴν ὅτι γ' ἦν ὁ σοφιστὴς τούτων πότερον, διωμολογημένον ἡμῖν ἐν τοῖς πρόσθεν ἦν.

ΘΕΑΙ. Ναί.

ΞΕ. Πάλιν τοίνυν ἐπιχειρῶμεν, σχίζοντες διχῇ τὸ E προτεθὲν γένος, πορεύεσθαι κατὰ τοὐπὶ δεξιὰ ἀεὶ μέρος τοῦ τμηθέντος, ἐχόμενοι τῆς τοῦ σοφιστοῦ κοινωνίας, ἕως ἂν αὐτοῦ τὰ κοινὰ πάντα περιελόντες, τὴν οἰκείαν λιπόντες φύσιν ἐπιδείξωμεν μάλιστα 265 μὲν ἡμῖν αὐτοῖς, ἔπειτα δὲ καὶ τοῖς ἐγγυτάτω γένει τῆς τοιαύτης μεθόδου πεφυκόσιν.

ΘΕΑΙ. Ὀρθῶς.

ΞΕ. Οὐκοῦν τότε μὲν ἠρχόμεθα ποιητικὴν καὶ κτητικὴν τέχνην διαιρούμενοι;

ΘΕΑΙ. Ναί.

ΞΕ. Καὶ τῆς κτητικῆς ἐν θηρευτικῇ καὶ ἀγωνίᾳ καὶ ἐμπορικῇ καί τισιν ἐν τοιούτοις εἴδεσιν ἐφαντάζεθ' ἡμῖν;

THEAET. You are right.

STR. And in the midst of our perplexity about that, we were overwhelmed by a still greater dizziness when the doctrine appeared which challenges everybody and asserts that neither likeness nor image nor appearance exists at all, because falsehood never exists anywhere in any way.

THEAET. True.

STR. But now, since the existence of false speech and false opinion has been proved, it is possible for imitations of realities to exist and for an art of deception to arise from this condition of mind.

THEAET. Yes, it is possible.

STR. And we decided some time ago that the sophist was in one of those two divisions of the image-making class.

THEAET. Yes.

STR. Then let us try again; let us divide in two the class we have taken up for discussion, and proceed always by way of the right-hand part of the thing divided, clinging close to the company to which the sophist belongs, until, having stripped him of all common properties and left him only his own peculiar nature, we shall show him plainly first to ourselves and secondly to those who are most closely akin to the dialectic method.

THEAET. Right.

STR. We began by making two divisions of art, the productive and the acquisitive, did we not?[1]

THEAET. Yes.

STR. And the sophist showed himself to us in the arts of hunting, contests, commerce, and the like, which were subdivisions of acquisitive art?

[1] See 219.

ΘΕΑΙ. Πάνυ μὲν οὖν.

ΞΕ. Νῦν δέ γ᾽ ἐπειδὴ μιμητικὴ περιείληφεν
αὐτὸν τέχνη, δῆλον ὡς αὐτὴν τὴν ποιητικὴν δίχα
B διαιρετέον πρώτην. ἡ γάρ που μίμησις ποίησίς
τίς ἐστιν, εἰδώλων μέντοι, φαμέν, ἀλλ᾽ οὐκ αὐτῶν
ἑκάστων· ἦ γάρ;

ΘΕΑΙ. Παντάπασι μὲν οὖν.

ΞΕ. Ποιητικῆς δὴ πρῶτον δύο ἔστω μέρη.

ΘΕΑΙ. Ποίω;

ΞΕ. Τὸ μὲν θεῖον, τὸ δ᾽ ἀνθρώπινον.

ΘΕΑΙ. Οὔπω μεμάθηκα.

49. ΞΕ. Ποιητικήν, εἴπερ μεμνήμεθα τὰ κατ᾽
ἀρχὰς λεχθέντα, πᾶσαν ἔφαμεν εἶναι δύναμιν ἥτις
ἂν αἰτία γίγνηται τοῖς μὴ πρότερον οὖσιν ὕστερον
γίγνεσθαι.

ΘΕΑΙ. Μεμνήμεθα.

C ΞΕ. Ζῷα δὴ πάντα θνητὰ καὶ φυτὰ ὅσα τ᾽ ἐπὶ
γῆς ἐκ σπερμάτων καὶ ῥιζῶν φύεται καὶ ὅσα ἄψυχα
ἐν γῇ ξυνίσταται σώματα τηκτὰ καὶ ἄτηκτα, μῶν
ἄλλου τινὸς ἢ θεοῦ δημιουργοῦντος φήσομεν ὕστερον
γίγνεσθαι πρότερον οὐκ ὄντα; ἢ τῷ τῶν πολλῶν
δόγματι καὶ ῥήματι χρώμενοι—

ΘΕΑΙ. Ποίω;

ΞΕ. Τῷ τὴν φύσιν αὐτὰ γεννᾶν ἀπό τινος αἰτίας
αὐτομάτης καὶ ἄνευ διανοίας φυούσης, ἢ μετὰ λόγου
τε καὶ ἐπιστήμης θείας ἀπὸ θεοῦ γιγνομένης;

D ΘΕΑΙ. Ἐγὼ μὲν ἴσως διὰ τὴν ἡλικίαν πολλάκις
ἀμφότερα μεταδοξάζω· νῦν μὴν [1] βλέπων εἰς σὲ
καὶ ὑπολαμβάνων οἴεσθαί σε κατά γε θεὸν αὐτὰ
γίγνεσθαι, ταύτῃ καὶ αὐτὸς νενόμικα.

ΞΕ. Καλῶς γε, ὦ Θεαίτητε· καὶ εἰ μέν γέ σε

[1] μὴν b ; μὴ ΒΤ.

THEAET. Certainly.

STR. But now, since imitative art has taken him over, it is clear that our first step must be the division of productive art into two parts; for imitative art is a kind of production—of images, however, we say, not of real things in each case. Do you agree?

THEAET. By all means.

STR. Then let us first assume two parts of productive art.

THEAET. What are they?

STR. The divine and the human.

THEAET. I don't yet understand.

STR. We said, if we remember the beginning of our conversation, that every power is productive which causes things to come into being which did not exist before.

THEAET. Yes, we remember.

STR. There are all the animals, and all the plants that grow out of the earth from seeds and roots, and all the lifeless substances, fusible and infusible, that are formed within the earth. Shall we say that they came into being, not having been before, in any other way than through God's workmanship? Or, accepting the commonly expressed belief—

THEAET. What belief?

STR. That nature brings them forth from some self-acting cause, without creative intelligence. Or shall we say that they are created by reason and by divine knowledge that comes from God?

THEAET. I, perhaps because I am young, often change from one opinion to the other; but now, looking at you and considering that you think they are created by God, I also adopt that view.

STR. Well said, Theaetetus; and if I thought you

ἡγούμεθα τῶν εἰς τὸν ἔπειτα χρόνον ἄλλως πως
δοξαζόντων εἶναι, νῦν ἂν τῷ λόγῳ μετὰ πειθοῦς
ἀναγκαίας ἐπεχειροῦμεν ποιεῖν ὁμολογεῖν· ἐπειδὴ
δέ σου καταμανθάνω τὴν φύσιν, ὅτι καὶ ἄνευ τῶν
E παρ' ἡμῶν λόγων αὐτὴ[1] πρόσεισιν ἐφ' ἅπερ νῦν
ἕλκεσθαι φῄς, ἐάσω· χρόνος γὰρ ἐκ περιττοῦ
γίγνοιτ' ἄν· ἀλλὰ θήσω τὰ μὲν φύσει λεγόμενα
ποιεῖσθαι θείᾳ τέχνῃ, τὰ δ' ἐκ τούτων ὑπ' ἀνθρώπων
ξυνιστάμενα ἀνθρωπίνῃ, καὶ κατὰ τοῦτον δὴ τὸν
λόγον δύο ποιητικῆς γένη, τὸ μὲν ἀνθρώπινον εἶναι,
τὸ δὲ θεῖον.

ΘΕΑΙ. Ὀρθῶς.

ΞΕ. Τέμνε δὴ δυοῖν οὔσαιν δίχα ἑκατέραν αὖθις.

ΘΕΑΙ. Πῶς;

266 ΞΕ. Οἷον τότε μὲν κατὰ πλάτος τέμνων τὴν
ποιητικὴν πᾶσαν, νῦν δὲ αὖ κατὰ μῆκος.

ΘΕΑΙ. Τετμήσθω.

ΞΕ. Τέτταρα μὴν αὐτῆς οὕτω τὰ πάντα μέρη
γίγνεται, δύο μὲν τὰ πρὸς ἡμῶν, ἀνθρώπεια, δύο
δ' αὖ τὰ πρὸς θεῶν, θεῖα.

ΘΕΑΙ. Ναί.

ΞΕ. Τὰ δέ γ' ὡς ἑτέρως αὖ διῃρημένα, μέρος μὲν
ἓν ἀφ' ἑκατέρας τῆς μερίδος αὐτοποιητικόν, τὼ δ'
ὑπολοίπω σχεδὸν μάλιστ' ἂν λεγοίσθην εἰδωλο-
ποιικώ· καὶ κατὰ ταῦτα δὴ πάλιν ἡ ποιητικὴ
διχῇ διαιρεῖται.

B ΘΕΑΙ. Λέγε ὅπη[2] ἑκατέρα αὖθις.

50. ΞΕ. Ἡμεῖς μέν που καὶ τἆλλα ζῷα καὶ ἐξ
ὧν τὰ πεφυκότ' ἐστί, πῦρ καὶ ὕδωρ καὶ τὰ τούτων
ἀδελφά, θεοῦ γεννήματα πάντα ἴσμεν αὐτὰ ἀπειργα-
σμένα ἕκαστα· ἢ πῶς;

---

[1] αὐτὴ W; αὕτη B; αυτη T.   [2] ὅπῃ inferior mss.; ὅποι BT.

were one of those who would think differently by
and by, I should try now, by argument and urgent
persuasion, to make you agree with my opinion; but
since I understand your nature and see that it of
itself inclines, without any words of mine, towards
that to which you say you are at present attracted, I
will let that go; for it would be a waste of time. But
I will assume that things which people call natural are
made by divine art, and things put together by man
out of those as materials are made by human art, and
that there are accordingly two kinds of art, the one
human and the other divine.

THEAET. Quite right.

STR. Now that there are two, divide each of
them again.

THEAET. How?

STR. You divided all productive art widthwise, as
it were, before; now divide it lengthwise.

THEAET. Assume that it is done.

STR. In that way we now get four parts in all;
two belong to us and are human, and two belong to
the gods and are divine.

THEAET. Yes.

STR. And again, when the section is made the
other way, one part of each half has to do with the
making of real things, and the two remaining parts
may very well be called image-making; and so
productive art is again divided into two parts.

THEAET. Tell me again how each part is distinguished.

STR. We know that we and all the other
animals, and fire, water, and their kindred elements,
out of which natural objects are formed, are one and
all the very offspring and creations of God, do we not?

PLATO

ΘΕΑΙ. Οὕτως.

ΞΕ. Τούτων δέ γε ἑκάστων εἴδωλα, ἀλλ᾽ οὐκ αὐτὰ παρέπεται, δαιμονίᾳ καὶ ταῦτα μηχανῇ γεγονότα.

ΘΕΑΙ. Ποῖα;

ΞΕ. Τά τε ἐν τοῖς ὕπνοις καὶ ὅσα μεθ᾽ ἡμέραν φαντάσματα αὐτοφυῆ λέγεται, σκιὰ μὲν ὅταν ἐν C τῷ πυρὶ σκότος ἐγγίγνηται, διπλοῦν δὲ ἡνίκ᾽ ἂν φῶς οἰκεῖόν τε καὶ ἀλλότριον περὶ τὰ λαμπρὰ καὶ λεῖα εἰς ἓν ξυνελθὸν τῆς ἔμπροσθεν εἰωθυίας ὄψεως ἐναντίαν αἴσθησιν παρέχον εἶδος ἀπεργάζηται.

ΘΕΑΙ. Δύο γὰρ οὖν ἐστι ταῦτα θείας ἔργα ποιήσεως, αὐτό τε καὶ τὸ παρακολουθοῦν εἴδωλον ἑκάστῳ.

ΞΕ. Τί δὲ τὴν ἡμετέραν τέχνην; ἆρ᾽ οὐκ αὐτὴν μὲν οἰκίαν οἰκοδομικῇ φήσομεν ποιεῖν, γραφικῇ δέ τιν᾽ ἑτέραν, οἷον ὄναρ ἀνθρώπινον ἐγρηγορόσιν ἀπειργασμένην;

D ΘΕΑΙ. Πάνυ μὲν οὖν.

ΞΕ. Οὐκοῦν καὶ τἆλλα οὕτω κατὰ δύο διττὰ ἔργα τῆς ἡμετέρας αὖ ποιητικῆς πράξεως, τὸ μὲν αὐτό, φαμέν, αὐτουργικῇ,[1] τὸ δὲ εἴδωλον εἰδωλοποιικῇ.[2]

ΘΕΑΙ. Νῦν μᾶλλον ἔμαθον, καὶ τίθημι δύο διχῇ ποιητικῆς εἴδη· θείαν [3] μὲν καὶ ἀνθρωπίνην [4] κατὰ θάτερον τμῆμα, κατὰ δὲ θάτερον τὸ μὲν αὐτῶν ὄν, τὸ δὲ ὁμοιωμάτων τινῶν γέννημα.

[1] αὐτουργικῇ Heindorf ; αὐτουργική BT.
[2] εἰδωλοποιικῇ Heindorf ; εἰδωλοποιική BT.
[3] θείαν Heindorf ; θεία B ; θείᾳ T.
[4] ἀνθρωπίνην Heindorf ; ἀνθρωπίνη B ; ἀνθρωπίνῃ T.

[1] This was the current explanation of reflection. Mirrors and smooth objects were supposed to contain a luminous principle which met on the smooth surface with the light

THEAET. Yes.

STR. And corresponding to each and all of these there are images, not the things themselves, which are also made by superhuman skill.

THEAET. What are they?

STR. The appearances in dreams, and those that arise by day and are said to be spontaneous—a shadow when a dark object interrupts the firelight, or when twofold light, from the objects themselves and from outside, meets on smooth and bright surfaces and causes upon our senses an effect the reverse of our ordinary sight, thus producing an image.[1]

THEAET. Yes, these are two works of divine creation, the thing itself and the corresponding image in each case.

STR. And how about our own art? Shall we not say that we make a house by the art of building, and by the art of painting make another house, a sort of man-made dream produced for those who are awake?

THEAET. Certainly.

STR. And in the same way, we say, all the other works of our creative activity also are twofold and go in pairs—the thing itself, produced by the art that creates real things, and the image, produced by the image-making art.

THEAET. I understand better now; and I agree that there are two kinds of production, each of them twofold—the divine and the human by one method of bisection, and by the other real things and the product that consists of a sort of likenesses.

coming from the object reflected. So in the act of vision the fire within the eye united with the external fire (*Timaeus*, 46 A). The words τῆς ἔμπροσθεν . . . ἐναντίαν αἴσθησιν refer to the transposition of right and left in the reflection (*cf. Theaetetus*, 193 c).

51. ΞΕ. Τῆς τοίνυν εἰδωλουργικῆς ἀναμνησθῶμεν ὅτι τὸ μὲν εἰκαστικόν, τὸ δὲ φανταστικὸν ἔμελ-
E λεν εἶναι γένος, εἰ τὸ ψεῦδος ὄντως ὂν ψεῦδος καὶ
τῶν ὄντων ἕν τι φανείη πεφυκός.

ΘΕΑΙ. Ἦν γὰρ οὖν.

ΞΕ. Οὐκοῦν ἐφάνη τε καὶ διὰ ταῦτα δὴ κατ-
αριθμήσομεν αὐτὼ[1] νῦν ἀναμφισβητήτως εἴδη
δύο;

ΘΕΑΙ. Ναί.

267 **ΞΕ.** Τὸ τοίνυν φανταστικὸν αὖθις διορίζωμεν
δίχα.

ΘΕΑΙ. Πῇ;

ΞΕ. Τὸ μὲν δι' ὀργάνων γιγνόμενον, τὸ δὲ αὐτοῦ
παρέχοντος ἑαυτὸν ὄργανον τοῦ ποιοῦντος τὸ
φάντασμα.

ΘΕΑΙ. Πῶς φής;

ΞΕ. Ὅταν, οἶμαι, τὸ σὸν σχῆμά τις τῷ ἑαυτοῦ
χρώμενος σώματι προσόμοιον ἢ φωνὴν φωνῇ
φαίνεσθαι ποιῇ, μίμησις τοῦτο τῆς φανταστικῆς
μάλιστα κέκληταί που.

ΘΕΑΙ. Ναί.

ΞΕ. Μιμητικὸν δὴ τοῦτο αὐτῆς προσειπόντες
ἀπονειμώμεθα[2]· τὸ δ' ἄλλο πᾶν ἀφῶμεν μαλακι-
B σθέντες καὶ παρέντες ἑτέρῳ συναγαγεῖν τε εἰς ἓν
καὶ πρέπουσαν ἐπωνυμίαν ἀποδοῦναί τιν' αὐτῷ.

ΘΕΑΙ. Νενεμήσθω, τὸ δὲ μεθείσθω.

ΞΕ. Καὶ μὴν καὶ τοῦτο ἔτι διπλοῦν, ὦ Θεαίτητε,
ἄξιον ἡγεῖσθαι· δι' ἃ δέ, σκόπει.

ΘΕΑΙ. Λέγε.

ΞΕ. Τῶν μιμουμένων οἱ μὲν εἰδότες ὃ μιμοῦνται

---

[1] αὐτὼ] αὐτῷ BT.

[2] ἀπονειμώμεθα W ; ἀπονειμόμεθα BT.

THE SOPHIST

STR. We must remember that there were to be two parts of the image-making class, the likeness-making and the fantastic, if we should find that falsehood really existed and was in the class of real being.

THEAET. Yes, there were.

STR. But we found that falsehood does exist, and therefore we shall now, without any doubts, number the kinds of image-making art as two, shall we not?

THEAET. Yes.

STR. Let us, then, again bisect the fantastic art.

THEAET. How?

STR. One kind is that produced by instruments, the other that in which the producer of the appearance offers himself as the instrument.

THEAET. What do you mean?

STR. When anyone, by employing his own person as his instrument, makes his own figure or voice seem similar to yours, that kind of fantastic art is called mimetic.

THEAET. Yes.

STR. Let us, then, classify this part under the name of mimetic art; but as for all the rest, let us be so self-indulgent as to let it go and leave it for someone else to unify and name appropriately.

THEAET. Very well, let us adopt that classification and let the other part go.

STR. But it is surely worth while to consider, Theaetetus, that the mimetic art also has two parts; and I will tell you why.

THEAET. Please do.

STR. Some who imitate do so with knowledge of that which they imitate, and others without such

PLATO

τοῦτο πράττουσιν, οἱ δ᾽ οὐκ εἰδότες. καίτοι τίνα
μείζω διαίρεσιν ἀγνωσίας τε καὶ γνώσεως θήσομεν;

ΘΕΑΙ. Οὐδεμίαν.

ΞΕ. Οὐκοῦν τό γε ἄρτι λεχθὲν εἰδότων ἦν μίμημα;
τὸ γὰρ σὸν σχῆμα καὶ σὲ γιγνώσκων ἄν τις μιμή-
σαιτο.

C ΘΕΑΙ. Πῶς δ᾽ οὔ;

ΞΕ. Τί δὲ δικαιοσύνης τὸ σχῆμα καὶ ὅλης ξυλλή-
βδην ἀρετῆς; ἆρ᾽ οὐκ ἀγνοοῦντες μέν, δοξάζοντες
δέ πῃ, σφόδρα ἐπιχειροῦσι πολλοὶ τὸ δοκοῦν σφίσι
τοῦτο ὡς ἐνὸν αὐτοῖς προθυμεῖσθαι φαίνεσθαι ποιεῖν,
ὅτι μάλιστα ἔργοις τε καὶ λόγοις μιμούμενοι;

ΘΕΑΙ. Καὶ πάνυ γε πολλοί.

ΞΕ. Μῶν οὖν πάντες ἀποτυγχάνουσι τοῦ δοκεῖν
εἶναι δίκαιοι μηδαμῶς ὄντες; ἢ τούτου πᾶν τοὐναντίον;

ΘΕΑΙ. Πᾶν.

ΞΕ. Μιμητὴν δὴ τοῦτόν γε ἕτερον ἐκείνου
D λεκτέον οἶμαι, τὸν ἀγνοοῦντα τοῦ γιγνώσκοντος.

ΘΕΑΙ. Ναί.

52. ΞΕ. Πόθεν οὖν ὄνομα ἑκατέρῳ τις αὐτῶν
λήψεται πρέπον; ἢ δῆλον δὴ χαλεπὸν ὄν, διότι τῆς
τῶν γενῶν κατ᾽ εἴδη διαιρέσεως παλαιά τις, ὡς
ἔοικεν, ἀργία [1] τοῖς ἔμπροσθεν καὶ ἀσύννους παρῆν,
ὥστε μηδ᾽ ἐπιχειρεῖν μηδένα διαιρεῖσθαι· καθὸ
δὴ τῶν ὀνομάτων ἀνάγκη μὴ σφόδρα εὐπορεῖν.
ὅμως δέ, κἂν εἰ τολμηρότερον εἰρῆσθαι, διαγνώσεως
ἕνεκα τὴν μὲν μετὰ δόξης μίμησιν δοξομιμητικὴν

---

[1] ἀργία Madvig; αἰτία BT.

knowledge. And yet what division can we imagine more complete than that which separates knowledge and ignorance?

THEAET. None.

STR. The example I just gave was of imitation by those who know, was it not? For a man who imitates you would know you and your figure.

THEAET. Of course.

STR. But what of the figure of justice and, in a word, of virtue in general? Are there not many who have no knowledge of it, but only a sort of opinion, and who try with the greatest eagerness to make this which they themselves think is virtue seem to exist within them, by imitating it in acts and words to the best of their ability?

THEAET. Yes, there are very many such people.

STR. Do all of them, then, fail in the attempt to seem to be just when they are not so at all? Or is quite the opposite the case?

THEAET. Quite the opposite.

STR. Then I think we must say that such an imitator is quite distinct from the other, the one who does not know from the one who knows.

THEAET. Yes.

STR. Where, then, can the fitting name for each of the two be found? Clearly it is not an easy task, because there was, it seems, among the earlier thinkers a long established and careless indolence in respect to the division of classes or genera into forms or species, so that nobody even tried to make such divisions; therefore there cannot be a great abundance of names. However, even though the innovation in language be a trifle bold, let us, for the sake of making a distinction, call the imitation which is

455

Ε προσείπωμεν, τὴν δὲ μετ' ἐπιστήμης ἱστορικήν τινα μίμησιν.

ΘΕΑΙ. Ἔστω.

ΞΕ. Θατέρῳ τοίνυν χρηστέον· ὁ γὰρ σοφιστὴς οὐκ ἐν τοῖς εἰδόσιν ἦν, ἀλλ' ἐν τοῖς μιμουμένοις δή.

ΘΕΑΙ. Καὶ μάλα.

ΞΕ. Τὸν δοξομιμητὴν δὴ σκοπώμεθα ὥσπερ σίδηρον, εἴτε ὑγιὴς εἴτε διπλόην ἔτ' ἔχων τινά ἐστιν ἐν ἑαυτῷ.

ΘΕΑΙ. Σκοπῶμεν.

268   ΞΕ. Ἔχει τοίνυν καὶ μάλα συχνήν. ὁ μὲν γὰρ εὐήθης αὐτῶν ἐστιν, οἰόμενος εἰδέναι ταῦτα ἃ δοξάζει· τὸ δὲ θατέρου σχῆμα διὰ τὴν ἐν τοῖς λόγοις κυλίνδησιν ἔχει πολλὴν ὑποψίαν καὶ φόβον, ὡς ἀγνοεῖ ταῦτα ἃ πρὸς τοὺς ἄλλους ὡς εἰδὼς ἐσχημάτισται.

ΘΕΑΙ. Πάνυ μὲν οὖν ἔστιν ἑκατέρου γένους ὧν εἴρηκας.

ΞΕ. Οὐκοῦν τὸν μὲν ἁπλοῦν μιμητήν τινα, τὸν δὲ εἰρωνικὸν μιμητὴν θήσομεν;

ΘΕΑΙ. Εἰκὸς γοῦν.

ΞΕ. Τούτου δ' αὖ τὸ γένος ἓν ἢ δύο φῶμεν;

ΘΕΑΙ. Ὅρα σύ.

Β   ΞΕ. Σκοπῶ· καί μοι διττὼ καταφαίνεσθόν τινε· τὸν μὲν δημοσίᾳ τε καὶ μακροῖς λόγοις πρὸς πλήθη δυνατὸν εἰρωνεύεσθαι καθορῶ, τὸν δὲ ἰδίᾳ τε καὶ βραχέσι λόγοις ἀναγκάζοντα τὸν προσδια- λεγόμενον ἐναντιολογεῖν αὐτὸν αὑτῷ.

ΘΕΑΙ. Λέγεις ὀρθότατα.

based on opinion, opinion-imitation, and that which is founded on knowledge, a sort of scientific imitation.

THEAET. Agreed

STR. We must therefore apply ourselves to the former, for we found that the sophist was among those who imitate but was not among those who know.

THEAET. Very true.

STR. Then let us examine the opinion-imitator as if he were a piece of iron, and see whether he is sound or there is still some seam in him.

THEAET. Let us do so.

STR. Well, there is a very marked seam. For some of these imitators are simple-minded and think they know that about which they have only opinion, but the other kind because of their experience in the rough and tumble of arguments, strongly suspect and fear that they are ignorant of the things which they pretend before the public to know.

THEAET. Certainly the two classes you mention both exist.

STR. Then shall we call one the simple imitator and the other the dissembling imitator?

THEAET. That is reasonable, at any rate.

STR. And shall we say that the latter forms one class or two again?

THEAET. That is your affair.

STR. I am considering, and I think I can see two classes. I see one who can dissemble in long speeches in public before a multitude, and the other who does it in private in short speeches and forces the person who converses with him to contradict himself.

THEAET. You are quite right.

457

ΞΕ. Τίνα οὖν ἀποφαινώμεθα τὸν μακρολογώτερον εἶναι; πότερα πολιτικὸν ἢ δημολογικόν;

ΘΕΑΙ. Δημολογικόν.

ΞΕ. Τί δὲ τὸν ἕτερον ἐροῦμεν; σοφὸν ἢ σοφιστικόν;

ΘΕΑΙ. Τὸ[1] μέν που σοφὸν ἀδύνατον, ἐπείπερ οὐκ
C εἰδότα αὐτὸν ἔθεμεν· μιμητὴς δ' ὢν τοῦ σοφοῦ δῆλον ὅτι παρωνύμιον αὐτοῦ τι λήψεται, καὶ σχεδὸν ἤδη μεμάθηκα ὅτι τοῦτον δεῖ προσειπεῖν ἀληθῶς αὐτὸν ἐκεῖνον τὸν παντάπασιν ὄντως σοφιστήν.

ΞΕ. Οὐκοῦν συνδήσομεν αὐτοῦ, καθάπερ ἔμπροσθεν, τοὔνομα συμπλέξαντες ἀπὸ τελευτῆς ἐπ' ἀρχήν;

ΘΕΑΙ. Πάνυ μὲν οὖν.

ΞΕ. Τὸ[2] δὴ τῆς ἐναντιοποιολογικῆς εἰρωνικοῦ μέρους τῆς δοξαστικῆς μιμητικόν, τοῦ φανταστι-
D κοῦ γένους ἀπὸ τῆς εἰδωλοποιικῆς οὐ θεῖον ἀλλ' ἀνθρωπικὸν τῆς ποιήσεως ἀφωρισμένον ἐν λόγοις τὸ θαυματοποιικὸν μόριον, ταύτης τῆς γενεᾶς τε καὶ αἵματος ὃς ἂν φῇ τὸν ὄντως σοφιστὴν εἶναι, τἀληθέστατα, ὡς ἔοικεν, ἐρεῖ.

ΘΕΑΙ. Παντάπασι μὲν οὖν.

[1] τὸ Stephanus ; τὸν BT.
[2] τὸ Schleiermacher ; τὸν BT.

STR. And what name shall we give to him who makes the longer speeches? Statesman or popular orator?

THEAET. Popular orator.

STR. And what shall we call the other? Philosopher or sophist?

THEAET. We cannot very well call him philosopher, since by our hypothesis he is ignorant; but since he is an imitator of the philosopher, he will evidently have a name derived from his, and I think I am sure at last that we must truly call him the absolutely real and actual sophist.

STR. Shall we then bind up his name as we did before, winding it up from the end to the beginning?

THEAET. By all means.

STR. The imitative kind of the dissembling part of the art of opinion which is part of the art of contradiction and belongs to the fantastic class of the image-making art, and is not divine, but human, and has been defined in arguments as the juggling part of productive activity—he who says that the true sophist is of this descent and blood will, in my opinion, speak the exact truth.

THEAET. Yes, he certainly will.

INDEX

INDEX

INDEX